Élise Lavoué · Hendrik Drachsler
Katrien Verbert · Julien Broisin
Mar Pérez-Sanagustín (Eds.)

Data Driven Approaches in Digital Education

12th European Conference
on Technology Enhanced Learning, EC-TEL 2017
Tallinn, Estonia, September 12–15, 2017
Proceedings

Springer

Editors
Élise Lavoué
Jean Moulin Lyon 3 University
Lyon
France

Julien Broisin
University of Toulouse
Toulouse
France

Hendrik Drachsler
German Institute for International Educational Research
Goethe University
Frankfurt
Germany

Mar Pérez-Sanagustín
Pontificia Universidad
Santiago de Chile
Chile

Katrien Verbert
KU Leuven
Leuven
Belgium

ISSN 0302-9743 ISSN 1611-3349 (electronic)
Lecture Notes in Computer Science
ISBN 978-3-319-66609-9 ISBN 978-3-319-66610-5 (eBook)
DOI 10.1007/978-3-319-66610-5

Library of Congress Control Number: 2017952878

LNCS Sublibrary: SL3 – Information Systems and Applications, incl. Internet/Web, and HCI

Printed on acid-free paper

This Springer imprint is published by Springer Nature
The registered company is Springer International Publishing AG
The registered company address is: Gewerbestrasse 11, 6330 Cham, Switzerland

Preface

We are pleased to welcome you to the 12th European Conference on Technology-Enhanced Learning (EC-TEL 2017). This year's conference is held in the beautiful city of Tallinn, Estonia, September 12–15, 2017.

The EC-TEL 2017 conference is supported by the European Association of Technology Enhanced Learning (EATEL), and this year is hosted by the University of Tallinn, a university with a young but very successful research program on Technology-Enhanced Learning and Learning Analytics.

Building on the momentum generated by previous EC-TEL conferences, this year's conference once again provides a multidisciplinary forum for different disciplines to discuss critical issues and challenges confronting the education sector of the future. Digitalization and data-driven research will probably be of major importance in upcoming years. It is rapidly growing in all facets and significantly changing how we conduct research in Technology-Enhanced Learning (TEL). Moreover, data-driven research is affecting our underlying theoretical constructs as well as government policies. The increasing amount of data that can be collected from learning environments, but also various wearable devices and new hardware sensors, offers plenty of opportunities to rethink educational practices and provides new innovative approaches to learning and teaching. This kind of data helps to investigate new insights about learning, inform on individual and group-based learning processes and contributes to a new kind of data-driven education for the 21st century.

For EC-TEL 2017, the Program Committee has selected contributions that explore how data can be used to change and enhance learning in different ways, and to highlight evidence for technological innovations in learning such as multimodal data, personal data stores, data visualizations for learner and teacher awareness, feedback processes, predictions of learning progress, personalization and adaptation, as well as data-driven learning designs, or ethics and privacy policies for the data-driven future.

The 12th EC-TEL conference on Data Driven Approaches in Digital Education aims to explore the multidisciplinary approaches that effectively illustrate what data-driven education combined with digital education systems can look like and what empirical evidence there is for the use of data-driven tools in educational practices. This theme is reflected in the workshops, papers, posters, panels, and especially our keynote talks. Stéphanie Teasley, from the University of Michigan, will give a presentation on "Creating the Institutional Capacity to Leverage Learning Analytics in Higher Education" and Gerhard Fischer, from the University of Colorado, will present on "Envisioning and Grounding New Educational Designs in Data Driven Approaches". Marco Marsella, from the European Commission, will detail the results of EU Actions, challenges and the future outlook of digital learning. The conference will culminate with a leadership panel featuring leaders from a spectrum of research societies dedicated to advancing education under the shadows of the data-driven society of the near future.

Continuing the trend from previous EC-TEL conferences, this year we worked to maintain the breadth and quality of the Program Committee and sought to include representation from related fields, bringing in prominent academics that are involved in data-driven education. We had a very high number of submissions that resulted in considerable competition among excellent research papers. A total of 141 valid paper submissions were received. We aimed to provide a high standard in our review process, providing at least three reviews for each full paper. All reviews were checked and discussed by the general chair, the PC and the poster and demonstration chairs. Out of the 95 full papers received, it has been quite a challenge to select 24 full papers for presentation, resulting in a 25.3% acceptance rate. Additionally, 26 papers were chosen as short papers, 6 as demonstrations, and 22 as posters. We also provided a pre-conference program consisting of a doctoral consortium including 19 students. Additionally, we accepted 7 workshops.

While we celebrate the vast interdisciplinary work within the EC-TEL community, and the continuous popularity of this conference in Europe and beyond, we are proud to be a community with diverse backgrounds and often intersecting research and theoretical approaches. Although this is already the 12th EC-TEL conference, interdisciplinary content is still a challenge and a source of innovation as well. We still need to work together to achieve a shared vision for the TEL field. We have also noticed that EC-TEL is facing a first generation change, where younger researchers take over what the experienced scholars have built up in the last 12 years. This is an important milestone for the EATEL society and the EC-TEL community in further maturing our research.

Our hope is that you will greatly benefit from your participation in EC-TEL 2017, and that it will both strengthen and deepen your network within the community. We explicitly want to stimulate young researchers to become pro-active members of the EATEL and the EC-TEL communities and to further shape the European research community on TEL, which is committed to high-quality research and international exchanges. We believe this community is urgently needed as a European fireplace to share knowledge, and to guide educational innovation and the use of technology and data for the European education systems of the future. The program has prepared a foundation for this vision, but the real value in the event will emerge through the interplay between the people behind the research and the interactions that will occur within the community.

We would like to thank all the authors who contributed to maintaining the high-quality level of the conference, as well as the PC members and reviewers who shared their expertise by giving constructive feedback to authors. We would also like to thank the local organization team for their great work and their warm welcome!

July 2017

Élise Lavoué
Hendrik Drachsler
Katrien Verbert
Mar Pérez-Sanagustín
Julien Broisin

Organization

Executive Committee

General Chair

Katrien Verbert	KU Leuven, Belgium

Program Chairs

Élise Lavoué	Jean Moulin Lyon 3 University, France
Hendrik Drachsler	Open University, The Netherlands

Workshop Chairs

Olga C. Santos	UNED, Spain
Luis-Pablo Prieto	Tallinn University, Estonia

Poster and Demonstration Chairs

Mar Pérez-Sanagustín	PUC, Chile
Julien Broisin	University of Toulouse, France

Doctoral Consortium Chairs

Katherine Maillet	Institut Mines-Télécom, Télécom Ecole de Management, France
Lone Dirckinck-Holmfeld	Aalborg University, Denmark
Ellen Rusman	Open University, The Netherlands

Dissemination Chair

Sharon Hsiao	Arizona State University, USA

Steering Committee Representative

Ralf Klamma	RWTH Aachen University, Germany

Industry Chair

Kadri-Liis Kusmin	Proekspert, and Tallinn University, Estonia

Local Organization Chairs

Tobias Ley	Tallinn University, Estonia
Kairit Tammets	Tallinn University, Estonia

Program Committee

Marie-Helene Abel	HEUDIASYC - Université de Technologie de Compiègne
Mohammad Al-Smadi	Jordan University of Science and Technology
Carlos Alario-Hoyos	Universidad Carlos III de Madrid
Liaqat Ali	SFU
Luis Anido-Rifon	Universidade de Vigo
Inmaculada Arnedillo-Sanchez	Trinity College Dublin
Antonio Balderas	University of Cadiz
Merja Bauters	Helsinki University
Jason Bernard	Athabasca University
Katrin Borcea-Pfitzmann	Technische Universität Dresden
Yolaine Bourda	LRI, CentraleSupélec
Andreas Breiter	Universität Bremen
Julien Broisin	University of Toulouse
Ilona Buchem	Beuth University
Manuel Caeiro	University of Vigo
Lorenzo Cantoni	Università della Svizzera Italiana
Manuel Castro	UNED
Sven Charleer	KU Leuven
Irene-Angelica Chounta	Carnegie Mellon University
Miguel Conde-González	University of León
Audrey Cooke	Curtin University
Mayela Coto	Universidad Nacional, Costa Rica
Raquel M. Crespo García	Universidad Carlos III de Madrid
Ulrike Cress	Knowledge Media Research Center
Alexandra Cristea	University of Warwick
Mihai Dascalu	University Politehnica of Bucharest
Paul De-Bra	TU/e
Carlos Delgado-Kloos	Universidad Carlos III de Madrid
Stavros Demetriadis	Aristotle University of Thessaloniki
Christian Depover	Université de Mons
Michael Derntl	University of Tübingen
Philippe Dessus	LSE, Université Grenoble Alpes
Darina Dicheva	Winston-Salem State University
Stefan Dietze	L3S Research Center
Daniele Dimitri	Open Universiteit Nederland
Yannis Dimitriadis	University of Valladolid
Vania Dimitrova	University of Leeds

Lone Dirckinck-Holmfeld	Aalborg University
Juan Manuel Dodero	Universidad de Cádiz
Peter Dolog	Aalborg University
Hendrik Drachsler	Open University
Benedict Du-Boulay	University of Sussex
Martin Ebner	University of Graz
Iria Estévez-Ayres	Universidad Carlos III de Madrid
Baltasar Fernandez-Manjon	Universidad Complutense de Madrid
Alejandro Fernández	LIFIA, Universidad Nacional de La Plata
Carmen Fernández-Panadero	Universidad Carlos III de Madrid
Christine Ferraris	Université Savoie Mont Blanc
Angela Fessl	Know-Center, Graz
Beatriz Florian	Universidad del Valle
Serge Garlatti	IMT Atlantique
Muriel Garreta	Universitat Oberta de Catalunya
Dragan Gasevic	University of Edinburgh
Sébastien George	Université du Maine
Denis Gillet	Swiss Federal Institute of Technology in Lausanne (EPFL)
Fabrizio Giorgini	eXact learning solutions
Carlo Giovannella	University of Tor Vergata
Christian Glahn	University of Applied Sciences HTW Chur
Frank Goldhammer	DIPF, ZIB
Sabine Graf	Athabasca University
Monique Grandbastien	LORIA, Université de Lorraine
Andrina Granić	University of Split
Wolfgang Greller	Vienna University of Education
David Griffiths	Institute for Educational Cybernetics, University of Bolton
Begona Gros	Universitat de Barcelona
Franka Grünewald	Bundespolizeipräsidium
Christian Gütl	Graz University of Technology
Joerg Haake	FernUniversitaet in Hagen
Cecilie Johanne Hansen	uniRes
Andreas Harrer	Clausthal University of Technology
Eelco Herder	L3S Research Center
Ángel Hernández-García	Universidad Politécnica de Madrid
Davinia Hernández-Leo	Universitat Pompeu Fabra, Barcelona
Knut Hinkelmann	FHNW University of Applied Sciences and Arts Northwestern Switzerland
Tore Hoel	Høgskolen i Oslo og Akershus
Teresa Holocher-Ertl	Centre for Social Innovation
Ulrich Hoppe	University Duisburg-Essen
Sharon Hsiao	Arizona State University
Seiji Isotani	University of Sao Paulo

Ioana Jivet	Open Universiteit Nederland
Srecko Joksimovic	Moray House School of Education, University of Edinburgh
Marco Kalz	Welten-Institute - Research Center for Learning, Teaching and Technology
Nikos Karacapilidis	University of Patras
Ulla Kask	Tallinn University
Michael Kickmeier-Rust	Graz University of Technology
Andrea Kienle	University of Applied Sciences Dortmund
Barbara Kieslinger	Centre for Social Innovation
Paul Kirschner	Open Universiteit Nederland
Ralf Klamma	RWTH Aachen University
Styliani Kleanthous-Loizou	University of Cyprus
Tomaz Klobucar	Jozef Stefan Institute
Johannes Konert	Beuth University of Applied Sciences
Vitomir Kovanovic	The University of Edinburgh
Milos Kravcik	DFKI GmbH
Mart Laanpere	Tallinn University
Lydia Lau	University of Leeds
Elise Lavoué	Université Jean Moulin Lyon 3
Effie Law	University of Leicester
Elisabeth Lex	Graz University of Technology
Tobias Ley	Tallinn University
Andreas Lingnau	Humboldt-Universität zu Berlin
Martin Llamas-Nistal	University of Vigo
Ulrike Lucke	University of Potsdam
Rose Luckin	The London Knowledge Lab
Vanda Luengo	Laboratoire d'informatique de Paris, LIP6, Université Pierre et Marie Curie
George Magoulas	Birkbeck College
Katherine Maillet	Institut Mines-Télécom, Télécom Ecole de Management
Nils Malzahn	Rhine-Ruhr Institute for Applied System Innovation e.V.
Schmitz Marcel	Zuyd Hogeschool
Estefanía Martin	Universidad Rey Juan Carlos
Jean-Charles Marty	LIRIS - équipe SICAL
Antonia Martínez-Carreras	University of Murcia
Manolis Mavrikis	London Knowledge Lab
Martin Memmel	DFKI GmbH
Agathe Merceron	Beuth University of Applied Sciences Berlin
Christine Michel	LIRIS, Université de Lyon, Insa-Lyon
Riichiro Mizoguchi	Japan Advanced Institute of Science and Technology
Inge Molenaar	Radboud University
Yishay Mor	Consultant
Pablo Moreno-Ger	Universidad Complutense de Madrid

Pedro Muñoz-Merino	Universidad Carlos III de Madrid
Rob Nadolski	Open University of the Netherlands-CELSTEC
Xavier Ochoa	Escuela Superior Politécnica del Litoral
Carmen L. Padrón-Nápoles	ATOS
Viktoria Pammer	Know-Center
Lucia Pannese	Imaginary
Pantelis Papadopoulos	Aarhus University
Abelardo Pardo	The University of Sydney
Denis Parra-Santander	Pontificia Universidad Catolica de Chile
Kai Pata	Tallinn University
Cesare Pautasso	University of Lugano, Switzerland
Zinayida Petrushyna	RWTH Aachen University
Hector Pijeiradiaz	University of Oulu
Niels Pinkwart	Humboldt-Universität zu Berlin
Kaska Porayska-Pomsta	UCL Knowledge Lab
Luis P. Prieto	School of Educational Sciences, Tallinn University, Estonia
Michael Prilla	Ruhr University of Bochum
Juan Pérez	Collaborative and Intelligent Systems Group, University of Valladolid
Mar Pérez-Sanagustín	PUC
Eric Ras	Luxembourg Institute of Science and Technology
Christoph Rensing	Technische Universität Darmstadt
Bart Rienties	Open University
Marc Rittberger	DIPF
Luz Stella Robles Pedrozo	Universidad Tecnológica de Bolívar
María Jesús Rodríguez-Triana	École Polytechnique Fédérale de Lausanne
Adolfo Ruiz-Calleja	Tallinn University
Ellen Rusman	Open University
Demetrios Sampson	Curtin University
Eric Sanchez	Université de Fribourg
Olga Santos	UNED
Maren Scheffel	Open Universiteit
Andreas Schmidt	Karlsruhe University of Applied Sciences
Ulrik Schroeder	RWTH Aachen University
Karim Sehaba	LIRIS - Université Lumière Lyon 2
Stylianos Sergis	University of Piraeus
Mike Sharples	The Open University
Bernd Simon	Knowledge Markets Consulting
Sergey Sosnovsky	Utrecht University
Fazeli Soude	OUNL
Marcus Specht	Open University, The Netherlands
Daniel Spikol	Malmö University
Slavi Stoyanov	Open University, The Netherlands
Kairit Tammets	Tallinna Ülikool

Stefano Tardini	USI
Deborah Tatar	VirginiaTech
Pierre Tchounikine	University of Grenoble
Stefaan Ternier	Open University, The Netherlands
Vladimir Tomberg	Tallinn University
Richard Tortorella	University of Eastern Finland
Christoph Trattner	MODUL University Vienna
Stefan Trausan-Matu	University Politehnica of Bucharest
Katrien Verbert	KU Leuven
Terje Väljataga	Tallinn University
Jo Wake	Uni Health, Uni Research
Barbara Wasson	University of Bergen
Wim Westera	CELSTEC-Centre for Learning Sciences and Technologies, Open University of the Netherlands
Denise Whitelock	Open University
Fridolin Wild	Oxford Brookes University
Raphael Zender	University of Potsdam

Additional Reviewers

Blees, Ingo
Chalco Challco, Geiser
Cukurova, Mutlu
Du Boulay, Benedict
Guţu, Marius-Gabriel
Hecking, Tobias
Itani, Alya
Jivet, Ioana
Kopeinik, Simone
Kusmin, Kadri-Liis
Lukarov, Vlatko
Manske, Sven
Paraschiv, Ionut Cristian
Paredes, Yancy Vance
Renner, Bettina
Roldán, David
Ross, Tamra
Röpke, René
Scheffel, Maren
Schulz, Sandra
Seitlinger, Paul
Sergis, Stylianos
Sun, Na
Treasure-Jones, Tamsin
Vozniuk, Andrii

Contents

Full Papers

Short Papers

Demo Papers

Poster Papers

Full Papers

The "Grey Area": A Computational Approach to Model the Zone of Proximal Development

Irene-Angelica Chounta[1(✉)], Patricia Albacete[2], Pamela Jordan[2], Sandra Katz[2], and Bruce M. McLaren[1]

[1] Human-Computer Interaction Institute, Carnegie Mellon University, Pittsburgh, PA, USA
{ichounta,bmclaren}@cs.cmu.edu
[2] Learning Research and Development Center, University of Pittsburgh, Pittsburgh, PA, USA
{palbacet,pjordan,katz}@pitt.edu

Abstract. In this paper, we propose a computational approach to model the Zone of Proximal Development (ZPD) using predicted probabilities of correctness while students engage in reflective dialogue. We employ a predictive model that uses a linear function of a variety of parameters, including difficulty and student knowledge, as students use a natural-language tutoring system that presents conceptual reflection questions after they solve high-school physics problems. In order to operationalize our approach, we introduce the concept of the "Grey Area", that is, the area of uncertainty in which the student model cannot predict with acceptable accuracy whether a student is able to give a correct answer without support. We further discuss the impact of our approach on student modeling, the limitations of this work and future work in systematically and rigorously evaluating the approach.

Keywords: Natural-language tutoring systems · Intelligent Tutoring Systems · Student modeling · Zone of Proximal Development

1 Introduction

Intelligent Tutoring Systems (ITSs) support students in grasping concepts, applying them during problem-solving activities, addressing misconceptions and in general improving students' proficiency in science, math, reading and other areas [1]. However, we still face the challenge of developing tutoring systems that emulate the interactive nature of human tutoring and that are just as effective – if not better – than human tutors. One approach for achieving this goal is to engage students in reflective discussions about scientific concepts [2]. To a large extent, these systems lack the ability to gauge students' level of mastery over the domain content that the tutoring system was designed to support. This is also challenging for human tutors, who roughly assess the level of knowledge and understanding of their tutees, although they are generally poor at diagnosing the specific causes of student errors [3]. We argue that a student model that maintains and dynamically updates a representation of students' ability level on targeted curriculum elements can help us bridge the gap between simulated and human tutors. Tutorial dialogue systems could be more effective if they are guided by the information

É. Lavoué et al. (Eds.): EC-TEL 2017, LNCS 10474, pp. 3–16, 2017.
DOI: 10.1007/978-3-319-66610-5_1

about the student's understanding of curriculum elements that is represented within a student model, along with other student characteristics such as demographic information and motivational factors such as interest in the targeted domain, self-efficacy, etc. [4].

1.1 Research Hypothesis and Impact

In order to provide meaningful instruction and scaffolding to students, a tutoring system should appropriately adapt the learning material with respect to both content and presentation. A way to achieve this is to dynamically assess the student's knowledge state and needs. Human tutors use their assessment of student ability to adapt the level of discussion to the student's "zone of proximal development" (ZPD) [5]. Adapting the conversation to the ZPD would mean asking the student questions just beyond their knowledge level – in other words, asking questions that students are able to answer correctly with adequate support. During tutorial dialogues, human teachers evaluate their students' learning state; a teacher judges whether a student will be able to answer a question correctly without any help (that is, the student is above the ZPD) or be able to answer correctly if given some help (that is, the student is in the ZPD) or unable to answer correctly even with help (that is, the student is below the ZPD). Depending on this judgment, the teacher will choose to ask this question, provide hints, or instead choose a more appropriate question for this student's ability level. We propose a computational approach for modeling students' ZPD as they carry out learning activities using a dialogue-based intelligent tutoring system, which replicates the pedagogical strategies of human tutors. The predictions of the student model serve as a proxy for human tutors' judgment. In particular, we employ a student model to assess students' changing knowledge state as they engage in a dialogue with the system. At each step of the dialogue, the student model predicts the probability of the student being able to answer the question posed by the computer tutor correctly. When the predicted probability is high, the student is likely to possess the knowledge needed to answer the question correctly. When the predicted probability is low, it is unlikely that the student has an adequate grasp of the necessary knowledge to give a correct response. An interesting case arises when the student model predicts that the student will be able to answer a question with a probability around 50%, because in this case there is greater uncertainty. In other words, the student may need some extra support to be able to give a correct response. Hence the region of predicted probabilities that reflects this area of uncertainly with regards to the student's abilities to give a correct answer without support is what we call the "Grey Area" [6]. Our research hypothesis is that we can use the fitted probabilities as predicted by the student model to model the ZPD. The core rationale is that if the student model cannot predict with acceptable accuracy whether a student will answer a question correctly, then it might be the case that the student is in the ZPD. To the best of our knowledge, this is a novel approach to modeling the ZPD, never before implemented or reported in the literature.

In the following section we discuss relevant research about the ZPD, Intelligent Tutoring Systems and student modeling. In Sect. 3, we present our approach and methodology. Analysis and results are presented in Sect. 4. Finally, in Sect. 5 we discuss the impact and implications of our approach and conclude by presenting the limitations of our study and future work.

2 Related Work

2.1 Zone of Proximal Development

The Zone of Proximal Development (ZPD) is one of the best known concepts in educational psychology, defined by Vygotsky as: "the distance between the actual developmental level as determined by independent problem-solving and the level of potential development as determined through problem-solving under adult guidance or in collaboration with more capable peers" [5]. This definition of the ZPD indicates the importance of appropriate assistance in relation to the learning and development process and thus it can be stated more simply as "the difference between what a learner can do without help and what he or she can do with help" [7]. Deriving ways to identify and formally describe the ZPD is an important step towards understanding the mechanisms that drive learning and development, gaining insights about learners' needs, and providing appropriate pedagogical interventions [8]. Approaches to identifying and/or modeling the ZPD typically depend on finding instances of successful assisted performance; for example, tasks that a student carries out successfully after having received some kind of scaffolding [8]. Various methods that derive from or build upon this notion have been developed for the dynamic assessment (DA) of the learning potential of students (or learners in general) [9]. Usually these approaches employ tests that measure the difference between unmediated and mediated performance [10] or the cognitive modifiability of learners (i.e., how students' cognitive structures change when they fail a task and the teacher/expert gives them help or remediation tasks) [11]. However, Dynamic Assessment focuses on assessing the learning or development potential of the learner rather than the actual level of development. Luckin and du Boulay proposed the use of domain knowledge representations and Bayesian Belief Networks (BBN) to construct the Zone of Proximal Adjustment (ZPA) [12], that is the tutor's adaptation mechanism to the ZPD of particular learners. Each student's knowledge is represented as an overlay model and the student model is compared to the domain knowledge representation.

2.2 Intelligent Tutoring Systems and Student Modeling

Intelligent Tutoring Systems (ITSs) commonly use student models to track the performance of students and choose appropriate content for practicing skills and fostering knowledge. Most student models developed for ITSs are based on the notion of mastery learning; that is, the student is asked to continue solving problems or answering questions about a concept until she has mastered it. Only then will the student be guided to move forward to other concepts [13]. Mastery learning is in line with the notion of learning curves [14] that is, how many opportunities a student needs to master a skill. One could argue that mastery learning is consistent with the ZPD, in the sense that the student is considered to have mastered a skill when she is able to successfully carry out a task that requires this particular skill without help. However, the ZPD does not directly address mastery but rather potential "development" under appropriate assistance; by identifying the ZPD not only can we assess the state of a student's knowledge but we also gain insight into how appropriate instruction can scaffold development [15]. Human tutors do not carry out detailed diagnoses of student knowledge and their assessments of students' knowledge are often inaccurate [3]. Nevertheless, they typically construct and dynamically update a normative mental representation of students' understanding, as reflected in tutors' adaptive responses to students' need for scaffolding or remediation [16]. Similarly, a tutorial dialogue system uses a student model to adapt to the student's needs. Otherwise, all students would be presented with the same topics, at the same level of detail or complexity. Moreover, if the student answers a question incorrectly and there is need for remediation, the simulated tutor will not be able to adapt the type of support that it provides. Indeed, it is the absence of information about the student that forces designers of tutorial dialogue systems to make a "best guess" about how to structure a dialogue—that is, what the main "line of reasoning" should be, what remedial or supplemental subdialogues to issue and when—and then to hard code these guesses into the dialogues. Consequently, with the "one size fits all" approach to dialogue that is implemented in most tutorial dialogue systems, students are often under-exposed to material that they don't understand and overexposed to material they have a firm grasp of. The first problem renders these systems ineffective in enabling students to achieve mastery over the focal content; the second makes them inefficient. Developing a computational model of students' ZPD takes an important step towards generating more adaptive tutorial dialogues.

3 Methods

3.1 Rimac: A Dialogue Tutor for Physics

In this study we explored the proposed approach using Rimac, a web-based natural-language tutoring system that engages students in reflective discussions about concepts after they solve quantitative physics problems [17]. Rimac has been used successfully to teach physics concepts to high-school students. We used data collected during three previous studies with Rimac to train a student model and predict students' performance. The three studies were conducted within high school physics classes at schools in the Pittsburgh, PA (U.S.) area, following a similar protocol. First, students took a pretest and were introduced to Rimac. Then they interacted with Rimac to discuss the physics knowledge associated with quantitative problems on dynamics. Finally, students took a post-test to measure learning gains. The tests aimed to test students' conceptual understanding of physics instead of their ability to solve quantitative problems. Rimac's dialogues were developed to present a directed line of reasoning, or DLR [18], in which the tutor presents a series of questions to the student. If the student answers a question correctly, she advances to the next question in the DLR. If the student responds incorrectly, the system launches a remedial sub-dialogue and then returns to the main line of reasoning after the sub-dialogue has completed. If the system is unable to understand the student's response, it completes the step for the student (for more details, see [19]). The knowledge components related to tutor question/student response pairings are logged during the system's interactions with students and were used to train the student model as described next. A short example of a dialogue with Rimac is presented in Table 1.

Table 1. A short example of an adaptive dialogue with Rimac

Tutor:	So, can you please tell me what the vertical forces on the arrow are?
Student:	Gravity
Tutor:	Very good. Since we know that the force of gravity is acting on the arrow, what does that mean about the arrow's vertical acceleration (zero, nonzero, etc)?
Student:	Nonzero

3.2 The Student Model

For this study, we used an Additive Factor Model (AFM), introduced by Cen et al. [20], to model students' knowledge. The model uses logistic regression to predict the probability of a student *i* completing a step *j* correctly as a linear function of student parameters (the student's proficiency θ_i), skill parameters β_k and the learning rates of skills γ_k, as shown in Eq. (1). AFM takes into account the frequency of prior practice and exposure to skills but not the correctness of responses since it assumes all students accumulate knowledge in the same way. In this paper we implemented the AFM model following the approach of Chi et al. [21] who modeled students working on physics problems using a dialogue-based tutor.

$$ln\frac{p_{ij}}{1-p_{ij}} = \theta_i + \sum_k \beta_k Q_{kj} + \sum_k Q_{kj}(\gamma_k N_{ik}) \tag{1}$$

The dataset was collected by training 291 students on Rimac over a period of 4 years (2011–2015). During students' interactions with Rimac, they answered reflection questions on physics problems about dynamics, such as: "*In our first question we will focus on the horizontal motion of the arrow. Let`s imagine a scenario in which an archer is standing at the edge of a high cliff. He shoots an arrow perfectly horizontally with an initial velocity of 60 m/s off this cliff. During the arrow's flight, how does its horizontal velocity change (increases, decreases, remains the same, etc.)? Remember that you can ignore air resistance*". Students worked on reflection questions about three physics problems that explored motion laws and addressed 88 knowledge components (KCs). The dataset contained in total 15,644 student responses. Each student response answers a question posed by the tutor and was classified as correct or incorrect. For the training of the model we split our dataset following an 80–20 rule [22]: 12,515 student responses were used for training the model and the remaining 3,129 were used for testing. On average, each student answered a total of 53 questions, stemming from several reflection questions. The test set contained on average 11 entries per student.

3.3 The Grey Area and the Study Setup

To predict the correctness of students' responses, we used the aforementioned AFM student model. Then, we classified the outcome as correct or incorrect based on the fitted probabilities provided by the model. In this study, the student model provided predictions at the step level (one step is one question/answer of the tutorial dialogue). A step might involve one or multiple KCs. The classification threshold in this case (i.e., the cutoff determining whether a response is classified as correct or incorrect) is 0.5 and was validated using the receiver operating characteristic (ROC) curve for the binary classifier (Fig. 1). For example, if the fitted probability for a step in the dialogue is 0.8 (above 0.5) then we expect that the student will be able to answer the corresponding dialogue step correctly; hence, it is classified as correct. Similarly, if the fitted probability for a step in the dialogue is 0.2 (below 0.5) then we expect that the student will not be able to answer correctly; hence it is classified as incorrect.

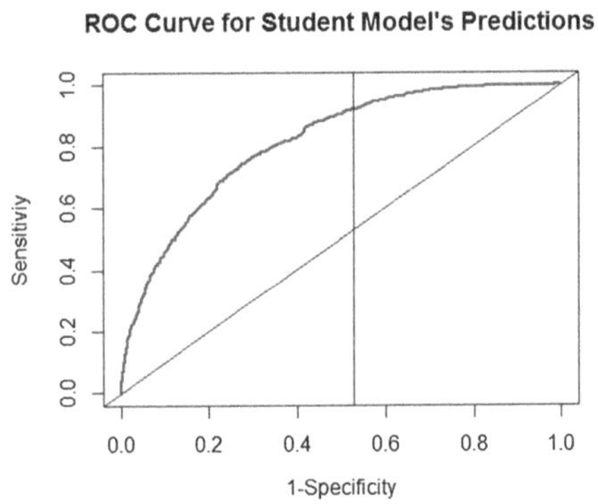

Fig. 1. ROC Curve for validating the classification threshold

We found that the predicted probabilities correlate with students' performance in the pre and post-tests: the student model will provide high probabilities of correctness (i.e., a high probability to answer a question correctly) for students who performed well on the pre and post-tests. Similarly, the model will provide low probabilities of correctness for students who performed poorly in the pre and post-tests. We argue that this correlation between students' performance in the pre and post-tests and predicted probabilities suggests that the predicted probabilities are appropriate indicators of the ZPD. In this study the pre and post-tests assessed conceptual knowledge associated with the questions that students were assigned to work on. Furthermore, we expect that the closer the prediction is to the classification threshold, the higher the uncertainty of the model and thus, the higher the prediction error. In other words, when the student model predicts that the student will be able to answer a question with a probability close to 0.5, we are more uncertain than with any other prediction as to whether or not the student will answer the question correctly. According to our hypothesis, the window where the prediction error is high (i.e. the "Grey Area") can be used to approximate the student's zone of proximal development. The concept of the Grey Area is depicted in Fig. 2.

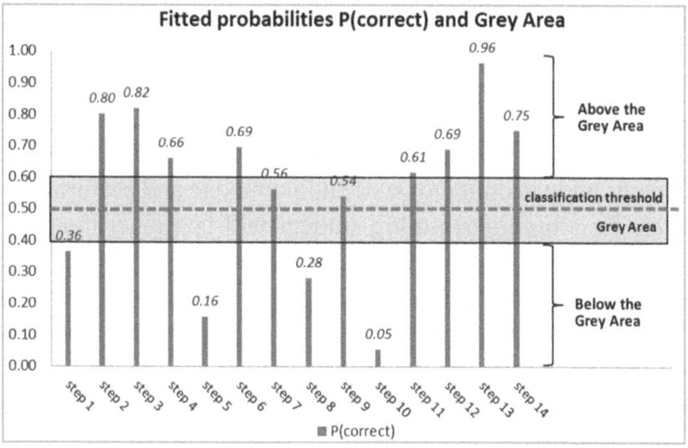

Fig. 2. The Grey Area concept with respect to the fitted probabilities as predicted by the student model for a random student and for the various steps of a learning activity. Here we depict the Grey Area ranging from 0.4 to 0.6 and extending on both sides of the classification threshold (dotted line).

The space "Above the Grey Area" denotes the region where the student is predicted to answer correctly (the fitted probability is considerably higher than the cutoff threshold) and consequently may indicate the area above the ZPD; that is, the area in which the student is able to answer a question without any assistance. Accordingly, the space "Below the Grey Area" denotes the area where the student is predicted to answer incorrectly (the fitted probability is considerably lower than the cutoff threshold) and consequently may indicate the area below the ZPD; that is, the area in which the student is not able to carry out the task either with or without assistance. In this paper, we model the Grey Area symmetrically around the classification threshold for simplicity and because the binary classifier was set to 0.5. However, the symmetry of the Grey Area is something that could change depending on the classification threshold and the learning objectives. This is also the case for the size of the Grey Area.

In this paper we present the concept of the Grey Area and the methodology to model the ZPD. We are exploring, but have not yet specified several design aspects (e.g. thresholds, the use of symmetrical or asymmetrical Grey Areas etc.). We do not propose a specific size but rather experiment with Grey Areas of different sizes and study how the student model behaves within these areas. We believe that the decision about the appropriate size (or shape) of the Grey Area is not only a modeling issue but also, and perhaps predominantly, a pedagogical one since it relies on the importance of the concepts taught, the teaching strategy and the learning objectives. That is, a teacher may consider it important to elicit an answer for a question even if it is predicted that the student is unable to correctly answer that question. The student may not be knowledgeable enough about the given topic or it might be of minor importance and thus even a low probability of correctness would be considered sufficient to classify the student as knowledgeable.

4 Analysis and Results

4.1 Model Behavior and Student Performance

Our research hypothesis is rooted in the belief that the predicted probabilities of the student model can provide insight into student knowledge and performance. That is, the fitted probabilities for a high-performing student will be higher than the fitted probabilities for a low-performing student. One could argue that predicted probabilities are a model's characteristic and may not be appropriate to describe students' performance. However, the fitted probability represents the probability that a student will correctly answer a dialogue question. Since high performers have a higher probability of correctly answering questions, the average of their fitted probabilities will be higher than those of low performing students.

We performed a correlation analysis to explore this hypothesis. We correlated the average fitted probability (i.e., the average value of the fitted probabilities for the answers of each student) per user with the students' knowledge pre-test scores. The correlation analysis showed that the average fitted probability correlates positively with the pre-test scores at a statistically significant level (Pearson's $r = 0.396^{**}$, $p < 0.01$). The positive correlation was also confirmed for the post-test scores (Pearson's $r = 0.46^{**}$, $p < 0.01$). This suggests that if a student scores high on the pre-test for a particular KC, the model will predict that this student is able to answer a question that deals with this KC. Similarly, a student who was predicted to answer correctly a question dealing with a KC will also have a high post-test score for this KC. This finding indicates that the model can predict a student's performance and may be further used to model the student's zone of proximal development. One might notice that the correlation between the average fitted probabilities and the pre and post-knowledge tests are not high (Pearson's $r < 0.5$). However, this might be due to the fact that in the pre and post knowledge tests we only test a small number of the knowledge components that are present in the dialogues. Therefore, the pre and post-knowledge scores can be suggestive of the student's knowledge state but they do not accurately represent it. Model Accuracy for cases inside the Grey Area

The Grey Area is defined as the area where the model cannot accurately predict whether a student will correctly answer a particular question. To operationalize the grey area with respect to size and threshold, we define areas of different sizes and further explore the model's behavior within these areas. For this study, we considered five grey areas of different sizes: Area 1 ($0.45 < p < 0.55$), Area 2 ($0.4 < p < 0.6$), Area 3 ($0.35 < p < 0.65$), Area 4 ($0.3 < p < 0.7$) and Area 5 ($0.25 < p < 0.75$). We chose these particular areas for symmetry and also to cover the range around the classification threshold for which one would expect low predictive accuracy. For these areas, we calculated how many times the model predicted the student answer accurately, where accuracy is defined as the total number of times (a) the student answered correctly and the model also predicted the student would answer correctly and (b) the student answered incorrectly and the model also predicted the student would answer incorrectly, divided by the total number of predictions. Table 2 presents the non-cumulative and the cumulative analysis of the data. For non-cumulative analysis, we mean the analysis of the cases that are contained only in the focal grey area under study (non-cumulative results) and exclude the cases that are also contained in preceding areas. For example, in Area 2 we examine 420 cases that are not contained in Area 1. The cumulative analysis presents the analysis of cases that are contained in the current area but can also be part of the preceding grey area (cumulative results). For example, Area 2 analyzes 814 cases out of which 394 are also contained in Area 1. The results of the non-cumulative analysis show that most predicted cases fall in Area 2 – Non Cumulative (the largest increase in uncertain cases is with Area 2) and that 42.6% of them are predicted incorrectly. This means that for 13.4% (420 cases) of the total number of cases (Total Number of Cases: 3,129), the model gave a prediction with a probability from 0.4 to .45 and .55 to 0.6. As we move away from the classification threshold (0.5), the number of additional fitted cases tends to decrease (fewer cases are predicted with probabilities far from the cutoff threshold) but the percentage of the correct predictions improves. This is depicted in Fig. 3. That finding was expected since the confidence of the model increases.

Table 2. Predictions' accuracy within grey areas of different sizes.

NC/(C)	Area 1	Area 2	Area 3	Area 4	Area 5
#Cases- NC/(*C*)	394/(*394*)	420/(*814*)	404/(*1218*)	369/(*1587*)	304/(*1891*)
Cases (%)- NC/(*C*)	12.6/(*12.6*)	13.4/(*26.0*)	12.9/(*38.9*)	11.8/(*50.7*)	9.7/(*60.4*)
#Correct- NC/(*C*)	213/(*213*)	241/(*454*)	259/(*713*)	250/(*963*)	221/(*1184*)
#Incorrect- NC/(*C*)	181/(*181*)	179/(*360*)	145/(*505*)	119/(*624*)	83/(*707*)
Correct (%)- NC/(*C*)	54.1/(*54.1*)	57.4/(*55.8*)	64.1/(*58.5*)	67.8/(*60.7*)	72.7/(*62.6*)
Incorrect (%)- NC/(*C*)	45.9/(*45.9*)	42.6/(*44.2*)	35.9/(*41.5*)	32.3/(*39.3*)	27.3/(*37.4*)

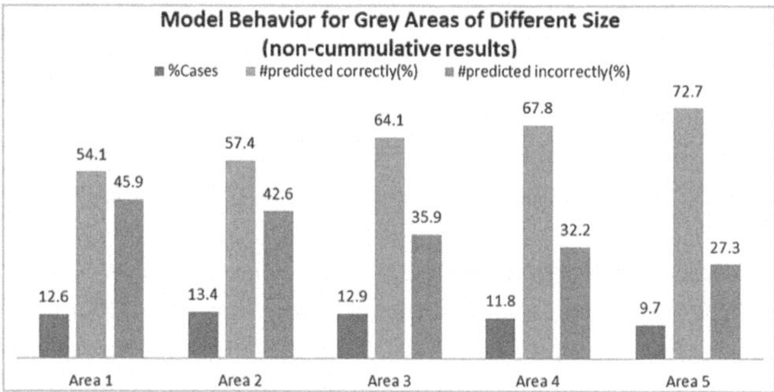

Fig. 3. Model behavior (percentage of total number of predicted cases, cases predicted correctly and cases predicted incorrectly) within the five grey areas of different sizes.

For Area 1, the prediction error is higher (45.9% of the cases were not predicted correctly) but the number of fitted cases is lower than Area 2. In Fig. 4 we depict the results for the cumulative analysis. As expected, more cases are predicted correctly as the size of the area increases. On one hand, choosing a narrow grey area to model the ZPD would limit the number of cases we scaffold since fewer cases would fall within the area. On the other hand, choosing a wide grey area would affect the accuracy; that is, some cases that could be predicted correctly would be falsely labeled as "grey". Our work to date does not aim to define the appropriate size for the Grey Area but rather to study how the model's behavior changes for areas of different size. It is worth mentioning that for the area that is not included in the five areas we study—that is, the area [0,0.25)U(0.75, 1]—the model predicted 89% of the cases correctly while the overall accuracy of the model was 73%.

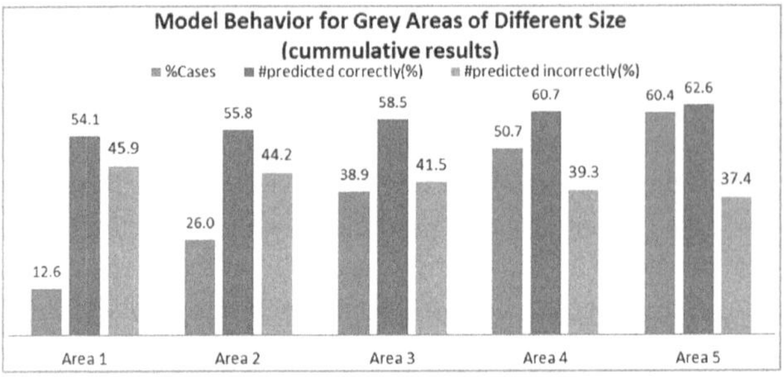

Fig. 4. Model behavior (percentage of total number of predicted cases, cases predicted correctly and cases predicted incorrectly) within the five grey areas of different sizes.

4.2 Grey Areas and Students' Performance

So far, we have studied how the model performs within grey areas of various sizes, but we have no indication of students' performance. One could argue that based on the way the grey zone was modeled—that is, symmetrical around the cutoff threshold of the binary classifier—correct and incorrect answers should be balanced and not vary significantly from one zone to the other. Again, here we only study students' performance; therefore "correctness" refers to the student's answers (i.e., whether a student answered a question correctly) and not whether the model predicted correctly (i.e., whether the model predicted that the student would answer the way she answered). For the five grey areas defined in 4.2, we have counted the number of correct and the number of incorrect student answers.

In Fig. 5 we present the distribution of correct and incorrect answers over the different grey areas and over correct and incorrect model predictions (as shown in the cumulative analysis in Fig. 4). For example, for Area 1, the model predicted 54.1% of the cases correctly- that is, the model predicted that a student would answer correctly and indeed the student answered correctly, or the model predicted that a student would answer incorrectly and indeed the student answered incorrectly. Out of these cases, 28.7% were correct answers to the question involved and 25.4% were incorrect. Likewise, for Area 1 the model predicted 45.9% cases incorrectly. Out of these cases, 18% were correct answers to the question involved and 27.9% were incorrect. It is evident that even though the accuracy of the prediction changes between areas of different sizes, the distributions of correct and incorrect answers are similar. Another thing that can be noted is that for cases that the model predicts correctly, the ratio of correct/incorrect answers is around 1.2 (correct answers are slightly more than incorrect). On the contrary, for cases that are not predicted correctly by the model the ratio of correct/incorrect answers are about 0.7 signifying that incorrect answers outnumber correct ones. Nonetheless this is a pattern that is maintained for all of the grey areas and most probably it reveals that the student model tends to provide positive predictions.

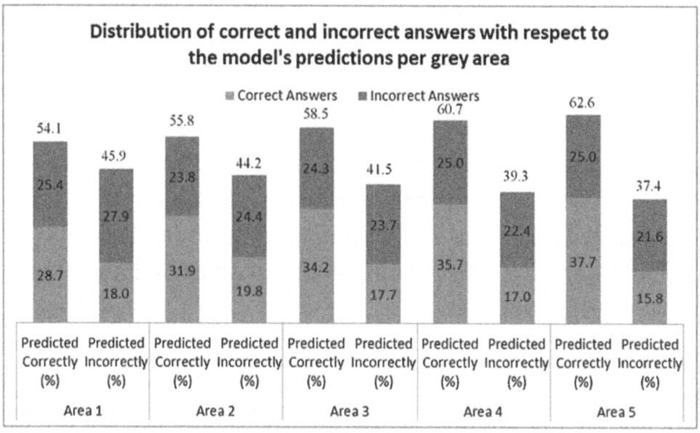

Fig. 5. Graphical representation of the distribution of correct and incorrect answers (percentage) with respect to the model's correct and incorrect predictions.

5 Discussion

5.1 Contribution of the Approach

We envision that the contribution of the proposed approach, besides its novelty, will be in defining and perhaps revising instructional methods to be implemented by ITSs. As noted previously, the most popular instructional method used to choose learning content (problems, activities, examples, etc.) is mastery learning. This means that the student goes through the same concept again and again until the probability of having mastered it is near certainty. Although mastery learning is highly effective—and might largely account for the effectiveness of human tutoring [1], it could lead to tedious repetition or frustration and eventually discourage the student from achieving the goal. Choosing the "next step" is a more prominent issue in the case of dialogue-based intelligent tutors. Not only should the task be appropriate with respect to the background knowledge of the student, but it should also be presented in an appropriate manner so that the student will not be overwhelmed and discouraged – if the task is hard for the student – or boring and not challenging – if the task is too easy. Another key distinction with Mastery Learning perhaps worth mentioning is the idea that ZPD focuses on the level of help. Mastery Learning implies that help might be needed to move the student forward, but it doesn't explicitly include it as part of the definition.

To address this issue, we need an assessment of the knowledge state of each student and insight into the appropriate level of support the student needs to achieve the learning goals. This is described by the notion of ZPD. We claim that our approach makes an explicit link between student modeling and the ZPD and that this approach is a reasonable and novel operationalization of the ZPD. It is evident that if we can model the ZPD then we can adapt our instructional strategy accordingly. For example, if a student is above the ZPD—that is, able to solve a problem on her own and without any help—the tutor will probably challenge the student with some questions that go beyond the current problem's level of difficulty. On the other hand, if a student is in the ZPD—that is, the student needs help and appropriate scaffolding to solve the current problem—the tutor will go slowly, perhaps clarifying step by step the knowledge the student seems to be lacking. Finally, if a student is below the ZPD—that is, the student completely lacks the necessary skills and will not be able to solve the problem, either with or without help—the tutor might choose to skip this problem or to select more appropriate (perhaps simpler) problems. Depending on the state of the student's knowledge, the tutorial dialogue may be directed and focus on particular curriculum elements (facts, concepts, skills, etc.) to discuss during a given problem and to determine the appropriate level at which to discuss these elements.

5.2 Validation of the Proposed Approach

In this paper, we provide preliminary support for our approach. It is also necessary to validate our approach. The challenge in doing so lies in the fact that there is no objective way to test that a student is (or is not) in the ZPD. One heuristic that could be used to explore this is to provide different levels of support to students using the proposed approach and then observe the outcome. Students who are expected to be in the ZPD and who receive appropriate scaffolding should be able to correctly answer the questions asked by the tutor. Thus, we plan to carry out larger scale studies where the dialogue will adapt to the student's knowledge according to the guidance provided by the student model and the represented Grey Area. The dialogue adaptation will take place on selected dialogue steps (in order to maintain the coherency of the dialogue) and will be implemented following three basic adaptation rules:

- Students who are above the Grey Area will receive more challenging questions, no help or even skip specific parts of the dialogue that the model predicts they have mastered;
- Students who are within the Grey Area will receive meaningful information, scaffolding and hints related to the step in question;
- Students who are below the Grey Area will either skip the step that the model predicts they are unable to answer or they will receive explicit information and instruction.

To evaluate our approach, we will study the learning gains of students who receive different levels of support (hints, worked out examples, explicit information, etc.) based on their performance in pre- and post- knowledge tests and their performance during activities within Rimac. We are optimistic that the dialogue adaptation according to the Grey Area concept will improve students' learning gains and motivation.

6 Conclusion

In this paper, we present a computational approach to model the Zone of Proximal Development in ITSs. To that end, we introduce the concept of the "Grey Area", that is the area of uncertainty in which the student model cannot predict with acceptable accuracy whether a student is able to give a correct answer without support. It is important to point out that we do not claim that the Grey Area is the ZPD. Instead, our proposal is that if the model cannot predict the state of a student's knowledge, it may be that the student's knowledge state falls withing the ZPD.

As an initial test to justify our hypothesis, we used data collected from classroom studies where students reflected on the concepts associated with physics problems, using a dialogue-based tutoring system (Rimac). We explored the operationalization of our approach by studying the behavior of the student model and the performance of students within grey areas of various sizes. We found that the accuracy of the model changes depending on the size of the grey zone but the distribution of correct and incorrect student responses remains fairly constant. Additionally, we showed that the average predicted probabilities per student—that is, the average value of the fitted probabilities for a particular student during her interaction with the Dialogue Tutor—correlates positively on a statistically significant level with the student's scores on pre- and post-knowledge tests. This suggests that the student model predictions can provide reliable indicators of students' performance. One limitation of our work is that we have not yet conducted a larger-scale and rigorous evaluation of the approach; however, plans to validate the model are being developed. Specifically, we plan to carry out extensive studies to explore the proposed approach to modeling the ZPD, as well as to better understand the strengths and limitations of using a student model to guide students through adaptive lines of reasoning.

Acknowledgements. This research was supported by the Institute of Education Sciences, U.S. Department of Education, through Grant R305A150155 to the University of Pittsburgh. The opinions expressed are those of the authors and do not necessarily represent the views of the Institute or the U.S. Department of Education.

We thank Sarah Birmingham, Dennis Lusetich, and Scott Silliman for their contributions.

References

1. VanLehn, K.: The relative effectiveness of human tutoring, intelligent tutoring systems, and other tutoring systems. Educ. Psychol. **46**, 197–221 (2011)
2. Graesser, A.C., Person, N., Harter, D., Group, T.R.: others: Teaching tactics and dialog in AutoTutor. Int. J. Artif. Intell. Educ. **12**, 257–279 (2001)
3. Chi, M.T., Siler, S.A., Jeong, H.: Can tutors monitor students' understanding accurately? Cogn. Instr. **22**, 363–387 (2004)
4. Chi, M., VanLehn, K., Litman, D., Jordan, P.: An evaluation of pedagogical tutorial tactics for a natural language tutoring system: a reinforcement learning approach. Int. J. Artif. Intell. Educ. **21**, 83–113 (2011)

5. Vygotsky, L.: Interaction between learning and development. Read. Dev. Child. **23**, 34–41 (1978)
6. Chounta, I.-A., McLaren, B.M., Albacete, P., Jordan, P., Katz, S.: Modeling the zone of proximal development with a computational approach. In: Proceedings of the 10th International Conference on Educational Data Mining (EDM 2017) (2017)
7. Reber, A.S.: The Penguin Dictionary of Psychology. Penguin Press, London (1995)
8. Chaiklin, S.: The zone of proximal development in Vygotsky's analysis of learning and instruction. Vygotsky's Educ. Theory Cult. Context **1**, 39–64 (2003)
9. Tzuriel, D.: Dynamic assessment of young children: educational and intervention perspectives. Educ. Psychol. Rev. **12**, 385–435 (2000)
10. Poehner, M.E., Lantolf, J.P.: Bringing the ZPD into the equation: capturing L2 development during Computerized Dynamic Assessment (C-DA). Lang. Teach. Res. **17**, 323–342 (2013)
11. Feuerstein, R., Rand, Y., Jensen, M.R., Kaniel, S., Tzuriel, D.: Prerequisites for assessment of learning potential: the LPAD model. Dyn. Assess., 35–51 (1987)
12. Luckin, R., Du Boulay, B.: others: Ecolab: The development and evaluation of a Vygotskian design framework. Int. J. Artif. Intell. Educ. **10**, 198–220 (1999)
13. Corbett, A.T., Koedinger, K.R., Anderson, J.R.: Intelligent tutoring systems. Handb. Hum.-Comput. Interact. **5**, 849–874 (1997)
14. Martin, B., Mitrovic, A., Koedinger, K.R., Mathan, S.: Evaluating and improving adaptive educational systems with learning curves. User Model. User-Adapt. Interact. **21**, 249–283 (2011)
15. Hedegaard, M.: 10 The zone of proximal development as basis for instruction. In: Introduction to Vygotsky, p. 227 (2005)
16. Katz, S., Allbritton, D., Connelly, J.: Going beyond the problem given: How human tutors use post-solution discussions to support transfer. Int. J. Artif. Intell. Educ. **13**, 79–116 (2003)
17. Katz, S., Albacete, P.L.: A tutoring system that simulates the highly interactive nature of human tutoring. J. Educ. Psychol. **105**, 1126 (2013)
18. Evens, M., Michael, J.: One-on-one tutoring by humans and computers. Psychology Press, New York (2006)
19. Jordan, P., Albacete, P., Katz, S.: Exploring contingent step decomposition in a tutorial dialogue system. In: The 24th Conference on User Modeling, Adaptation and Personalization (UMAP)
20. Cen, H., Koedinger, K., Junker, B.: Comparing two IRT models for conjunctive skills. In: Woolf, B.P., Aïmeur, E., Nkambou, R., Lajoie, S. (eds.) ITS 2008. LNCS, vol. 5091, pp. 796–798. Springer, Heidelberg (2008). doi:10.1007/978-3-540-69132-7_111
21. Chi, M., Koedinger, K.R., Gordon, G.J., Jordan, P., VanLehn, K.: Instructional factors analysis: a cognitive model for multiple instructional interventions. In: Proceedings of the 4th International Conference on Educational Data Mining, pp. 61–70 (2011)
22. Kiremire, A.R.: The application of the Pareto principle in software engineering. Consult. January 13, 2016 (2011)

Machine and Human Observable Differences in Groups' Collaborative Problem-Solving Behaviours

Mutlu Cukurova[1(✉)], Rose Luckin[1], Manolis Mavrikis[1], and Eva Millán[2]

[1] UCL Knowledge Lab, University College London, London, UK
m.cukurova@ucl.ac.uk
[2] University of Málaga, Málaga, Spain

Abstract. This paper contributes to our understanding of how to design learning analytics to capture and analyse collaborative problem-solving (CPS) in practice-based learning activities. Most research in learning analytics focuses on student interaction in digital learning environments, yet still most learning and teaching in schools occurs in physical environments. Investigation of student interaction in physical environments can be used to generate observable differences among students, which can then be used in the design and implementation of Learning Analytics. Here, we present several original methods for identifying such differences in groups CPS behaviours. Our data set is based on human observation, hand position (fiducial marker) and heads direction (face recognition) data from eighteen students working in six groups of three. The results show that the high competent CPS groups spend an equal distribution of time on their problem-solving and collaboration stages. Whereas, the low competent CPS groups spend most of their time in identifying knowledge and skill deficiencies only. Moreover, as machine observable data shows, high competent CPS groups present symmetrical contributions to the physical tasks and present high synchrony and individual accountability values. The findings have significant implications on the design and implementation of future learning analytics systems.

Keywords: Collaborative learning · Problem-solving · Learning analytics

1 Introduction

Open-ended, collaborative, practical learning activities are an essential part of STEM education and are employed as part of many common teaching approaches, including problem-based learning, inquiry-based learning, project-based learning, and practice-based learning. Such constructivist teaching approaches have potential to help foster the 21st century learning skills we require of young people across subject domains [1]. However, existing evidence on the effective- ness of these methods to satisfy common learning outcomes is rare [2, 3]. As argued by Blikstein and Worsley [4], one reason for this is that evaluation in this context is notoriously laborious and requires measurement methods that the current standardized testing strategies and psychometrics cannot provide. On the other hand, multimodal learning analytics (MMLA) research can yield novel methods that can generate distinctive information about what happens when

É. Lavoué et al. (Eds.): EC-TEL 2017, LNCS 10474, pp. 17–29, 2017.
DOI: 10.1007/978-3-319-66610-5_2

students are engaged in practice-based learning activities [4]. This information can be used to inform student models, which allow to automate the support and continuous evaluation of student skills [5]. In this paper, we focus on students collaborative problem solving (CPS) ability. CPS is one of the fundamental teaching and learning strategies involved in constructivist pedagogies, such as practice-based learning. We present an empirical study through which we explored CPS behaviours in six groups of three students (aged 11–12 years) while they were working on a practice-based activity. The main goal of this study is to investigate observable differences between groups of students during CPS (both human observable and machine observable). These differences can be used to provide support for behaviours that lead to effective CPS and help automate the identification of patterns of effective CPS behaviours. In this vein, there are already some research efforts to automate the discovery of patterns of interaction that can be associated with different collaboration strategies, which can lead to more effective collaboration [5, 6]. However, overwhelming majority of these approaches collect data from students interaction in digital learning environments. Differently in our approach, we focus on data from face-to-face learning environments.

2 What is Collaborative Problem-Solving?

It is important that we make clear what we mean by the term CPS, because, as learning analytics developers, we rely on clear definitions of complex terms to drive the analysis of our data. The research questions are themselves shaped by theoretical understanding, which enables researchers to make sense of their data [8]. Drawing from these considerations, we initially start by the OECD's definition. Collaborative problem-solving competency is the capacity of an individual to effectively engage in a process whereby two or more agents attempt to solve a problem by sharing the understanding and effort required to come to a solution and pooling their knowledge, skills and efforts to reach that solution [7]. However, the OECD approach is not complete in its reflection of CPS. It should be noted that the OECD approach was developed for assessment purposes, which results in a couple of limitations. First, the process of CPS is only considered from an individual capacity perspective. This makes sense from the OECDs perspective since PISA assessments are done at the individual level. However, CPS is a multilevel process and needs to be considered from different perspectives, which must reflect the needs of individuals, groups and communities and these different perspectives should be taken into account in the design and investigation of CPS processes [9]. Second, the OECDs approach does not include some components of problem-solving, which are considered as important when CPS is considered as a tuition approach [11]. For example, it does not take into account the element of identifying each participants knowledge deficiency [10]. In this research study, we, therefore, use a theoretical framework that is based on PISAs exhaustive work on CPS, combined with research that has considered CPS as a tuition process.

3 Experiment and Methodology

3.1 Participants

The participants were eighteen secondary school students in the first year of their secondary education (aged 11–12 years) from a girls-only secondary school in the UK. All students were recruited from a computer science class. We obtained written consent from both students and their parents/guardians in line with our institutions ethics procedures.

3.2 Learning Activity

The activity was conducted as part of students computer science school curriculum activity with physical computing kits. However, due to the practical issues of the transport of the learning analytics system, students and the teachers were invited to the leading author's institute to undertake the activity. Students were set the task of building a working prototype of an interactive toy using an Arduino-based physical computing kit, called TALKOO, that was created as part of an EU-funded project (www.pelars.eu). The TALKOO kit comprises hardware modules, a visual IDE and prototyping material. Sensor and actuator modules are pluggable and do not require soldering, and no prior knowledge of electronics is needed. The students were also provided with craft materials (coloured paper, paper cups, wooden sticks, glitter, glue, etc.) with which to create their working prototypes in combination with the physical computing kit.

3.3 Sessions

The session lasted about four hours and involved:

1. A refresher session, during which students worked through predefined ac- tivities that exemplified the functions of TALKOO components and logic functions (as in Session 1) - 30 min
2. An open-ended activity to build an interactive toy 2 h
3. A brief activity to demonstrate the function of a motor 15 min
4. An open-ended activity to build an artefact using a motor 1 h

Activities (1) and (3) were led by a researcher in collaboration with the class teacher, who demonstrated how to connect and program the components. During activities (2) and (4) groups worked independently, but each group was supported by an adult, who assisted the students with troubleshooting the TALKOO kit and debugging the visual programming.

3.4 Research Questions, Data Sources and Research Variables

The overarching research aim of this study was to identify human and machine observable differences in student behaviours in groups during CPS. This aim was shaped into three research questions:

- (RQ1) What are the human observable differences between groups, in terms of the amount of time spent in different CPS competencies?
- (RQ2) What are the machine observable differences between groups, in terms of nonverbal indexes of students physical interactivity?
- (RQ3) What constructs of CPS can be identified using the nonverbal indexes of students physical interactivity?

Data sources and research variables for the first research question
The data source for the first research question takes the form of human collected observation data. The collection of this observation data was structured by a theoretical framework developed through previous empirical work: the PELARS CPS framework [11]. This framework was informed by the OECDs CPS assessment and encompasses three collaboration competencies (namely, establishing and maintaining shared understanding, taking appropriate actions to solve the problem, establishing and maintaining group organisation) and six problem-solving competencies (namely, identifying facts, representing and formulating knowledge, generating hypothesis, planning and executing, identifying knowledge and skill deficiencies, monitoring-reflecting-applying). The framework has been used to develop an observation protocol and mobile application that runs on phones, tablets and laptops.

During activities (2) and (4), each group was observed by an adult, who used the mobile application to code the instantiates of collaboration and problem solving, as defined by the protocol in the PELARS CPS framework. In order to ensure high level of agreement between different coders, all coders were trained in a day-long, hands-on workshop about the CPS competencies and the observation tool we built based on the framework. The human observers watched student activity and used the tool to mark the critical incidents that relate to the key dimensions for collaboration and problem-solving as they occurred. The tool recorded the exact date and time each dimension was marked by the hu- man observer and we calculated the total amount of time spent on different dimensions of the CPS competencies.

The data collected with this observation tool was used to define two related research variables:

TPS (G, Ci) = Percentage of time each group G spent in each competence level Ci relative to problem-solving, where G = Red, Green, Purple, Blue, Yellow, Black and i = 1, 2, 3, 4, 5, 6.

TCL (G, Ci) = Percentage of time each group G spent in each competence level Ci related to collaboration, where G = Red, Green, Purple, Blue, Yellow, Black and i = 1, 2, 3.

Data sources and research variables for the second research question
In addition to the human observation data, we also collected video recordings of all of the empirical sessions. We analysed the video data using two variables that can also be automatically observed using our multimodal learning analytics system [12]:

(a) students' hand positions, that can be used to represent their physical engagement with objects; (b) students face directions, that might indicate their degree of involvement in the activity (depending on whether they are looking at the manipulated objects, at other students in their group, or at something outside the activity being carried out).

Video data analysis was performed by two researchers using a coding scheme, that is used to inform the future development of the automatic data capture facilities of our computer vision system. The coding scheme makes use of three digits, 0, 1 and 2 to represent passive, semi-active and active student states. The active code (2) was used whenever a student's hand was active with an object; the semi-active code (1) was used when a student was not physically active, but their head was directed towards a peer who was active; and the passive code (0) was used for the rest of the situations. Students behaviours were coded using ten-second windows. To validate the coding, two coders applied this coding scheme to all groups video data using the 10- second window. This procedure was used as a way of testing the reliability of the coding system generated. Where there was disagreement, the researchers discussed the data and agreed a revised coding accordingly. Although, there was no objective measure for the inter-coder reliability, thanks to the simplicity of the coding scheme (0, 1 and 2 codes), there were only a few disagreements between coders.

To use this information in our research questions 2 we defined two research variables, designed to account for the physical activity for the group and for each individual student, respectively.

N(G, i) = Percentage of i states in group G, where i = 0, 1, 2 and G = Red, Green, Purple, Blue, Yellow, Black.

Nj(G, i) = Percentage of i states for student j in group G, where j = 1, 2, 3; i = 0, 1, 2 and G = Red, Green, Purple, Blue, Yellow, Black.

Data sources and research variables for the third research question

Finally, for the third research question we to represent the situation of each group at a given time by concatenating the activity code for each of its student at a given moment.

Fig. 1. Photos that show examples of situations coded as 012, 121, 002, 202

For example, coding examples for the situations pictured in each of the four photographs are shown in Fig. 1.

The use of active, semi-active and passive codes provides 27 potential combinations for three students working together could be at any particular point in time. We categorized these positions into groups of 10 situations and identified potential predictors of CPS. Table 1 below presents this categorization (position and situations).

Table 1. Positions, situations and predictors

Potential positions of three students CPS	Categorised situations of three students CPS
000	Only 0s (000)
100, 010, 001	Two 0, one 1 (001)
200, 020, 002	Two 0, one 2 (002)
011, 101, 100	Two 1, one 0 (011)
012, 021, 102, 120, 201, 210	One of each (012)
111	Only 1s (111)
002, 020, 200	One 0, two 2s (022)
112, 121, 211	One two, two 1s (211)
122, 212, 221	One 1, two 2s (221)
222	Only 2s (222)

Next, we studied how we can use the learning sciences theories to make sense of students nonverbal indexes of physical interactions to create further signifiers of students CPS processes. To this end, we have investigated two concepts, namely (1) group synchrony and (2) individual accountability.

(1) Group Synchrony: The quality of the collaboration is related with the quality of the relationships of the students within the groups [13]. This relationship quality is dependent on multiple aspects of group dynamics including reciprocity, impressions about others in the group, the feeling of being a community with other group members, and the perceptions about mutual dependency to achieve the aim [13]. Some of these psychosocial processes of social interactions might be interpreted through observation of students physical interactions. For instance, when groups are working well, students appear to converge their actions such that they move in unison [14]. In the learning analytics research context, Schneider and Pea [15] found that students visual synchrony, measured with eye-trackers, positively correlated with students learning gains. However, this finding was contradicted when it came to body synchrony. Schneider and Blikstein [16] found that even though gaze synchrony can be a strong predictor of student learning, body synchrony does not hold the same properties. In our study, we propose the use of a variable to account for synchrony in each group, which we define as Syn(G) = percentage of 222 states in group G, where G = Red,…, Black

(2) Individual Accountability: Individual accountability refers to students making sure that they undertake their share of the work ad feel personally responsible for the groups success while others are also undertaking their share in completing the task. As argued by Slavin [17] in his synthesis of research so far undertaken in the domain

group goals and individual accountability are the two key features of any successful group work. In groups that present high collaboration, students engage in promotive interaction and show a willingness to support each other in their joint efforts to complete the task and achieve the goal [17]. Therefore there appear to be two main requirements of individual accountability (1) students should undertake their share in completing the task, (2) each students share is promoted and acknowledged by other members of the group. In a learning analytics context, individual accountability is often considered to be measured with the amount of input generated by individual students. This satisfies the first requirement of individual accountability. However, individual students promotion and acknowledgement should also be taken into account in considerations of individual accountability. In order to interpret students promotion and acknowledgment of each others contribution, we added the percentage of those situations in which at least one member student is purposefully observing the action taken by a member of the group (221 + 211) and subtracted those situations in which at least one student is ignoring an action taken by a member of the group (220, 210, 200). That is, to represent individual accountability we have defined the following variable: IA(G) = percentage of 222 and 221 percentage of 220, 210 and 200, where G = Red,…., Black

Independent variable: Classroom Teacher and Facilitators Judgement of Groups CPS

In order to create an independent variable to categorise the differences between groups of students, the class teacher and facilitators involved in the activity were asked to use their expertise and experiences as teachers to judge each groups CPS competence. They were all asked to watch the video recordings of the six group sessions and to independently rank groups as high, medium and low competence CPS groups. Then, teachers and facilitators were brought together to discuss their individual judgments. In their individual judgments of the CPS competency of the groups, there were only discrepancies for two groups. Discussion between teachers and facilitators was used to agree a final competency value for these two groups. Table 2 below shows the results of this expert evaluation of groups CPS levels (see Table 2 below).

Table 2. Classification of students' groups according to their level of CPS

Colour code of group	Teachers' judgement of CPS competency
Green	Low
Red	High
Purple	Medium
Blue	Medium
Yellow	High
Black	Low

4 Results

4.1 Identifying Observable Differences in Terms of the Amount of Time Spent by Student Groups on Different CPS Competencies

As Figs. 2 and 3 present, the red and yellow groups (which were identi- fied as high competency CPS groups by their teachers) show a more balanced segregation of different problem-solving activities: they spend their time fairly equally on the different dimensions of collaboration and problem-solving. By contrast, the other groups show unbalanced segregation of time spent in different CPS competencies. It appears that green and black groups (which were identified as low CPS groups by their teachers) spend most of their time on identifying knowledge and skill deficiencies. They spent very little or no time on the some of the important stages of problem solving, such as representing and formulating knowledge, generating hypotheses, and planning and executing.

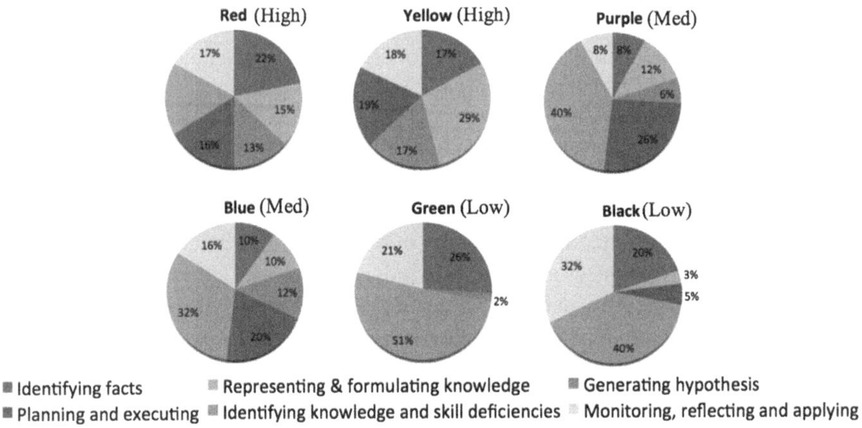

Fig. 2. Results for TPS (percentage of time each group devoted to each competency)

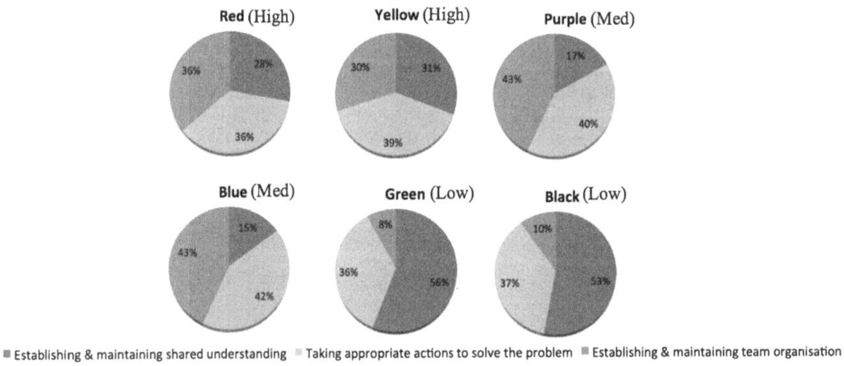

Fig. 3. Results for TCL (percentage of time each group devoted to each competency)

These behaviours might therefore be indicative of a less effective problem-solving pattern. The data from the red and yellow groups also evidences that they spent similar shares of time on different aspects of collaboration competencies. The green and purple groups, by comparison, present a greater difference in terms of the amount of time spent on the different aspects of collaboration. It appears that groups who had been evaluated as low CPS competent by human experts spent very little time on establishing and maintaining team organization, com- pared to other groups.

The experts rated the red and yellow groups to be the high CPS competent groups, and it may, therefore, be the case that a balance between the different types of problem solving and collaboration activities is an indicator of effective CPS. Measuring the different amounts of time spent of key dimensions of CPS appears to be an effective method for identifying CPS competencies. However, it heavily relies on human observation of critical incidents. Next, we investigate machine observable features of CPS behaviours as part of our second and third research questions.

4.2 Identifying Observable Differences in Nonverbal Indexes of Student Interactivity

Figure 4 above illustrates that the percentage of active states (2) was similar across all six groups and ranged from 46.4% (Black) to 66.4% (Yellow). It is interesting to observe that the group with the highest percentage of active code (2), yellow group with 66.4%, was judged as a high CPS group by human experts. Similarly, the group with the lowest of active codes (2), black group with 46.4%, was rated by human experts as a low CPS competency group. However, this result does not lead to the conclusion that high active code percentage leads to high CPS competency. The other group rated by our experts as having low CPS competency (green group) had the second highest percentage of active codes (2), and the other group rated as being high CPS competency (red group) has the second lowest percentage of active codes (2). This result suggests that the crude measure of the percentage of active states may not be a suitable indicator for differentiating the quality of the collaboration in the group (i.e. just individual students activity with objects may not be contributing to CPS overall). However, we also considered if students passive codes (0) might be a predictor. The red and yellow groups had the lowest percentages of passive codes (0). By contrast, the green and black groups had the highest

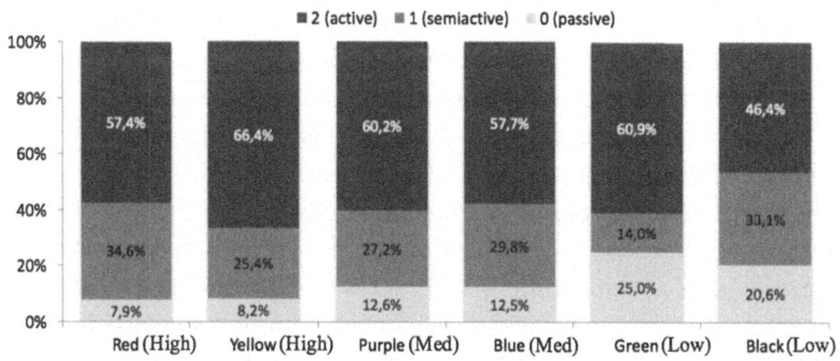

Fig. 4. Percentage of total number of passive 0, semi-active 1, and active 2 codes

percentages of passive codes (0). *This result is surprising because the most researched and tracked indicators used in learning analytics research are often related to what students are doing. Our results suggest observing what students are not doing might be also informative.*

We show in Fig. 5 the values obtained for the research variables Nj(G, i). It illustrates that the individual students in the red and yellow groups get similar values for all the codes. The rest of the groups, by contrast, show greater differences between each students individual contributions. In the red group all three partners show a similar degree of involvement in the activity (2 code), ranging from 53,1% to 62,2%. However, in the green group there is a greater difference in the degree of involvement (for S3 it is s 23.1% to and for S2 is 82,1%). Clearly, in the red and yellow groups all members were contributing to the task similarly active ways, while in the other two groups students physical interactions were more passive and varied more.

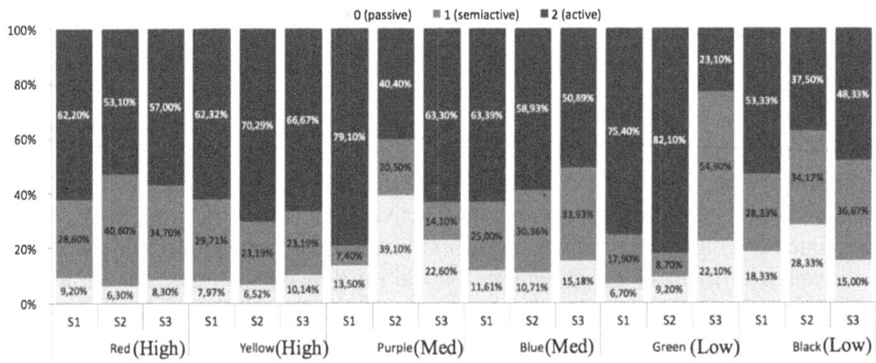

Fig. 5. Percentage of individual students number of passive 0, semi-active 1, and active 2 codes

4.3 Identifying Potential Predictors of CPS

Figure 6 presents the CPS rating of our human experts for each group and the percentages of different categories of situations. Note that the last two rows in this table correspond to the values of the proposed variables to measure the synchrony Syn(G) and individual accountability IA(G), as defined previously.

The first feature that can be identified in Fig. 6 is the total percentage of time that each group spent off-task (represented by the code 000) and the total percentage of time each group spent observing their teacher or a facilitator intervention (represented by the code 111). We can see that the percentage of off- task situations is very low, ranging from 0.4% in the yellow group to 7,4% in the purple one. Also, the low percentage of 111 states indicates little intervention from facilitators or teachers occurred. Perhaps more interestingly, the respective values of the two proposed measures, synchrony SYN(G) and individual accountability IA(G), show that groups rated by experts as being high CPS competent appear to have high percentages for both constructs. For instance, the red group spent 24.50% of their time in synchronized activity, whereas the green group only spent 5.4% of their time in synchronized activity. Similarly, for individual

	Red	Yellow	Purple	Blue	Green	Black
000	2.40%	0.50%	7.4%	6.4%	3.6%	4.2%
111	5.50%	0.00%	0.0%	0.0%	0.0%	2.5%
001	0.90%	1.00%	0.0%	0.0%	0.9%	2.5%
002	3.10%	5.10%	7.4%	11.2%	8.0%	16.7%
011	0.90%	1.00%	0.0%	0.0%	0.0%	1.7%
012	5.00%	10.30%	9.6%	11.2%	7.1%	8.3%
022	2.80%	12.80%	18.8%	8.0%	27.7%	25.8%
211	24.90%	15.90%	25.7%	26.4%	24.1%	18.3%
221	30.10%	36.40%	20.1%	24.8%	23.2%	11.7%
SYN (G)	24.50%	16.90%	11.0%	12.0%	5.4%	8.3%
IA (G)	44.10%	24.10%	10.15%	20.80%	4.46%	-20.83%
Expert Evaluation of CPS competency	High	High	Medium	Medium	Low	Low

Fig. 6. Percentages of the different situations across the six groups

accountability, yellow groups calculated value is 24.10%, whereas for the green group this value is 4.5%. These results reveal an interesting correlation between the CPS quality of a group as judged by our human experts and their synchronization and individual accountability values calculated via nonverbal indexes of students physical interactivity. In the previously cited study [16], the researchers studied dyads collaborating remotely and found that body synchrony might not correlate with collaboration. However, the dynamics of three students working together in the same physical space on an open-ended task appear to be different.

5 Discussion and Conclusions

This paper reports an empirical study of young students engaging with CPS activities. We present several methods for identifying differences in groups CPS behaviour in PBL activities, based on human observation and students hand and head position data. We show that machine observable nonverbal indexes of student behaviours may be used to interpret certain educational constructs that are fundamental to CPS processes, such as individual accountability and synchronisation. The differences in group behaviours, presented by our data, provide evidence to support the suggestion that there might be a relationship between the competency of a groups CPS and their human and machine observable behaviours. This relationship requires further investigation, but our initial results are encouraging for those involved in the design of Learning Analytics. In this section, we discuss the answers to our research questions based on the three results sections presented above.

Our initial research question was to identify whether there are observable differences between group behaviours in terms of the amount of time spent on different CPS competencies. We used human observation data to answer this question and our results show clear differences between groups. Specifically, the high CPS competent groups spent more or less an equal distribution of time on their problem-solving stages. Whereas, the low CPS competent groups spent most of their time in identifying knowledge and skill deficiencies, whilst spend- ing very little time or no time on other important aspects of problem-solving including, identifying facts, generating hypotheses, and representing knowledge. Although, appear to be effective, such human judgment based methods are hard to detect via learning analytics tools. However, such investigations of fine-grained actions of CPS can be used as tools to support the identification of knowledge distributions, to support the communication of knowledge inside groups, and, as a consequence of the cognitive group awareness, to facilitate organizational tasks. They can also be used to inform open learner models, to improve students reflective practice.

Our second research question required that we investigated the potential of students physical activity data, which is based on their hand and head positions. The results show that our coding scheme can provide useful data to identify group differences. First, these differences can be used to identify which students were left out or excluded from the CPS process. Second, and perhaps more importantly, the results show that, in high competent CPS groups, all students percentages of active, semi-active and passive scores overlapped and presented similar figures. However, in low CPS competent groups, individual students data did not illustrate similarities. In their early research Damon and Phelps [18] introduce two terms: equality and mutuality. Equality is a situation where participants are equal in status and participate in a two-way dialogue taking direction from one another; and mutuality is a situation where high mutuality means that discourse is extensive, intimate and connected. Authors argue that CPS should be high in both equality and mutuality. Looking at the results presented in Fig. 6, some groups present more symmetrical individual contributions than others, which might reflect their effective CPS competencies in terms of their equality and mutuality.

Finally, our results show that students hand and head position data can be used to interpret group synchrony and individual accountability. Groups who were rated by human experts as having high CPS also presented a high percentage in group synchrony and individual accountability. We argue that the results of such differences, particularly, when they are triangulated with the data from other sources, may be used to identify effective CPS in an analytical and subjective way.

This exploratory study was limited to a small number of groups and, there- fore, the results reported in this research paper should be approached with caution and we do not suggest that they are conclusive. However, we see the work presented here as an opportunity to lay the groundwork for future studies researching CPS in real-world environments under three research themes. First, our simple coding scheme of students active, semi-active and passive positions can inform the design of automated analysis systems of CPS from video data. Second, this study can inform the research in supervised machine learning approaches to automatically categorise students' CPS competences based on acquired multimodal data [19]. The observable features of CPS identified here can be used to label training data for algorithms. Third, human and machine observable features of CPS can be visualised with the purpose of improving reflective practice of students during their skill development activities.

Acknowledgements. This work is co-funded by the European Union under the PELARS project. The fourth author was partially supported by Agencia Estatal de Investigacion (AEI) y el Fondo Europeo de Desarrollo Regional (FEDER), TIN2016-80774-R.

References

1. Banks, F., Barlex, D.: Teaching STEM in the secondary school: Helping teachers meet the challenge. Routledge, London (2014)
2. Kirschner, P.A., Sweller, J., Clark, R.E.: Why minimal guidance during instruction does not work: an analysis of the failure of constructivist, discovery, problem-based, experiential, and inquiry-based teaching. Educ. Psychol. **41**(2), 75–86 (2006)
3. Klahr, D., Nigam, M.: The equivalence of learning paths in early science instruction effects of direct instruction and discovery learning. Psychol. Sci. **15**(10), 661–667 (2004)
4. Blikstein, P., Worsley, M.: Multimodal learning analytics and education data mining: using computational technologies to measure complex learning tasks. J. Learn. Anal. **3**(2), 220–238 (2016)
5. Rodríguez, F.J., Boyer, K.E.: Discovering individual and collaborative problem-solving modes with hidden Markov models. In: Conati, C., Heffernan, N., Mitrovic, A., Verdejo, M.F. (eds.) AIED 2015. LNCS, vol. 9112, pp. 408–418. Springer, Cham (2015). doi: 10.1007/978-3-319-19773-9_41
6. Martinez-Maldonado, R., Kay, J., Yacef, K.: An automatic approach for mining patterns of collaboration around an interactive tabletop. In: Lane, H.C., Yacef, K., Mostow, J., Pavlik, P. (eds.) AIED 2013. LNCS, vol. 7926, pp. 101–110. Springer, Heidelberg (2013). doi: 10.1007/978-3-642-39112-5_11
7. OECD: Draft Collaborative Problem Solving Framework (2015). http://www.oecd.org/pisa/pisaproducts/Draft. PISA 2015 Collaborative Problem Solving Framework.pdf
8. Luckin, R., Baines, E., Cukurova, M., Holmes, W.: Solved! Making the case for collaborative problem-solving. London, NESTA (2017)
9. Dillenbourg, P., Jermann, P.: Designing integrative scripts. In: Fischer, F., Kollar, I., Mandl, H., Haake, J.M. (eds.) Scripting Computer-Supported Collaborative Learning: Cognitive, Computational and Educational Perspectives, pp. 275–301. Springer, Boston (2007)
10. Hmelo-Silver, C.E.: Problem-based learning: what and how do students learn. Educ. Psychol. Rev. **16**(3), 235–266 (2004)
11. Cukurova, M., Avramides, K., Spikol, D., Luckin, R., Mavrikis, M.: An analysis framework for collaborative problem solving in practice-based learning activities: a mixed-method approach. In: LAK 2016, pp. 84–88. ACM (2016)
12. Ruffaldi, E., Dabisias, G., Landolfi, L., Spikol, D.: Data collection and processing for a multimodal learning analytic system. In: SAI 2016, pp. 858–863 (2003)
13. Kreijns, K., Kirschner, P.A., Jochems, W.: Identifying the pitfalls for social interaction in computer-supported collaborative learning environments: a review of the research. Comput. Hum. Behav. **19**(3), 335–353 (2003)
14. Lakens, D., Stel, M.: If they move in sync, they must feel in sync. Soc. Cogn. **29**(1), 1–14 (2011)
15. Schneider, B., Pea, R.: Real-time mutual gaze perception en- hances collaborative learning and collaboration quality. Int. J. Comput. Support. Collab. Learn. **8**(4), 375–397 (2013)
16. Schneider, B., Blikstein, P.: Unraveling students' interaction around a tangible interface using multimodal learning analytics. J. Educ. Data Min. **7**(3), 89–116 (2015)
17. Slavin, R.E.: Synthesis of research of cooperative learning. Educ. Leadersh. **48**(5), 71–82 (1991)
18. Damon, W., Phelps, E.: Critical distinctions among three approaches to peer education. Int. J. Educ. Res. **13**(1), 9–19 (1989)
19. Spikol, D., Ruffaldi, E., Cukurova, M.: Using Multimodal Learning Analytics to Identify Aspects of Collaboration in Project-Based Learning. In: CSCL 2017, Philadelphia, PA (2017)

Diagnosing Collaboration in Practice-Based Learning: Equality and Intra-individual Variability of Physical Interactivity

Mutlu Cukurova[1(✉)], Rose Luckin[1], Eva Millán[2], Manolis Mavrikis[1], and Daniel Spikol[3]

[1] UCL Knowledge Lab, University College London, London, UK
m.cukurova@ucl.ac.uk
[2] University of Málaga, Málaga, Spain
[3] University of Malmo, Malmö, Sweden

Abstract. Collaborative problem solving (CPS), as a teaching and learning approach, is considered to have the potential to improve some of the most important skills to prepare students for their future. CPS often differs in its nature, practice, and learning outcomes from other kinds of peer learning approaches, including peer tutoring and cooperation; and it is important to establish what identifies collaboration in problem-solving situations. The identification of indicators of collaboration is a challenging task. However, students physical interactivity can hold clues of such indicators. In this paper, we investigate two non-verbal indexes of student physical interactivity to interpret collaboration in practice-based learning environments: equality and intra-individual variability. Our data was generated from twelve groups of three Engineering students working on open-ended tasks using a learning analytics system. The results show that high collaboration groups have member students who present high and equal amounts of physical interactivity and low and equal amounts of intra-individual variability.

Keywords: Collaborative learning · Problem-solving · Indexes of physical interaction · Behaviour patterns

1 Introduction and Research Questions

Collaborative problem solving (CPS), as a teaching and learning approach, has potential to provide opportunities to learners to practice and improve skills that are key to their future success in life. In addition to skill development, CPS can allow students to apply their knowledge, to explain it clearly to others, to synthesize it with fresh knowledge and knowledge from other subject areas [1]. CPS, therefore, helps learners acquire important subject knowledge. However, the research evidence from meta-level reviews shows that such improvement in skills and knowledge specific to CPS is rare. There is good evidence that well designed and managed peer learning, conducted by learners who have sufficient knowledge and skill and supported by teachers who also have the requisite skills, has a positive impact on learning including attainment in science [2, 3], mathematics [4], literacy [5] and upon learner attitudes [6]. However,

É. Lavoué et al. (Eds.): EC-TEL 2017, LNCS 10474, pp. 30–42, 2017.
DOI: 10.1007/978-3-319-66610-5_3

this evidence is generated from meta-analyses and reviews of research based on studies examining peer-tutoring, cooperative learning, collaborative learning and collaborative problem-solving all together.

Although, these concepts are related, they are not synonymous. Clear distinctions were drawn between such group work pedagogies in theory (See for instance [7, 8]). These distinctions are seldom found in research papers and reviews of empirical work. However, they are important as different pedagogical approaches to students learning together, have different quality and degree of interaction and differ in their likelihood of achieving certain learning outcomes. For instance, collaborative and cooperative peer instructions are found to be more suited to students conceptual understanding, whereas peer-tutoring activities were found to be more appropriate for practice using concepts already acquired [9]. If the learning outcome of a session is to master a particular task that can be divided into sub-tasks, which can be achieved by individual students, cooperative learning, in which the learning group tackles the problems by dividing up the responsibility, may be more appropriate. Examples of such cooperative approaches involve jigsaw method [10] or the Sharan method [11].

On the other hand, if the task or the problem at hand cannot be achieved by any individual students on their own, then a collaborative learning approach is required, because it is particularly effective when solving problems that impose a high cognitive load [12]. As argued by Kirschner et al. [12] cognitive load theory suggests that collaborative learning may be effective for solving such problems and tasks that cannot be solved by any of the individuals in the group on their own, because it reduces load at the level of working memory within the minds of the individuals concerned. It was also showed in an experimental study [13] that collaborative learning was superior for high-complexity tasks, but inferior for low-complexity tasks. However, in practice, there is wide variation in group work with a lack of clarity regarding the impact of such variations on the intended learning outcomes and as argued by Damon and Phelps [7] "such lack of clarity places the credibility and educational usefulness of the entire enterprise of peers learning together at risk". This lack of clarity becomes even more ambiguous in practice-based teaching and learning environments due to the dynamic nature of the educational setting.

In this research study, we investigate two research questions aiming to provide more clarity to this variation in implementation of group learning in practice-based learning environments.

- RQ1. Can equality of physical interactivity and intra-individual variability be used as non-verbal indexes of collaboration in practice-based learning? Related to the first research question, our second research question is;
- RQ2. What amounts of physical interactivity and intra-individual variability represent collaboration in practice-based learning?

The proxies of student collaboration are often studied with verbal indexes [14, 15]. Nevertheless, the work discussed in this paper is based on a European project (PELARS) in which one of the aims is to develop learning analytics tools for hands-on, open-ended STEAM (Science, Technology, Engineering and Maths teaching through the means of Art) learning activities using physical computing. The project has developed a software system that includes customized furniture with an integrated

Learning Analytics System (LAS), that includes devices for tracking hands, faces and objects, and an Arduino platform with a visual web-based Integrated Development Environment (IDE), that captures information about interactions with these physical computing objects [16]. In this paper, we study non-verbal indexes of students physical interactivity. This is due to the challenges related to the collection and analysis of students' verbal indexes in dynamic practice-based learning environments.

2 The Importance of Collaboration and Problem-Solving Skills

One of the fundamental purposes of education is to support the teaching and learning process, so that each person is supported to achieve their potential. Although there are differences of opinion about what should be taught and how the teaching process should be conducted, there is some sense of agreement that the aim of education is to ensure that learners are equipped to meet their future needs, both in employment and generally in life. This perspective on education highlights the important role played by the skills that will be needed during the lifetime of students. More recently, these skills have been referred to as the 21st century skills [17], referring to the century in which current students will be living. There is no unanimously recognized definition of 21st century skills and various different suggestions exist. For example, the World Economic Forum (WEF) has proposed 16 skills [18], including collaboration and problem solving. A recent report from the UK Institute of Directors (2016) [19] stressed the need for schools to move away from the skills that are easiest to teach and test, because these are also the easiest to automate and therefore likely to be the least in demand in the workplace. They identified various skills as important including communication, collaboration and teamwork. These skills are essential for current and future work environments and they are key requirements of future education and training across the globe. Peer learning is intertwined with all the aforementioned key skills and is an increasingly common teaching approach to improve students 21st century skills. However, as we discussed in the introduction different practices of peer learning may lead to different learning outcomes, including different levels and types of skill development, as they involve different types and levels of student interactivity.

For instance, equality and mutuality are two indexes of student interactivity used to distinguish between three approaches to peer learning: peer tutoring, cooperative learning and collaborative learning. Equality refers to a situation where participants are equal in status and participate in a two-way dialogue taking direction from one another, while mutuality refers to a situation where high mutuality means that discourse is extensive, intimate and connected. As argued by Damon and Phelps [7] peer tutoring tends to foster dialogues that are relatively low on equality and varied in mutuality; cooperative learning foster ones that are relatively high in equality and low to moderate in mutuality; and peer collaboration fosters ones that are high in both. More recent researchers echo similar ideas. For instance, Dillenbourg et al. [20] use the concept of symmetry and argues that collaborative learning requires some sense of symmetry in terms of students knowledge and skills as well as their contribution to interactions. Identification of different approaches is key to create and apply learning tasks that achieve their intended learning outcomes (both in terms of skill development and knowledge) with more precision. One potential solution to identifying and differentiating these different approaches to students working together as a group in practice-based learning environments is to use indexes of students physical interactions. In this paper, we investigate two indexes of physical interactivity in order to identify unique features of collaborative problem solving in practice-based learning: (a) equality of students physical interactivity, and (b) intra-individual variability in students physical interactivity in practice-based learning activities.

The concept of equality is fairly self-explanatory and not novel to this research domain. However, students' intra-individual variability to our knowledge has not been investigated in the contexts of students' CPS in practice-based learning. As emphasised by various other researchers CPS tends to be inherently interactive, interdependent, and dynamic [21, 22]. CPS can only occur if the students attempt to create a common ground about the problem/task they are dealing with [23]. The establishment of such shared understanding occurs through students communication and interaction with each other about the meaning of the problem/task. Creation of a common ground among group members is based on students ability to understand behaviours, cognitions, and attitudes of other participants and oneself and to translate this understanding into appropriate behaviour in social situations [24]. In this dynamic context, the establishment of a common ground involves continuous correction of students performance based on reactions of others during social exchanges [25]. This continuous correction and change in behaviours require a dynamic systems approach [26] to students physical interactions, as therefore we argue that the investigation of students' intra-individual variability may generate insights into students' CPS in practice-based learning activities.

3 Methodology

3.1 Participants

The study discussed in this paper involves 12 sessions of groups of 3 Engineering students at a European University (average age 20 years old, with 17 men and 1 woman). Students were volunteers to take part in the research and they had no formal CPS training in the past. However, they all declared that they have experience of working in groups as part of their university courses. Each student group used the PELARS project system hardware, software and desk over 3 days, to complete 3 open-ended tasks.

3.2 The Task

The students were introduced to the PELARS project system and introduced to their first task. Task 1 required students to design and prototype an inter-active toy. Task 2 required students to design and prototype a colour sorting machine, and Task 3 required students to design and prototype an autonomous automobile. No specific instructions about the timing of these phases were given to students and sessions lasted between 33 and 75 min (with the median of 63 min).

3.3 Data Collection and Analysis

All sessions were video recorded through the PELARS learning analytics system. This video data was analysed by two researchers using a very simple coding scheme, which was designed to inform future automatic video analysis.

The coding scheme makes use of three digits, 0, 1 and 2 to represent passive, semi-active and active student physical states, respectively. The active code (2) was used whenever a student's hand was active with an object; the semi-active code (1) was used when a student was not physically active but their head was directed towards a peer who was active, or to the object he/she was manipulating, or to the screen; and the passive code (0) was used if a students hands were not physically active with any object and their head was directed towards a different position than any of their peers who were active. Students behaviours were coded using thirty seconds windows. Therefore the variable used for our research questions is the activity index AI, which takes values 0, 1, 2 and is defined in Eq. 1:

$$\mathrm{AI}(\mathrm{S}, \mathrm{G}, \mathrm{t}) := \text{Activity code of student S of group G at time t} \tag{1}$$

where S = 1, 2, 3; G = A, …, L and t = 30, 60, 90…

For example, in the situation represented by the photo shown in Fig. 1, the student to the left is coded as 2, while the other two students are coded as 1. To validate the coding, two coders applied this coding scheme to all groups video data using 30-second windows. Where there was disagreement, the researchers discussed the data and revised their coding accordingly. Thanks to the simplicity of the coding scheme, there were only a few differently coded 30 s windows, and these were resolved easily through discussion. This discussion involved playing the window again together to decide on the final code.

Fig. 1. A moment during students' work to exemplify the coding scheme

3.4 Observer Analysis of Collaborative Problem Solving Competencies

In addition to the data capture facilitated by the project system, human observers analysed student interactions as they happened using an analysis framework [27], based on OECDs work on CPS [28]. The analysis framework has three key dimensions of collaboration (Establishing and maintaining shared understanding, Taking appropriate actions to solve the problem, Establishing and maintaining team organisation), and six key dimensions of problem-solving (Identifying facts, Representing and formulating knowledge, Generating hypotheses, Planning and executing, Identifying knowledge and skill deficiencies, Monitoring, reflecting and applying). The human observer watches student activity and uses a mobile tool to mark the critical incidents that relate to the key dimensions of collaboration and problem solving as they occur [29]. The tool also records the exact date and time each dimension was marked by the human observer. Using this framework student groups were ranked as high, medium and low-level collaboration groups. The ranking was done based on threshold values of the frequency of critical incidents, and this ranking was used as an independent variable for the analysis presented in this paper.

4 Results

Table 1 shows the classification of the different groups using the observer coding. Groups D, F and J were coded as the highest CPS groups, whereas B and K were coded as the lowest CPS groups.

Table 1. Classification of students' groups according to their level of CPS

Group Code	Level of CPS competency
A	Medium
B	Low
C	Medium
D	High
E	Medium
F	High
G	Medium
H	Medium
I	Medium
J	High
K	Low
L	Medium

4.1 Equality of Students Physical Interactivity

In order to answer our first research question, we first investigated the extent to which the degree of equality observable in the students physical interactivity can be used as a non-verbal index to interpret collaboration in practice-based learning activities. To this end, we defined new research variables (Eq. 2):

$$\mathrm{Nj(G,i)} := \text{Percentage of i states for student j in group G} \tag{2}$$

where i, j = 1, 2, 3 and G = A, …, L

Figure 2 presents the coding of each students physical interactivity and illustrates that some groups showed more equality (e.g. groups I, J, D) than others. The distribution is irregular (e.g. groups B, E) and identifies the students who were more engaged (e.g., student S1 in group F) and students who were less engaged (e.g. student 1 in the A group). In order to have a better idea about the equality of students physical interactivity, we looked at the mean scores of their codes. Table 2 presents these results and indicates in dark grey the groups which were identified by the observer as high CPS groups. The groups identified as lower CPS are indicated by a lighter shade of grey.

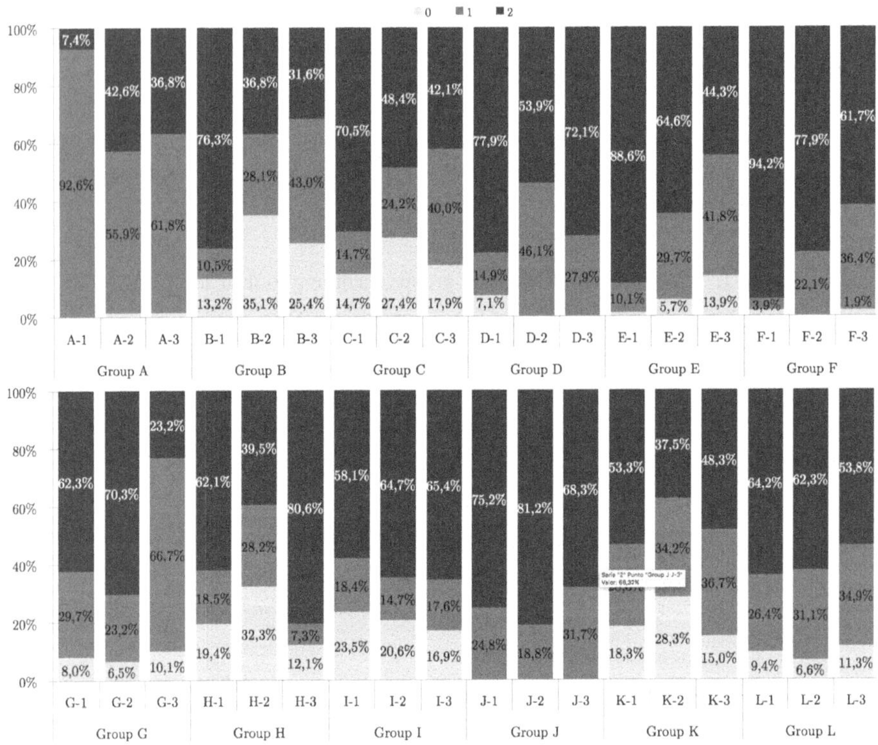

Fig. 2. Percentages of individual student's number of passive 0, semi-active 1, and active codes 2

As the results above show, those groups coded as high collaboration groups by human observers had higher mean scores for physical interactivity than those coded as

Table 2. Mean activity index per student, standard deviations, average mean and total mean differences

	Group A			Group B			Group C			Group D			Group E			Group F		
	A.s1	A.s2	A.s3	B.s1	B.s2	B.s3	C.s1	C.s2	C.s3	D.s1	D.s2	D.s3	E.s1	E.s2	E.s3	F.s1	F.s2	F.s3
Mean AI	1,07	1,41	1,35	1,71	1,07	1,12	1,63	1,29	1,33	1,70	1,60	1,75	1,87	1,60	1,31	1,92	1,78	1,60
Sd AI	0,26	0,53	0,51	1,71	1,07	1,12	0,64	0,78	0,65	0,61	0,49	0,43	0,37	0,59	0,70	0,33	0,42	0,53
Av. Mean	*1,28*			*1,30*			1,41			**1,68**			1,59			**1,77**		
Max. diff.	*0,68*			*1,27*			0,68			**0,31**			1,12			**0,65**		
	Group G			Group H			Group I			Group J			Group K			Group L		
Mean AI	G.s1	G.s2	G.s3	H.s1	H.s2	H.s3	I.s1	I.s2	I.s3	J.s1	J.s2	J.s3	K.s1	K.s2	K.s3	L.s1	L.s2	L.s3
Sd AI	1,54	1,64	1,13	1,45	1,10	1,71	1,43	1,55	1,58	1,75	1,81	1,68	1,35	1,09	1,33	1,55	1,56	1,42
Av. Mean	0,64	0,60	0,56	0,77	0,83	0,63	0,77	0,72	0,67	0,43	0,39	0,47	0,77	0,81	0,73	0,66	0,62	0,69
Max. diff.	1,44			1,42			1,52			**1,75**			*1,26*			1,51		
	1,01			1,23			0,29			**0,26**			*0,52*			0,26		

low collaboration groups. Considering the practice-based structure of the learning activity these results are not surprising. However, a finding that becomes clear from Table 2 is that the groups rated as high collaboration groups have member students whose physical interactivity mean scores are similar. By contrast, the groups rated as low collaboration groups have member students whose mean scores for the physical interactivity of each student are more varied. For instance, in group D, which was coded as a high collaboration group, the mean scores for the member students physical interactivity were s1 = 1.60, s2 = 1.70, and s3 = 1.75; and the average of differences between the three students physical interactivity scores was 0.31. On the other hand, the mean physical interactivity scores for member students of group B, which was coded as one of the low collaboration groups, were s1 = 1.07, s2 = 1.12, and s3 = 1.71 and the average of the differences between the three students physical interactivity was 1.27. The difference in physical interactivity scores for group B is approximately four times bigger than the average differences in the high collaboration group D. These results suggest that equality of students physical interactivity is a potential indicator of collaboration in practice-based learning activities. It is important to note that when the students physical interactivity is low, for instance, as in the case of the group K, which had the lowest average mean score for physical interactivity among all groups, then the ratio of the differences in scores by member students between low collaboration and high collaboration groups does not hold. The level of activity is too low.

4.2 Intra-individual Variability of Students Physical Interactivity

The second potential non-verbal indicator of collaboration we investigated is the intra-individual variability of students physical interactivity. Intra-individual variability refers to the amount of change in every single students behaviour between two sequential time windows. The cause of these changes were not taken into account and we used a simple statistical formula to calculate it as the mean sequential squared difference M. This formula is presented in Eq. 3:

$$M := \frac{1}{N-1}\sum_{k=1}^{N-1}(x_{k-1} - x_k)^2 \tag{3}$$

We consider M as a good method to calculate students intra-individual variability, as it represents the mean value of the total amount of changes in students physical interactivity. Table 3 shows the computed M for each student, together with the total group differences. Then the total differences values T are calculated by summing the differences of three students M values using the formula defined in Eq. 4.

$$T := (M_{max} - M_{mid}) + (M_{max} - M_{min}) + (M_{mid} - M_{min}) \tag{4}$$

Results show that high collaboration groups show lower M values, whereas low collaboration groups show higher M values. If we look at the average differences of individual students M scores, high collaboration groups appear to have the smallest three figures (Group D = 0.09, Group F = 0.33, Group J = 0.10), whereas low collaboration groups have the highest two figures (Group B = 0.64, Group K = 1.11). The low M values can be achieved if students continue their level of physical interactivity for longer periods of times, rather than having frequent changes in their interactivity. Figure 3 illustrates the chronological changes in M value for Group F, assessed as being a high CPS group and Group K, assessed as a low CPS group.

Table 3. M values per group and student and group M differences

	Group A			Group B			Group C			Group D			Group E			Group F		
	A.s1	A.s2	A.s3	B.s1	B.s2	B.s3	C.s1	C.s2	C.s3	D.s1	D.s2	D.s3	E.s1	E.s2	E.s3	F.s1	F.s2	F.s3
MSSD	0.54	0.61	0.83	0.52	0.61	0.84	0.68	0.89	0.51	0.29	0.27	0.24	0.27	0.53	0.42	0.20	0.25	0.38
Total diff.	*0.57*			*0.64*			*0.58*			**0.09**			*0.51*			**0.33**		
	Group G			Group H			Group I			Group J			Group K			Group L		
	G.s1	G.s2	G.s3	H.s1	H.s2	H.s3	I.s1	I.s2	I.s3	J.s1	J.s2	J.s3	K.s1	K.s2	K.s3	L.s1	L.s2	L.s3
MSSD	0.60	0.41	0.63	0.73	0.76	0.45	0.77	0.58	0.72	0.22	0.22	0.27	0.98	0.92	0.43	0.82	0.60	0.54
Total diff.	*0.44*			*0.63*			*0.38*			**0.10**			*1.11*			*0.55*		

One potential explanation for continuing on the same action is that, students have a sense of mutual understanding of the task/problem they are working on. When such mutual understanding does not occur among group members, their actions may appear to vary more often as they stop and start their physical activities more frequently. The importance of mutual understanding as a dimension of collaboration has been recognized by other researchers (e.g. [30–32]). And the magnitude of change in physical interactivity measurement may be one option to interpret this mutual understanding. Our results suggest that the intra-individual variability of students physical interactivity is another potential indicator of collaborative problem solving in practice-based learning activities.

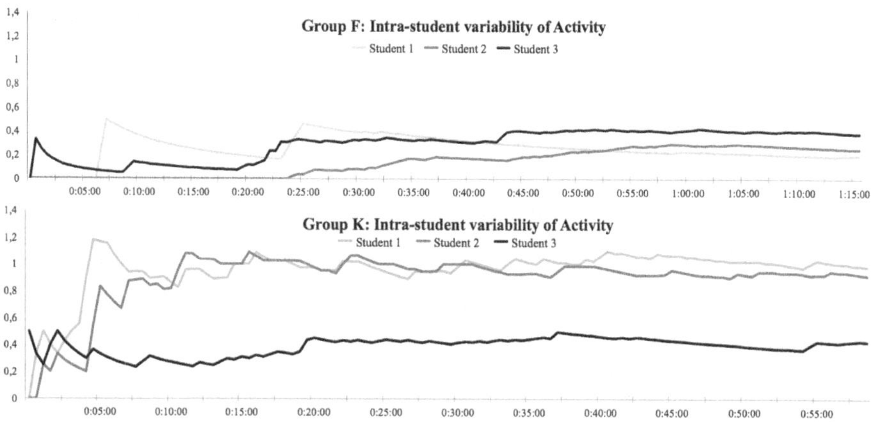

Fig. 3. Chronological changes of M in high and low CPS groups

5 Discussion

Students knowledge acquisition is important. However, students must also be able to apply this knowledge, to explain it clearly to others, to synthesize it with newly acquired knowledge from the same or other subject areas. They must also be able to use their knowledge to solve problems collaboratively. Subject specific knowledge and routine cognitive skills are the easiest to be automated with technology and these alone are no longer enough in the modern workplace. As science and technology continue to progress the notion of a body of knowledge will increasingly be something that will be distributed amongst multiple intelligences, both human and machine. It is therefore of great importance that young people should acquire appropriate collaboration skills to be able to solve problems and tasks that neither of the multiple agencies (including human and machine) of the future would be able to solve on their own.

However, acquisition of CPS skills requires purposeful practice of collaboration in settings that differ from uncollaborative group work or other peer learning settings including cooperation and peer tutoring approaches. Hence, the identification of indicators of collaborative problem-solving and their support have great importance to the researchers and practitioners of the research community. In this paper, we investigate the potential of two non-verbal indexes of students physical interactivity, to identify the level of collaboration in groups of students. Our first research question was: Can equality of physical interactivity and intra-individual variability be used as non-verbal indexes of collaboration in practice-based learning? Our results show that both the measures of students equality of physical interactivity and measures of intra-individual variability are useful indexes of students physical interactivity that can be used to evaluate the level of collaboration in a group. Related to this question our second research question was: What amounts of physical interactivity and intra-individual variability represent collaboration in practice-based learning? Analysing the data from twelve groups of Engineering students working in groups of three in open-ended practice-based activities, we found that students in groups that had been evaluated by a human observer as being high collaboration groups have member students who have high and equal scores for physical interactivity and low and equal scores for intra-individual variability.

These results are aligned with the existing research findings in the field. For instance, earlier research on peer learning shows that collaborative groups are high in equality and mutuality [7], they move in unison [33, 34], they present symmetry in terms of their status and contributions [35], and they are synchronised in their gaze [36]. In addition to these concepts, we argue that, students intra-individual variability in their physical interactivity is an important indicator of collaboration in practice-based learning and it may reflect the mutual understanding between students in a group.

We must point out the limitations of this work as well as its potential benefits. The evaluation of student performance through concepts such as, equality and intra-individual variability is only one small part of understanding how good a student is at CPS. The CPS process is much more complicated than any of the existing statistical measures of performance, particularly when it comes to complex learning environments of practice-based learning. However, these statistical measurements can act as useful indicators of potential success or failure of collaboration. Although our results are derived from twelve groups of three students, which can be considered as a small sample size, they are promising and we aim to investigate them further with larger sample sizes.

6 Conclusions

In this research paper, we present two non-verbal indexes of students physical interactivity that can be used to interpret the collaborative nature of their practice-based activities. Students in collaborative problem-solving groups show high levels of physical interactivity and low levels of intra-individual variability. Both of these indexes present smaller ranges in high collaboration groups when compared with low collaboration groups. Our simple coding scheme of students active, semi-active and passive positions is a practical and valuable approach that can inform the design of automated analysis systems. Hence, future research could involve attempts to automate this process of coding and provide real-time feedback to students and teachers about the collaborative or non-collaborative patterns of their physical interactivity during their learning activities. These results would have multiple implications both for the design and implementation of peer learning activities in classrooms and they would increase the accuracy and timeliness of teacher interventions. We argue that the most effective and efficient education can be provided through combining the statistical analyses of student performances with teachers expert instinctive judgment of the learning situations. Nevertheless, it would be wrong to rely only on such instinctive judgment, in the same way that it would be wrong to rely only on similar statistical calculations to these presented in this paper.

Acknowledgements. This work is co-funded by the European Union under the PELARS project. Third author was partially supported by Agencia Estatal de Investigaci´on (AEI) y el Fondo Europeo de Desarrollo Regional (FEDER), TIN2016-80774-R.

References

1. Luckin, R., Baines, E., Cukurova, M., Holmes, W.: Solved! Making the case for collaborative problem-solving. A report for Nesta. Nesta, London (2017)
2. Johnson, D.W., Johnson, R.T.: Learning together and alone: overview and meta-analysis. Asia Pac. J. Educ. **22**, 95–105 (2002)
3. Kyndt, E., Raes, E., Lismont, B., Timmers, F., Cascallar, E., Dochy, F.: A meta-analysis of the effects of face-to-face cooperative learning: do recent students verify or falsify earlier findings? Educ. Res. Rev. **10**, 133–149 (2013)
4. Nunnery, J.A., Chappel, S., Arnold, P.: A meta-analysis of a cooperative learning model: effects on student achievement in mathematics. Cypriot J. Educ. Sci. **8**(1), 34–48 (2013)
5. Puzio, K., Collby, G.T.: Cooperative learning and literacy: a meta-analytic review. J. Res. Educ. Eff. **6**(4), 339–360 (2013)
6. Roseth, C.J., Johnson, D.W., Johnson, R.T.: Promoting early adolescents' achievement and peer relationships: the effects of cooperative, competitive, and individualistic goal structures. Psychol. Bull. **134**(2), 223 (2008)
7. Damon, W., Phelps, E.: Critical distinctions among three approaches to peer education. Int. J. Educ. Res. **13**(1), 9–19 (1989)
8. Dillenbourg, P.: What do you mean by 'collaborative learning'? In: Cognitive and Computational Approaches, pp. 1–19 (1999)
9. Sharan, S.: Cooperative learning in small groups: recent methods and effects on achievement, attitudes, and ethnic relations. Rev. Educ. Res. **50**(2), 241–271 (1980)
10. Clarke, J.: Pieces of the puzzle: the jigsaw method. In: Sharan, S. (ed.) Handbook of Cooperative Learning Methods. Pearson, London (1994)
11. Sharan, S.: Cooperative Learning: Theory and Research. Praeger Publishers, New York (1990)
12. Kirschner, F., Paas, F., Kirschner, P.A., Janssen, J.: Differential effects of problem-solving demands on individual and collaborative learning outcomes. Learn. Instr. **21**(4), 587–599 (2011)
13. Kirschner, F., Paas, F., Kirschner, P.A.: Task complexity as a driver for collaborative learning efficiency: The collective working-memory effect. Appl. Cogn. Psychol. **25**(4), 615–624 (2011)
14. Metcalf, S., Kamarainen, A., Tutwiler, M.S., Grotzer, T., Dede, C.: Ecosystem science learning via multi-user virtual environments. Int. J. Gaming Comput. Mediat. Simul. (IJGCMS) **3**(1), 86–90 (2011)
15. Rouet, J.F.: The Skills of Document Use. Erlbaum, Mahwah (2006)
16. Spikol, D., Avramides, K., Cukurova, M., Vogel, B., Luckin, R., Mavrikis, M., Ruffaldi, E.: Exploring the interplay between human and machine annotated multimodal learning analytics in hands-on stem activities. In: Proceedings of the 6th International Learning Analytics & Knowledge Conference (2016)
17. Trilling, B., Fadel, C.: 21st Century Skills: Learning for Life in Our Times. Wiley, Hoboken (2009)
18. WEF: New vision for education: fostering social and emotional learning through technology. World Economic Forum: Industrial Agenda Report (2016)
19. Nevin, S.: Lifelong learning: reforming education for an age of technological and demographic change. Institute of Directors Policy Report, March 2016
20. Dillenbourg, P., Lemaignan, S., Sangin, M., Nova, N., Molinari, G.: The symmetry of partner modelling. Int. J. Comput. Support. Collab. Learn. **11**(2), 227–253 (2016)

21. Blech, C., Funke, J.: Dynamis review: an overview about applications of the dynamis approach in cognitive psychology. German Institute for Adult Education (DIE), Bonn (2005)
22. Wirth, J., Klieme, E.: Computer-based assessment of problem solving competence. Assess. Educ. Princ. Policy Practice **10**(3), 329–345 (2004)
23. Clark, R.E.: Using Language. Cambridge University Press, Cambridge (1996)
24. Marlowe, H.A.: Social intelligence: evidence for multidimensionality and construct independence. J. Educ. Psychol. **78**(1), 52–58 (1986)
25. Argyle, M.: New Developments in the Analysis of Social Skills, pp. 139–158. Academic Press, New York (1979)
26. Vallacher, R.R., Read, S.J., Nowak, A.: The dynamical perspective in personality and social psychology. Pers. Soc. Psychol. Rev. **6**(4), 264–273 (2002)
27. Cukurova, M., Avramides, K., Spikol, D., Luckin, R., Mavrikis, M.: An analysis framework for collaborative problem solving in practice-based learning activities: a mixed-method approach. In: Proceedings of the International Conference on Learning Analytics and Knowledge, Edinburgh, United Kingdom, pp. 84–88. ACM (2016)
28. OECD: Draft collaborative problem solving framework. Report (2015)
29. Cukurova, M., Avramides, K., Luckin, R., Mavrikis, M.: Revealing behaviour pattern differences in collaborative problem solving. In: Verbert, K., Sharples, M., Klobučar, T. (eds.) EC-TEL 2016. LNCS, vol. 9891, pp. 563–569. Springer, Cham (2016). doi:10.1007/978-3-319-45153-4_64
30. Andriessen, J., Baker, M., Suthers, D.: Arguing to Learn: Confronting Cognitions in Computer-Supported Collaborative Learning Environments, vol. 1. Springer Science & Business Media, Berlin (2013)
31. Barkley, E.F., Cross, K.P., Major, C.H.: Collaborative Learning Techniques: A Handbook for College Faculty. Wiley, Hoboken (2014)
32. Engestrom, Y.: Learning by Expanding. Cambridge University Press, Cambridge (2014)
33. Lakens, D.: Movement synchrony and perceived entitativity. J. Exp. Soc. Psychol. **46**(5), 701–708 (2010)
34. Lakens, D., Stel, M.: If they move in sync, they must feel in sync: movement synchrony leads to attributions of rapport and entitativity. Soc. Cogn. **29**(1), 1–14 (2011)
35. Dillenbourg, P., Zufferey, G., Alavi, H., Jermann, P., Do-Lenh, S., Bonnard, Q.: Classroom orchestration: the third circle of usability. In: International Conference on Computer Supported Collaborative Learning, CSCL 2011, ISLS, pp. 510–517 (2011)
36. Schneider, B., Pea, R.: Real-time mutual gaze perception enhances collaborative learning and collaboration quality. Int. J. Comput. Support. Collab. Learn. **8**(4), 375–397 (2013)

How Well Do Student Nurses Write Case Studies? A Cohesion-Centered Textual Complexity Analysis

Mihai Dascalu[1,2,3](✉), Philippe Dessus[3], Laurent Thuez[4], and Stefan Trausan-Matu[1,2]

[1] University Politehnica of Bucharest, Bucharest, Romania
{mihai.dascalu,stefan.trausan}@cs.pub.ro
[2] Academy of Romanian Scientists, Splaiul Independenţei 54, 050094 Bucharest, Romania
[3] Laboratoire des Sciences de l'Éducation, Univ. Grenoble Alpes, 38000 Grenoble, France
philippe.dessus@univ-grenoble-alpes.fr
[4] IFSI, Centre Hospitalier Annecy-Genevois, 74374 Metz-Tessy, Pringy, France
lthuez@ch-annecygenevois.fr

Abstract. Starting from the presumption that writing style is proven to be a reliable predictor of comprehension, this paper investigates the extent to which textual complexity features of nurse students' essays are related to the scores they were given. Thus, forty essays about case studies on infectious diseases written in French language were analyzed using *ReaderBench*, a multi-purpose framework relying on advanced Natural Language Processing techniques which provides a wide range of textual complexity indices. While the linear regression model was significant, a Discriminant Function Analysis was capable of classifying students with an 82.5% accuracy into high and low performing groups. Overall, our statistical analysis highlights essay features centered on document cohesion flow and dialogism that are predictive of teachers' scoring processes. As text complexity strongly influences learners' reading and understanding, our approach can be easily extended in future developments to e-portfolios assessment, in order to provide customized feedback to students.

Keywords: Health care · Nursing school · Textual complexity · Infectious diseases and hygiene · Case analysis

1 Introduction

The reflective turn in nurse training has gained popularity and interest, as in any professional fields pertaining to the "helping professions", such as teachers, midwives, psychological counseling or social work [1]. The instructional models guiding their training have progressively abandoned the *apprenticeship* image, where the trainee has to do what the mentor does or tells. Even though simulations can be used to train nurses, higher-level mentoring models, involving either *reflections* – the trainees understand why they perform certain tasks, and which ones –, or *competencies* – the trainees do what they can, in reference to a set of "best practices" or a competency framework, are most often promoted to support the building of sound nursing practices [2].

É. Lavoué et al. (Eds.): EC-TEL 2017, LNCS 10474, pp. 43–53, 2017.
DOI: 10.1007/978-3-319-66610-5_4

In consequence, and towards a more meaningful articulation between theoretical and practical knowledge, the assessment of complex professional skills is processed through critical thinking-based examinations of case studies [3], or creation of portfolios of actual competencies [4]. This approach of assessment aims at capturing the professional reflection of students when mastering their skills.

In addition, critical thinking has become a key skill in many professional training sectors [5], like nursing. This profession requires a wide range of skills (e.g., patient care, interpersonal skills, hygienic precautions, drug calculations, and safe lifting) [6]. Some of these skills are highly anchored in body and motor experience; others require accurate observations, analysis and problem-solving skills. For instance, the French curriculum of nursing schools requires students to write reflective essays, so-called "situation analyses", which refer to their professional placements. The main pedagogical goal of this activity is to foster students' abilities to extract the main variables of the situation, so that they solve problems and elaborate the most adequate solutions. In brief, they become able to use scientific, technical, procedural knowledge in order to develop fully professional nursing abilities. However, as many researchers pointed out [7], developing portfolios or critical thinking without mentoring is useless: students need guidance to extract and analyze relevant pieces of knowledge, manage plans for improvement, and link assessment and practice [8].

Despite its interest in developing professional expertise, the assessment of portfolios or essays stemming from case studies is seldom performed for two reasons. First, the cognitive processes engaged by teachers during assessments are subject to little research [9]. Second, essay grading is time-consuming and there is a limited set of potential computer-based procedures to support this demanding process. Recent advances in Natural Language Processing (NLP) make it possible, at least partially, to automatically assess students' skills through some proxies, like the textual formulation of their abilities or reflective thoughts on a professional situation. Teachers would use these proxies, once identified, to assess the quality of essays in large-scale educational contexts, like university exams or MOOCs. Moreover, this would encourage course designers to progressively abandon the frequently-used Multiple Choice Questionnaires (also used in nurse training [10]), which are less prone to capture higher-level thinking processes.

Thus, our aim is to create and validate an extensible and adaptive automated method of evaluating student's case studies. More specifically, our approach is to consider that the analysis of the students' textual production can predict their teachers' grades. This approach is in line with the reflective approach, which prescribes that professionals are able to verbalize their thoughts and decisions, and that, in turn, their verbalizations are subject to a fine-grained analysis to predict which competence is acquired. Therefore, our research question is to examine to what extent an automated assessment approach of nurse students' essays can help teachers assess their professional abilities. Within the conducted analyses, we used *ReaderBench*, a multi-language and multi-purpose system to assess the textual complexity of the students' essays [11, 12]. Moreover, we chose to focus in this study on the domain of infectious diseases and hygiene, of crucial importance in nurse training. This domain is closely related to the quality of the care persons receive, their health and their well-being, as well as biology (relationships with infectious agents).

In the rest of this paper, we focus on ways to automatically assess health care training (medical and nurse studies), as well as on textual complexity measures to quantify students' essay quality. Afterwards, we introduce to the main components of our study, followed by results, discussions, and conclusions.

2 Automated Assessment Approaches in Health Care

A posteriori semi-automated e-portfolios assessments are frequent in the literature [13], but they rely on qualitative research-focused systems like *NVivo* [14]. However, systems that rely on more integrated, automated, and quantitatively oriented data are considerably scarcer. *CONSPECT* [15] is a blog-based automated assessor which uses NLP and Network Analysis techniques to evaluate the conceptual development of medical students. The system takes as input students' blog writings and displays a network of the main concepts they used. It also can automatically compare the evolution of the terms used by a given learner to other students, or domain experts.

A more recent study [16] aimed at devising an LMS-based system to provide an automated assessment of e-portfolios, upon raw statistical features like word count or number of images. A first comparison of human vs. machine grades of 12 e-portfolios yielded promising results ($r = .67$). Another study [17] argues that e-portfolios enhanced with learning analytics can potentially increase the quality and efficiency of workplace-based assessment and feedback in professional education.

However, none of the previous approaches models the extent to which teachers are sensible to textual features encountered while reading, nor accounts for more sophisticated and semantically-related textual features.

3 Textual Complexity and Assessment

The complexity of texts, or their level of sophistication, is an important educational issue, either for the selection of texts for reading purposes [18], for understanding academic materials [19], or merely for assessing text difficulty [20]. Despite some attempts [21], little has been done so far to uncover the relationships between the students' writings (e.g., essays, reflective thoughts, portfolios) and the grades that were given by teachers or experts.

Seminal research [22, 23] showed that very shallow textual features of a document (e.g., number of characters, words, sentences, paragraphs and length of words and sentences) are good predictors of human grades. More extensive research on lexical, syntactic, and semantic levels [24] showed that essay quality increases as both lexical and syntactic text levels increase, whereas semantic-based cohesion indices (word or sentence-based) are negatively correlated with essay quality. Moreover, a recent research [25] processed about 560 master and bachelor theses, analyzing a wide range of textual complexity features (from lexical to semantic levels), and linking them to their assigned grades. The results showed that the correlation between these two variables was low, but this was mainly due to the skewed grade distribution and to the difficulty in selecting the most adequate criteria beforehand, which would best predict the assigned grades.

Since teachers, while scoring an essay, have access to the reading material assigned through the reading task, it is now well documented that its textual features may likely influence their scoring. So far, lexical and syntactic levels' quality is known to positively influence human judgments; more investigations are to be performed on semantic levels (i.e., cohesion-based).

4 Research Question

While perusing students' essays for assessment and scoring purposes, teachers are mostly focused on the usage of domain concepts and the manner in which they are related to the task at hand. Our research question is to understand to what extent teachers are also sensitive to other features, like textual complexity at several levels (lexical, syntactic, semantic, dialogical). To that aim we first computed a wide range of complexity indices, followed by a Discriminant Function Analysis (DFA) to analyze to which extent our model can classify students' grades. As Attali [26] put it, we can consider this large number of complexity indices as "black boxes" that are related to essay quality, though not individually interpretable per se.

5 Method

5.1 Participants

Forty essays written by 1st-year nurse students as case studies of 'infectious diseases and hygiene' were randomly selected. For homogeneity purposes, we excluded essays from repeating students and essays from students having completed medicine studies during the previous year.

5.2 Textual Complexity Assessment with *ReaderBench*

We used *ReaderBench* [11], a multi-language and multi-purpose NLP framework, designed to be an educational helper for students, teachers, and tutors. *ReaderBench* takes as input a wide range of educational productions (e.g., essays, explanations, discussions) and automatically assesses features, like the main concepts used, knowledge-building contributions, comprehension prediction, topic extraction, or textual complexity assessment. *ReaderBench* makes use of Cohesion Network Analysis [27] which harmoniously integrates semantic distances from WordNet with similarity measures derived from semantic models (i.e., Latent Semantic Analysis, LSA, and Latent Dirichlet Allocation, LDA), trained on our custom text corpora. Thus, we gathered a nurse-centered corpus for the analyses to account for the specificity of the vocabulary usage. We selected 9 documents on infectious diseases and hygiene, of about 273 pages comprising of 133,000 words, compliant with the French nurse training competencies framework. This corpus was added on top of a more general corpus (one-year issues of the French newspaper *Le Monde*; http://lsa.colorado.edu/spaces.html), and was used to train new semantic models integrated in the *ReaderBench* framework.

Of particular importance to the rest of this paper is the measure of *document flow*, coined in [28]: a "measure of a document's structure derived from the order of different paragraphs and of the manner in which they combine to hold the text together". (id., p. 765) This is an aggregated measure based on the identification of paragraph relationships in terms of semantic relatedness that captures global cohesion. Besides a wide variety of textual complexity indices presented in detail in previous papers [11, 29], *ReaderBench* integrates specific measures derived from the polyphonic model [30], inspired from Bakhtin's dialogism [31]. According to this model, interanimating 'voices', in a generalized way, are coherent points of view over semantically related concepts. Therefore, these indices take into account the distribution of 'voices' as well as their co-occurrence patterns [32]. Derived from dialogism, voices are operationalized as semantic chains and can be perceived as recurrent points of view or emerging topics that span throughout the document.

We ran on *ReaderBench* a multi-dimensional analysis of textual complexity indices adapted for French language, integrating classic surface metrics derived from automatic essay scoring techniques, morphology and syntax factors [33], as well as semantics and discourse factors [11]. In the end, subsets of factors were aggregated through a Discriminant Function Analysis in order to predict student performance.

5.3 Procedure

The main characteristics of students' selected essays are as follows: mean length: 1,342 words ($SD = 293$ words); minimum length: 680 words; maximum length: 2,179 words. Each essay was distributed randomly to one teacher who graded it. Afterwards, the essays were typed and corrected for spelling, followed by their automated assessment with *ReaderBench* (Table 1).

Table 1. Grader allocation and information on essay grades.

Grader	No. graded essays	Grade range (max: 20)	Mean	*SD*
A	14	[5.0; 16]	11.3	2.5
B	9	[8.0; 17]	13.5	2.1
C	5	[10.5; 19]	16.4	2.3
D	12	[5.3; 18]	12.6	2.5
Overall	40	[5.0; 19]	12.9	3.5

6 Results

We split the students into two equal-sized groups, namely high-performance students with scores greater or equal to 13 (in France, a [1; 20] scale is used), while the rest were catalogued as low-performance students (see Fig. 1 for correspondent frequency histogram). The textual complexity indices from *ReaderBench* that lacked normal distributions were discarded. Pearson correlations were then calculated for the remaining indices to decide whether there was a statistical ($p < .05$) and meaningful relation (at least a small effect size, $r > .3$) between the selected indices and the dependent variable (the students' essay scores). Indices that were highly collinear ($r \geq .90$) were flagged, and the index with the strongest correlation with the essay scores was kept, while the other indices were removed. The remaining indices were included as predictor variables in a stepwise multiple regression to explain the variance in the students' essay scores, as well as predictors in a Discriminant Function Analysis used to classify students based on their performance.

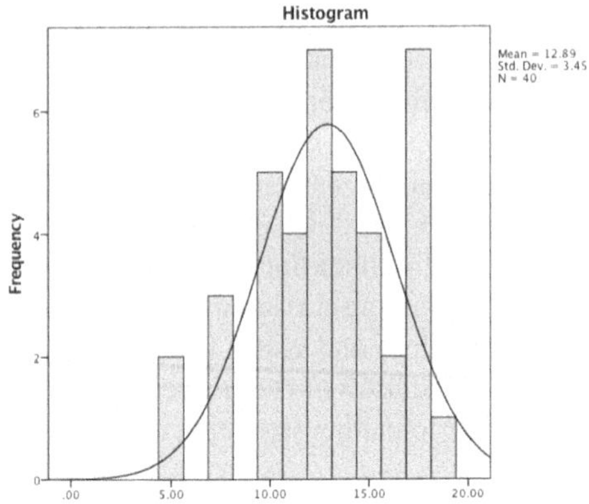

Fig. 1. Essay scores distribution.

Medium sized effects for Pearson correlation coefficients ($.3 < |r| < .5$) were found for *ReaderBench* textual complexity indices, as presented in Table 2 and relating to: document cohesion flow (e.g., adjacent accuracy), global cohesion (e.g., paragraph-document and start-middle relatedness) and dialogism (e.g., 'voice' entropy as a measure of diversity in terms of semantic chains that contain related concepts). The effects of each index are presented in detail in the next section. The negative correlations denote a wider range of introduced topics, a more diverse vocabulary for essays with higher

Table 2. Correlations between *ReaderBench* textual complexity indices and essay scores.

Indices	*r*	*p*
Document cohesion flow adjacent accuracy using Wu-Palmer distance and maximum criterion	.496	.001
Document cohesion flow adjacent accuracy using path distance and above plus standard deviation criterion	.451	.004
Content words (i.e., nouns, verbs, adjective and adverbs that are not considered stop-words by providing contextual information)	.448	.004
Average start-middle cohesion using path distance	–.446	.004
Average paragraph-document cohesion using path distance	–.436	.005
Average 'voice' paragraph entropy	.431	.005
Average paragraph-document cohesion using Wu-Palmer distance	–.405	.010

scores, thus a lower average global cohesion while relating each paragraph to the entire document.

We conducted a stepwise regression analysis using the first three most significant indices as the independent variables. This yielded a significant model, $F(1, 38) = 12.367$, $p < .001$, $r = .496$, $R^2 = .246$. One variable was selected as a significant and positive predictor of essay scores: document cohesion flow adjacent accuracy using Wu-Palmer distance and maximum criterion. This variable explained 25% of the variance in the students' essay scores.

Afterwards, a multivariate analysis of variance (MANOVA) was conducted to examine whether the lexical and semantic properties differed between high and low performing students. For all the variables presented in Table 3, Levene's test of equality of error variances was not significant ($p > .05$); thus, the MANOVA assumption that the variances of each variable are equal across the groups was met. There was a significant difference among the two groups, Wilks' $\lambda = .295$, $p < .001$ and partial $\eta^2 = .705$. The textual complexity indices from Table 3 present the effect sizes of the variable introduced in Table 2; all indices were significantly different between the two groups of students.

Table 3. Tests of between-subjects effects for significantly different indices.

Dependent variable	Mean (SD) low	Mean (SD) high	F	Sig.	Partial η^2
Document cohesion flow adjacent accuracy using Wu-Palmer distance and maximum criterion	0.98 (0.61)	1.74 (0.54)	17.33	< .001	0.313
Document cohesion flow adjacent accuracy using path distance and above mean plus standard deviation criterion	1.07 (0.63)	2.07 (0.85)	18.07	< .001	0.322
Content words	472.79 (122.10)	655.24 (139.67)	19.16	< .001	0.335
Average start-middle cohesion using path distance	0.48 (0.07)	0.41 (0.07)	9.03	.005	0.192
Average paragraph-document cohesion using path distance	0.76 (0.02)	0.74 (0.02)	6.27	.017	0.142
Average 'voice' paragraph entropy	1.14 (0.11)	1.26 (0.10)	15.15	< .001	0.285
Average paragraph-document cohesion using Wu-Palmer distance	0.863 (0.015)	0.855 (0.010)	4.18	.048	0.099

The stepwise Discriminant Function Analysis (DFA) retained two variables as significant predictors (Content words, and Document cohesion flow adjacent accuracy using path distance and above plus standard deviation criterion) and removed the remaining variables (Document cohesion flow adjacent accuracy using Wu-Palmer distance and maximum criterion) as non-significant predictors. These two indices correctly allocated 33 of the 40 students, $\chi^2(df = 2, n = 40) = 19.015$, $p < .001$, for an accuracy of 82.5% (the chance level for this analysis is 50%). For the leave-one-out cross-validation (LOOCV), the discriminant analysis allocated 31 of the 40 students for an accuracy of 77.5% (see the confusion matrix reported in Table 4). The measure of agreement between the actual student performance and that assigned by the model produced a weighted Cohen's Kappa of .652, demonstrating substantial agreement.

Table 4. Confusion matrix for DFA classifying students based on performance.

		Predicted performance group		Total
		Low	High	
Whole set	Low	17	2	19
	High	5	16	21
Cross-validated	Low	17	2	19
	High	7	14	21

7 Discussion and Conclusions

The results of this study shed light on the essay features, in terms of complexity, that influence teachers' scoring processes of nurse students' case studies. First, we showed that one discriminant function, based on document cohesion flow using Wu-Palmer distance, significantly differentiated the two student groups (of low and high performance). The correlation between this variable and the teachers' scoring is moderate (.50), and higher than the values found in another study [28] with regards to the process of scoring the overall quality of essays.

Moreover, the analysis of textual complexity indices that correlate the most with human scores brings added information on teachers' focus. Essays with higher scores tend to be longer and contain more content words. They inherently introduce more varied concepts, additional ideas (thus, more 'voices' are encountered), which determines a decrease in global cohesion perceived in terms of paragraph-document cohesion, start-middle cohesion (i.e., the semantic similarity between the introduction versus the essay body), as well as a higher entropy determined by the presence of additional semantic chains. Essays that received higher scores have a better organization in terms of paragraph structure, and a more suitable cohesion flow among adjacent paragraphs with two distance functions and both criteria; this leads to a more coherent discourse.

As a consequence, this study showed that human categorization of professional case studies can be partly predicted in analyzing document flow features. This study leads to the use of systems that would help teachers assess students' portfolios or case studies; in a parallel way, students would benefit from an automated support during writing. We strongly believe that the series of activities case studies promote can be supported by systems like *ReaderBench*: help students make connections to content, let them focused on the grade-influential textual features, collect and analyze data, write multiple drafts against standards towards the development of contextual features, prompt specific and timely feedback [34].

However, this study has some limitations. First, the number of essays is rather low, though comparable with that of other studies [35], and each essay is assessed by only one rater. Second, the way specific words are used in essays should have been subject to a more detailed analysis; for instance, the Age of Exposure model [36] would account for a more developmental view of word acquisition. Unfortunately, the model is not currently available for French language. Although semantic models like LSA and LDA were trained on specific corpora that were designed to properly conceptualize nurses' vocabulary, in further studies, we plan to adopt a more developmental view, capturing students' reflection evolution in assessing, for each student, a set of essays along the university year, independently assessed by at least two raters. We also plan to undertake a study in which students can freely assess their essays upon a series of textual complexity features, concurrently trying to improve their writing skills. Eventually, this approach might be applied to other domains and contexts, like teacher training, where reflective written accounts on activity foster professional development as well.

To our knowledge, this study is one of the few in which cohesion-centered indices proved to be predictive of human grading scores. Similarly, *ReaderBench* is one of the rare tools that provide as many and as varied textual complexity indices for languages other than English (in this study, French).

Acknowledgements. The authors wish to thank Patrice Lombardo, head of the IFSI, Centre Hospitalier Annecy-Genevois, who helped make this research possible, and Jean-Luc Rinaudo, University of Rouen, for his valuable input all along the phases of this research. This research was partially supported by the FP7 2008-212578 LTfLL project, by the 644187 EC H2020 *Realising an Applied Gaming Eco-system* (RAGE) project, as well as by University Politehnica of Bucharest through the "Excellence Research Grants" Programs UPB–GEX 12/26.09.2016.

References

1. Powell, J.H.: The reflective practitioner in nursing. J. Adv. Nurs. **14**, 824–832 (1989)
2. Maynard, T., Furlong, J.: Learning to teach and models of mentoring. In: Kerry, T., Mayes, A.S. (eds.) Issues in Mentoring, pp. 10–24. Routledge, New York (1995)
3. Simpson, E., Courtney, M.: Critical thinking in nursing education: literature review. Int. J. Nurs. Pract. **8**(2), 89–98 (2002)
4. Jasper, M.A.: The potential of the professional portfolio for nursing. J. Clin. Nurs. **4**(4), 249–255 (1995)
5. Popil, I.: Promotion of critical thinking by using case studies as teaching method. Nurs. Educ. Today **31**, 204–207 (2011)
6. Schober, J., Ash, C. (eds.): Student nurses' guide to professional practice and development. CRC Press, Boca Raton (2005)
7. Driessen, E.: Do portfolios have a future? Adv. Health Sci. Educ. **22**(1), 221–228 (2016)
8. Eva, K.W., Bordage, G., Campbell, C., Galbraith, R., Ginsburg, S., Holmboe, E., Regehr, G.: Towards a program of assessment for health professionals: from training into practice. Adv. Health Sci. Educ. **21**(4), 897–913 (2016)
9. Brooks, V.: Marking as judgment. Res. Pap. Educ. **27**(1), 63–80 (2012)
10. Green, S.M., Weaver, M., Voegeli, D., Fitzsimmons, D., Knowles, J., Harrison, M., Shephard, K.: The development and evaluation of the use of a virtual learning environment (Blackboard 5) to support the learning of pre-qualifying nursing students undertaking a human anatomy and physiology module. Nurs. Educ. Today **26**(5), 388–395 (2006)

11. Dascalu, M., Dessus, P., Bianco, M., Trausan-Matu, S., Nardy, A.: Mining texts, learner productions and strategies with ReaderBench. In: Peña-Ayala, A. (ed.) Educational Data Mining: Applications and Trends, pp. 345–377. Springer, Cham (2014). doi: 10.1007/978-3-319-02738-8_13
12. Dascalu, M.: Analyzing Discourse and Text Complexity for Learning and Collaborating. Studies in Computational Intelligence, vol. 534. Springer, Cham (2014). doi: 10.1007/978-3-319-03419-5
13. Nielsen, K., Pedersen, B.D., Helms, N.H.: Reflection and learning in clinical nursing education mediated by ePortfolio. J. Nurs. Educ. Pract. **5**(12), 63 (2015)
14. QSR International Pty Ltd.: NVivo (2017)
15. Wild, F.: Learning Analytics in R with SNA, LSA, and MPIA. Springer, Berlin (2016). doi: 10.1007/978-3-319-28791-1
16. Müller, W., Rebholz, S., Libbrecht, P.: Automatic inspection of E-portfolios for improving formative and summative assessment. In: Wu, T.-T., Gennari, R., Huang, Y.-M., Xie, H., Cao, Y. (eds.) SETE 2016. LNCS, vol. 10108, pp. 480–489. Springer, Cham (2017). doi: 10.1007/978-3-319-52836-6_51
17. van der Schaaf, M., Donkers, J., Slof, B., Moonen-van Loon, J., van Tartwijk, J., Driessen, E., Badii, A., Serban, O., Ten Cate, O.: Improving workplace-based assessment and feedback by an E-portfolio enhanced with learning analytics. Educ. Technol. Res. Dev. **65**(2), 359–380 (2017)
18. Fitzgerald, J., Elmore, J., Koons, H., Hiebert, E.H., Bowen, K., Sanford-Moore, E.E., Stenner, A.J.: Important text characteristics for early-grades text complexity. J. Educ. Psychol. **107**(1), 4–29 (2015)
19. Frantz, R.S., Starr, L.E., Bailey, A.L.: Syntactic complexity as an aspect of text complexity. Educ. Res. **44**(7), 387–393 (2015)
20. Collins-Thompson, K.: Computational assessment of text readability: a survey of current and future research. Int. J. Appl. Linguist. **165**(2), 97–135 (2014)
21. Page, E.B.: The imminence of… grading essays by computer. Phi Delta Kappan **47**, 238–243 (1966)
22. Larkey, L.S.: Automatic essay grading using text categorization techniques. In: Proceedings of SIGIR 1998, Melbourne (1998)
23. Page, E.B., Paulus, D.H.: The analysis of essays by computer. U.S. Department of Health, Education, and Welfare, project No. 6-1318, Washington (1968)
24. Crossley, S.A., McNamara, D.S.: Understanding expert ratings of essay quality: coh-metrix analyses of first and second language writing. Int. J. Contin. Eng. Educ. Life Long Learn. **21**(2/3), 170–191 (2011)
25. Mosallam, Y., Toma, L., Adhana, M.W., Chiru, C.-G., Rebedea, T.: Unsupervised system for automatic grading of bachelor and master thesis. In: Proceedings of the International Conference on eLearning and Software for Education (eLSE 2014), pp. 165–171 (2014)
26. Attali, Y.: Validity and reliability of automated essay scoring. In: Shermis, M.D., Burstein, J. (eds.) Handbook of Automated Essay Evaluation: Current Applications and New Directions, pp. 181–198. Routledge, New York (2013)
27. Dascalu, M., McNamara, D.S., Trausan-Matu, S., Allen, L.K.: Cohesion network analysis of CSCL participation. In: Behavior Research Methods, pp. 1–16 (2017)
28. Crossley, S.A., Dascalu, M., Trausan-Matu, S., Allen, L., McNamara, D.S.: Document cohesion flow: striving towards coherence. In: 38th Annual Meeting of the Cognitive Science Society, pp. 764–769. Cognitive Science Society, Philadelphia (2016)

29. Dascalu, M., Stavarache, L.L., Trausan-Matu, S., Dessus, P., Bianco, M.: Reflecting comprehension through French textual complexity factors. In: 26th International Conference on Tools with Artificial Intelligence (ICTAI 2014), pp. 615–619. IEEE, Limassol (2014)
30. Trausan-Matu, S.: A polyphonic model, analysis method and computer support tools for the analysis of socially-built discourse. Roman. J. Inf. Sci. Technol. **16**(2–3), 144–154 (2013)
31. Bakhtin, M.M.: The Dialogic Imagination: Four Essays. The University of Texas Press, Austin and London (1981)
32. Dascalu, M., Allen, K.A., McNamara, D.S., Trausan-Matu, S., Crossley, S.A.: Modeling comprehension processes via automated analyses of dialogism. In: Proceedings of the 39th Annual Meeting of the Cognitive Science Society (CogSci 2017). Cognitive Science Society, London (2017, in press)
33. Dascălu, M., Trausan-Matu, S., Dessus, P.: Towards an integrated approach for evaluating textual complexity for learning purposes. In: Popescu, E., Li, Q., Klamma, R., Leung, H., Specht, M. (eds.) ICWL 2012. LNCS, vol. 7558, pp. 268–278. Springer, Heidelberg (2012). doi:10.1007/978-3-642-33642-3_29
34. Darling-Hammond, L., Hammerness, K.: Toward a pedagogy of cases in teacher education. Teach. Educ. **13**(2), 125–135 (2002)
35. Crossley, S.A., McNamara, D.S.: Say more and be more coherent: how text elaboration and cohesion can increase writing quality. J. Writ. Res. **7**(3), 351–370 (2016)
36. Dascalu, M., McNamara, D.S., Crossley, S.A., Trausan-Matu, S.: Age of exposure: a model of word learning. In: 30th AAAI Conference on Artificial Intelligence, pp. 2928–2934. AAAI Press, Phoenix (2016)

Towards Automatic Assessment of Argumentation in Theses Justifications

Jesús Miguel García-Gorrostieta[1(✉)], Aurelio López-López[1], and Samuel González-López[2]

[1] National Institute of Astrophysics, Optics and Electronics, Tonantzintla, Puebla, México
{jesusmiguelgarcia,allopez}@inaoep.mx
[2] Technological Institute of Nogales, Nogales, Sonora, México
samuelgonzalezlopez@gmail.com

Abstract. Argumentation during the academic life is a critical skill when writing. This skill is needed to communicate clearly ideas and to convince the reader of the presented claims. However, not many students are good arguers and this is a skill difficult to master. This paper presents advances in the development of an argument assessment module. Such module supports students to identify argumentative paragraphs and determine the level of argumentation in the text. The task is achieved employing machine learning techniques with lexical features such as unigrams, bigrams, and argumentative markers categories. We based the module on an annotated collection of student writings, that serves for training. We performed an initial experiment to evaluate argumentative paragraph identification in the justification section of theses, reaching encouraging results, when compared against previously proposed approaches. The module is one component of a Thesis Writing Tutor, an Internet-based learning software for academic writing.

Keywords: Computer-assisted argument analysis · Argumentation studies · Academic writing · Corpus analysis · Intelligent tutoring system

1 Introduction

Writing an academic text such as a thesis can be a challenge for students. This writing requires argumentation skills to support presented claims with solid arguments. An argument is a set of statements (e.g. premises) that individually or collectively provide support to a claim (conclusion). There are several computational tools which use diagrams to analyze the argumentation (e.g. Belvedere [31], LARGO [25], ARGUNAUT [7], LASAD [18], ArgumentPeer [20], and ALES [1]). These argumentation tools have been conceived and developed to help in the visual mapping and analysis of arguments, assisting students to achieve a deeper understanding of argument construction [2]. For an academic review of essays, systems like Criterion [3], Writing Pal [27], or SWORD [5] are used to provide general support in several linguistic dimensions. For argument analysis,

É. Lavoué et al. (Eds.): EC-TEL 2017, LNCS 10474, pp. 54–66, 2017.
DOI: 10.1007/978-3-319-66610-5_5

there are tools like MARGOT [17] to identify argument components or an argument assessment system [13] which uses keywords to analyze natural language texts. Still, we have not found systems aimed to analyze automatically textual argumentation in larger academic works such as theses. Theses are often written at the end of college as one of the requirements for the degree, being in consequence quite important for students. For this reason, an argument assessment tool for theses is necessary to support students in this challenging task.

In this paper, we present an extension to a previous system TURET[1] 2.0, that consists of a new argumentation assessment module for the framework, that previously only considered an analysis of lexical richness. This module supports students to identify argumentative paragraphs using machine learning techniques with representations of diverse lexical features, and determines the level of argumentation in the text. To apply machine learning, we create a corpus of thesis sections (problem statement, justification, conclusions) with argumentative paragraphs annotated. We annotated 300 sections and performed experiments on justification section to automatically identify paragraphs with arguments, showing better efficacy than other approaches. The argument assessment module is presented as part of the Tutor for Thesis Writing (TURET), an Internet-based software for academic writing. TURET2.0 is a tutoring system that aims to support students with the requirement to write a thesis. Also, the results of a pilot test (prior version of the system) with students of a public university showed encouraging results. Students who used the tutor had better results when writing their thesis (regarding Lexical Richness) compared to those who did not use the tutor [10]. With this new module on the system, we expect to provide support in argumentation to students when drafting their theses.

The paper is structured as follows. In Sect. 2, we detail the related work of argument identification found so far. We explain our proposed architecture of argument assessment module in the TURET framework in Sect. 3. In Sect. 4, we present an exploratory analysis of the argumentative annotated corpus. Section 5 reports the result of argument identification in justification section using our corpus. Finally, in Sect. 6, we conclude with some final remarks and work in progress.

2 Related Work

In this section, we present previous research in argument mining in particular for the tasks of corpus creation and argument detection. We require these tasks to develop the argument assessment module. Argument mining involves automatic argument extraction from unstructured text. The first task is the corpus creation to validate the efficacy of the proposed method. As found in the literature, most researchers in the field of argument analysis create their annotated corpus, using certain argumentative scheme. We found few annotated corpus available for our purpose. One of the corpus most used among researchers to identify the presence of arguments is Araucaria [14]. This corpus has several types of documents with

[1] In Spanish: TURET: Tutor para la Redacción de Tesis.

annotated premises, conclusions, and the argument scheme used, however it did not include the level of agreement between annotators.

Corpus creation is done in different types of text, as well as in various domains. In [21], an experimental collection was built with ten legal documents from the ECHR (European Court of Human Rights) corpus, with annotated premises and conclusions. In this corpus, the level of agreement between the two annotators is a Kappa of 0.80. In a further study [22], the number of annotators was increased to three and the number of documents in the corpus to 47, where the level of agreement among annotators decreased to a Kappa of 0.75. It is important to note that dealing with legal texts with a clear structure facilitates the annotation process and increases the level of agreement. On the other hand, in [29], 90 persuasive essays on randomly-chosen topics are annotated by three persons. They annotated argumentative components with a level of agreement for the component of major conclusions of 0.83 (stance of the author), premises with 0.70 and conclusions with 0.65. In a more recent work [30], they increased the corpus to 402 essays, and manually analyzed 80 essays with three annotators. They reported an inter-rate agreement of Fleiss Kappa of 0.877 for major claims, 0.635 for claims and 0.833 for premises. In [15], the authors created a corpus with 24 scientific articles in education for the sections of introduction and discussion. Four participants annotated argument components as premises or conclusions, as well as four relationships (support, attack, sequence and detail) between these argumentative components, with an average in the level of agreement of Fleiss Kappa of 0.41. Therefore, we observed that obtaining acceptable levels of annotation agreement in scientific texts is a complex task, which depends on an appropriate annotation guide and regularly monitoring annotators during the corpus construction. For our research, the closest kind of document are scientific articles since theses share a similarly complex structure and scientific vocabulary. However, undergraduated theses have a longer extension for each section, and student writings present very often several argumentative errors. On the other hand, scientific articles are often written by researchers with more experience in the task.

Once a corpus is built, it is necessary to detect the presence of arguments in paragraphs, sentences, or clauses. In [23], an automatic identification of argumentative and non-argumentative sentences in Araucaria corpus was performed. They represented sentences with features like combinations of pairs of words, verbs and text statistics before applying a naive Bayes classifier, achieving a 73.75% of accuracy. In a research with legal texts of the ECHR corpus [22], they reached an 80% of accuracy. In this domain, legal texts have a specific structure which allows lawyers to identify arguments more easily. Another approach to identify the presence of arguments in texts was reported in [8], extracting a set of discourse markers and features based on mood and tense of verbs. They achieved an F1 measure of 0.764 using a decision tree classifier. In [11], they performed identification of argumentative sentences, employing structural, lexical, contextual and grammatical features to represent each sentence. With a logistic regression classifier, they reached an F1 measure of 0.771 on a corpus of 204 documents collected from social media and written in Greek. They also considered the identification of argument components (claim and premise). For this task, they applied a Conditional Random Field (CRF) classifier to obtain an F1 measure of 0.423. Also, [28] presented a similar approach with CRF and distributed representations of words to identify segments that correspond to argument components. For this task, an F1 measure of 0.322 was reported.

For argumentative writing revision, we found the methodology presented in [32] to identify jointly the location and type of revisions, using two versions of essays. They recognized different types of changes in the text such as surface or reasoning. To minimize error propagation of the task, a representation for edit sequences was proposed, which was optimized using a mutation approach. First, a segmentation of essays in sentences was done, and then a sentence alignment between the two versions was obtained. Subsequently, the alignments were transformed into edit sequences according to criteria established by the author; then multiple solutions were generated using a Long Term Short Memory (LSTM) network. These sequences were labeled with the type of revision using a CRF. Finally, the best edit sequence was chosen. This method could be a further improvement for our module in the future, to indicate the student's changes and how their writings are improving.

3 System Architecture

This section describes the architecture of the Tutor for Thesis Writing (TURET) extended with the argument assessment module, as shown in Fig. 1. The framework consists of three parts: (1) The student model, that keeps track of the student performance; (2) The argumentation model, which contains resources and the argument assessment module with 3 main parts: a vector space model, an argumentative paragraph classifier, and an argument level detection; (3) The lexical richness model with two components: an assessment module and a list of common words (the 1000 common words, according to SRA[2]), previously developed and tested.

So, TURET2.0 is a tool that integrates two modules that work independently. However, they complement each other since the results of both modules collaborate to identify if the text under evaluation has desirable features in a thesis, allowing the student to improve his writing draft through evaluation and feedback. The suggested evaluation for the student begins with the Lexical Richness Model (LR), which serves as a first filter in the student's document. The LR model integrates the evaluation of three features: density, variety and lexical sophistication [10]. If the student reaches a medium or high level of the three features, it means that the document has lexical richness levels similar to gold standard documents.

After using the LR model, the student is encouraged to move to the Argument Assessment Module. The argumentation feature is of higher level, compared to the lexical model. Here, we describe in more detail the Argumentation model

[2] Spanish royal academy.

since the LR has been reported previoulsy [10]. As mentioned, the student model keeps track of the progress in each of the models described above to provide the student with a detailed report and feedback.

TURET2.0 was developed in Python with the Django+HTML5 Web framework, to display the user interface and evaluation results. Also, the open-source relational database management system MySQL was used to store the results of each evaluation of students. Finally, Freeling tool was installed as a server, such that the lemmatization process was performed under a service scheme, i.e., when a student requests an evaluation in the tutor, the system requests the lemmatization service of Freeling.

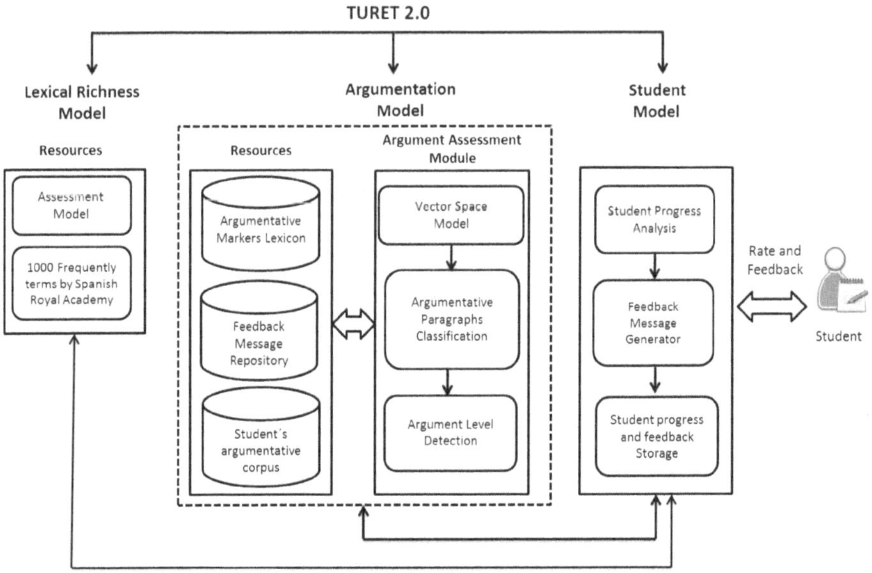

Fig. 1. System architecture

3.1 The Argumentation Model

The argumentation model identifies the proportion of argumentative paragraphs, assigns a level of this proportion, and provides a textual feedback to the student. Our approach relies on certain processes of the methodology used in argument mining [24]. First, a paragraph segmentation is required. Secondly, as presented in Fig. 1, we generate a vector space model to represent each paragraph with lexical features. Then, we supply these vectors to the argumentative paragraph classifier, where we use machine learning techniques to identify all argumentative paragraphs. Once we identify all the argumentative paragraphs, this information is shared for the argument level detection. This module identifies the proportion of argumentative paragraphs. With this proportion, the argumentative level of the text is assessed, according to our corpus statistics. Finally, a textual feedback is supplied to the student, according to the level obtained in the submitted text. Our goal is to provide an assessment along with recommendations, to support students with a clear identification of paragraphs with arguments, so help them to improve the argumentation in their writings.

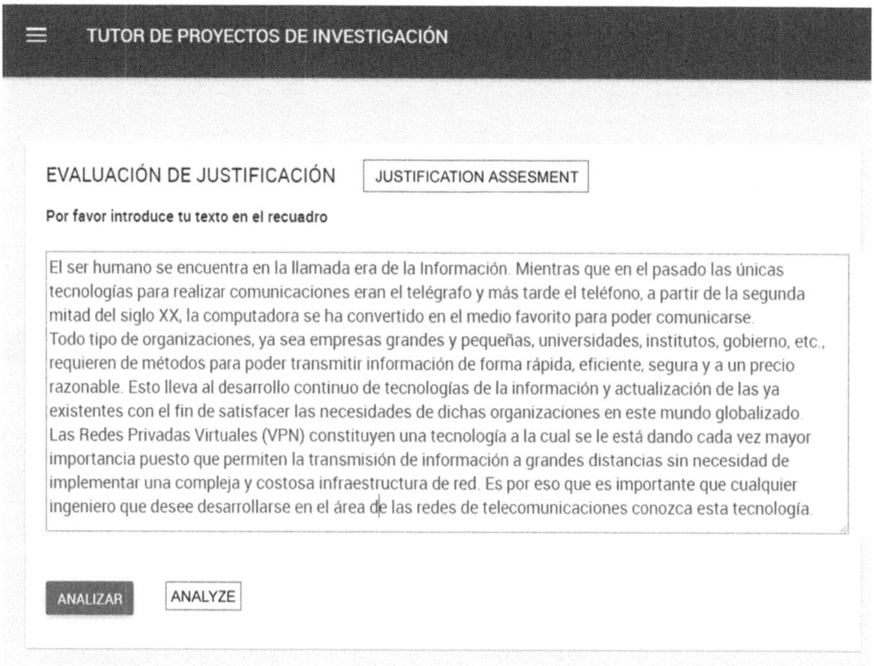

Fig. 2. Argument assessment module input

Figure 2 shows the interface of the argumentative module used to assess the justification section of theses. In this text box, the student writes or brings his justification for analysis. Then, he can trigger the analysis of the text by clicking on the button (labeled "ANALIZAR" in Spanish). The text appearing in the input interface is from a justification section of an undergraduate thesis, and consists of three paragraphs submitted for evaluation.

In Fig. 3, the argumentative assessment output is presented, where we can notice the identified argumentative paragraphs in blue and non-argumentative in red. So two argumentative paragraphs were found with a 66.6% proportion of argumentative paragraphs. Finally, a textual feedback is also provided, which for now is static. This feedback is defined depending on the level achieved by the student. We observe a medium level of argumentation assessment, with a textual recommendation for the student to improve his writing: "Very well, your text has argumentation; But try to improve the arguments of paragraphs indicated without argumentation" (in Spanish).

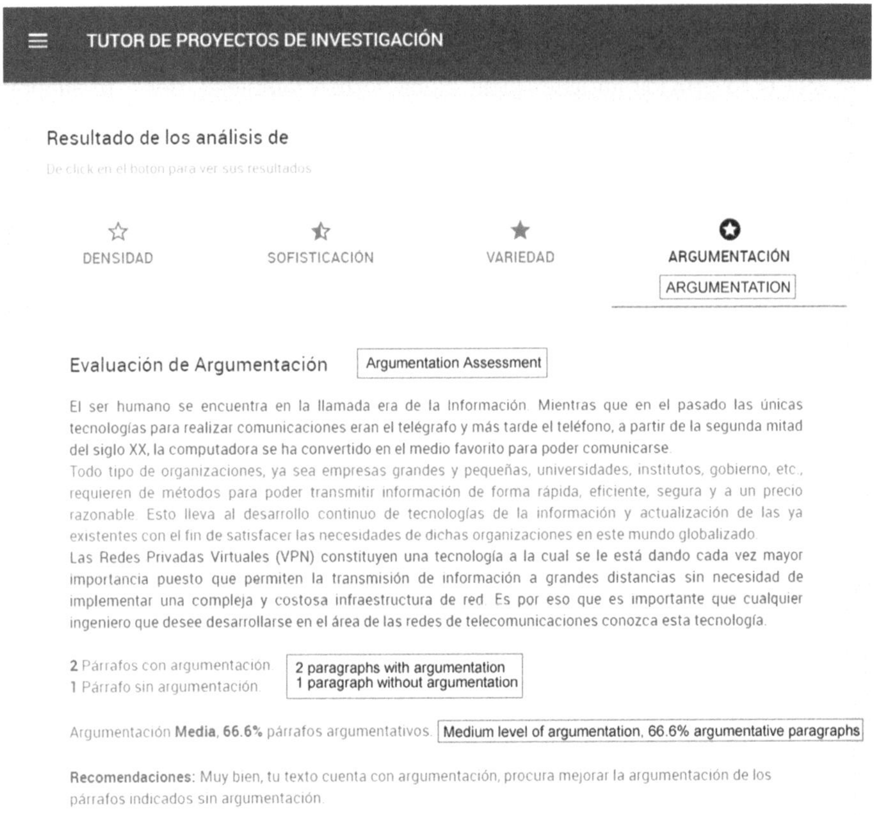

Fig. 3. Argument assessment module output (Color figure online)

4 Corpus Creation and Analysis

Corpus analysis is done to understand the argumentative characteristics in writings of undergraduate and graduate level. For this analysis, we used the collection Coltypi [9] consisting of 468 theses and research proposals in the computer and information technologies domain, in Spanish. This corpus has undergraduate (TSU[3] and Bachelor Degree) and graduate level (M.Sc. and Ph.D.) texts. According to [19], the sections of the problem statement, justification and conclusions are considered highly argumentative, so we focused the analysis on them.

By analyzing the collection, we observed that each section contains an average of 11 sentences. Each sentence contains 35 words on average with a total of 398 words per section. The length of sentences for the undergraduate level is 38 words per sentence which turn them slightly more difficult to follow when reading, in contrast to the doctoral level, which has an average of 30 words. Based on this,

[3] Advanced College-level Technician degree, study program offered in some countries.

we considered that doctoral writings are better, and we can take them as a reference.

To conduct the annotation study, we formulated an annotation guide. In this guide, we described the different argumentative structures, along with examples. The annotators were instructed to read the title and objectives of the thesis first, and then move to identify and mark all argumentative paragraphs. We performed the annotation of 300 sections (100 of each section) with the help of two instructors who have experience reviewing theses.

The analysis of inter-annotator agreement (IAA) was done considering the paragraphs with observed agreement (i.e. different of zero) in the identification of argumentative components (e.g. premises or conclusions). A total of 890 paragraphs were used to analyze the IAA with Cohen Kappa [6]. Table 1 presents the IAA for the different sections with a Kappa measure above 0.81, that is interpreted as “Almost perfect”, according to [16].

Table 1. Kappa level by section

Problem statement	Justification	Conclusion
0.867	0.935	0.817

As shown in Table 2, most sections have more than half of the paragraphs with arguments. We selected only the paragraphs where the two annotators agreed. This restriction reduces the number of paragraphs to 837, that once analyzed, led to 565 argumentative paragraph, corresponding to a proportion of 68%. From this analysis, we observed that a large proportion of paragraphs in theses have arguments. One characteristic of this corpus is that the conclusion section includes more paragraphs per section, when compared to the sections of the problem statement or justification. Moreover, we observed a higher number of paragraphs with arguments in the conclusion section.

Table 2. Class distribution per section

	Paragraphs with arguments	Paragraphs without arguments
Problem statement	164	93
Justification	151	81
Conclusion	250	98
Total	565 (68%)	272 (32%)

We have presented the class distribution of argumentative paragraphs of the three sections. However, in this study, we focus first on the Justification section (i.e. only in 100) to identify the intervals to determine the argumentative levels: low, medium and high. In Table 3 we present intervals for each level based on the proportion of argumentative paragraphs found in the one hundred sections

Table 3. Level ranges for argumentative paragraphs in justification section

Low	Medium	High
0%–42%	43%–82%	83%–100%

analyzed. We found a mean of 63% of paragraphs with arguments per section, with a standard deviation of 40. To assign the limit between low and medium level, we take half standard deviation below the mean (63 – 40/2), to get 43%. Similarly, to assign the limit between medium and high levels, we add to the mean half of the standard deviation (63 + 40/2), to obtain 83%. With these intervals, we assess the level of argumentation in the student text and provide a textual feedback.

5 Argumentative Paragraph Identification

To evaluate the efficacy of the Argument Assessment Module to detect argumentative paragraphs, we used 232 paragraphs of the justification section (See Table 4), where we have 65% of paragraphs with arguments. The problem was approached as a binary classification for each paragraph, i.e. identify if it has arguments or not. To perform the validation, we used a stratified 10-fold cross-validation.

Table 4. Class distribution among instances in justification section

Paragraphs with arguments	Paragraphs without arguments
151 (65%)	81 (35%)

To perform the classification, we employed the Weka machine learning toolkit [12]. In particular, we applied Support Vector Machine (SVM) [29], Random Forest (RF) [4] and Simple Logistic Regression (SLR) [22] classifiers since they have been previously used in argument mining. Also, these classifiers achieved the best results in this section of the corpus.

Vector representations were built to identify paragraphs with arguments. In Table 5, we present three representations used to compare the efficacy of our proposed representation in this task. The first representation consists of bigrams, i.e. pairs of consecutive terms, taken as a baseline. The second representation is a set of features previously proposed by Florou [8], consisting of discourse markers and mood and tense of verbs. The third representation was proposed by Moens [23], consisting of combinations of all possible pairs of words, main verbs, and text statistics. The fourth representation is our proposal with the following set of features: (1) unigrams, i.e. all single terms in the paragraph; (2) bigrams; (3) categories of argumentative markers, which are the number of argumentative markers in each category found in the paragraph using our argumentative markers lexicon. The categories of argumentative markers are $c = \langle justification, explanation, deduction, refutation, conditional \rangle$.

We built the four representations taking into account all words and punctuation symbols. Then, we trained the classifiers with the data set for training and applied them to the test data set. Table 5 shows the averages of F-measure, recall and precision of each representation for the ten folds. We present the best combination of classifier and feature set obtained by feature selection with information gain for each representation. As we can notice, our representation achieves the best F-measure with 0.887, 0.885 of precision and 0.854 of accuracy to identify paragraphs with arguments with a Simple Logistic Regression (SLR) classifier and a feature selection using only attributes with some information gain (i.e. IG > 0). The baseline consisting of bigrams and a Support Vector Machine showed the best recall, just above the recall of the proposed representation.

Table 5. Classification of argumentative paragraphs results. FS stands for feature selection configuration

	Classifier	FS	F-measure	Recall	Precision	Accuracy
Bigrams	SVM	None	0.843	**0.900**	0.798	0.784
Florou	SLR	25	0.817	0.847	0.797	0.755
Moens	RF	IG > 0	0.860	0.887	0.842	0.814
Our representation	SLR	IG > 0	**0.887**	0.894	**0.885**	**0.854**

With these initial results, we provide support to use the proposed representation to perform the identification of argumentative paragraphs in the argument assessment module in the justification section.

6 Conclusion

The system presented in this paper aims to support students to improve their argumentative writing by identifying which paragraphs do not seem to have arguments. After using the system and following suggestions, this can also benefit academic advisors/instructors by reviewing improved writings, with better content.

As we observed in the experimental collection, there were enough arguments in theses to exploit. With the analysis of the corpus, we realized that more than half of the paragraphs include arguments, so it is important to make further progress in building systems that support the argumentative assessment of this type of academic texts.

According to the results, the best accuracy and F-measure observed in our experiments to identify paragraphs with arguments was achieved by the Simple

Logistic Regression classifier with our proposed representation, consisting of n-grams and the number of argumentative markers per categories.

In future work, we plan to complete the analysis of problem statement and conclusion sections to identify their particular level ranges for the assessment of such sections, and whether the features and classifier have a similar efficacy. After we complete the analysis of these two sections, we intend to conduct a pilot test in several groups of undergrad students to assess the performance of the module. Also, we plan to work on the identification of argumentative components (e.g. premises, conclusions) to indicate precisely to the students their deficiencies, for instance in the case of a paragraph with a conclusion but without supporting premises. Afterward, we can aim for relation identification, i.e. to determine whether a premise is supporting or attacking the conclusion.

A further improvement in terms of system support for students that we foresee is the use of a rubric to offer a better textual feedback, as presented in [26]. As part of this feedback, we also consider showing an example of an argument retrieved from our corpus with the same argumentation type and similar or closely related topic.

Acknowledgement. We thank the annotators for the assistance in the corpus creation. The first author was partially supported by CONACYT, México, under scholarship 357381.

References

1. Abbas, S., Sawamura, H.: Ales: An innovative argument-learning environment. Online Submission **7**(9), 58–67 (2010)
2. Buckingham Shum, S.: The Roots of Computer Supported Argument Visualization, pp. 3–24. Springer London, London (2003)
3. Burstein, J., Chodorow, M., Leacock, C.: Criterionsm online essay evaluation: an application for automated evaluation of student essays. In: IAAI, pp. 3–10 (2003)
4. Carstens, L., Toni, F.: Towards relation based argumentation mining. In: NAACL HLT 2015, p. 29 (2015)
5. Cho, K., Schunn, C.D.: Scaffolded writing and rewriting in the discipline: a web-based reciprocal peer review system. Comput. Educ. **48**(3), 409–426 (2007)
6. Cohen, J.: A coefficient of agreement for nominal scales. Educ. Psychosoc. Measur. **20**(1), 37–46 (1960)
7. De Groot, R., Drachman, R., Hever, R., Schwarz, B.B., Hoppe, U., Harrer, A., De Laat, M., Wegerif, R., McLaren, B.M., Baurens, B.: Computer supported moderation of e-discussions: the argunaut approach. In: Proceedings of the 8th International Conference on Computer Supported Collaborative Learning, pp. 168–170. International Society of the Learning Sciences (2007)
8. Florou, E., Konstantopoulos, S., Koukourikos, A., Karampiperis, P.: Argument extraction for supporting public policy formulation. In: Proceedings of the 7th Workshop on Language Technology for Cultural Heritage, Social Sciences, and Humanities, pp. 49–54 (2013)
9. González-López, S., López-López, A.: Colección de tesis y propuesta de investigación en tics: un recurso para su análisis y estudio. In: XIII Congreso Nacional de Investigación Educativa, pp. 1–15 (2015)

10. González-López, S., López-López, A.: Lexical analysis of student research drafts in computing. Comput. Appl. Eng. Educ. **23**(4), 638–644 (2015)
11. Goudas, T., Louizos, C., Petasis, G., Karkaletsis, V.: Argument extraction from news, blogs, and social media. In: Likas, A., Blekas, K., Kalles, D. (eds.) SETN 2014. LNCS, vol. 8445, pp. 287–299. Springer, Cham (2014). doi:10.1007/978-3-319-07064-3_23
12. Hall, M., Frank, E., Holmes, G., Pfahringer, B., Reutemann, P., Witten, I.H.: The weka data mining software: an update. ACM SIGKDD Explor. Newsl. **11**(1), 10–18 (2009)
13. Huang, C.J., Wang, Y.W., Huang, T.H., Liao, J.J., Chen, C.H., Weng, C.H., Chu, Y.J., Chien, C.Y., Shen, H.Y.: Implementation and performance evaluation of an intelligent online argumentation assessment system. In: 2010 International Conference on Electrical and Control Engineering (ICECE), pp. 2560–2563. IEEE (2010)
14. Katzav, J., Reed, C., Rowe, G.W.A.: Argument research corpus. In: Proceedings of the 2003 Conference on Practical Applications in Language and Computers, pp. 229–239 (2004)
15. Kirschner, C., Eckle-Kohler, J., Gurevych, I.: Linking the thoughts: analysis of argumentation structures in scientific publications. In: Proceedings of the 2nd Workshop on Argumentation Mining, pp. 1–11 (2015)
16. Landis, J.R., Koch, G.G.: The measurement of observer agreement for categorical data. Biometrics **33**, 159–174 (1977)
17. Lippi, M., Torroni, P.: Margot: a web server for argumentation mining. Expert Syst. Appl. **65**, 292–303 (2016)
18. Loll, F., Pinkwart, N.: Lasad: flexible representations for computer-based collaborative argumentation. Int. J. Hum. Comput. Stud. **71**(1), 91–109 (2013)
19. López Ferrero, C., García Negroni, M.: La argumentación en los géneros académicos. In: Actas del Congreso Internacional La Argumentación, pp. 1121–1129. Universidad de Buenos Aires, Buenos Aires (2003)
20. Lynch, C., Ashley, K.D.: Modeling student arguments in research reports. In: Proceedings of the 4th AHFE Conference, pp. 191–201 (2012)
21. Mochales, R., Moens, M.F.: Study on the structure of argumentation in case law. In: Proceedings of the 2008 Conference on Legal Knowledge and Information Systems, pp. 11–20 (2008)
22. Mochales, R., Moens, M.F.: Argumentation mining. Artif. Intell. Law **19**(1), 1–22 (2011)
23. Moens, M.F., Boiy, E., Palau, R.M., Reed, C.: Automatic detection of arguments in legal texts. In: Proceedings of the 11th International Conference on Artificial Intelligence and Law, pp. 225–230. ACM (2007)
24. Peldszus, A., Stede, M.: From argument diagrams to argumentation mining in texts: a survey. Int. J. Cogn. Inf. Nat. Intell. (IJCINI) **7**(1), 1–31 (2013)
25. Pinkwart, N., Aleven, V., Ashley, K., Lynch, C.: Evaluating legal argument instruction with graphical representations using largo. Front. Artif. Intell. Appl. **158**, 101 (2007)
26. Rahimi, Z., Litman, D., Correnti, R., Wang, E., Matsumura, L.C.: Assessing students use of evidence and organization in response-to-text writing: using natural language processing for rubric-based automated scoring. Int. J. Artif. Intell. Educ., 1–35 (2017)
27. Roscoe, R.D., Allen, L.K., Weston, J.L., Crossley, S.A., McNamara, D.S.: The writing pal intelligent tutoring system: usability testing and development. Comput. Composit. **34**, 39–59 (2014)

28. Sardianos, C., Katakis, I.M., Petasis, G., Karkaletsis, V.: Argument extraction from news. In: NAACL HLT 2015, p. 56 (2015)
29. Stab, C., Gurevych, I.: Identifying argumentative discourse structures in persuasive essays. In: EMNLP, pp. 46–56 (2014)
30. Stab, C., Gurevych, I.: Recognizing the absence of opposing arguments in persuasive essays. In: ACL 2016, p. 113 (2016)
31. Suthers, D.D.: Architectures for computer supported collaborative learning. In: Proceedings of the IEEE International Conference on Advanced Learning Technologies, pp. 25–28. IEEE (2001)
32. Zhang, F., Litman, D.: A joint identification approach for argumentative writing revisions. arXiv preprint arXiv:1703.00089 (2017)

Contextualizing the Co-creation of Artefacts Within the Nested Social Structure of a Collaborative MOOC

Stian Håklev[1(✉)], Kshitij Sharma[1,2], Jim Slotta[3], and Pierre Dillenbourg[1]

[1] École Polytechnique Fédérale de Lausanne, Lausanne, Switzerland
stian.haklev@epfl.ch
[2] Faculty of Business and Economics, University of Lausanne, Lausanne, Switzerland
[3] Boston College, Newton, USA

Abstract. MOOCs have traditionally been seen as providing an individual learning experience, however there is an increasing trend towards enabling social learning in MOOCs. To make online learning at scale more social and collaborative, some MOOCs have introduced cohorts. The interaction between a smaller number of learners, within a cohort, facilitates a richer exchange of experiences and ideas as compared to the effect of "drinking from the fire hose" felt in MOOCs without cohorts. Traditionally, these cohorts have been formed randomly. In this paper, we examine the MOOC "Inquiry and Technology for Teachers", where we formed cohorts based on student demographics relevant to our course design. Furthermore, these cohorts (which we called Special Interest Groups, SIGs) contained a nested social structure of small teams that worked together on co-creating a final artifact. The different social planes (whole course, SIGs, teams, and individuals) were linked together by pedagogical scripts that orchestrated the movement of ideas and artifacts vertically and horizontally. In this contribution, we analyzed the interaction between these social planes to contextualize the co-creation of artefacts.

Keywords: Inquiry-based learning · Orchestration at scale · MOOCs · Massive Open Online Courses · Group formation · Learning analytics · Multi-level analysis · Scripting collaboration · CSCL

1 Introduction

Massive Open Online Course (MOOC) platforms like Coursera and EdX have gradually added certain social features to their courses, such as peer reviews, discussion forums, and cohorts. Cohorts are course sub-communities, implemented by partitioning forum threads such that participants in a given cohort are only able to see thread replies by other members of the same cohort, to support more

É. Lavoué et al. (Eds.): EC-TEL 2017, LNCS 10474, pp. 67–81, 2017.
DOI: 10.1007/978-3-319-66610-5_6

intimate and less overwhelming discussions. These cohorts are typically formed by random assignment.[1]

In [9], we have described in detail the design of a MOOC for teacher education, in which we sought to create a collaborative knowledge community, where teachers would be able to connect with relevant peers and share professional resources. While inspired by the connectivist MOOCs, we were simultaneously concerned about providing enough support and scaffolding to lead the students to meet specific learning goals, and not get confused in a too open-ended learning environment. To support a diverse learner population, we designed semantically meaningful cohorts (called Special Interest Groups, SIGs), such as "Secondary Science", or "Elementary English, History, and Social Studies".

These SIGs formed disciplinary sub-communities that supported participants in reflecting on and applying general course theories to their own specific contexts. The design of the course relied on an integration between EdX functionality, and external LTI[2] components, to enable students to benefit from their larger disciplinary community, while engaging in the co-creation of lesson design documents in small teams. This was formalized through collaborative scripts that described the flow of ideas between different levels, both explicit and implicit.

The initial bootstrapping of lesson design groups was informed by SIG-level brainstorming around relevant resources, and commenting upon lesson design documents from previous courses. The in-progress lesson designs were regularly circulated out to the broader SIG community for constructive peer-review, with prompts informed by the weekly themes. In addition to these formal interdependencies, work by participants in their small design groups was also naturally informed by their own participation in forum discussions and other collaborative knowledge building activities in the broader SIG.

A clearly explicated learning design calls for a targeted approach to learning analytics. In this paper, we will use learning analytics approaches to investigate the extent to which these various groups could make the MOOC their own, and benefit from appropriate learning trajectories and a personally relevant community experience. We will contextualize the co-creation of course artefacts within a multi-level social context, analyzing the impact of the SIGs, the design groups, and individual behaviour on lesson design quality, as indicated by a coding scheme.

In this contribution, we present the design of a MOOC with a nested social structure (Sect. 3). Furthermore, we present a new coding scheme to assess the quality of the collaborative artifact generated by the MOOC participants, and an analysis framework to analyse the relationships among the different social granularities in the nested structure (Sect. 4). Finally, we present the relationships among various social levels based on our multi-level analysis framework (Sect. 5).

---

[1] A separate use case for cohorts, not discussed here, is to present different content to different populations, such as on-campus learners and informal learners.

[2] Learning Tools Interoperability, a protocol for embedding components in a Learning Management System.

2 Related Work

Cohorts in Computer Supported Collaborative Learning (CSCL): The idea of scripting collaboration in forums/asynchronous chats/discussion groups has been studied in detail over many years in CSCL. One central idea to manage a large number of students, is to scaffold the collaborative learning processes using cohorts [5]. The cohorts can be based upon many factors, such as: roles [22], tasks [4,18], learning context [15], or learners' experience [24]. In the present contribution, we propose a design based on semantically meaningful cohorts, based on the contextual (learning) interests of the participants. In the MOOC, "Inquiry and Technology for Teachers", the SIGs were created based on the disciplines the participants used to teach in their respective institutions.

Online activities as a measure of student behaviour: Previous research has shown that there is a close relation between students' online behaviour and their success in MOOCs. We list a few examples here. El Badrway et al. [6] used collaborative multi-regression with online activities (form views, comments. posts, videos watched, quizzes answered) to predict students' grade. Similarly, Pardo and colleagues [19] used weekly data from on-line activities, such as, number of play/pause events, number of quizzes submitted number of exercises answered correctly/incorrectly to predict students' performance. Kenneedy et al. [11] used the success rate in the previous assignments to predict students' success in the next assignments. Coffrin et al. [3] used on-line access routines (videos and assessment submission), to predict students' success. Ren et al. [21] used number of sessions, average session length, number log in, number of quiz, number of videos, pauses, total view time, homework problems (time, sessions) to predict students' performance. Sharma et al. [23] showed that delay in video watching, assignment and quiz submission, correlated negatively to grade.

Social Network and/or forum text mining: Another stream of research has used the Social Network Analysis (SNA) based methods to predict final grades of students. For example Brown et al. [1] found that certain cliques in SNA perform better than the others. Other SNA based variables such as betweenness, upvotes, centrality, degree [2,10]; density, centrality, efficiency, content richness [20]; forum questions, answers, reads, contributions [25]; forum text [16]; were found to be correlated with students' performance. Khan and colleagues [12] showed that there is a correlation between students' grade and their forum access routines. Some researchers have found the forum or Learning Management Systems (LMS) access routines are predictive of students' grades. For example, reading forums [8], number of forum/LMS visits and time spent on LMS [7,13,17], were found to be good predictors of students' performance in a MOOC.

In this paper, we combine the online activities and the SNA based variables to quantify the participant activities at different levels of social scales of the MOOC (Sect. 4). We also show how scaffolding the co-creation of the collaborative artifact, and the peer-review process helps the participants produce high quality artifacts (Sect. 5).

3 MOOC on Inquiry and Technology for Teachers

The MOOC featured in this study was designed to support in-service teachers in their efforts to integrate inquiry and technology into their lessons. Although open to anyone, it was explicitly marketed to in-service teachers, and was designed to build upon their professional experience and respond to their real challenges, providing tools, examples and approaches that could be directly applied within their professional settings.

The course came out of a collaboration between the University of Toronto Schools (UTS), a university-affiliated private secondary school, and the Encore research group led by Dr. Jim Slotta, enabling us to provide an integration of academic and theoretical ideas, with applied practice. Both the UTS principal, as well as a number of their experienced teachers, contributed to the design and the contents of the MOOC. In particular, we wanted to showcase the specific cases of technology-enhanced inquiry that were happening at UTS, including some that were the result of research collaborations with Dr. Slotta's group, and some that had occurred spontaneously within the school.

3.1 Course Design

The following weekly themes were chosen to bring participants into contact with a variety of technologies and pedagogical topics relevant to their teaching: (1) Inquiry and student-centred pedagogy; (2) Designing inquiry activities and assessments; (3) Collaborative learning; (4) Handheld/mobile devices; (5) Knowledge co-construction and student-contributed content; and (6) Inquiry enactment.

The participants engaged with these weekly topics in a number of ways, on different social planes, as depicted in Fig. 1. Each week began with a selection of videos, ranging from theoretical and academic to applied and practical. Participants were asked to write an individual reflection on the topic, to connect the theory with their own experience. This was followed by a forum discussion within the SIG, shaped by prompts appropriate to each week's topic, and an individual evaluation of participants' own discussion forum activity.

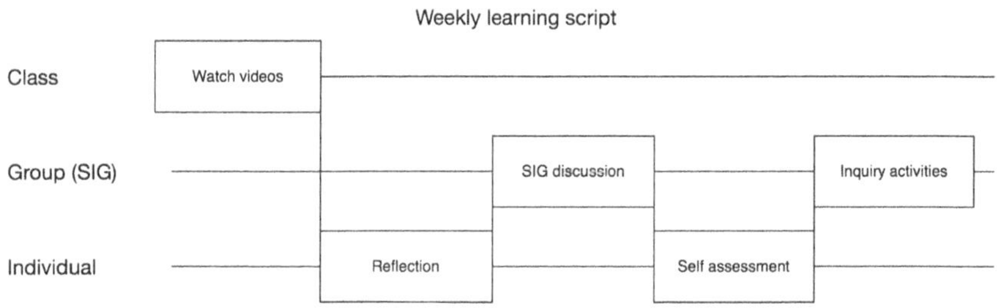

Fig. 1. Pedagogical graph of weekly activities.

Finally, there were a set of inquiry activities each week, which began by contributing to the SIG knowledge base, by for example commenting on old lesson designs, crowd-sourcing relevant technology resources, or brainstorming ideas through voting and commenting. The second part of the inquiry activities centered around the lesson design groups.

3.2 Design Groups

The organizing principle of the course was the co-creation of a lesson design, utilizing principles and resources from the course, but adapted to the teacher's own interests and needs. Participants suggested lesson topics, and formed small teams of 2–6 members during the first week of the course. We developed a "collaborative workbench" tool to support group collaboration and coordination, which contained all the information and tools needed by the small groups (see Fig. 2).

Each week, groups received new prompts and suggestions relevant to the weekly theme, gradually increasing in sophistication. Some sections of the collaborative workbench were private to the group, such as chat, messaging, and scratchpad, while others were bringing in relevant resources from the broader

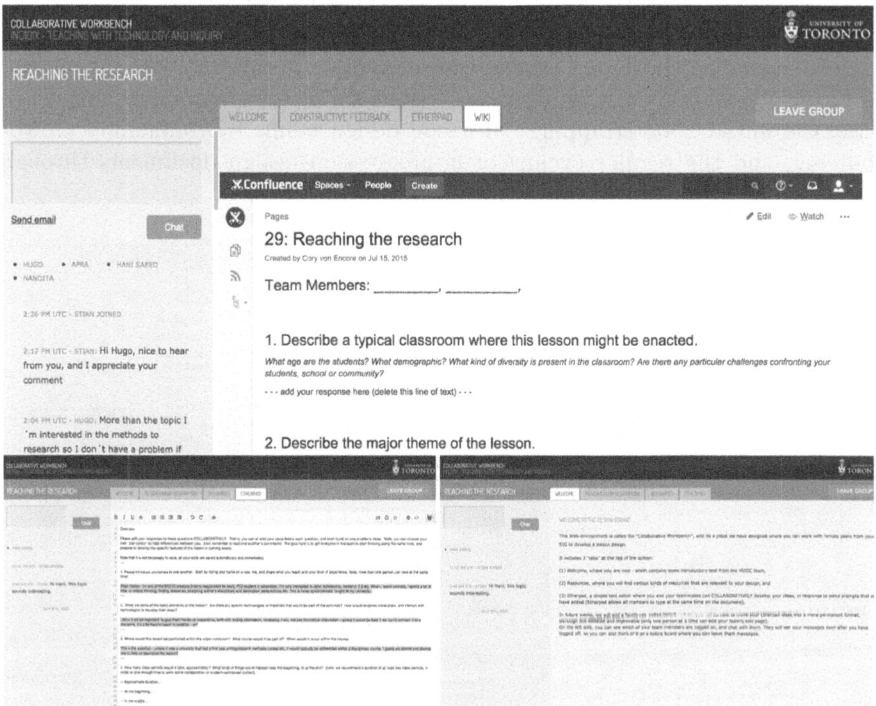

Fig. 2. The collaborative workbench, a unified interface to multiple components.

community, such as constructive peer review, and brainstormed resources. Finally, the wiki page, where the group drafted the lesson design, was a public resource, available to the rest of the SIG for review.

The lesson design document was built around a template with the prompts listed below. These were not all made available to the students in the first week, but rather incrementally added to the document.

1. Describe a typical classroom where this lesson might be enacted.
2. Describe the major theme of the lesson.
3. What are the learning goals of the technology-enhanced lesson?
4. Aspects of the design: Student-Centered Design/Peer Collaboration/Use of Handheld or Mobile Computers/Supporting Equity and Diversity
5. What is the activity structure of the lesson?
6. Assessment notes.
7. Enactment notes, and ethics or enactment concerns.

Most weeks, the inquiry activities included peer reviewing lesson design documents in progress. Participants were not asked to rate the quality of unfinished products, but rather to suggest ways of improving the documents, informed by the weekly theme. Given that only a subset of students were actively engaged in the authoring of lesson designs, each lesson design group would receive a large number of aggregated suggestions to inform their regular work.

Figure 3 shows a systematic depiction of the various pedagogical scripts in the MOOC, including the flow of artefacts from previous iterations of the course, and to future iterations, the way activities contribute to the community knowledge base, the initial "bootstrapping" of lesson design teams by community crowdsourcing, and the regular cycling of in-progression design documents through

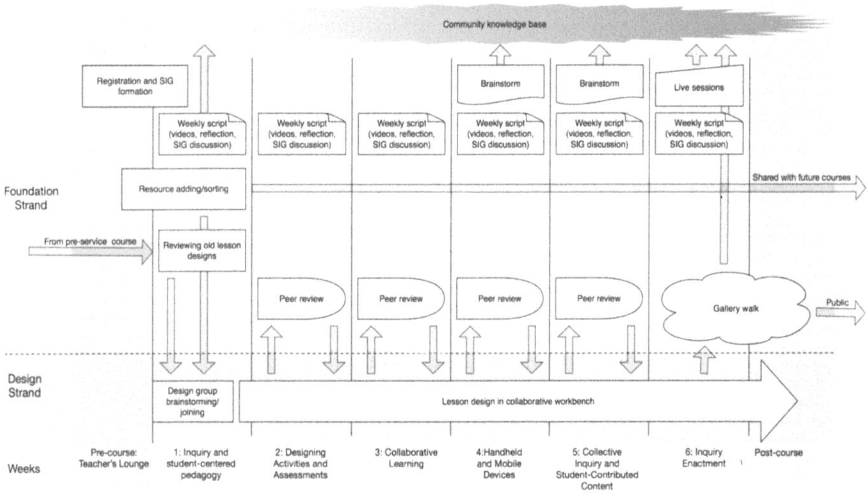

Fig. 3. Pedagogical graph of weekly activities.

the SIG community for review, and back to the design groups. The script was intentionally developed to account for the fact that one group of participants would want to engage deeply in sustained co-creation, and another group would want a more "traditional" MOOC experience, but that these two groups could not only both be catered to, but also made to be positively interdependent on each other.

4 Variables

Figure 4 shows the nested social structure of the MOOC and the variables we measure at different levels. The top-most level is the whole MOOC learners' population. The second level is the cohorts or, as we will refer to them in the rest of this paper, "Special Interest Groups (SIGs)". The third level contains the design groups. Finally, the fourth level is comprised of the individual learners.

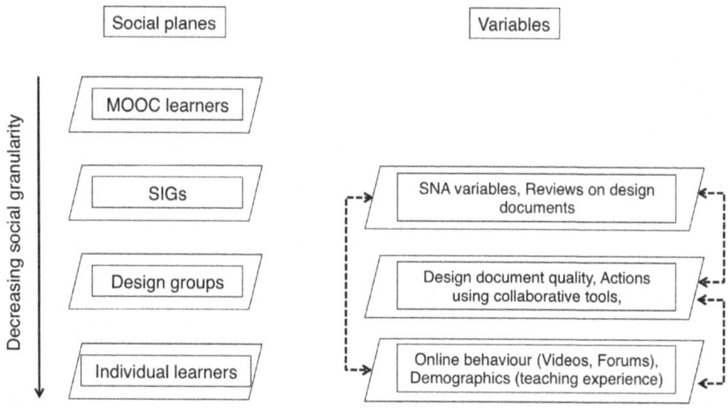

Fig. 4. Social planes (left) and the variables defined at different planes (right). **Left:** the number of members in a social plane decreases as we move from the MOOC participants at the top to the individual learners at the bottom. **Right:** we define variables at three levels, the dashed arrows represent the different relations among the variables computed at the three different social planes.

Each social plane has a set of variables that are either collected at a specific plane or represents the flow of the information between the two levels. The different variables according to their respective planes or the interaction between two planes are as follows: **SIGs in terms of teaching levels (SIG level):** We categorised the SIGs into three categories based on the levels of the education they addressed: K1-6, K7-12, and HighED.

Social Network Variables (SIG level): in the MOOC's forum, each SIG had its own social network. We computed the Social Network Analysis (SNA) variables for each SIG: in-degree, out-degree, and network centrality.

Design document quality (design group level): the final artifact produced by the learners in each design group was the design document, where the members provided details of a course that they were teaching in their respective institutions. Two of the authors coded the quality of these design document (inter-rater reliability = 0.82) based on the following quality metrics, which were derived from the learning objectives of the MOOC. Each criteria was scored from 1–5, with 0 indicating total absence.

- *Learning Objective (LO):* Level of detail put in the learning objectives mentioned.
- *Activity Design (AD):* Richness in the design of the activities according to the learning objectives.
- *Coherence (CO):* Level of coherence in the various parts of the design document.
- *Innovative use of technology (DT):* Depth of thought put into the innovative use of technology in the design document.
- *Incorporating inquiry-based learning (IB):* The use of inquiry based learning principles in the design document.

Reviews on the design documents (interaction between SIG and design group levels): in different weeks of the course, the SIG members were given a set a questions to comment on different design documents. For each week that the reviews were requested, the $reviewMetric$ measures how many questions the reviewers answered, and in what detail.

Collaborative actions (design group level): while collaborating on the design documents, the design group members could use various collaborative tools; for example group wiki page, chat tool, and group Etherpad (for collaborative note taking). We measured the amount of activity on these tools per design group.

Video watching behaviour (individual level): there were four different types of videos each week.

- Fireside: Informal weekly introduction, recorded as the course progressed, and reflecting community evolution and emerging questions.
- Academic: Theoretical and conceptual introduction to the weekly theme by Dr. Slotta.
- Principal: Introduction to the weekly theme by principal or vice-principal of a middle school (UTS).
- Practitioner: Interviews with teachers and mini-documentaries from classroom exercises implementing ideas from the weekly theme.

For each video type and each week, we computed: the number of new and old videos watched and the time difference between two video viewing. Besides this, we also counted the different video watching actions from the click stream data: play, pause, seek-back, seek-forward, and speed-change.

Forum access behaviour (individual level): besides computing the SNA variables, we also computed the individual forum actions in terms of the viewing, posting, commenting, and searching behaviour for the whole course.

5 Results and Discussion

In the previous section, we presented 6 different sets of variables based on the activities and the social planes. In this section, we report the relations we found among these variables based on the social plans or the interaction between the two social planes.

5.1 SIG-Individual

Video Watching Behaviour for different SIG types. We divided the video watching behaviour into two level: (1) the number of videos watched in the same week as they were released; (2) the number of videos watched in the later weeks as they were released. For the number of videos watched in the same week as they were released, overall, members in HighEd SIGs watch the most Fireside ($F[2,4819] = 6.80$, $p = .001$) and Academic ($F[2,4819] = 10.10$, $p < .0001$) videos. Whereas, members in K7-12 SIGs watch the least number of Fireside and Academic videos. On the other hand, members in K7-12 SIGs watch the most number of Principal ($F[2,4819] = 5.13$, $p = .005$) and those in K1-6 the least. Members in the K1-6 SIGs watch the most Practitioner ($F[2,4819] = 10.50$, $p < .0001$) videos; where as, members of HighEd SIGs watch the least number of Practitioner videos. For the number of videos watched in the later weeks than they were released, overall, members in the HighEd SIGs watch the most Academic ($F[2,4850] = 8.95$, $p = .006$), Principal ($F[2,3979] = 14.69$, $p < .0001$), and Practitioner ($F[2,4291] = 7.00$, $p = .0009$) videos; and the members of the

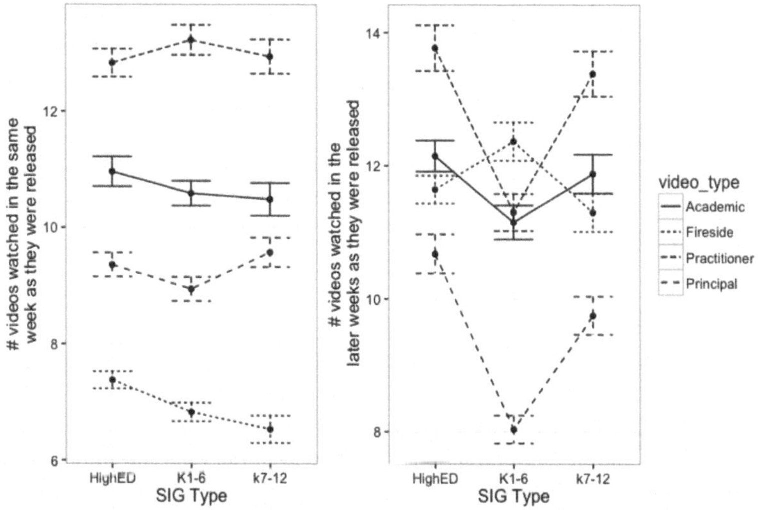

Fig. 5. Left: Number of videos watched in the same week as they were released by the members of different SIG types. **Right:** Number of videos watched in the week later than the week they were released by the members of different SIG types.

K1-6 watch the least number of Academic, Principal, and Practitioner videos. While the members of the K1-6 SIGs watch the most Fireside ($F[2,4819] = 5.07$, $p = .006$) videos, in this case those in K7-12 SIGs watch the least number of Fireside videos. (See Fig. 5).

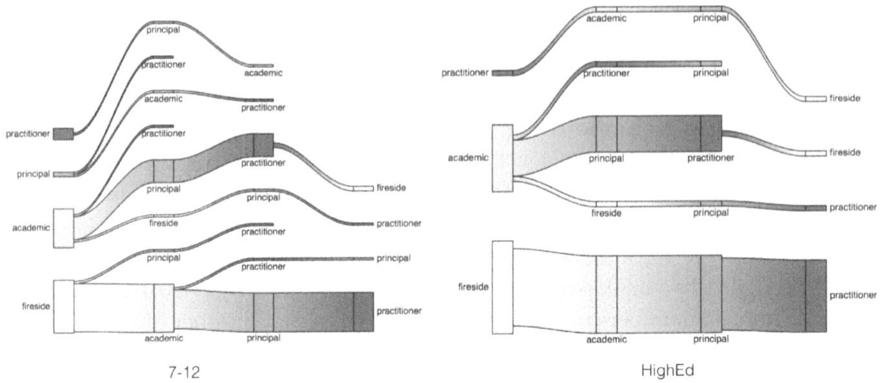

Fig. 6. Sequence of first watches of each video (width indicates number of students).

Student flow through videos. Most participants followed the default ordering of the videos in the EdX interface, but to see how these pathways could subtly differ between differently categorized SIGs, we chose a SIG, Secondary Sciences, whose members are representative of the 7–12 mean (SIGs where most members taught between 7th to 12th grade), and another SIG representative of the HighEd population (Foreign Languages and English as a Second Language). Plotting the pathways of participants through the videos (only first views of each videos are taken into account) for week 4, as an example, we can see that HighEd participants are more likely to follow the standard pathway, and focus attention on the academic video. Whereas the 7–12 participants show a much larger diversity of paths, and more focus on school-based videos (practitioner and principal) (see Fig. 6).

5.2 SIG-Design Group

Reviews and design document quality. Table 1 shows the relations between the *reviewMetric* and the design document quality. We observe that the *reviewMetrics* from weeks 2 and 3 are correlated to all the quality codes. However, we observe no such relation for the other two weeks. One plausible explanation for this could be the fact that the review questions from weeks 2 and 3 were about generating/brainstorming the ideas and incorporating collaboration in the student activities. These were higher level concepts, which could have been more significant for high ratings in the quality indicators. On the other hand, the review questions from week 4 were about specific topics, for example, using smart phones and tablets in the activity design. This might not had any effect on the design document, as many learners did not plan their activity around such devices. Finally, the review questions from week 5 were about incorporation of inquiry based learning in the lesson plans. This, we hypothesize, was too late in the course time-line to have any effect on the design document quality, as after receiving an insightful feedback from week 5, the design groups might have had to change the whole lesson design to incorporate the new ideas.

SNA and design document quality. We observe a significant correlation between the design document quality and the network centrality from weeks 1 and 5 (Table 1). This might be due to the fact that these two weeks correspond to the initial and final weeks of the collaborative work on the design document. High network centrality depicts the fact that all the learners in a SIG were equally contributing to the forums. This could entail the brainstorming conversations among the peers.

Discussion - SIG-Design group. The two aforementioned results indicate that the scripting of the course might have an effect on the activities of the learners, as well as the interactions between the different social planes. The review questionnaires scripted to be abstract in the beginning of the course, gradually become more concrete. The relationships we found reflect this process. The first two review weeks (1 and 3) had an impact on the quality of the final artifact and the last two did not. Moreover, the script of the course from weeks 1 (initiating collaboration) to 5 (finalising the collaborative artifact) has corresponding actions in the forums as well.

5.3 Within Design Group

Collaborative tools and design document quality There were many collaborative tools provided to the design groups to facilitate the group work. For example, collaborative etherpads, wikis, and chat-tools. We observed a significant correlation between both the number of wiki-edits, and chat events, with the design document quality. This is not surprising for us, as wiki-edits and chat-activities depict the offline and online sharing and discussing of ideas, respectively. This relation can also be attributed to the design of the course and availability of the collaborative/cooperative tools (Table 1).

5.4 Design Group - Individual

Video watching behaviour and design document quality. We observe a significant negative correlation between the number of seeking-back events on the videos and the design document quality (Table 1). This might have stemmed from the fact that the seeking-back behaviour is indicative of higher perceived difficulty [14]. Those groups who had difficulties in understanding the content also had lower design document quality. Moreover, there was a significant positive correlation between the number of new videos watched and the design document quality. Those groups who watched more videos also had higher design document

Table 1. Correlations between variables and quality metrics. All the correlations are have at least p-value < 0.1. In the following the significance level is as follows: $* < 0.05$, $** < 0.01$, $*** < 0.001$

Ind.	Social level	Variable	Estimate	Std.err.
LO	Individual (video)	Seek.Back	-0.007288**	0.002670
		newVideos	0.125865***	0.030932
	Individual (forum)	Forum.Load	-0.020290***	0.008753
		Forum.Search	0.029055	0.016544
	Design group (collaboration)	Collab.Chat	0.081835*	0.034158
		Collab.WikiEdit	0.928531***	0.180442
	SIG (SNA)	Centrality week 1	2.930e+02**	1.098e+02
		Out degree week 1	-1.609e+02**	5.829e+01
		Centrality week 5	5.046e-04*	2.219e-04
	SIG (reviews)	Review Week 1	0.0011257**	0.0003933
		Review Week 3	0.0009519**	0.0004802
AD	Individual (video)	Seek.Back	-0.006289**	0.002604
		newVideos	0.083227**	0.030372
	Individual (forum)	Forum.Load	-0.017708*	0.008426
		Forum.Search	0.033812*	0.015926
	Design group (collaboration)	Collab.Chat	0.0914995**	0.0331748
		Collab.WikiEdit	0.7468573***	0.1752467
	SIG (SNA)	Centrality week 1	2.381e+02*	1.116e+02
		Out degree week 1	-1.331e+02*	5.924e+01
		Centrality week 5	4.746e-04*	2.256e-04
	SIG (reviews)	Review Week 1	0.0010307**	0.0003605
		Review Week 3	0.0009525*	0.0004401
CO	Individual (video)	Seek.Back	-0.006224	0.002739*
		newVideos	0.089395**	0.031171
	Individual (forum)	Forum.Load	-0.020801**	0.008726
		Forum.Search	0.031160	0.016494
	Design group (collaboration)	Collab.Chat	0.087815**	0.035658
		Collab.WikiEdit	0.736609***	0.188362
	SIG (SNA)	Centrality week 1	2.685e+02*	1.159e+02
		Out degree week 1	-1.479e+02**	6.155e+01
		Centrality week 5	5.105e-04*	2.343e-04
	SIG (reviews)	Review Week 1	0.0009799**	0.0003760
		Review Week 3	0.0011245**	0.0004591
DT	Individual (video)	Seek.Back	-0.0055070*	0.0024674
		newVideos	0.075931**	0.028272
	Individual (forum)	Forum.Load	-1.770e-02*	7.781e-03
		Forum.Search	3.490e-02*	1.471e-02
	Design group (collaboration)	Collab.Chat	0.0843472**	0.0306641
		Collab.WikiEdit	0.6282267***	0.1619840
	SIG (SNA)	Centrality week 1	2.308e+02*	1.031e+02
		Out degree week 1	-1.268e+02*	5.474e+01
		Centrality week 5	5.424e-04**	2.084e-04
	SIG (reviews)	Review Week 1	0.0010294**	0.0003357
		Review Week 3	0.0010323**	0.0004098
IB	Individual (video)	Seek.Back	-0.0049693*	0.0024701
		newVideos	0.066964*	0.028568
	Individual (forum)	Forum.Load	-0.013087	0.007833
		Forum.Search	0.035876*	0.014805
	Design group (collaboration)	Collab.Chat	0.0828273**	0.0295544
		Collab.WikiEdit	0.6955376***	0.1561218
	SIG (SNA)	Centrality week 1	2.248e+02*	1.030e+02
		Out degree week 1	-1.235e+02*	5.472e+01
		Centrality week 5	5.496e-04**	2.083e-04
	SIG (reviews)	Review Week 1	0.0009621**	0.0003382
		Review Week 3	0.0008912*	0.0004129

quality. These relations show the contribution of having a mutual-understanding, achieved by watching videos, of the video material while co-creating the artifact.

Forum behaviour and design document quality. We observed a positive correlation between number of forum searches and the design document quality. However number of forum visits were negatively correlated to the design document quality. These two relations indicate that only visiting/reading/contributing to the meaningful threads was helpful in co-creation of the design document.

6 Conclusions

In this paper we have described an innovative MOOC design, with novel technologies and pedagogical scripts that allowed participants with similar disciplinary interests to find each other, and which supported both intensive small-group co-creation, while at the same time letting participants benefit from a larger community of peers (Sect. 3). We introduced a new qualitative coding scheme to assess the co-created design documents produced by the different design groups. Finally we have introduced a framework for multilevel analysis, where the design document quality is considered as a dependent variable, and we have used various process variables from different social planes of the course to explain the relationship among these social planes as well as the different design document quality levels (Sect. 4).

Having semantically meaningful SIGs in the course had two effects: (1) on participants' actions, and (2) on the design document quality. We provided evidence for these two effects in two different ways: (1) by showing the differences in actions of SIG members, and (2) by showing the relationship between actions of design group members, and the quality of their design document (Sect. 5).

One of the interesting observations we found was that some of the review prompts did not show the strong positive correlation with high quality design documents that we had expected. We observed that the prompts with high levels of abstraction (brainstorming and collaboration) were positively correlated with design document quality while prompts related to specific technologies and pedagogies (mobile devices and student generated content) were not correlated with the quality. One plausible explanation for the latter could be the timing of the prompts. The specific prompts were towards the end of the MOOC, when the design groups were too advanced in their documents to be able to incorporate new ideas. We plan to investigate the feedback uptake by the design groups in the future.

There is a growing interest towards MOOCs with complex social structures, where participants benefit from small group collaboration, as well as larger scale communities of interest. This contribution presents one such example and shows the contextualisation of data within the nested social structure. The authors hope that this contribution exemplifies forthcoming MOOCs with innovative social and pedagogical scenarios. In conclusion, this multi-level analysis has opened a few new directions for further investigations and interventions. For example, review uptake as mentioned above, as well as focusing on individual learning gains and small group collaborative mechanisms.

References

1. Brown, R., Lynch, C.F., Eagle, M., Albert, J., Barnes, T., Baker, R., Bergner, Y., McNamara, D.: Good communities and bad communities: does membership affect performance. In: Proceedings of the 8th International Conference on Educational Data Mining, pp. 612–614 (2015)
2. Bydžovská, H.: Towards freshmen performance prediction. In: Proceedings of the 8th International Conference on Educational Data Mining (2015)
3. Coffrin, C., Corrin, L., de Barba, P., Kennedy, G.: Visualizing patterns of student engagement and performance in MOOCs. In: Proceedings of the Fourth International Conference on Learning Analytics and Knowledge, pp. 83–92. ACM (2014)
4. Cramphorn, C.: An evaluation of formal and underlying factors influencing student participation within e-learning web discussion forums. In: Proceedings of the Fourth International Conference on Networked Learning, pp. 417–423 (2004)
5. Dillenbourg, P.: Over-scripting CSCL: the risks of blending collaborative learning with instructional design. In: Kirschner, P.A. (ed.) Three Worlds of CSCL: Can We Support CSCL?. Open Universiteit Nederland, Heerlen (2002)
6. Elbadrawy, A., Studham, R.S., Karypis, G.: Collaborative multi-regression models for predicting students' performance in course activities. In: Proceedings of the Fifth International Conference on Learning Analytics and Knowledge, pp. 103–107. ACM (2015)
7. García-Saiz, D., Zorrilla, M.: A promising classification method for predicting distance student' s performance. In: Proceedings of the 5th International Conference on Educational Data Mining (2012)
8. Gunnarsson, B.L., Alterman, R.: Predicting failure: a case study in co-blogging. In: Proceedings of the 2nd International Conference on Learning Analytics and Knowledge, pp. 263–266. ACM (2012)
9. Håklev, S., Slotta, J.D.: A principled approach to the design of collaborative MOOC curricula. In: Delgado Kloos, C., Jermann, P., Pérez-Sanagustín, M., Seaton, D.T., White, S. (eds.) EMOOCs 2017. LNCS, vol. 10254, pp. 58–67. Springer, Cham (2017). doi:10.1007/978-3-319-59044-8_7
10. Joksimović, S., Manataki, A., Gašević, D., Dawson, S., Kovanović, V., De Kereki, I.F.: Translating network position into performance: importance of centrality in different network configurations. In: Proceedings of the Sixth International Conference on Learning Analytics & Knowledge, pp. 314–323. ACM (2016)
11. Kennedy, G., Coffrin, C., de Barba, P., Corrin, L.: Predicting success: how learners' prior knowledge, skills and activities predict MOOC performance. In: Proceedings of the Fifth International Conference on Learning Analytics and Knowledge, pp. 136–140. ACM (2015)
12. Khan, T.M., Clear, F., Sajadi, S.S.: The relationship between educational performance and online access routines: analysis of students' access to an online discussion forum. In: Proceedings of the 2nd International Conference on Learning Analytics and Knowledge, pp. 226–229. ACM (2012)
13. Kim, J.H., Seodaemun-Gu, S., Park, Y., Song, J., Jo, I.-H.: Predicting students' learning performance by using online behavior patterns in blended learning environments: comparison of two cases on linear and non-linear model. In: Proceedings of the 7th International Conference on Educational Data Mining (2014)

14. Li, N., Kidzinski, L., Jermann, P., Dillenbourg, P.: Characterising MOOC video behaviours with video interaction styles: what do they tell. In: Proceedings of the 10th European Conference on Technology Enhanced Learning (2015)
15. Lim, W.-Y., Hedberg, J.G., Yeo, J.A.-C., Hung, D.: Fostering communities of practice-a case study of heads of it departments. In: The Annual Convention of the Association for Educational Communications and Technology (2005)
16. Luo, J., Sorour, S.E., Goda, K., Mine, T.: Predicting student grade based on free-style comments using Word2Vec and ANN by considering prediction results obtained in consecutive lessons. In: Proceedings of the 8th International Conference on Educational Data Mining (2015)
17. McCuaig, J., Baldwin, J.: Identifying successful learners from interaction behaviour. In: Proceedings of the 5th International Conference on Educational Data Mining (2012)
18. McDougall, M.J., Nason, R.A., McRobbie, C.J.: Growth of teacher knowledge: the promise of CSCL. In: AARE 2004 International Education Research Conference, Melbourne, Australia. Australian Association for Research in Education (2004)
19. Pardo, A., Mirriahi, N., Dawson, S., Zhao, Y., Zhao, A., Gašević, D.: Identifying learning strategies associated with active use of video annotation software. In: Proceedings of the Fifth International Conference on Learning Analytics And Knowledge, pp. 255–259. ACM (2015)
20. Paredes, W.C., Chung, K.S.K.: Modelling learning & performance: a social networks perspective. In: Proceedings of the 2nd International Conference on Learning Analytics and Knowledge, pp. 34–42. ACM (2012)
21. Ren, Z., Rangwala, H., Johri, A.: Predicting performance on MOOC assessments using multi-regression models. In: Proceedings of the 9th International Conference on Educational Data Mining (2016)
22. Schellens, T., Van Keer, H., De Wever, B., Valcke, M.: Scripting by assigning roles: does it improve knowledge construction in asynchronous discussion groups? Int. J. Comput. Support. Collab. Learn. **2**(2), 225–246 (2007)
23. Sharma, K., Jermann, P., Dillenbourg, P.: Identifying styles and paths toward success in MOOCs. International Educational Data Mining Society (2015)
24. Stephens, A.C., Hartmann, C.E.: Using an online discussion forum to engage secondary mathematics teachers in teaching with technology. In: American Educational Research Association Annual Meeting (2002)
25. Tomkins, S., Ramesh, A., Getoor, L.: Predicting post-test performance from online student behavior: a high school MOOC case study. In: Proceedings of the 9th International Conference on Educational Data Mining (2016)

Awareness Is Not Enough: Pitfalls of Learning Analytics Dashboards in the Educational Practice

Ioana Jivet[1(✉)], Maren Scheffel[1], Hendrik Drachsler[1,2,3], and Marcus Specht[1]

[1] Open Universiteit, Valkenburgerweg 177, 6419 AT Heerlen, Netherlands
{ioana.jivet,maren.scheffel,hendrik.drachsler,marcus.specht}@ou.nl
[2] Goethe University Frankfurt, Frankfurt, Germany
[3] German Institute for International Educational Research (DIPF), Frankfurt, Germany
drachsler@dipf.de

Abstract. It has been long argued that learning analytics has the potential to act as a "middle space" between the learning sciences and data analytics, creating technical possibilities for exploring the vast amount of data generated in online learning environments. One common learning analytics intervention is the learning dashboard, a support tool for teachers and learners alike that allows them to gain insight into the learning process. Although several related works have scrutinised the state-of-the-art in the field of learning dashboards, none have addressed the theoretical foundation that should inform the design of such interventions. In this systematic literature review, we analyse the extent to which theories and models from learning sciences have been integrated into the development of learning dashboards aimed at learners. Our critical examination reveals the most common educational concepts and the context in which they have been applied. We find evidence that current designs foster competition between learners rather than knowledge mastery, offering misguided frames of reference for comparison.

Keywords: Learning dashboards · Learning theory · Learning analytics · Systematic review · Learning science · Social comparison · Competition

1 Introduction

Learning Analytics (LA) emerged from the need to harness the potential of the increasingly large data sets describing learner data generated by the widespread use of online leaning environments and it has been defined as "the measurement, collection, analysis, and reporting of data about learners and their contexts, for purposes of understanding and optimising learning and the environments in which it occurs" [37]. Ferguson [13] identified two main challenges when it comes to learning analytics: (i) building strong connections to learning sciences and (ii) focusing on the perspectives of learners.

É. Lavoué et al. (Eds.): EC-TEL 2017, LNCS 10474, pp. 82–96, 2017.
DOI: 10.1007/978-3-319-66610-5_7

There is a common notion in the LA community that learning analytics research should be deeply grounded in learning sciences [28,29]. Suthers and Verbert [38] labelled LA the "middle space" as it lies at the intersection between technology and learning sciences. Moreover, LA should be seen as an educational approach guided by pedagogy and not the other way around [19]. However, there is a strong emphasis on the "analytics", i.e. computation of the data and creation of predictive models, and not so much on the "learning", i.e. applying and researching LA in the learning context where student outcomes can be improved [17].

One of the focuses of LA research is to empower teachers and learners to make informed decisions about the learning process, mainly by visualising the collected learner data through dashboards [9]. Learning analytics dashboards are "single displays that aggregate different indicators about learner(s), learning process(es) and/or learning context(s) into one or multiple visualizations" [35]. Dashboards have been developed for different stakeholder groups, including learners, teachers, researchers or administrative staff [35]. Charleer et al. [5] suggest that LA dashboards could be used as powerful metacognitive tools for learners, triggering them to reason about the effort invested in the learning activities and learning outcomes. However, a large majority of dashboards are still aimed at teachers, or at both teachers and learners [35]. Moreover, there has been very little research in terms of what effects such tools have on learning [26].

As a first step towards building effective dashboards for learners, we need to understand how learning sciences can be considered in the design and pedagogical use of learning dashboards. Following Suther and Verbert's [38] position that learning analytics research should be explicit about the theory or conception of learning underlying the work, we sought out to investigate which educational concepts constitute the theoretical foundation for the development of learning dashboards aimed at learners.

A number of previous works reviewed LA dashboards from different perspectives, including their design and evaluation. Verbert et al. [42] introduced a conceptual framework for analysing LA applications and reviewed 15 dashboards based on the target users, displayed data and the focus of the evaluation. A follow-up review [43] extended this analysis to 24 dashboards, examining the context in which the dashboards had been deployed, the data sources, the devices used and the evaluation methodology. Yoo et al. [47] reviewed the design and evaluation of 10 educational dashboards for teachers and students through their proposed evaluative tool based on Few's principles of dashboard design [15] and Kirkpatrick's four-level evaluation model [25]. A more recent systematic review by Schwendimann et al. [35] of 55 dashboards looked at the context in which dashboards had been deployed, their purpose, the displayed indicators, the technologies used, the maturity of the evaluation and open issues.

The scope of all these reviews included learning analytics dashboards, regardless of their target users. Focusing on the challenges identified by Ferguson [13], we narrow down our scope to LA dashboards aimed at learners in order to focus on their perspective. A closely related work to this paper was published by

Bodily and Verbert [4]. They provided a systematic review that focused exclusively on student-facing LA systems, including dashboards, educational recommender systems, EDM systems, ITS and automated feedback systems. The systems were analysed based on functionality, data sources, design analysis, perceived effects on learners and actual effects.

Although other works looked into the learning theory foundations of game-based learning [46], one major limitation of previous dashboard reviews is that none investigate the connection to learning sciences. Moreover, [4,35] provide recommendations for the design of learner dashboards, but none suggest the use of educational concepts as a basis for the design or evaluation of the dashboards. Through this systematic literature review we aim to bridge this gap by investigating the relation between educational concepts and the design of learning dashboards. Dashboard design was previously examined by looking at the type of data displayed on the dashboard and the type of charts or visualisation that were used. However, in this study, we will specifically focus on how the data presented on the dashboard is contextualised and framed to ease the sense-making for the learners.

Throughout this literature review, we explore how educational concepts are integrated into the design of learning dashboards. Our study is guided by the following research question: *According to which educational concepts are learning analytics dashboards designed?*

2 Methodology

Prior to the systematic review, we conducted an informative literature search in order to get an overall picture of the field. We ran the systematic literature review following the PRISMA statement [31] and we selected the following databases which contain research in the field of Technology Enhanced Learning: ACM Digital Library, IEEEXplore, SpringerLink, Science Direct, Wiley Online Library, Web of Science and EBSCOhost. Additionally, we included Google Scholar to cover any other sources, limiting the number of retrieved results to 200. We searched the selected databases using the following search query: *"learning analytics" AND (visualization OR visualisation OR dashboard OR widget)*. The first term narrows down the search field to *learning analytics*, while the second part of the query is meant to cover different terminologies used for this type of intervention, addressing one of the limitations identified in [35]. Although the scope of this review is limited to visualisations that have learners as end-users, it was not possible to articulate this criterion in relevant search terms. Therefore, the approach that we took was to built a query that retrieves all dashboards, regardless of their target end-users, and remove the ones that fall out of our scope in a later phase.

The queries were run on February 20th, 2017, collecting 1439 hits. Each result was further screened for relevance, i.e. whether it described a learning dashboard aimed at learners, by examining the title and the abstract, thus reducing the list of potential candidate papers to 212. Eleven papers that we came across during the informal check and fit the scope of our survey were also added to the set of papers to be further examined. Next, we accessed the full text of each of these 223 studies in order to assess whether they are eligible for our study considering the following criteria:

1. the paper's full text is available in English;
2. the paper describes a fully developed dashboard, widget or visualisation, i.e. we excluded theoretical papers, essays or literature reviews;
3. the target user group of the dashboard is learners;
4. the authors explicitly mention theoretical concepts for the design;
5. the paper includes an evaluation of the dashboard.

We identified 95 papers that satisfied the first three criteria. Only half of these papers have theoretical grounding in educational concepts, suggesting a large gap between learning sciences and this type of learning analytics interventions. The focus of this study is set on *26 papers* that describe dashboards that both rely on educational concepts (criterion 4) and were empirically evaluated (criterion 5). The list of papers included in this review is available at bit.ly/LADashboards.

3 Results

We started this investigation by collecting the theoretical concepts and models used in the dashboards and analysing the relationships between the purpose of the dashboards and the concepts that were employed in the development of the dashboard. Next, we looked at how the design of these dashboards integrate different concepts from learning sciences.

3.1 Learning Theories and Models

By analysing the introduction, background and dashboard design sections of each of the papers included in this study, we identified 17 theories, models and concepts that we bundled into six clusters (see Table 1).

EC1: Cognitivism cluster relies upon the cognitivism paradigm which posits that learning is an internal process, involving the use of memory, thinking, metacognition and reflection [1]. This is the most represented category through self-regulated learning (SRL), 16 papers citing the works of Zimmerman [48], Pintrich [33] or Winne [44]. Deep vs surface learning theory explains different approaches to learning, where deep learners seek to understand the meaning behind the material and surface learners concentrate on reproducing the main facts [21]. *EC2: Constructivism cluster* is rooted in the assumption that learners are information constructors and learning is the product of social interaction [1]. Social constructivist learning theory [24] and Paul-Elder's critical thinking model [11] have been used mostly in dashboards aimed to offer learner support in collaborative settings, while Engeström's activity theory [12] was used as a pedagogical base for supporting university students overcome dyslexia. *EC3:*

Table 1. Six clusters presentation of educational concepts identified and the papers in which they appear. The list of papers included in this review is available at bit.ly/LADashboards

Cluster	Educational concept	Freq.	Papers
EC1: Cognitivism	Self-regulated learning	16	D1; D4; D5; D7; D9; D11; D12; D14; D15; D18; D20; D21; D22; D23; D25; D26
	Deep vs surface learning	2	D16; D19
EC2: Constructivism	Collaborative learning	6	D12; D13; D14; D16; D24; D26
	Social constructivist learning theory	4	D7; D13; D19; D22
	Engeström activity theory	1	D12
	Paul-Elder's critical thinking model	1	D19
EC3: Humanism	Experiential learning	2	D4; D13
	Learning dispositions	1	D2
	21st century skills	4	D2; D11; D13; D19
	Achievement goal orientation	3	D15; D19; D24
EC4: Descriptive models	Engagement model	1	D10
EC5: Instructional design	Universal Design for Learning instructional framework	1	D19
	Formative assessment	3	D3; D6; D19
	Bloom's taxonomy	3	D3; D4; D22
EC6: Psychology	Ekman's model for emotion classification	1	D23
	Social comparison	3	D8; D15; D25
	Culture	1	D25

Humanism cluster puts the learner at the centre of the learning process, seeking to engage the person as a whole and focusing on the study of the self, motivation and goals [8]. More recent works focus on developing 21st century skills [40] and learning dispositions [36]. Achievement goal orientation theory is concerned with learners' motivation for goal achievement [32]. *EC4: Descriptive models* cluster includes the engagement model [16] which differentiates between behavioural, emotional and cognitive engagement. Several papers also cover the pedagogical use of dashboards, aligning the *EC5: Instructional design* in which the dashboard is embedded with Bloom's taxonomy [3], formative assessment [34] or Universal Design for Learning framework [6]. While the majority of these clusters contain concepts belonging to the learning sciences field, we also identified three concepts that originate in the broader field of *EC6: Psychology*: Ekman's model of emotions and facial expressions [10], social comparison [14] and culture [18,22].

3.2 Dashboard Goals and Educational Concepts

In order to understand the reasons behind using these educational concepts, we analysed the goals of the dashboards and looked at how their use was explained in the papers. We extracted the goals of each dashboard and categorised them based on the competence they aimed to affect in learners: metacognitive, cognitive, behavioural or emotional (see Table 2). Most of the dashboards do not serve only one goal, but rather aim to catalyse changes in multiple competencies. A fifth category *C5: Self-regulation* was also added to account for papers that explicitly described their goal as supporting self-regulation, a concept that involves all four competencies [48].

Figure 1 illustrates the relation between the goals of the dashboards and the educational concept clusters listed in Table 1. We can draw some interesting observations from these connections. Firstly, the largest part of the visualisations aim to influence learners' *metacognitive* competence, with the purpose of supporting awareness and reflection. This aim is often motivated by SRL theory, a learning concept that heavily relies on the assumption that actions are consequences of thinking as SRL is achieved in cycles consisting of forethought, performance and self-reflection [49]. SRL also motivates the goal of monitoring progress and supporting planning, but to a lesser extent. Social constructivist learning theory and collaborative learning also appear quite frequently in relation to metacognition, due to the collaborative setting in which the dashboards were used. Dashboard developers argue that for effective collaboration, learners need to be aware of their teammates' learning behaviour, activities and outcomes. Other concepts used for affecting the metacognitive level are formative assessment as it implies evaluation of one's performance, 21st century skills with the focus on *learning how to learn* and social comparison as a means for framing the evaluation of one's performance.

Secondly, there is a strong emphasis on supporting the *self-regulation* competence by using cognitivist concepts. The design of these dashboards is usually informed by SRL theory. Constructivist concepts are also commonly used for the development of these dashboards because the context in which these dashboards were deployed is the online collaborative learning setting. Less used are instructional design concepts, more notable being the use of formative assessment as a means for reflection and self-evaluation.

Thirdly, in order to affect the *behavioural* level, SRL is again one of the most commonly used concepts, alongside social constructivism and collaborative learning. Social comparison has a stronger presence on this level as it is used to reveal the behaviour of peers as a source of suggestions on how learners could improve. Surprisingly, very few dashboards aim to support learners on the *cognitive* level, i.e. acquiring knowledge and improving performance, and the few

Table 2. Competencies, the goals that are intended to affect each competence and the papers in which they appear. The list of papers included in this review is available at bit.ly/LADashboards

Competence	Goal	Freq.	Papers
C1: Metacognitive	Improve metacognitive skills	4	D6; D7; D20; D23
	Support awareness and reflection	20	D1; D2; D3; D4; D6; D7; D9; D10; D11; D12; D13; D14; D17; D18; D20; D21; D22; D23; D25; D26
	Monitor progress	8	D7; D8; D11; D15; D19; D20; D22; D23
	Support planning	2	D20; D22
C2: Cognitive	Support goal achievement	3	D9; D18; D25
	Improve performance	3	D16; D23; D24
C3: Behavioural	Improve retention or engagement	2	D10; D25
	Improve online social behaviour	7	D7; D13; D14; D16; D19; D24; D26
	Improve help-seeking behaviour	1	D17
	Offer navigational support	2	D8; D15
C4: Emotional	Deactivate negative emotions	1	D9
	Increase motivation	4	D2; D8; D15; D19
C5: Self-regulation	Support self-regulation	13	D1; D4; D7; D9; D11; D12; D15; D19; D20; D21; D22; D23; D25

that do, rely mostly on SRL and social comparison. Finally, in order to animate changes on the *emotional* level, dashboards build mostly on social comparison and the modelling of learning dispositions and 21st century skills.

3.3 Reference Frames

According to the framework for designing pedagogical interventions to support student use of learning analytics proposed by Wise [45], learners need a "*representative reference frame*" for interpreting their data. We analysed this aspect by looking at how the information was contextualised on the dashboard based on the dashboard goals. We identified three types of reference frames: (i) social, i.e. comparison with other peers, (ii) achievement, i.e. in terms of goal achievement, and (iii) progress, i.e. comparison with an earlier self (see Table 3).

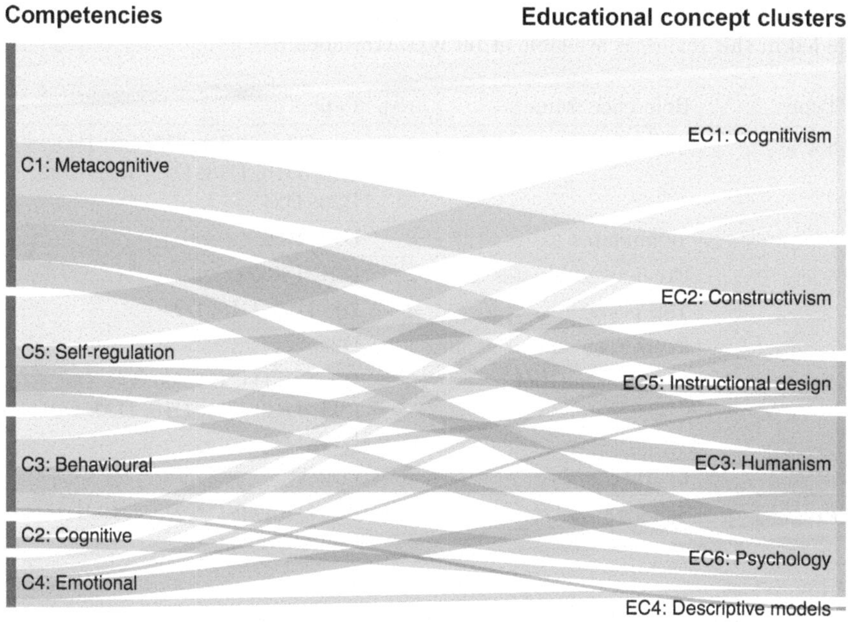

Fig. 1. The competence level targeted by the dashboards included in the review in relation to the educational concept clusters that were used as a theoretical basis for their development.

Apart from the origin of the reference frame, the three types are also characterised by where in time the anchor for comparison is set. The social reference frame focuses on the present, allowing learners to compare their current state to the performance levels of their peers at the same point in time. The achievement reference frame directs learner' attention to the future, outlining goals and a future state that learners aim for. Finally, the progress reference frame is anchored in the past, as the learners use as an anchor point a past state to evaluate what they achieved so far. In the following paragraphs we discuss in detail each type.

Social. The most common frame was showing learners their data in comparison to the whole class. We also identified cases where learners had access to the data of individual members of their working groups in collaborative learning settings. In other cases, learners compared themselves to previous graduates of the same course. In order to avoid the pitfalls of averages in heterogeneous groups, D22 allowed learners a more specific reference: peers with similar goals and knowledge. A few dashboards compared learners to the "top" students, while on some dashboards learners had the option to choose against which group they compare themselves. On one dashboard, learners compared their self-assessment of group work performance with the assessment made by their peers. We also looked at how the data of the reference groups is aggregated. Most of the dashboards

Table 3. The reference frames for comparison and their frequency. The list of papers included in this review is available at bit.ly/LADashboards

Type	Reference frame	Freq.	Papers
Social	Class	15	D1; D3; D4; D5; D7; D8; D11; D15; D16; D18; D19; D21; D22; D23; D24
	Teammates	2	D14; D26
	Previous graduates	2	D21; D25
	Top peers	4	D8; D15; D16; D24
	Peers with similar goals	1	D22
Achievement	Learning outcomes	15	D2; D3; D4; D5; D6; D8; D9; D11; D12; D15; D16; D20; D21; D22; D24
	Learner goals	1	D22
Progress	Self	10	D1; D2; D3; D4; D5; D10; D18; D23;D25; D26

displayed averages (16 dashboards), while only six showed data of individuals and three presented a learner's ranking within the reference group.

Achievement. The second way of framing the information displayed on the dashboard is in terms of the achievement of the learning activity. Here, we distinguish between two types of goals: (i) learning outcomes set by the teachers and (ii) learner goals set by the learners themselves. One purpose of presenting learners' performance in relation to *learning outcomes* was to illustrate mastery and skillfulness achievement. Content mastery was expressed through the use of key concepts in forum discussion (D16, D24), performance in quizzes covering topics (D5, D8, D9, D15) or different difficulty levels (D3). The acquisition of skills was quantified through the number of courses covering those skills in the curriculum objectives (D21), while learning dispositions were calculated from self-reported data collected through questionnaires (D2). A second purpose for using teacher defined goals is to support learners in planning their learning by offering them a point of reference as to how much effort is required for the completion of a learning activity (D11). Concerning the *learner goals*, our results were surprising. Only one dashboard allowed learners enough freedom to set their own goals: on D22, learners could establish their aimed level of knowledge and time investment and follow their progress in comparison to their set targets.

Progress. The third frame of reference refers to whether dashboards allow learners to visualise their progress over time, by having access to their historical data. This functionality directly supports the "execution and monitoring" phase of the SRL cycle [48]. Our results show that only 10 dashboards offered this feature, while the rest displayed only the current status of the learners.

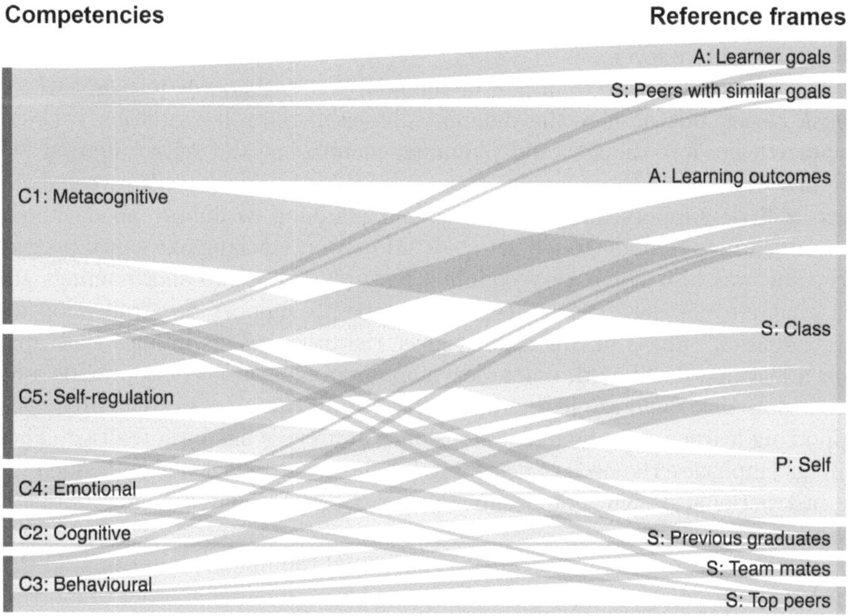

Fig. 2. The competence level targeted by the dashboards in relation to the three reference frames identified: social (S: red), achievement (A: blue) and progress (P: yellow). (Color figure online)

4 Discussion

Through this literature review, we seek to investigate the relation between learning sciences and learning analytics by looking into which educational concepts inform the design of learning analytics dashboards aimed at learners. Our investigation revealed that only 26 out of the 95 dashboard designs identified by our search have grounding in learning sciences and have been evaluated. This might indicate that the development of these tools is still driven by the need to leverage the learning data available, rather than a clear pedagogical focus of improving learning. The most common foundation for LA dashboard design is *self-regulated learning* theory, used frequently to motivate dashboard goals that aim to support awareness and trigger reflection. Two findings related to the use of SRL are striking.

Firstly, very few papers have a secondary goal besides fostering awareness and reflection. However, being aware does not imply that remedial actions are being taken and learning outcomes are improved. Moreover, awareness and reflection are not concepts that can be measured objectively, making the evaluation of such dashboards questionable. According to McAlpine and Weston, reflection should be considered a mechanism through which learning and teaching can be improved rather than an end in itself [30]. Thus, we argue that LA dashboards should be designed and evaluated as pedagogical tools which catalyse changes also in the cognitive, behavioural or emotional competencies, and not only on the metacognitive level.

Secondly, since more than half of the analysed dashboards rely on SRL, we took a closer look at how the different phases of the self-regulation cycle are supported, i.e. fore-thought and planning, monitoring and self-evaluation [49]. The investigation of the reference frames used on the dashboards revealed that there is little support for goal setting and planning as almost no dashboard allowed learners to manage self-set goals. Moreover, tracking one's own progress over time was also not a very common feature. These two shortcomings suggest that current dashboards are built mostly to support the "reflection and self-evaluation" phase of SRL and neglect the others. This implies that apart from a learning dashboard, online learning environments need to provide additional tools that facilitate learners to carry out all the phases of the SRL cycle, supporting learners in subsequent steps once awareness has been realised. These findings emphasise the need of designing LA dashboards as a tool embedded into the instructional design, potentially solving problems related to low uptake of LA dashboards [28].

Furthermore, our analysis revealed that social framing is more common than achievement framing. Comparison with peers is usually used in order to motivate students to work harder and increase their engagement, sometimes by "inducing a feeling of being connected with and supported by their peers" [41]. When looking at the theoretical concepts that inform the design of the studied dashboards, only two theories would justify the use of comparison with peers: social comparison theory and achievement goal orientation theory.

Social comparison. [14] states that we establish our self-worth by comparing ourselves to others when there are no objective means of comparison. However, empirical research in the face-to-face classroom has shown that comparison to self-selected peers who perform slightly better has a beneficial effect on middle school students' grades, whereas no effects were found when there was a bigger gap in performance [23]. Despite the availability of such research, social comparison theory is rarely used to inform the design of dashboards. Only 3 works rationalise the use of comparison by grounding it on social comparison theory and validations of this theory in educational sciences [7,20,27]. Moreover, learners usually got to see their data in comparison to the average of their peers. Averages are often misleading because they are skewed by data of inactive learners and the diversity of learning goals among learners, offering a misguided reference frame.

A second theory that might support the use of social comparison is *achievement goal orientation theory*. This theory distinguishes between mastery and performance orientations as the motivation behind why one engages in an achievement task [32]. In contrast to learners who set mastery goals and focus on learning the material and mastering the tasks, learners who have performance goals are more focused on demonstrating their ability by measuring skill in comparison to others. We found few dashboards that contextualised the data in terms of goals achieved, while the majority used different groups of peers as a frame of reference. This finding suggests that the design of current dashboards is more appealing to performance oriented learners, neglecting learners who have a tendency towards mastery. Indeed, as Beheshitha et al. [2] observed, learners that considered the subject matter of the course more motivating than competition between students were more inclined to rate negatively the visualisation based on social comparison. We found only one dashboard proposal that catered to the needs of learners with different achievement goal orientations. Mastery Grids [20] provides an open learner model for mastery oriented learners on which they can monitor their progress, as well as social comparison features for performance oriented learners.

The lack of support for goal achievement and the prevalence of comparison fosters competition in learners. On the long-term, there is the threat that by constantly being exposed to motivational triggers that rely on social comparison, comparison to peers and "being better than others" becomes the norm in terms of what defines a successful learner. We argue that learning and education should be about mastering knowledge, acquiring skills and developing competencies. For this purpose, comparison should be used carefully in the design of learning dashboards, and research needs to investigate the effects of social comparison and competition in LA dashboards. More attention should be given to the different needs of learners and dashboards should be used as pedagogical tools to motivate learners with different performance levels that respond differently to motivating factors. As Tan [39] envisioned, "differentiated instruction can become an experienced reality for students, with purposefully-designed LA serving to compress, rather than exacerbate, the learning and achievement gap between thriving and struggling students".

5 Conclusion

This paper presents the results of a systematic survey looking into the use of educational concepts in learning analytics dashboards for learners. Our main findings show that, firstly, *self-regulated learning* is the core theory that informs the design of LA dashboards that aim to make learners aware of their learning process by visualising their data. However, just making learners aware is not enough. Dashboards should have a broader purpose, using awareness and reflection as means to improve cognitive, behavioural or emotional competencies. Secondly, effective support for online learners that do not have well developed SRL skills should also facilitate goal setting and planning, and monitoring and self-evaluation. As dashboards mostly aim to increase awareness and trigger self-reflection, different tools should complement dashboards and be seamlessly integrated in the learning environment and the instructional design. Thirdly, there is a strong emphasis on comparison with peers as opposed to using goal achievement as reference frame. However, there is evidence in educational sciences that disproves the benefits of fostering competition in learning. Our findings suggest that the design of LA dashboards needs better grounding in learning sciences.

Finally, we see the need to investigate the effectiveness of using educational concepts in the design of LA dashboards by looking at how these tools were evaluated, what are the effects perceived by learners and how learning was improved. Our study was limited by a narrow focus set within the LA field, a relatively recent research area. Valuable proposals could also be found in related fields, e.g. educational data mining. We plan to answer these research questions in the future by extending this work.

References

1. Anderson, T.: The Theory and Practice of Online Learning. Athabasca University Press, Edmonton (2008)
2. Beheshitha, S.S., Hatala, M., Gašević, D., Joksimović, S.: The role of achievement goal orientations when studying effect of learning analytics visualizations. In: Proceedings of LAK 2016, pp. 54–63. ACM (2016)
3. Bloom, B., Krathwohl, D., Masia, B.: Bloom Taxonomy of Educational Objectives. Allyn and Bacon, Pearson Education, Boston (1984)
4. Bodily, R., Verbert, K.: Trends and issues in student-facing learning analytics reporting systems research. In: Proceedings of LAK 2017, pp. 309–318. ACM (2017)
5. Charleer, S., Klerkx, J., Duval, E., Verbert, K., De Laet, T.: Creating effective learning analytics dashboards: lessons learnt. In: Verbert, K., Sharples, M., Klobučar, T. (eds.) EC-TEL 2016. LNCS, vol. 9891, pp. 42–56. Springer, Cham (2016). doi:10.1007/978-3-319-45153-4_4
6. Corey, M.L., Leinenbach, M.T.: Universal design for learning: theory and practice. In: Proceedings of 2004 Society for Information Technology and Teacher Education International Conference, pp. 4919–4926 (2004)
7. Davis, D., Jivet, I., Kizilcec, R.F., Chen, G., Hauff, C., Houben, G.J.: Follow the successful crowd: raising MOOC completion rates through social comparison at scale. In: Proceedings of LAK 2017, pp. 454–463. ACM (2017)
8. DeCarvalho, R.J.: The humanistic paradigm in education. Hum. Psychol. **19**(1), 88 (1991)
9. Durall, E., Gros, B.: Learning analytics as a metacognitive tool. In: CSEDU, vol. 1, pp. 380–384 (2014)
10. Ekman, P., Friesen, W.V.: Facial action coding system (1977)
11. Elder, L., Paul, R.: Critical thinking: why we must transform our teaching. J. Dev. Educ. **18**(1), 34 (1994)
12. Engeström, Y.: Expansive visibilization of work: an activity-theoretical perspective. Comput. Support. Coop. Work (CSCW) **8**(1), 63–93 (1999)
13. Ferguson, R.: Learning analytics: drivers, developments and challenges. Int. J. Technol. Enhanc. Learn. **4**(5–6), 304–317 (2012)
14. Festinger, L.: A theory of social comparison processes. Hum. Relat. **7**(2), 117–140 (1954)
15. Few, S.: Information Dashboard Design: Displaying Data for At-a-Glance Monitoring. Analytics Press, Berkeley (2013)
16. Fredricks, J.A., Blumenfeld, P.C., Paris, A.H.: School engagement: potential of the concept, state of the evidence. Rev. Educ. Res. **74**(1), 59–109 (2004)
17. Gašević, D., Dawson, S., Siemens, G.: Lets not forget: learning analytics are about learning. TechTrends **59**(1), 64–71 (2015)
18. Gelfand, M.J., Raver, J.L., Nishii, L., Leslie, L.M., Lun, J., Lim, B.C., Duan, L., Almaliach, A., Ang, S., Arnadottir, J., et al.: Differences between tight and loose cultures: a 33-nation study. Science **332**(6033), 1100–1104 (2011)

19. Greller, W., Drachsler, H.: Translating learning into numbers: a generic framework for learning analytics. Educ. Technol. Soc. **15**(3), 42–57 (2012)
20. Guerra, J., Hosseini, R., Somyurek, S., Brusilovsky, P.: An intelligent interface for learning content: combining an open learner model and social comparison to support self-regulated learning and engagement. In: Proceedings of IUI 2016, pp. 152–163. ACM (2016)
21. Haggis, T.: Constructing images of ourselves? A critical investigation into 'approaches to learning' research in higher education. Br. Educ. Res. J. **29**(1), 89–104 (2003)
22. Hofstede, G.: Cultures and Organizations: Software of the Mind. McGraw-Hill, London (1991)
23. Huguet, P., Galvaing, M.P., Monteil, J.M., Dumas, F.: Social presence effects in the Stroop task: further evidence for an attentional view of social facilitation. J. Pers. Soc. Psychol. **77**(5), 1011 (1999)
24. Kim, B.: Social constructivism. Emerg. Perspect. Learn. Teach. Technol. **1**(1), 16 (2001)
25. Kirkpatrick, D.L.: Evaluating Training Programs. Tata McGraw-Hill Education, San Francisco (1975)
26. Klerkx, J., Verbert, K., Duval, E.: Enhancing learning with visualization techniques. In: Spector, J., Merrill, M., Elen, J., Bishop, M. (eds.) Handbook of Research on Educational Communications and Technology, pp. 791–807. Springer, New York (2014)
27. Loboda, T.D., Guerra, J., Hosseini, R., Brusilovsky, P.: Mastery grids: an open source social educational progress visualization. In: Rensing, C., de Freitas, S., Ley, T., Muñoz-Merino, P.J. (eds.) EC-TEL 2014. LNCS, vol. 8719, pp. 235–248. Springer, Cham (2014). doi:10.1007/978-3-319-11200-8_18
28. Lonn, S., Aguilar, S.J., Teasley, S.D.: Investigating student motivation in the context of a learning analytics intervention during a summer bridge program. Comput. Hum. Behav. **47**, 90–97 (2015)
29. Marzouk, Z., Rakovic, M., Liaqat, A., Vytasek, J., Samadi, D., Stewart-Alonso, J., Ram, I., Woloshen, S., Winne, P.H., Nesbit, J.C.: What if learning analytics were based on learning science? Australas. J. Educ. Technol. **32**(6), 1–18 (2016)
30. McAlpine, L., Weston, C.: Reflection: issues related to improving professors' teaching and students' learning. Instr. Sci. **28**(5), 363–385 (2000)
31. Moher, D., Liberati, A., Tetzlaff, J., Altman, D.G., PRISMA Group, et al.: Preferred reporting items for systematic reviews and meta-analyses: the PRISMA statement. PLoS Med. **6**(7), 1000097 (2009)
32. Pintrich, P.R.: Multiple goals, multiple pathways: the role of goal orientation in learning and achievement. J. Educ. Psychol. **92**(3), 544 (2000)
33. Pintrich, P.R., De Groot, E.V.: Motivational and self-regulated learning components of classroom academic performance. J. Educ. Psychol. **82**(1), 33 (1990)
34. Sadler, D.R.: Formative assessment and the design of instructional systems. Instr. Sci. **18**(2), 119–144 (1989)
35. Schwendimann, B., Rodriguez-Triana, M., Vozniuk, A., Prieto, L., Boroujeni, M., Holzer, A., Gillet, D., Dillenbourg, P.: Perceiving learning at a glance: a systematic literature review of learning dashboard research. IEEE Trans. Learn. Technol. **10**(1), 30–41 (2016)
36. Shum, S.B., Crick, R.D.: Learning dispositions and transferable competencies: pedagogy, modelling and learning analytics. In: Proceedings of LAK 2012, pp. 92–101. ACM (2012)

37. Siemens, G., Gašević, D.: Guest editorial-learning and knowledge analytics. Educ. Technol. Soc. **15**(3), 1–2 (2012)
38. Suthers, D., Verbert, K.: Learning analytics as a middle space. In: Proceedings of LAK 2013, pp. 1–4. ACM (2013)
39. Tan, J.P.L., Yang, S., Koh, E., Jonathan, C.: Fostering 21st century literacies through a collaborative critical reading and learning analytics environment: user-perceived benefits and problematics. In: Proceedings of LAK 2016, pp. 430–434. ACM (2016)
40. Trilling, B., Fadel, C.: 21st Century Skills: Learning for Life in Our Times. Wiley, Hoboken (2009)
41. Venant, R., Vidal, P., Broisin, J.: Evaluation of learner performance during practical activities: an experimentation in computer education. In: Proceedings of ICALT 2016, pp. 237–241. IEEE (2016)
42. Verbert, K., Duval, E., Klerkx, J., Govaerts, S., Santos, J.L.: Learning analytics dashboard applications. Am. Behav. Sci. **57**(10), 1500–1509 (2013)
43. Verbert, K., Govaerts, S., Duval, E., Santos, J.L., Van Assche, F., Parra, G., Klerkx, J.: Learning dashboards: an overview and future research opportunities. Pers. Ubiquit. Comput. **18**(6), 1499–1514 (2014)
44. Winne, P.H., Zimmerman, B.J.: Self-regulated learning viewed from models of information processing. Self Regul. Learn. Acad. Achiev. Theor. Perspect. **2**, 153–189 (2001)
45. Wise, A.F.: Designing pedagogical interventions to support student use of learning analytics. In: Proceedings of LAK 2014, pp. 203–211. ACM (2014)
46. Wu, W.H., Hsiao, H.C., Wu, P.L., Lin, C.H., Huang, S.H.: Investigating the learning-theory foundations of game-based learning: a meta-analysis. J. Comput. Assist. Learn. **28**(3), 265–279 (2012)
47. Yoo, Y., Lee, H., Jo, I.-H., Park, Y.: Educational dashboards for smart learning: review of case studies. In: Chen, G., Kumar, V., Kinshuk, Huang, R., Kong, S.C., et al. (eds.) Emerging Issues in Smart Learning. LNET, pp. 145–155. Springer, Heidelberg (2015). doi:10.1007/978-3-662-44188-6_21
48. Zimmerman, B.J.: Self-regulated learning and academic achievement: an overview. Educ. psychol. **25**(1), 3–17 (1990)
49. Zimmerman, B.J., Boekarts, M., Pintrich, P., Zeidner, M.: A social cognitive perspective. In: Handbook of Self-Regulation, vol. 13, No. 1, pp. 695–716 (2000)

Examining Interaction Modality Effects Toward Engagement in an Interactive Learning Environment

Bo Kang(✉), Joseph J. LaViola Jr., and Pamela Wisniewski

University of Central Florida, Orlando, FL, USA
{bkang,jjl}@cs.ucf.edu, pamwis@ucf.edu

Abstract. The primary goals of interactive learning environments (ILEs) are to improve student engagement and learning outcomes. In this paper, we examine different tablet-based user interaction strategies within the domain of analytical geometry (i.e., the intersection of algebra and geometry) that supports active learning for math problem solving. From a learning technology view, we ground our work using cognitive engagement theory and apply usability to evaluate and further infer user engagement by using different interaction metaphors. We propose two ILE features: (1) self-constructed graphing, which provides a Cartesian coordinate interface so that students can graph toward a solution and (2) system-generated graphing, where the ILE automatically translates written algebraic equations into their geometric equivalents. We recruited 24 college students and conducted a 2×2 mixed factorial experimental design by varying two levels (with & without) for each condition (self-constructed & system-generated graphing). We found that these two features combined optimally increased student engagement and solving performance. More importantly, letting students control multi-modal user interactions (given the self-constructed graphing feature) should be provided before introducing automated user interactions (given the system-generated graphing feature).

Keywords: Interactive learning environments · Multiple representations · Student engagement · Technology-enhanced learning

1 Introduction

Research has shown that interactive learning environments (ILEs) can improve students math concept comprehension and problem solving skills [1]. However, designing such systems is a nontrivial and iterative process. ILE developers must model domain knowledge, analyze cognitive processes [2], and implement appropriate instructional methodologies [3, 4] within the design of ILE systems. Further, designing for educational user experiences is difficult because there are a number of different goals and concerns that need to be balanced, as well as trade-offs that must be made [5]. In addition, learning engagement is a key factor that should be considered when designing such ILE user interfaces [6]. To improve students learning engagement, numerous techniques have been illustrated and integrated into intelligent tutoring systems, digital games or other learning systems [7–10]. For instance, Oviatt et al. showed the tablet pen-input

É. Lavoué et al. (Eds.): EC-TEL 2017, LNCS 10474, pp. 97–110, 2017.
DOI: 10.1007/978-3-319-66610-5_8

effectiveness to support students reasoning and further engage into math problem solving [11]. Marrikis et al. integrated automatic speech recognition into an interactive learning environment to support children's exploration and reflection [12].

In terms of concept understanding and knowledge acquisition, researchers have shown the power of using *multiple representations* to understand certain concepts [13], such as arithmetic fractions [14] and chemical bonds [15]. ILE designers consider multi-modal inputs toward representations to let students interact with each one. Some existing tools automate the connection between representations to demonstrate certain concepts. For example, Desmos automatically translates algebraic expressions into the corresponding geometric graph [16]. However, it does not allow students to enter or edit geometric shapes.

In this paper, with the aim of understanding how user interaction affects students' engagement, we demonstrate a case study to design and evaluate the *multiple representation* learning technique from one interactive learning environment. The sketch-based ILE helps students to learn analytical geometry concepts by connecting algebraic and geometric representations. To quantify the property of multiple representations, we ground our experimental design from educational psychology research, mapped as two ILE features: (1) *self-constructed graphing* – A feature that allows students to graph geometric shapes on their own, and (2) *system-generated graphing* – A feature that automatically translates the equations students write on an algebraic canvas to their geometric equivalents on a geometry canvas. We conduct an empirical study with 24 college students to evaluate the different combinations of these two features (with or without) across four experimental conditions, as well as comparing to a baseline condition of using pen and paper.

To our knowledge, there has been no prior study to apply multiple learning representations to evaluate student engagement. Our work presents a grounded approach to extract and differentiate features. We show evidence that a dependency between self-controlled and system-generated exists. It is recommended that before introducing automatic system-generated features, ILEs should maximally support user self-controlled features.

2 Related Work

2.1 Math ILEs with Multiple Representations

Since our proposed math-based ILE is bi-modal (allowing students to engage in both algebraic equation solving and graphing geometry concepts), we reviewed the literature related to math-learning strategies using multiple representations, in general, and within the context of math ILEs. *Multiple representations* allow the same object or entity to be described or displayed in multiple formats. This instructional technique has been used widely across different learning domains, such as within chemistry [17], and specifically for math learning, such as understanding arithmetic fractions [14] and algebraic equation solving [18]. For algebraic equation solving, previous work has shown the importance of using *multiple representations* to understand math functions, which treat both algebra and geometry as two representations [14, 17]. Our ILE integrates tablet pen-input for writing and recognizes handwritten algebraic equations as knowledge patterns [19].

2.2 Engagement and ICAP Framework

We draw from the educational psychology literature related to how different user interaction features can incrementally escalate engagement in the user experience. Chi et al. [20] conceptualized and validated the ICAP framework, which links cognitive engagement to active learning outcomes. The ICAP framework postulates that student engagement increases across four modes as students' progress through learning activities: *passive*, *active*, *constructive*, and *interactive* engagement. Passive engagement represents receiving instruction without any action, such as listening to a lecture or reading a textbook. Active engagement means students' self-manipulative actions, such as repeating or rehearsing material during note-taking. Constructive engagement produces additional externalized outputs by synthesizing and applying concepts that have been learned, such as reflecting out-loud and self-explaining. Finally, interactive engagement requires defending and negotiating one's conceptual understanding in relation to others, such as through debating problem-solutions with a partner or group [20]. The ICAP framework presents this taxonomy of engagement modes hierarchically, where passive engagement impacts learning the least, and interactive discourse enhances learning outcomes the most optimally. Further, the hierarchy exists such that higher modes subsume lower modes. This framework has been empirically validated in the domain of material science [20]. We apply this framework in the analytical geometry math problem solving domain.

3 Methods

3.1 Self-constructed Graphing and System-Generated Graphing

Albert needs to set up a light perpendicular to a stage. He knows the equation for the stage is $2x - 3y = 9$. *Also, he knows the stage goes through a point* $(-4, -1)$. *Give the equation of line in the slope-intercept form if it is perpendicular to the stage.*

Given the analytical geometry math problem above, students are required to understand and manipulate algebraic expressions to quantitatively reason about the problem [21]. Further they can use geometric forms as a qualitative view to facilitate their quantitative reasoning using algebra. Then, students should link these expressions as geometric forms on the Cartesian coordinate system. To help students consolidate this cognitive problem-solving process, the basic ILE design should allow students to enter algebraic expressions to support quantitative reasoning (Fig. 1 right canvas).

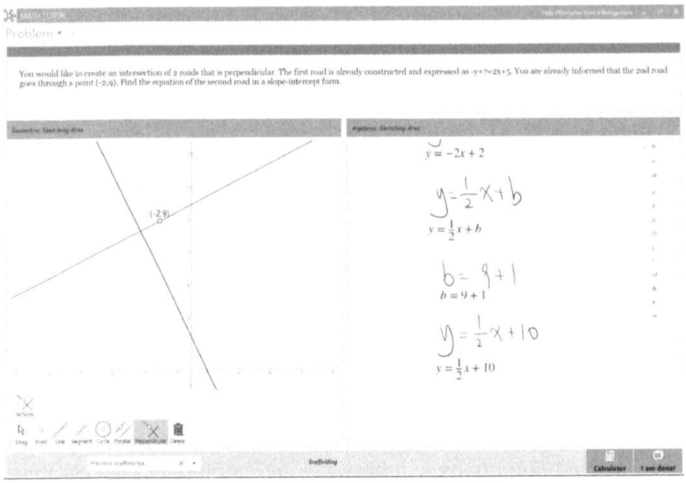

Fig. 1. Math ILE with self-constructed and system-generated graphing features

Further, *self-constructed graphing* lets students externally construct and directly manipulate geometric shapes and relations on a geometry canvas (Fig. 1 left canvas). This modality provides additional qualitative assistance that allows students to conduct quantitative reasoning using visual representations of the algebraic equations. For example, graphing a line to determine its slope. Relating this feature to the ICAP framework, the bi-modal interface facilitates students in reflective activities on both the algebra and geometry canvases, enhancing cognitive engagement from an *active* to a *constructive* mode of learning.

Last, *system-generated graphing* supports multiple representations by automatically translating written equations on the algebraic canvas to their visual equivalents on the geometry canvas. When students enter an algebraic expression that matches a knowledge pattern (e.g., a point, a line or a circle), the ILE translates and graphs that shape automatically. However, this feature does not allow students to interact directly with the geometry canvas, only through writing interpretable equations on the algebraic canvas that are then translated for them. Therefore, *system-generated graphing* supports a *passive* to *active* mode of learning related to the geometry representation, and a *constructive* learning mode only as it relates to algebraic conceptual learning. Systems, such as Desmos, support this type of *system-generated graphing* without *self-constructed graphing*.

Combining Two Graphing Features. We argue that the combination of *self-constructed* and *system-generated* graphing within our bi-modal ILE (Fig. 1) will optimally support learning via multiple representations and by bringing learning activities to an *interactive* mode of engagement. In our proposed ILE [22], students have the flexibility of using either algebra or geometry canvases to work toward solving a given problem. This would allow them to engage in constructive learning activities for both algebra and geometry learning outcomes. Yet, when students write an equation on the algebra canvas, it will automatically graph the equation for them on the geometry canvas. Then, students can directly manipulate the *system-generated* geometric shapes as to negotiate with the ILE how to best solve the problem. As such, the ILE acts as a simulated conversation partner in co-constructing the solution to a given problem with the student. In our ILE, it is important to note that we intentionally chose to implement multiple representations unidirectional from algebraic to geometry representations and not the reverse. Our rationale for this decision is that algebraic knowledge is mandatory for solving analytical geometry problems, while geometry conceptual knowledge is helpful but not required. As such, allowing students to graph towards a solution, further letting the system generate the algebraic output based on graphical input would potentially allow them to arrive at the correct answer without demonstrating mastery of the underlying concepts.

3.2 Study Design

The aim of our experimental design is to evaluate two graphing features (*self-constructed* and *system-generated* graphing) and their relations based on ICAP cognitive engagement theory. Our study utilized a 2 × 2 mixed factorial design with a baseline control (i.e., pen and paper). We assumed that *self-constructed* graphing is the pre-requisite feature to further add the *system-generated* graphing feature. Thus, the *self-constructed* graphing feature was modeled as a between-subject factor, and the *system-generated* graphing feature was implemented as a within-subject factor. Table 1 varies the inclusion of the two features in various implementations of an ILE and maps each version of the system to theory based on: (1) whether the ILE includes *multiple representations* (MR) via a bi-modal algebra and geometry interface, and (2) the stage of learning engagement as specified by the ICAP framework. For instance, in condition 2 (Non-MR), the ILE supports unimodal interaction without containing both features, which only shows one algebraic canvas without the geometric coordinate canvas. In the study, each participant solved math problems using three conditions separately: (1) Pen and Paper, (2) an ILE without *system-generated* graphing, and (3) an ILE with *system-generated* graphing.

Table 1. Summary of experimental conditions

#	MR*	ICAP	ILE systems/features
1	N/A	N/A	Pen & Paper (Baseline)
2	No	Algebra constructive	Algebra ILE only
3	Yes	Algebra constructive	Bi-modal ILE with *system-generated* graphing only
4	Yes	Algebra & geometry constructive	Bi-modal ILE with *self-constructed* graphing only
5	Yes	Algebra & geometry interactive	Bi-modal ILE with *self-constructed* & *system-generated graphing*

3.3 System Implementation

We developed four different ILE systems by varying the inclusion or exclusion of the two graphing features. All ILEs had some common features, which included the problem description area on the top and a sketched-based canvas to draw algebraic expressions. Students could sketch any notes or math expressions. Written expressions can be recognized using a math expression parser [19]. Students could touch to manipulate the algebraic canvas to manage their writing space and erase their writings by performing a scribble pen-gesture. Three versions of the ILEs provided bi-modal interfaces with both algebra (positioned to the right) and geometry (positioned to the left) canvases. In the version without either graphing feature, the geometry canvas was rendered useless, thus removed. For *system-generated* graphing when the system detected pattern matches between a written algebraic expression and a known knowledge pattern (such as point, line slope intercept form, line general form, circle standard form), it automatically graphed its corresponding geometric shape on the geometric canvas. The system could perform real-time geometric shape drawing from student input, including when they modified or deleted an algebraic expression. For *self-constructed* graphing, students could zoom and translate the visualized coordinate interface through single or double contact touch interactions. Students could enter geometric shapes upon the geometric canvas using a structured visual widget toolbar on the bottom of the canvas. The visual widget toolbar contained icons for creating a point, line, circle, two parallel lines, and two perpendicular lines [23]. Dragging and deleting visual widgets were also provided. Students could execute a command by first selecting a visual widget, and then pointing onto the geometric canvas to finish the input task.

3.4 Stimuli Design

We chose analytical geometry math word problems as the stimuli for our experiment, since solving word problems is considered both challenging and interesting to students [21]. Students might pay more attention to the problems, which allows us to capture students' implicit perception toward study conditions and user interface. We modeled problem-solving tasks to cover two main analytical geometry concepts: (1) Solving for a perpendicular line given the equation of an existing line, and (2) Solving for two points on a circle given an intersecting line. Both concepts required students to construct the relationship between two geometric entities. Since participants need to solve a word problem per concept and per condition, we found six math story-based problems from a high school geometry textbook [24]. We modeled the problems so that they were constructed using hybrid language that included both algebra- and geometry-oriented cues. Problems were randomly assigned across the experimental conditions.

3.5 Participants

Prior to recruiting participants, we conducted a priori power analysis to determine our target sample size. Using G*Power [25], to detect a medium effect size with a power of 0.80, we needed a total of 24 participants. Twenty-four adults, 14 females and 10 males, aged 19 to 21-years-old, participated in our experiment. All participants were college freshmen at our university. Participants had taken Algebra 1 and Geometry 1 in high school. 20 out of 24 participants previously used graphical calculators, such as the TI-84 and TI-89.

3.6 Procedure and Apparatus

Participants were invited to the user experience lab in our university to perform the experiment. After participants agreed with our IRB consent form, they began the study by first taking a pre-survey. Participants were then asked to solve the first two problems using Pen and Paper. Next, they were randomly assigned to the *self-constructed* graphing between-subjects condition or not. All participants engaged with the within-subjects factor of *system-generated* graphing (with and without) in a randomized order. The study design was counter-balanced to avoid order effects for both factors. Thus 12 participants experienced two ILEs with *self-constructed* graphing. Problems were also assigned randomly. During problem solving, participants were asked to talk aloud and try their best to solve each problem. After solving one problem, participants click the "Done" button, which directed them to the next problem. After finishing problem solving for one condition, participants took a web-based survey to evaluate the current condition of ILE in which they just used. After using all conditions to solve problems, a post-survey was administered to ask debriefing questions. The entire experimental session was video/audio recorded. The apparatus used was a Microsoft Surface Pro 3 with a digitizer. The experiment window was set in full-screen mode. Participants used the stylus to work on the system and could hold the tablet any way that they felt more comfortable.

4 Dependent Variables and Hypotheses

Based on the engagement literature, we accessed engagement through evaluating students problem-solving behavior under the cognitive category [6]. Though many forms of measurement coexist, we believed that most of them were too generalized which cannot fit for our own need. Thus, derived from human computer interaction, we accessed student engagement in three aspects: usability, cognitive load and perceived learning. Since usability testing plays a critical role to evaluate any system in HCI, we used perceived usability to partially infer engagement. Usability was measured by self-reported rankings on a pre-validated questionnaire that assessed four dimensions of usability: usefulness, ease of use, ease of learning, and satisfaction [26]. Each dimension contained four items. In term of cognitive evaluation, previous HCI research has been using cognitive load theory to measure user interface affordance [27–29], we evaluated self-reported cognitive load to infer engagement in a different aspect. We measured cognitive load using a pre validated seven item survey scale for mental effort [30]. A high score on this scale equated to lower levels of cognitive load. Though evaluating perceived usability and cognitive load can deduce engagement, we also wanted to know our ILE's perceived learning effect, which might influence student engagement. Thus, we created a new construct to operationalize perceived learning at the intersection of algebra and geometry concepts. This construct was developed as a six-item measure on 7-point Likert scale. To specifically test the user interface's effect to help students link two representations, we devised the perceived learning construct with 6-items, which is shown below:

- *The interface helped me relate algebra + geometric concepts.*
- *The interface gave me a better understanding of how equations are represented.*
- *The interface could link my understanding of geometry algebra concepts.*
- *The interface encouraged me to utilize geometry as well as algebra to solve the problem.*
- *The system encouraged me to figure out how I was going to solve problems.*
- *The system motivated me to apply my knowledge to solve problems efficiently.*

Other than evaluating engagement, we also examined learning performance across different experimental conditions. which was scored based on correctness of the problem solution using a pre-validated grading rubric. The rubric contains: (1) translating the word problem correctly to either canvas, (2) recalling the appropriate knowledge (i.e., equations) needed to solve the problem, (3) meaningful progress toward problem completion, and (4) arriving at the correct answer [31]. To ensure reliability in grading for solving performance, we recruited two math tutors to grade participants' solutions. The inter-rater agreement between two graders was good (Cohen's Kappa = 0.87). We averaged the two graders' scores as learning performance. To infer student engagement into the ILE, we hypothesize:

Hypothesis 1 (Perceived Usability): An ILE with *self-constructed* and *system-generated graphing* will be perceived as significantly more usable than ILEs without either or both features.
Hypothesis 2 (Cognitive Load): An ILE with *self-constructed graphing* and *system-generated graphing* will require significantly less mental effort than an ILE without either or both features.
Hypothesis 3 (Perceived Learning): An ILE with *self-constructed graphing* and *system-generated graphing* will significantly improve perceived learning over an ILE without either or both features.
Hypothesis 4 (Learning Performance): An ILE with *self-constructed graphing* and *system-generated graphing* will significantly improve learning performance over an ILE without either or both features.

5 Results

We present our results by describing the validity and reliability of our dependent measures. We report MANOVA results for our perceived measures and a mixed factorial ANOVA for solving performance. We also analyze data from self-reported surveys, recorded video and supplemented quantitative findings with qualitative insights from participants' feedback. Table 2 presents the descriptive statistics for dependent measures. Normality checking showed that all dependent measures are normally distributed. All scale reliabilities calculated as Cronbach's alpha are above the 0.70 threshold of acceptability. The results of hypotheses testing are presented in Table 3. To evaluate our hypotheses (which posit that both features will out-perform the other four conditions), we interpret both the main effects of each feature, as well as the interaction effects between the two features. Compared to the baseline condition of Pen and Paper the ILE with both features are perceived to be significantly more useful (t(11) = 2.68, $p < 0.05$), easier to use (t(11) = 2.31, $p < 0.05$), easier to learn (t(11) = 2.85, $p < 0.05$), more satisfying (t(11) = 3.74, $p < 0.01$), required less mental effort (t(11) = 2.34, $p < 0.05$), and improved perceived learning (t(11) = 3.68, $p < 0.01$). Actual solving performance is also significantly enhanced by our ILE system (t(11) = 4.14, $p < 0.01$).

Table 2. Descriptive statistics

Dependent measure	With self-constructed graphing				Without self-constructed graphing			
	With system-generated		Without system-generated		With system-generated		Without system-generated	
	M	SD	M	SD	M	SD	M	SD
Usefulness	6.33	0.66	5.73	0.93	5.54	0.79	4.87	1.29
Ease of use	5.88	0.75	5.50	0.90	5.06	0.91	5.33	0.92
Ease of learning	6.29	0.72	6.04	0.77	5.40	0.95	5.90	0.83
Satisfaction	6.02	0.82	5.35	0.88	5.29	0.82	4.52	1.01
Cognitive load	5.78	0.82	5.37	1.08	4.93	1.04	4.52	1.12
Perceived learning	6.35	0.73	5.56	1.13	5.58	0.77	4.25	1.27
Solving performance	77.08	30.16	59.37	26.16	63.95	35.12	52.50	36.57

5.1 Main Effects of Self-constructed Graphing

As shown in Table 3, we found a significant ($p < 0.05$) main effect of *self-constructed* graphing on all but two of our perceived usability measures (ease of use and ease of learning). Overall, participants found the versions of the ILE that included this feature to be significantly more usable (useful and satisfying). They also experienced less cognitive load and felt that the ILE helped them relate and understand algebra and geometry concepts more effectively. However, we did not find a significant main effect of self-constructed graphing on actual solving performance.

5.2 Main Effects of System-Generated Graphing

We also found a significant ($p < 0.05$) main effect of *system-generated* graphing (Table 3) on all but two of our perceived usability measures (ease of use and ease of learning). Overall, the perceived effects of system-generated graphing were all in the same direction as self-constructed graphing. We also found a significant main effect of system-generated graphing on solving performance. When participants had this within-subjects feature, they performed significantly better than when the feature was not available to them. Based on these results, we can say that we found partial support for **H1** (perceived usability) and that our data fully supported **H2** (cognitive load), and **H3** (perceived learning). We consider our results as providing partial support for **H4** (solving performance) and discuss the implications of our findings in more detail in our discussion.

Table 3. Hypothesis testing results

Measures		Statistical results
Self-constructed	**Usefulness**	$\mathbf{F(1, 22) = 6.84, p < 0.02, \eta_p^2 = 0.24}$
	Ease of use	$F(1, 22) = 2.24, p = 0.15, \eta_p^2 = 0.09$
	Ease of learning	$F(1, 22) = 2.89, p = 0.10, \eta_p^2 = 0.12$
	Satisfaction	$\mathbf{F(1, 22) = 5.84, p < 0.02, \eta_p^2 = 0.21}$
	Cognitive load	$\mathbf{F(1, 22) = 5.05, p < 0.04, \eta_p^2 = 0.19}$
	Perceived learning	$\mathbf{F(1, 22) = 9.70, p < 0.01, \eta_p^2 = 0.31}$
	Solving performance	$F(1, 22) = 0.70, p = 0.41, \eta_p^2 = 0.03$
System-generated	**Usefulness**	$\mathbf{F(1, 22) = 8.13, p < 0.01, \eta_p^2 = 0.27}$
	Ease of use	$F(1, 22) = 0.13, p = 0.72, \eta_p^2 = 0.01$
	Ease of learning	$F(1, 22) = 0.84, p = 0.37, \eta_p^2 = 0.04$
	Satisfaction	$\mathbf{F(1, 22) = 19.35, p < 0.01, \eta_p^2 = 0.47}$
	Cognitive load	$\mathbf{F(1, 22) = 5.02, p < 0.04, \eta_p^2 = 0.19}$
	Perceived learning	$\mathbf{F(1, 22) = 19.57, p < 0.01, \eta_p^2 = 0.47}$
	Solving performance	$\mathbf{F(1, 22) = 13.14, p < 0.01, \eta_p^2 = 0.37}$
Interaction effect	Usefulness	$F(1,22) = 0.02, p = 0.89, \eta_p^2 = 0.001$
	Ease of use	$\mathbf{F(1, 22) = 4.90, p = 0.04, \eta_p^2 = 0.18}$
	Ease of learning	$\mathbf{F(1, 22) = 7.52, p = 0.01, \eta_p^2 = 0.26}$
	Satisfaction	$F(1, 22) = 0.10, p = 0.75, \eta_p^2 = 0.01$
	Cognitive load	$F(1, 22) = 0.00, p = 1.0, \eta_p^2 = 0.00$
	Perceived learning	$F(1, 22) = 1.27, p = 0.27, \eta_p^2 = 0.06$
	Solving performance	$F(1, 22) = 0.60, p = 0.45, \eta_p^2 = 0.027$

Note: Significant *p*-values (< 0.05) are shown in bold

5.3 Interactions Effects

We detected significant interaction effects between the two features for ease of use and ease of learning (medium to large effect size), which were the two dimensions of perceived usability that we previously did not detect significant main effects. Figure 2 illustrates the interaction effect for ease of use, which was similar to that of ease of learning. While our ILE with two features was still perceived as significantly easier to use and easier to learn than the other conditions, we found an unanticipated result, which suggests that *system-generated* graphing without *self-constructed* graphing was considered significantly harder to use and harder to learn than the other four conditions.

Participants preferred the ILE that only provided an algebraic canvas without the geometry canvas or two features over this option.

Fig. 2. Interaction effect for ease of use

6 Discussion

For the *system-generated* graphing, students felt that the ILE helped them to relate and better understand algebra and geometry concepts. For example, one student said:

> *"I was able to see the geometric representation of my algebra which greatly helped in solving/ checking work especially if I was solving the equation right."*

This finding was consistent with the intelligent novice cognitive model that suggests that students can improve their conceptual understanding through self-checking capabilities [32]. However, the fact that we only found a significant main effect of *system-generated* graphing on actual solving performance is an area of potential concern. This finding suggests that the *system-generated* feature may be giving students too much help by partially solving the problem for them. Therefore, future research should further examine the potential learning benefits versus the potential negative "enabling" effects of this feature. Adaptive graphing features should be investigated based on students prior learning experience. In the current experiment, besides the system-generated graphing effect for certain conditions, all conditions do not have a cognitive tutor that provide procedural scaffolds or hints to guide students' problem solving. Another experiment to incorporate a cognitive tutor to verify this finding might be essential.

The results provided additional empirical validation for the ICAP framework as it applies to the context of ILEs for analytical geometry math work problem-solving. We confirmed that two-feature ILE system increased usability, reduced cognitive load and increased their perceive learning, which indirectly improve students engagement. The system with such features also improve learning outcomes. This finding coincided with the previous research that the combined set of multimodal features is most predictive, indicating an additive effect [33]. One student explained:

"I enjoyed editing geometric shapes by myself. I also enjoyed the effect of the automation as it encouraged me and engaged me in solving such problems. The automation helps me check and keep on going with my problem solving, which was greatly helpful."

The most unique finding from this experiment was the interaction effect for ease of use and ease of learning between the two features. From a theoretical view, it confirmed the hierarchical nature of ICAP's learning modes. *System-generated* graphing proved to be a less engaged learning mode without allowing students to reach a *constructive* level of engagement on the geometry canvas. Only with the combination of *both* features was an *interactive* level of engagement reached as students began to co-construct the problem solution with the ILE. Indeed, both features achieve the same goal to construct the geometric shapes linking to algebraic expressions. However, the result implied that students wanted to manipulate and interact with geometric shapes before introducing the automated graphing feature. This finding reveals that ILE designers should consider all modality input and features in the first place. Automated mechanisms should be considered after supporting all modality interaction features to give students more smooth user interaction and engaged user experience. Though we did find certain significant effects through the current sample size (N = 24), future work can widen it to verify the findings in a large scale.

7 Conclusion

In this paper, we illustrated a human computer interaction approach to extract two user interface features and ground them in the ICAP cognitive engagement framework to access student engagement. We further conducted a mixed-factorial experiment to evaluate the system with or without each feature. We found the same result as previous research that the combination of graphing features accumulates student engagement level. More surprisingly, we found that two features do depend on each other, which meets the ICAP hierarchical view. This finding suggests that ILE designers should let students maximally manipulate and interact with each input modality before adding automated features.

Acknowledgements. This work is supported in part by NSF Award IIS-1638060, Lockheed Martin, Office of Naval Research Award ONRBAA15001, Army RDECOM Award W911QX13C0052, and Coda Enterprises, LLC. We thank the ISUE lab members at UCF for their support as well as the anonymous reviewers for their helpful feedback.

References

1. Moreno, R., Mayer, R.: Interactive multimodal learning environments. Educ. Psychol. Rev. **19**, 309–326 (2007)
2. Ritter, S., Anderson, J.R., Koedinger, K.R., Corbett, A.: Cognitive tutor: applied research in mathematics education. Psychon. Bull. Rev. **14**, 249–255 (2007)
3. Dunlosky, J., Rawson, K.A., Marsh, E.J., Nathan, M.J., Willingham, D.T.: Improving students' learning with effective learning techniques promising directions from cognitive and educational psychology. Psychol. Sci. Public Interest **14**, 4–58 (2013)

4. Koedinger, K.R., Booth, J.L., Klahr, D.: Instructional complexity and the science to constrain it. Science **342**, 935–937 (2013)
5. Rau, M.A., Aleven, V., Rummel, N., Rohrbach, S.: Why interactive learning environments can have it all: resolving design conflicts between competing goals. In: Proceedings of the SIGCHI Conference on Human Factors in Computing Systems, pp. 109–118. ACM, New York (2013)
6. Henrie, C.R., Halverson, L.R., Graham, C.R.: Measuring student engagement in technology-mediated learning: a review. Comput. Educ. **90**, 36–53 (2015)
7. Lim, C.P., Nonis, D., Hedberg, J.: Gaming in a 3D multiuser virtual environment: engaging students in science lessons. Br. J. Edu. Technol. **37**, 211–231 (2006)
8. Anderson, A., Huttenlocher, D., Kleinberg, J., Leskovec, J.: Engaging with massive online courses. In: Proceedings of the 23rd International Conference on World Wide Web, pp. 687–698. ACM (2014)
9. Guo, P.J., Kim, J., Rubin, R.: How video production affects student engagement: an empirical study of MOOC videos. In: Proceedings of the First ACM Conference on Learning @ Scale Conference, pp. 41–50. ACM, New York (2014)
10. Sabourin, J.L., Lester, J.C.: Affect and engagement in game-based learning environments. IEEE Trans. Affect. Comput. **5**, 45–56 (2014)
11. Oviatt, S., Cohen, A., Miller, A., Hodge, K., Mann, A.: The impact of interface affordances on human ideation, problem solving, and inferential reasoning. ACM Trans. Comput. Hum. Interact. (TOCHI) **19**, 22 (2012)
12. Mavrikis, M., Grawemeyer, B., Hansen, A., Gutierrez-Santos, S.: Exploring the potential of speech recognition to support problem solving and reflection. In: Rensing, C., de Freitas, S., Ley, T., Muñoz-Merino, Pedro J. (eds.) EC-TEL 2014. LNCS, vol. 8719, pp. 263–276. Springer, Cham (2014). doi:10.1007/978-3-319-11200-8_20
13. Ainsworth, S., Bibby, P., Wood, D.: Examining the effects of different multiple representational systems in learning primary mathematics. J. Learn. Sci. **11**, 25–61 (2002)
14. Rau, M.A., Aleven, V., Rummel, N.: Intelligent tutoring systems with multiple representations and self-explanation prompts support learning of fractions. In: AIED, pp. 441–448 (2009)
15. Rau, M.A.: Enhancing undergraduate chemistry learning by helping students make connections among multiple graphical representations. Chem. Educ. Res. Pract. **16**, 654–669 (2015)
16. Desmos|Beautiful, Free Math. https://www.desmos.com/
17. Rau, M.A., Michaelis, J.E., Fay, N.: Connection making between multiple graphical representations: a multi-methods approach for domain-specific grounding of an intelligent tutoring system for chemistry. Comput. Educ. **82**, 460–485 (2015)
18. Brenner, M.E., Mayer, R.E., Moseley, B., Brar, T., Duran, R., Reed, B.S., Webb, D.: Learning by understanding: the role of multiple representations in learning algebra. Am. Educ. Res. J. **34**, 663–689 (1997)
19. Zeleznik, R., Miller, T., Li, C., LaViola, Joseph J.: MathPaper: mathematical sketching with fluid support for interactive computation. In: Butz, A., Fisher, B., Krüger, A., Olivier, P., Christie, M. (eds.) SG 2008. LNCS, vol. 5166, pp. 20–32. Springer, Heidelberg (2008). doi: 10.1007/978-3-540-85412-8_3
20. Chi, M.T., Wylie, R.: The ICAP framework: linking cognitive engagement to active learning outcomes. Educ. Psychol. **49**, 219–243 (2014)
21. Koedinger, K.R., Nathan, M.J.: The real story behind story problems: effects of representations on quantitative reasoning. J. Learn. Sci. **13**, 129–164 (2004)

22. Kang, B., Kulshreshth, A., LaViola Jr., J.J.: AnalyticalInk: an interactive learning environment for math word problem solving. In: Proceedings of the 21st International Conference on Intelligent User Interfaces, pp. 419–430. ACM (2016)
23. Kang, B., LaViola Jr., J.J., Wisniewski, P.: Structured input improves usability and precision for solving geometry-based algebraic problems. Presented at the (2017)
24. David Gustafson, R., Frisk, P.D.: Elementary Geometry, 3rd edn. Wiley, Chichester (1991)
25. Faul, F., Erdfelder, E., Lang, A., Buchner, A.: G*Power 3: a flexible statistical power analysis program for the social, behavioral, and biomedical sciences. Behav. Res. Meth. **39**, 175–191 (2007)
26. Lund, A.M.: Measuring usability with the USE questionnaire. Usability Interface **8**, 3–6 (2001)
27. Paas, F., Tuovinen, J.E., Tabbers, H., Van Gerven, P.W.: Cognitive load measurement as a means to advance cognitive load theory. Educ. Psychol. **38**, 63–71 (2003)
28. Van Merriënboer, J.J., Ayres, P.: Research on cognitive load theory and its design implications for e-learning. Educ. Tech. Res. Dev. **53**, 5–13 (2005)
29. Oviatt, S.: Human-centered design meets cognitive load theory: designing interfaces that help people think. In: Proceedings of the 14th ACM International Conference on Multimedia, pp. 871–880. ACM, New York (2006)
30. Hart, S.G., Staveland, L.E.: Development of NASA-TLX (Task Load Index): results of empirical and theoretical research. Adv. Psychol. **52**, 139–183 (1988)
31. Huntley, M.A., Marcus, R., Kahan, J., Miller, J.L.: Investigating high-school students' reasoning strategies when they solve linear equations. J. Math. Behav. **26**, 115–139 (2007)
32. Mathan, Santosh A., Koedinger, Kenneth R.: An empirical assessment of comprehension fostering features in an intelligent tutoring system. In: Cerri, Stefano A., Gouardères, G., Paraguaçu, F. (eds.) ITS 2002. LNCS, vol. 2363, pp. 330–343. Springer, Heidelberg (2002). doi:10.1007/3-540-47987-2_37
33. Grafsgaard, J.F., Wiggins, J.B., Vail, A.K., Boyer, K.E., Wiebe, E.N., Lester, J.C.: The additive value of multimodal features for predicting engagement, frustration, and learning during tutoring. In: Proceedings of the 16th International Conference on Multimodal Interaction, pp. 42–49. ACM (2014)

Using Embodied Learning Technology to Advance Motor Performance of Children with Special Educational Needs and Motor Impairments

Panagiotis Kosmas[1(✉)], Andri Ioannou[1], and Symeon Retalis[2]

[1] Cyprus Interaction Lab, Cyprus University of Technology, 3075 Limassol, Cyprus
pk.kosmas@edu.cut.ac.cy
[2] University of Piraeus, Athens, Greece

Abstract. Embodied learning, under the lens of Embodied Cognition theory, emphasizes on the inseparable link between brain, body and the world; it considers that the active human body can alter the function of the brain and therefore the cognitive process. From this perspective, the exploration of learning environments that promote bodily activity in relation to cognitive tasks are gaining the attention of the research community in the recent days. One such case is the use of multimodal, motion-based games mediated by sensors like a Kinect camera to enable learning through active and embodied interaction with learning content. This paper presents findings from an empirical investigation of using embodied touchless interactive games to enhance motor performance for children with learning disabilities and motor impairments. Young children, mainly attending special units within mainstream elementary schools, participated in a five-month intervention. Kinetic analytics, together with teachers' self-reported observations and interviews, revealed improvements in children's motor performance, particularly psychomotor ability and psychomotor speed. The paper contributes to the technology-enhanced learning community by providing insights into the use of embodied learning technology in special education.

Keywords: Embodied cognition · Embodied learning · Motion-based games · Kinect · Natural interaction · Learning disabilities · Special education · Technology-enhanced learning

1 Introduction

In the age of technological imperative, massive efforts are underway to transform traditional teaching and learning to something that is enriched and mediated by technology with the prospect of advancing learning. In this spirit, motion-based interactive environments are gaining the attention of interaction designers and learning scientists who have considered the role of the active body in the functioning of the brain. In this direction, the emerging field of embodied learning, offers new ways of understanding learning which builds upon the inseparable link between brain, body, and the world.

Embodied learning takes into consideration that the human body can play a significant role in the cognitive process, in thinking and in acting in the world [1, 2]. Advocates

É. Lavoué et al. (Eds.): EC-TEL 2017, LNCS 10474, pp. 111–124, 2017.
DOI: 10.1007/978-3-319-66610-5_9

of embodied learning believe that the involvement of the physical body and activity in the learning process has the capacity to change the cognitive process [3]. Although a good deal of research in the field of education has investigated how the integration of bodily movements and senses can influence learning [4], there is still insufficient evidence about this link based on which firmed conclusions can be drawn [4, 5].

The present study investigates how the use of embodied touchless interactive games can advance the motor performance of children with learning disabilities and motor impairments. The study is part of a larger investigation of embodied learning addressing a range of skills, yet the present manuscript focuses on motor performance, particularly:

1. Gains in (a) Psychomotor Abilities (Gp) - the ability to perform physical body motor movements with precision, coordination, or strength, and (b) Psychomotor Speed (Gps) - the speed and fluidity with which physical body movements can be made, based on the Cattell-Horn-Carroll Integrated Model classification of skills, which is widely accepted as the most comprehensive and empirically supported model of cognitive abilities [6].
2. Perceived experiences of the special education teachers and therapists regarding the development of the abovementioned skills, through embodied learning.

In the sections below, we first provide an overview of the relevant literature and previous empirical work related to embodied learning using technology. Subsequently, the method of the present investigation is detailed, followed by major findings and implications for research and practice in the intersection of technology-enhanced learning, special education and multimodal, motion-based technologies.

2 Background

2.1 Embodied Cognition Theory and Technology Enhanced Learning

Embodied cognition has become a significant learning paradigm in contemporary theory of cognitive sciences. The fascinating insight of this theory is that behavior is not simply the output of someone's isolated brain [7]. Rather, embodied cognition holds that cognitive processes are deeply rooted in the body's interactions with the world [1]. Consequently, the body plays a central role in shaping the mind and therefore, learning scientists should consider ways of engaging the body in the learning activity [8], known as embodied learning. As Nguyen, and Larson [9] noted, in embodied learning environments where learners use their bodies "learners are simultaneously sensorimotor bodies, reflective minds, and social beings".

Theories such as embodied cognition serve as an interesting foundational approach to technology-enhanced learning research. Indeed, the progress of multimodal, interactive spaces and motion-based technologies in the field of education has brought to light a lot of interesting considerations, pointing to the need to reconsider teaching practices and educational settings. Embodied cognition also became prominent in the fields of human computer interaction and interaction design with the work of Dourish [10] who first suggested the term "embodied interaction". Since then, lots of research aims to explore the role of the body in learning to create appropriate design strategies and environments in the service of learning. For example, tangible computing and Tangible User Interfaces (TUIs) [5, 11], as well as the use of multi-sensor artifacts, gesture technologies, and whole-body interaction [12] aim to create innovative and interactive learning experiences.

Overall, embodied cognition theory and embodied learning practices have brought to light essential considerations on how to develop appropriate learning environments for interactions between people and learning content [13]. Yet, little prior work has focused on the integration and evaluation of technologies that mediate embodied learning with specific learning goals in mind [14], such as the advancement of Psychomotor Abilities (Gp) and Psychomotor Speed (Gps) for children with special educational needs. That said, this work aims to push the boundaries of new learning technologies, teaching methods and evaluation techniques for the investigation and exploitation of the embodied learning field.

2.2 Related Empirical Work

In the last few years, innovative embodied interaction technologies are replacing the traditional human-computer interface modalities like mouse and keyboard [15]. Motion-based, interactive games such as Wii, Wii Fit or Wii Balance Board, Kinect-based games and exergames have received the researchers' attention investigating their potential for learning. These types of interactive games require active participation and physical engagement by the participants. In doing so, players can practice their motor skills in addition to others (e.g., cognitive skills depending on the goals of the game). Without a doubt, education is a research area in which the theory of embodied cognition has strong implications [15]. However, there is limited empirical research that studies the use of embodied games in general education as well as special education [16].

Within the limited empirical evidence in special education, motion-based interactive games appear to enhance the motor skills of children with disabilities [17, 18]. For example, in a relevant study [19] a total of 15 children with cerebral palsy with limited motor control of arms, experienced increased physical activity during the interventions with motion-based interactive games, compared to children in the control group. In another study conducted with 40 children diagnosed with cerebral palsy spastic diplegia, the practice with Nintendo Wii Fit games showed significant improvement in children's motor performance, when the control group exhibited no significant changes in the respective measures [20]. Moreover, a study conducted with 10 children with motor impairments using Nintendo Wii (Wii), showed significant improvement in upper limb functions for children in the intervention group [21]. It should be noted that all above-mentioned studies used motion-based interactive games in home settings (rather than in school environments or therapy centers) with children with motor impairments.

Along the same lines, a series of studies has been conducted to support both children and adults with attention problems and motor impairments [22–26]. In one study [27] children with gross motor skills problems were actively engaged in learning and, as a result of playing, improved their motor performance. In another recent study [28], a total of 20 children with special educational needs used a suite of Kinect-based learning games for a number of weeks; results showed significant improvement in children's motor, cognitive and academic skills. Moreover, previous findings from research on exergames suggest that their use in rehabilitation interventions is pleasant in addition to being effective in helping people to improve their motor skills [29]. Yet, other studies have shown limited effects of exergames in participants' performance [23].

Outside the field of special education, Lee et al. [30] used Kinect-based games to facilitate conversational language learning with 39 non-English speaking college students. Their findings suggested that gestures grasped the attention of the learners and stimulated their thinking about language. The study of VanDam et al. [31], showed that word meaning was linked to sensorimotor experience and therefore, the embodied approach resulted in language comprehension. The study of Chang et al. [32] claimed that the embodied learning experience facilitated students' cognitive learning outcomes and gave opportunities for more active learning engagement.

All things considered, a few empirical studies in the last decade, have shown that bodily movement can enhance learning and motor performance, whilst it appears to help with attention levels during the task. In all studies, researchers have emphasized the need for conducting more work to provide compelling evidence for the effectiveness of motion-based, multimodal interactive technologies for embodied learning.

3 Method

3.1 Participants

This present piece of investigation involved 10 elementary students (seven boys and three girls) with special education needs and motor impairments. Most of them (n = 7) attended mainstream elementary schools with special education units. The remaining children (n = 3) attended a special school. The participants had comorbid learning disabilities and disorders which influenced their motor performance, such as dyspraxia, brain paralysis, Down syndrome and ADHD. Five children were diagnosed with brain paralysis, spastic diplegia or quadriplegia which are subsets of spastic cerebral palsy that affects arms and legs. One child was diagnosed with dyspraxia which is a disorder that makes it hard to plan and coordinate physical movement. The rest four children had motor impairments combined with other disorders such as Down Syndrome, autism and ADHD (see Table 1). Inclusion criteria were age (6–14 years old) and ability to use Kinect-based, multimodal interactive games, even from a seated position. Exclusion criteria included severe motor or mental disorders to the extent that no engagement with the activities would be possible, according to the participating educators/therapist. Nine special educators and one occupational therapist were involved in the study, who were responsible for implementing the interventions during five-month period.

Table 1. Children participating in the study

Child	Age	Diagnosis
1	8	Motor impairments (seated on a wheelchair)
2	8	Down Syndrome and motor impairments
3	11	Brain paralysis
4	8	Motor impairments and ADHD
5	9	Dyspraxia and motor impairments
6	8	Autism and motor impairments
7	10	Brain paralysis - Spastic diplegia
8	12	Brain paralysis - Spastic quadriplegia (seated on a wheelchair)
9	14	Brain paralysis - Spastic diplegia (seated on a wheelchair)
10	14	Brain paralysis and motor impairments

3.2 Kinect Movement-Based Multimodal Interactive Games

Building on the idea of embodied learning, we used the commercial suite of Kinect movement-based interactive educational games, known as Kinems [33]. Kinems games engage students in learning related to verbal, math, and motor skills among others, through natural interaction, using only hands and body, via the Microsoft Kinect camera. Previous research has found evidence of many positive effects Kinems games have on children to develop a variety of skills [28, 34]. A unique aspect of Kinems is that children's interaction, performance and movements during the intervention sessions are recorded on a cloud server, therefore the researcher or practitioner can extract conclusions about the participant's progress. As of 2017, the Kinems suite includes 18 interactive games. In the present study, we focused on games which can enhance Psychomotor Abilities (Gp) and Psychomotor Speed (Gps), based on Cattell-Horn-Carroll Integrated Model classification of skills [6]. These are the "Walks" and "River Crossing". The study is part of a larger investigation addressing a range of skills through embodied learning using the complete Kinems suite.

To provide a better picture of the embodied learning games, "Walks" is a game that takes place in an imaginary farm. A farmer should walk along a path and collect carrots, without straying off the path into the mud or colliding with moving critters. The game can be made more/less challenging by selecting various path directions (horizontal, vertical, diagonal or zigzag) or by adding/removing obstacles to be avoided (see Fig. 1, left). On the other hand, in "River Crossing" (see Fig. 1, right), the child undertakes the task to lead a boat in a river and transfers animals and items of the food chain from one shore to the other. The child should be very careful so as not to crash the boat on rocks that exist. Sometimes the passage for the boat becomes narrower or wider, depending on the difficulty level of the game, that the teacher/therapist can adjust [33].

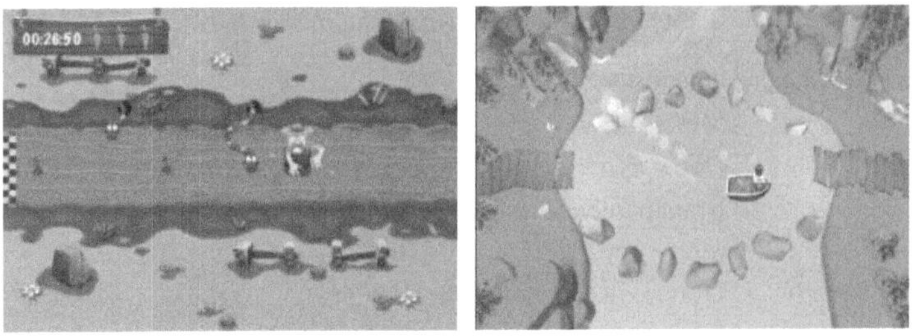

Fig. 1. "Walks" game (left) and "River Crossing" game (right)

3.3 Procedures and Data Collection

Special education teachers/therapists with their students were invited to participate in the study, upon ethical review of the proposed work. Once all parental permissions were obtained, a training workshop was conducted for teachers/therapists to practice the use of Kinems games and understand how to implement the method effectively with their special education children.

The intervention was conducted in a five-month period. In mainstream elementary schools with a special education unit (n = 7 students) the interventions took place in the unit. In this case, the teacher prepared personalized intervention based on the needs of their students. Children in the special school (n = 3) also received personalized instruction. On average, students received two sessions of 40-minutes Kinems interaction per week and completed between 12 and 40 sessions in the duration of the study (see Fig. 2). Children did not play the games in the same order, duration, or configuration settings; the personalized programme of each participating child involved different game settings as decided by the child's special teacher/therapist.

Fig. 2. Children using Kinect-based games by Kinems

In terms of data collection, system log-file data of children's interaction were automatically recorded in the Kinems platform. For example, depending on the game, the system recorded hand movements and stability, number of times the child completed the game, number of obstacles avoided (e.g., snakes and worms in "Walks" and rocks in "River Crossing" game) and speed of completing the game. In other words, the Kinect sensor recorded tracking data as the game progressed to enable the teachers' and researchers' understanding of children's progress on the variables of interest, in this case Psychomotor ability (Gp) and Psychomotor speed (Gps).

The dataset also included teachers' typed observations regarding children's performance, behavior and participation in the learning process; per researchers' instructions, these observations was noted by teachers at the end of each session in a specific notes-area for typing within the Kinems software. Furthermore, at the end of the programme, semi-structured interviews were conducted with all participating teachers. As shown in Table 2, questions focused on teachers' perceptions of students' improvement through their participation in the programme and the value of the Kinems games for embodied learning for students with motor impairments and educational needs.

Table 2. List of some questions asked in semi-structured interviews

Question	
1	How was the mood and motivation of the children during the sessions?
2	How children increase or not their participation during the intervention?
3	In what ways did the games support children's motor needs and learning needs?
4	Were the games hard, easy, and usable for the children and the teacher/therapist?
5	Please describe the general performance of children across sessions (motivation, completion time, body and hand movement etc.).
6	How do you see embodied games helping children to improve their skills?

4 Findings

4.1 Gains in Psychomotor Abilities (Gp) and Speed (Gps)

Initially, the analysis focused on understanding how the use of embodied touchless interactive games can enhance children's Psychomotor Abilities (Gp) and Psychomotor Speed (Gps). Based on the Cattell-Horn-Carroll Integrated Model classification of skills [6], Psychomotor Ability (Gp) is the ability to perform physical body motor movements with precision, coordination, or strength, operationalized in this study as the motor stability of the hand. Psychomotor Speed (Gps) is the speed and fluidity with which physical body movements can be made, operationalized in this work as the time for successful completion of the task.

With regards to Gps, we examined the speed-related analytics recorded in "Walks" which was used by all 10 participants for a different number of sessions, using configuration settings within the personalized programme of each child. Table 3 presents sequences of "Walks" usage by each child with the same configuration settings. As shown in Table 3, the overall completion time of the game improved across intervention sessions. In fact, there was a statistically significant difference on children's speed ($t(9) = 4.35$, $p = .002$), with children completing the task in shorter time in their last session ($M = 1.67$, $SD = .78$) compared to their first session ($M = 3.57$, $SD = 1.85$), with a large effect size (Cohen's d = 1.37) suggesting the practical significance of this finding.

Table 3. Completion time from the first to the last session in "Walks"

	Time in Walks session 1	Time in Walks last session	Number of sessions with same settings
Child 1	2.37	1.4	4
Child 2	5.1	2.12	4
Child 3	7.33	2.39	6
Child 4	5.8	3.34	8
Child 5	1.58	1.3	4
Child 6	2.19	1.51	7
Child 7	3.19	1.29	4
Child 8	2.42	1.7	4
Child 9	3.34	1.18	9
Child 10	2.4	0.49	7

With regards to Gp, we present the case of two children, while similar gains were evident across the majority children of Table 3. Child 2 played "Walks" for four consecutive sessions with the same configuration settings. As Fig. 3 shows, this child progressively improved his hand stability along a combination of horizontal and vertical movement, in only four sessions. Also, as the child was increasingly more capable of performing more accurate hand movement, success in completing the task was achieved in progressively shorter time (see Table 3). This child did not play other consecutive sessions of Walks with more advanced configuration settings.

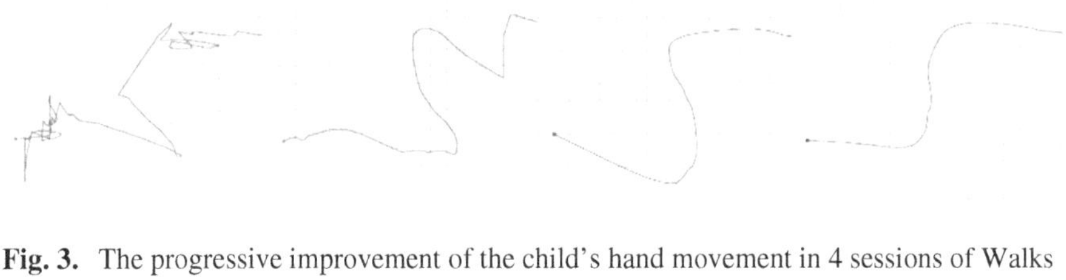

Fig. 3. The progressive improvement of the child's hand movement in 4 sessions of Walks

In "River Crossing", we present the case of Child 9 who played the game for twelve consecutive sessions with the same configuration settings. Figure 4 shows progressive improvement of the horizontal movement of his hand for four different routes from left to right during the game. The charts of the first session (left side), show that child faces kinetic instability during the execution of the right to drive left. Instead, looking at the figures of the last session (right side) one can see the child's improvement in comparison with the hand movement of the respective first session. Overall, the child's Gp ability for hand movements from left to right improved over time. Meanwhile, the game completion time of the child (Gps ability) was improved across sessions. In the first session, the child finished the "River Crossing" game in ten seconds; in the fourth session, he finished the game in four seconds and maintained this speed for the remaining sessions in "River Crossing".

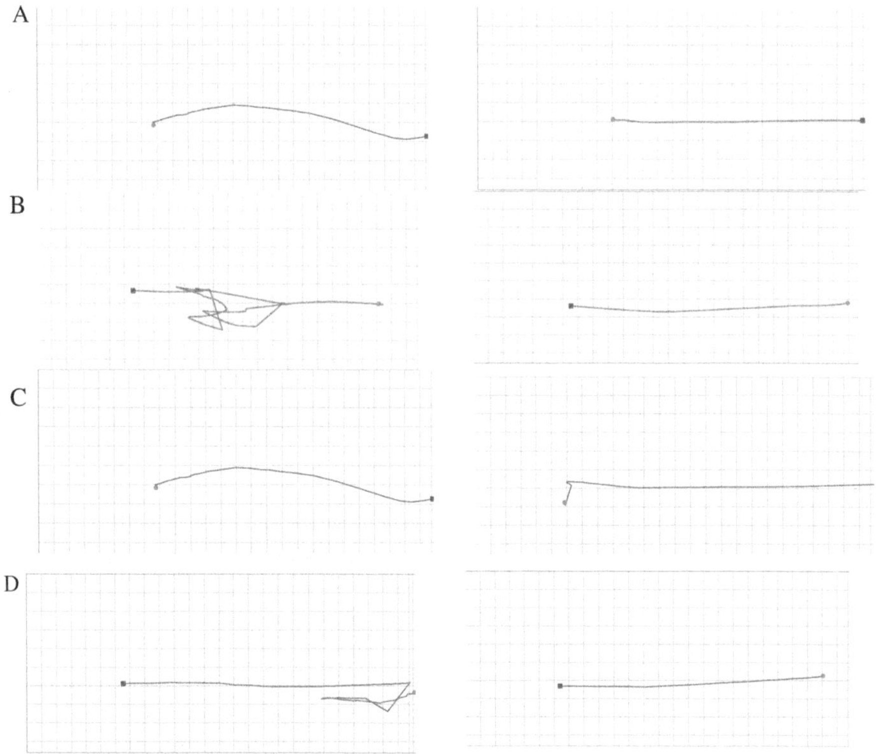

Fig. 4. A: Hand movement from 1st session to 12th session - route 1; B: Hand movement from 1st session to 12th session - route 2; C: Hand movement from 1st session to 12th session - route 3; D: Hand movement from 1st session to 12th session - route 4.

4.2 Teachers' Perceived Experiences of Embodied Learning

Teachers' observation notes taken upon each intervention session were analyzed in conjunction with the semi-structured interviews conducted at the end of five-month period. The interview data was transcribed and coded as described in Saldana [35]. Coding was done by two researchers (authors) who worked closely together on coding the interview transcripts, while considering the observation notes of the respective teachers. Following an iterative coding approach [35], a total of 18 thematic codes were identified until saturation was reached. These were then classified into four larger themes associated with the embodied learning experience from the teachers' perspective. Next, we report on one theme – "Improvement of motor skills" –which is directly linked to variables of interest in the present study– Gp and Gps. A detailed analysis of all four themes is beyond the scope of this manuscript.

According to the teachers, the method of touchless interaction enabled children to engage in physical activity and improve their body and hand movement. The clear majority of teachers discussed progress in vision-motor coordination, hand stability and speed improvement, as illustrated in Table 4.

Table 4. Teachers talk about visual-motor coordination, hand stability and speed

Participant	Visual-motor coordination	Hand stability	Speed improvement in task completion
p1	√	√	√
p2	√	√	√
p3	√		√
p4	√	√	√
p5	√	√	√
p6	√		√
p7	√	√	√
p8		√	√
p9	√	√	
p10	√	√	√

A few teachers went on to discuss that the embodied interaction with the games helped the children improve their gross motor and fine motor skills, body position in the space and ability coordinate thought and movement. Some indicative quotes on the matter are presented below to express the depth of the experience:

(p1) "*With the interactive games I saw that [child's name] was more concentrated and improved her movement. I think that this interactivity is very helpful especially for these children who have a lot of disabilities which affect their movement.*"

(p2) "*In the beginning, it was very difficult for my students to play the interactive games, but after a few sessions, they became much more confident in their movements.*"

(p4) "*I saw a significant improvement in the gross motor skills of my students. I saw that during the intervention my children could coordinate their hands better as well as their body position in front of the game.*"

(p9) "*I believe that this learning experience helped the children to coordinate their thinking and how to materialize it; thought - movement coordination for these children is very important.*"

(p5) "*One of my students has issues with his balance and hand-movement coordination. He has also a lot of difficulties in physical activities and for this reason he cannot participate in the gym class. However, this student managed to complete all the interventions. I saw significant improvement in his balance, hand stability and hand-movement coordination. I think that the games helped him a lot.*"

(p7) "*I saw improvement even with children who do not have severe mobility problems. Children with severe motor impairments had stress at the beginning, but during the programme they became capable of controlling their movement and their balance.*"

(p10) "*My children were seated on a wheelchair while playing. I saw an improvement especially in hand movement. I saw, for example, improvement in their hand stability and in their visual-motor coordination in the game. Playing these games, which require physical effort, I helped my students practice and learn to control their movements improving the fluidity of their hand and fingers movements*".

Some yet more promising feedback was related to the transfer of motor skills. One of teachers reported improvement in his student's writing, although the study did not have the data to triangulate this finding. In the teacher's own words:

(p9) "*During the programme, I noticed that one of my students improved the way of his writing; his grapho-kinetic skill improved significantly. Before the intervention, his movements were more steel and often without control; I noticed that after these sessions his movements are more limited around the body and are more controlled*".

Overall, the teachers' perceptions were fully consistent with the findings from the Kinetic analytics reported earlier. All the participating teachers felt that the embodied learning games can have an impact on children with motor impairments and special educational needs.

5 Discussion and Implications

A few studies in the field of educational technology have recently focused on exploring the potential of engaging the body in the learning process. This paper presents findings from an empirical investigation of using embodied touchless interactive games to enhance motor performance for children with learning disabilities and motor impairments. In sum, analysis of system analytics data from the Kinems embodied learning sessions revealed that children experienced significant gains in (i) psychomotor abilities (Gp) operationalized as stability of hand movement and (ii) psychomotor speed (Gps) operationalized as the time needed to successfully complete the task. These findings were consistent with the experiences and impressions of the teachers-participants.

In general, the results of the study are encouraging as they not only support our initial expectations driven by the theory of embodied cognition but also, confirm results of previous works making use of motion-based technologies to achieve learning goals including motor performance for children with special needs and learning disabilities [15, 16, 19–21, 27, 28]. Moreover, although many previous works make use of embodied learning technology in (isolated) home settings, the present study suggests that such methods can be used in traditional educational settings, including special schools, mainstream schools with special units and personalized education programmes, enriching the way of teaching and learning and enhancing the motor performance of children.

Nonetheless, empirical research in the field of embodied interactive games in special education for children with developmental coordination disorders are still limited [27, 28], not allowing for firm conclusions to be drawn. More investigation is needed to demonstrate how learning content and methods of embodied learning are best integrated in different domains [36]. Furthermore, theoretical frameworks need to be elaborated to explain the idea of body being active in the cognitive process and to establish the limitations of the relationship between the body and the mind.

One limitation of this study is the use of a large suite of games. Because of the many options to choose from, the teachers did not make extensive use of each single game. For example, most of them used "Walks" with the default settings, while after several sessions when the child mastered the game (within 4 to 9 sessions as in Table 3), the teachers chose to switch to a different game, rather than continue with "Walks" configured with more difficult settings. Therefore, from the perspective of the researchers, the study lacked data from consecutive sessions in a single game with increasing levels of difficulty. Future work in this area, should aim to track progressive improvement of skills across time and increasing difficulty. Therefore, although encouraging, the results of the present investigation require replication and extension to inform scientists about the value of embodied experiences linked to specific (learning) goals.

Future efforts could also involve clusters of participants with very similar needs so that gains in specific skills can also be clustered. To elaborate, in this work we studied the complete pool of participants as one unit of analysis. Yet, it is our next aim to explore the different impact of Kinect-based games on different clusters of participants such as participants with mild brain paralysis, as well as in different intervention settings such as, receiving personalized intervention in special units in mainstream classrooms vs. special schools vs. being part of class-wide embodied learning interventions. Furthermore, given the initial teacher-reported evidence of skills transfer, future studies would do well to investigate whether any competence developed during the programme will last beyond its duration and even transfer to other domains. In other words, it would be essential to examine if good scores in the embodied games are linked to good skills in real life.

Overall the study contributes to the technology-enhanced learning community by providing a better understanding of the potential of using embodied learning technology in special education. The study suggests that the use of touchless, multimodal interactive games can help enact embodied learning and result to the advancement of motor performance for children with special learning needs and motor impairments. The findings from the study can inform and further encourage the integration of embodied learning experiences mediated by motion-based technology in different learning environments.

Acknowledgments. We would like to thank all who voluntary participated in this study, especially the teachers, for their active involvement and collaboration, and the children for their hard work and engagement. We also thank Kinems and Microsoft Cyprus for providing the learning games and Kinect cameras respectively, free of charge.

References

1. Wilson, M.: Six views of embodied cognition. Psychon. Bull. Rev. **9**(4), 625–636 (2002)
2. Price, S., Roussos, G., Falcão, T.P., Sheridan, J.G.: Technology and embodiment: relationships and implications for knowledge, creativity and communication. Beyond Curr. Horiz. **29**, 1–22 (2009)
3. Foglia, L., Wilson, R.A.: Embodied cognition. Wiley Interdisc. Rev. Cogn. Sci. **4**(3), 319–325 (2013)

4. Antle, A.N.: Exploring how children use their hands to think: an embodied interactional analysis. Behav. Inf. Technol. **32**(9), 938–954 (2013)
5. Antle, A.N., Wise, A.F.: Getting down to details: Using theories of cognition and learning to inform tangible user interface design. Interact. Comput. **25**(1), 1–20 (2013)
6. Schneider, W.J., McGrew, K.S.: The Cattell-Horn-Carroll model of intelligence. Contemp. Intellect. Assess. Theor. Tests **3**, 99–144 (2012)
7. Clark, A.: An embodied cognitive science? Trends Cogn. Sci. **3**(9), 345–351 (1999)
8. Abrahamson, D.: Building educational activities for understanding: an elaboration on the embodied-design framework and its epistemic grounds. Int. J. Child-Comput. Interact. **2**(1), 1–16 (2013)
9. Nguyen, D.J., Larson, J.B.: Don't forget about the body: exploring the curricular possibilities of embodied pedagogy. Innov. High. Educ. **40**, 331–344 (2015)
10. Dourish, P.: Where the Action Is: The Foundations of Embodied Interaction, vol. 36. The MIT Press, London (2001)
11. Shaer, O., Hornecker, E.: Tangible user interfaces: past, present, and future directions. Found. Trends Hum.-Comput. Interact. **3**(1–2), 1–137 (2009)
12. Birchfield, D., Thornburg, H., Megowan-Romanowicz, M. C., Hatton, S., Mechtley, B., Dolgov, I., Burleson, W.: Embodiment, multimodality, and composition: convergent themes across HCI and education for mixed-reality learning environments. Adv. Hum.-Comput. Interact., 1–19 (2008)
13. Hornecker, E., Buur, J.: Getting a grip on tangible interaction: a framework on physical space and social interaction. In: Proceedings of the SIGCHI Conference on Human Factors in Computing Systems, pp. 437–446. ACM, New York (2006)
14. Li, K.H., Lou, S.J., Tsai, H.Y., Shih, R.C.: The effects of applying game-based learning to webcam motion sensor games for autistic students' sensory integration training. Turkish Online J. Educ. Technol. TOJET **11**(4), 451–459 (2012)
15. Leitan, N.D., Chaffey, L.: Embodied cognition and its applications: a brief review. Sensoria: J. Mind Brain Cult. **10**(1), 3–10 (2014)
16. Bartoli, L., Corradi, C., Garzotto, F., Valoriani, M.: Exploring motion-based touchless games for Autistic children's learning, In: Proceedings of Interaction Design and Children (IDC) Conference, New York, NY, USA (2013)
17. Barnhart, R.C., Davenport, M.J., Epps, S.B., Nordquist, V.M.: Developmental coordination disorder, physical therapy. J. Am. Phys. Ther. Assoc. **83**(8), 722–731 (2003)
18. Chang, Y.-J., Chen, S.-F., Huang, J.-D.: A Kinect-based system for physical rehabilitation: A pilot study for young adults with motor disabilities. Res. Dev. Disabil. **32**(6), 2566–2570 (2011)
19. Sandlund, M., Lindh Waterworth, E., Häger, C.: Using motion interactive games to promote physical activity and enhance motor performance in children with cerebral palsy. Dev. Neurorehabil. **14**(1), 15–21 (2011)
20. AlSaif, A.A., Alsenany, S.: Effects of interactive games on motor performance in children with spastic cerebral palsy. J. Phys. Ther. Sci. **27**(6), 2001–2003 (2015)
21. Sajan, J. E., John, J. A., Grace, P., Sabu, S. S., Tharion, G.: Wii-based interactive video games as a supplement to conventional therapy for rehabilitation of children with cerebral palsy: a pilot, randomized controlled trial. Dev. Neurorehabil., 1–7 (2016)
22. Deutsch, J.E., Borbely, M., Filler, J., Huhn, K., Guarrera-Bowlby, P.: Use of a lowcost, commercially available gaming console (wii) for rehabilitation of an adolescent with cerebral palsy. Phys. Ther. **88**(10), 1196–1207 (2008)

23. Hsu, J.K., Thibodeau, R., Wong, S.J., Zukiwsky, D., Cecile, S., Walton, D.M.: A “Wii” bit of fun: The effects of adding Nintendo Wii Bowling to a standard exercise regimen for residents of long-term care with upper extremity dysfunction. Physiother. Theory Pract. **27**(3), 1–9 (2010)
24. Joo, L.Y., Yin, T.S., Xu, D., Thia, E., Chia, P.F., Kuah, C.W.K., He, K.K.: Feasibility study using interactive commercial off-the-shelf computer gaming in upper limb rehabilitation in patients after stroke. J. Rehabil. Med. **42**, 437–441 (2010)
25. Loureiro, R.C.V., Valentine, D., Lamperd, B., Collin, C., Harwin, W.S.: Gaming and social interactions in the rehabilitation of brain injuries: a pilot study with the Nintendo Wii console. In: Designing Inclusive Interactions, Part V, pp. 219–228 (2010)
26. Saposnik, G., Teasell, R., Mamdani, M., Hall, J., McIlroy, W., Cheung, D., Bayley, M.: Effectiveness of virtual reality using Wii gaming technology in stroke rehabilitation: a pilot randomized clinical trial and proof of principle. Stroke **41**, 1477–1484 (2010)
27. Altanis, G., Boloudakis, M., Retalis, S., Nikou, N.: Children with motor impairments play a kinect learning game: first findings from a pilot case in an authentic classroom environment. J. Interact. Des. Architect. **19**, 91–104 (2013)
28. Kourakli, M., Altanis, I., Retalis, S., Boloudakis, M., Zbainos, D., Antonopoulou, K.: Towards the improvement of the cognitive, motoric and academic skills of students with special educational needs using Kinect learning games. Int. J. Child-Comput. Interact. **11**, 28–39 (2016)
29. Vernadakis, N., Papastergiou, M., Zetou, E., Antoniou, P.: The impact of an exergame-based intervention on children’s fundamental motor skills. Comput. Educ. **83**, 90–102 (2015)
30. Lee, W., Huang, C., Wu, C., Huang, S., Chen, G.: The effects of using embodied interactions to improve learning performance. In: 12th IEEE International Conference on Advanced Learning Technologies (ICALT), pp. 557–559. IEEE, New York (2012)
31. Van Dam, W.O., Van Dijk, M., Bekkering, H., Rueschemeyer, S.A.: Flexibility in embodied lexical-semantic representations. Hum. Brain Mapp. **33**(10), 2322–2333 (2012)
32. Chang, C.Y., Chien, Y.T., Chiang, C.Y., Lin, M.C., Lai, H.C.: Embodying gesture-based multimedia to improve learning. British J. Ed. Technol. **44**(1), E5–E9 (2013)
33. Kinems Learning Games. http://www.kinems.com/
34. Retalis, S., Korpa, T., Skaloumpakas, C., Boloudakis, M., Kourakli, M. Altanis, I., Siameti, F., Papadopoulou, P., Lytra, F., Pervanidou, P.: Empowering children with ADHD 21 learning disabilities with the Kinems kinect learning games. In: 8th European Conference on Games Based Learning, vol. 1, pp. 469–477 (2014)
35. Saldaña, J.: The Coding Manual for Qualitative Researchers. Sage, London (2009)
36. Dijkstra, K., Eerland, A., Zijlmans, J., Post, L.S.: Embodied cognition, abstract concepts, and the benefits of new technology for implicit body manipulation. Front. Psychol. **5**(757) (2014)

Teacher Dashboards in Practice: Usage and Impact

Inge Molenaar(✉) and Carolien Knoop-van Campen

Behavioral Research Institute, Radboud University, Montessorilaan 3, Nijmegen, The Netherlands
i.molenaar@pwo.ru.nl

Abstract. Even though the recent influx of tablets in primary education goes together with the vision that educational technologies will revolutionize education, empirical results supporting this claim are scarce. The adaptive educational technology in this research is used daily in primary classrooms and includes teacher dashboards. While students practice on the tablet, the technology displays real-time data of learner progress and performance in teacher dashboards. This study examines how teachers use the dashboards during lessons applying the Verberts' learning analytic process model. Teacher dashboard consultations and resulting pedagogical actions were observed in mathematics lessons. In a following stimulated recall interview, a teacher was asked to elaborate on the knowledge he/she activated and his/her reasoning in interpreting the dashboard. The results indicate that teachers consult the dashboard on average 8,3 times per lesson, but great variation among teachers was found. Teachers activate existing knowledge about the class and students to interpret dashboard data. The pedagogical actions teachers take after dashboard consultation are mainly providing individual feedback and additional instruction. The results show that pedagogical actions preformed at teachers' own initiative are mostly directed to low ability students, whereas actions after consulting the dashboard are more directed at middle and high ability students. These results indicate that extracted learning analytics, in the form of teacher dashboards are indeed influencing teachers' pedagogical actions in daily classroom activities and may initiate behavior changes in teaching practices.

Keywords: Educational technologies · Primary education · Dashboards · Ability levels

1 Introduction

Even though the recent influx of tablets in primary education goes together with the vision that educational technology empowered with learning analytics will revolutionize education, empirical results supporting this claim are scarce [1]. Specifically, advances are expected in adapting learning materials to the needs of individual students, leading to enhanced educational effectiveness [2, 3]. Learning analytics are expected to play and important role in driving adaptive learning and are often conceptualized by the distinction between embedded and extracted learning analytics [4]. On the one hand, embedded analytics refer to cases where the data is used directly by

É. Lavoué et al. (Eds.): EC-TEL 2017, LNCS 10474, pp. 125–138, 2017.
DOI: 10.1007/978-3-319-66610-5_10

the learning technology, for example providing different practice assignments to different students based on their ability profiles. On the other hand, extracted learning analytics refer to instances in which data are made available for different actors, such as teacher or students. Teacher dashboards are an often-used example of extracted analytics [5]. Dashboards can be conceptualized as new instruments that help teachers to improve their daily practice. However, we know very little about how teachers are using dashboards and how this affects their pedagogical actions such as the feedback they provide or the instruction they give.

A way to theoretically ground teachers' dashboard usage is through the distributed cognition theory. This theory states that instruments can indeed support professionals, when these instruments fit seamlessly into the activities of a professional [7]. Extensive research in domains ranging from aviation to medicine shows that the connection between instruments and the professional's routine is of great importance for the successful usage of new tools [8]. For example, a new tool in an aircraft must fit seamlessly into the daily routine of the pilot and his crew to prevent accidents. In classrooms dashboards can be considered a 'new' instrument for teachers to support them in selecting effective pedagogical actions [6]. Where the distributed cognition theory provides a research paradigm to view the use of instruments during professional functioning, the Verberts' learning analytics process model can be used to investigate how teachers use dashboards specifically in their daily classroom contexts.

Verberts' learning analytics process model specifies the stages users go through from interpretation of the data on the dashboards towards meaningful actions [5]. Four stages are distinguished in this learning analytic process model. First, in the awareness stage the user becomes aware of the dashboard and the data available. Second, in the reflection stage the user interprets the data by asking questions and evaluating the relevance of these questions. In the third, sense making stage the user answers the relevant questions to further understand the value of the data. Finally, in the impact stage, the user's understanding of the data is employed to change his/her behavior. Hence, this model applies to teachers and their use of dashboards in their teaching practices [5]. Teacher dashboards are directed at teachers to better understand students' ability, learning process and progress. Often these dashboards represent information about students' progress on different learning goals and show correct and incorrect answers students have given on assignments [5]. In the awareness stage teachers become consciously aware of the data in the dashboards. For example, they explore which information is shown. Next, in the reflection stage, teachers start asking themselves questions about the data, such as "how can I see if students are understanding the material?". In the sense making stage teachers try to answer their questions, and try to understand how the data are informative for their teaching and how they relate to their pedagogical actions, for example, how do the data show that a student is struggling which would call for feedback or additional instruction. Finally in the impact stage teachers determine pedagogical actions that respond to the data in de dashboard. Pedagogical actions are interventions teachers take to support students' learning, for example providing additional instruction to improve individual students' progress.

Generally, teachers constantly make decisions leading to pedagogical actions [9]. These pedagogical actions are based on teachers' pedagogical knowledge base that consists of knowledge, skills, perceptions, and personal characteristics and entail knowledge on both student and class level. Important knowledge elements are understanding of individual students' abilities, students' domain knowledge and skills, but also common developmental problems students face during learning and how they are indicated by particular errors students make. Furthermore, knowledge on the class level deals with social dynamics within the group and understanding of the knowledge and skill development at the group level. All these knowledge elements can be used to select appropriate pedagogical actions. Information on the dashboards can add to teachers' knowledge base on both student and class level. Therefore, when teachers go through the stages of the learning analytics process model to interpret data on the dashboards, it is likely that they activate their pedagogical knowledge base. To understand how dashboard data affect teaching, it is important to understand which additional knowledge teachers activate to understand the data and reason towards pedagogical actions.

Both on a class and student level, teachers can use data to adjust pedagogical actions such as instruction and feedback. Teachers in Dutch primary schools often follow the direct instruction model [10]. In this model a lesson consists of 7 phases. First teachers present the general topic of the lesson and assess students' prior knowledge in the introduction phase. Second, in the goal setting phase, teachers elaborate on the learning goal of the lesson and their expectation of students' learning. Third, during the instruction phase, teachers give class-wide instruction adjusted to the class's knowledge and skills. Fourth, in the guided practice phase, students practice together with the teacher. This stage is important for teachers to determine if all students understand the instruction provided. Fifth, in the independent practice phase, students work on practice assignments individually. Sixth, during the independent practice phase, teachers may give extended instruction to low ability students. After the extended instruction, all students are working in the independent practice phase and teachers provide help to individual students using a range of pedagogical actions. Often they provide additional instruction or they give students feedback. Feedback is defined as individual support, which helps the student progress. It can be directed at the task, person, progress, metacognition, or social aspects of learning [11]. Teachers' pedagogical actions can also entail selecting different learning material for a student, or changing the pace for students depending on their needs and progress. The seventh and last phase of the lesson is the reflection phase, in which the teacher reflects on students' practice and progress.

The dashboard information can have different functions in different phases of the lesson. For example, if a teacher sees that a number of students are making similar mistakes during independent practice, he/she can give additional instruction to this particular group. However, if this information is provided during guided practices, the teacher might change the instruction. Moreover data on learning phase may be viewed in a different light during the guided practices phase as compared to during the independent practice phase. For example, if a particular student is much slower compared to the other students, in the guided practice phase where the strategy is discussed together this could indicate a problem with prior skills and knowledge, whereas during the independent practices phase this could indicate an individual problem, for instance this student is using a less effective strategy. Additional insight provided by clicking in the dashboard to show the type of errors and mistakes this student is making can support the teacher to investigate the students' errors and define an appropriate pedagogical action.

To conclude, extracted learning analytics in the form of dashboards provide teachers with concurrent information about students' abilities, progress, performance, and errors made. This information can be useful to adjust pedagogical actions and teaching behavior, but only when teachers are aware of the data and able to interpret the data properly and translate this understanding into appropriate pedagogical actions. Consequently different stages of the learning analytics process model are a prerequisite for effective teacher usage of dashboards in different phases of the lesson. Accordingly, this study explores how teachers go through the different stages of the learning analytics process model in their use of extracted analytics, thereby increasing our understanding of the usage of dashboards by teachers in the classroom context. The following research questions are examined:

1. How often do teachers consult the dashboards during a lesson and in which phases of the lesson?
2. Which pedagogical knowledge do teachers activate to interpret the data on the dashboards?
3. What pedagogical actions do teachers take after consulting the dashboards?
4. How do teachers' teaching practices change in response to the usage of dashboards?

In this study, the awareness stage of the learning analytics process model is operationalized by how often teachers consult the dashboards during lessons. The reflection and sense making stage are combined by assessing which pedagogical knowledge teachers activate to interpret the data provided on the dashboard. The pedagogical actions that teachers take after consulting the dashboards provide first insights of the potential impact dashboards can have. Finally, changes in teaching practices are determined by comparing teachers' pedagogical actions after consulting the dashboard to teachers' pedagogical actions that are initiated without dashboard consultation. It is important to note that consultation and pedagogical actions are directly observed in the classroom context, whereas the reflection and sense making are assessed through a stimulated recall interview with the teachers.

2 Method

2.1 Sample

In total, 38 teachers of 8 different primary schools participated in this study. 30 teachers were female and 8 were male. The participating teachers each taught a different class, ranging from Grade 2 (8-year-old students) to Grade 6 (12-year-old students). On average teachers had 19 years of teaching experience and 2 years experience with tablet education. Each teacher was observed during a 50-minute mathematics lesson, dealing with the topics of the math curriculum the school follows. Teachers agreed to participate in the study and were interviewed directly after the lesson.

2.2 Adaptive Educational Technology

The adaptive educational technology used in this research is called 'Snappet'. This technology is mainly used for mathematics and spelling across primary schools in the Netherlands. The mathematics and spelling assignments in 'Snappet' are comparable to those used in traditional paper workbooks. This educational technology operates on tablet computers and features both adaptive assignments (embedded analytics) and dashboards (extracted analytics). Children receive immediate (knowledge of results) feedback after finishing each assignment. Next to pre-selected assignments that are the same for all students in a class, the technology features adaptive assignments, which are adjusted, automatically to students' performance levels. The technology uses a derivative of the Elo rating system to adapt assignments to the current ability level of the individual student [10]. The system uses the algorithm to model the probability of a student answering a question correctly. The algorithm calculates a student's ability score, which is the representation of a student's ability on a particular learning objective. The ability score represents an expected outcome for a given assignment with a specific difficulty level. Once the student finishes an assignment, the ability score is re-calculated using the difference between the expected and actual outcome. Based on the ability score the next assignment with matching difficulty level is selected.

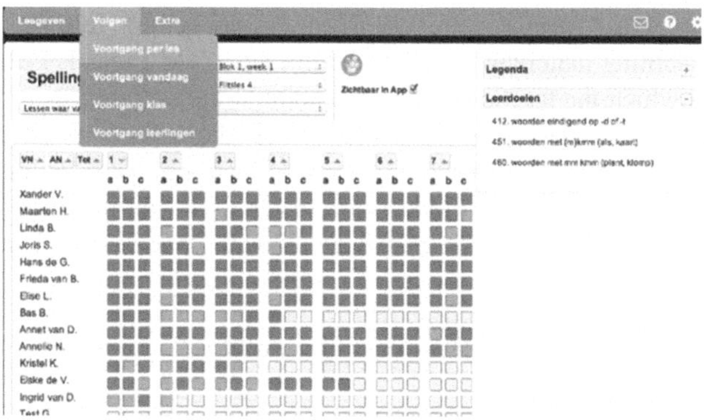

Fig. 1. Teacher dashboard lesson overview.

Teachers use this technology in a blended educational scenario in which traditional instruction is combined with practice on the tablet computer. Class wide teacher instruction plays an important role in this scenario. After the teacher has explained a new topic to all students, students first practice with the same pre-selected assignments. In the next phase, students work with adaptive assignments. This adaptive practice supports individual practice at the students' own ability level.

The dashboards. The technology captures real-time data of learner performance, which are concurrently displayed to the teachers on dashboards. The system includes three different dashboards for teachers. The *lesson overview* dashboard indicates the performance of students on the pre-selected assignments, see Fig. 1. Teachers can monitor this dashboard to see the progress of the individual students. Green blocks indicate that a student has answered an assignment correctly. Orange blocks denote that a student eventually answered the question correctly after one or more incorrect attempts. Finally, red blocks indicate that the student did not manage to give a correct answer. As this dashboard is updated concurrently during the class it also provides information on students' pace. The *class overview* dashboard provides an overview of the performance of the students compared to all other students using the system, indicating to which norm group each student belongs (10% best students, 20% best students, etc.). Finally the *progress dashboard* is used when students work on adaptive assignments. This dashboard indicates which students are progressing on their learning goals, are stable, or slow down in their progress.

2.3 Measurements

The observations. To examine how often teachers consult the dashboards during a lesson classroom observations were performed by trained research assistant that were seated in the classroom. They observed the teacher's tablet or computer screen and were logged in the adaptive educational technology being able to see the teachers' dashboard. Every time the teacher consulted a dashboard, the observer wrote down the time, made a screen shot of the dashboard and coded the pedagogical action that followed. Pedagogical actions were classified as: no action, feedback, instruction, adjustment of learning materials, or adjustment of pace, see Table 1. Feedback actions were actions in which the teacher gave information to the students about their learning process. Instruction actions were instances where the teacher provided additional instruction to one or more students. Adjustment of learning materials included actions in which the teacher customized the learning materials for an individual student or a group of students. Adjustment of pace included allowing one or more students to work

Table 1. Pedagogical actions

Pedagogical actions	Explanation	Example
Feedback	Actions in which the teacher provided feedback to student(s) about their learning process	"You are working very hard, well done"
Additional instruction	Actions in which the teacher provides additional explanations or examples to student(s)	"Please do not forget to add the numbers you have to keep in mind"
Adjustment of learning materials	Actions in which the teacher adapted the material (assignments or learning goal) of student(s)	"Tim, please make the assignments I put in a work package for you"
Adjustment of pace	Actions in which the teacher adapted the pace of the lesson for student(s)	"The star group should now continue with the next lesson"
No action	Teacher did not perform a didactic action after consulting the dashboard	The teacher takes no clear action

shorter or longer on a particular section of learning materials. The Cohens' Kappa on all categories was acceptable to good, ranging from .71 to .90. Finally, in case an action was directed at an individual student, the research assistant also wrote down the ability level of the student that was addressed. This was done by using classroom plans indicating the ability level of children based on the seating arrangement.

Stimulated recall interviews. After each observation, the research assistant discussed all dashboard consultations in a stimulated recall interview with the teacher. The teacher was asked to indicate which knowledge he/she used to assess the data in the dashboard. By means of a grounded analysis the teachers' answers were classified in the following categories: knowledge of the student, characteristics of the student, progress of the student, error analysis, knowledge of the class, characteristics of the class, and agreements with the class, see Table 2. The Cohens' Kappa was acceptable to good, ranging .69 to .94 for different categories.

Table 2. Teacher pedagogical knowledge activation

Pedagogical actions	Explanation	Example
Knowledge of the student	Refers to the teachers' knowledge about students' knowledge or personal characteristics	"This student is weak in math but has a high general intelligence"
Error analyses	Refers to the analysis of mistakes to determine the reason of these errors	"Peter has a wrong conceptualization of double digit numbers"
Progress of the student	Refers to students' advancement, for example, the number of assignments made	"This student made less assignments compared to the other students"
Characteristics of the class	Refers to the teachers' knowledge of the class' characteristics and knowledge	"This class has many dyslexic students"
Agreements made with the class	Refers to the agreements that were made with a class, for example, we respect each other's opinion	"Every lesson consult with your neighbor student for 5 min"
Progress of the class	Refers to the class' advancements	"The whole class has worked well today"

Children's mathematics ability was determined by using the national standardized mathematics assessment, CITO Mathematics [*CITO Rekenen-Wiskunde*]. Students were divided in three ability levels. The high ability group represented the top 25%, the middle ability group contained the middle 50% and the low ability group represented the lowest scoring 25%.

3 Results

3.1 Awareness: Dashboard Consultation

The first research question addressed how often teachers consult the dashboards during a lesson. In the 38 lessons that were observed, teachers consulted the dashboards a total of 317 times. On average, teachers looked at the dashboards 8.34 times per lesson with a standard deviation of 5.22 times. There was quite some difference in how often teachers consulted the dashboards, ranging from 2 to 22 times per lesson. Three groups of teachers could be distinguished: −1 SD and below (between 0 and 5 dashboard consultations in a lesson) consisting of 13 teachers, between −1 SD and +1 SD (between 6 and 10 dashboard consultations) consisting of 15 teachers, and +1SD and above (between 10 and 22 dashboard consultations) consisting of 10 teachers. These groups are further distinguished as the low, medium and high consultation group.

With respect to the positioning of dashboard consultations during the 7 phases of the direct instruction model, 69% of the dashboard consultations were during the independent practice phase, see Fig. 2. Teachers also consulted the dashboard during the reflection phase to evaluate how the class performed. During other phases consultation was minimal.

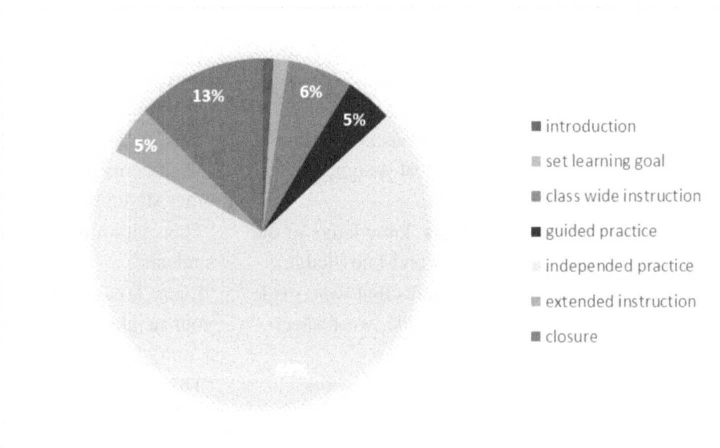

Fig. 2. Percentage of dashboard consultations during the phases of the direct instruction model

3.2 Reflection and Sense Making: Pedagogical Knowledge Activation and Data Interpretation

The data from the stimulated recall interviews showed that teachers indeed reflect on the data when consulting dashboards. Teachers did activate their existing pedagogical knowledge to interpret the data in the dashboards. For example, teachers would activate knowledge of a particular student to interpret why his pace was different from the other students. Based on the teacher's knowledge that this student was often very accurate, he could determine if the current information on the dashboard was different than expected and create new meaning. Figure 3 provides an overview of the types of pedagogical knowledge teachers activated. Knowledge of the student (66 of the 317 dashboard consultations) was activated mostly to understand the data in the dashboards. Furthermore, teachers often made an analysis of the type of errors students made (56 dashboard consultations) and of students' progress (55 consultations) to determine which particular type of support a student needed. Teachers also activated pedagogical knowledge on progress of the class (46 consultations), knowledge of the class (37 consultations) and agreements with the class (34 consultations) to interpret the data and determine pedagogical actions. Teachers mostly activated knowledge on the individual student level, namely 60% of the time versus 40% knowledge at class level.

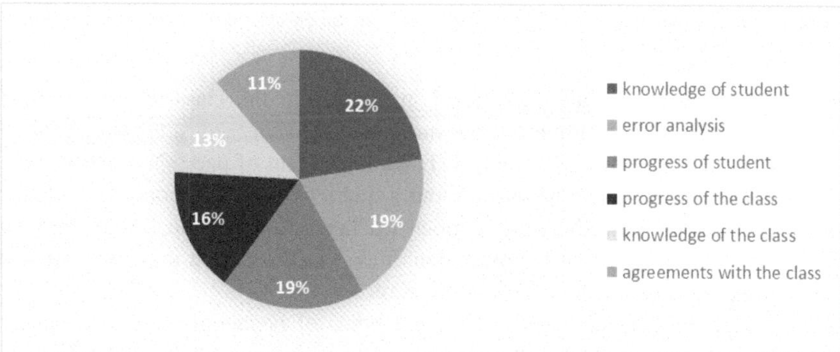

Fig. 3. Percentage of types of pedagogical knowledge activated.

On average teachers activated 4 different knowledge types during a lesson. We examined if the dashboard consultation rate was associated with the diversity of the activated knowledge. A three-way ANOVA analysis indicated that there was a significant difference between teachers in the low, medium, and high consultation group, $F(2,35) = 30.94$, $p = .001$. Post-hoc Bonferroni analysis indicated that there were significant differences between all three groups. Teachers in the low consultation group on average activated 2.54 different types of knowledge, teachers in the medium consultation group activated 4.00 types of knowledge, and teachers in the high consultation group activated 5.00 different types of knowledge. Additionally a difference was found between the three groups in the types of knowledge that teachers activated. Low consulting teachers mostly relied on knowledge of student and class. Medium and high consulting teachers also engaged in error analysis and used progress information of both class and students more frequently.

3.3 Impact: Pedagogical Actions

The actions that followed dashboard consultation are outlined in Fig. 4. The action that was most likely to follow after a teacher looked at the dashboard, was providing feedback to a student (N = 118). For example, "*you are doing really well, keep this up*

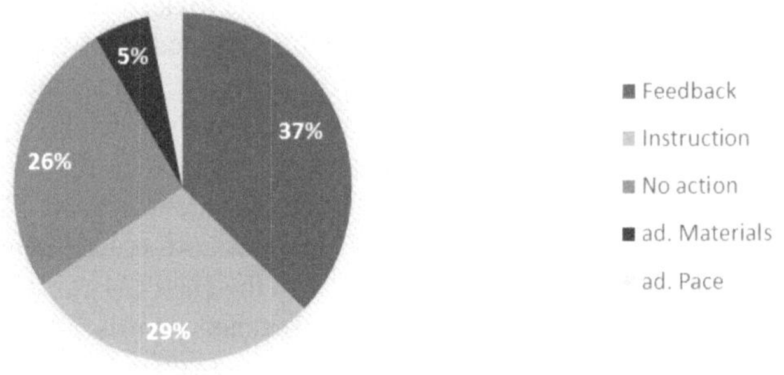

Fig. 4. Percentage of types of pedagogical actions taken after dashboard consultation

Ann". Often teachers provided additional instruction to the class or to a particular student (N = 90). For example, "*you need to remember to add that number*". Adjustment of learning materials (N = 17) and adjustment of pace (N = 10) were less frequently taken pedagogical actions. About a quarter of the dashboard consultations (N = 82) were not followed by any explicit teacher action. Of the actions that were performed following dashboard consultation, 50% was directed at individual students, 7% at a group of students, and 43% at the class level.

On average teachers activated 3 different types of pedagogical actions during a lesson. We determined whether the number of consultations of the dashboards was associated with the diversity of the pedagogical actions. Possibly teachers that consulted the dashboards more frequently, were also more likely to show more diversity in pedagogical actions. Indeed a three-way ANOVA analysis indicated that there was a significant difference between the low, medium, and high consulting teachers $F(2,35) = 20.31$, $p = .001$. Post-hoc Bonferroni analysis indicated that there were significant differences between all three groups. Low consulting teachers on average took 2.08 different actions, medium consulting teachers took 2.80 different actions, and high consulting teachers took 3.90 different actions. Additionally a difference was found between the three groups in the types of pedagogical actions. Low consulting teachers mostly gave additional instruction or did not engage in any action. Medium and high consulting teachers gave feedback more often and high consulting teachers also adjusted materials and pace.

3.4 Sense Making: Relation Between Knowledge Activation and Pedagogical Action

In order to further understand teachers sense making proces, the relation between knowledge activation and the three most likely following pedagogical actions were assessed. Table 3 shows the correlations between activated knowledge types and pedagogical actions. Instruction was related to activation of knowledge about the class or students which indicated that teachers need to augment the information in the

Table 3. Correlations between pedagogical actions and teacher activated knowledge

Pedagogical actions	Feedback	Instruction	No action
Knowledge of students	0.24	0.69***	−0.60*
Error analysis	0.59**	0.16	0.51**
Progress of students	0.54***	0.30	0.15
Progress of the class	0.27	−0.25	0.73***
Knowledge of the class	0.17	0.35	−0.01
Agreements with the class	0.67***	−0.01	−0.04

*significant at 0.05, **0.01, ***0.001 *note.* N = 317 dashboard views

dashboard with existing knowledge to be able to determine which instructional actions are appropriate. Feedback actions were driven by agreement with the class, for example, "you are working according to our agreement, well done!" Also error analysis and progress of students drove feedback actions. This indicated that individual feedback actions were supported by data on mistakes made and progress and augmented by reasoning on the types of mistakes and meaning thereof. Finally, in cases where no action was taken, teachers often simply confirmed that the class was making appropriate progress or they assessed errors and felt no immediate need to intervene.

3.5 Prolonged Impact: Changing Teacher Behavior After Dashboard Consultation

Teachers naturally initiate pedagogical actions during their lessons and now they also initiate pedagogical actions after dashboard consultation. To determine whether teachers alter their practices due to the dashboard information, we examined if teachers' pedagogical actions after dashboard consultation were directed at students with different abilities compared to teacher actions that were initiated naturally (i.e. without dashboard consultation). We found that indeed there was a marginally significant difference $\chi^2(2, 329) = 5.84$, $p = .054$. Naturally initiated teacher actions were mostly directed at low ability student, which (see Fig. 5). However, after dashboard consultation teachers supported medium and high ability students more often. The dashboard information seemed to guide teachers to support students that normally would have received less support.

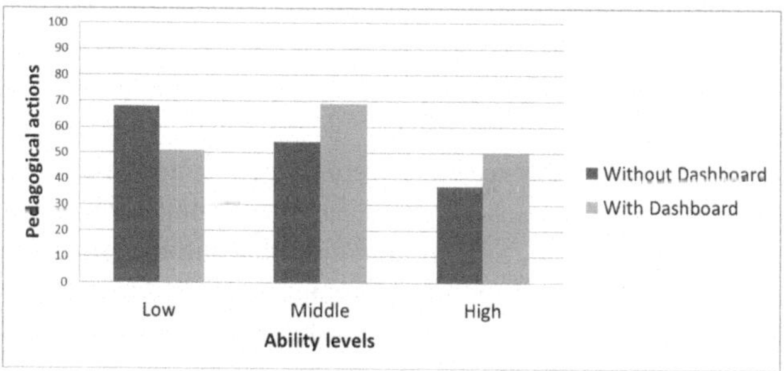

Fig. 5. The division of pedagogical actions directed at different ability groups

4 Conclusion

This study examined how teachers use teacher dashboards, a form of extracted learning analytics, during mathematics and spelling lessons. The results showed that teachers were aware of the dashboards and consulted them on average over 8 times in a 50-minute lesson. However, a large diversity in consultation was found. Low, medium and high consulting teachers were distinguished. As expected dashboard consultations were mostly occurring during the independent practice phase of the lessons, but also during the reflection phase the dashboard was consulted. Typically in the independence practice phase teachers were giving additional feedback or instruction to students. In the closure phase teachers would provide additional feedback reflection on the student or class progress as input to discuss problems students' faced.

Teachers indeed reflected on the data and activated additional pedagogical knowledge to interpret the data as suggested by Verberts' learning analytics process model [5] and Roelofs' pedagogical knowledge bases model [8]. Knowledge on the individual student level was activated more often, but also knowledge on the class level was used by teachers to make sense of the dashboard data. In line with these results, 50% of the pedagogical actions following dashboard consultation were directed at individual students, about 7% was directed at a small group, and 43% at the class level. At the individual student level, pedagogical actions taken were feedback and providing students with additional instruction, whereas at the class level teachers most often gave additional instruction. Surprisingly, about a quarter of the dashboard consultation were not followed by any explicit teacher action. This seems to indicate that the dashboard was also used as a tool by which teachers confirm their own assessment of students' and class progress.

The analyses showed that Verberts' learning analytics process model can be used to progressively study teachers' use of dashboard data. Teachers, who consulted the dashboard more often, also activated more and different types of pedagogical knowledge to interpret the data. Consequently, they also engaged in more diverse pedagogical actions. In line with this development, teachers who view the dashboards more often also analyzed students' errors and progress more often. This was associated with more feedback and adjustment of students' pace and learning materials. This suggests that more diverse teaching practices are associated with awareness, reflecting and sense making of the dashboard data. Moreover, behavior change was evidenced by a shift in the type of students that were directed by teachers' pedagogical actions. Middle and high ability students received support more often after teachers looked at the dashboard. We expect that the data on the dashboard highlighted the need for support for these groups of students. Possible consequences of this shift in teacher attention an important focus of future research.

Overall, this study shows that teachers were indeed using the dashboards and this seemed to influence their daily teaching practices. Interpreting our results in the light of the distributed cognition theory, we can conclude that information in the dashboard connects to teachers' professional routine and teachers are indeed able to successfully usage these new tools. The stages of Verbert's learning analytics model support the analysis how teachers use dashboards. The data drove reflection and sense making and teachers used their existing pedagogical knowledge to come to new understandings, which lead to pedagogical actions. This study indicates that there were changes in teacher behavior due to using the dashboard. These actions can potentially support educational effectiveness, but future research needs to investigate this further. Moreover, developments in teacher usage of dashboards over time as well as the role of experience and possible interactions with professional skills need to be explored in future research.

Consequently, we conclude that dashboards seem to impact the way teachers teach. The diversity among teachers as indicated by the differences between low, medium and high consulting teachers and related differences in reflection, sense making and impact could be indicative of a development in the usage of the dashboards, but this hypothesis needs future research to be tested. Naturally more research is needed to further explore the way teachers are using dashboards and to come to a more profound understanding of the associations found in this exploratory study. Yet there are ample opportunities to improve the human-technology interaction and the usage of dashboards. As indicated by the learning analytics process model, it starts by making teachers more aware of the data. Moreover, training teachers to interpret data with their existing pedagogical knowledge might help teachers forward. Moreover, as suggested by the distributed cognition theory, a good connection between the instrument (dashboard) and the repertoire of the professional can support successful usage in daily classroom practice. This connection can be improved by adding new services to the existing dashboards, for example highlighting important dashboard information and making potential pedagogical actions more explicit with recommender services.

Acknowledgements. We thank the team of bachelor students of Radboud University for collecting data, as well as master student Liset Onnink and post-doc Karly van Gorp.

References

1. Papamitsou, A., Economides, Z., Anastasios, A.: Learning analytics and educational data mining in practice: a systematic literature review of empirical evidence. J. Educ. Technol. Soc. **17**(4), 49–64 (2014)
2. Tempelaar, D., Rienties, B., Giesbers, B.: In search for the most informative data for feedback generation: learning analytics in a data-rich context. Comput. Hum. Behav. **47**, 157–167 (2015)
3. Fullan, M.: Systems Thinkers in Action. DfES Innovation with NCSL, London (2004)
4. Wise, A., Yuting, Z., Hausknecht, S.: Learning analytics for online discussions: embedded and extracted approaches. J. Learn. Anal. **1**(2), 48–71 (2014)
5. Verbert, K., et al.: Learning analytics dashboard applications. Am. Behav. Sci. **57**, 1500–1509 (2013)
6. Molenaar, I., van Schaik, A.: A methodology to investigate classroom usage of educational technologies on tablets. In: Aufenanger, S., Bastian, J. (eds.) Tablets in Schule und Unterricht. Forschungsergebnisse zum Einsatz digitaler Medien, pp. 87–116. Springer, Wiesbaden (2016)
7. Hutchins, E.: Distributed cognition. In: International Encyclopedia of the Social and Behavioral Sciences. Elsevier Science (2000)

8. Norman, D.A.: Cognitive Artifacts. Department of Cognitive Science, University of California, San Diego (1990)
9. Roelofs, E., Sanders, P.: Towards a framework for assessing teacher competence. Eur. J. Vocat. Training **40**(1), 123–139 (2007)
10. Gersten, R., Keating, T., Becker, W.: The continued impact of the direct instruction model: longitudinal studies of follow through students. Educ. Treat. Children **11**(4), 318–327 (1988)
11. Keuvelaar-van den Bergh, L.: Teacher Feedback During Active Learning: The Development and Evaluation of a Professional Development Program. Technische Universiteit, Eindhoven (2013)

MAGAM: A Multi-Aspect Generic Adaptation Model for Learning Environments

Baptiste Monterrat[1(✉)], Amel Yessad[1], François Bouchet[1], Élise Lavoué[2], and Vanda Luengo[1]

[1] Sorbonne Universités, UPMC Paris 6, CNRS, LIP6 UMR 7606, Paris, France
{baptiste.monterrat,amel.yessad,francois.bouchet, vanda.luengo}@lip6.fr

[2] IAE Lyon, Université Jean Moulin Lyon 3, LIRIS UMR CNRS 5205, Lyon, France
elise.lavoue@univ-lyon3.fr

Abstract. Adaptation in learning environments can be performed according to various aspects, such as didactics, pedagogy or game mechanics. While most current approaches propose to adapt according to a single aspect, this paper proposes a Multi-Aspect Generic Adaptation Model (MAGAM). Based on the Q-matrix, this model aims at taking into account heterogeneous data to select adapted activities. It has been implemented and used into an experiment which allowed the adaptation of learning activities for 97 students based on both knowledge and gaming profiles. This experiment has shown the usefulness of MAGAM to combine various aspects of adaptation in ecological conditions.

Keywords: Adaptation · Learner model · Recommender system

1 Introduction

Adaptive systems are often defined by three characteristics: (1) the *source* (what will it adapt to), (2) the *target* (what will be adapted) and (3) the *pathway* (how to adapt the target to the source). In this paper, we call the combination between the source and the target an *aspect* of adaptation. For an adaptation to be successful, the source should bring information that is relevant with regard to the target. For example, a system adapting didactic contents relies on cognitive profiles, while a system adapting the game mechanics of a serious game relies on player profiles.

In a review of the state of the art of adaptation for learning, Vandewaetere *et al.* [1] identified over ten sources of adaptation, such as the learners' knowledge and culture, and over twenty targets of adaptation such as content and feedback. However, most proposed systems in the literature are limited to one aspect of adaptation. The diversity of adaptation technics could be an explanation for this limitation. Indeed, Vandewaetere *et al.* [1] also identified over twenty pathways such as rule-based systems or Bayesian networks. This wealth of techniques could also be the reason why Naik and Kamat [2] think it is not feasible to take into account a large number of sources for adaptation. However, we believe a multi-aspect adaptation is not only advisable but also feasible if it is supported by a model designed to be generic enough.

É. Lavoué et al. (Eds.): EC-TEL 2017, LNCS 10474, pp. 139–152, 2017.
DOI: 10.1007/978-3-319-66610-5_11

We make the hypothesis that a model with generic variables and operators could federate different aspects of adaptation. To this end, we developed a model called MAGAM (*Multi-Aspect Generic Adaptation Model*) which relies on properties that are common to the learners and to the activities to be adapted. After a brief state of the art of adaptation techniques in Sect. 2, we present this model in Sect. 3. Then we present in Sect. 4 an experiment performed to evaluate the model and its usage.

2 Approaches for Adaptation of Learning Environments

2.1 The Adaptation Loops

Aleven *et al.* [3] distinguish three types of adaptation loops: design, task and step. The design loop adaptation relies on an analysis of the learner and learning data that is taken into account for new design iterations. In task loop adaptation, the system has to select the task that suits best the learner. Finally, the step loop is responsible for several adaptations within a task, in reaction to the learner's actions. Systems based on the design loop adapt the learning design to the common characteristics of learners, while systems based on the task and step loop adapt to the differences between learners. The model we present here is developed mainly for the task loop.

The adaptation loops rely on two operations: selecting/setting the activities adapted to the learners, and initializing/updating the learners' profiles. The model we propose applies to selecting/setting activities. It can be used in conjunction with various methods for initializing/updating the learners' profiles – a point not considered here.

2.2 Aspects of Adaptation

Several types of sources have been found to positively impact learning outcomes. Through a literature review, Aleven *et al.* [3] classified into five categories the sources that have been experimentally validated: (1) knowledge, (2) problem-solving strategies and errors, (3) affect and motivation, (4) self-regulated learning and metacognition and (5) learning styles. We detail here six aspects of adaptation, five of which are related to these sources. We consider the gaming profile as another aspect of adaptation.

Didactic Aspect. The learner's knowledge level was one of the first lines of research for adaptation. In 1972, Atkinson [4] improved the students' performances in language learning by selecting their tasks according to their previous answers. In 1995, Anderson *et al.* [5] proposed *Cognitive Tutor*, a system that evaluates the knowledge state of a learner, represented in a Bayesian network. The model is then used to select the tasks not mastered by the learner, leading to a better improvement of the students' performances than when no model is used. Other kinds of knowledge dimensions may be considered for adaptation. For example, Luengo *et al.* [6] consider the nature of the knowledge (e.g. perception, gesture, procedural) to adapt the learning task in orthopedic surgery based on a didactical analysis implemented by a Bayesian network.

Pedagogic Aspect. Melero *et al.* [7] proposed a system that recommends activities of a serious game to the learners. It takes into account both the learner's cognitive profile and teaching strategies (advancing, reinforcing and deepening) set by the teachers. This system relies on the Competence-based Knowledge Space Theory (CbKST) [8] to identify the space of knowledge states learners go through. Field experiments showed a concordance between the teachers' choices and those of the adaptation system.

Affective and Motivational Aspect. Walkington [9] developed an environment for learning algebra that adapts to the learners' interests. This system has enabled learners to better understand the problems and to obtain better results. In their research on the links between personality and emotions, Harley *et al.* [10] also made several proposals to make learning environments adapted to emotions, in particular to reduce anxiety.

Strategic Aspect. In MetaTutor [11], a learning environment designed to encourage students to deploy self-regulated learning strategies, pedagogical agents' interventions are triggered by a rule-based system to encourage students to use these processes at the appropriate moment. Experimental evaluations have shown that students who received agents' prompts obtained better results than students who did not.

Learning Styles Aspect. Mampadi *et al.* [12] worked on two learners' cognitive styles: holistic and serialist. In their experiment, participants who learned using an environment adapted to their cognitive style performed better than those in the control group. Learners' profile can be initialized through a questionnaire [12] or through an automatic detection of learning styles from learners' traces [13].

Gaming Aspect. Proposals for adaptation among the gaming aspect appear less often in literature reviews, although some experiments gave positive results. Natkin *et al.* [14] made one of the first proposals of game mechanics adaptation. They relied on personality types (e.g. introvert, resilient) to select quests in a serious game which mechanics were adapted to the players. Inspired by their method, Monterrat *et al.* [14] developed an adaptive system to gamify an existing learning environment. They relied on player types (e.g. socializer, achiever [16]) to select gamification features adapted to the students. During an experiment with 223 learners, those with adapted elements used more the environment than those with a counter-adapted environment.

2.3 Multi-Aspect Adaptation

Some articles report research based on a multi-aspect adaptation. Heilman *et al.* [17] present a system that considers both the learners' interests and competences. It was evaluated in an English vocabulary course with 22 learners and showed positive results on the learners' performance. As another example, the system proposed by Yarandi *et al.* [18] adapts the learning path based on learners' knowledge model and the presentation based on their learning styles, abilities and preferences. These systems are not easily generalizable, as they are specific to the combined aspects and their related adaptation techniques.

For a more generic approach, Murray *et al.* [19] propose an approach based on decisions theory to model adapted pedagogical actions. This approach uses a Bayesian dynamic decision network to model tutor actions and several student adaptation aspects (knowledge, focus and affect, ibid. p. 241). The authors evaluate (with historical data) one or two dimensions of the decision network in the framework of tutoring systems. Even if the model is generic enough, the problem of tractability is still a challenge. Indeed, the model can include hundreds of nodes, their specification and calibration is difficult and not accessible to non-experts. In addition, the tutor actions are still dependent of the system.

In gaming contexts, Göbel et al. [20] proposed a model that uses both a didactic adaptation model based on learners' knowledge and a gaming adaptation model based on learners' player types. They propose a weight system to merge the two aspects at the same time to choose an activity. The model presented in this paper can be seen as a generalization of the one proposed by Göbel *et al.* [20].

3 MAGAM: Presentation of a Multi-Aspect Generic Model

In this section, we present MAGAM (*Multi-Aspect Generic Adaptation Model*). This model is based on three entities: the users-learners (U), the pedagogic activities (A) and the properties (P) applied to both users and activities.

3.1 A Generic Model

The main goal of the adaptation model is to propose activities adapted to each learner according to several aspects. Each aspect is embodied in a set of properties. The properties are linked (1) to the users through a system of values with their own semantic, and (2) to the activities with another semantic and system of values. For example:

- If the properties are skills (e.g. add, multiply), the values can express the level of mastery of the user in each skill on the one hand, and express how well the activity helps learning each skill on the other hand.
- If the properties are game mechanics (e.g. competition, exploration), the values can express how much the user appreciates these mechanics on the one hand, and to what degree the activity includes these mechanics on the other hand.

To visualize the model, we propose a representation on the three visible faces of a cuboid (see Fig. 1). The user profile is the set of values that link the properties to the user, represented into the matrix M. The values that link the properties to the activities are represented into the matrix Q. Finally, the system provides a recommendation matrix called R representing how well each activity is adapted to each learner.

The values of the user profiles (M) can be collected using various methods, such as questionnaires or interaction traces analysis, either in real time or from previously collected data. Matrix Q is inspired by the Q-matrix of Barnes [18], but it can apply to other aspects than skills and contain other values than 0 and 1. There are also several ways to obtain the matrix Q, such as relying on domain experts [14] or data analysis [22].

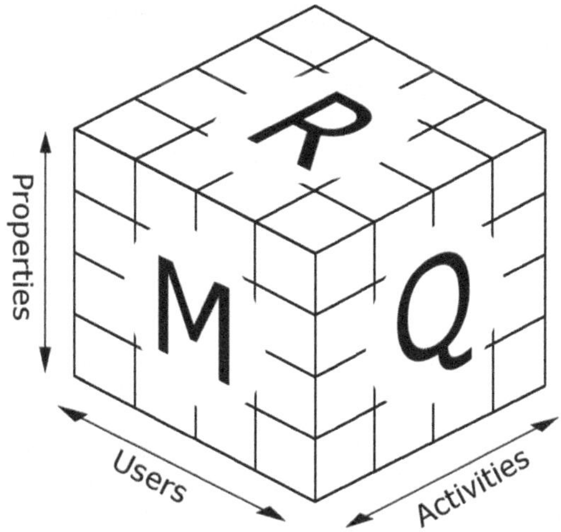

Fig. 1. Three-dimensional representation of MAGAM.

To obtain the recommendation matrix, we define a *Calculation* (Eq. 1), denoted C, as an application that builds R from Q and M:

$$C(Q, M) \rightarrow R \tag{1}$$

Several examples from the literature described in Sect. 2.2 are compatible and can be described as use cases of MAGAM. As previously mentioned, in [11] (see Fig. 2), the learners were classified according to whether they were holist or serialist. We can represent these two sides of the same personality trait as one property with the value 1 (*Holist*) or −1 (*Serialist*). The matrix M represents the results of the personality survey. In some cases, the model can recommend characteristics of the learning environment rather than activities. In this case, the adaptive characteristics of the activities were (1) next/previous buttons, (2) hyperlinks, (3) a hierarchical map and (4) an index. The matrix Q links these characteristics with the personality traits (e.g. a *holistic* user would prefer content that is structured as a hierarchical map). Finally, a calculation provides the matrix R, that contains 1 when the activity matches the learner's profile and 0 when it does not.

$$\forall u \forall a,\ R_{ua} = \Sigma_{p=1}^{pmax} \frac{|Q_{pa} + M_{up}|}{2}$$

Fig. 2. Representation of the adaptation system in [11] through MAGAM.

Walkington [8] gave students algebra problems based on the users' interests. 27 algebra problems were developed, with 4 versions for each corresponding to different interests, which makes 108 activities in total. The authors do not provide the details of the calculation, however when applying MAGAM, a calculation can be deduced from their adaptation logic. We propose on Fig. 3 a possible representation of their adaptation system (calculation C_1). It includes four problems that belong to three different types of interests, and assumes the survey provided scores from zero to five.

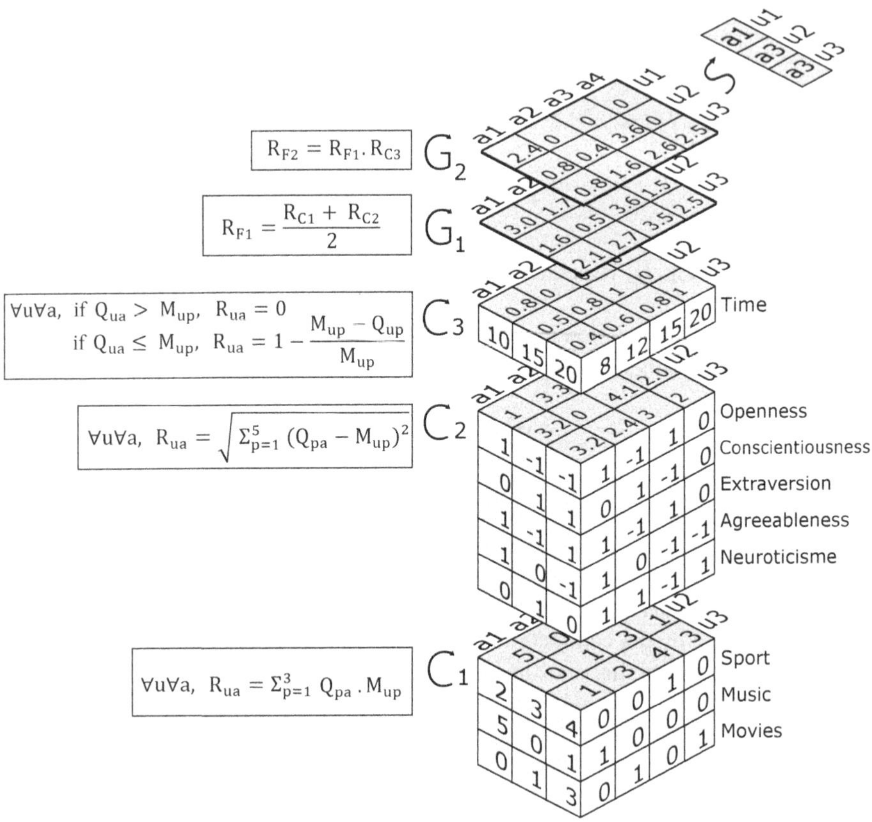

Fig. 3. Example of successive mergers.

The model used by Natkin *et al.* [13] is also compatible with MAGAM. Their adaptation is based on the Five Factor Model [23], composed of five dimensions expressed in values from −1 to 1 for both users and activities. The recommendation comes from a distance measurement between the vector of the user and the vector of the activity. We can express this distance with a calculation in MAGAM. It is shown in Fig. 3 (calculation C_2).

3.2 Merging for a Multi-Aspect Adaptation

The calculation system described in the previous section builds an adaptation on several properties that belong to the same aspect. To build an adaptation on several aspects, we need to combine the recommendations obtained from different calculations. To this end, we define the *merGer* (Eq. 2) as an application that builds a matrix R from other matrices Ri.

$$G(R1, R2, \ldots, Rn) \rightarrow R \tag{2}$$

Several types of calculations can be used as a merger. For example, we can take a weighted average of the matrices as proposed by Göbel *et al.* [20]. Alternately we can take the minimum for each value. Thus, if a calculation gives a very low value in Ri, then it is sure this low value will persist in the final matrix R, which prevents selecting activities evaluated as unsuitable on one aspect. We can also take the maximum of each value to select activities that suit the user very well on, at least, one of the aspects.

Finally, to identify which activity will be recommended to the learner, we define the *Selection* (Eq. 3) as an application that builds a one-column matrix R′ from R. The matrix R′ contains the id of each activity that has been selected for each user.

$$S(R) \rightarrow R' \tag{3}$$

To illustrate the possibilities of mergers, Fig. 3 represents an example of application of MAGAM including three calculations: by the motivational aspect (C_1), by the gaming aspect (C_2) and by the pedagogical aspect C_3).

The first calculation is derived from [8] and the second from [13]; they are described in details in Sect. 3.1. For the third calculation, we propose to apply a pedagogical constraint by considering the learner's available time. In matrix M, the user expresses how much time (in minutes) he/she had for the learning session. The matrix Q represents how much time is required to complete each activity. We design a calculation that rejects activities longer than the user's available time and accepts shorter ones. Figure 3 shows that the activity a1 takes 8 min, it suits extroverts and talks about music.

Firstly, we merge R_{C1} and R_{C2} into R_{G1} by taking the average values, giving them the same weight. Secondly, we merge R_{G1} and R_{C3} into R_{G2} by taking the product of the values. Indeed, a zero value in R_{C3} means the corresponding activity cannot be done by the user and merging with the product of values maintains the zeros into the final R.

3.3 Implementation of MAGAM

We implemented the MAGAM framework using web technologies (HTML, MySQL, PHP), with an interface allowing to manually specify the entities, write the values in the matrices M and Q, choose the operations and finally read the results of the adaptation (see Fig. 4).

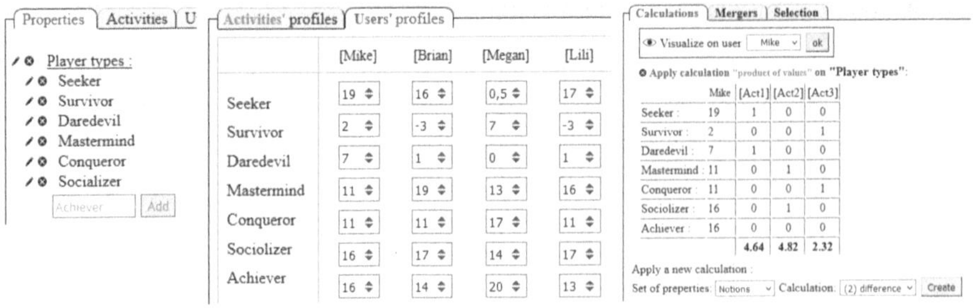

Fig. 4. Screenshot extracts from an implementation of MAGAM. *Left: page to create/edit a list of properties. Middle: page to edit the values of matrix M. Right: page to apply a calculation and visualizing the results for one user.*

4 Experiment

We organized a four-week experiment to evaluate MAGAM and its implementation. The experiment proposed a didactic and gaming adaptation for students of a methodology course for written and oral expression. Paper activities are carried out in the classroom and Moodle activities are performed individually outside of the classroom.

4.1 Method

Participants. The participants were 176 1st year science students from a French public university, distributed into ten groups initially composed of 13 to 20 students. They were following a class to help improve and develop their writing skills in French, in particular in science, where writing correctly can be an issue even for some university-level students, foreign or not. The number of participants has fallen sharply because some students dropped the class and others did not receive some mandatory e-mails for the experiment. Finally, the 98 considered students are 19 years old on average and 53% of them are women. Each participant was randomly assigned to one of the four following conditions:

[c] No adaptation (control group): 29 students
[g] Gaming Adaptation: 26 students
[d] Didactic Adaptation: 24 students
[gd] Gaming and Didactic Adaptation: 19 students

Material. The participants answered two surveys before the experiment. The first one (pretest) was a knowledge test based on scores from 0 to 1 on six areas: spelling, grammar, syntax, time concordance, conjugation and vocabulary. It was built by one of the teachers. The second survey was the BrainHex test [16], returning scores from −10 to 20 on seven player types: Seeker, Survivor, Daredevil, Mastermind, Conqueror, Socializer et Achiever. The validity of the Brainhex typology and survey was investigated recently. Busch et al. [24] measured the internal consistency of each of the seven factors underlying the test with Cronbach's Alpha (n = 592) and found acceptable reliability coefficients. Finally, the participants answered a posttest based on the same six knowledge areas as for the pretest.

In collaboration with teachers, we created 46 paper activities to be used in the classroom and 58 Moodle activities to be used independently. The type of most activities was multiple choice questions, text to be completed and table to be completed. Each activity was made to improve knowledge on one of the six areas. It included zero, one or several gamification mechanics. The integrated mechanics are presented in Table 1.

Table 1. Implemented gamification mechanics.

Player type	Classroom activities	Moodle activities
Seeker	Activity based on an article including scientific knowledge	Activity based on an article including scientific knowledge
Survivor	Activity ending at an unexpected moment	–
Daredevil	Limited time activity	Time and number of trials are limited
Mastermind	–	–
Conqueror	Competitive activity	–
Socializer	Cooperative activity	Discussion on the forum included into the activity
Achiever	–	A check mark for each activity achieved

Procedure. The experiment took place on a four-week period with two hours of class each week. The students had to work on Moodle activities between the classroom lessons. The students' distribution into the four conditions ([c], [g], [d] and [gd]) divided each of the ten groups in four sub groups. These steps took place each week:

1. Two days before the classroom session, the classroom recommendations were calculated and sent to the teacher by e-mail.
2. During the first 20 min of the classroom session, the students carried out the recommended activities in subgroups.
3. After each classroom session, the students' profiles were updated according to whether they performed the classroom activities or not.
4. The same day, the Moodle recommended activities were calculated and sent to the students by e-mail. Each student was offered two mandatory activities and one optional activity. They were given three days to perform them. They had no recommended activity the fourth week.
5. Three days before the classroom session, the students' profiles were updated according to the score that they obtained on each Moodle activity.
6. The same day, the teachers were informed of the number of mandatory Moodle activities done by their students, in order to take it into account for their mark.

Applying MAGAM. For the group [c], the recommended activities were selected randomly. For the group [g], the recommendations were based on the calculation (C_g) applied to the seven player types. This calculation gives a high recommendation value for the activities with gamification mechanics adapted to the user player types. For the group [d], the recommendations were based on calculation (C_d) applied to the six knowledge areas. This calculation gives a high recommendation value for the activities that teach knowledge the learner does not master yet. If the mastery value for a knowledge area *p* is weak (i.e. M_{ua} low) and the activity *a* teaches this knowledge area (i.e. Q_{ua} is high), then the activity is more likely to be recommended (i.e. $R2_{ua}$ is high). For the group [gd], the calculations (C_g) and (C_d) were applied successively and merged using (G_{gd}).

$$\forall u \forall a, \quad R1_{ua} = \frac{\sum_{p=1}^{7} M_{ua} \cdot Q_{ua}}{7} \qquad (\mathbf{C_g})$$

$$\forall u \forall a, \quad R2_{ua} = \sum_{p=1}^{6} (1 - M_{ua}) \cdot Q_{ua} \qquad (\mathbf{C_d})$$

$$\forall u \forall a, \quad R3_{ua} = R1_{ua} \cdot R2_{ua} \qquad (\mathbf{G_{gd}})$$

Three selections were used to recommend the Moodle activities. They selected the activities with the higher recommendation values independently for each student. One selection was used to recommend the classroom activities. It selected the activity with the highest average value for all the students of each subgroup, as they had to work on the same activity. During the experiment, the player profiles of the users (player types) were considered as static. However, their learner profiles (knowledge areas) were updated according to their results. After each activity, the value of each knowledge area changed according to this formula: $value_{t+1} = (value_t + score) / 2$.

When a learner finished an activity, it could no longer be recommended to him/her.

4.2 Results

Table 2 presents the scores obtained by the students of each condition for the pretest and posttest. We took the average value of the six areas to get a score between 0 and 1. The progress of each student was calculated with the formula: *progression = (posttest − pretest) / (1 − pretest)*. The value reported in Table 2 is the medium progression value of each group. Contrary to the original teacher's expectation, the posttest appeared to be more difficult than the pretest, which explains the negative values of progression.

Table 2. Progression between pretest and posttest and p values.

Condition	N	Pretest	Posttest	Progression	[c]	[g]	[d]
[c]	28	0.66	0.50	−0.044			
[g]	26	0.68	0.52	−0.050	p = 0.603		
[d]	24	0.66	0.48	−0.058	p = 0.190	p = 0.153	
[gd]	19	0.73	0.55	−0.042	p = 0.849	p = 0.306	p = 0.034

The difference between each condition was evaluated with a bilateral Student t-test. We performed six tests with a 5% threshold. The participants in conditions [g] and [gd] did not have a progression superior to the control group. Also, the participants in condition [gd] progressed more than the participants in condition [d] ($p = 0.034$). However, after applying the correction of Bonferroni, this difference does not pass the threshold of the test at $p = 0.0085$.

For each week, we observed the number of participants who carried out the optional activities (see Table 3). The numbers obtained were compared using a Khi^2 test. Only the comparison of conditions [d] and [gd] showed a significant difference ($p = 0.006$) for the first week. This result could mean that the gaming adaptation indeed motivates the learners to carry out more activities. However, further experiments would be required to confirm this observation.

Table 3. Percentage of participants who carried out the optional activity each week.

Condition	N	Week 1	Week 2	Week 3
[c]	28	52%	55%	50%
[g]	26	53%	45%	45%
[d]	24	26%	40%	41%
[gd]	19	73%	75%	62%

4.3 Discussion

The participants with didactic adaptation performed a very low number of optional activities compared to the others. We believe this is because calculation (C_d) recommended activities on areas that the students did not master, thus the activities that would appear as the most difficult for them. This may have caused a difficulty peak in the beginning that affected the participants' motivation.

When comparing the gaming adaptation condition lg] with the control one [c], it seems the gaming adaptation failed to increase the students' progression (Table 2) or their motivation (Table 3). However, when the gaming adaptation was merged to the didactic adaptation, it seems the gamification mechanics had a positive impact on the students' performances. This may also be related to the difficulty the students were facing because of the calculation (C_d). Thus, the impact of the gaming adaptation is not as clearly identified as in [15]. This could be explained by the lack of a competition mechanic in the Moodle activities (see Table 1), as competition is an important component of many player profiles. It could also be due to the absence of mechanics related to the player type *Mastermind*.

Concerning the use of MAGAM, this paper brings a proof of concept on its genericity. Indeed, we have presented several adaptation cases from the literature as instantiations of MAGAM. An implementation of this model was used for an unprecedented (to the authors' knowledge) multi-aspect adaptation case, in particular considering the ecological conditions of the experiment.

Although the current implementation of MAGAM is functional, the experiment highlighted some of its limitations, mainly a lack of interoperability. It takes a lot of time to fill the M and Q matrices by hand from the survey results and updating them. It also takes time to read the recommendations and send them by e-mail. For its second version, MAGAM should be implemented as a library that would be used into an existing learning environment. The learning environment would automatically fill and update the profiles, and use the resulting recommendations.

5 Conclusion

We have presented MAGAM, a generic model that can adapt learning activities according to various aspects of adaptation. Through a brief literature review and an experiment in ecological conditions, we have shown that using MAGAM is a way to adapt learning activities along multiple aspects.

MAGAM is based on the Q-matrix model [21], thus it represents each aspect of adaptation as a simple list of properties. The choice of the Q-matrix model also implies some limitations. For example, it does not represent the prerequisite relations between skills as the Competence-based Knowledge State Theory (CbKST) does. Also, it does not manage uncertainty as Bayesian networks do [25].

Many avenues of research are opening up following this work. First, several extensions could develop and complete MAGAM, such as:

- Limiting the number of times an activity is recommended.
- When there are too much constraints and some users do not have any suitable activity, releasing some constraints automatically.
- Taking into account pedagogical constraints such as the number of students required to work on the same collaborative activity.

The interest of taking into account several aspects of adaptation still has to be empirically tested, as few experiments can be found in the literature. MAGAM should help driving the tests to identify which set of properties and calculations work and which ones do not. Upon these findings, another set of experiments could explore which types of mergers and selections give the best results on learning outcomes.

Finally, some work still has to be done to give the teachers access to an interface allowing them to handle this model, as the choice of an operation remains highly technical for now. We should develop a library of calculations, mergers and selections and specifying their semantic in educational terms. For example, a teacher setting the system would not select "a weighted average merger" but rather "an adaptation giving priority to the didactic aspect over the gaming aspect". This effort should come with a more ergonomic management tool.

Acknowledgements. We would like to thank Sorbonne Universités for funding this research project and teachers, but also students, who accepted to participate to this experiment.

References

1. Vandewaetere, M., Desmet, P., Clarebout, G.: The contribution of learner characteristics in the development of computer-based adaptive learning environments. Comput. Hum. Behav. **27**(1), 118–130 (2011). doi:10.1016/j.chb.2010.07.038

2. Naik, V., Kamat, V.: Adaptive and gamified learning environment (AGLE). In: 2015 IEEE Seventh International Conference on Technology for Education (T4E), pp. 7–14 (2015)
3. Aleven, V., McLaughlin, E.A., Glenn, R.A., Koedinger, K.R.: Instruction based on adaptive learning technologies. In: Handbook of Research on Learning and Instruction. Routledge, London (1997)
4. Atkinson, R.C.: Optimizing the learning of a second-language vocabulary. J. Exp. Psychol. **96**(1), 124–129 (1972). doi:10.1037/h0033475
5. Anderson, J.R., Corbett, A.T., Koedinger, K.R., Pelletier, R.: Cognitive tutors: lessons learned. J. Learn. Sci. **4**(2), 167–207 (1995)
6. Luengo, V., Mufti-Alchawafa, D.: Target the controls during the problem solving activity, a process to produce adapted epistemic feedbacks in ill-defined domains. The case of a TEL system for orthopaedic surgery. In: Workshop on Formative Feedback in Interactive Learning Environments, in conjunction with AIED 2013 (2013)
7. Melero, J., El-Kechai, N., Yessad, A., Labat, J.-M.: Adapting learning paths in serious games: an approach based on teachers' requirements. In: Zvacek, S., Restivo, M.T., Uhomoibhi, J., Helfert, M. (eds.) CSEDU 2015. CCIS, vol. 583, pp. 376–394. Springer, Cham (2016). doi: 10.1007/978-3-319-29585-5_22
8. Augustin, T., Hockemeyer, C., Kickmeier-Rust, M.D., Podbregar, P., Suck, R., Albert, D.: The simplified updating rule in the formalization of digital educational games. Journal of Computational Science **4**(4), 293–303 (2013). doi:10.1016/j.jocs.2012.08.020
9. Walkington, C.A.: Using adaptive learning technologies to personalize instruction to student interests: the impact of relevant contexts on performance and learning outcomes. J. Educ. Psychol. **105**(4), 932 (2013)
10. Harley, J.M., Carter, C.K., Papaionnou, N., Bouchet, F., Landis, R.S., Azevedo, R., Karabachian, L.: Examining the predictive relationship between personality and emotion traits and students' agent-directed emotions: towards emotionally-adaptive agent-based learning environments. User Model. User-Adap. Inter. **26**(2–3), 177–219 (2016). doi: 10.1007/s11257-016-9169-7
11. Taub, M., Azevedo, R., Bouchet, F., Khosravifar, B.: Can the use of cognitive and metacognitive self-regulated learning strategies be predicted by learners' levels of prior knowledge in hypermedia-learning environments? Comput. Hum. Behav. **39**, 356–367 (2014)
12. Mampadi, F., Chen, S.Y., Ghinea, G., Chen, M.-P.: Design of adaptive hypermedia learning systems: a cognitive style approach. Comput. Educ. **56**(4), 1003–1011 (2011). http://doi.org/10.1016/j.compedu.2010.11.018
13. Bousbia, N., Labat, J.M., Balla, A., Rebai, I.: Supervised classification on navigational behaviours in web-based learning systems to identify learning styles. Int. J. Learn. Technol. **6**(1), 24–45 (2011)
14. Natkin, S., Yan, C., Jumpertz, S., Market, B.: Creating multiplayer ubiquitous games using an adaptive narration model based on a user's model. In: Digital Games Research Association International Conference (DiGRA 2007) (2007)
15. Monterrat, B., Desmarais, M., Lavoué, É., George, S.: A player model for adaptive gamification in learning environments. In: Conati, C., Heffernan, N., Mitrovic, A., Verdejo, M.F. (eds.) AIED 2015. LNCS, vol. 9112, pp. 297–306. Springer, Cham (2015). doi: 10.1007/978-3-319-19773-9_30
16. Nacke, L.E., Bateman, C., Mandryk, R.L.: BrainHex: preliminary results from a neurobiological gamer typology survey. In: Anacleto, J.C., Fels, S., Graham, N., Kapralos, B., Saif El-Nasr, M., Stanley, K. (eds.) ICEC 2011. LNCS, vol. 6972, pp. 288–293. Springer, Heidelberg (2011). doi:10.1007/978-3-642-24500-8_31

17. Heilman, M., Collins-Thompson, K., Callan, J., Eskenazi, M., Juffs, A., Wilson, L.: Personalization of reading passages improves vocabulary acquisition. Int. J. Artif. Intell. Educ. **20**(1), 73–98 (2010)
18. Yarandi, M., Jahankhani, H., Tawil, A.-R.H.: Towards adaptive E-learning using decision support systems. Int. J. Emerg. Technol. Learn. (iJET), **8**(S1) (2013). https://doi.org/10.3991/ijet.v8iS1.2350
19. Murray, R.C., Vanlehn, K., Mostow, J.: Looking ahead to select tutorial actions: a decision-theoretic approach. Int. J. Artif. Intell. Educ. **14**(3,4), 235–278 (2004)
20. Göbel, S., Wendel, V., Ritter, C., Steinmetz, R.: Personalized, adaptive digital educational games using narrative game-based learning objects. In: 5th International Conference on E-learning and Games (Edutainment 2010), Changchun, Chine, pp. 438–445 (2010)
21. Barnes, T.: The Q-matrix method: mining student response data for knowledge. In: American Association for Artificial Intelligence 2005 Educational Data Mining Workshop (2005)
22. Desmarais, M.C., Naceur, R.: A matrix factorization method for mapping items to skills and for enhancing expert-based Q-matrices. In: Lane, H.C., Yacef, K., Mostow, J., Pavlik, P. (eds.) AIED 2013. LNCS, vol. 7926, pp. 441–450. Springer, Heidelberg (2013). doi: 10.1007/978-3-642-39112-5_45
23. McCrae, R.R., Costa, P.T.: Validation of the five-factor model of personality across instruments and observers. J. Pers. Soc. Psychol. **52**(1), 81 (1987)
24. Busch, M., Mattheiss, E., Orji, R., Fröhlich, P., Lankes, M., Tscheligi, M.: Player type models: towards empirical validation. In: Proceedings of the 2016 CHI Conference Extended Abstracts on Human Factors in Computing Systems, pp. 1835–1841. ACM Press (2016). https://doi.org/10.1145/2851581.2892399
25. Pearl, J.: Probabilistic Reasoning in Expert Systems: Networks of Plausible Inference. Morgan Kaufmann Publishers Inc., San Francisco (1988)

Automatic Assessment of Programming Assignments Using Image Recognition

Eerik Muuli[1,2], Kaspar Papli[1], Eno Tõnisson[1(✉)], Marina Lepp[1], Tauno Palts[1], Reelika Suviste[1], Merilin Säde[1], and Piret Luik[1]

[1] University of Tartu, Liivi 2, Tartu, Estonia
{kaspar.papli,eno.tonisson,marina.lepp,tauno.palts, reelika.suviste,merilin.sade,piret.luik}@ut.ee

[2] Software Technology and Applications Competence Center (STACC), Ülikooli 2, Tartu, Estonia
eerik.muuli@stacc.ee

Abstract. Automatic assessment of programming tasks in MOOCs (Massive Open Online Courses) is essential due to the large number of submissions. However, this often limits the scope of the assignments since task requirements must be strict for the solutions to be automatically gradable, reducing the opportunity for solutions to be creative. In order to alleviate this problem, we introduce a system capable of assessing the graphical output of a solution program using image recognition. This idea is applied to introductory computer graphics programming tasks whose solutions are programs that produce images of a given object on the screen. The image produced by the solution program is analysed using image recognition, resulting in a probability of a given object appearing in the image. The solution is accepted or rejected based on this score. The system was tested in a MOOC on 2,272 solution submissions. The results contained 4.6% cases of false negative and 0.5% cases of false positive grades. The method introduced in this paper saved approximately one minute per submission of the instructors' time compared to manual grading. A participant survey revealed that the system was perceived to be functioning well or very well by 82.1% of the respondents, with an average rating of 4.4 out of 5.

Keywords: Automatic assessment · Automatic grading · MOOC · Programming · Image recognition · Computer graphics

1 Introduction

Programming MOOCs (Massive Open Online Course) have become very popular alongside other MOOCs. The central part of a programming course is the programming task. It is essential that the MOOCs' tasks would be automatically assessable, because manual grading is not possible with a large volume of participants. Programming tasks can be automatically assessed by checking the program's code and/or the output produced. As a rule of thumb the assessable output is textual. In our MOOC "Introduction to programming" most of the tasks have textual output but there are some tasks where the solution program produces a graphical object on the screen. A certain object,

É. Lavoué et al. (Eds.): EC-TEL 2017, LNCS 10474, pp. 153–163, 2017.
DOI: 10.1007/978-3-319-66610-5_12

like a flag or a house, is required on the screen. In previous years the solutions with graphical output were assessed manually. A new assessment system was created to alleviate the problem and reduce the time spent on assessing the solutions with graphical output.

The purpose of this paper is to describe the system created. The system takes a participant's solution code as an input and sends it to the virtual machine's sandbox, a security mechanism for separating running programs, where an image is generated from the code. The system sends the image to an online service that provides image recognition. The service responds with a probability of a certain object (for example, a house) being present on the image. The participant's submission is graded based on that probability. Another aim of this paper is to evaluate the usefulness of the system and summarise the key aspects of the participants' feedback.

The paper is divided into 6 sections. After introduction, a theoretical background is given, and also a brief overview of different means of assessment is presented in the second section. The third section focuses on the programming MOOCs held at the University of Tartu and gives a general understanding about the MOOCs and describes the tasks in them. The fourth section discusses the system that was implemented within our MOOCs. A detailed summary is given on what happens with the participant's solution and how it gets automatically assessed. The fifth section summarises and analyses the feedback gathered from the participants. The article ends with a conclusion in which the key points are repeated.

2 Theoretical Background

2.1 Automated Assessment

Automated assessment is essential in the case of MOOCs as it is impossible to assess thousands of solutions by hand [15]. In this section we briefly discuss the general aspects of automated assessment and the specific automated assessment of programming assignments with graphical output.

The importance of good feedback can never be over-estimated. Beginner programmers need precise and personal feedback on their solutions in order to understand their mistakes, learn from them and become better at coding. The solutions can be improved based on quality feedback [12]. As usually the organizers of MOOC could not assess and give feedback themselves personally it is possible to organize peer and self-assessment [9]. Peer assessment is a means of assessment where participants grade each other's submissions. At the same time the participants are revising and getting better at understanding the topic during the process [21]. Peer assessment could also be used in programming courses [20].

Different means of automated assessment can be highlighted. As opposed to the peer assessment, quizzes are mainly content based and are used with questions that have defined right and wrong answers [3]. A MOOC's assessment system should not only consist of quizzes [14]. In case of learning programming, feedback on the solution code is necessary. Immediate results and feedback provided by automated assessment is extremely valuable [8]. Automated assessment is one of the key issues in MOOCs, because it is very time-consuming to check task solutions from a large number of participants by hand [15]. The most common means of assessment in MOOCs is automated assessment. The feedback provided should be very detailed and go hand in hand with unlimited number of submissions. This gives the participants an opportunity to improve and correct their solution based on the feedback given. It has been observed that learners recognise the benefits in peer assessment but they prefer automated assessment [10] and especially programming MOOC can benefit from automated assessment tools [18]. Designing good test cases for automated assessment can be as challenging as creating good multiple choice questions. Every little issue in a marking definition can cause problems. It often happens that the time spent earlier on manual assessment is now entirely taken up with the creation of automated assignments. A notable surplus of time will occur only when the test cases are being re-used throughout the courses [12]. The participants' solution output is usually compared with the instructor's. Besides the correctness of the solution there are some other metrics that can be evaluated: difficulty, style, design, and effectiveness [11].

2.2 Automatic Assessment of Programming Assignments with Graphical Output

Technical tasks, such as programming, require extremely detailed description in order to be automatically assessed. There can be no ambiguity in the task description, otherwise the participants can misinterpret the assignment, causing different solutions, even though test cases mostly accept only one correct solution [16]. Then again, providing only one correct answer conflicts with participants' general interest – they have bigger interest in creative graphical tasks [5]. Meanwhile, developing automated assessment for graphical tasks presents the greatest challenge. It is usually too difficult for both the participants and the instructors to generate good test cases for programming tasks with graphical output [17]. A system to automatically assess tasks with graphical output was created at the University of Brighton. They are using a framework called JEWL to automatically assess GUI (graphical user interface) programs written in Java. The JEWL framework is a GUI toolkit that supports both development and automatic assessment. In JEWL the GUI is replaced by a test harness that can then interpret instructions that the program under test executes. It is possible to check all the functionality of the GUI but they have not found a way to verify if a particular drawing meets a given specification and therefore assessing canvases has been avoided [5].

Although no out-of-the-box system that could be used was discovered, the literature review showed that, given adequate need, interest and competence, a system that automatically assesses the solutions with graphical output can be created. This paper reports a solution for automated assessment of the programming tasks with graphical output. The system is described in the fourth section.

3 Assignments with Graphical Output in MOOC "Introduction to Programming"

This section introduces the MOOC "Introduction to Programming" and particularly the tasks with graphical output. The MOOCs of introductory programming have been organized by the Institute of Computer Science at the University of Tartu since 2014. Three MOOCs – a 4-week course "About Programming"; an 8-week course "Introduction to Programming"; and an 8-week course "Introduction to Programming II" – are provided in Estonian language and intended primarily for adults. 3,835 people have taken part in the MOOC "Introduction to programming" during the past year. The course has been held four times. The courses held from March to May 2016 and from January to March 2017 are relevant for this paper. Usually, four tasks and a weekly test must be taken each week. The topic of graphics is introduced in the 4th week of the course. There are three tasks in total from which the participants can choose. In order to pass they need to submit and pass at least one of them. In each of the tasks, participants must draw an image with a Python library called Tkinter [7]. They can choose from three different tasks: drawing (a) a flag, (b) a traffic sign or (c) a house.

The first task is drawing a flag. The task is to create a program that would draw a flag of an Estonian rural municipality. The flag has to include at least three different colours or have an interesting shape (see Figs. 1 and 2). It is suggested to choose a cyclic flag so that cycles could be used in the code.

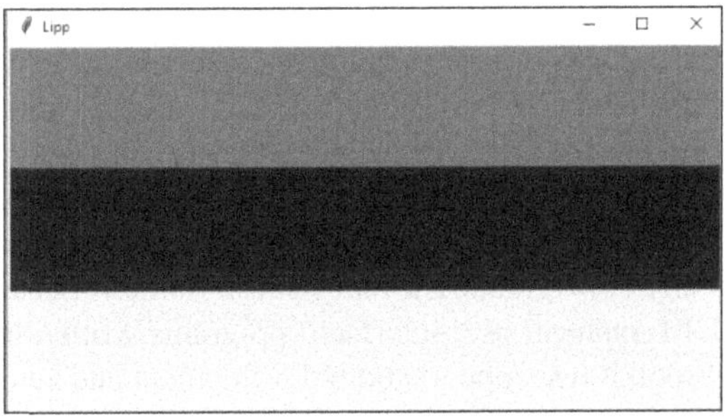

Fig. 1. A participant's solution of the flag task from the year 2016.

The second task is drawing a traffic sign. The task is to draw a freely chosen traffic sign. There are no other restrictions or compulsory constraints. The only suggestion is to draw a traffic sign where cycles would be relevant.

The third task is drawing a house. The task is to draw a house containing at least three different elements. There are no restrictions on which elements to choose. Some of the elements can be the following: a door, a window, a roof, a chimney. Also, at least three different colours must be used (see Figs. 3 and 4).

Fig. 2. A participant's solution of the flag task from the year 2016.

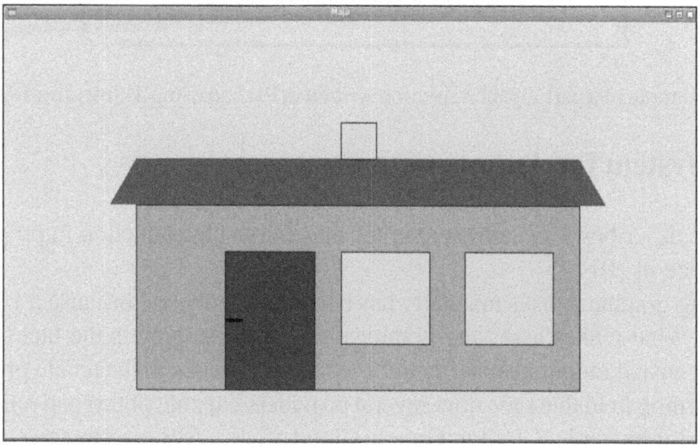

Fig. 3. An example of a participant's solution written in Python using Tkinter from the year 2017.

The need for automatic assessment came from the course in 2016 where more than 1,200 solutions had to be assessed manually. If the solution had any faults, the author was informed about it. One of the main faults was that the picture of the code was submitted instead of the textual code. Manual assessment took a lot of time and effort. In 2016 all the solutions including code and the graphical output image had to be submitted to a forum where everybody could see each other's work after submitting their own solution. A few downsides of the forum were that not all participants wanted to share their artwork and the forum became very slow after hundreds of submissions had been made.

Fig. 4. An example of a participant's solution written in Python using Tkinter from the year 2017.

4 New System for Automatic Assessment

Section four describes a system created for the course "Introduction to programming" that took place in 2017.

Assessing graphical tasks manually has become a challenge because it is very time-consuming. What makes assessing graphical tasks challenging is the fact that besides the code, the visual output also needs to be assessed. Thanks to the recent growth in the machine learning field there are now several providers capable of fast and reliable image recognition, for example, Clarifai, Google Cloud Vision API, and Imagga.

The following steps were taken in order to develop the new system:

- Analyse the previous means of assessment;
- Collect the previous submissions;
- Analyse the image recognition service providers;
- Implement the new system;
- Test the new system on the previous submissions.

The process of creating the automatic assessment system began with analysing the solutions from 2016. The first thing that had to be changed was the forum format. The downsides were mentioned before. Looking into the submissions, another idea popped up: the automated assessment could generate the image from the participant's code so that the image does not have to be uploaded at all. That also ensures that the submitted code compiles and the required graphical output is generated. Before implementing the system, it was necessary to choose the image recognition service provider. Various criteria were evaluated, including service speed, pricing, customer support, documentation, and image recognition based on keyword(s). After choosing the appropriate provider and implementing the system, it was tested on the previous year's solutions.

The graphical tasks are used in the MOOC "Introduction to Programming". The tasks are located in the open source learning management system Moodle [4]. The programming assignments are created and assessed with VPL (Virtual Programming Lab) [13]. It allows the user to define test cases for each task that contains the input and expected output of the program and feedback messages for different situations. After submitting the solution via Moodle, it is then sent to the VPL execution server which is installed onto one of the university's virtual machines. Each time a participant's solution is sent to the VPL execution server, a temporary sandbox is created in the virtual machine to ensure safety [19].

The user is expected to use a Python library called Tkinter for drawing the required images. The correction of the code is verified via using Python's abstract syntax trees (AST) [1]. After verifying correctness of the code, it is renamed to remove any special characters in the file name. In order to carry out any actions with the submitted code (for example, execution) in the virtual machine, the Tkinter library requires a display to work. In order to simulate having a display connected to the virtual machine, a display server called Xvfb was installed onto it. The result was that the virtual machine's operating system presumed it had a display connected, but in fact all the graphical operations were performed in memory [22].

If a correct solution was submitted it had to be manipulated to create an image based on the submission. Some extra code was injected into the participant's solution to create a PostScript (.ps) file. A software program called GhostScript was used to convert the PostScript file into a .JPG or .PNG file [6]. One of its features is converting PostScript files into raster images (png, tiff, jpg etc.). The resulting image was sent to the Clarifai image recognition service via their API [2]. Clarifai is the market leader in visual recognition since winning the ImageNet 2013 competition. A keyword representing the recognisable object is also attached to the image. For example, if the assignment was about drawing a house, then the keyword "house" would be sent with the submission. The Clarifai API then responds via JSON, indicating the probability of the image containing an object corresponding to the keyword. It was decided to pass the

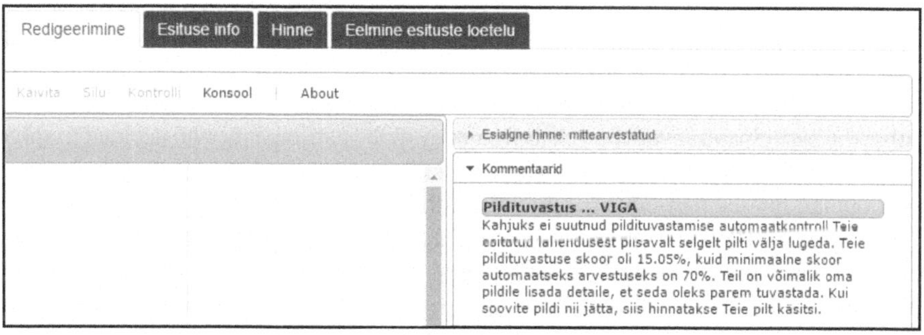

Fig. 5. A participant's submission that did not pass the automated assessment. The solution scored 15.05% out of the minimal 70%.

submissions that received a probability higher than 0.7. The probability can be adjusted for upcoming courses as needed. The participants that passed the submission successfully, received a message of passing the test. The participants who did not pass received a message with their result (the probability of the image containing an object) and were asked to resubmit their code or wait for manual assessment (see Fig. 5). The number of submissions was not limited so that the participants could improve their solution.

The following actions are performed to assess a solution and provide feedback:

1. Participant submits the code via Moodle;
2. The submission is sent to the VPL Execution Server;
3. The submission is analysed with Python's AST;
4. The submission is renamed;
5. Special code is injected into the submission;
6. PostScript file is created from the submission;
7. PostScript file is converted into an image file;
8. The image is sent to Clarifai;
9. Clarifai responds with a probability score;
10. Participant's submission is graded based on the probability.

In order to let participants share their artwork, a forum was created where they could upload their solution code and also the image created from their code. Sharing their code and graphical output was not mandatory but was required in order to see the solutions of others.

5 Results

This section highlights some results based on the analysis of participants' feedback and summarises the key issues.

A nonmandatory survey was conducted after the fourth week of the course. The participants were requested to answer 14 questions, some of which were relevant for this paper. 766 participants answered the questionnaire.

The first relevant question was about the complexity of the graphical tasks (see Table 1). The scale was from 1 (too simple) to 5 (too difficult). Firstly, the respondents had to give feedback on the "Draw a house" task. Secondly, they had to give feedback on the "Draw a traffic sign" task. Thirdly, they had to give feedback on the "Draw a house" task. On average the tasks were moderately difficult or even more complex than moderately difficult. Interestingly the "Draw a flag" task was the most popular task within the participants, even though the majority of the participants who decided to solve the task found it very difficult. The "Draw a traffic sign" and "Draw a house" tasks were less popular, but the participants found the difficulty to be more feasible for them.

Next, they were asked to give general feedback on the graphical tasks. The main ideas of their answers are the following: participants like graphical tasks because they can choose a suitable level of complexity; participants like to see and compare each other's artwork; participants find it somewhat difficult to draw the geometrical objects with coordinates. Interestingly, some participants invested a lot more time doing the graphical tasks than others in order to amend and complete their "drawing".

Table 1. Complexity of the graphical tasks.

Task/Difficulty	Drawing a flag	Drawing a traffic sign	Drawing a house
1 (Too simple)	7 (1.2%)	3 (1.1%)	9 (3.2%)
2	49 (8.6%)	25 (9.5%)	34 (11.9%)
3	241 (42.3%)	123 (46.6%)	144 (50.7%)
4	244 (42.8%)	101 (38.3%)	86 (30.3%)
5 (Too difficult)	29 (5.1%)	12 (4.5%)	11 (3.9%)
Did not solve the task	196	502	482

404 (52.7%) participants out of 766 found the graphical tasks the most interesting out of the 8 tasks that were given in weeks three and four. The last question was about the general implementation of automated assessment of the graphical tasks. The average score was 4.43 out of 5 where 1 means "does not work at all" and 5 means "works really well". The overall impression from the participants was great but there were some aspects that clearly emerged: the automatic assessment is fast and working well; some people encountered problems but their solution passed nonetheless – therefore they did not mention anything to the instructors; the feedback from the automatic assessment is really vague and does not benefit the participant much; the participants do not know how the automatic assessment for graphical tasks works and therefore do not know what is expected of them.

There were 1,828 participants in the course and 2,272 graphical task submissions were made and automatically assessed. The submissions contained 4.6% of false negative cases and 0.5% of false positive grades. In order to evaluate the system's quality and ensure the reliability, all the submissions were also manually checked. It was estimated that 28 h of work was saved using the system introduced in this paper although the implementation of the system took at least twice the effort. It is worth mentioning that the efficiency of the system will unfold during repeated usage of the system.

The submissions that received a probability higher than 0.7 were passed. The number was chosen by testing the system on the previous year's submissions and the instructors' practice. It worked out really well based on the false positive grades. The number could be adjusted as needed, but it is not advisable to lower it due to the increasing number of false positives.

6 Conclusion

The purpose of this paper was to describe a system that automatically assesses the programming tasks that have a graphical output. The system takes a participant's solution code as an input and sends it to a virtual machine with a temporary sandbox in it. The submission is analysed and modified to generate an image file from the code. The image is sent to an image recognition service called Clarifai that responds with a probability of a certain object being in that image. Based on that probability the submission is either accepted or not.

What makes the system handy and special is the fact that only the solution code needs to be submitted. The participants were pleased with the overall performance of the automated assessment. Participants still have an opportunity to share their artwork through a special forum created for it.

The system was used and tested in a programming MOOC called "Introduction to programming". Based on the feedback of the participants and also on the fact that the instructors save time using the system, it will certainly be used henceforward.

References

1. Abstract Syntax Trees. https://docs.python.org/3.6/library/ast.html. Last accessed 1 April 2017
2. Clarifai Homepage. https://clarifai.com/. Last accessed 1 April 2017
3. Doherty, I., Harbutt, D., Sharma, N.: Designing and developing a MOOC. Med. Sci. Educ. **25**(2), 177–181 (2015)
4. Dougiamas, M., Taylor, P.C.: Moodle: Using learning communities to create an open source course management system. In: Proceedings of the EDMEDIA 2003 Conference, Honolulu, Hawaii (2003)
5. English, J.: Automated assessment of GUI programs using JEWL. ACM SIGCSE Bull. **36**(3), 137–141 (2004)
6. Ghostscript Homepage. https://www.ghostscript.com/. Last accessed 1 April 2017
7. Graphical User Interfaces with Tk. https://docs.python.org/3/library/tk.html. Last accessed 1 April 2017
8. Higgins, C.A., Gray, G., Symeonidis, P.: Automated assessment and experiences of teaching programming. J. Educ. Resour. Comput **5**(3), 5 (2005)
9. Kulkarni, C., Wei, K.P., Le, H., Chia, D., Papadopoulos, K., Cheng, J., Koller, D., Klemmer, S.R.: Peer and self assessment in massive online classes. In: Plattner, H., Meinel, C., Leifer, L. (eds.) Design Thinking Research. UI, pp. 131–168. Springer, Cham (2015). doi: 10.1007/978-3-319-06823-7_9
10. Papathoma, T., Blake, C., Clow, D., Scanlon, E.: Investigating learners' views of assessment types in massive open online courses (MOOCs). In: Conole, G., Klobučar, T., Rensing, C., Konert, J., Lavoué, É. (eds.) EC-TEL 2015. LNCS, vol. 9307, pp. 617–621. Springer, Cham (2015). doi:10.1007/978-3-319-24258-3_72
11. Pears, A., Seidman, S., et al.: A survey of literature on the teaching of introductory programming. ACM SIGCSE Bull. **39**(4), 204–223 (2007)
12. Pieterse, V.: Automated assessment of programming assignments. In: Proceedings of the 3rd Computer Science Education Research Conference on Computer Science Education Research, pp. 45–56. Open Universiteit, Heerlen, Arnhem, Netherlands (2013)
13. Rodríguez-del-Pino, J.C., Rubio-Royo, E., Hernández-Figueroa, Z. J.: A virtual programming lab for Moodle with automatic assessment and anti-plagiarism features. In: Proceedings of The 2012 International Conference on e-Learning, e-Business, Enterprise Information Systems, & e-Government (2012)
14. Sánchez-Vera, M.M., Prendes-Espinosa, M.P.: Beyond objective testing and peer assessment: alternative ways of assessment in MOOCs. Int. J. Educ. Technol. High. Educ. **12**(1), 119–130 (2015)

15. Siemens, G.: Massive open online courses: innovation in education? Open Educ. Resour: Innov. Res. Prac. **5**, 5–15 (2013)
16. Staubitz, T., Klement, H., Renz, J., Teusner, R., Meinel, C.: Towards practical programming exercises and automated assessment in Massive Open Online Courses. In: IEEE International Conference on Teaching, Assessment, and Learning for Engineering (TALE), 2015, pp. 23–30. IEEE (2015)
17. Thornton, M., Edwards, S.H., Tan, R.P., Pérez-Quiñones, M.A.: Supporting student-written tests of GUI programs. ACM SIGCSE Bull. **40**(1), 537–541 (2008)
18. Vihavainen, A., Luukkainen, M., Kurhila, J.: Multi-faceted support for MOOC in programming. In: Proceedings of the 13th annual conference on Information technology education, pp. 171–176. ACM (2012)
19. VPL Homepage. http://vpl.dis.ulpgc.es/. Last accessed 1 April 2017
20. Wang, Y., Liang, Y., Liu, L., Liu, Y.: A multi-peer assessment platform for programming language learning: considering group non-consensus and personal radicalness. Interact. Learn. Environ. **24**(8), 2011–2031 (2016)
21. Wulf, J., Blohm, I., Leimeister, J.M., et al.: Massive open online courses. Bus. Inf. Syst. Eng. (BISE) **6**(2), 111–114 (2014)
22. Xvfb Homepage. https://www.x.org/archive/X11R7.6/doc/man/man1/Xvfb.1.xhtml. Last accessed 1 April 2017

Learning Analytics for Professional and Workplace Learning: A Literature Review

Adolfo Ruiz-Calleja[1(✉)], Luis P. Prieto[1], Tobias Ley[1], María Jesús Rodríguez-Triana[1,2], and Sebastian Dennerlein[3]

[1] Tallinn University, Narva road 29, 10120 Tallinn, Estonia
adolfo@tlu.ee
[2] École Polytechnique Fédérale de Lausanne, 1015 Lausanne, Switzerland
[3] Graz University of Technology, Inffeldgasse 13, 8010 Graz, Austria

Abstract. Despite the ubiquity of learning in the everyday life of most workplaces, the learning analytics community only has paid attention to such settings very recently. One probable reason for this oversight is the fact that learning in the workplace is often informal, hard to grasp and not univocally defined. This paper summarizes the state of the art of Workplace Learning Analytics (WPLA), extracted from a systematic literature review of five academic databases as well as other known sources in the WPLA community. Our analysis of existing proposals discusses particularly on the role of different conceptions of learning and their influence on the LA proposals' design and technology choices. We end the paper by discussing opportunities for future work in this emergent field.

Keywords: Workplace Learning · Professional development · Learning Analytics · Learning metaphors

1 Introduction

Workplace Learning (WPL) occurs across different formal and informal settings where professionals advance their competence, often through self-directed exploration or social exchange that is tightly connected to the processes and places of work [17]. Unlike learning in educational settings, WPL is often driven by personal interest or problems that appear in the work context, and typically lacks a pedagogical design to guide the learning process [24]. WPL typically consists of a strong interaction between formal training and informal learning, where both are motivated by job-based demands and contribute to workplace performance.

Despite the known importance of this kind of learning, Learning Analytics (LA) applications that focus specifically on workplace settings are rare. Some applications have been proposed under more general, overlapping denominations (e.g., 'community analytics' [23] or 'social learning analytics' [10]). Other proposals have focused on specific domains or professions, such as teaching [30] or healthcare [19]. Recent attempts have sought to unify and systematize these different efforts [27], under the term 'Workplace Learning Analytics' (WPLA).

É. Lavoué et al. (Eds.): EC-TEL 2017, LNCS 10474, pp. 164–178, 2017.
DOI: 10.1007/978-3-319-66610-5_13

The aforementioned fragmentation can also be related with the different conceptions of learning existing within the emergent WPLA community, which can well be explained by the three metaphors of learning defined by Paavola and Hakkarainen [29]: some researchers conceive learning as individual process of acquiring or constructing knowledge (knowledge acquisition metaphor); others see it rather as a matter of social enculturation (participation metaphor); while for others learning is a collaborative and systematic development of common objects of activity (knowledge creation metaphor). These conceptions influence how learning is analyzed, leading to different kinds of LA technological proposals.

However, the recent emergence of this community and the lack of a systematic analysis of existing WPLA proposals, make it difficult to understand how LA can support different kinds of WPL. This paper provides such an overview by systematically reviewing WPLA literature and analyzing the different conceptions of learning underlying existing proposals. Our review (whose methodology is presented in Sect. 2) tackles three main goals:

1. Provide a descriptive overview of existing WPLA proposals: the work domains covered, target users, LA functionalities and data models, theoretical approaches to learning, research methods, barriers and limitations (Sect. 3).
2. Analyze the relationship between the different conceptions of WPL underlying WPLA -as defined by the aforementioned learning metaphors-, and the design and technological choices made (Sect. 4).
3. Elicit over- and under-explored areas of WPLA research, in order to outline potential lines of future research work (Sect. 5).

2 Methodology

In our review, we have followed the methodological guidelines proposed by Kitchenham and Charters [22]. We queried four academic databases for works in WPLA: Science Direct[1], IEEE Xplore[2], Springer Link[3] and ACM Digital Library[4]. Additionally, we used Google Scholar[5] to find grey literature and other references we might have overlooked. We also searched manually in specific literature sources in the area, namely the Journal of Learning Analytics[6] and a recent workshop on WPLA [27].

Our review focuses on LA studies devoted to support WPL and professional development. Given the recent emergence of the term and the fragmentation of this research community, other overlapping terms were also added to the query we used on these literature databases: 'educational data mining' (very related to LA and with a slightly longer history), 'adaptive learning systems' and 'intelligent tutoring systems' (to catch earlier works which have many commonalities

[1] http://www.sciencedirect.com.
[2] http://ieeexplore.ieee.org/Xplore/home.jsp.
[3] http://link.springer.com.
[4] http://dl.acm.org/dl.cfm.
[5] https://scholar.google.com.
[6] http://learning-analytics.info.

with what we now denominate LA). However, we did not include terms related to the transition between vocational schools or higher university and workplace learning, nor the use of LA to assess higher education activities outside the classroom. The query string we used to query those databases was:

("Learning Analytics" OR "Educational Data Mining" OR "educational datamining" OR "adaptive learning systems" OR "intelligent tutoring systems") AND ("workplace" OR "professional development")

The query was launched on September 2016. The references were obtained from the four databases were collected, as well as the 100 first results (out of 7520) from Google Scholar. Furthermore, we added resources known to us from previous work on the area of WPLA and we obtained a total amount of 1320 references. It should be noticed that there maybe variations in the way each search engine applies the query (e.g., some of them only search in title, abstract and keywords, others in the full text, and others also include metadata coming from reviews). Thus, once the papers were downloaded, we ran the query restricting it to the title, abstract and keywords to guarantee the same filtering criteria. As a result we obtained a subset of 263 articles and we considered the rest to be out of the scope of the review. We then manually removed duplicates and preliminary versions of other papers, ending up with a subset of 90 papers. Finally, we went through the 90 papers and we discarded those that were out of scope (e.g., the paper does not describe any data analysis or is not related to WPL), those that were not mature enough (e.g., papers whose length is less than 4 pages) and those of very low credibility or quality (e.g., papers whose low quality prevents understanding and assessing the contribution).

After this filtering, 30 papers were left to be reviewed in detail, forming the dataset for the rest of the analysis in the following sections. These 30 papers included 7 journal publications, 19 conference papers and 4 book chapters. The descriptions of these papers are summarized in Table 1.

Note that the reduction from 1320 initial results to 30 reviewed papers is mainly due to four aspects. First, we launched the same query in five different search engines so many of the results obtained were duplicated. Second, the search engines of some academic databases do not allow to search only the terms included in the title, keywords and abstract; hence, in many reference the terms that are relevant for us were cited but were not too relevant for the paper. Third, we added the keywords 'adaptive learning systems' and 'intelligent tutoring systems', thus obtaining an important number of papers related to these aspects but not to WPLA. Fourth, there was a significant percentage of very short and low quality papers, due to the immaturity of WPLA field.

3 Descriptive View of WPLA

This section provides a descriptive overview of existing WPLA proposals (first goal of the review). We analyzed the work domains covered in the proposals and their main target users (Subsect. 3.1); the technological approaches and the LA functionalities provided in the solutions (Subsect. 3.2); the theoretical approaches

Table 1. Overview of the reviewed papers in terms of type of their type of contribution (E. evaluation, I. implementation, M. methodological, T. theoretical), domain, target group (S. students, T. trainers, W. workers), data sources (I. interviews, Q. questionnaires, P. physical world data, S.L. system logs, U.G.D. user-generated documents, U.P. user profiles), functionality (A. awareness, A.S. adaptive system, C.P.F. communities of practice formation, F. activity feedback, I.P. improve participation, R. recommendations, P. predictions, S.N.V. social network visualization, Ta.V. task visualization, ToV. topic visualization, U.A. system use analysis, U.M. user modelling), information model (F. folksonomies, R.M. relational model or ontologies, S.M. statistical model, S.N. social network), technical context, learning metaphor (K.A. knowledge acquisition, K.C. knowledge creation, P. participation), evaluation type (A.D. validation using an artificial dataset, C.S. case study, E. experimental study, I.E. informal evaluation, O.S. observational study, P.C. proof of concept), evaluation methodology (M. mixed, Q. quantitative) and evaluation data (D. demographics, L. logs, O. observations, P. predictions, R. recordings, U.F. user feedback).

Ref	Cont	Domain	Target group	Data sources	Functionality	Inf. model	Tech. context	Metaphor	E. type	E. meth	E. data
[1]	T.	Generic	W.	U.P.	C.P.F.	S.N.	-	P.	A.D.	Q.	L.
[2]	I.	Education	W.	S.L.	I.P.	S.M.	-	P.	-	Q.	L.
[3]	I.	Public Services	S., T.	S.L., U.G.D.	S.N.V.	S.N.	MOOC	K.C.	-	-	-
[5]	I.	Education	W.	S.L., U.G.D.	U.A.	S.M.	Platform	P.	P.C.	Q.	L.
[6]	I.	Software dev	W.	S.L., U.G.D.	A.	R.M.	Platform	K.C.	O.E.	M.	O., U.F.
[7]	T.	Education	W.	S.L., U.G.D.	S.N.V.	S.N., F.	Application	P.	-	-	-
[9]	E.	Education	S.	U.P., Q.	S.N.V.	S.M.	LA Inf.	K.A.	A.D.	Q.	L.
[11]	T.	Education	W.	S.L., U.G.D.	-	S.N.	-	P.	P.F.	-	-
[12]	I.	Education	W.	U.G.D.	Ta.V.	-	Application	K.A.	P.F.	Q.	L.
[14]	M.	Education	W.	S.L., I.	S.N.V.	S.N.	Other tool	P.	C.S.	M.	U.F.
[13]	I.	Education	W	Q.	S.N.V.	S.N.	Application	P.	C.S.	M.	U.F.
[15]	I.	Research	W.	U.G.D.	To.V.	R.M.	-	K.C.	P.F.	Q.	L.
[16]	E.	Education	W.	P.	F.	S.M.	Application	K.A.	C.S.	M.	O., R.
[19]	T.M.	Medicine	S.	-	-	S.N.	-	P.	-	-	-
[20]	I.	Engineering	T.	S.L.	A.S.	-	Other tool	K.A.	I.E.	-	-
[21]	T.M.	Medicine	T.	U.P., Q.	S.N.V.	S.N.	VLE.	P.	E.S.	Q.	L.
[25]	I.	Business consultancy	T.	S.L.	A.S.	R.M.	VLE.	K.A.	-	-	-
[26]	I.	Medicine	W.	U.G.D.	Co.V.	S.M.	Other tool	K.A.	A.D.	Q.	L.
[28]	E.	Business consultancy	S.	U.G.D.	P.	R.M.	VLE.	K.A.	C.S.	-	P.
[31]	E.	Generic	S.	U.G.D.	R.	S.M.	Application	K.C.	C.S.	M.	U.F.
[33]	I.	Construction, Medicine	T.	S.L.	-	S.N., R.M.	LA Inf.	K.C.	C.S.	-	-
[32]	I.	Education	S.	S.L.	S.N.V., TaV., ToV.	S.N., R.M., F.	LA Inf.	K.C.	C.S.	M.	O., U.F.
[34]	T.I.	Medicine	T.	S.L.	R.	S.N.	LA Inf.	P.	C.S.	M.	O., U.F.
[35]	I.	Education	T.	S.L.	U.M.	F.	LA Inf.	K.C.	E.S.	Q.	L.
[40]	I.	Medicine, Education	S.	S.L.	Ta.V.	R.M.	LA Inf.	K.A.	-	-	-
[38]	I.	Generic	W.	S.L.	S.N.V.	R.M.	LA Inf.	K.A.	C.S.	M.	D., U.F., L.
[39]	E.	Education, manufacture	W.	S.L.	S.N.V.	R.M.	LA Inf.	K.A.	C.S.	M.	U.F., L.
[41]	E.	Education, manufacture	W.	S.L.	S.N.V.	S.N.	Other tool	K.A., P.	E.S.	M.	U.F.
[42]	E.	Education	S.	S.L., U.G.D.	To.V.	S.N., S.M.	Other tool	K.C.	A.D., C.E.	Q.	L.
[44]	T.	Education	W.	S.L., U.P.	-	S.N., S.M.	–	K.C.	P.C.	Q.	L.

to learning adopted by the authors (Subsect. 3.3); the research and evaluation methods (Subsect. 3.4); and finally the barriers and limitations (Subsect. 3.5).

3.1 Domain and Target Users

Although the papers analyzed cover applications of LA in several work domains, a large part of the proposals (16 papers) focus on education, aiming to analyze or support teacher learning. We can also find multiple proposals in the domain of medicine (6). The rest of the papers apply WPLA to very diverse domains, including business consultancy (2), car manufacture (2), software development (1), research (1), public service (1), engineering (1) and construction (1). Three of the papers apply proposals to multiple (or generic) professional domains.

More than half of the analyzed workplace LA proposals target workers themselves as learners (16), in informal learning situations. The rest of the proposals consider more formal settings (e.g., training courses) and the LA solutions are aimed at trainers (5), students/apprentices (6) or both (3).

3.2 Technological Approaches and LA Functionalities

In order to understand existing technological approaches to WPLA, we should first understand the different kinds of contributions that make up the set of analyzed papers. Most of the analyzed papers (20) are proposals of technological systems, often focusing on data visualization aspects (15), the data collection infrastructure (12), or other aspects such as recommender systems (2). Seven of the contributions proposed analysis methods for WPLA (without necessarily proposing a technological application in the workplace setting). Another group of proposals (5) focused on the analysis of a particular WPL situation (e.g., correlational analyses). Finally, only one instance was found of proposals for conceptual frameworks, or data models.

The LA proposals that have been made in WPL purportedly provide a wide variety of benefits for its use (which are also closely linked to the functionalities offered by the system implementations). Among the most common benefits cited are: understanding and supporting communities of practice and other informal social networks occurring in the workplace (12); tracking of work practices (e.g., to infer the evolution of learners' competences – 6). Additionally, other benefits were also cited including supporting assessment, self- and team-awareness, the understanding of learning situations and the adaptation of training.

Regarding the technical context (i.e. the technical ecosystem used at the workplace), we can see that, in many cases, there is only one tool used by the learners or whose data is exploited. In some cases (5) such tool is the contribution of the paper where in other cases (5) it is other application whose data is collected and processed. In other cases, the technological environment counts on an infrastructure that allows (at least potentially) to coherently process data from different applications. In some cases (8), the environment counts on an infrastructure that was explicitly designed for LA. In other situations the infrastructure is not explicitly meant for LA: it may be a Virtual Learning Environment (VLE) (3), a MOOC (1) or other kind of platforms (2).

WPLA systems follow the general trends found in other sub-areas of LA regarding data sources [36]: system logs are by far the most commonly used data source (19). The analysis of learning artifacts (alone or in combination with logs – 11) is also common. Profile data (4), questionnaires (3), interviews (1) or audio input (1) are far less common. Nevertheless, it is noteworthy that quite a few proposals use more than one kind of data source, or from more than one platform (11). These proposals include infrastructures specifically designed to collect and integrate data for WPLA (needed in many cases in which work practices and WPL processes lack a clear central data source). WPLA proposals also represent and model their information in a variety of ways, being the most common: as social networks, tied to the social network analyses and visualizations, and the focus on workplace communities of practice (13); as ontological or relational models, used for a variety of purposes, from recommendations to assessment or awareness (9); as statistical models, used often in analyses of learning settings or analytic method proposals, aimed to track practices or understand a WPL situation (8); or as folksonomies, used to collect the emerging and unexpected concepts that appear in a community of learners (3).

3.3 Theoretical Approaches

To start untangling the reasons behind the technological choices summarized above, we have looked at how proposals' focus on a particular learning theory guides the processes of collecting, managing and representing data to extract meaningful information. This is not only a major challenge in the LA community [18]; it is even more critical in the workplace, where often a curriculum or pedagogical design are not available to guide the analytics. Nonetheless, some contributions (6) do not make their theoretical stance explicit at all. For this reason it is sometimes difficult to understand the assumptions that guide the creation of existing WPLA applications and infrastructures. In order to solve this difficulty and allow the synthesis of the proposals, we used the three metaphors of learning proposed by Paavola and Hakkarainen [29] -knowledge acquisition, participation and knowledge creation- as an analytical lens to classify the papers. These metaphors are "closely connected to the way knowledge is understood in different conceptions of learning" [29]. The paper classification was an overall qualitative assessment, emitted by looking at their theoretical stance, technical realisation (especially the information model they employ) and the general stance authors took towards learning in the solution they proposed. Whenever possible we related each paper to a learning metaphor.

The **knowledge acquisition metaphor** includes theories that assume individuals as the basic unit of learning. Learners have to acquire, construct and represent the concepts of the domain in their internal memory [29]. The acquisition metaphor is therefore concerned with the construction of internal representations. This construction of existing knowledge is seen as an individualistic process that leads to the transmission and possession of knowledge [29]. It is connected to an understanding of the mind as a container, which is filled by the learning process [4].

Eleven proposals were classified as following the knowledge acquisition metaphor. We included all the papers based on theories of assessment (3), as well as papers focusing on self-regulated learning theories (4). Other theories cited are cognitive apprenticeship (1), assessment design (1), self-regulated learning (1), learning by doing (1) and competence-based knowledge-space theory (1).

The **participation metaphor** and its related theories (e.g., communities of practice and situated learning) assume that learning happens by participating in cultural practices that shape cognitive activity in manifold ways [29,37]. It represents a continuous, interactive and discourse-based process that includes the negotiation of norms [37]. Through this contextualized and activity-based socialization, learners adopt the skills that are recognized in the community. Thus, learning is understood as a form of enculturation.

The 11 papers that followed the participation metaphor all drew on social learning theories, especially communities of practice or situated learning theories. In line with the social character of workplace and professional learning, a variety of social learning theories motivated many of the analyzed WPLA approaches. Among these theories, the most cited ones are communities of practice (4), learning networks (4) and social networks (2). Other theories include collective learning (1), learning communities (1), connectivism (1) and social constructivism (1).

Finally, the **knowledge creation metaphor** deals with the collaborative and systematic development of common objects of activity [29], such as in theories of knowledge building [4], organizational knowledge creation, meaning making [43] and knowledge maturing. This metaphor focuses on the creation, uptake [43] and development of new materials and conceptual artifacts. Hence, this metaphor is concerned with the way individuals collaboratively develop these mediating artifacts in interaction with the learning community. Its focus is on the temporal evolution of objects and practices emerging in concrete object-mediated reciprocal communication and collaboration. Hence, these theories follow socio-constructivist approaches, in which knowledge is socially constructed.

Theories that have motivated the 9 papers in this category include knowledge building and knowledge creation theories, but also informal WPL and social learning theories. Knowledge creation models (e.g., knowledge building, maturing, scaling-up informal learning) were mentioned by 5 papers, and networked learning and connectivism were the starting point for another 4. Other theories cited were group awareness (1), scaffolding (1) and situated learning (1).

3.4 Research Methods and Evaluation

The methodological approaches followed in the 30 papers under review can be broadly classified in four categories. The largest set of papers (13) follows the traditional methodological approach of presenting and evaluating a proposal. Another significant cluster (8) spans several research iterations, combining top-down and bottom-up approaches, which allow them to carry out exploratory and evaluative work. There are also papers (4) that explore certain aspects in a bottom-up fashion, inferring theory or trends from available datasets. Finally, 5 papers are exclusively theoretical proposals that draw from previous literature.

Concerning their evaluation, 6 of the analyzed papers do not portray an evaluation. In other examples (9), the purpose of the evaluation is merely to provide a proof of concept, or to illustrate the potential of the proposal. The proposals describe more formal evaluations that often assess rather technical aspects such as the performance, accuracy, or efficacy of the proposal (6), or constructs related with acceptance and adoption: usability (3), user interest and perceived usefulness (2), impact on users (4), or the applicability of the proposal in an authentic setting (1).

The evaluation methodologies shows a balance between quantitative methods (11) and mixed methods that combined qualitative and quantitative techniques (10). A wide variety of data sources are also used. Most of the papers rely on either artificial (4) or real data sets and logs (10). In addition, these sources are often triangulated mainly with user feedback (9) and observations (4).

Regarding user involvement in the evaluations, it is noteworthy that only 13 of the reviewed papers report on the user involvement. The addressed users are typically workplace learners, labeled as 'employees' (9) or 'students' (2). Trainers (2) or company managers (1) are also involved in some of the evaluations.

3.5 Barriers and Limitations

To better understand the current state and maturity of existing WPLA proposals, we extracted the limitations highlighted by the authors, and the barriers they found when applying LA in a workplace. Five of the papers reported limitations related to the data gathering (e.g., [14,16]). According to the authors, part of the learning process is not tracked, and therefore, the analyses are built on incomplete data. Another typical limitation is that the volume of data is insufficient due to low number of users or scarce interaction with the systems (e.g., [2,31]). These two obstacles -incomplete and scarce data- have a crucial impact on the accuracy of the results.

Regarding the data processing, several papers (6) mention limitations on the automation of the data analyses (e.g., [7,12]). In some cases, the analysis process required manual human intervention (e.g., providing or curating data). Apart from being time consuming, such manual steps make the success of the proposal dependent on the motivation and quality of the users' work. Other technical problems refer to time (1 - [41]) and scalability (1 - [44]) constraints.

In those cases where the analytics outputs were fed back to users, the authors sometimes highlighted limitations due to the usability of the proposed solution (e.g., [13,25]), especially regarding the understanding of indicators and visualizations. This hints to crucial role of users' data literacy: to make data-driven decisions, consumers of LA solutions need to be aware of the limitations of the analyses, and have the skills to interpret the results in their own context.

Finally, as it is often the case in research efforts in their early stages, several papers (7) acknowledge limitations in terms of generalizability of the results (e.g., [2,38]). To address this issue, they propose to conduct long-term evaluations with larger or different user groups in the future.

4 Discussion: The Three Metaphors of Learning in WPLA

In our previous analysis we used the three learning metaphors [29] to group the proposals that share similar conceptions of learning (see Sect. 3.3). We also realized that these conceptions of learning had an impact on the LA services offered and the design and implementation decisions taken to develop the LA services (see Table 1). Current section further discusses this impact grouping the proposals according to the learning metaphors they followed. Thus, we tackle the second goal of the review.

A first group of proposals followed the **knowledge acquisition metaphor**. They used ontologies or other relational information models more often, in order to represent the knowledge that was to be acquired. The main use cases of this kind of proposals were related to the building of user models from work activities in order to diagnose work-related competences. This information was then used either to give formative feedback for reflection (e.g., about tracked activities or progression along some learning goal), or to make automatic adaptation decisions (e.g., recommending items to learn, or suggesting scaffolding). Feedback was typically given in the form of visualizations (e.g., dashboards or open learner models). In several cases, the learning goals were derived from business or workplace demands (e.g., workplace tasks) that had then be turned into an ontology or similar model allowing the tracking of progression along these goals.

These approaches are limited because they are usually built upon a fixed model of the learning domain. Hence, there are less opportunities of detecting emergent learning. Besides, this kind of proposals have a stronger potential for guiding learners through diverse forms of scaffolding. Knowledge acquisition approaches would benefit from research into transitions between educational institutions and the workplace. They could be using ontologies developed as part of educational curricula or for professional certification, rather than building on frameworks developed ad-hoc, as this would enhance their scope and impact.

Another group of proposals followed the **participation metaphor**. In almost all these cases, the information collected was represented as a social network and several different Social Network Analysis (SNA) techniques were used. The information inferred from the analyses is used to promote the participation among learners, either by identifying similarities that help to build groups, by creating awareness of learning networks or by giving community managers tools to improve participation.

Well in line with the idea of learning as participation, the main use cases were on fostering participation in communities, building groups by identifying similarities, creating awareness of the professional network and giving community managers tools to improve participation. Participation approaches create awareness for emerging learning and possibilities for collaboration. However, these approaches sometimes assume that mere participation will improve learning. And while those approaches built on knowledge acquisition can usually draw on self-regulated learning theory to explain how explicating learning goals benefits metacognitive strategies, it is not clear whether the awareness of the social network has any impact on learning.

Another issue with social networks is that they are usually built on similarity, but learning sometimes benefits from dissimilar others. An interesting proposal in this direction is made by one of the reviewed papers [31] who suggest dissimilar users to provoke learning. For the future, we see a good opportunity for participation oriented approaches to explore similarity and dissimilarity of learners in social networks and the effect on learning and forming of the community.

The third group of proposals followed the **knowledge creation metaphor**. The technologies employed in these proposals were very diverse. They included social networks, ontologies and folksonomies, but also analyses of natural language texts and topic modeling. In several cases their data models create implicit or explicit networks of actors and artifacts (e.g., documents or concepts) that are sometimes enriched with semantic relationships. This is because in "trialogical learning" relations need to be established between learners and their mediating artefacts (e.g., documents or concepts). In several cases, a number of different technologies were used at the same time which might suggest that in order to understand knowledge creation, a broader range of technologies are needed.

The downside of the proposals building in the knowledge creation metaphor are the very small numbers of participants. While this is a general problem in WPL settings, it is likely to be especially prevalent in knowledge creation approaches, as these originate from research in group cognition and, hence, take smaller groups as a unit of analysis. Hence, it would be interesting to see proposals focusing on large scale communities, on knowledge building in organizations, or even in cross-organizational networks.

5 Conclusions and Future Lines of Research

This section summarizes the conclusions of the paper and reflects on the underexplored areas and the potential lines of future research work. Thus, we tackle the third goal of the review.

Our analysis of 30 Workplace Learning Analytics (WPLA) proposals highlights several conclusions about the state of the art in this area. A first insight is that the field is still in an early stage of development, when compared to other areas of LA. The number of existing WPLA proposals is still relatively small, and features many contributions with a limited evaluation. However, the fact that most of the publications available appeared in the last few years is a clear symptom that WPLA is a growing community. The analysis also shows that the WPLA community is still somewhat fragmented. Many of the papers analyzed were published under different keywords, some of which we collected when querying research databases (e.g., 'adaptive learning systems' or 'teaching analytics'). Nonetheless, there may be other terms that we did not consider and can provide further insight on this and other related fields.

The provision and adoption of WPLA solutions are higher in education and healthcare sectors. In both cases, the professionals involved share some routines that contribute to the applicability of WPLA (e.g., need for being up to date, need for reflection processes). On the contrary, other sectors (e.g., construction) could be more challenging in order to receive LA support due to the lack of trackable evidence in their current activity. Additionally very few existing proposals are targeted at, and evaluated in, multiple domains. These facts put into question the generalizability of current proposals' results, but also poses an interesting challenge for future WPLA research.

We can also draw insights from the technological makeup of current WPLA proposals. Most of the proposals only collect and process one type of data (e.g., system logs), while WPLA could potentially be enriched by exploring other types of data sources. We foresee a big potential in MultiModal Learning Analytics (MMLA) [8], although they are still very rare in WPLA. MMLA may help to overcome the problems of incomplete and scarce data caused by the low number interactions between users and a systems, thus reducing the burden that the manual data gathering may entail and increasing the chances of WPLA adoption. The data analyses and visualization also require special attention by the WPLA community. It is required to identify relevant indicators for the target users. Furthermore, the users' data literacy and their data-consuming experience should be taken into account when designing visualization interfaces. With respect to the evaluation of the proposals, most of them support the learning process indirectly, either promoting awareness, scaffolding the community of practice, or recommending resources. However, there are few evaluations that measure learning-related constructs directly, maybe due to the difficulty of accessing learners and their data. Further studies that demonstrate the effectiveness of WPLA solutions for learning are needed.

A very positive aspect of the WPLA community is the strong focus on theory that most of the analyzed papers have. As our previous discussion shows, the theoretical approaches taken by the proposals –which we grouped into three learning metaphors– have a big impact on the functionalities they offer, and on the technologies chosen to provide them. This impact is especially notorious on the data models of the proposals, as the way learning is understood conditions which data should be retrieve to analyze a learning situation and how these data should be structured. The relatively low occurrence of WPLA proposals based on knowledge creation assumptions is surprising if we take into account their importance for WPL, but it also indicates a promising path for future research.

Acknowledgements. This research has been partially funded by the European Union in the context of CEITER and the Next-Lab (Horizon 2020 Research and Innovation Programme, grant agreements no. 669074 and 731685).

References

1. AbuKhousa, E., Atif, Y.: Virtual social spaces for practice and experience sharing. In: Li, Y., Chang, M., Kravcik, M., Popescu, E., Huang, R., Kinshuk, Chen, N.-S. (eds.) State-of-the-Art and Future Directions of Smart Learning. LNET, vol. 9240, pp. 86–104. Springer, Singapore (2016). doi:10.1007/978-981-287-868-7_49
2. Ahn, J., Weng, C., Butler, B.S.: The dynamics of open, peer-to-peer learning: what factors influence participation in the P2P university? In: Proceedings of the 46th Hawaii International Conference on System Sciences (HICSS), Hawaii, USA, pp. 3098–3107 (2013)
3. Attwell, G., Kieslinger, B., Blunk, O., Schmidt, A., Schaefer, T., Jelonek, M., Kunzmann, C., Prilla, M., Reynard, C.: Workplace learning analytics for facilitation in European public employment services. In: Proceedings of the CrossLAK 2016: Learning Analytics Across Physical and Digital Spaces, Edinburgh, UK, pp. 91–97. CEUR (2016)
4. Bereiter, C.: Education and Mind in the Knowledge Age. Routledge, Hillsdale (2005)
5. Berendt, B., Vuorikari, R., Littlejohn, A., Margaryan, A.: Learning analytics and their application in technology-enhanced professional learning. In: Littlejohn, A., Margaryan, A. (eds.) Technology-Enhanced Professional Learning: Processes, Practices and Tools, pp. 144–157. Routledge, London (2014)
6. Biehl, J.T., Czerwinski, M., Smith, G., Robertson, G.G.: FASTDash: a visual dashboard for fostering awareness in software teams. In: Proceedings of the SIGCHI Conference on Human Factors in Computing Systems, San Jose, California, USA, pp. 1313–1322. ACM (2007)
7. Bieke, S., Maarten, D.L.: Network awareness tool - learning analytics in the workplace: detecting and analyzing informal workplace learning. In: Proceedings of the 2nd International Conference on Learning Analytics and Knowledge (LAK), pp. 59–64. ACM, New York (2012)
8. Blikstein, P., Worsley, M.: Multimodal learning analytics and education data mining: using computational technologies to measure complex learning tasks. J. Learn. Anal. **3**(2), 220–238 (2016)
9. Buckingham-Shum, S., Crick, R.D.: Learning dispositions and transferable competencies: pedagogy, modelling and learning analytics. In: Proceedings of the 2nd International Conference on Learning Analytics and Knowledge (LAK), pp. 92–101. ACM, New York (2012)
10. Buckingham-Shum, S., Ferguson, R.: Social learning analytics. J. Educ. Technol. Soc. **15**(3), 3–26 (2012)
11. Cambridge, D., Pérez López, K.: First steps towards a social learning analytics for online communities of practice for educators. In: Proceedings of the 2nd International Conference on Learning Analytics and Knowledge (LAK), pp. 69–72. ACM, New York (2012)
12. Chen, G., Clarke, S.N., Resnick, L.B.: Technology and teacher professional development: promoting teachers' reflection on orchestrating classroom discussions. In: Proceedings of the 20th Global Chinese Conference on Computers in Education, Hong Kong, China, pp. 947–950 (2016)
13. de Laat, M., Schreurs, B., Sie, R.: Utilizing informal teacher professional development networks using the network awareness tool. In: Carvalho, L., Goodyear, P. (eds.) The Architecture of Productive Learning Networks, pp. 239–256. Routledge, London (2014)

14. De Laat, M.F., Schreurs, B.: Professional development networks: building a case for learning analytics in the workplace. Am. Behav. Sci. **57**(10), 1421–1438 (2013)
15. Derntl, M., Günnemann, N., Klamma, R.: A dynamic topic model of learning analytics research. In: Proceedings of the LAK Data Challenge, held at the 3rd Conference on Learning Analytics and Knowledge (LAK), Leuven, Belgium, pp. 1–5 (2013). CEUR
16. Donnelly, P.J., Blanchard, N., Samei, B., Olney, A.M., Sun, X., Ward, B., Kelly, S., Nystran, M., D'Mello, S.K.: Automatic teacher modeling from live classroom audio. In: Proceedings of the 2016 Conference on User Modeling Adaptation and Personalization (UMAP), pp. 45–53. ACM, New York (2016)
17. Eraut, M.: Informal learning in the workplace. Stud. Contin. Educ. **26**(2), 247–273 (2004)
18. Gašević, D., Dawson, S., Siemens, G.: Let's not forget: learning analytics are about learning. TechTrends **59**(1), 64–71 (2015)
19. Gray, K., Elliott, K., Barnett, S., Chang, S., Li, X.: A conceptual model for analysing informal learning in online social networks for health professionals. Stud. Heal. Technol. Inf. **204**, 80–85 (2014)
20. Hilem, Y., Futtersack, M.: COMPANION: an interactive learning environment based on the cognitive apprenticeship paradigm for design engineers using numerical simulations. In: Proceedings of the World Conference on Educational Multimedia and Hypermedia, Vancouver, British Columbia, Canada, pp. 281–286 (1994)
21. Khousa, E.A., Atif, Y., Masud, M.M.: A social learning analytics approach to cognitive apprenticeship. Smart Learn. Environ. **2**(1), 1–23 (2015)
22. Kitchenham, B., Charters, S.: Guidelines for performing systematic literature reviews in software engineering. Technical report, Keele University (UK) (2007)
23. Klamma, R.: Community learning analytics – challenges and opportunities. In: Wang, J.-F., Lau, R. (eds.) ICWL 2013. LNCS, vol. 8167, pp. 284–293. Springer, Heidelberg (2013). doi:10.1007/978-3-642-41175-5_29
24. Kooken, J., Ley, T., de Hoog, R.: How do people learn at the workplace? investigating four workplace learning assumptions. In: Duval, E., Klamma, R., Wolpers, M. (eds.) EC-TEL 2007. LNCS, vol. 4753, pp. 158–171. Springer, Heidelberg (2007). doi:10.1007/978-3-540-75195-3_12
25. Kump, B., Seifert, C., Beham, G., Lindstaedt, S., Ley, T.: Seeing what the system thinks you know - visualizing evidence in an open learner model. In: Proceedings of the 2nd International Conference on Learning Analytics and Knowledge (LAK), pp. 153–157, Vancouver, Canada. ACM (2012)
26. Lee, H., Weerasinghe, A., Barnes, J., Oakden-Rayner, L., Gale, W., Carneiro, G.: CRISTAL: adapting workplace training to the real world context with an intelligent simulator for radiology trainees. In: Micarelli, A., Stamper, J., Panourgia, K. (eds.) ITS 2016. LNCS, vol. 9684, pp. 430–435. Springer, Cham (2016). doi:10.1007/978-3-319-39583-8_52
27. Ley, T., Klamma, R., Lindstaedt, S., Wild, F.: Learning analytics for workplace and professional learning. In: Proceedings of the 6th International Conference on Learning Analytics & Knowledge (LAK), pp. 484–485. ACM, New York (2016)
28. Ley, T., Kump, B.: Which user interactions predict levels of expertise in work-integrated learning? In: Hernández-Leo, D., Ley, T., Klamma, R., Harrer, A. (eds.) EC-TEL 2013. LNCS, vol. 8095, pp. 178–190. Springer, Heidelberg (2013). doi:10.1007/978-3-642-40814-4_15
29. Paavola, S., Hakkarainen, K.: The knowledge creation metaphor-an emergent epistemological approach to learning. Sci. Educ. **14**(6), 535–557 (2005)

30. Prieto, L.P., Sharma, K., Dillenbourg, P., Rodríguez, M.J.: Teaching analytics: towards automatic extraction of orchestration graphs using wearable sensors. In: Proceedings of the 6th International Conference on Learning Analytics & Knowledge (LAK), pp. 148–157, Edinburgh, UK. ACM (2016)
31. Rajagopal, K., van Bruggen, J.M., Sloep, P.B.: Recommending peers for learning: matching on dissimilarity in interpretations to provoke breakdown. Br. J. Educ. Technol. **48**(2), 385–406 (2017)
32. Ruiz-Calleja, A., Dennerlein, S., Ley, T., Lex, E.: Visualizing workplace learning data with the SSS Dashboard. In: Proceedings of the CrossLAK 2016: Learning Analytics Across Physical and Digital Spaces, pp. 79–86, Edinburgh, UK. CEUR (2016)
33. Ruiz-Calleja, A., Dennerlein, S., Tomberg, V., Ley, T., Theiler, D., Lex, E.: Integrating data across workplace learning applications with a social semantic infrastructure. In: Li, F.W.B., Klamma, R., Laanpere, M., Zhang, J., Manjón, B.F., Lau, R.W.H. (eds.) ICWL 2015. LNCS, vol. 9412, pp. 208–217. Springer, Cham (2015). doi:10.1007/978-3-319-25515-6_19
34. Santos, P., Dennerlein, S., Theiler, D., Cook, J., Treasure-Jones, T., Holley, D., Kerr, M., Attwell, G., Kowald, D., Lex, E.: Going beyond your personal learning network, using recommendations and trust through a multimedia question-answering service for decision-support: a case study in the healthcare. J. Univers. Comput. Sci. **22**(3), 340–359 (2016)
35. Schoefegger, K., Seitlinger, P., Ley, T.: Towards a user model for personalized recommendations in work-integrated learning: a report on an experimental study with a collaborative tagging system. Procedia Comput. Sci. **1**(2), 2829–2838 (2010)
36. Schwendimann, B.A., Rodríguez, M.J., Vozniuk, A., Prieto, L.P., Boroujeni, M.S., Holzer, A., Gillet, D., Dillenbourg, P.: Perceiving learning at a glance: a systematic literature review of learning dashboard research. IEEE Trans. Learn. Technol. **10**(1), 30–41 (2017)
37. Sfard, A.: On two metaphors for learning and the dangers of choosing just one. Educ. Res. **27**(1), 4–13 (1998)
38. Siadaty, M., Gašević, D., Hatala, M.: Associations between technological scaffolding and micro-level processes of self-regulated learning: a workplace study. Comput. Hum. Behav. **55**(1), 1007–1019 (2016)
39. Siadaty, M., Gašević, D., Hatala, M.: Measuring the impact of technological scaffolding interventions on micro-level processes of self-regulated workplace learning. Comput. Hum. Behav. **59**, 469–482 (2016)
40. Siadaty, M., Gašević, D., Jovanović, J., Milikić, N., Jeremić, Z., Ali, L., Giljanović, A., Hatala, M.: Learn-B: a social analytics-enabled tool for self-regulated workplace learning. In: Proceedings of the 2nd International Conference on Learning Analytics and Knowledge (LAK), pp. 115–119. ACM, New York (2012)
41. Song, E., Petrushyna, Z., Cao, Y., Klamma, R.: Learning analytics at large: the lifelong learning network of 160,000 European teachers. In: Kloos, C.D., Gillet, D., García, R.M.C., Wild, F., Wolpers, M. (eds.) EC-TEL 2011. LNCS, vol. 6964, pp. 398–411. Springer, Heidelberg (2011). doi:10.1007/978-3-642-23985-4_31
42. Southavilay, V., Yacef, K., Reimann, P., Calvo, R.A.: Analysis of collaborative writing processes using revision maps and probabilistic topic models. In: Proceedings of the 3rd International Conference on Learning Analytics and Knowledge (LAK), pp. 38–47, Leuven, Belgium. ACM (2013)

43. Suthers, D.: Collaborative knowledge construction through shared representations. In: Proceedings of the 38th Annual Hawaii International Conference on System Sciences (HICSS), pp. 1–10, Hawaii, USA. IEEE (2005)
44. Vuorikari, R., Scimeca, S.: Social learning analytics to study teachers' large-scale professional networks. In: Ley, T., Ruohonen, M., Laanpere, M., Tatnall, A. (eds.) Open and Social Technologies for Networked Learning. IFIP AICT, vol. 395, pp. 25–34. Springer, Berlin (2013). doi:10.1007/978-3-642-37285-8_3

Automatic Group Formation in a MOOC Based on Students' Activity Criteria

Luisa Sanz-Martínez(✉), Alejandra Martínez-Monés, Miguel L. Bote-Lorenzo, Juan A. Muñoz-Cristóbal, and Yannis Dimitriadis

GSIC-EMIC Research Group, Universidad de Valladolid, Valladolid, Spain
luisa@gsic.uva.es

Abstract. Although there is significant evidence regarding benefits of small group collaboration in small-scale contexts, several challenges have been detected about the use of collaborative learning in MOOCs. Group formation, which is a crucial activity in order to achieve effective collaboration, is scarcely covered in MOOC platforms, which do not allow the formation of teams using criteria defined by the instructors. This paper presents an exploratory study conducted in a seven-week MOOC, comparing our group formation proposal, based on students' activity criteria, to a baseline grouping function provided by the platform. We analyse the impact of each grouping approach over group performance, group activity, and student satisfaction. The results show initial evidence about the advantages of using the criteria-based group formation approach regarding student satisfaction and group interactions.

Keywords: MOOC · Collaborative Learning · Automatic group formation · Criteria-based group formation

1 Introduction

The increasing popularity of MOOCs (Massive Open Online Courses), as a new and powerful medium to access knowledge, has fostered many discussions within the higher education domain. Several authors are concerned about their low instructional quality [18] or their high dropout rate [21], while others highlight the variety of research challenges triggered by the massive scale feature [8]. Some of these challenges are related to the promotion of social interactions that can generate knowledge [17] or the development of new pedagogical approaches which take advantage of the benefits of large scale [28].

Over the last decades, active pedagogies, such as Collaborative Learning (CL), have been largely studied at small-scale educational contexts. These studies have shown positive effects, *e.g.*, that collaboration enriches learning with social and cognitive dimensions that maintain student motivation and elicit verbal communication [26].

Currently, most MOOCs follow a behaviorist pedagogical approach where the instructors add the educational content to the course stream and the students

É. Lavoué et al. (Eds.): EC-TEL 2017, LNCS 10474, pp. 179–193, 2017.
DOI: 10.1007/978-3-319-66610-5_14

self-assess their learning with questionnaires [7], limiting the interaction between participants and instructors to discussion forums. However, since the appearance of the first MOOC in 2008 (Connectivism and Connective Knowledge - CCK08), many authors have explored the benefits of using active pedagogies in this type of courses claiming that these pedagogies have a positive influence in various facets such as students' engagement [10]. The analysis of collaboration among students shows that social participation has a positive influence into student performance [1]. Some studies have focused on the students' preferences [11] finding that learners demand more opportunities for discussing in groups. Nevertheless, the inclusion of effective collaboration in MOOCs is still a challenge [15] due to the specific characteristics of the MOOC context. At the moment, collaboration and social interactions are mostly pragmatically limited to peer reviews, forum interactions [4] or external social tools [2]. The massive scale and its variability, caused by latecomers and dropouts, the heterogeneity of the enrolled students or their low engagement level [3] hinder effective implementation and uptake of CL strategies.

Several studies on CL have showed that group formation is a crucial factor to put in practice collaboration [20,23] because successful collaboration depends, to a large extent, on the suitability of the peers included in the group [13,14]. However, group formation presents particular difficulties at massive scale that deserve a deeper analysis. Thus, we decided to address this question by investigating the issues involved in the group formation problem at massive and variable scale. To that aim, we deem it necessary to further study the criteria that can be used in group formation in MOOC contexts and analyze the impact of these group formation strategies on the groups themselves and their members. Based on the outcome of this study, we aim to provide support to teachers interested in introducing collaborative activities performed in groups in MOOCs. In previous studies [27], we have proposed a framework that considers the factors that could be taken into account in group formation, when the scale is large and suffers significant variations during the course enactment. Based on this framework, appropriate advice for MOOC design and supporting tools for deployment may be provided.

In this paper, we present an exploratory study, where a criteria-based group formation approach was compared to a baseline grouping function provided by the platform that hosts the intervened MOOC. In our proposal, students were grouped in homogeneous groups based on their previous activity in the course. We analyzed the impact of each grouping approach over group performance, group activity, and students satisfaction. This analysis seeks to show differences, benefits and drawbacks of each grouping approach.

The rest of the paper presents, firstly, an analysis of the group formation problem delving into the scalability issues. Then, we continue explaining the study carried out in a MOOC deployed in the Canvas Network platform. We conclude showing the experiment results and exposing our conclusions and future work.

2 Group Formation Scalability

A basic definition of group formation in educational contexts could be "to put students together in groups with an educative purpose" [23], but effective CL usually requires planning in advance the collaboration to foster the relevant interactions that can better promote learning [9]. Group formation is an essential activity in CL and the method used to define the group composition is a critical function in Computer Supported Collaborative Learning (CSCL) environments [13]. The adequacy of the peers included in a team is a major factor for effective collaboration, and the group composition may affect the group performance and the individual student benefits [14]. Poorly formed groups can lead to many possible negative peer group influences: conformity, anti-intellectualism, intimidation, and leveling-down of quality, which lead to detrimental effects for learning [23]. In her thesis, Ounnas [23] exposed three approaches that can be used to create groups in educational contexts:

- **Random selection of groups**, where the formation is initiated by the teacher who assigns students randomly to groups. It is a simple way of forming groups because there are no constraints to enforce.
- **Self-selection groups**, where students decide the group they want to join and they can negotiate the peers to work with. The allocation of members requires the identification of potential peers which meet the requirements to join the group. This approach is commonly used in communities and networks where participants join together based on common interests. It can also be used in teams where students select their teammates based on interests, (*e.g.*, friendship or confidence, technical capabilities, skills to complete the task). This type of groups have a tendency to homogeneity.
- **Teacher selected groups**, also known as **criteria-based grouping**. This is a very popular approach in task-oriented grouping. The teacher's criteria can be applied in different ways, so that formed groups may have: (i) an homogeneous structure, including members with similarities regarding the criteria, (ii) an heterogeneous structure, including members with differences regarding the criteria, or (iii) a structure based on rules, i.e. several constraints are applied that group members have to meet.

Criteria-based group formation has been largely explored at small-scale educational environments [12,13,20,24], employing different types of criteria (e.g., student's profile, student's learning style), targeting both homogeneity and heterogeneity, as well as applying different types of rules. In the CSCL field, several tools and systems have been proposed to support automatic group formation using different techniques and algorithms [16]. However, MOOCs have particular characteristics, such as their massive and variable scale which hamper a direct extrapolation of conclusions derived in small-scale studies.

Due to the interest for including CL in MOOCs, several authors have tackled the group formation problem in these contexts [5,29–32] addressing the challenge through different perspectives. These perspectives include a variety of criteria (*e.g.*, knowledge, personality, preferences, affinities, location, motivation), grouping approaches (e.g., criteria-based homogeneity or heterogeneity, random grouping) and technological aspects (*e.g.*, social network metrics, natural language processing, classification algorithms) which suggests there are different factors that can be considered for group management in MOOC contexts. Figure 1 shows a hierarchical representation included in our previous framework proposal [27], which depicts four dimensions where grouping factors can be framed: (i) learning design, (ii) student's static data, (iii) course-activity dynamic data and (iv) technological implementation.

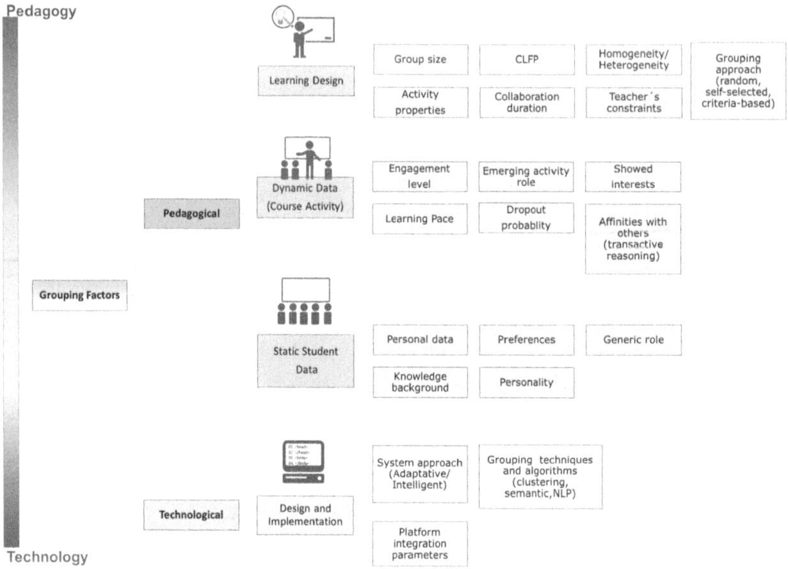

Fig. 1. Categories and factors to be considered for group management in MOOCs.

The **course-activity dynamic data** can be obtained from the course analytics and may allow us to know *when* and *how* the students work, so these data can reflect some particular features (*e.g.*, irregular level of engagement, variable learning paces) which distinguish MOOCs from other contexts. Therefore, these course-activity dynamic data may be interesting criteria to be considered in the group formation process.

Currently, only a few platforms offer facilities to collaborate in teams (i.e., Canvas, NovoEd, edX), while the students of other platforms (e.g., Coursera, Udacity, FutureLearn), which do not provide these group facilities, have even formed external networks to meet and create study groups. The grouping facilities offered by the aforementioned MOOC platforms include features for students to self-select the teams to join (mostly by the topic). The group may be created by the teacher or by the students. This method leaves out many students who can't manage to join a team [31]. Some platforms also allow teachers to assign manually the members of each group, but this solution is not efficient in a course with a massive number of registered students. Canvas Network includes a function for splitting students into random teams. All students are distributed in groups with equal number of members. This is a convenient way of ensuring every student will belong to a team. Nevertheless, the criteria-based approach for grouping, which is the preferred method at small-scale context for its pedagogic capabilities, is not covered by MOOC platforms at the moment.

3 Description of the Study

Our research work follows a Design Science Research Methodology (DSRM) [25]. The study reported in this paper is part of the initial iteration of the process. Its main goal is to evaluate the initial ideas of the proposal in order to improve them in the next iterations. We collected quantitative and qualitative data, in order to gain a deeper understanding of the results of the intervention by means of complementarity. This approach is a consequence of our underpinning pragmatic worldview, centered in the problem and oriented to real world practice [6].

3.1 Context

The course was initially designed by teachers of the Faculty of Translation at University of Valladolid and its topic was an introduction to translation from Spanish to English over economic and financial texts. It was originally conceived as an instructor-led MOOC of seven weeks. We formed a co-design team composed of instructors and researchers, and this team redesigned the course to incorporate CL activities in order to identify the emerging challenges [22]. To meet this end, a community glossary and several peer reviewed translation tasks were integrated as optional activities. Moreover, the main collaborative activity included in the MOOC learning design, basis for our experimental study, was a compulsory task presented in the fourth week (see Sect. 3.2 for a full description). All mandatory activities should be completed (one per week) to obtain the certificate, although no grades were included in the assessment of the students.

The course was deployed in the Canvas Network platform and began on February the 6th, 2017. The total number of students enrolled was 1031, but only 875 remained registered when the course ended. Two surveys were employed: an optional welcome survey during the first week, that was completed by 668 students, and a mandatory final satisfaction survey completed by 152 (17,37% of the remaining registered students). 130 students applied for the certificate (12,61% of the initially enrolled students or 14.86% of the students registered at the end of the course).

3.2 Collaborative Activity

We used different data gathering techniques (i.e., questionnaires, interviews and meetings with the MOOC's teachers, and observation) to codesign the compulsory collaborative activity, which was the basis of the grouping experiment. The activity consisted in terminology extraction from some given texts in teams of six. Each team should create a group artifact including 20 economic or financial English terms and their corresponding Spanish translation referencing the source. The teams should use some of the group-oriented Canvas platform tools (*i.e.*, discussion forums and announcements) for organizing their work, sharing opinions, discussing and reaching agreements in order to select the required terms and choose a spokesman who would be in charge of the task submission. Finally, the activity would be considered as completed, when all members of a team perform an individual revision of the artifact produced by another team. This way, the non-active members of a team would not pass the activity, even if the task was submitted by a member of their group, since the non-active members did not carry out the individual review. The task was assessed as passed/not passed for all the students that completed it and there were no individual or group grades.

3.3 Intervention

This subsection describes the main decisions taken for the design of the experiment. One of the most important decisions was the selection of the criteria to be used for creating the experimental groups. We used dynamic factors (*i.e.*, data from the activity of the students in the platform) to respond to our research question regarding the relevance of these data to reflect some peculiarities of the context (*i.e.*, the variable engagement level). Therefore, we chose three variables to cover three aspects regarding the student engagement level [10]:

- **page views**, to measure their activity,
- **submitted tasks**, to estimate their commitment, and
- **posted messages**, to reveal their active participation.

Another major decision was the application of homogeneity over the criteria instead of heterogeneity. The underlying reason was that, taking into account the group size (six members) and MOOC statistics in literature (5–15% of completion rates), heterogeneity over student's activity criteria could be very similar to a random grouping (feature already covered in the Canvas platform) and could result in many teams with only one active student. The fact that the activity was assessed as pass/not pass and there were no grades strengthened this decision, because this type of homogeneity would have affected the grades.

For the composition of the control group, we chose random grouping because that option can be performed automatically in Canvas and guarantees that all students would be included in a group. However, the fact that in our approach the students with an activity profile type of no-shows [1] were clustered together could be a big advantage over the random teams, where the no-shows students would be spread over the teams. Therefore, we decided to improve the baseline to compare with in order to obtain richer conclusions about the impact of using a criteria-based approach for grouping. Hence, in the control group, we segregated the students with zero page views by grouping them together prior to the creation of the random teams.

The algorithm selected for implementing the homogeneous grouping was k-means clustering because it is a well known, effective technique that works with big datasets [31]. We combined it with a balancing algorithm to obtain clusters with exactly the same number of members (same size k-means variation[1]). To carry out the experiment the following steps were followed:

1. Finding out the statistical distribution of the selected variables (page views, submitted tasks and forum messages). Using the Kolmogorov & Smirnov, and the D'Agostino & Pearson tests, we found out that all three variables followed a non-gaussian distribution.
2. Data preprocessing. Prior to the clustering process the data was standardized in order to assign the same weight to the three selected variables (page views had a dimension much bigger than the other two) as recommended in [19].
3. Creation of two subsets (the experimental group and the control group) checking their uniformity regarding the variables used as grouping criteria. As a consequence of the non-gaussian distribution of the three variables, a Wilcoxon test was selected to verify that the subsets do not differ regarding them. The array of students was shuffled and splitted in two equal size subsets until the Wilcoxon test returned a p value greater than 0.5 in the three variables used as grouping criteria (if $p < 0.05$, the samples would be different with 95% confidence; if $p > 0.05$ we cannot say that the samples differ; we required a $p > 0.5$ to strengthen the non-difference between samples).
4. Creation of the teams in the control group. Firstly, students with zero page views were segregated, grouping them together in 11 teams and then, the rest of the students in the control group were distributed randomly in 70 six-members teams.
5. Creation of the teams in the experimental group. The selected clustering algorithms were used to obtain 81 clusters of six members based on homogeneity on the three standardized variables.

3.4 Analysis Methods

To measure the intervention effects we collected data from several sources (i.e., the platform API, the final satisfaction survey and the communications between students and teachers during the collaborative activity) in order to triangulate and complement the results. We monitored team performance during the activity retrieving data about: (i) messages exchanged in each group space, (ii) active participants in each team, and (iii) teams that complete the task submission. On the other hand, the messages that students sent to teachers regarding this activity were collected. Finally, after the end of the activity, we gathered quantitative and qualitative data about student satisfaction by means of open and close ended questions in a survey.

We analyzed the aforementioned data to find out the differences between the experimental (criteria-based) and the control (random) groups regarding:

[1] https://elki-project.github.io/tutorial/same-size_k_means.

(i) active teams, (ii) active participants per team, (iii) interactions within a team, (iv) task completion rate, (v) student complaints, and (vi) student satisfaction level. This analysis may provide initial evidence about the impact of using criteria-based group formation in order to achieve effective CL in MOOC contexts.

4 Results

4.1 Analysis of the Activity of the Teams Gathered from the Platform

After the end of the activity, we collected available data through the Canvas LMS API about the activity within each team. A summary of the gathered information is shown in Table 1. We captured data about the total number of messages (posts and replies in the group discussion forums and announcements) exchanged within each team, as well as the students that produced these messages, in order to detect the team members that were indeed participating in the activity.

Table 1. Data about teams' activity gathered from the Canvas LMS API.

Data gathered from the API	Control	Experimental
Teams with registered activity	47/81 = 58.02%	25/81 = 30.86%
Teams that submitted the task	46/81 = 56.79%	26/81 = 32.1%
Teams with activity which do not submit the task	4	1
Teams without activity which submit the task	3	2
Total number of messages	300	372
Total number of active users	76	78
Average number of messages per active user	3.95	4.77
Standard deviation of messages per active user	2.69	3.67
Average number of messages per active team	6.38	14.88
Standard deviation of messages per active team	5.87	14.92
Median number of messages per active team	3	10

The method used for the creation of the two subsets ensured a similar number of active users in both subsets (76/78). Due to the homogeneous activity criteria in the experimental group, students with a low activity level were joined together, giving as a result 56 teams with no registered activity (vs. 34 in the control group, out of which 11 were formed in the prior segregation process for no-shows students). This is an expected result, since there were a big quantity of inactive or low-activity students in the MOOC, and therefore homogeneous groups composed by students with a previous low level of activity will tend to even show less activity, due to negative interdependence. On the contrary, since active users were scattered in the random process, the randomly assigned groups may include some dispersed high-activity members, who will show some activity, even in the presence of inactive team teammates. Nevertheless, there were also 25 experimental teams with a significantly more intense exchange of messages (average of 14.88 messages per team vs. 6.38 in the control group). Moreover, the active users in the experimental group sent a higher number of messages each (mean of 4.77 vs. mean of 3.95). In this case, the homogeneous teams with active members have higher chances of developing a higher activity due to the positive influence of their teammates. In the control group there were four teams (vs. one in the experimental group) with registered activity which did not manage to complete the task and therefore, could not obtain the course certificate. All these teams had registered a single active member, which suggests that these students might have felt isolated due to negative interdependence and their motivation regarding the course decreased.

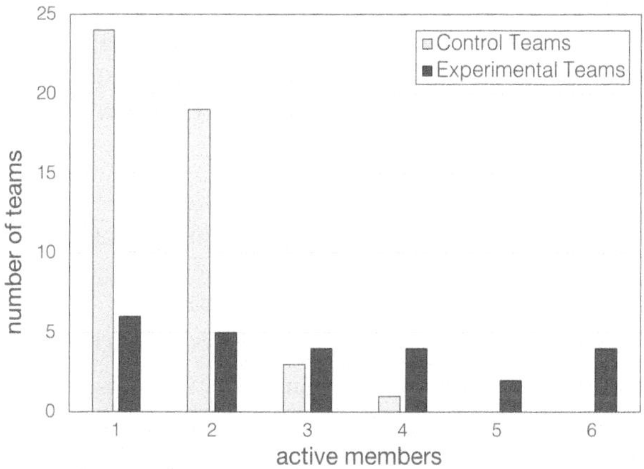

Fig. 2. Number of teams (y axis) with a registered number of active members (x axis).

In Fig. 2 a significant observation is depicted: the high number of teams with only one or two active participants in the control group (almost fourfold than in the experimental group). We can also observe that full active teams (with five or six active members) can only be found in the experimental group. In this case, due to the homogeneity criterion of the experimental group, it is more likely that all members of some groups may be active. This result confirms that homegeneous group formation may favor some groups, since the most active students are grouped together.

The aforementioned conclusion is further supported by Table 2 which presents data structured according to the number of active participants registered in the team, which we called *team size*. The average number of messages per active user

Table 2. Data about teams and users regarding *team size* (num. of active members).

Team size (active members)	1			2			3			4			5			6		
Total/Control/ Experiment	T	C	E	T	C	E	T	C	E	T	C	E	T	C	E	T	C	E
Number of teams	31	24	6	24	19	5	7	3	4	5	1	4	2	0	2	4	0	4
Msg/Active user - Avg	1.8	1.9	1.3	4.6	5.0	3.2	5.5	5.0	5.8	4.5	5.3	4.2	5.5	–	5.5	5.8	–	5.8
Msg/Active user - StdDev	1.0	1.1	0.5	2.7	2.8	2.1	3.4	2.2	4.1	3.0	2.2	3.2	3.5	–	3.5	4.5	–	4.5

increases with the size of the team with a correlation coefficient of 0.78 stating a strong positive correlation.

4.2 Analysis of the Students Opinions

A summary of the results of the closed-ended questions of the final survey regarding the collaborative activity on the fourth week is shown in Table 3. The responses *Agree* and *Strongly Agree* in the survey have been agreggated in the category **Agree** in the table, and the responses *Disagree* and *Strongly Disagree* have been agreggated in the categorie **Disagree**. The *Don't Know/No Answer* responses are not included in the table.

Table 3. Quantitative data collected from the final satisfaction survey.

Subset	Control		Experimental	
	Agree	Disagree	Agree	Disagree
Satisfaction with the collaboration in my team	35.3%	59.1%	55.0%	36.6%
Inactive students in my team hindered collaboration	78.9%	12.7%	52.1%	32.4%
Inactive students in my team affected negatively to my satisfaction	57.7%	31.0%	40.9%	38.0%
Collaboration in this activity enhanced my motivation	42.3%	42.3%	40.9%	38.0%
Collaboration in this activity enhanced my participation	60.5%	26.7%	67.6%	19.7%

The students of the homogeneous teams (experimental group) are more satisfied with the collaboration carried out in their teams, while the students in the random teams complain about the presence of inactive students in their group. On the other hand, the collaborative activity was valued as positive regarding participation for both subsets, while collaboration had a neutral effect on motivation for both subsets. These observations confirm previous findings (appeared in the communications between students and teachers during the activity development) regarding the negative effect of inactive students in groups (something that is less prominent in homegenous groups), as well as the positive effect of collaborative activities on participation, even in MOOC contexts.

A finer analysis regarding the *team size* (number of active participants registered in the team) shows that the survey respondents belonging to teams with five or six active members (32 students) were the most satisfied with the collaborative activity (expressing high satisfaction in 75% of the cases), and the survey respondents belonging to teams with one or two active members (68 students) were the less satisfied with the collaborative activity (expressing dissatisfaction in 69,12% of the cases). This result reinforces the need to find the best strategy (based on the most suitable criteria for group formation) in order to include several active members in each group.

The final satisfaction survey also included open-ended questions about the mandatory collaborative activity where the students could explain the aspects they most or less liked of this activity. We used this information together with the messages that students sent to the teachers in the Canvas Network platform to perform an initial content analysis aiming to gain a deeper understanding of what happened in the experiment.

The majority of complaints came from students who were the only active learner of a given group. In many cases the students in teams with one or two active members expressed frustration due to the lack of participation in their group, as well as feelings of having lost the opportunity of an enriching activity. We illustrate the previous observation through a set of comments expressed by students that belonged to groups with only one or two active students:

"I wish my teammates would have been more active, or at least they had contacted me". "My colleagues were noted for their absence. At least they could have introduced themselves and said that they would not participate instead of keep us waiting to see if they appeared". "No teammates showed up, although I sent them messages in the forum asking for their availability. I should say that it was an especially upleasant experience." "In fact, the most interesting aspects of the activity were related to its content and not to the collaborative work, since my teammates did not show any interest for the activity".

The most positive comments belonged to students in teams with five or six active members who expressed their satisfaction of having the opportunity of meeting their mates, helping each other and knowing different points of view. We provide below a characteristic set of comments expressed by this type of students in teams with five or six active members:

"We have been able to learn from each other and to correct the mistakes committed by our colleagues, a process that leads to a higher level of learning". "This group has enchanted me because we have all collaborated and we have fit perfectly, something difficult to achieve". "Everything has been very simple. Each one has contributed the terms that he could and when he could, without any pressure". "Although we are partners from all over the world, we managed to finish the activity and maintain a good communication". "What I liked the most

was the possibility of having real contact with the classmates. I loved reading many of the translations and the points of view provided by colleagues! There were frankly good translations. In my group there were no inactive students". "We were able to distribute the work and see the way that the other colleagues had to work. We learned from each other".

Teams with three or four active members registered more positive comments than negative ones. On the positive side, the students of these teams show their satisfaction in similar terms than the students of full active teams, but in the negative side they express some frustration for the absence of some teammates.

5 Conclusions and Future Work

In this paper we have presented the results of a study in which a small group collaboration activity was introduced in a MOOC. More concretely, a criteria-based group formation strategy was compared to the baseline option of random assignment of students to groups provided by the learning platform. On the other hand, we used the dynamic data of previous activity of each student in the course, since such type of data reflects better the large and varying scale context of MOOCs. Such study has provided some insights regarding the introduction of small group collaboration in MOOCs, and the relative advantages of two group formation strategies. After analyzing the results, we can conclude that the new strategy selected for the creation of the teams (homogeneous groups based on prior activitiy) had a positive impact on student satisfaction and group interactions. We also observe a slight positive impact regarding students dropout.

A key aspect regarding the measures of participation and regarding students' satisfaction is the number of active members in the team (what we called *team size*). Teams with five or six active members registered the most intense activity and the most satisfied students of the experiment. The correlation between the number of messages per active user and the *team size* was relatively high (0.78), which indicates a strong correlation. Therefore, the higher the *team size* the more active the members, probably as an effect of the positive interdependence. As expected, teams with five or six active members promote collaboration, registering the highest number of interactions and a high student satisfaction. This type of teams were only achieved through the grouping strategy that promoted homegeneous groups based on the dynamic activity data. On the other hand, teams with only one active member did not allow collaboration and generated student frustration, giving as a result several cases of dropout. This fact occurred fourfold less frequently in the homogeneous teams.

This experience has served to gain insight about grouping solutions which may run smoothly at massive or variable scale. The findings of this study may serve as a seed of the knowledge base to support MOOCs teachers by giving them advice regarding the course design and by developing tools which can help them in the design and deployment of group activities.

Given the iterative nature of the DSRM methodology, we plan to carry out new iterations, in which we plan to study several aspects, such as: (a) other alternatives of criteria-based strategies, (b) other types of data (dynamic or static) according to the factors included in our framework, (c) the impact and usability of a user interface for the instructors - instructional designers regarding the criteria to be used for group formation. These studies will be performed in the context of real MOOCs, that have been scheduled in the upcoming months.

Acknowledgements. This research has been partially supported by the Junta de Castilla y León, Spain (VA082U16) and Ministerio de Economía y Competitividad, Spain (TIN2014-53199-C3-2-R). The authors thank the rest of the GSIC/EMIC research team, as well as Roberto Castellanos and the Canvas team for their valuable ideas and support. The authors also thank the Spanish network of excellence SNOLA (TIN2015-71669-REDT).

References

1. Alario-Hoyos, C., Pérez-Sanagustín, M., Delgado-Kloos, C., Parada, G., Hugo, A., Muñoz-Organero, M.: Delving into participants' profiles and use of social tools in MOOCs. IEEE Trans. Learn. Technol. **7**(3), 260–266 (2014)
2. Alario-Hoyos, C., Pérez-Sanagustín, M., Delgado-Kloos, C., Parada G., H.A., Muñoz-Organero, M., Rodríguez-de-las-Heras, A.: Analysing the impact of built-in and external social tools in a MOOC on educational technologies. In: Hernández-Leo, D., Ley, T., Klamma, R., Harrer, A. (eds.) EC-TEL 2013. LNCS, vol. 8095, pp. 5–18. Springer, Heidelberg (2013). doi:10.1007/978-3-642-40814-4_2
3. Blom, J., Li, N., Dillenbourg, P.: MOOCs are more social than you believe. eLearning Papers **33**, 1–3 (2013)
4. Brinton, C.G., Chiang, M., Jain, S., Lam, H., Liu, Z., Wong, F.M.F.: Learning about social learning in MOOCs: from statistical analysis to generative model. IEEE Trans. Learn. Technol. **7**(4), 346–359 (2013)
5. Cheng, H.F., Yu, B., Park, Y.H., Zhu, H.: ProjectLens: supporting project-based collaborative learning on MOOCs (2017)
6. Creswell, J.W.: Research Design: Qualitative, Quantitative, and Mixed Methods Approaches. SAGE Publications, Thousand Oaks (2014)
7. Daniel, J.: Making sense of MOOCs: musings in a maze of myth, paradox and possibility. J. Interact. Media Educ. **2012**(3), 18 (2012)
8. Dillenbourg, P., Fox, A., Kirchner, C., Wirsing, M.: Massive open online courses: current state and perspectives. Technical report 1 (2014)
9. Dillenbourg, P., Tchounikine, P.: Flexibility in macro-scripts for computer-supported collaborative learning. J. Comput. Assist. Learn. **23**(1), 1–13 (2007)
10. Ferguson, R., Clow, D., Beale, R., Cooper, A.J., Morris, N., Bayne, S., Woodgate, A.: Moving through MOOCS: pedagogy, learning design and patterns of engagement. In: Conole, G., Klobučar, T., Rensing, C., Konert, J., Lavoué, É. (eds.) EC-TEL 2015. LNCS, vol. 9307, pp. 70–84. Springer, Cham (2015). doi:10.1007/978-3-319-24258-3_6
11. Grünewald, F., Meinel, C., Totschnig, M., Willems, C.: Designing MOOCs for the support of multiple learning styles. In: Hernández-Leo, D., Ley, T., Klamma, R., Harrer, A. (eds.) EC-TEL 2013. LNCS, vol. 8095, pp. 371–382. Springer, Heidelberg (2013). doi:10.1007/978-3-642-40814-4_29
12. Inaba, A., Supnithi, T., Ikeda, M., Mizoguchi, R., Toyoda, J.: How can we form effective collaborative learning groups? In: Gauthier, G., Frasson, C., VanLehn, K. (eds.) ITS 2000. LNCS, vol. 1839, pp. 282–291. Springer, Heidelberg (2000). doi:10.1007/3-540-45108-0_32

13. Isotani, S., Inaba, A., Ikeda, M., Mizoguchi, R.: An ontology engineering approach to the realization of theory-driven group formation. Int. J. Comput. Support. Collab. Learn. **4**(4), 445–478 (2009)
14. Konert, J., Burlak, D., Steinmetz, R.: The group formation problem: an algorithmic approach to learning group formation. In: Rensing, C., de Freitas, S., Ley, T., Muñoz-Merino, P.J. (eds.) EC-TEL 2014. LNCS, vol. 8719, pp. 221–234. Springer, Cham (2014). doi:10.1007/978-3-319-11200-8_17
15. Mackness, J., Mak, S.F.J., Williams, R.: The ideals and reality of participating in a MOOC. In: Proceedings of the 7th International Conference on Networked Learning, Aalborg, Denmark, 3–4 May 2009, vol. 10, pp. 266–274 (2010)
16. Magnisalis, I., Demetriadis, S., Karakostas, A.: Adaptive and intelligent systems for collaborative learning support: a review of the field. IEEE Trans. Learn. Technol. **4**(1), 5–20 (2011)
17. Manathunga, K., Hernández-Leo, D.: Has research on collaborative learning technologies addressed massiveness? A literature review. Educ. Technol. Soc. **4522**, 1–14 (2015)
18. Margaryan, A., Bianco, M., Littlejohn, A.: Instructional quality of massive open online courses (MOOCs). Comput. Educ. **80**, 77–83 (2015)
19. Mohamad, I.B., Usman, D.: Standardization and its effects on K-means clustering algorithm. Res. J. Appl. Sci. Eng. Technol. **6**(17), 3299–3303 (2013)
20. Muehlenbrock, M.: Learning group formation based on learner profile and context. In: Duval, E., Ternier, S., Assche, F.V. (eds.) Learning Objects in Context, pp. 19–25. AACE (2008)
21. Onah, D.F., Sinclair, J., Bollat, R.: Dropout rates of massive open online courses: behavioural patterns. In: Proceedings of the 6th International Conference on Education and New Learning Technologies, Barcelona, Spain, 7–9 July 2014, pp. 14–15 (2014)
22. Ortega-Arranz, A., Sanz-Martínez, L., Álvarez-Álvarez, S., Muñoz-Cristóbal, J.A., Bote-Lorenzo, M.L., Martínez-Monés, A., Dimitriadis, Y.: From low-scale to collaborative, gamified and massive-scale courses: redesigning a MOOC. In: Delgado Kloos, C., Jermann, P., Pérez-Sanagustín, M., Seaton, D.T., White, S. (eds.) EMOOCs 2017. LNCS, vol. 10254, pp. 77–87. Springer, Cham (2017). doi:10.1007/978-3-319-59044-8_9
23. Ounnas, A.: Enhancing the automation of forming groups for education with semantics. Ph.d. thesis, University of Southampton (2010)
24. Paredes, P., Ortigosa, A., Rodriguez, P.: A method for supporting heterogeneous-group formation through heuristics and visualization. J. Univ. Comput. Sci. **16**(19), 2882–2901 (2010)
25. Peffers, K., Tuunanen, T., Rothenberger, M.A., Chatterjee, S.: A design science research methodology for information systems research. J. Manag. Inf. Syst. **24**(3), 45–77 (2007)
26. Roschelle, J., Teasley, S.D.: The construction of shared knowledge in collaborative problem solving. In: O'Malley, C. (ed.) Computer-Supported Collaborative Learning, vol. 128, pp. 69–97. Springer, Heidelberg (1995)
27. Sanz-Martínez, L., Dimitriadis, Y., Martínez-Monés, A., Alario-Hoyos, C., Bote-Lorenzo, M.L., Rubia-Avi, B., Ortega-Arranz, A.: Influential factors for managing virtual groups in massive and variable scale courses. In: 2016 International Symposium on Computers in Education (SIIE), pp. 1–4 (2016)
28. Sharples, M., Delgado-Kloos, C., Dimitriadis, Y., Garlatti, S., Specht, M.: Mobile and accessible learning for MOOCs. J. Interact. Media Educ. **4**, 1–8 (2014)

29. Sinha, T.: Together we stand, together we fall, together we win: dynamic team formation in massive open online courses. In: Proceedings of the 5th International Conference on the Applications of Digital Information and Web Technologies (ICADIWT 2014), pp. 107–112 (2014)
30. Spoelstra, H., Van Rosmalen, P., Sloep, P.: Toward project-based learning and team formation in open learning environments. J. Univ. Comput. Sci. **20**(1), 57–76 (2014)
31. Wen, M.: Investigating virtual teams in massive open online courses: deliberation-based virtual team formation, discussion mining and support. Ph.d. thesis proposal, Carnegie Mellon University (2015)
32. Zheng, Z., Vogelsang, T., Berlin, B., Pinkwart, N.: The impact of small learning group composition on student engagement and success in a MOOC. In: Proceedings of the 8th International Conference of Educational Data Mining, pp. 500–503 (2015)

The Proof of the Pudding: Examining Validity and Reliability of the Evaluation Framework for Learning Analytics

Maren Scheffel[1(✉)], Hendrik Drachsler[1,2,3], Christian Toisoul[1], Stefaan Ternier[1], and Marcus Specht[1]

[1] Open Universiteit, Valkenburgerweg 177, 6419AT Heerlen, Netherlands
{maren.scheffel,hendrik.drachsler,christian.toisoul,stefaan.ternier, marcus.specht}@ou.nl

[2] Goethe University Frankfurt, Frankfurt, Germany

[3] German Institute for International Educational Research (DIPF), Frankfurt, Germany

Abstract. While learning analytics (LA) is maturing from being a trend to being part of the institutional toolbox, the need for more empirical evidences about the effects for LA on the actual stakeholders, i.e. learners and teachers, is increasing. Within this paper we report about a further evaluation iteration of the Evaluation Framework for Learning Analytics (EFLA) that provides an efficient and effective measure to get insights into the application of LA in educational institutes. For this empirical study we have thus developed and implemented several LA widgets into a MOOC platform's dashboard and evaluated these widgets using the EFLA as well as the framework itself using principal component and reliability analysis. The results show that the EFLA is able to measure differences between widget versions. Furthermore, they indicate that the framework is highly reliable after slightly adapting its dimensions.

Keywords: Learning analytics · Evaluation · Validity · Reliability

1 Introduction

By using learning analytics (LA), i.e. by measuring, collecting, analysing and reporting the learners' data from a course in a useful and meaningful way, awareness and reflection about the learning and teaching processes can be stimulated [11,14]. During the last few years the amount of LA-related research, publications and events has increased steadily [9]. Learning analytics, however, is not to be seen as pure 'number-crunching' on a strictly institutional level or as only being used to improve retention. Instead, it is about creating a holistic view on all learning and teaching processes involved [10]. Therefore, as LA should stimulate the self-regulating skills of the learners [16] and foster awareness and reflection processes for learners and teachers, it is recognised that a good way to present

É. Lavoué et al. (Eds.): EC-TEL 2017, LNCS 10474, pp. 194–208, 2017.
DOI: 10.1007/978-3-319-66610-5_15

LA to users is through a visual representation [22]. Kim, Jo and Park [13] indicate that learners' achievement could be increased by allowing them access to a learning analytics dashboard, i.e. a collection of visualisations. They also point out that LA visualisations should be carefully designed if interest in and usage of the dashboard and analytics is to be maintained by the main stakeholders, i.e. learners and teachers.

With the need for empirical studies growing and more and more discussions about the effect of learning analytics coming up [8,21], a number of studies investigating the impact of LA dashboards have been published in the last few years. Lonn et al. [15] for example have shown that seeing their academic performance in a LA applications could affect students' interpretation of their data and their success. They stress that LA interventions need to be designed carefully with student goal perception in mind. Beheshita et al. [2] randomly assigned LA visualisations to students of a blended learning course and showed that it depended on the students' achievement goal orientation whether the effect of the visualisations on learning progress was positive or negative. They stress that students' achievement goal orientation and other individual differences need to be taken into account during the LA design process. Finally, Khan and Pardo [12] showed that depending on the students' information needs and the types of learning activities different kinds of LA dashboards and visualisations are needed for them to be effective. From all three studies it is thus clear that LA visualisations need to be embedded into the instructional design to have a positive effect.

An important aspect that thus needs to be kept in mind when using LA to address issues such as the ones mentioned above is the following: How can we make sure that the learning analytics are valid, reliable, understandable and supportive for the involved stakeholders? We have thus developed an evaluation instrument that allows a standardised approach to the evaluation of LA tools: the Evaluation Framework for Learning Analytics (EFLA) [17,19]. The framework consists of four dimensions (Data, Awareness, Reflection, Impact) for learners and teachers.

Taking all of this into account, we designed and developed new versions for two widgets from the LA dashboard of the ECO MOOC platform and investigated in a lab experiment whether the current structure of the EFLA appropriately reflects the questionnaire's underlying components and whether the evaluation instrument can be used to measure changes between different versions of widgets. The lab setting was chosen as low numbers of teachers in the ECO environment would not give us sufficient input from that stakeholder group and because it allowed for a controlled experimental setting. We conducted our study with the following research questions in mind:

(RQ-A) Can the EFLA measure differences between iterations of a widget?
(RQ-B1) Do the four current EFLA dimensions validly represent the underlying components?
(RQ-B2) Do the items within the dimensions reliably measure the underlying component?

The next section describes the ECO platform's widgets and the evaluation instrument and elaborates on the method of analysis. After the presentation of results, the discussion section sets the results in relation to the research questions while the final section concludes the paper.

2 Method

2.1 Participants

Fifteen PhD candidates (eight women and seven men) and fifteen assistant, associate or full professors (seven women and eight men) from the Faculty of Psychology and Education of the Open University of the Netherlands voluntarily participated in the experiment. The PhD candidates were assigned the role of students while the post-docs were assigned the role of teachers during the experiment. All participants had at least basic knowledge about what LA is. Informed consent was obtained from all participants.

2.2 Materials

The Learning Analytics Widgets. Massive Open Online Courses (MOOCs) have the potential to provide education at a low cost for a wide and diverse public [6]. The European project ECO (Elearning Communication Open-Data)[1] has therefore created a platform that gives free access to MOOCs based on Open Educational Resources. A learning analytics dashboard containing several visualisations is part of the ECO platform to support the ECO users. The visualisations are based on interaction data of the users with the platform and with the MOOCs, e.g. launching a course, accessing pages, watching videos, posting in a forum, uploading homework, etc. All users of the portal, i.e. the students as well as the teachers of the MOOCs, see the same visualisations.

Two of the existing ECO LA visualisations were chosen for the experiment: the Activity Widget and the Resources Widget. The Activity Widget shows how active the learners are in a MOOC according to the number of actions done in that MOOC. The Resources Widget shows what types of resources are present in this course and how often all users together have accessed the various resources in the MOOC (see Appendix A at *bit.ly/EFLApudding* for the screenshots and more detailed descriptions of all widget versions).

The second version of the Activity Widget again shows the total activity per user. Additionally a user's own position is highlighted. Users can choose between two types of clustering: the Median with quartiles and an artificial intelligence algorithm. Both create four clusters in reference to Cobo et al.'s four activity types [5]. In order to protect the users' privacy, none of the users are able to identify who the other users are in the visualisation as the ECO LA dashboard does not distinguish between students and teachers of the course. The updated version of the Resources Widget compares a user's MOOC path with the ideal

[1] https://ecolearning.eu.

path of the course and the paths of other participants. A user can see which activities he has accessed and which ones not. Teachers could use this tool to identify if learners are using the MOOC as planned by discovering if activities are accessed too early, too late, or not at all. Students could compare themselves to other users and to the model line. Again, in order to protect the users' privacy, none of the other users are identifiable.

Table 1. Dimensions and items of the learner and the teacher section of the EFLA.

EFLA items for learners/teachers	
Data:	**D1** For this LA tool it is clear what data is being collected **D2** For this LA tool it is clear why the data is being collected **D3** For this LA tool it is clear who has access to the data
Awareness:	**A1** This LA tool makes me aware of my/my students' current learning situation **A2** This LA tool makes me forecast my/my students' possible future learning situation given my/their (un)changed behaviour
Reflection:	**R1** This LA tool stimulates me to reflect on my past learning/teaching behaviour **R2** This LA tool stimulates me to adapt my learning/teaching behaviour if necessary
Impact:	**I1** This LA tool increases my motivation to study/teach **I2** This LA tool stimulates me to study/teach more efficiently **I3** This LA tool stimulates me to study/teach more effectively

The Evaluation Framework. An institution's need for reflection on how ready they are to implement LA solutions is addressed by the Learning Analytics Readiness Instrument (LARI) [1]. While LARI has been shown to be an effective instrument to evaluate institutional readiness, there is no standardised instrument so far to evaluate the LA tools once implemented. However, more and more LA tools are being designed, developed and implemented. In order to close this gap, we have therefore developed the Evaluation Framework for Learning Analytics (EFLA). Inspired by the System Usability Scale (SUS), a "reliable, low-cost usability scale that can be used for global assessments of system usability" [3], the EFLA aims to provide similar facilities for the LA domain. Using the subjective assessments by their users is a quick and simple way to get a general indication of the overall quality of a tool in comparison to other tools or other versions of the same tool as Brooke [3] points out.

The first version was constructed through a group concept mapping (GCM) study with experts from the LA community and consisted of five dimensions (Objectives, Learning Support, Learning Measures and Output, Data Aspects, and Organisational Aspects) with four items each [19]. After a small evaluation study with LA experts [17] as well as a revisit of the GCM data and a thorough look at related literature, the second EFLA version was developed. Split into two parts, one for learners and one for teachers, the framework now consisted of four dimensions (Data, Awareness, Reflection and Impact) with three items each. This version was turned into an applicable tool, i.e. a questionnaire for students and teachers, and then used in an online course [18]. Based on a subsequent evaluation of the EFLA-2, the third version was created. While the dimensions stayed the same, the items were slightly reduced and further refined. Table 1 shows version 3 of the EFLA that was used in this study. All items are rated on a scale from 1 for no agreement to 10 for high agreement.

2.3 Procedure

All participants were invited to an individual face-to-face session for the experiment. At the beginning of each session, every participant received an introduction to the experiment and was asked to give their informed consent to take part in the study. Following an experimental script, each participant first received some introductory information about the ECO platform and its LA dashboard before getting detailed explanations about the four LA widgets while being shown a screenshot of the corresponding widget. For the two updated widget versions a live demo was also provided. After each widget explanation, participants were asked to evaluate the widget using the EFLA while assuming either the role of a student (all PhD candidates) or a teacher (all post docs). At the end of each EFLA survey participants had the option to add comments. When all four widgets had been evaluated, participants were asked to supply some demographic information (gender and age range) and were given a final opportunity to enter comments about the experiment. Once all data was collected from the participants, several statistical analyses were calculated using IBM's SPSS Statistics and graphs showing the average evaluation of each EFLA item for the different widgets from both stakeholder groups were created. The statistical analyses included t-tests for the widget evaluation and principal component analysis as well as reliability analysis for the EFLA evaluation.

3 Results

3.1 Widget Evaluation

Figure 1 shows the average scores of the ten EFLA items from students and teachers for both versions of the widgets. On average students and teachers gave better ratings to the second versions of both widgets. The only item students rated lower in an updated widget version is D1 for the Resources Widget. The items that teachers rated lower in an updated widget version are D3 and R2 for the Activity Widget and also D1 for the Resources Widget. While the original versions of the widgets received higher ratings from the teachers, the updated widget versions received higher ratings from the students.

Conducting paired sample t-tests for the ten EFLA items allowed us to see whether the differences in ratings between the two versions of the widgets were significant or not (see Appendix B at *bit.ly/EFLApudding* for detailed results tables). For the student participants there are several EFLA items where the difference between the ratings of the widgets' two versions is significant. The second version of the Activity Widget received significantly higher ratings for the items A1 ($p = .019$), R1 ($p = .044$), R2 ($p = .008$) and I2 ($p = .022$) while the Resources Widget received significantly higher ratings for all items (p ranges between .000 and .048) except D1. In case of the teachers, each widget only has one item where the difference between the two versions is significant: for item I2 of the Activity Widget $t(14) = -2.942, p = .011$ and for item A2 of the Resources Widget $t(14) = -2.839, p = .013$.

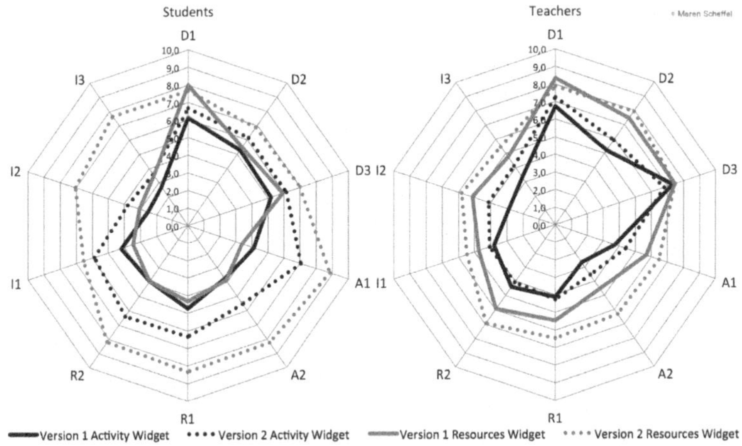

Fig. 1. Average scores of the EFLA items for students (left) and teachers (right) for both versions of both widgets.

Table 2. Descriptive statistics of all EFLA items from all widgets combined for students (left) and teachers (right).

	Students						Teachers					
	N	Min.	Max.	Mean	St.D.	Var.	N	Min.	Max.	Mean	St.D.	Var.
D1	60	1	10	7.12	2.450	6.003	60	3	10	7.55	1.908	3.642
D2	60	1	10	5.93	2.968	8.809	60	2	10	6.63	2.091	4.372
D3	60	1	10	6.07	3.194	10.199	60	2	10	7.27	3.162	9.995
A1	60	1	10	5.87	3.105	9.643	60	1	10	5.07	2.642	6.979
A2	60	1	10	5.35	2.839	8.062	60	1	9	4.27	2.421	5.860
R1	60	1	10	5.93	2.711	7.351	60	1	10	5.08	2.438	5.942
R2	60	1	10	5.62	2.853	8.139	60	1	9	5.33	2.319	5.379
I1	60	1	10	5.02	2.902	8.423	60	1	8	4.52	2.259	5.101
I2	60	1	10	4.12	2.811	7.901	60	1	10	4.48	2.411	5.813
I3	60	1	10	4.38	2.946	8.681	60	1	9	4.42	2.309	5.332

3.2 EFLA Evaluation

Every participant completed the EFLA survey for both versions of the two LA widgets which gives us a total N of 120 for each EFLA item (60 per stakeholder group, 30 per widget, 15 per widget version). All statistical analyses were conducted separately for the students' and teachers' data due to the different semantics, i.e. different wording leading to different meaning, of the ten EFLA items. The highest N within one analysis is thus 60.

Table 2 shows the descriptive statistics, i.e. N, minimum value, maximum value, mean, standard deviation and variance, for all ten EFLA items for the students (left) and the teachers (right). Two values seem to be slightly different from the rest: the variance of EFLA item D3 for students as well as for teachers is noticeably higher than all other variance values.

First Analysis. Before conducting the principal component analysis (PCA) we first looked at the factorability of the ten EFLA items for students and teachers. For the students' EFLA only few correlations were below .3 and all ten items correlated at least .6 with at least two other items. Additionally, the Kaiser-Meyer-Olkin measure of sampling adequacy was .836, i.e. above the recommended value of .6, and Bartlett's test of sphericity was $\chi^2(45) = 462.515, p < .000$. All diagonals of the anti-image correlation matrix were above .7. For the teachers' EFLA there were also few correlations below .3 and nine items correlated at least .4 with at least two other items (only D3 did not). Additionally, the Kaiser-Meyer-Olkin measure of sampling adequacy was .848, i.e. above the recommended value of .6, and Bartlett's test of sphericity was $\chi^2(45) = 405.841, p < .000$. Nine diagonals of the anti-image correlation matrix were above .7 (except D3 where it was .486). Due to these results, none of the items were discarded at this point and we continued with the PCA using Varimax rotation in order to identify the factors underlying the EFLA. As we had structured the EFLA with four dimensions in mind (Data, Awareness, Reflection, Impact), the solution with four components was examined first, followed by those with three and with two components (see Appendix C at *bit.ly/EFLApudding* for details of all analyses).

First Principal Component Analysis – Students. For the students' four-components solution all communalities were above .8 except I1 which was .749. Together the four components explained 85.824% of the variance (80.805 for the three components with primary loadings). All items in the four-components solution (rotated matrix) had a primary loading of .6 or above. However, only three of the four components contained primary loads. Component 1 was clearly formed by items I1, I2 and I3, component 2 consisted of items A1, A2 and R1 and component 3 was clearly formed by items D1, D2 and D3. Item R2 had two possible primary loads (.636 and .634) and could be part of either component 1 or component 2. Looking at the three-components solution for the students' data, the communalities were all above .736. The three components cumulatively explained 81.427% of the variance. Also, the distinction between the components was clearer than in the four-components solution: component 1 contained items

I1, I2 and I3, component 2 contained items A1, A2, R1 and R3 and component 3 contained items D1, D2 and D3. Again all items had a primary loading of .6 or above. The two-components solution for the students' data had communality values above .7 except for A2 (.660) and I1 (.672). Cumulatively the two components explained 75.238% of the variance. This solution had primary loadings for nine items above .8 and one item at .796 with component 1 containing A1, A2, R1, R2, I1, I2 and I3 and component 2 containing the items D1, D2 and D3.

To sum up, the three-components solution seems to be the best result as all components contain primary loads (the four-components solution does not) and as it explains more variance than the two-components solution.

First Principal Component Analysis – Teachers. The PCA of the teachers' data provided somewhat less clearly structured solutions. In the four-components solution all communalities were above .7. Together the four components explained 83.866% of the variance. All items had a primary loading of at least .6. Component 1 contained items R1, R2, I1, I2 and I3, while component 2 contained items D2, A1 and A2. Items D1 and D3 each formed their own component. The Data items thus did not form one component but were spread over three different ones. The three-components solution for the teachers' data had communality values of at least .7 for all values except for D2 (.589) and I3 (.691). Cumulatively 77.409% of variance were explained by the three components. This solution had one clear component containing items R1, R2, I1, I2 and I3 with all primary loadings above .7. D1, D2 and A1 formed one component, as did D3 and A2, all with primary loadings above .5. Both A1 and A2, however, had rather high cross-loads: while A1 had a primary load of .677 in component 2 (together with D1 and D2) it had a cross-load of .580 for component 3 (where it would join A2 and D3). A2 (primary load of .586) on the other hand also had a high cross-load of .551 in component 1 (where it would join R1, R2, I1, I2 and I3). Finally, in the two-components solution for the teachers' data, the communalities were above .6 except for D1 (.489), D2 (.526) and A1 (515). The two components explained 68.146% of the variance. Component 1 contained D2, A1, A2, R1, R2, I1, I2 and I3 (all with primary loads above .6), while the second component was comprised of items D1 and D3. Again, the Data items did not form one clear component. Item D1 (primary load of .503 in component 2), however, had a rather high cross-load of .486 in component 1 and could thus possibly be positioned there leaving D3 to form its own component.

To sum up, the three-components solution seems to be the best result as all components have at least two primary loads (the four-components solution does not) and as it explains more variance than the two-components solution.

First Reliability Analysis. In order to see how reliable the scales are and to check whether any of the items should be excluded, we calculated the reliability values, i.e. Cronbach's Alpha, for several item combinations based on the PCA results: the four EFLA dimensions Data, Awareness, Reflection and Impact individually (D,A,R,I), the combination of the Awareness and Reflection items (A+R), the combination of the Awareness, Reflection and Impact items (A+R+I), and the combination of the Reflection and Impact items (R+I).

Only one scale, i.e. the teachers' three Data items on their own, received a low reliability score (.397). All other scales had a reliability score of .8 or higher. For two scales a substantial increase (>.05) in Cronbach's Alpha could be achieved by eliminating an item. For the students' EFLA eliminating item I1 in the Impact-items-only scale would result in a Cronbach's Alpha of .954 while an elimination of item D3 in the Data-items-only scale of the teachers' EFLA would result in a Cronbach's Alpha of .574.

As the items D3 and I1 seemed to cause problems and hindered a clear component solution, we decided to delete them and to re-do the analysis with the remaining eight items D1, D2, A1, A2, R1, R2, I2 and I3.

Second Analysis. Before doing the PCA, we again looked at the factorability of the EFLA items. For the students' data there were again few correlations between the items that were below .3 and all items correlated at least .6 with at least one other item. The Kaiser-Meyer-Olkin measure of sampling adequacy was .799 (which is above the recommended value of .6) and Bartlett's test of sphericity was $\chi^2(28) = 359.650, p < .000$. All diagonals of the anti-image correlation matrix were above .7 (except for D1 which was .526). The teachers' data also showed few correlations below .3 and, except for D1 and D2 which correlated at .4 with three other items, all other items correlated at .6 with at least one other item. Additionally, the Kaiser-Meyer-Olkin measure of sampling adequacy was .826 and Bartlett's test of sphericity was $\chi^2(28) = 338.879, p < .000$. All diagonals of the anti-image correlation matrix were above .7.

Table 3. PCA using Varimax rotation for four, three and two components for students' EFLA (primary loads are light grey) and teachers' EFLA (primary loads are grey).

	four components								three components						two components			
	students				teachers				students			teachers			students		teachers	
	1	2	3	4	1	2	3	4	1	2	3	1	2	3	1	2	1	2
D1	.070	.048	.936	.301	.210	.120	.934	.176	.077	.008	.903	.171	.100	.928	.054	.904	.103	.940
D2	.162	.151	.377	.878	.292	.205	.199	.895	.156	.184	.862	.451	.262	.524	.226	.864	.466	.572
A1	.840	.300	.049	.220	.220	.881	.297	.135	.845	.289	.184	.202	.878	.329	.839	.197	.566	.443
A2	.849	.266	-.013	.157	.481	.767	-.120	.216	.853	.254	.096	.506	.786	-.029	.824	.109	.823	.091
R1	.780	.436	.246	-.153	.874	.218	.067	.240	.798	.386	.087	.893	.236	.144	.863	.100	.876	.213
R2	.717	.540	.063	.123	.834	.226	.152	.348	.731	.523	.131	.869	.247	.265	.896	.142	.849	.333
I2	.380	.891	.052	.112	.869	.230	.167	.199	.405	.881	.115	.872	.241	.221	.864	.121	.852	.289
I3	.419	.863	.049	.126	.785	.339	.246	-.001	.443	.853	.122	.741	.332	.220	.876	.129	.783	.293

Second Principal Component Analysis – Students. Table 3 shows the results of the PCA using Varimax rotation for these different settings. For the students' four-components solution all communalities were above .8. Together the four components explained 89.975% of the variance. All items in the four-components solution had a primary loading of .7 or above. Component 1 was clearly formed by items A1, A2, R1 and R2, component 2 consisted of items I2 and I3, component 3 only contained D1 and component 4 only contained D2. Looking at the three-components solution for the students' data, the communalities were all above .793. The three components cumulatively explained 84.559% of the variance. Again, component 1 was clearly formed by items A1, A2, R1 and R2 and component 2 consisted of items I2 and I3. Component 3 was made up of D1 and D2. All primary loadings were above .7. The two-components solution for the students' data had communality values above .7 except for A2 (.691). Cumulatively the two components explained 77.195% of the variance. This solution had primary loadings for all items above .8 with component 1 containing A1, A2, R1, R2, I2 and I3 and component 2 containing the items D1 and D2.

To sum up, the three-components solution seems to be the best result as all components have at least two primary loads (the four-components solution does not) and as it explains more variance than the two-components solution.

Second Principal Component Analysis – Teachers. The PCA of the teachers' data provided the following results. In the four-components solution all communalities were above .792. Together the four components explained 89.644% of the variance. All items had a primary loading of at least .7. Component 1 contained items R1, R2, I2 and I3, while component 2 contained items A1 and A2. Items D1 and D2 each formed their own component. The three-components solution for the teachers' data had communality values of at least .7 for all items except for D2 (.547). Cumulatively 82.201% of variance were explained by the three components. This solution had one clear component containing items R1, R2, I2 and I3 with all primary loadings above .7. A1 and A2 formed component 2, and D1 and D2 formed component 3, all with primary loadings above .7 except for D2 (.524). Finally, in the two-components solution for the teachers' data, the communalities were either just below or well above .7 except for D2 (.545) and A1 (.517). The two components explained 72.445% of the variance. Component 1 contained items A1, A2, R1, R2, I2 and I3, all with primary loads above .7 except for A1 (.566), while the second component was comprised of items D1 (.940) and D2 (.572).

To sum up, the three-components solution seems to be the best result as all components have at least two primary loads (the four-components solution does not) and as it explains more variance than the two-components solution.

Second Reliability Analysis. Again, we calculated reliability values, i.e. Cronbach's Alpha, for several item combinations: the four EFLA dimensions Data, Awareness, Reflection and Impact individually (D,A,R,I), the combination of the Awareness and Reflection items (A+R), the combination of the Awareness, Reflection and Impact items (A+R+I), and the combination of the Reflection and Impact items (R+I). Table 4 gives an overview of these analyses for the students' as well as the teachers' EFLA. Only one scale, i.e. the teachers' Data items on their own, receives a noticeably lower reliability score (.574). All other scales have a reliability score of .7 or higher. For none of the scales a substantial increase (>.05) in Cronbach's Alpha could be achieved by eliminating an item.

Table 4. Reliability statistics and scale statistics of different item groups for students' EFLA (left) and teachers' EFLA (right)

Items	Students					Teachers				
	N	Cron.α	Mean	Var.	St.D.	N	Cron.α	Mean	Var.	St.D.
D	2	.745	13.05	23.608	4.859	2	.574	14.18	11.237	3.352
A	2	.852	11.22	30.851	5.554	2	.814	9.33	21.650	4.653
R	2	.890	11.55	27.913	5.283	2	.945	10.42	21.468	4.633
I	2	.954	8.50	31.712	5.631	2	.881	8.90	19.922	4.463
A+R	4	.916	22.77	105.945	10.293	4	.870	19.75	69.513	8.337
A+R+I	6	.936	31.27	226.029	15.034	6	.916	28.65	149.214	12.215
R+I	4	.925	20.05	104.794	10.237	4	.935	19.32	75.135	8.668

4 Discussion

4.1 Widget Evaluation

The evaluation of the widgets using the EFLA questionnaire shows that there are indeed significant differences in evaluation results between the different widget versions. RQ-A can thus be answered with "yes". However, the differences are not significant for all items of all widgets from both stakeholders. Students really seemed to appreciate the second versions of the widgets much more than the first versions. Especially the Resources Widget received significantly higher evaluation results for its second version. Taking into account the open comments from the questionnaire as well as the questions and comments uttered during the experiment by both stakeholder groups, these results are not really surprising. The teacher participants were much more hesitant and held back by the lab setting of the experiment while the student participants could easily put themselves in the mindset of an online course participant. Another factor that is likely to play a role in influencing the teachers' widget evaluations is that due to the ECO platform's not distinguishing between the user types of learners and teachers, the personalisation aspect of the widgets' second versions was rather pointless for the teachers. That is, they might feel disregarded.

4.2 EFLA Evaluation

Although none of the items were discarded before conducting the first PCA, the descriptive statistics (variance) as well as the factorability check (correlations and anti-image correlations for the teachers' data) hinted at possible issues with item D3. We began the first PCA assuming that EFLA consisted of four distinct dimensions. For the students' data, however, only three components had primary loadings in the four-components solution thus indicating that there are only three underlying components to EFLA. This was also supported by the other two solutions (the variance explained was higher for the three-components solution compared to the two-components solution).

The first analysis of the teachers' data also showed that a four-components solution did not best represent the data. It also became apparent that D1, D2 and D3 and to some extent A1 and A2 seemed to be problematic for the teachers. Their PCA results for those items were much less clear than those of the students. This had already been foreshadowed during the experiment. The teacher participants asked considerably more questions than the student participants and voiced uncertainty about how to answer some of the questions. This insecurity about the items is likely to be reflected in their answers resulting in partially inconclusive PCA results. The students did not seem to have such issues with the items and their results are thus more confident and possibly more credible.

The reliability analysis confirmed that several items might hinder a clear component solution. Two items, D3 and I1, had to be discarded. The fact that it was precisely those two items that were problematic is reasonable if we look at the actual questions behind those items. D3 says "For this LA tool it is clear who has access to the data". In comparison to this item, D1 and D2 much more clearly address the micro level of the immediately involved learners and teachers themselves [11] which is what EFLA is about. Both of those items are much more connected to the user's personal point of view whereas D3 could be (mis)interpreted so as to cover the whole learning environment instead of an individual LA tool despite the statement saying "For this LA tool...". Additionally, in order to interpret a visualisation it is important to know what data it is based on and why (i.e. what the purpose is) but to know who else has access to the data does not affect the interpretation. Instead, it is more an issue of an institution's LA policy than an individual visualisation to make sure that privacy and transparency regulations are in place and transparently communicated.

Already during the experiment, student as well as teacher participants mentioned that they had difficulties answering item I1 due to its generality. The item says "This LA tool increases my motivation to study/teach". Whereas I2 and I3 cover the specific aspects of efficiency and effectiveness, item I1 covers motivation in general. Many participants said that their being motivated by a visualisation very much depended on the contents of the widget. For example, if a student sees that he is the lowest performing student, he might not be motivated to study by such a visualisation, while the opposite might be true if he sees himself in the top-performing group. On other days, the same student might feel very motivated to study when seeing that he is lagging behind. General motivation is thus too context-dependent to receive a reliable rating for one visualisation.

The second PCA without the two discarded items confirmed the previous indication that there are three underlying components for the EFLA items. In this solution each component was loaded by at least two items and explained more of the variance than the two-components solution. There is, however, a difference in how the items are spread across the components. For the students' data, D1 and D2 form one component, A1, A2, R1 and R2 form a second one and I2 and I3 form a third. The teachers' data resulted in one component containing D1 and D2, a second one containing A1 and A2 and another one containing R1, R2, I2 and I3. Even though some of the items of the student and teacher EFLA are semantically different, the two EFLA versions are still to be seen as two sides of the same coin.

Thus, in order to decide which of the three-components solutions to use for the next version of the EFLA, we took several aspects into account. First, the teacher participants of our study voiced more insecurities than the student participants did which leads us to put more confident in the students' results. Second, the reliability results for the students' data showed higher Cronbach's Alpha values than those of the teachers and the explained variance was higher for the students' three component solution. And third, supporting awareness and reflection processes in users in order to impact the learning or teaching processes is an important aim of LA. Awareness and reflection go hand in hand, with the former being a prerequisite of the latter [4,7,20].

Based on this, the new version of EFLA now consists of three dimensions: Data, Awareness & Reflection, Impact. The Data dimension contains items D1 and D2 and the Impact dimension contains items I2 and I3. Finally, the Awareness & Reflection dimension contains the four items A1, A2, R1 and R2 (see Appendix D at *bit.ly/EFLApudding* for the full framework structure).

RQ-B1 thus has to be answered with "no" as the assumed four-components structure did not turn out to be the best solution. However, the three-components solution we settled on does provide a fairly similar EFLA structuring to the one we envisioned as the items were not completely re-arranged within new clusters but two of the original dimensions were combined into one. RQ-B2 also has to be answered with "no" as not all ten EFLA items turned out to reliably measure their component. However, eight of the items did and will thus constitute the new EFLA.

5 Conclusion

This paper presented the results of an empirical lab study where we developed and implemented several widgets for a MOOC platform's LA dashboard and evaluated them using the Evaluation Framework for Learning Analytics (EFLA). We also evaluated said framework using principal component analysis and reliability analysis. The results of the widget analysis showed that the EFLA can indeed be used to measure differences between different widget iterations. The results of the EFLA analysis show that there are three underlying dimensions in the EFLA instead of four and that not all items in version 3 of the EFLA reliably measured these dimensions. A new and improved fourth version of the EFLA has thus been created that can be used to validly and reliably evaluate LA tools. All items are to be rated on a scale from 1 for 'strongly disagree' to 10 for 'strongly agree'. In order to calculate a LA tool's EFLA score, i.e. a number between 0 and 100, the following steps are needed per stakeholder group: (1) calculate the average value for each item based on the answers given for that item, (2) calculate the average value for each dimension based on the average of its items, (3) calculate the dimensional scores by rounding the result of $((x-1)/9)*100$ where x is the average value of a dimension, and (4) calculate the overall EFLA score by taking the average of the three dimensional scores.

The learning analytics community now has the opportunity to verify the EFLA's applicability and benefit, i.e. the proof of the pudding is now in the eating. The framework has been published as open access and the framework's template flyer as well as an interactive spreadsheet to automatically calculate the EFLA scores and create visualisations of the scores are available for download via the LACE website at http://www.laceproject.eu/evaluation-framework-for-la/.

References

1. Arnold, K.E., Lonn, S., Pistilli, M.D.: An exercise in institutional reflection: the learning analytics readiness instrument (LARI). In: Proceedings of the 4th International Conference on Learning Analytics and Knowledge, LAK 2014, pp. 163–167. ACM, New York (2014)
2. Beheshitha, S., Hatala, M., Gašević, D., Joksimovic, S.: The role of achievement goal orientations when studying effect of learning analytics visualizations. In: Proceedings of the 6th International Conference on Learning Analytics and Knowledge, LAK 2016, pp. 54–63. ACM, New York (2016)
3. Brooke, J.: SUS: a quick and dirty usability scale. In: Jordan, P.W., Weerdmeester, B., Thomas, A., Mclelland, I.L. (eds.) Usability evaluation in industry. Taylor and Francis, London (1996)
4. Butler, D., Winne, P.: Feedback and self-regulated learning: a theoretical synthesis. Rev. Educ. Res. **65**(3), 245–281 (1995)
5. Cobo, A., Rocha, R., Rodriguez-Hoyos, C.: Evaluation of the interactivity of students in virtual learning environments using a multicriteria approach and data mining. Behav. Inf. Technol. **33**(10), 1000–1012 (2014)
6. Drachsler, H., Kalz, M.: The MOOC and learning analytics innovation cycle (MOLAC): a reflective summary of ongoing research and its challenges. J. Comput. Assist. Learn. **32**(3), 281–290 (2016)
7. Endsley, M.R.: Toward a theory of situation awareness in dynamic systems. Hum. Factors **37**(1), 32–64 (1995)
8. Ferguson, R., Clow, D.: Learning analytics community exchange: evidence hub. In: Proceedings of the 6th International Conference on Learning Analytics and Knowledge, LAK 2016, pp. 520–521. ACM, New York (2016)
9. Gašević, D., Dawson, S., Mirriahi, N., Long, P.: Learning analytics - a growing field and community engagement. J. Learn. Anal. **2**(1), 1–6 (2015)
10. Gašević, D., Dawson, S., Siemens, G.: Let's not forget: learning analytics are about learning. TechTrends **59**(1), 64–71 (2015)
11. Greller, W., Drachsler, H.: Translating learning into numbers: a generic framework for learning analytics. Educ. Technol. Soc. **15**(3), 42–57 (2012)
12. Khan, I., Pardo, A.: Data2U: scalable real time student feedback in active learning environments. In: Proceedings of the 6th International Conference on Learning Analytics and Knowledge, LAK 2016, pp. 249–253. ACM, New York (2016)
13. Kim, J., Jo, I.H., Park, Y.: Effects of learning analytics dashboard: analyzing the relations among dashboard utilization, satisfaction, and learning achievement. Asia Pac. Educ. Rev. **17**(1), 13–24 (2016)
14. Long, P., Siemens, G.: Penetrating the fog: analytics in learning and education. EDUCAUSE Rev. **46**(5), 31–40 (2011)
15. Lonn, S., Aguilar, S., Teasley, S.: Investigating student motivation in the context of a learning analytics intervention during a summer bridge program. Comput. Hum. Behav. **47**, 90–97 (2015)

16. Persico, D., Pozzi, F.: Informing learning design with learning analytics to improve teacher inquiry. Br. J. Educ. Technol. **46**(2), 230–248 (2014)
17. Scheffel, M., Drachlser, H., Specht, M.: Developing an evaluation framework of quality indicators for learning analytics. In: Proceedings of the 5th International Conference on Learning Analytics and Knowledge, LAK 2015, pp. 16–20. ACM, New York (2015)
18. Scheffel, M., Drachsler, H., Kreijns, K., de Kraker, J., Specht, M.: Widget, widget as you lead, i am performing well indeed!: using results from an exploratory offline study to inform an empirical online study about a learning analytics widget in a collaborative learning environment. In: Proceedings of the 7th International Conference on Learning Analytics and Knowledge, LAK 2017, pp. 289–298. ACM, New York (2017)
19. Scheffel, M., Drachsler, H., Stoyanov, S., Specht, M.: Quality indicators for learning analytics. Educ. Technol. Soc. **17**(4), 117–132 (2014)
20. Schön, D.: The Reflective Practitioner: How Professionals Think in Action. Temple Smith, London (1983)
21. Siemens, G., Dawson, S., Lynch, G.: Improving the quality and productivity of the higher education sector - policy and strategy for system-level deployment of learning analytics. Discussion paper for the Australian Government, Society for Learning Analytics Research (SoLAR) (2013)
22. Verbert, K., Govaerts, S., Duval, E., Santos, J.L., Assche, F., Parra, G., Klerkx, J.: Learning dashboards: an overview and future research opportunities. Pers. Ubiquit. Comput. **18**(6), 1499–1514 (2014)

Opportunities and Challenges in Using Learning Analytics in Learning Design

Marcel Schmitz[1(✉)], Evelien van Limbeek[1(✉)], Wolfgang Greller[2(✉)], Peter Sloep[3(✉)], and Hendrik Drachsler[3,4,5(✉)]

[1] Zuyd University of Applied Sciences, Nieuw Eyckholt 300, 6419 AT Heerlen, The Netherlands
{marcel.schmitz,evelien.vanlimbeek}@zuyd.nl
[2] Vienna University of Education, Vienna, Austria
wolfgang.greller@gmail.com
[3] Open University, Valkenburgerweg 177, 6419 AT Heerlen, The Netherlands
{peter.sloep,hendrik.drachsler}@ou.nl
[4] Goethe University, Frankfurt, Germany
[5] German Institute for International Educational Research (DIPF), Frankfurt, Germany

Abstract. Educational institutions are designing, creating and evaluating courses to optimize learning outcomes for highly diverse student populations. Yet, most of the delivery is still monitored retrospectively with summative evaluation forms. Therefore, improvements to the course design are only implemented at the very end of a course, thus missing to benefit the current cohort. Teachers find it difficult to interpret and plan interventions just-in-time. In this context, Learning Analytics (LA) data streams gathered from 'authentic' student learning activities, may provide new opportunities to receive valuable information on the students' learning behaviors and could be utilized to adjust the learning design already "on the fly" during runtime. We presume that Learning Analytics applied within Learning Design (LD) and presented in a learning dashboard provide opportunities that can lead to more personalized learning experiences, if implemented thoughtfully.

In this paper, we describe opportunities and challenges for using LA in LD. We identify three key opportunities for using LA in LD: (O1) using on demand indicators for evidence based decisions on learning design; (O2) intervening during the run-time of a course; and, (O3) increasing student learning outcomes and satisfaction. In order to benefit from these opportunities, several challenges have to be overcome. Following a thorough literature review, we mapped the identified opportunities and challenges in a conceptual model that considers the interaction of LA in LD.

Keywords: Learning design · Learning analytics · Learning dashboards · Metacognitive competences · Feedback · Reflection

1 Introduction

Providing high quality education to students becomes increasingly challenging due to the high diversity of the student population that signs up for a study programme [1]. Due

É. Lavoué et al. (Eds.): EC-TEL 2017, LNCS 10474, pp. 209–223, 2017.
DOI: 10.1007/978-3-319-66610-5_16

to the increasing demands for professionalization, as well as new competences and skills, lifelong learning has become more important than ever before [2, 3]. Higher education institutions (HEI) need to adapt to these changes and make their educational offers more open and flexible for students from heterogeneous backgrounds. This is challenging since different types of students enroll for a study course, such as students from secondary school with no previous work experience, students that aim for a career switch and combine their study with their job, or students that prefer to be educated in close relation to their workplace pursuing further professionalization in their current practice [4, 5]. Therefore, HEI study programmes need to take the individual needs and life situation of their learners into account and provide better customized educational possibilities. Traditional HEI struggle with fulfilling this mission which resulted in a large variety of commercial providers such as Coursera and edX aiming to fill the gap with open and flexible educational offers such as online courseware that often is open or designed for the masses (i.e. MOOCs). Recently, more and more traditional universities in the Netherlands have adjusted their educational models towards these needs, where strong investments have been made in flexible and personalized educational offers [6]. One result of this is that many traditional and applied sciences universities extend their education with more malleable and distance education offers. Among changing and adjusting the educational model also technology innovations are explored that can foster these new requirements. Among various technologies to facilitate blended and distance learning models, Learning Analytics (LA) has been identified as a most promising technology to aid the personalization of learning and also change the educational model or even a course design due to insights gained from data. FitzGerald et al. [48] illustrate the different important dimensions to take into consideration for personalization of technology enhanced learning. In terms of their framework, using LA in LD tends to provide a cognitive-based and whole-person personalization.

In the rise of LA globally and in the Netherlands specifically, institutions use a number of data sources to gather 'authentic' data regarding student learning behavior: electronic learning environments, digital assessment methods, and student information systems, to name a few. Furthermore, digital devices like mobile phones, tablets and laptops are being used to collect activities of students. It is this insight into the students' learning processes and behaviors that, when presented in a user-friendly way, enables teachers to adapt their course and learning activities "on the fly", during the course's run-time. Additionally, these data provide students with insight into their own learning behavior in comparison with the course goals, achievements or the performance of their fellow students. This could – if guided properly and if the student is able to reflect and act upon the information using metacognitive competences [7] – enable them to adapt their learning behavior to become more effective or efficient.

In this paper, we identify and present three main opportunities for using LA in LD, with nine sub-opportunities and six sub-challenges based on the main opportunities, by critically studying current scientific literature on LA, LD, learning dashboards and metacognitive competences. These will be presented in table format and discussed in the sections below.

2 Identifying Opportunities and Challenges for LD and LA

In order to find and extrapolate the main opportunities for using Learning Analytics in Learning Design, we thoroughly and comprehensively analysed the current scientific literature on LA, LD, learning dashboards and meta-cognitive competences. In Table 1 and the remainder of this article, these opportunities and challenges are presented and marked with identifiers such as 'O+Number' for the opportunities, 'SO+Number' for

Table 1. Overview opportunities and challenges of LA of LD.

	Learning Design	Learning Analytics	Learning Dashboards	Metacognitive Competences	References
O1. Using on demand indicators for evidence based decisions on LD	X	X	X		[19]
SO1. Observing the effects of LD	X	X			[18, 33]
SO2. Sharing knowledge on LD	X		X		[18, 33]
SO3. Involving the students	X		X		[18, 33]
SC1. Interoperability of LD	X				[14, 46]
SC2. Interoperability of LA		X			[34, 35, 46]
O2. Intervening during the run-time of a course	X	X	X	X	[18, 33]
SO1. Delivering information/feedback on demand		X	X		[18, 33]
SO2. Creating and using interventions	X	X	X	X	[27, 30, 32, 35]
SO3. Changing learning behavior	X	X	X	X	[31, 32, 35]
SC1. Presenting relevant information the right way	X	X	X		[35]
SC2. Improving ability to act on information				X	[30, 56]
O3. Increasing student learning outcome and satisfaction	X	X	X	X	[31, 34, 35]
SO1. Making learning outcomes visible	X		X		[53, 55]
SO2. Making learning information accesible	X	X	X		[52, 56]
SO3. Improving learning to learn	X	X	X	X	[54, 55]
SC1. Understanding learning dashboards			X	X	[47]
SC2. Coping with the diversity of students	X	X	X	X	[1, 4–6]
References	[8–10, 13–16]	[18, 19, 23–29, 31, 32]	[18, 31–35]	[7, 11, 35]	
References aligning LA and LD	[40, 42, 44–47]				

sub-opportunities and 'SC+Number' for the sub-challenges. If an opportunity or challenge is linked to a key opportunity in the text, the identifier is concatenated, for example O1.SC2. is sub-challenge number 2 related to opportunity 1.

2.1 Learning Design

To define LD it is necessary to understand the definition of a learning activity. In this research, a learning activity is seen as a task that a student can do that involves interaction with teachers, fellow students, or content items in order to increase their knowledge. The LD is the description of all elements of the course's design in such a way that teachers can understand it and can use it. Elements of LD are the description of the learning activities that students have to do, the resources needed and the support actions a teacher can provide to facilitate the learning process [8]. Teachers can use help in the evaluation of the design and in the revision of courses. This is currently methodologically done by formative assessment during the course, but mostly by summative assessments and qualitative surveys at the end of the course as instructional design models like ADDIE propose [9]. This brings us directly to our main opportunities for LA supported LD: **O1. Using on demand indicators for evidence based decisions on learning design** by using authentic data in student behavior. In parallel, these, on demand insights in data on student behavior create possibilities for teachers to make alterations in the LD of the current course and for students to adjust their learning behavior. We call this second opportunity: **O2. Intervening during the run-time of a course.**

Although there have been various attempts to standardize LD like IMS-LD [51], these standardisation approaches are seldom implemented in educational practice. Therefore, a common widely accepted language to discuss LD within education is currently lacking. The same holds for frameworks regarding the use and evaluation of LDs [10, 13–16]. They often differ in their approaches. For instance, a framework that is using LORI, a tool for eliciting learning object evaluations, has nine different aspects like: content quality, learning goal alignment, motivation, presentation, each individually based on several theories from different researchers, while Baker [10] presents a framework based on Bloom's Taxonomy [11] and Tyler's Basic Principles [12]. Another approach is chosen by Bundsgaard and Hansen, who claim to combine several frameworks into a holistic view where learning potential plays a big role [13]. Falconer et al. [14] illustrate the diversity by presenting an overview of LD frameworks that focus on either: "stages of a learning cycle; degree of embeddedness of information on LD; representation, medium and format; mode of use based on Laurillard's conversational model; and degree of adaptation." Considering this plethora of approaches and available standards for LD leads us to our first challenge, which is the absence of a commonly accepted language in which learning activities based on different LD frameworks can be discussed **O1.SC1. Interoperability of LD**.

LD is not a static field. As HEI are trying to facilitate different target groups with their education, changes in the LD become necessary. Examples of relatively new target groups for traditional universities are workers, the unemployed and part-time students that are part of projects developing innovative LD's. As the group of students is becoming more diverse by these efforts, the challenge **O3.SC2. Coping with the diversity of students** becomes something to take into consideration when developing education.

2.2 Learning Analytics

Over the last years, sources to collect data in the context of learning are becoming increasingly available, which leads to large amounts of learning data [17]. The availability and accessibility of data that learners produce during learning activities is an additional identification of the learning behavior of a student and could be of great value regarding feedback and evaluation of courses and consequently has potential for the (re)design of learning activities. LA describes all aspects of collecting, cleaning, analyzing and visualizing this data. The use of LA to inform decision-making in education is not new, predecessors of LA have been used to inform students in choosing study programs, curriculum development, design of learning outcomes, get insight into behavior of students and their learning process, personalize learning, improve instructor performance, acquire insight in employment opportunities after graduation, and enhance research [18]. But the scope and scale of its potential has increased enormously with the rapid adoption of technology over the last few years and the dependent growth of tracking data that comes with the use of technology. We are now at a stage where data can be automatically harvested, and analysis of these data opens up the opportunity for transforming learning insights into learner abilities and patterns of behavior, cognition, motivation, and emotions [19], and, therefore, studying the effects of design choices within higher education. We identify this as a sub-opportunity: **O1.SO1. Observing effects of LD**.

Frameworks for LA are used to bring structure to all relevant topics [20–23, 26]. A diverse selection of frameworks can be found, varying from Open Learning Analytics [20] to a framework on characteristics of LA [21] and a framework of quality indicators for LA [22, 50]. The differences between the frameworks and the dedicated work that each framework is based on delivers a large amount of research, but makes it difficult to talk about LA on one level between all stakeholders. We call this challenge **O1.SC2. Interoperability of LA.** A comprehensive introduction to different domains that are affected by LA was provided by Greller and Drachsler [23]. They developed a generic design framework that can serve as a guide in developing LA applications in support of educational practice. The framework addresses six fields of attention that have to be addressed in every LA design: 1. Stakeholders, 2. Objectives, 3. Data, 4. Instruments, 5. External constraints, 6. Internal limitations. For the implementation of LA it is very important to make all stakeholders aware of the aspects of LA and find a common understanding to communicate LA findings. Organizations struggle with the complexity of the field of LA. Considering the five step LA sophistication model developed by the Society of Learning Analytics Research (SoLAR) [19], there is still a lot of work to be done in order to transform the educational sector to a data-driven educational science. Most organizations in Europe are still on level one (Aware) of the sophistication model and only very few more advanced organizations are heading towards levels two (Experimentation) and three (Institution wide use). In the various LA reviews [18, 19, 24], there is little mention about experiences of using LA supported LD in educational practice. Despite the great potential surrounding LA, most attempts to implement LA in educational organizations are still at the initiation phase [25, 26].

Rienties and Toetenel [27] state that the challenge in the field of LA is how to put the power of LA into the hands of teachers so that they are able to use it and act upon it. Although an increasing body of literature has become available regarding how researchers and institutions have experimented with interventions using LA [28, 29] and first steps of a conceptual model (Analytics4Action) [30] are made, no comprehensive conceptual model, nested within a strong evidence-base, is available that describes how teachers and administrators can use LA to make successful interventions in their own educational practice. We define this challenge as: **O2.SC2. Improving ability to act on information**, and believe that more research into the use of a learning dashboard as part of the LD would provide some opportunities to overcome this challenge.

2.3 Learning Dashboards

A dashboard can be defined as a visual display of the most important information needed to achieve one or more objectives; consolidated and arranged on a single screen so the information can be monitored at a glance [31]. A learning dashboard can provide both teachers and students with insights into study progress and potential for improvement. Learning dashboards give opportunities for awareness, reflection, sense making, recommendations, and, therefore, could improve learning by helping users raising their ability to act on information [32]. From a teacher perspective we call this opportunity **O2.SO2. Creating and using interventions,** while from a student centered perspective, we derive the opportunity **O2.SO3. Changing learning behavior.** Presenting learning data in the context of LD provides the opportunity **O1.SO2. Sharing knowledge on LD**. Insight in which design choices work and which don't in comparable contexts enables institutions to increase educational quality and help to grasp the opportunity of **O1. Using on demand indicators for evidence based decisions on learning design** [18, 33].

A diversity of learning dashboards have been reviewed in several studies [34, 35]. In the review by Bodily and Verbert [34], the most mentioned goal for developing a learning dashboard for the student is creating awareness and reflection on their learning process (37% out of 94 articles). Awareness and reflection of their educational process leads to two opportunities: first, the opportunity of **O3.SO2 Making learning information accessible** as reflection amplifiers for self-directed learners, or: as benchmarking of student progress against others, which can also be used by teachers if it is in actionable format [52], second, the opportunity of **O1.SO3. Involving the students** in the educational process. The recommendation of resources was the second highest goal (29% out of 94 articles) while 19% of the articles stated that the improvement of retention or engagement is the main goal for implementing a learning dashboard. All these goals contribute to an opportunity we named **O3. Increasing student learning outcome and satisfaction**. Bodily and Verbert show how articles did report on effects of using learning dashboards with regard to the effect of using the dashboard on student behavior (15 out of 94), student skills (14 out of 94) or student achievement (2 out of 94). These elements of the review illustrate that learning dashboards are developed for different goals from different perspectives and it also shows that there is an opportunity to improve student learning outcomes, satisfaction **(O3.),** and behavior **(O2.SO3.)**. Bodily and Verbert conclude that more research is needed on the actual effects of these reporting systems on student behavior, student achievement and skills.

Schwendimann, Rodrıguez-Triana, Vozniuk, Prieto, Boroujeni, Holzer, Gillet, and Dillenbourg [35], present an overview of the state of the art of learning dashboards. They reviewed 53 scientific papers and identified more than 200 indicator types, divided them into the categories: learner, action, content, result, context and socially related. This many indicator types that can be used in analyses mean an enormous potential for LA. It is great to see that there are plenty of indicators for LA, but it is a challenge to select the right indicators for a specific learning activity to provide meaningful insights into the learning process, and for the teacher to select and use the right indicators that influence the LD. For us, this is part of a challenge we named **O2.SC1. Presentation of relevant information the right way**. The review of Schwendimann et al. also showed that, research on the effects of learning dashboards is still young, demonstrated by the considerable amount of exploratory work and limited number of proof-of-concept studies that were rarely implemented (and evaluated) in educational practice. Most of the 53 articles Schwendimann reviewed describe future work and open issues as repeating their research on different targets (students instead of teachers and vice versa) and they also address more usability research in educational practice. The granularity, visualization and interpretation of the information are mentioned as important issues in that type of research.

One of the mentioned goals for using learning dashboards are increasing student learning outcomes. Traditional HEI in the Netherlands are using learning outcomes as a starting point while rethinking LD to reach new target groups [6]. **O3.SO1. Making learning outcomes visible** [53, 55] is an opportunity applied within these new LDs to be able to create workplace related education, where competences can be proved by a portfolio of work related products or enable students to choose their own learning path. Either option improves student's learning outcome and satisfaction **(O3.)** by boosting confidence in their own achievement and progress.

2.4 Metacognitive Competences Used in LD and LA

Park and Jo [47] found that students' overall satisfaction on learning dashboards is correlated with both the degree of understanding and students' capability to change their behavior. This presents the challenge of building a learning dashboard in a way that is understandable for users, which we called **O3.SC1. Understanding learning dashboards.** In order to achieve this, supporting attributes have to be added in such a way that the metacognitive competences of students and teachers are enforced so that they are able to understand and interpret the information, and are able to act on it **(O2.SO1, O2.SO2. and O2.SO3.)**. Most recently, Jivet et al. [49] conducted a study on pitfalls for LA dashboards and showed that most dashboards only consider the reflection process very roughly They conclude that they are not designed apt enough to meet the needs of their actual stakeholders; the teacher and learners.

A definition of metacognitive knowledge is given by Flavell [7]: "*metacognitive knowledge consists primarily of knowledge or beliefs about what factors or variables act and interact in what ways to affect the course and outcome of cognitive enterprises*". In the context of this research, cognitive experiences are understood as learning experiences. Awareness and interpretation of the information presented from learning experiences and critical thinking on actions and behavior that can be applied on the elements of the learning experience are metacognitive competences. These are competences needed to think of factors necessary to act adequately on the information provided [23]. Awareness, however, is not the only aspect that influences the process of feedback, reflection and behavioral change, i.e. of self-efficacy and self-regulated learning [36]. Winne [37] describes self-regulated learning as "*principally comprised of knowledge, beliefs, and learned skills, malleable in response to environmental influences*" and as something that learners inherently do. Zimmerman [38] adds to this that self-regulated learning is indeed about more than knowledge and skills and that metacognitive competences are also influenced by emotions, one's behavior and one's social environment play an important role. Learners thus have different ways to construct knowledge and they have different ways to think about how that construction took place on the basis of the information given to them when learning in a self-regulated way [39]. Learners can act and react in different ways based on that information.

So not only, a clear and user-friendly presentation of the LA information is a challenge (**O2.SC1.Understanding learning dashboards**), but it also is a challenge to train and use the metacognitive competences of teachers and students. We identified this as challenge **O2.SC2. Improving ability to act on information** so that they are able to make use of the information and act directly on the information they are provided with. This challenge is seldomly addressed in research practice of learning dashboards, just 3 of the 53 articles reviewed by Schwendimann et al. [35] talk about competences or how to enforce them. We believe that acquisition of knowledge and skills on using LA in practice will be key for the uptake of LA by end users. Doing so will enable us to use the opportunity **O3.SO3. Improving learning to learn.**

3 Aligning LA and LD in Frameworks and Dashboards

The potential value of using LA as a purposeful element in the LD of modules, is described by several researchers [40–42]. In developing a specific LD, a teacher or educational designer works on all phases of an instruction; starting from the definition of prior knowledge prerequisites of the particular target student group, the learning objectives and outcomes, and the design of assessments to test if the outcomes have been achieved. In between are many choices for appropriate learning activities and sequences, content, teaching methods, materials and other resources that contribute to achieving the learning objectives of the design. The teaching activities and resources are provided increasingly over IT infrastructures and are most of the time also digitally available. This offers the possibility to use LA as part of the learning environment and the LD [27, 40].

The alignment of LA and LD changes the design process of learning activities from a post-evaluation design process into a permanent monitoring process of adaptation. In this way, teachers should already consider measurements at the design phase of their learning activities and they should select most suitable LA indicators that can be used to monitor if the selected learning activities of a course are going as intended or not. But the alignment also changes the monitoring process of courses into a learning design-aware monitoring process. It is of crucial importance for a LA supported LD to consider potential LA indicators already while designing the learning objectives and related activities [40]. Like assessment procedures, LA indicators should be considered in the very beginning of the development of the LD. In that way, e.g. a 'forum discussion' is not only an effective learning activity by itself, but LA can also provide a much more efficient and effective overview of e.g. student participation through social network analysis tools [41] that can provide students with self-monitoring information and make teachers more aware of the learning process of their students and adds possibilities for personalized feedback. Using LA while scripting LD and thinking about LD when initializing LA indicators makes it necessary to use a more unified way of talking and thinking about LD **(O1.SC1.)** and LA **(O1.SC2.)**. By collecting data from learners on learning activities in a LA dashboard that is designed according to LD intentions will enable teachers and educational designers to make improvements to their courses on demand during run-time **(O2.)** [42]. Only few studies on the alignment of LA and LD have been done to date. Wise et al. [43] sums up a list of studies that "*underscore the idea that the use of a combined approach of LD, teacher inquiry into student learning and LA can produce effective new pedagogies*" [43]. Rodriguez et al. [44] are trying to combine scripting and monitoring and vice versa. To take advantage of this potential, teachers and instructional designers need to keep LA in mind while designing learning activities to select the most appropriate LA indicators for the dashboard solution [44]. Rienties et al. [30] are developing a framework to enable teachers to create interventions by using LA for LD. All frameworks that incorporate LA and LD [10, 14, 15, 30, 45, 46] describe roughly three elements: resources, learning tasks and supporting mechanisms that can be monitored in learning contexts. Each framework mentions some type of timing where the monitoring takes place. This can be during a course, after a course and after several courses. The conceptual framework of Bakhari et al. [45] describes this timing item as a temporal analysis, which makes a distinction in the frequency of the analysis event: recurring events (weekly workspace meeting), submission events (assignments), single events (guest lectures). Timing is an opportunity we called **O2.SO1. Delivering information/feedback on demand.** Further work needs to be done to create frameworks and tools and research the effect of using them to establish an evidence base.

4 Conclusion

In this paper, we presented several opportunities and challenges for aligning and incorporating LA into LD to innovate and improve higher education and achieve a more personalized and "just-in-time" learning culture with more on-demand feedback mechanisms. In Fig. 1, below, a tentative model for the implementation of LA supported LD is shown. It maps the identified opportunities and challenges from this study to the model.

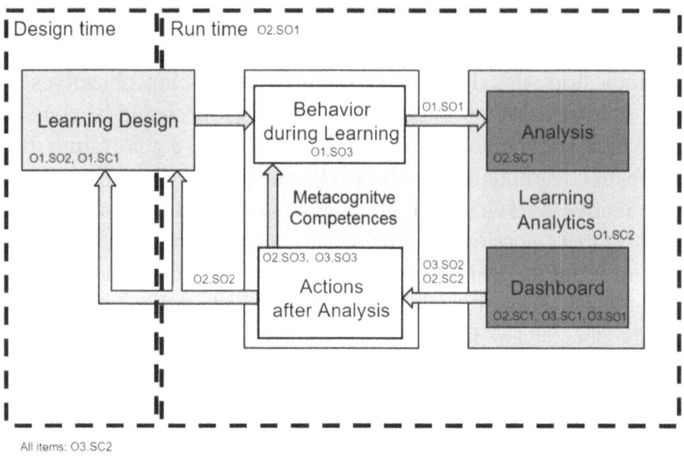

Fig. 1. Proposed LA in LD model, including opportunities and challenges of Table 1.

From a course design perspective, LA can be used to take the measurement of quality of learning activities into consideration which delivers the opportunity **O1.SO1. Observing the effects of LD**. Collecting this information enables users to use opportunity **O1.SO2. Sharing knowledge on LD** so that the design can be improved and made more efficient, effective and reusable. Two challenges here are **O1.SC1. Interoperability of LD** and **O1.SC2. Interoperability of LA**. Because of the large amount of frameworks and tools for both LD and LA, some type of order is necessary to be able to collaborate with colleagues in designing learning activities and to be successful with opportunity **O1.SO3. Involving students**. The observations, the possibility to share knowledge, the learner centered way of involving the students and the coping with the challenges of interoperability of LD and LA make it possible to build a base for future research and thereby addressing the key opportunity **O1. Using on demand indicators for evidence based decisions on learning design** Steps are made on this subject with the development of frameworks, but practical research is needed. When striving for more personalized education, evidence based choices on which learning activities are most fit for an individual student are essential for educational designers.

From a user perspective, LA for LD creates the opportunity **O2.SO1. Delivering information/feedback on demand.** For teachers this means getting timely feedback on the effects of decision in de LD which makes it possible to seize the opportunity of **O2.SO2. Creating and using interventions** to help students. For students this means receiving feedback and personal support from teachers and the opportunity to **O2.SO3. Change learning behavior** with regard to the course. Neither teachers nor students are able to do this without a visualization that adresses the challenge **O2.SC1. Presenting the relevant information the right way.** Furthermore, teachers and students should be able to view, interpret and act based on the information they have received. In our opinion, the biggest challenge is **O2.SC2. Improving the ability to act on information.** Some research mentions addressing metacognitive competences to tackle this challenge, but very little has been done in this field, which therefore provides opportunities for further research. If teachers and students are trained and facilitated in using their meta-cognitive competences to not only understand the relevant information delivered to them on demand, but to also change their behavior or use interventions accordingly, then the main opportunity **O2. Intervening during the run-time of a course** can become a reality. But as Jivet et al. [49] laid out in a recent study, this objective is only seldom reached and, therefore, the LA dashboard applications often fail in supporting the students and teachers in the way that is intended. An instrument that delivers on-demand information enables adaptations of the learning experiences and thereby an effect of improved personalization.

From an HEI perspective, **O3.SO1. Making learning outcomes visible** creates an opportunity to change the educational process and make it attainable for new target groups. This automatically presents the challenge of **O3.SC2. Coping with the diversity of students** that higher education institutions are confronted with. Tools like a learning dashboard enable **O3.SO2. Making learning information accessible** by using reflection amplifiers for self-directed learners, or as benchmarking of student progress. Both elements improve personalized self-regulated learning and regulatory teaching. Bringing well-designed user-friendly learning dashboards (**O3.SC1. Understanding learning dashboards**), as instruments for application of LA in LD, into the playing field and enabling both students and teachers is using these information by increasing meta-cognitive competences, would add to the opportunity **O3.SO3. Improving learning to learn.** We believe that if students and teachers are enabled and facilitated to understand the data that is brought to them and are motivated to act on their learning process or learning design, HEI's are a step closer to delivering personalized content and processes enforced by LA in LD. Only then the key opportunity of **O3. Increasing student learning outcome and satisfaction** becomes achievable.

In the upcoming future, and following on from this model, we want to further investigate how LA supported LD can be implemented in authentic teaching situations. Key for this implementation will be the empowerment of teachers and learners with meta-cognitive competences to directly think along LA indicators for the use in their LD and interaction with their students. Part of this future investigation is whether our suggested solution affects the described opportunities and challenges with the aim of making education more personalized.

A first attempt towards the practical part of this research is currently conducted in the REFLECTOR project that is funded by the SURF foundation in the Netherlands. Within the REFLECTOR project we are mainly focusing on the following opportunities and challenges: **O1.SO1, O1.SO3, O2.SO1, O2.SC2, O3.SO1, O3.SO2, O3.SC1.** We are designing and implementing an LA dashboard into a ICT-course design in close colaboration with the end users. We will address teachers'as well as students'needs related to their capability to reflect and act upon their teaching and learning behavior. To study whether the teachers followed their intended LD and students their planned performance, teachers will be interviewed about the intended LD of the course and argumentation for their learning activities. We will also survey students'intended study behavior within the particular course by using a Dutch version of the MSLQ [57]. Both information sources will than be monitored during the course runtime to study the effects of on-demand feedback provided from the LA dashboard on the intended teaching or learning behavior.

Acknowledgements. We would like to thank the SURF Foundation & NRO for supporting the efforts of Marcel Schmitz, Evelien van Limbeek and Hendrik Drachsler under the REFLECTOR project grant.

References

1. Altbach, P., Reisberg, L., Rumbley, L.: Tracking a global academic revolution. Change **42**(2), 30–39 (2010)
2. Field, J.: Lifelong learning and the multigenerational workforce. In: Burke, R.J., Cooper, C.L., Antoniou, A.-S.G. (eds.) The multi-generational and Aging Workforce: Challenges and Opportunities, pp. 311–325. Edward Elgar Publishing, Cheltenham (2015)
3. Volles, N.: Lifelong learning in the EU: changing conceptualisations, actors, and policies. Stud. High. Educ. **41**(2), 343–363 (2014)
4. Nonis, S., Hudson, G.: Academic performance of college students: influence of time spent studying and working. J. Edu. Bus. **81**(3), 151–159 (2006)
5. Tuononen, T., Parpala, A., Mattsson, M., Lindblom-Ylänne, S.: Work experience in relation to study pace and thesis grade: investigating the mediating role of student learning. High. Educ. **72**(1), 41–58 (2016)
6. Ministerie van Onderwijs, Cultuur & Wetenschap: De waarde(n) van weten: strategische agenda hoger onderwijs en onderzoek 2015–2025. Den Haag (2015)
7. Flavell, J.: Metacognition and cognitive monitoring: a new area of cognitive–developmental inquiry. Am. Psychol. **34**(10), 906–911 (1979)
8. Donald, C., Blake, A., Girault, I., Datt, A., Ramsay, E.: Approaches to learning design: past the head and the hands to the HEART of the matter. Distance Edu. **30**(2), 179–199 (2009)
9. Peterson, C.: Bringing ADDIE to life: instructional design at its best. J. Edu. Multimed. Hypermedia **12**(3), 227–241 (2003)
10. Baker, R.: A framework for design and evaluation of internet-based distance learning courses: Phase one–Framework justification design and evaluation. Online J. Distance Learn. Admin. **6**(2), 43–51 (2003)
11. Bloom, B., Engelhart, M., Furst, E., Hill, W., Krathwohl, D.: Taxonomy of Educational Objectives: The Classification Of Educational Goals. Handbook I: Cognitive Domain. David McKay Company, New York (1956)
12. Tyler, R.: Basic Principles of Curriculum and Instruction. University of Chicago Press, Chicago (1949)
13. Bundsgaard, J., Hansen, T.: Evaluation of learning materials: a holistic framework. J. Learn. Des. **4**(4), 31–45 (2011)
14. Falconer, I., Beetham, H., Oliver, R., Littlejohn, A.: Mod4L final report: representing learning designs. Final report for the JISC-funded MOD4L project. Glasgow (2007)
15. Leacock, T., Nesbit, J.: A framework for evaluating the quality of multimedia learning resources. Edu. Technol. Soc. **10**, 44–59 (2007)
16. Falconer, I.: Mediating between practitioner and developer communities: the learning activity design in education experience. Alt-J **15**(2), 155–170 (2007)
17. Masie, E.: Big Learning Data. ASTD Press, Alexandria (2014)

18. Avella, J., Kebritchi, M., Nunn, S., Kanai, T.: Learning analytics methods, benefits, and challenges in higher education: a systematic literature review. Online Learn. J. **20**(2), 13–29 (2016)
19. Siemens, G.: Learning analytics: the emergence of a discipline. Am. Behav. Sci. **57**(10), 1380–1400 (2013)
20. Siemens, G., Gasevic, D., Haythornthwaite, C., Dawson, S., Shum, S., Ferguson, R., Duval, E., Verbert, K., Baker, R.: Open learning analytics: an integrated and modularized platform. Educause Rev. **42**(4), 53–54 (2007)
21. Cooper, A.: A framework of characteristics for analytics. CETIS Anal. Ser. **1**(7), 1–17 (2012)
22. Scheffel, M., Drachsler, H., Stoyanov, S., Specht, M.: Quality indicators for learning analytics. Edu. Technol. Soc. **17**(4), 124–140 (2014)
23. Greller, W., Drachsler, H.: Translating learning into numbers: a generic framework for learning analytics. Edu. Technol. Soc. **15**(3), 42–57 (2012)
24. Ferguson, R.: Learning analytics: drivers, developments and challenges. Int. J. Technol. Enhanced Learn. **4**(5/6), 304–317 (2012)
25. Bichsel, J.: Analytics in Higher Education: Benefits, Barriers, Progress, and Recommendations. Educause Center for Applied Research, Louisville (2012)
26. Colvin, C., Rogers, T., Wade, A., Dawson, S., Gasevic, D., Shum, S., Nelson, K., Alexander, S., Lockyer, L., Kennedy, G., Corrin, L., Fisher, J.: Student retention and learning analytics: a snapshot of Australian practices and a framework for advancement. Australian Office for Learning and Teaching, Sydney (2015)
27. Rienties, B., Toetenel, L.: The impact of 151 learning designs on student satisfaction and performance: social learning (analytics) matters. In: Proceedings of LAK 2016 6th International Conference on Analytics and Knowledge, pp. 339–343 (2016)
28. Clow, D., Cross, S., Ferguson, R.: Evidence hub review. LACE Project, Milton Keynes (2014)
29. Papamitsiou, Z., Economides, A.: Learning analytics and educational data mining in practice: a systematic literature review of empirical evidence. Edu. Technol. Soc. **17**(4), 49–64 (2014)
30. Rienties, B., Boroowa, A., Cross, S., Kubiak, C., Mayles, K., Murphy, S.: Analytics4Action evaluation framework: a review of evidence-based learning analytics interventions at the Open University UK. J. Interact. Med. Edu. **1**, 2 (2016)
31. Few, S.: Information dashboard design: the effective visual communication of data. O'Reilly Media, Sebastopol (2006)
32. Verbert, K., Duval, E., Klerkx, J., Govaerts, S., Santos, J.: Learning analytics dashboard applications. Am. Behav. Sci. **57**(10), 1500–1509 (2013)
33. Mor, Y., Ferguson, R., Wasson, B.: Editorial: learning design, teacher inquiry into student learning and learning analytics: a call for action. Br. J. Edu. Technol. **46**(2), 221–229 (2015)
34. Bodily, R., Verbert, K.: Trends and issues in student-facing learning analytics reporting systems research. In: Proceedings of the Seventh International Learning Analytics & Knowledge Conference, pp. 309–318. ACM, New York (2017)
35. Schwendimann, B., Rodriguez-Triana, M., Vozniuk, A., Prieto, L., Boroujeni, M., Holzer, A., Gillet, D., Dillenbourg, P.: Perceiving learning at a glance: a systematic literature review of learning dashboard research. IEEE Trans. Learn. Technol. **10**(1), 30–41 (2017)
36. Butler, D., Winne, P.: Feedback and self-regulated learning: a theoretical synthesis. Rev. Edu. Res. **65**(3), 245–281 (1995)
37. Winne, P.: Inherent details in self-regulated learning. Edu. Psychol. **30**(4), 173–187 (1995)
38. Zimmerman, B.: Self-regulation involves more than metacognition: a social cognitive perspective. Edu. Psychol. **30**(4), 217–221 (1995)
39. Winne, P.: How software technologies can improve research on learning and bolster school reform. Edu. Psychol. **41**(1), 5–17 (2006)

40. Lockyer, L., Heathcote, E., Dawson, S.: Informing pedagogical action: aligning learning analytics with learning design. Am. Behav. Sci. **57**(10), 1439–1459 (2013)
41. Bakharia, A., Dawson, S.: SNAPP: a bird's-eye view of temporal participant interaction. In: Proceedings of LAK 2011 1st International Conference on Analytics and Knowledge, pp. 168–173 (2011)
42. Persico, D., Pozzi, F.: Informing learning design with learning analytics to improve teacher inquiry. Br. J. Edu. Technol. **46**(2), 230–248 (2015)
43. Wise, A., Shaffer, D.: Why theory matters more than ever in the age of big data. J. Learn. Anal. **2**(2), 5–13 (2015)
44. Rodríguez-Triana, M., Martínez-Monés, A., Asensio-Pérez, J., Dimitriadis, Y.: Scripting and monitoring meet each other: aligning learning analytics and learning design to support teachers in orchestrating CSCL situations. Br. J. Edu. Technol. **46**(2), 330–343 (2015)
45. Bakharia, A., Corrin, L., Barba, P. De, Kennedy, G., Gasevic, D., Mulder, R., Williams, D., Dawson, S., Lockyer, L.: A conceptual framework linking learning design with learning analytics. In: Proceedings of LAK 2016 6th International Conference on Analytics and Knowledge, pp. 329–338 (2016)
46. Verbert, K., Govaerts, S., Duval, E., Santos, J., Van Assche, F., Parra, G., Klerkx, J.: Learning dashboards: an overview and future research opportunities. Pers. Ubiquit. Comput. **18**(6), 1499–1514 (2014)
47. Park, Y., Jo, I.: Development of the learning analytics dashboard to support students' learning performance. J. Univ. Comput. Sci. **21**(1), 110–133 (2015)
48. FitzGerald, E., Kucirkova, N., Jones, A., Cross, S., Ferguson, R., Herodotou, C., Hillaire, G., Scanlon, E.: Dimensions of personalisation in technology-enhanced learning: a framework and implications for design. Br. J. Edu. Technol. (2017, in press)
49. Jivet, I., Scheffel, M., Drachsler, H., Specht, M.: Awareness is not enough: pitfalls of learning analytics dashboards in the educational practice. In: Proceedings of the 12th European Conference on Technology Enhanced Learning (EC-TEL 2017) (in press)
50. Scheffel, M., Drachsler, H., Toisoul, C., Ternier, S., Specht, M.: The proof of the pudding: examining validity and reliability of the evaluation framework for learning analytics. In: Proceedings of the 12th European Conference on Technology Enhanced Learning (EC-TEL 2017) (in press)
51. Koper, R., Olivier, B.: Representing the learning design of units of learning. Edu. Technol. Soc. **7**(3), 97–111 (2004)
52. Prinsloo, P., Slade, S.: An elephant in the learning analytics room: the obligation to act. In: LAK 2017 Proceedings of the Seventh International Learning Analytics & Knowledge Conference, pp. 46–55 (2017)
53. Trigwell, K., Prosser, M.: Improving the quality of student learning: the influence of learning context and student approaches to learning on learning outcomes. High. Educ. **22**(3), 251–266 (1991)
54. De La Fuente, J., Sander, P., Martínez-Vicente, J.M., Vera, M., Garzón, A., Fadda, S.: Combined effect of levels in personal self-regulation and regulatory teaching on meta-cognitive, on meta-motivational, and on academic achievement variables in undergraduate students. Front. Psychol. **8**, 232 (2017)
55. Gašević, D., Jovanović, J., Pardo, A., Dawson, S.: Detecting learning strategies with analytics: links with self-reported measures and academic performance. J. Learn. Anal. **4**(1), 113–128 (2017)

56. Pardo, A., Martinez-Maldonado, R., Buckingham Shum, S., Schulte, J., McIntyre, S., Gašević, D., Gao, J., Siemens, G.: Connecting data with student support actions in a course: a hands-on tutorial. In: LAK 2017 Proceedings of the Seventh International Learning Analytics & Knowledge Conference, pp. 522–523 (2017)
57. Pintrich, P., Smith, D., Garcia, T., Mckeachie, W.: Reliability and predictive validity of the Motivated Strategies for Learning Questionnaire (MSLQ). Educ. Psychol. Measur. **53**(3), 801–813 (1993)

Evaluating Student-Facing Learning Dashboards of Affective States

Gayane Sedrakyan[1(✉)], Derick Leony[2], Pedro J. Muñoz-Merino[2], Carlos Delgado Kloos[2], and Katrien Verbert[1]

[1] Department of Computer Science, KU Leuven, Leuven, Belgium
gayane.sedrakyan@kuleuven.be, katrien.verbert@cs.kuleuven.be
[2] Department of Telematics Engineering, Universidad Carlos III de Madrid, Madrid, Spain
{dleony,pedmume,cdk}@it.uc3m.es

Abstract. Detection and visualizations of affective states of students in computer based learning environments have been proposed to support student awareness and improve learning. However, the evaluation of such visualizations with students in real life settings is an open issue. This research reports on our experiences from the use of four different types of dashboard visualizations in two user studies ($n = 115$). Students who participated in the studies were bachelor and master level students from two different study programs at two universities. The results indicate that usability, measured by interpretability, perceived usefulness and insight, is overall acceptable. However, the findings also suggest that interpretability of some visualizations, in terms of the capability to support emotion awareness, still needs to be improved. The level of students awareness about their emotions during learning activities based on the visualization interpretation varied depending on previous knowledge on visualization techniques. Furthermore, simpler visualizations resulted in better outcomes than more complex techniques.

Keywords: Learning dashboards · Human-computer interface · Interactive learning environments · Learning analytics · Emotion visualization · Visualization evaluation

1 Introduction

The interplay between emotions and learning has been recognized in many studies [16,30]. Recent research has highlighted the importance of supporting awareness of these emotions [2]. For example, students can reflect about the type of emotions they felt, the activities that generated certain emotions or their evolution over time. By analyzing their emotions, students can take decisions to improve their learning process, based for instance on information from studies that relate learning outcomes with affective states (e.g. [4]). As students' emotions are an important aspect of the learning process that has been proved to have an impact on learning achievements, different methodologies and detectors

É. Lavoué et al. (Eds.): EC-TEL 2017, LNCS 10474, pp. 224–237, 2017.
DOI: 10.1007/978-3-319-66610-5_17

of emotions have been proposed in different learning contexts. There are detectors of emotions based on facial and gesture recognition [7], based on signals such as brainwaves captured with headsets [3], and students actions in different learning environments such as Intelligent Tutoring Systems [23], MOOCs [19] or active programming environments [17]. In other cases, emotion data are entered manually in the system by students [21].

Information about students' affective states, such as the type and intensity of the experienced emotion, should be presented in an intuitive way to the different stakeholders, including teachers, students and managers. One of the most used techniques to present such information is through visualizations in the context of so-called learning dashboards [32]. An important issue is that stakeholders can gain insight from these visualizations, and that the information can be of utility, for instance to support awareness and reflection, or to support decision-making [31]. There are some works about visualizations of emotions in computer based learning environments [18]. However, to our knowledge, existing literature lacks in empirical studies evaluating different visualizations with regard to their capabilty to support emotion awareness in learning environments. In addition, most evaluations of learning visualizations are done by teachers [32]. Only a few works focus on evaluation of visualizations by students to gain insight into the utility of these visualizations.

In this paper, we focus specifically on evaluating the usability of visualizations of affective states for students using well-known constructs such as the perceived usefulness and insight that is supported by different visualizations. Usability of the visualizations refers to ease of use of the visualizations. We define perceived usefulness as the perception of students about the importance of each visualization for the learning process. Insight is considered as an important measure to evaluate visualizations [22] and is defined as the extent to which students can interpret correctly the presented visualizations. This paper presents the first experiences from the use of visualizations of affective states for students and attempts to identify future research directions in this domain. The paper addresses the following research question:

How usable are the visualizations of affective states that we have developed for students in terms of perceived usefulness and insight?

We present the results of our user studies that assess the usability of different visualizations using different student groups in higher education. The pilot study was conducted with a first group of students with a background in visualization techniques, whereas the second study was conducted with a second group of students with little knowledge about visualization techniques. The insights from the first user study ($n = 10$) were used to improve the visualizations. We used suggestions of these students to create additional visualizations. The second user study was conducted with the enhanced environment with a larger group of students ($n = 105$).

The rest of the paper is organized as follows: Sect. 2 presents related work on visualizations of affective states in the context of learning dashboards. Section 3 presents the AffectVis dashboard with four different visualizations of affective states. Sections 4 and 5 present our two user studies in two different courses, detailing the participants, data collection, data analysis and post-study interview results. Finally Sect. 6 concludes the work with a discussion of the obtained results and suggestions for possible future research directions.

2 Background: Affective State Visualizations in the Context of Learning Analytics Dashboards

Detecting affective states in educational settings has been explored previously by researchers in the field [3,4,7,15,23]. Leony et al. presented a concrete case of inference of emotions from interaction data with a programming environment [17]. The approach consists of a set of Hidden Markov Models (HMMs). Each HMM receives as observations all the events generated by the learners during a programming laboratory, such as correct compilation, erroneous compilation, text edition and access to web resources. During the programming task students are asked several times to provide information about their affective state in the form of an input. This information is used to train the HMMs that are then used to infer emotions at other moments.

In another approach and educational environment, Leony et al. use a rule-based model for each emotion of interest, contextualizing emotion detection in MOOCs [19]. For instance, frustration is understood to occur in this context when students either frequently fail exercises or fail an exercise about a topic that was already considered as controlled. In addition, all of the models take into account the recency of the events, i.e. recent activities of learners registered in the system, that can potentially cause an emotion. Thus, recent negative results of an exercise will have a higher effect on the level of frustration.

In this paper, we focus specifically on visualizing data about affective states of learners and evaluating the usability (usefulness and insight) of visualizations to support students. Data acquisition is done in a manual way.

A series of studies have explored the affective states that occur during learning [9]. These studies have shown that the basic emotions identified by [12], such as anger, fear, sadness, joy, disgust, and surprise, typically do not play a significant role in learning [16]. The authors investigated the effect of a set of affective states that typically do play significant role in learning, at least in the case of college students learning. Craig et al. [8] found evidence for a link between learning and the affective states of confusion, flow and boredom. D'Mello et al. [11] found significant overall relationships for happiness (eureka), confusion, and frustration, but not for boredom. In this paper, we used visualizations for this set of five affective states Frustration, Confusion, Boredom, Happiness, Motivation in a learning dashboard for college students and present results of user studies that assess the usability, measured by usefulness and insight of different visualizations of these affective states.

There are a few interesting observations in the literature on learning analytics dashboards that are relevant to the content of this paper. The first observation is that usability and usefulness evaluations have been conducted most often with teachers [1,14,24], indicating that perceived usefulness is often higher for teachers than for students. In this paper, we focus therefore explicitly on evaluations with students. In addition, most dashboards focus on performance/resource/time utility information [32]. To the best of our knowledge, only one dashboard has been presented that focuses on the representation of student emotions [13]. Also in this work, the focus is on the utility of such a dashboard for instructors.

In our work, we focus on visualization of affective data, as such data has shown to be an important player in learning behaviour [4], and evaluate the usability of such a dashboard with students. Finally, little is known about the effectiveness of different visualization techniques to give students insight into their data. Different visualizations have been proposed in earlier work, but to which extent these visualizations can be interpreted in a correct way by students and which techniques work better than others still require further research.

3 AffectVis: A Learning Dashboard of Affective States and Learning Activities in Projects

We have developed four visualizations with the general objective of allowing learners to reflect on their affective states and their connection with course work and learning activities. The visualizations are web-based, thus the only tool needed to access them is a web browser with JavaScript capabilities. The first visualization, shown in Fig. 1, uses a set of polar bars to present the average frequency of each learner affective state for each of the learning activities. Affective states of each learner are indicated through the color of each bar while labels are used to indicate the associated activity. The solid line shows the average value of the class for each emotion and activity. This visualization is an improved version of the radial visualization presented by [20].

The next visualization is a timeline that presents the evolution of time dedication of the student during the course and the average time dedication of the whole class. Figure 2 presents a capture of this visualization. The visualization represents the accumulated time dedication of students: when the student selects a point of time in the horizontal axis, then the values of the vertical axis will indicate the accumulated levels of time dedicated until that moment. In addition, the timeline shows the evolution of each emotion during the course.

The third visualization is a heat-map in which columns represent time units (e.g., days, weeks, months) and rows represent students. Each affective dimension is represented by a cell, while the frequency level of each emotion is represented through the intensity of the cell color (more intensity represents higher levels of this emotion). A portion of this visualization is shown in Fig. 3.

Lastly, we designed a scatter-plot visualization. Each affective dimension has a different scatter-plot associated to it. The X-axis corresponds to the exact date and time when the emotion takes place and the Y-axis presents the frequency value of the emotion associated to the scatter plot. Bubble sizes represent the amount of work dedication indicated in the given submission, and bubble colors

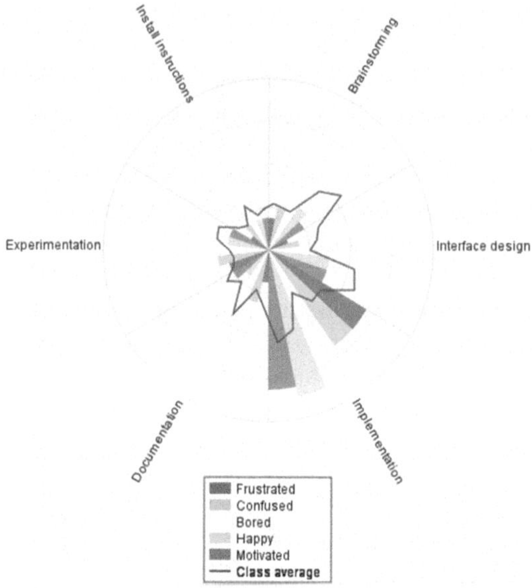

Fig. 1. Visualization showing the frequency of each affective state for each activity. Polar bars show the values for the active student while solid line shows the values for the class average. (Color figure online)

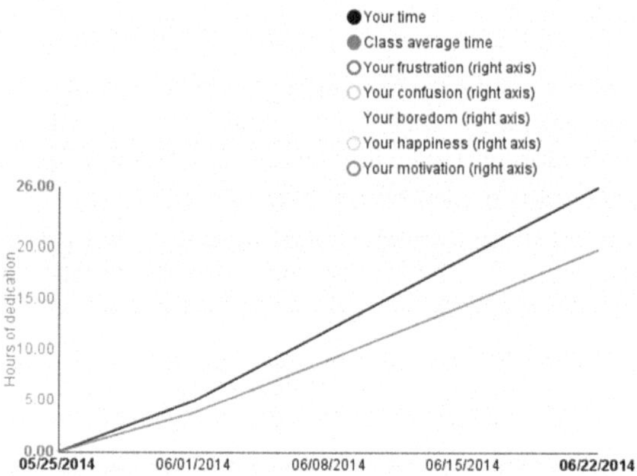

Fig. 2. Visualization of the accumulated amount of time dedication and frequency of affective dimension. Students can also see the time dedication average of the class.

indicate whether it belongs to the viewer or to another learner. Figure 4 presents an example scatter-plot for "confusion".

In its current form the visualizations in the AffectVis dashboard rely on data based on think-aloud sessions and surveys of students reporting on their emotion

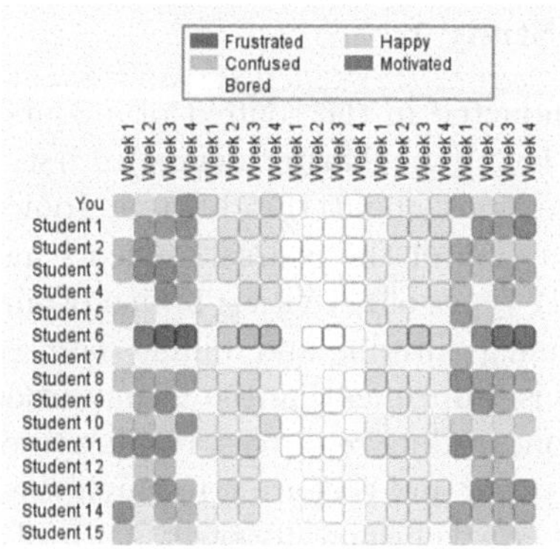

Fig. 3. Heat-map of emotion frequency for each learner and each week.

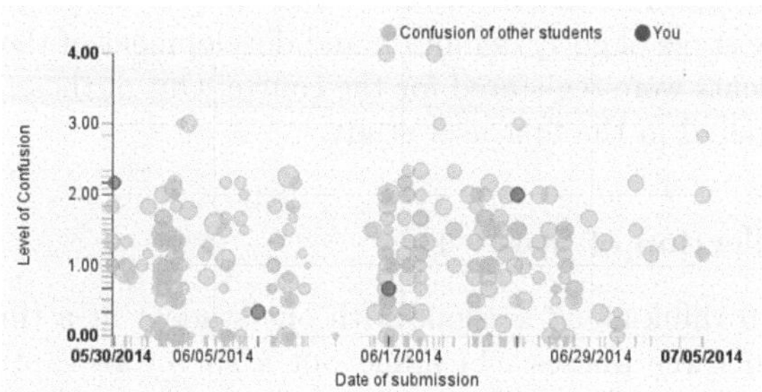

Fig. 4. One of the scatter-plot showing the relation between the emotion frequency and work dedication along time.

levels per different learning activity (see further details in the next sections on user studies).

4 Pilot Study with a Small Group of Students with Expertise in Visualizations: User Study 1

The main purpose of this user study was to perform an exploratory analysis of the developed visualizations with a small number of students. Thus, the feedback obtained from students would help to improve these visualizations for a more elaborate second user study. The first study was conducted with master-level students at Vrije Universiteit Brussel in Belgium. The profile of students, having knowlege about visualizations, was beneficial for obtaining this type of feedback. In addition, this first user study can serve to observe differences between students with knowledge on visualizations and students without knowledge about it (the profile of students in user study 2). In the first user study, we evaluated the two first visualizations presented in Sect. 3: the average emotion level per activity and the timeline.

4.1 Participants of Study 1

This user study was conducted in the context of a course on information visualization at a graduate level (i.e., Master degree). First, students received theoretical and practical sessions about the different topics of the course. Next, and as part of the evaluation of the course, students had to do and present a project which included 12 types of activities: brainstorming, designing visualization, gathering data, parsing, filtering and mining data, getting started with the visualization library D3.js, implementing the visualization, implementing interaction in the visualization, reading resources, reading research papers, preparing questions for a research paper and preparing research presentations. The project lasted five weeks, from late February to early April of 2014. The user study took place during this period. As participants were registered for an information visualization course, they all had a relevant knowledge of principles and theories involved in the creation of visualizations. Thus, their feedback was highly interesting during the stage of early definition and development of the visualizations. In total, 42 students were registered for the course. Out of these 42 students, 10 students participated in the first user study.

4.2 Data Collection of Study 1

We conducted 10 think-aloud sessions with one student at a time. The session was organized in three phases: (1) filling out a survey to capture data about their work during the project, (2) conducting tasks with the two visualizations, and (3) filling out an evaluation survey about the visualizations. The survey to capture data about students' activities during the project asked explicitly about the students' affective state for each type of activity. This way, for each type of activity, students had to indicate how frequently they have experienced the five affective dimensions known to occur in learning scenarios: motivation, happiness, boredom, confusion and frustration [10]. It also included a question about the amount of time dedicated to the project during the course for each of the weeks.

The usability evaluation survey included questions about the perceived usefulness and the insights of the generated visualizations. The usability was measured with the System Usability Scale (SUS) method [6]. Students evaluated the usability through two 5-point Likert scale direct questions, rating the two visualizations from not useful at all to very useful.

Students were also asked about the utility of other information of interest that could be represented through visualizations. They could rate the utility of five types of information on a 5-point Likert scale: (1) types of used resources (e.g., forums, blogs or files), (2) detailed information of one student, (3) comparing actions between two students, (4) detailed statistics of most used resources and (5) information about content creation by students.

Insight was assessed through direct questions regarding information that visualizations intended to provide. The objective was to assess whether students can interpret the presented information on their affective states in the visualizations. For instance, students were asked to assess the intensity of their affective states using a 5-point Likert scale, such as "much below", "below", "average", "above the average", "much above the average". They were also asked to indicate what their most frequently occuring emotion was and the activity during which they were most different compared to their peers. In addition, they had to select the time periods in which they had worked the most and the least.

4.3 Data Analysis and Results of Study 1

The usability results obtained from the evaluation of the SUS questions averaged 72.5 points which can be assessed as positive [5]. The timeline was the visualization perceived as the most useful by the students. The emotion per activity visualization (Fig. 1) was graded as very useful (score above three on a scale from one to five). Among the information types that were found to be of interest for the students the detailed information for one student, the comparison of students positionining a student with respect to a peer and the information about content creation were the top priorities. The information related to types of used resources and the usage of top resources were the least prioritized. The correlation coefficients comparing the answers of students about their affective states based on the provided visualizations and the real values were found to be high and positive in general ($r > 0.5$), which suggests that students' perceptions about the information of the visualizations were according to the reality. The analysis of students' answers to the post-study interview questions provided useful insights with respect to the improvement needs of the presented visualizations. The results suggested that the students also experienced difficulties in interpreting the visualizations. For instance, some students found it difficult to identify the values on the radial bars mainly due to user interface related issues such as having adjacent bars with similar colors or to a low level contrast making them not easily distinguishable in the chart, etc. In general, students expressed that they *"liked the timeline and the comparison with their peers"* and prefer its use. On the other hand, the generated visualization of affective states per activity was difficult to understand by some students (*"it's hard to see the information of all students"*, *"the red color [of bars representing frustration] is too distracting"* and *"it's confusing that bars don't start from zero"*) which suggests that interpretability of visualizations need to be further improved to provide more intuitive understanding.

5 Extended Study with a Larger Group: User Study 2

The second study was conducted with bachelor-level students at the Eindhoven University of Technology in the Netherlands. For the second user study, we improved the two visualizations based on the findings and suggestions of students from the pilot study. The contrast of colors and the visibility of elements in both visualizations were improved. Interactivity was added to clarify the details of the visualizations: the affective states per type of activity showed the value of each bar when the mouse cursor hovered over it. The timeline was adjusted to offer the option to hide and show data series, etc. In addition, we have added two new visualizations with emphasis on individual and detailed information, as such information was identified as relevant by students of the first user study. These visualizations include the heat-map and scatter-plots described in Sect. 3. The purpose of this study was to evaluate the usability of the four visualizations measured by usefulness, ease of use and insight, namely, the improved versions of the two visualizations used in user study 1, and the two new visualizations.

5.1 Participants of Study 2

Overall 105 first-year bachelor students enrolled in technological programs took part in the study 2. The study was conducted in the context of the course Human-technology Interaction. In the beginning of the course, an introduction was provided about all the concepts and processes involved in the design of usable interfaces for technological artefacts. At the end of the semester, students had to complete a project about the design of a thermostat. The project duration was four weeks from late April to early June of 2014. At the end, students presented their project to the teaching staff and their peers. For this project, we defined six types of activities in collaboration with the instructors: brainstorming, interface design, implementation, writing documentation, experiment with users and writing installation instructions.

5.2 Data Collection of Study 2

Every week during the course project, students completed the following tasks: (1) filling out a survey about their activities during the week, (2) exploring this data in relation to data of other students with several interactive visualizations, and (3) filling out a survey about their perceiptions and judgements on the visualizations. The survey included questions to the students about their activities. Students were asked to indicate how frequently they had experienced each affective state while performing each of the project activities and the time dedicated to the project. Students were allowed to report activities for a week different than the current one. After the data was submitted, the student could use a web application to access the visualizations.

In this study, the students were also asked to answer an evaluation survey to assess the usability, usefulness and insight of the visualizations continuously. As in the final survey of the first user study, the usability was evaluated through SUS questions, while the usefulness was evaluated using 5-point Likert scales to rank each visualization from not useful at all to very useful. In addition, we also used questions to objectively assess the insight of the visualizations as follows:

- 5-point Likert scale to indicate whether the student is much below, below, average, above or much above the class for each emotion and time dedication.
- Indicate the most frequent emotion experienced during the project.
- Identify the activity that motivated students (the whole class) the most.
- Identify the activity that frustrated the student the most.
- Identify the activity during which the student is most different from the rest.

Overall, we received 298 submissions from 95 students for the data gathering survey, with 91% of the responses coming from male students and 9% from females. Most of the submissions (78.5%) belonged to students 20 years old or younger, 17.4% between 21 and 25, 1.7% between 26 and 30, 0.7% between 31 and 35, and 1.7% between 36 and 40. The survey for weekly evaluations received 218 responses from 85 students while only 52 students participated in the final evaluation.

5.3 Data Analysis and Results of Study 2

The average SUS score for the set of visualizations was 60.1. The obtained results for the usability were found to be lower than in the user study 1, namely 2.5 on average on a 5-point Likert scale. The reason for that can potentially be attributed to the profile of the students having little or no knowledge about information visualization techniques.The perceived differences of students' affective states with respect to the mean of the classroom based on the visualizations and the real differences in students' affective states with respect to the mean of the classroom was tested using the Pearson correlation with $N = 34$, which resulted in the following findings: frustration ($r = 0.634$, $p = 0.000$), confusion ($r = 0.620$, $p = 0.000$), boredom ($r = 0.551$, $p = 0.000$), happiness ($r = 0.684$, $p = 0.000$), motivation ($r = 0.829$, $p = 0.000$) and time dedication ($r = 0.374$, $p = 0.040$). For all the relationships, a significant correlation was found ($r > 0.5$), with the exception of the time dedication. This suggests that in general students were able to correctly interpret the provided visualizations. However, there is also a room for improvement of the interpretability of visualizations as suggested by moderate coefficient values.

Interview comments were very heterogeneous in the second user study. Some students valued the affective state per activity as more useful. *"I liked the states per activity the most. After that will go the timeline, followed by the heat map. Finally the scatter plots."*. Other students considered the timeline the most useful: *"The timeline is easiest to interpret, since it is in a form I am used to and since it doesn't contain that much data at the same time, which the others do. Especially the heat map and scatter plot are containing too much detailed and deviating information, which makes it hard to get an overview. The emotion per activity is okay, but also not readable very easily, because some coloured areas are very small and it is not always clear which colour is represented at what place of the grey line."* For others the combination of data and design used in complex visualizations such as the heat map were perceived as more useful.

6 Discussion and Future Work

This study addresses the lack of empirical studies for evaluating different visualizations with regard to their capabilty to support emotion awareness in learning environments. The results of study 1 indicate that the visualizations are easy to use for students with knowledge of visualization techniques. A SUS score of 72.5

can generally be assessed as very positive [5]. The same results could not be confirmed by user study 2, but the usability results were still found to be acceptable as the average SUS score of 60.1 in this user study still reflect positive beliefs. Since students participating in the second study had little or no knowledge of information visualization techniques, the results could potentially be attributed to difficulties with using/interpreting the visualizations. Insight was measured by correlations between the actual data meaning and student perceptions. In addition, we measured how well students were able to interpret the visualizations with the use of objective questions. All the correlations were significant with more than 0.5 but less than 0.7. This suggests that, in many occasions, students were able to correctly interpret the provided visualizations.

Students were highly aware of the difference betweeen their real affective states and the mean of the classroom, their most frequent emotions along their learning project, the activity that frustrated them the most and the relationship between their time dedication and boredeom. They were less aware about their time dedication, the activity that motivated them the most and differences with peers. Simpler techniques such as timeline visualization resulted in higher positive perceptions than more complex techniques such as heatmap or radial visualizations.

While students in the user study 1 showed interest in more detailed data about individual students, the representation of such data remains a challenge. Evaluation results of user study 2 indicate that there were some difficulties in interpreting more complex visualizations by users with no background in information vesualizations. The differences between students with knowledge about visualizations and those without knowledge about visualizations suggest that the fact of having knowledge about visualizations might have an influence on the usability, perceived usefulness and insight.

Despite the positive results, some limitations of our studies should be also articulated. First and foremost, in contrast to our earlier work [17,19], data collection was performed in a manual way in both user studies, thus the accuracy of affective states could be subject to subjective judgments of students. In this paper, we focus on visualization aspects by evaluating representation of such data with different visualization techniques. While manual data acquisition works to evaluate the visualizations based on real student data provided by a student, the acquisition process may also have an influence on perceived usefulness and interpretation of data. Second, the evaluation is limited to perceived usefulness and insight, and does not provide any insight related to potential impact on learning improvements.

In summary, the evaluation presented in this paper suggests that usability of the proposed dashboards both in terms of perceived usefulness and insight was acceptable (SUS scores and comparative correlations above average), thus showing the potential of visualizations to support students awareness of affective information and reflection. Students showed particular interest in visualizations positioning their emotion-related information with respect to their peers in the context of different learning activities. The simpler techniques seemed to offer the highest potential with respect to usability. However, the results also suggest that visualizations need to be designed with care to address the needs of students. More research will be needed to examine further improvements needs in the domain of affective visualizations and their effects on learning processes.

Our future work will focus on more generic representations to enable use by a general audience. Initial modifications will be based on the feedback received during the interviews. The ultimate goal is the inclusion of affective visualizations in the context of learning process analytics [25,26,29] and educational dashboards for generic learning goals that will be expanded with textual feedback [27,28]. Such a feedback will support timely teacher interventions and learner self-regulation (councious change in behaviour) for the emotional context of learning (e.g. with respect to motivations, engagement, etc.) and thus improved learning outcomes.

Acknowledgements. This work is partially supported by the eMadrid project (funded by the Regional Government of Madrid) under grant no S2013/ICE-2715, the Commin project (funded by the Spanish Ministry of Economy and Competitiveness) under grant no IPT-2012-0883-430000 and the RESET project (Ministry of Economy and Competiveness) under grant RESET TIN2014-53199-C3-1-R. The research has been partially financed by the SURF Foundation of the Netherlands and the KU Leuven Research Council (grant agreement no. C24/16/017).

References

1. Ali, L., Hatala, M., Gašević, D., Jovanović, J.: A qualitative evaluation of evolution of a learning analytics tool. Comput. Educ. **58**(1), 470–489 (2012)
2. Ashkanasy, N.M., Dasborough, M.T.: Emotional awareness and emotional intelligence in leadership teaching. J. Educ. Bus. **79**(1), 18–22 (2003)
3. Azcarraga, J., Marcos, N., Suarez, M.T.: Modelling EEG signals for the prediction of academic emotions. In: Workshop on Utilizing EEG Input in Intelligent Tutoring Systems (2014)
4. Baker, R.S., D'Mello, S.K., Rodrigo, M.T., Graesser, A.C.: Better to be frustrated than bored: The incidence, persistence, and impact of learners cognitive affective states during interactions with three different computer-based learning environments. Int. J. Hum. Comput. Stud. **68**(4), 223–241 (2010)
5. Bangor, A., Kortum, P.T., Miller, J.T.: An empirical evaluation of the system usability scale. Intl. J. Hum.-Comput. Interact. **24**(6), 574–594 (2008)
6. Brooke, J.: Sus-a quick and dirty usability scale. Usability Eval. Ind. **189**, 194 (1996)
7. Burleson, W.: Aective Learning Companions: strategies for empathetic agents with realtime multimodal affective sensing to foster meta-cognitive and meta-affective approaches to learning, motivation, and perseverance. Ph.D. thesis, Massachusetts Institute of Technology (2006)
8. Craig, S., Graesser, A., Sullins, J., Gholson, B.: Affect and learning: an exploratory look into the role of affect in learning with autotutor. J. Educ. Media **29**(3), 241–250 (2004)
9. DMello, S.: Monitoring affective trajectories during complex learning. In: Seel, N.M. (ed.) Encyclopedia of the Sciences of Learning, pp. 2325–2328. Springer, New York (2012)

10. D'Mello, S., Picard, R., Graesser, A.: Towards an affect-sensitive autotutor. IEEE Intell. Syst. **22**(4), 53–61 (2007)
11. D'Mello, S.K., Craig, S.D., Sullins, J., Graesser, A.C.: Predicting affective states expressed through an emote-aloud procedure from autotutor's mixed-initiative dialogue. Int. J. Artif. Intell. Educ. **16**(1), 3–28 (2006)
12. Friesen, E., Ekman, P.: Facial action coding system: a technique for the measurement of facial movement, Palo Alto (1978)
13. GhasemAghaei, R., Arya, A., Biddle, R.: A dashboard for affective e-learning: data visualization for monitoring online learner emotions. In: EdMedia: World Conference on Educational Media and Technology, vol. 2016, pp. 1536–1543 (2016)
14. Govaerts, S., Verbert, K., Duval, E., Pardo, A.: The student activity meter for awareness and self-reflection. In: CHI 2012 Extended Abstracts on Human Factors in Computing Systems, pp. 869–884. ACM (2012)
15. Jaques, P.A., Vicari, R.M.: A BDI approach to infer students emotions in an intelligent learning environment. Comput. Educ. **49**(2), 360–384 (2007)
16. Kort, B., Reilly, R., Picard, R.W.: An affective model of interplay between emotions and learning: reengineering educational pedagogy-building a learning companion. In: ICALT, vol. 1, pp. 43–47 (2001)
17. Leony, D., Muñoz-Merino, P.J., Pardo, A., Delgado Kloos, C.: Modelo basado en hmm para la deteccin de emociones a partir de interacciones durante el aprendizaje de desarrollo de software. In: XI Jornadas de Ingeniera Telemtica (2013)
18. Leony, D., Muñoz-Merino, P.J., Pardo, A., Delgado Kloos, C.: Provision of awareness of learners' emotions through visualizations in a computer interaction-based environment. Expert Syst. Appl. **40**, 5093–5100 (2013)
19. Leony, D., Muñoz-Merino, P.J., Pardo, A., Ruiperez-Valiente, J., Arellano Martin-Caro, D., Delgado Kloos, C.: Detection and evaluation of emotions in massive open online courses. J. Univ. Comput. Sci. **21**(5), 638–655 (2015)
20. Leony, D., Parada Gélvez, H.A., Muñoz-Merino, P.J., Pardo, A., Delgado Kloos, C.: A generic architecture for emotion-based recommender systems in cloud learning environments. J. Univ. Comput. Sci. **19**(14), 2075–2092 (2013)
21. Muñoz-Merino, P.J., Fernández Molina, M., Muñoz Organero, M., Delgado Kloos, C.: Motivation and emotions in competition systems for education: an empirical study. IEEE Trans. Educ. **57**(3), 182–187 (2014)
22. North, C.: Toward measuring visualization insight. IEEE Comput. Graph. Appl. **26**(3), 6–9 (2006)
23. Pardos, Z.A., Baker, R.S.J.D., San Pedro, M.O.C.Z., Gowda, S.M., Gowda, S.M.: Affective states and state tests: investigating how affect throughout the school year predicts end of year learning outcomes. In: Proceedings of the Third International Conference on Learning Analytics and Knowledge, LAK 2013, pp. 117–124. ACM, New York (2013)
24. Santos, J.L., Verbert, K., Govaerts, S., Duval, E.: Addressing learner issues with stepup!: an evaluation. In: Proceedings of the Third International Conference on Learning Analytics and Knowledge, pp. 14–22. ACM (2013)
25. Sedrakyan, G.: Process-oriented feedback perspectives based on feedback-enabled simulation and learning process data analytics. Ph.D. thesis (2016)
26. Sedrakyan, G., De Weerdt, J., Snoeck, M.: Process-mining enabled feedback: tell me what i did wrong vs. tell me how to do it right. Comput. Hum. Behav. **57**, 352–376 (2016)
27. Sedrakyan, G., Järvelä, S., Kirschner, P.: Conceptual framework for feedback automation and personalization for designing learning analytics dashboards. In: Conference EARLI SIG 27, Online Measures of Learning Processes (2016)

28. Sedrakyan, G., Malmberg, J., Noroozi, O., Verbert, K., Järvelä, S., Kirschner, P.: Designing a learning analytics dashboard for feedback to support learning regulation (2017, submitted)
29. Sedrakyan, G., Snoeck, M., De Weerdt, J.: Process mining analysis of conceptual modeling behavior of novices-empirical study using jmermaid modeling and experimental logging environment. Comput. Hum. Behav. **41**, 486–503 (2014)
30. Trigwell, K., Ellis, R.A., Han, F.: Relations between students' approaches to learning, experienced emotions and outcomes of learning. Stud. High. Educ. **37**(7), 811–824 (2012)
31. Verbert, K., Duval, E., Klerkx, J., Govaerts, S., Santos, J.L.: Learning analytics dashboard applications. Am. Behav. Sci. **57**(10), 1500–1509 (2013)
32. Verbert, K., Govaerts, S., Duval, E., Santos, J., Van Assche, F., Parra, G., Klerkx, J.: Learning dashboards: an overview and future research opportunities. Pers. Ubiquit. Comput. **18**(6), 1499–1514 (2014)

Looking THROUGH versus Looking AT: A Strong Concept in Technology Enhanced Learning

Kshitij Sharma[1,2], Hamed S. Alavi[1,3(✉)], Patrick Jermann[1], and Pierre Dillenbourg[1]

[1] École Polytechnique Fédérale de Lausanne, Lausanne, Switzerland
[2] Faculty of Business and Economics, University of Lausanne, Lausanne, Switzerland
[3] Human-IST Research Center, University of Fribourg, Fribourg, Switzerland
hamed.alavi@unifr.ch

Abstract. When watching an educational video, our eyes look for relevant information related to the topic that is being explained at that particular moment. Studying the learners' gaze behavior and particularly how it correlates with their performance, we have found a series of results, which converge to an understanding about learner behavior that is more abstracted than the use situation or the studied learning contexts. In this contribution we present "Looking Through vs. Looking At" as a generative intermediate-level body of knowledge, and show how it can construct a Strong Concept (as developed by Höök [10]) in technology enhanced learning (TEL). "Looking At", simply put, refers to missing the relevant information because of either looking at the incorrect place or lagging behind the teacher in time. "Looking Through", on the other hand, is the success in finding the relevant displayed information at the right moment such that the communication, through verbal and visual channels, becomes synchronous. The visual medium becomes transparent and the learning experience shifts from interacting with the material to interacting with the teacher. We define formally and show how to quantify the proposed strong concept in dyadic interaction scenarios. This concept is applicable to MOOC video interaction, but also to other learning scenarios such as (collaborative) problem solving. We put a particular emphasis on the generative aspect of the concept and demonstrate, with examples, how it can help designing solutions for interactive learning situations.

Keywords: Eye-tracking · Dual eye-tracking · Collaborative learning · Computer supported collaborative learning · CSCL · Strong concepts · MOOCs · Collaborative problem solving · Video based learning · Strong TEL Concepts

1 Introduction

The retrospective analysis of gaze patterns has proved that it can contribute to understanding the users' behavior, contextual expertise, and cognitive processes

É. Lavoué et al. (Eds.): EC-TEL 2017, LNCS 10474, pp. 238–253, 2017.
DOI: 10.1007/978-3-319-66610-5_18

(for details see [18]). The challenge, however, manifests itself in making sense out of the gaze data and relate eye movement patterns to the task-related cognitive activity. Typically, following three approaches address this issue [11]:

1. **Top-down based on a cognitive theory:** Grounded in predefined high-level theories that relate eye movements to cognitive activity, the researcher interprets different gaze behaviors and relates them to the learning context.
2. **Top-down based on a design hypothesis:** This is similar to the first method, with two differences. First, the interpretation is based on a hypothesis that might not be fully established. Second, the hypothesis is specific to a learning scenario, which is created and used to validate hypotheses that are context-specific and produce knowledge at the scope of of the studied scenarios.
3. **Bottom-up:** The analysis begins with detecting interesting eye movements patterns, followed up by an attempt to uncover the meanings and to conjecture possible reasons.

This contribution builds on a series of eye-tracking studies which individually fall in the second category, but together push its boundaries *upward* (i.e. first method). More precisely, we use the results of these studies to construct knowledge that is more abstracted than instances and is applicable across a class of learning contexts, though does not reach the generalisability of cognitive theories.

We present four eye-tracking studies that while vary in terms of learning practice and design intervention, draw congruent conclusions, suggesting a particular learning behavior pattern. In Interaction Design terms, this pattern translates to an intermediate-level body of knowledge known as "Strong Concept" [10]. Höök [10] proposes that a strong concept sits between the general theories and the specific instances. It is particularly generative in the sense that it can be appropriated to be used in the design of new interactive solutions, and in the practice of design-oriented research. Furthermore, the TEL research community has recently begun to adopt the notion of Strong Concept and develop it in the context of technology-enhanced learning design, titled as "Strong TEL Concepts" [15].

The source of the strong concept that we propose is the user-studies that instantiate a specific theory of learning behavior, and its application extends to the scope of design for collaborative learning and learning at distance.

In the course of the following sections, we describe a set of studies whose results merge into an intermediary body of knowledge (Sects. 3–6). Then we elaborate on its connections to the high-level theories (Sect. 9) and the other related intermediary bodies of knowledge (Sect. 8). In Strong Concept terminology, the former is known as "Vertical Grounding" and the latter as "Horizontal Grounding".

2 Formal Definitions

This section sketches a formalization for the essential elements and concepts that we will use to describe our strong concept.

Shared Visual Content: is a composition of pieces of information arranged on a screen in a way that does not require reading in a specific ordering.

The receiver: Is the person who "reads" the shared visual content, by looking at the displayed information that is supported by a verbal communication channel.

The transmitter: Is the person who uses the shared visual content to send a particular message. She might enrich the communication by using other channels such as dialogue.

Perceptual with-me-ness: Is the extent to which the receiver succeeds in following the transmitter's explicit deictic gestures. In Sect. 5, we show how this metric is quantified.

Conceptual with-me-ness: Is the extent to which the receiver succeeds in following the content that is being explained through other channels such as dialogue. In Sect. 5, we show how this metric is quantified.

Gaze similarity: In a collaborative learning context, gaze similarity is the extent to which the collaborating partners (transmitters and receivers) look at the similar set of objects in the same temporal window. In Sect. 3, we show how this metric is quantified.

Looking through: In a context where at least one receiver and one transmitter, for a common purpose, use a shared visual content, the receiver *looks through* the shared artifact if she, with her eyes, follows the content that is being explained by the transmitter. In other words, the receiver can look through the artifact and communicate with the transmitter if she has similar gaze patterns as that of the transmitter, with a small time lag. Looking through entails high perceptual and conceptual with-me-ness or high gaze similarity. In Sects. 3 and 4 we describe design instances that use high gaze similarity as indicatives of "looking through".

Looking at: Defined as the opposite of looking through, it refers to the situation where the receiver fails (or decides not) to follow the transmitter. In this scenario, the receiver interacts only with the artifact and the transmitter's remote presence remains only marginally relevant. In Sects. 5 and 6, we describe design instances that use high with-me-ness as indicative of "looking at".

We would like to point out that we restricted ourselves from calling shared visual content as learning material, receiver as learner, and transmitter as teacher. The reason is that in collaborative learning scenarios these roles (learner, teacher) are not statically identifiable. In the next four sections, we very briefly describe four eye-tracking experiments that we designed to study particular learning practices, the results of which have created the bases for our proposed strong concept; and we refer to them as "Design Instance" 1–4.

3 Design Instance I: Collaborative Program Comprehension

Pair programming is a method by which the two co-located programmers share a display while performing various programming tasks [20]. We take pair programming as a special case of collaborative learning, a process that involves coordination between participants and the construction of shared understanding. Pair programming is usually done with co-located programmers. However, spatially remote pair programming has been studied with satisfactory results showing that the distance factor can be neglected [3]. In this section, we present a dual eye-tracking experiment with spatially separated pair programming configuration.

3.1 Experiment

In a dual eye-tracking experiment, we asked pairs of subjects to understand and describe the rules of a game implemented as a Java program (e.g., initial situation, valid moves, winning conditions, and other rules). 82 students from École Polytechnique Fédérale de Lausanne, Switzerland, were recruited to participate in the study. The participants were paired into 40 dyads irrespective of their level of expertise, gender, age or familiarity. The participants' gaze was recorded with two synchronised Tobii 1750 eye-trackers at 50 Hz. The eye-trackers were placed back to back and separated from each other by a wooden wall (Fig. 1).

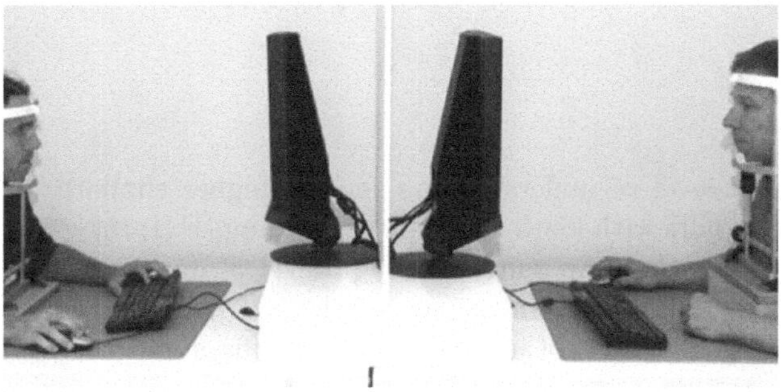

Fig. 1. The setup for the dual eye-tracking experiments, where the participants are separated by a wooden wall. They could not see each other, but they were asked to discuss with each other and the two screens were completely synchronized.

3.2 Dependent Variable

Level of Understanding: We distinguished between two levels of understanding based on how well the pair performed the task. Pairs with high level of understanding are those who described correctly and completely the rules of the game including initial situation, valid moves, and winning conditions.

3.3 Process Variables

Gaze Similarity: The program is comprised of tokens. For example, a line of code "location = array [c] ;" contains 13 tokens (location, c, = , array, ; , 2 brackets and 6 spaces). Fixations on the individual tokens were detected using a probabilistic model (for details see [14,19]). We computed the proportion of time spent on the different tokens. In order to characterise the individual visual focus, we computed the "token density vector" over a given time window. This vector is computed by aggregating gaze data over a 10-second time window and we computed the amount of gaze time that was accumulated for each token. Next, for each 10-second window, we defined the pair's visual focus coupling (Fig. 2) as the *similarity* between the tokens looked at by the two subjects. We quantified this coupling using the cosine between the two token density vectors.

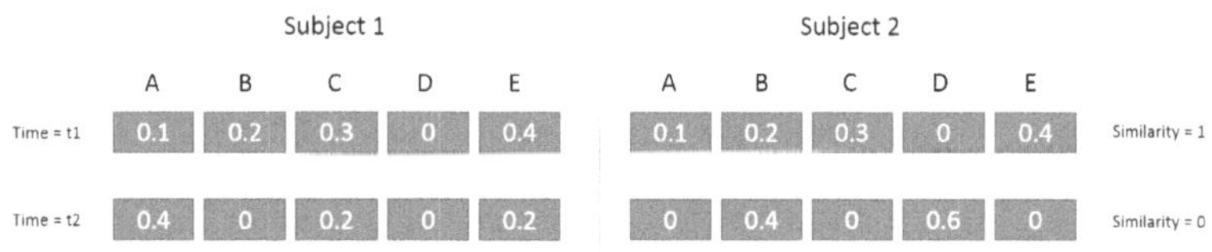

Fig. 2. A typical example of computing gaze similarity for a pair. The letters are symbolic semantic tokens. The numbers inside the boxes represent the proportion of the time window spent on the respective semantic tokens. We show the two extreme cases with highest an lowest possible values of gaze similarity.

3.4 Result

Pairs with high level of understanding showed higher similarity in their gaze behaviour than pairs with low level of understanding ($F[1,15] = 7.580, p = 0.01$). This demonstrates that the pairs with high level of understanding spent more time looking together at the similar parts of the program. This could have helped them to attain a high level of mutual understanding about the program's functionality.

3.5 Summary

In this experiment, both peers played receiver and transmitter, during the collaboration. The shared visual content was a program and the task was to make a correct mutual understanding of what the program does. The results show that the synchrony between the gaze patterns of the receiver and the transmitter was indicative of the the collaboration outcome. Here, the pair's gaze similarity depicts the behaviour which exemplifies "looking through".

4 Design Instance II: Collaborative Concept Map

In this experiment we describe a collaborative concept mapping experiment which differs from collaborative learning task (described in the last section) in two aspects. First, in terms of cognitive processing required: collaborative program understanding is based on mutual understanding built upon what the pair learns from the program; on the other hand, while creating a collaborative concept map the peers use already learnt content to synthesise the understanding of the content in a collaborative manner. Second, in terms of the eye-tracking stimulus: a program is textual and static, while the shape and size of a concept map changes over time as peers keep on adding new concepts and relations between various concepts during the course of the task.

4.1 Experiment

In a dual eye-tracking experiment, we asked pairs of subjects to collaboratively create a concept map about "resting membrane potential". Before collaborating on the concept map, the peers watched a "Khan Academy" video about the same topic individually. Before the video and after the collaborative task, they took a multiple choice pretest and posttest. 98 students from École Polytechnique Fédérale de Lausanne, Switzerland, were recruited to participate in the study. The participants were paired into 49 dyads irrespective of their level of expertise, gender, or age. The participants' gaze was recorded with two synchronised SMI RED eye-trackers at 250 Hz. The physical setup of the experiment was similar to that of the first experiment (Sect. 3, Fig. 1).

4.2 Dependent Variable

Learning Gain: We computed the learning gain as the difference between the pretest and the posttest scores. The minimum and maximum for each test were 0 and 10.

4.3 Process Variables

Gaze Similarity: It was calculated using the same procedure as described in Sect. 3.

4.4 Results

We observed a significant positive correlation between the gaze similarity and the average learning gain of the pairs ($R^2 = 0.34, F(1,1) = 17.23, p < .001$). The pairs that had higher gaze similarity also had higher average learning.

4.5 Summary

In this experiment, both peers played receiver and transmitter, during the collaboration. The shared visual content was a concept map being created and the task was to make a correct mutual understanding of how to best represent the learnt material. The results show that the synchrony between the gaze patterns of the receiver and the transmitter was indicative of the learning gain. Here, the pair's gaze similarity depicts the behaviour which exemplifies "looking through".

5 Design Instance III: MOOC-1

Massive open online courses (MOOCs) are online learning resources with the following features: (a) massive unlimited number of participants as opposed to relatively smaller number in distance learning; (b) the courses are designed to be open to global audience, with none to a few prerequisites for participants and no participation fees; (c) the courses are designed to be conducted strictly online and location-independent.

5.1 Experiment

In this experiment, the participants watched two MOOC videos from the course "Functional Programming Principles in Scala" and answered programming questions after each video. Participants' gaze was recorded, using SMI RED 250 eye-trackers at 250 Hz, while they were watching the videos. The participants were not given controls over the video for two reasons. First, the eye-tracking stimulus for every participant was the same which facilitated the same kind of analysis for each participant. Second, the "time on task" remained the same for every participant. 40 university students from École Polytechnique Fédérale de Lausanne, Switzerland, participated in the experiment. The only criterion for selecting participants was that they took the Java course in the previous semester.

5.2 Dependent Variable

Posttest Score: After each video the learners answered programming questions based on the video content. The score for these questionnaires was the dependent variable for this experiment.

5.3 Process Variable

With-me-ness: With-me-ness is defined at two levels: perceptual and conceptual. There are two ways a teacher may refer to an object: with deictic gestures, generally accompanied by words ("here", "this variable") or only by verbal references ("the counter", "the sum"). Deictic references were recorded using two cameras during MOOC recording: first, that captured the teacher's face; and

second, above the writing surface, that captured the hand movements. In some MOOCs, the hand is not visible but teacher used a digital pen whose traces on the display (underlining a word, circling an object, adding an arrow) act as a deictic gestures.
Perceptual with-me-ness measures if the students looked at the items referred to by the teacher through deictic acts. It is defined as combination of three components.

- *Entry time* is the temporal lag between the time a referring pointer appeared on the screen and stops at the referred site (x,y); and the time student first looked at (x,y).
- *First fixation duration* is how long the student's gaze stopped at the referred site for the first time.
- *Revisits* are the number of times the student's gaze came back to the referred site.

Conceptual With-me-ness measures how often a student looked at the object (or the set of objects) verbally referred to by the teacher during the whole course of time (the complete video duration). In order to have a consistent measure of conceptual with-me-ness, we normalised the time a student looked at the overlapping content (the verbal reference and the slide content) by slide duration.

5.4 Results

We observed significant correlations between the two levels of with-me-ness and the posttest score. The details are as follows:
Perceptual With-me-ness [Entry time]: We observed no correlation between entry time and the posttest score ($r(40) = 0.1, p > 0.5$). This can be explained using the saliency of the teacher's pointer. When a moving object appears on the screen, it constituted a salient visual feature to which gaze was always attracted. This attraction did not reflect a deeper cognitive process and this is probably why it was not predictive of learning.
Perceptual With-me-ness [First fixation duration]: We observed a significant correlation between the posttest score and the first fixation duration ($r(40) = 0.35, p < .05$). The students who scored high in the posttest paid more attention to the teacher's pointers. This behaviour is indicative of more attention during the moments of deictic references.
Perceptual With-me-ness [Number of revisits]: We observed a significant correlation between the posttest score and the number of times the students looked at the referred site ($r(40) = 0.31, p < .05$). Students who scored high in the posttest came back to the referred sites more often than the students who scored less in the posttest. Having more revisits also resulted in having more fixations and thus more aggregated fixation duration as well. The revisiting behaviour indicates rereading. Moreover, having more overall fixation duration on the referred sites indicated more reading time.
Conceptual with-me-ness: We observed a significant correlation between the

posttest score and the time spent by the student following teachers' dialogues on the content of the slide ($r(40) = 0.36, p < .05$). The students who scored high in the posttest were paying more attention to the teacher's dialogue. This behaviour was indicative of more attention during the whole video lecture.

5.5 Summary

In this experiment the students are the receivers; the teacher is the transmitter; the shared visual content is the course's slides; and the task for students is to understand the video content. The results show that the synchrony between the eye movement patterns of the receiver and the visual deixis and dialogue of the transmitter is indicative for the learning outcome. Here, the students' high with-me-ness (both perceptual and conceptual) depicts the behaviour which exemplifies "looking through", whereas the students' low with-me-ness exemplifies "looking at".

6 Design Instance IV: MOOC-2

In the experiment described in Sect. 5, the participants could neither pause the video nor they could navigate back and forward in the video timeline. This restricted the ecological validity of the experiment. Moreover, the slides of the video lecture were textual. However, the experiment served as a "proof of concept" that we can measure learners' attention while they watch a lecture video and this measure of attention ("with-me-ness") was correlated with the learning gain. In order to validate the positive correlation between the "with-me-ness" and the learning gain in a more ecologically valid settings, we conducted another eye-tracking experiment with video lectures.

6.1 Experiment

There were 98 students from École Polytechnique Fédérale de Lausanne, Switzerland, participating in the present study. The participants took a pretest about the video content. Then they watched two videos about "resting membrane potential". Finally, they took a posttest. The videos were taken from "Khan Academy". The total length of the videos was 17 min and 5 s. While watching the videos, the participants had full control over the video player. They had no time constraint to finish the videos. The video slides were a mixture of both textual and schematic contents. Both the pretest and the posttest had questions where the participants had to indicate whether a given statement was either true or false. Participants' gaze was recorded, using SMI RED 250 eye-trackers at 250 Hz, while they were watching the videos.

6.2 Dependent Variable

Learning gain: The learning gain was calculated simply as the difference between the individual pretest and posttest scores. The minimum and maximum for each test were 0 and 10.

6.3 Process Variable

With-me-ness: It was calculated using the same procedure as described in Sect. 5.

6.4 Results

Both components of with-me-ness were significantly correlated with the learning gain. We observed a significant positive correlation between the perceptual with-me-ness and the learning gain ($R^2 = 0.21, F(6.17, 7.30) = 3.85, p < .001,$). The participants who had high perceptual with-me-ness, also had high learning gain. We also observed a significant positive correlation between the conceptual with-me-ness and the learning gain ($R^2 = 0.06, F(1, 1) = 6.43, p < .05$). The participants with high conceptual with-me-ness, had high learning gain.

6.5 Summary

In this experiment, the students are the receivers; the teacher is the transmitter; the shared visual content is the course's slides; and the task for students is to understand the video content. The results show, the synchrony between the eye movement patterns of the receiver and the visual deixis and dialogue of the transmitter is indicative of the learning gain, and exemplifies looking either "through" the video.

7 Looking THROUGH vs. Looking AT

From the presented studies, what emerged is a body of understanding that, we argue here, embodies a strong concept. The quality of communication, in the learning situations, highly depends on the coordinated movements of the participants' eyes. The more synchronized are the gaze patterns of the receiver and the transmitter, the higher is the learning gain.

The difference between the coordinated and uncoordinated eye movements suggests two distinct interaction styles:

- Some receivers "looked at" the stimulus as we look at a magazine. They interact primarily with the content only, very often because they lag in following the transmitter.
- Some receivers established a synchronous communication with the transmitter, by "looking through" the shared visual content. In this case the stimulus becomes only a support for gaining a deeper engagement, and hence a better quality and output of communication, as opposed to the stimulus being the main focus of interaction.

The concepts of "looking through" and "looking at" could be seen as new set of interaction style categories. "Looking at" the interface/display indicates that the learner is engaged with the material only, which is presented to her. "Looking through" the interface/display indicates that the learner is engaged with the peer. The peer in the MOOC experiments is the teacher and in the collaborative concept map/pair programming is the collaborating partner.

In order not to be misunderstood, we would like to mention that togetherness does not always lead to higher performance, for example in situations such as brain storming sessions, collaborative visual search, or when the verbal communication channel has a high level of abstraction. However, in the contexts where the togetherness is hypothesized that it can lead to higher performance, the presented studies suggest that through similar quantitative methods one can study and even improve the gaze-togetherness and hence the learning gains.

8 Related Works (Horizontal Grounding)

This section relates the proposed strong concept to some of the similar concepts in the domains of educational technologies. The key idea is to connect "looking through" and "looking at" with other concepts that are based upon the synchrony in collaborative as well as in pseudo-cooperative settings. We give a few examples where a specific kind of information was provided/collected to support/analyze the quality/outcome of collaboration.

In the context of classroom lecturing Raca and colleagues studied students' body posture and head motion metrics, using computer vision algorithms. They showed that the direct synchrony between the student's head motion and the teachers' movement has positive correlation with the level of reported attention. Moreover, he found correlation between level of students' attention and indirect-synchrony, that is, the extent to which one student's head motions follow the others' [16] .

Alavi and colleagues [1] created an ambient awareness tool to increase togetherness in university lab sessions, that is, when students in teams, work on a set of exercises while receiving on-demand help from the tutors. In this setting every team has an interactive lamp on their study desk that shows which exercise the team is currently working on. Their studies showed that merely having a shared object, that displays the status of the whole group, could encourage students to work more synchronously within their group; and thus increase the quality and throughput of collaboration.

Richardson and colleagues [17] proposed the *eye-eye span* as the difference between the time when the speakers started looking at the referred object and the time when listeners looked at it. In a dual eye-tracking experiment, the authors [17] asked one of the participants in each pair to narrate the relationship between the characters in the TV series Friends to the other participant in the pair. The authors measured the time lag between the speakers looking and referring at a specific actor and the listeners looking at the same actor. This time lag was termed as the "cross-recurrence" between the participants. The results showed that the cross-recurrence was correlated with the correctness of the answers given by the listeners in a comprehension quiz. The average cross-recurrence was found to be between 1200 and 1400 ms. This time was consistent with the additions of *eye-voice* span [9] and *voice-eye* span [2].

Jermann and Nüssli [12] extended the concept of cross-recurrence in a pair programming task, by enabling remote collaborators to share their selections on the screen. The authors found the similar levels of cross-recurrence as it was found by Richardson et. al. [17]. The participants in this dual eye-tracking experiment were asked to collaboratively understand a JAVA program of about 200 lines of code. The selections made by one participant in each pair were also shown to the other participant in the pair. The authors [12] found that the cross-recurrence levels were higher when there was a selection present on the screen than the times when there were no selections. Furthermore, the cross-recurrence levels were correlated to the quality of collaboration [12].

Duchowski [5] compared three modalities of assisting a referee's deictic references to his partner in a virtual collaborative environment. The three assisting cues were: head rotation, head and eye rotation, head and eye rotation with the light-spot over the target. Participants were asked to verbally identify the target selected by the referee. The authors concluded that the reference disambiguation is fastest when the light-spot was shown along with the head and eye rotations.

Cherubini and colleagues [4] explored the relation between the ability to explicitly refer at something in a collaborative map annotation task, and the success in the task. Participants were asked to plan a music festival around a university campus by annotating a map with parking spots, places for drinks and stages. The participants were given a chat tool. The chat application had two modalities, (1) the participants could link the places they were talking about in the map with what they wrote in the chat; (2) there was no such facility. The results showed that with the explicit referencing enabled the pairs were faster in completing the task; and they had more concrete references in terms of message length, compared to the modality without the facility of explicit referencing.

The first three studies ([1,16,17]) show that the "togetherness" was correlated with the outcome and the quality of collaboration. The last three studies

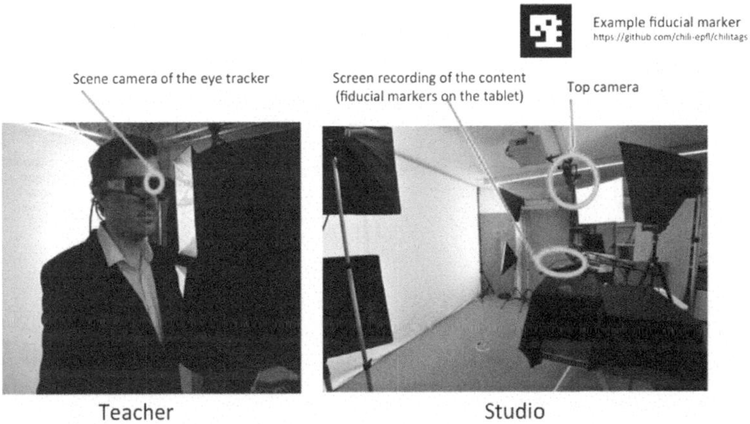

Fig. 3. The setup for recording the teacher's gaze while he was recording the MOOC content.

([4,5,12]) shows that by providing the collaborating partners with tools that help them in "being together" one can have a positive effect on the quality of collaboration.

9 Vertical Grounding

In this section, we show how the proposed strong concept can add to the high level theories of cognition and communication (i.e. upward vertical grounding); and how the idea can be implemented in other design instances (i.e. downward vertical grounding).

9.1 Upward Vertical Grounding

There are two major information processing strategies, to build up the understanding of the visual content: top-down [8] and bottom-up [7]. In the bottom-up strategy, the gaze of the receiver is driven by the displayed content, while in the top-down strategy the gaze is driven by cognition, prior knowledge, or other factors that are external to the displayed content. "Looking through" is an exemplar behavior for top-down approach, where the gaze of the receiver is driven by the explicit visual deixis and/or the dialogue of the transmitter. On the other hand, "looking at" is an example for the bottom-up approach, where the gaze of the receiver is driven mostly by the displayed content. By introducing this perspective to the theory of visual cognition, we provide a generic and concrete method to quantify different information processing strategies.

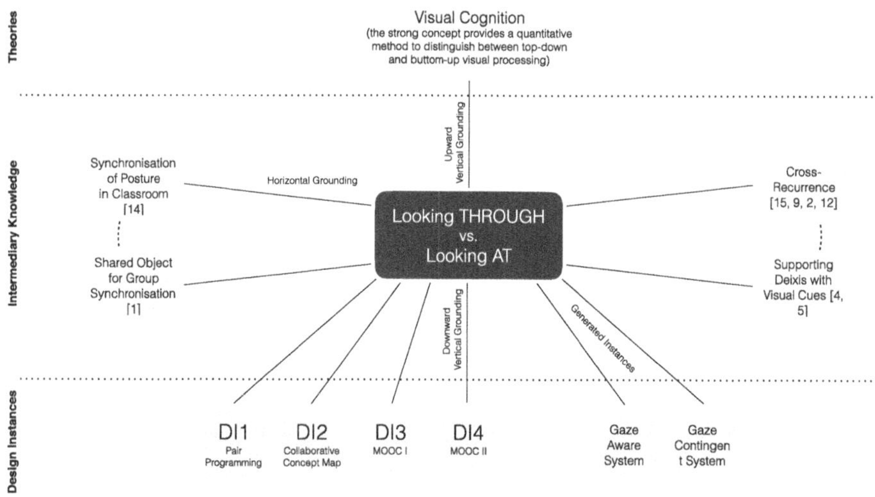

Fig. 4. Looking THROUGH versus looking AT: a TEL strong concept. The different relations of the proposed strong concepts with the general theories, parallel bodies of knowledge, the learning contexts and the generated scenarios

9.2 Downward Vertical Grounding

In the following, we give two concrete examples, where the presented strong concept guided the design of TEL systems.

Gaze Aware Feedback is a tool that we designed to provide feedback to the students about their with-me-ness levels. The feedback was displayed on the screen as red rectangles circumscribing the area of the screen where the teacher was talking about. The feedback was shown only when the with-me-ness levels of participants went below a baseline. This baseline was calculated for each second of the video lecture. To calculate the baseline we took the gaze data of the participants from a previous experiment (Sect. 6). In the following this group is called "baseline group". We conducted an eye-tracking study where the participants attended a MOOC lecture while receiving the gaze aware feedback.

There were 27 students from École Polytechnique Fédérale de Lausanne, Switzerland, participating in this study. The participants took a pretest about the video content. Then they watched two videos about "resting membrane potential". Finally, they took a posttest. The videos were the same as the experiment described in Sect. 6. The participants were told that the feedback would appear only when they were not paying attention to the teacher's deixis and/or dialogues. We observed a significant improvement in learning gain for the experimental group over that for the baseline group ($t\ (df = 49.88) = -2.50$, $p = .02$).

The fact that the students had higher learning gains with the gaze-aware feedback system than those without it, suggests that the gaze-awareness made it easier for students (receivers) to maintain the synchrony with the teacher (transmitter) and "look through" the shared visual content.

Gaze Contingency is a tool that we designed to display teacher's gaze on the MOOC video and we carried out a study in order to explore its effects on the students' video interaction patterns. The teacher's gaze was captured while he was recording the MOOC video (see Fig. 3). Our prime hypothesis was that displaying the teacher's gaze on the video would facilitate reference disambiguation in highly ambiguous situations [6], and thus making students' behaviour more linear in terms of following the content (fewer pauses and fewer backward jumps). We compared students' behaviour across different videos in the weeks succeeding and preceding the week of the experimental video. We observed the following trends.

- *The proportion of the replayed length* of video was the lowest for the experimental video ($F[9, 4202] = 2.12, p = .03$).
- *The average number of pauses* was the lowest for the experimental video ($F[9, 4202] = 2.89$, $p = .002$).
- *The average number of seek backs* was the lowest for the experimental video ($F[9, 4202] = 1.92$, $p = .04$).
- *The ratio of pause time and video length* was the lowest for the experimental video ($F[9, 4202] = 2.58$, $p = .005$).

The fact that the students did not need to check back the previously told content (fewer seeking-back events) suggests that making visible the teacher's gaze made it easier (also shown by [13]) for students (receivers) to maintain the synchrony with the teacher (transmitter) and "look through" the shared visual content.

10 Conclusions

The four studies that we briefly presented in this paper produced results that together create a body of knowledge about gaze behavior in different learning scenarios. This body of knowledge, though coming out of empirical design instances, sits at a more abstracted level than the individual findings. By connecting to the similar works in the same level, to the higher level cognitive theories, and to the lower level design instances, we constructed a strong concept that is generative both in terms of completing the theories and being applicable to different technology enhanced learning problems. Figure 4 shows the different relations of the proposed strong concepts with the general theories, parallel bodies of knowledge, the learning contexts and the generated scenarios.

More experimentation will enrich the knowledge about "looking through v. looking at". For example, whether it is a binary concept or a spectrum; what is the temporal nature of the proposed strong concept; do peers switch between these two interaction styles in a single learning session; what is the relation between expertise and these interaction styles; is it possible that during different episodes of learning processes expert learners choose to "look through" or "look at".

References

1. Alavi, H.S., Dillenbourg, P.: An ambient awareness tool for supporting supervised collaborative problem solving. IEEE Trans. Learn. Technol. **5**(3), 264–274 (2012)
2. Allopenna, P.D., Magnuson, J.S., Tanenhaus, M.K.: Tracking the time course of spoken word recognition using eye movements: Evidence for continuous mapping models. J. Mem. Lang. **38**(4), 419–439 (1998)
3. Baheti, P., Williams, L., Gehringer, E., Stotts, D.: Exploring pair programming in distributed object-oriented team projects. In: Educator's Workshop, OOPSLA, pp. 4–8. Citeseer (2002)
4. Cherubini, M., Dillenbourg, P.: The effects of explicit referencing in distance problem solving over shared maps. In Proceedings of the 2007 International ACM conference on Supporting group work, pp. 331–340, ACM (2007)
5. Duchowski, A.T., Cournia, N., Cumming, B., McCallum, D., Gramopadhye, A., Greenstein, J., Sadasivan, S., Tyrrell, R.A.: Visual deictic reference in a collaborative virtual environment. In Proceedings of the 2004 Symposium on Eye Tracking Research and Applications. ACM (2004)
6. Gergle, D., Clark, A.T.: See what i'm saying?: using dyadic mobile eye tracking to study collaborative reference. In: Proceedings of the ACM 2011 Conference on Computer Supported Cooperative Work, pp. 435–444. ACM (2011)

7. Gibson, J.J.: The perception of the visual world
8. Gregory, R.L.: Perceptions as hypotheses. Philos. Trans. Royal Soc. B: Biol. Sci. **290**(1038), 181–197 (1980)
9. Griffin, Z.M., Bock, K.: What the eyes say about speaking. Psychol. Sci. **11**(4), 274–279 (2000)
10. Höök, K., Löwgren, J.: Strong concepts: Intermediate-level knowledge in interaction design research. ACM Trans. Comput. Hum. Interact. **19**(3), 23 (2012)
11. Jacob, R., Karn, K.S.: Eye tracking in human-computer interaction and usability research: Ready to deliver the promises. Mind **2**(3), 4 (2003)
12. Jermann, P., Nüssli, M.-A.: Effects of sharing text selections on gaze cross-recurrence and interaction quality in a pair programming task. In: Proceedings of the ACM 2012 Conference on Computer Supported Cooperative Work, pp. 1125–1134. ACM (2012)
13. Li, N., Kidzinski, L., Jermann, P., Dillenbourg, P.: How do in-video interactions reflect perceived video difficulty. In: The third MOOC European Stakeholders Summit, EMOOCs 2015 (2015)
14. Nüssli, M.-A.: Dual eye-tracking methods for the study of remote collaborative problem solving. École polytechnique fédérale de lausanne (2011)
15. Prieto, L.P., Alavi, H., Verma, H.: Strong technology-enhanced learning concepts. In: Accepted at the 12th European Conference on Technology Enhanced Learning (EC-TEL 2017)
16. Raca, M., Kidzinski, L., Dillenbourg, P.: Translating head motion into attention-towards processing of students body-language. In: Proceedings of the 8th International Conference on Educational Data Mining (2015)
17. Richardson, D.C., Dale, R., Kirkham, N.Z.: The art of conversation is coordination common ground and the coupling of eye movements during dialogue. Psychol. Sci. **18**(5), 407–413 (2007)
18. Sharma, K.: Gaze analysis methods for learning analytics. Ph.d. thesis, Chapter 2. École polytechnique fédérale de lausanne (2015)
19. Sharma, K., Jermann, P., Nüssli, M.-A., Dillenbourg, P.: Gaze evidence for different activities in program understanding. In: 24th Annual Conference of Psychology of Programming Interest Group (2012)
20. Williams, L.A., Kessler, R.R.: All I really need to know about pair programming I learned in kindergarten. Commun. ACM **43**(5), 108–114 (2000)

A New Theoretical Framework for Curiosity for Learning in Social Contexts

Tanmay Sinha(✉), Zhen Bai, and Justine Cassell

School of Computer Science, Carnegie Mellon University, Pittsburgh, USA
{tanmays,zhenb,justine}@cs.cmu.edu

Abstract. Curiosity is a vital metacognitive skill in educational contexts. Yet, little is known about how social factors influence curiosity in group work. We argue that curiosity is evoked not only through individual, but also interpersonal activities, and present what we believe to be the first theoretical framework that articulates an integrated sociocognitive account of curiosity based on literature spanning psychology, learning sciences and group dynamics, along with empirical observation of small-group science activity in an informal learning environment. We make a bipartite distinction between individual and interpersonal functions that contribute to curiosity, and multimodal behaviors that fulfill these functions. We validate the proposed framework by leveraging a longitudinal latent variable modeling approach. Findings confirm positive predictive relationship of the latent variables of individual and interpersonal functions on curiosity, with the interpersonal functions exercising a comparatively stronger influence. Prominent behavioral realizations of these functions are also discovered in a data-driven way. This framework is a step towards designing learning technologies that can recognize and evoke curiosity during learning in social contexts.

1 Introduction and Motivation

Curiosity pertains to the strong desire to learn or know more about something or someone, and is an important metacognitive skill to prepare students for lifelong learning [42]. Traditional accounts of curiosity in psychology and neuroscience focus on how it can be evoked via underlying mechanisms such as novelty (features of a stimulus that have not yet been encountered), surprise (violation of expectations), conceptual conflict (existence of multiple incompatible pieces of information), uncertainty (the state of being uncertain), and anticipation of new knowledge ([18,24]). These knowledge seeking experiences create positive impact on students' beliefs about their competence in mastering scientific processes, in turn promoting greater breadth and depth of information exploration [43]. These theories have inspired the development of several computer systems aiming to facilitate task performance via enhancing an individual's curiosity (e.g. [16,27,43]), simulating human-like curiosity in autonomous agents [34], and aiding in game theory development [9]. Evoking curiosity in these systems mainly focuses on directing an individual to a specific new knowledge component, followed by facilitating knowledge acquisition through exploration. Such a linear

É. Lavoué et al. (Eds.): EC-TEL 2017, LNCS 10474, pp. 254–269, 2017.
DOI: 10.1007/978-3-319-66610-5_19

approach largely ignores the how learning is influenced when working in social contexts. Here, a child's intrinsic motivation, exploratory behaviors, and subsequent learning outcomes may be informed not only by materials available to the child, but also the active work of other children, social and cultural environment, and presence of facilitators [22,35]. For example, an expression of uncertainty or of a hypothesis about a phenomenon made by one child may cause peers to realize that they too are uncertain about that phenomenon, and therefore initiate working together to overcome the cause of uncertainty, in turn positively impacting their curiosity [20]. While prior literature has extensively studied the intrapersonal origins of curiosity, there seems to be very little prior work on how social factors contribute to moment by moment changes in an individual's curiosity when learning in social contexts (except for rare exceptions such as [13] that primarily focused on coarse-grained study of adult-child interaction).

As learning in small group becomes prevalent in today's classrooms [35], it is critical to understand curiosity beyond the individual level to an integrated knowledge-seeking phenomenon shaped by social environment. Embodied Conversational Agents (ECAs) have demonstrated special capacity in supporting learning and collaborative skills for young children [7]. Knowing how social factors influence curiosity allows researchers to design ECAs and other learning technologies to support curiosity-driven learning before children naturally support each other. To address the above goal, we first propose an integrated socio-cognitive account of curiosity based on literature spanning psychology, learning sciences and group dynamics, and empirical observation of an informal learning environment. We make a bipartite distinction between putative functions that contribute to curiosity, and multimodal behaviors that fulfill these functions. These functions comprise (i) "knowledge identification and acquisition (helps humans realize that there is something they desire to know, and leads to acquisition of the desired new knowledge), and (ii) "knowledge intensification" (escalates the process of knowledge identification or acquisition by providing favorable environment, attitude etc.) - at individual and interpersonal level. Second, we perform a statistical validation of this theoretical framework to illuminate predictive relationships between multimodal behaviors, functions (latent variables because they cannot be directly observed) and ground truth curiosity (as judged by naive annotators). A longitudinal latent variable modeling approach called "continuous time structural equation model" [12] is used to explicitly account for group structure and differentiate fine-grained behavioral variations across time.

The main contributions of this work are two-fold: First, it begins to fill the research gap of how social factors, especially interpersonal peer dynamics in group work, influence curiosity. Second, the model is designed to lay a theoretical foundation to inform the design of learning technologies, a virtual peer in the current study, that employ pedagogical strategies to evoke and maintain curiosity in social environments. Findings derived from the current analyses of human-human interaction can be informative in guiding the design of human-agent interaction. Section 2 describes the putative underlying mechanisms of curiosity and associated multimodal behaviors. Section 3 discusses the study context and the annotation approach. Section 4 discusses empirical validation of the theoretical framework of curiosity, with results of the latent variable model fit to our corpus. Section 5 discusses implications and conclusions of our work.

2 Theoretical Framework Development

We initiated development of a theoretical framework for curiosity in learning in social contexts with several iterations of literature review that gradually shifted from individual- to interpersonal-level curiosity. This led us to describe: (i) a set of putative functions that contribute to curiosity, and (ii) multimodal behaviors that provide evidence for potential presence of an individual's curiosity in the current time-interval because of their fulfillment of these functions.

2.1 Putative Functions that Contribute to Curiosity

The iterative process described above led to emergence of three function groups at the individual and interpersonal level. Each of these functions can be realized in several different behavioral forms. We call the first function group **Knowledge Identification**. As curiosity arises from a strong desire to obtain new knowledge that is missing or doesn't match with one's current beliefs, a critical precondition of this desire is to realize the existence of such knowledge. At an **individual** level, knowledge identification contributes to curiosity by increasing awareness of gaps in knowledge [29], as well highlighting relationships with related or existing knowledge in order to assimilate new information [8]. Furthermore, exposure to novel and complex stimulus can raise uncertainty, subsequently resulting in conceptual conflict [4,36]. At an **interpersonal** level, knowledge identification contributes to curiosity by developing awareness of somebody else in the group having conflicting beliefs [4] and awareness of the knowledge they possess [33], so that a shared conception of the problem can be developed [5].

We call the second function group **Knowledge Acquisition**. This is because knowledge seeking behaviors driven by curiosity not only contribute to the satisfaction of the initial desire for knowledge, but also potentially lead to further identification of new knowledge. For example, question asking may help close one's knowledge gap by acquiring desired information from another group member. Depending on the response received, however, it may also lead to escalated uncertainty or conceptual conflict relating to the original question, thus consequently reinforcing curiosity. At an **individual** level, knowledge acquisition involves finding sensible explanation and new inference for facts that do not agree with existing mental schemata [8,39], and can be indexed by generation of diverse problem solving approaches [39]. It also comprises comparison with existing knowledge or search for relevant knowledge through external resources to reduce simultaneous opposing beliefs that might stem from the investigation [6]. At an **interpersonal** level, knowledge acquisition comprises revelation of uncertainties in front of group members [40], joint creation of new interpretations and ideas, engagement in argument to reduce dissonance among peers [19], and critical acceptance of what is told [40].

Finally, we call the third function group **Intensification of Knowledge Identification and Acquisition**. The intensity of curiosity, or the desire for new knowledge is influenced by factors such as the confidence required to acquire it [29], its incompatibility with existing knowledge, existence of a favorable environment [6] etc. At an **individual** level, intensification of knowledge identification and acquisition can stem from factors such as anticipation of knowledge discovery [11], interest in the topic [23], willingness to try out tasks beyond ability without fear of failure [21], taking ownership of own learning and being inclined to see knowledge as a product of human inquiry [40]. These factors can subsequently result in a state of increased pleasurable arousal [4]. At an **interpersonal** level, intensification of knowledge identification and acquisition is influenced by the willingness to get involved in group discussion and the tendency to be part of a cohesive unit [6], and can span from the spectrum of merely continuing interacting to pro-actively reacting to the information others present [5]. Various interpersonal factors play out along different portions of this spectrum. Salient ones include interest in knowing more about a group member [37], promotion of an unconditional positive and non-evaluative regard towards them [11], and awareness of one's own uncertainty being shared or considered legitimate by those peers [20], all of which can subsequently result in cooperative effort to overcome common blocking points for the group to proceed [11].

2.2 Behaviors that Fulfill Putative Functions of Curiosity

Our review of prior research in psychology and learning sciences led us to link the behaviors with their functions in evoking curiosity, and organize these behaviors into four clusters. **Cluster 1** corresponds to behaviors that enable an individual to get exposed to and investigate physical situations, which may spur socio-cognitive processes that are beneficial to curiosity-driven learning [4,8]. Examples include orientation (using eye gaze, head, torso etc.) and interacting with stimuli (for e.g. - manipulation of objects). **Cluster 2** corresponds to behaviors that enable an individual to actively make meaning out of observation and exploration [4,8,30]. Examples include idea verbalization, justification, generating hypotheses etc. **Cluster 3** corresponds to behaviors that involve joint investigation with other group members [4,8,30]. Examples include arguing, evaluating problem-solving approach of a partner (positive or negative), expressing disagreement, making suggestions, sharing findings, question asking etc. Finally, **Cluster 4** corresponds to behaviors that reveal affective states of an individual [22,31] including expressions of surprise, enjoyment, confusion, uncertainty, flow and sentiment towards task. Table 1 illustrates examples of these behavior clusters from empirical observation of informal group learning activities.

We hypothesize that behaviors across these clusters will map onto one or more putative functions of curiosity, since there can be many different functions or reasons why a communicative behavior occurs. For example, in knowledge-based conflict in group work, attending to differing responses of others compared to one's own may raise simultaneous opposing beliefs *(knowledge identification)*. This awareness might in turn activate cognitive processes, wherein

Table 1. Corpus examples of behavior sequences. P1 is the child with high curiosity

Behavior cluster	Empirical observation (Example 1)	Empirical observation (Example 2)
Cluster 1,2	**P1**: Hey let's..wait I have an idea *[idea verbalization]* **P1**: Let's see what this is, but let me just, let me just.. *[proposes joint action, co-occurs with physical demonstration, initiates joint inquiry]* **P2**: I have no idea how to do this, but it's making my brain think *[positive attitude towards task]*	**P1**: So the chain has to be like this *[idea verbalization with iconic gesture]* **P1**: How would that be? *[question asking followed by orienting towards stimulus]* **P1**: Well, I don't want it to break, so I want it to be about...no, let's say half an...half an inch *[causal reasoning to justify actions being taken]*
Cluster 1,3	**P1**: Wait we need to raise it a bit higher *[making suggestions]* **P1**: Maybe if we put it on..Umm.. this thing maybe..this is high enough? *[co-occurs with joint stimulus manipulation]* **P2**: Why? W-Why do we need to make it that high? *[disagreement and asking for evidence]*	**P2**: And the funnel can drop it into one of um..those things **P1**: If the funnel can drop it... **P1**: Okay but then..even if it hits this, then we need what is this going to hit? *[challenge]* **P1**: Here- let- just- make sure that it's going to hit it *[followed by physical demonstration/verification]*
Cluster 2,3,4	**P1**: Roll off into here and go in there *[hypothesis generation]* **P1**: Okay, so how are we going to do that? *[question asking]* **P2**: It looks like something should hit the ball *[making suggestion]*	**P2**: We could use this if we wanted *[making suggestion]* **P1**: Let's figure this quickly...so we at least have this part done *[preceded by expression of surprise and followed by trying to connect multiple objects to create a more complex object]*

an individual may seek social support for one's original belief by emphasizing its importance and validating one's idea by providing justification, or, engaging in a process of back and forth reasoning to come to a common viewpoint *(knowledge acquisition)*. Furthermore, this awareness may as well impact social and emotional processes, where an individual may perceive a conflict differently and their emotions felt and expressed might vary depending on relation with and perception of the source of conflict, for e.g., is it a friend/stranger, more competent/less competent, more cooperative/less cooperative group member that raises conflict, and therefore take the next action of resolving that conflict differently *(intensification of knowledge identification and acquisition)*. We intend to discover prominent mappings between functions described in Sect. 2.1 and behaviors described in Sect. 2.2 more formally in a data-driven way in Sect. 4.

3 Annotation of Curiosity and Multimodal Behaviors

In preparation for empirical validation of the theoretical framework of curiosity, we annotated audio and video data that was collected for 12 groups of children (aged 10–12, 3–4 children per group, 44 in total) engaged in a hands-on activity commonly used in informal learning contexts, and that is to collaboratively build a Rube Goldberg machine (RGM). A RGM includes building several chain reactions that are to be triggered automatically for trapping a ball in a cage, using simple objects. This paper describes fine-grained analyses from a convenience sample of the first 30 min (out of 35–40 min given each group), of the RGM task for half of the sample; that is, 22 children across 6 groups. Table 2 provides a summary of all coding metrics used in this study.

3.1 Ground Truth Curiosity Coding

Person perception research has demonstrated that judgments of others based on brief exposure to their behaviors is an accurate assessment of interpersonal dynamics [1]. We used Amazon's MTurk platform to obtain ground truth for curiosity via such a thin-slice approach, using the definition "curiosity is a strong desire to learn or know more about something or someone", and a rating scale comprising 0 (not curious), 1 (curious) and 2 (extremely curious). Four naive raters annotated every 10 s slice of videos of the interaction for each child presented to them in randomized order. To post-process the ratings for use, we removed those raters who used less than 1.5 standard deviation time compared to the mean time taken for all rating units (HITs). We then computed a single measure of Intraclass correlation coefficient (ICC) for each possible subset of raters for a particular HIT, and then picked ratings from the rater subset that had the best reliability for further processing. Finally, inverse-based bias correction [25] was used to account for label overuse and underuse, and to pick one single rating of curiosity for each 10 s thin-slice. The average ICC of 0.46 aligns with reliability of curiosity in prior work [10, 32].

3.2 Verbal Behavior Coding

We adopted a mix of semi-automatic and manual annotation procedures to code 11 verbal behaviors, in line with the curiosity-related behavioral set described

Table 2. A summary of coding methods used for the annotation. Detailed coding scheme for verbal behaviors can be found at http://tinyurl.com/codingschemecuriosity

Construct	Definition used to code/infer the construct	Coding method
Ground Truth Curiosity	A strong desire to learn or know more about something or someone.	Four MTurk raters annotated each 10-sec thin slice; average ICC=0.46; used inverse-based bias correction to pick the final rating.
Verbal Behavior		
1. Uncertainty	Lack of certainty about ones choices or beliefs, and is verbally expressed by language that creates an impression that something important has been said, but what is communicated is vague, misleading, evasive or ambiguous. e.g - *"well maybe we should use rubberbands on the foam pieces"*	Used a semi-automated annotation approach: after automatic labeling of these verbal behaviors, two trained raters (Krippendroff's alpha >0.6) independently corrected machine annotated labels; average percentage of machine annotation that remained the same after human correction was 85.9 (SD=12.71).
2. Argument	A coherent series of reasons, statements, or facts intended to support or establish a point of view. e.g - *"no we got to first find out the chain reactions that it can do"*	
3. Justification	The action of showing something to be right or reasonable by making it clear. e.g - *'wait with the momentum of going downhill it will go straight into the trap"*	
4. Suggestion	An idea or plan put forward for consideration. e.g - *"you are adding more weight there which would make it fall down"*	
5. Agreement	Harmony or accordance in opinion or feeling; a position or result of agreeing. e.g - *"And we put the ball in here..I hope it still works, and it goes..so it starts like that, and then we hit it" [Quote] — "Ok that works" [Response]*	
6. Question Asking (On-Task/Social)	Asking any kind of questions related to the task or non-task relevant aspects of the social interaction. e.g - *"why do we need to make it that high?", "do you two go to the same school?"*	Used manual annotation procedure due to unavailability of existing training corpus (Krippendroff's alpha >0.76 between two raters).
7. Idea Verbalization	Explicitly saying out an idea, which can be just triggered by an individual's own actions or something that builds off of other peer's actions. e.g - *"yeah that ball isn't heavy enough"*	
8. Sharing Findings	An explicit verbalization of communicating results, findings and discoveries to group members during any stage of a scientific inquiry process. e.g - *"look how I'm gonna see I'm gonna trap it"*	
9. Hypothesis Generation	Expressing one or more different possibilities or theories to explain a phenomenon by giving relation between two or more variables. e.g - *"okay we need to make it straight so that the force of hitting it makes it big"*	
10. Task Sentiment (Positive/Negative)	A view of or attitude (emotional valence) toward a situation or event; an overall opinion towards a subject matter. We were interested in looking at positive or negative attitude towards the task that students were working on. e.g - *"oh it's the coolest cage I've ever seen, I'd want to be trapped in this cage", "I'm getting very mad at this cage"*	
11. Evaluation (Positive/Negative)	Characterization of how a person assesses a previous speaker's action and problem-solving approach. It can be positive or negative. e.g - *'oh that's a pretty good idea", "no it can't go like that otherwise it will be stuck"*	
Non-verbal Behavior (AU - facial action unit)		
1. Joy-related	AU 6 (raised lower eyelid) *and* AU 12 (lip corner puller).	Used an open-source software OpenFace for automatic facial landmark detection, and a rule-based approach post-hoc to infer affective states
2. Delight-related	AU 7 (lid tightener) *and* AU 12 (lip corner puller) *and* AU 25 (lips part) *and* AU 26 (jaw drop) *and not* AU 45 (blink).	
3. Surprise-related	AU 1 (inner brow raise) *and* AU 2 (outer brow raise) *and* AU 5b (upper lid raise) *and* AU 26 (jaw drop).	
4. Confusion-related	AU 4 (brow lower) *and* AU 7 (lid tightener) *and not* AU 12 (lip corner puller).	
5. Flow-related	AU 23 (lip tightener) *and* AU 5 (upper lid raise) *and* AU 7 (lid tightener) *and not* AU 15 (lip corner depressor) *and not* AU 45 (blink) *and not* AU 2 (outer brow raise).	
6. Head Nod	Variance of head pitch.	Used OpenFace to extract head orientation, and computed variance post-hoc
7. Head Turn	Variance of head yaw.	
8. Lateral Head Inclination	Variance of head roll.	
Turn Taking		
1. Indegree	A weighted product of number of group members whose turn was responded to (*activity*) and total time that other people spent on their turn before handing over the floor (*silence*).	Used two novel metrics constructed using an application of social network analysis for weighted data.
2. Outdegree	A weighted product of number of group members to whom floor was given to (*participation equality*), and the amount of time spent when holding floor before allowing a response (*talkativeness*).	

in Sect. 2.2. Five verbal behaviors were coded using a semi-automatic approach - *uncertainty, argument, justification, suggestion* at the clause level, and *agreement* at the turn level. First, a particular variant of neural language models called paragraph vector or doc2vec [28] was used to learn distributed representations for a clause/turn. The motivation for this approach stems from - (i) lack of available corpora of verbal behaviors that are large enough, and collected in similar settings as ours (groups of children engaged in open-ended scientific inquiry), and hence (ii) limited applicability of traditional n-gram based machine learning models to cross-domain settings, which would result in a very high-dimensional representation with poor semantic generalization, (iii) limitations of other popular neural language models such as word2vec that do not explicitly represent word order and surrounding context in the semantic representation, and (iv) our desire to reduce manual annotation due to how long it takes for a corpus such as this where each child's behaviors must be annotated.

Based on empirical analysis and recommended procedure in [28], we used concatenated representations of two fixed size vectors of size 100 that we learned for each sentence as input to a machine learning classifier (L2 regularized logistic regression) - one learned by the standard paragraph vector with distributed memory model, and one learned by the paragraph vector with distributed bag of words model. Training data for the five verbal behaviors annotated using this process is shown in the right column of Table 3, along with standard performance metrics. Robustness of machine annotated labels was ensured by using human annotators. Two raters first coded presence or absence of verbal behaviors on a random sample of 100 clauses/turns following a coding manual given to them for training, and computed inter-rater reliability using Krippendorff's alpha. Once raters reached a reliability of >0.7 after one or more rounds of resolving disagreements, they independently rated a different set of 50 clauses/turns independently, and we computed the final reliability on these (left column of Table 3, and >0.6 for all behaviors). Subsequently, the raters independently de-noised or corrected machine annotated labels for the full corpus.

Compared with this human ground truth, the average of ratio of false positives to false negatives in the machine prediction was 14.18 (SD = 12.31) across all behaviors, meaning that the machine learning models over-identified presence of verbal behaviors. We found that the most common false positives were cases where a clause or turn comprised one word (e.g. - okay), backchannels (e.g. - hmmm..) and very short phrases lacking enough context to make a correct prediction. The average percentage of machine annotated labels that did not change even after the human de-noising step was 85.9 (SD = 12.71), meaning majority of labels were correctly predicted in the first place. This was also reflected in a good cross validation training performance of the models (right column of Table 3). Six other verbal behaviors (*question asking (on-task, social)* ($\alpha = 1$), *idea verbalization* ($\alpha = 0.761$), *sharing findings* ($\alpha = 1$), *hypothesis generation* ($\alpha = 0.79$), *attitude towards task (positive, negative)* ($\alpha = 0.835$), *evaluation sentiment (positive, negative)* ($\alpha = 0.784$)) were coded using a traditional manual annotation procedure due to unavailability of existing training corpus. Overall, our approach of combining machine annotation with human judgment favors reproducibility, speed and scalability, without compromising on reliability.

3.3 Assessment of Nonverbal Behaviors

The motivation for coding nonverbal behaviors is inspired by prior theoretical and empirical research, which has identified the facial action units accompanying the experience of certain emotions that often co-occur with curiosity [32], and has discovered consistent associations (correlations as well as predictions) between particular facial configurations and human emotional or mental states [17,31,32]. We used automated visual analysis to construct five feature groups corresponding to emotional expressions that provide evidence for presence of the affective states of *joy, delight, surprise, confusion* and *flow* (a state of engagement with a task such that concentration is intense). A simple rule-based approach was followed (see Table 2) to combine emotion-related facial landmarks, which were previously extracted on a frame by frame basis using a state-of-the-art open-source software OpenFace [2]. We then selected the most dominant (frequently occurring) emotional expression for every 10 s slice of the interaction for each group member, among all the frames in that time interval. While facial expressions have the advantage of being observable and being detected using current computer vision approaches with high accuracy, we acknowledge that they can often be polysemous, ambiguous, and be voluntarily camouflaged.

Automated visual analysis was also used to capture variability in head angles for each child in the group, which correspond to *head nods (i.e. pitch), head turns (i.e. yaw)*, and *lateral head inclinations (i.e. roll)*. The motivation for using head movement in our curiosity framework is inspired by prior work in the multimodal analytics [15,38] that has emphasized contribution of nonverbal cues in inferring behavioral constructs such as interest and involvement that are closely related to the construct of curiosity. By using OpenFace [2], we first performed frame by frame extraction of head orientation, and then calculated the variance post-hoc to capture intensity in head motions for every 10 s of the interaction for each group member. Since head pose estimation takes as input facial landmark detection, we only considered those frames for calculation that had a face tracked and facial landmarks detected with confidence greater than 80%.

3.4 Assessment of Turn Taking Dynamics

The motivation for capturing turn taking stems from prior literature that has used measures such as participation equality and turn taking freedom as indicators of involvement in small-group interaction [26]. Specifically, we designed two novel metrics using a simple application of social network analysis for weighted data. By representing speakers as nodes and time between adjacent speaker turns as edges, the following two features are computed for each group member (see definition in Table 2) for every 10 s: (i) $TurnTakingIndegree = activity^{1-\alpha} * silence^{\alpha}$. Since high involvement is likely to be indexed by higher activity and lower silence, α was set to -0.5, (ii) $TurnTakingOutdegree = participation\ equality^{1-\alpha} * talkativeness^{\alpha}$. Since higher participation equality and talkativeness are favorable, α was set to $+0.5$.

Table 3. Results from semi-automatic verbal behavior annotation. Right column describes external corpus used for training machine learning classifiers & depicts their predictive performance using 10-fold cross validation. Left column depicts inter-rater reliability for human judgment that was used to denoise these behaviors

Verbal Behavior [Krippendorff's α for human judgment]	**Training Data for Semi-Automated Classification [Weighted F1, AUC (10-fold cross validation)]**
1. Uncertainty [0.78]	Wikipedia corpus manually annotated for 3122 uncertain 7629 certain instances (Farkas et al., 2010) [0.695, 0.717]
2. Argument [0.792]	Internet Argument Corpus manually annotated for 3079 argument and 2228 non argument instances (Swanson et al., 2015). Argument quality score split at 70% to binarize class label [0.658, 0.706]
3. Justification [process (0.936), causal (0.905), model (0.821), example (0.731), definition (0.78), property (0.847)]	AI2 Elementary Science Questions corpus manually annotated for 6 kinds of justification - process, causal, model, example, definition, property (Jansen et al., 2016). Reported performance is the average performance of 6 binary machine learning classifiers [0.766, 0.696]
4. Suggestion [0.608]	Product reviews (Negi, 2016) and Twitter (Dong et al., 2013) corpuses manually annotated for 1000 explicit suggestion and 13000 explicit non-suggestion instances [0.938, 0.865]
5. Agreement [0.935]	LiveJournal forum and Wikipedia discussion corpuses manually annotated for 2754 agreement and 8905 disagreement instances based on quote and response pairs (Andreas et al., 2012) [0.717, 0.696]

4 Empirical Validation of the Theoretical Framework

We used a "multiple-group" version of continuous time structural equation models (CTSEM) [12] to evaluate the proposed theoretical framework of curiosity, and statistically verify the predictive relationships between ground truth curiosity (that we formalized as our manifest variable), functions described in our theoretical framework (that we formalized as latent variables) and multimodal behaviors (that we formalized as time-dependent predictors). By using multivariate stochastic differential equations to estimate an underlying continuous process and recover underlying hidden causes linking entire behavioral sequence, this approach allows investigation of group level differences, while accounting for the autocorrelated nature of the behavioral time series. A Kalman filter was used to fit CTSEM to the data and obtain standardized estimates for the influence of behaviors on latent functions, and in turn these latent functions on curiosity.

4.1 Description of the Approach

Since knowledge identification and acquisition are closely intertwined with knowledge seeking behaviors and it is hard to draw a distinction between these putative underlying mechanisms based on observable or inferred multimodal behaviors, we formalized them under the same latent variable. The final set of latent functions for our theoretical framework that we statistically verified therefore included: (i) **individual** knowledge identification and acquisition, (ii) **interpersonal** knowledge identification and acquisition, (iii) **individual** intensification of knowledge identification and acquisition, (iv) **interpersonal** intensification of knowledge identification and acquisition. Two versions of CTSEM were run. In first version, we specified a model where only factor loadings between the manifest variable and latent variables were estimated for each group distinctly (average and standard deviation reported in Fig. 1), but all other model parameters were constrained to equality across all groups ($\text{Model}_{constrained}$) and then estimated freely. Since the form of a behavior does not uniquely determine its function, nor vice-versa, we did not pre-specify the exact pattern of relationships between behaviors and functions to look for/estimate. In second version of the model, all parameters for all groups were estimated distinctly (Model_{free}).

The decision to separately run these two models was based on the intuition that while the relationships between appearance of behaviors and their contribution to the latent functions of curiosity would remain the same across groups, the relative contribution of interpersonal or individual tendencies for knowledge identification, acquisition and intensification would vary based on learning dispositions of people towards seeking the unknown. This intuition stemmed from prior literature of measuring learning dispositions [40], an important dimension of which is the ability of learners to balance between being sociable and being private in their learning work interdependently. We hypothesized that this dimension will impact curiosity differently when working in group, and therefore expected $\text{Model}_{constrained}$ to fit the data better than Model_{free}. An empirical validation confirmed this hypothesis. The Akaike Information Criterion (AIC) for $\text{Model}_{constrained}$ (933.48) was ~3x lower than Model_{free} (2278.689).

4.2 Model Results and Discussion

We illustrate results of the CTSEM ($\text{Model}_{constrained}$) in Fig. 1, depicting links with top ranked standardized estimates between behaviors and latent variables. In few cases, we also added links with the second highest standardized estimate if they clarified our interpretation of the latent function. Overall, these results provide confirmation of correctness of the theoretical framework of curiosity along three main aspects: (i) The grouping of behaviors under each latent function and their contribution to individual and interpersonal aspects of knowledge identification, acquisition and intensification aligns with prior literature on the intrapersonal origins of curiosity, but also teases apart the underlying interpersonal mechanisms, (ii) There exists strong and positive predictive relationships between these latent variables and thin-slice curiosity, (iii) Knowledge identification and acquisition have stronger influence to curiosity than knowledge intensification, and interpersonal-level functions have stronger influence compared to individual-level functions. We now discuss latent functions and associated behaviors, ordered by the degree of positive influence on curiosity.

First, "Interpersonal Knowledge Identification and Acquisition" shows the strongest influence to curiosity among the four latent functions (2.612 ± 0.124). The natural merging of knowledge identification and knowledge acquisition corroborates with the notation that one person's knowledge seeking may draw attention of another group member to a related knowledge gap and escalate collaborative knowledge seeking. Behaviors that positively contribute to this function are mainly from cluster 3 (*sharing findings, task related question asking, argument, and evaluation of other's idea*). In addition, nonverbal behaviors including *head turn* and *turn taking dynamics (indegree)* are also related to this function, which support the idea that higher degree of group members' interest and involvement in the social interaction stimulates awareness of peer's ideas, subsequently leading to knowledge-seeking via social means in order to gain knowledge from the experience of others and add that onto one's own direct experiences.

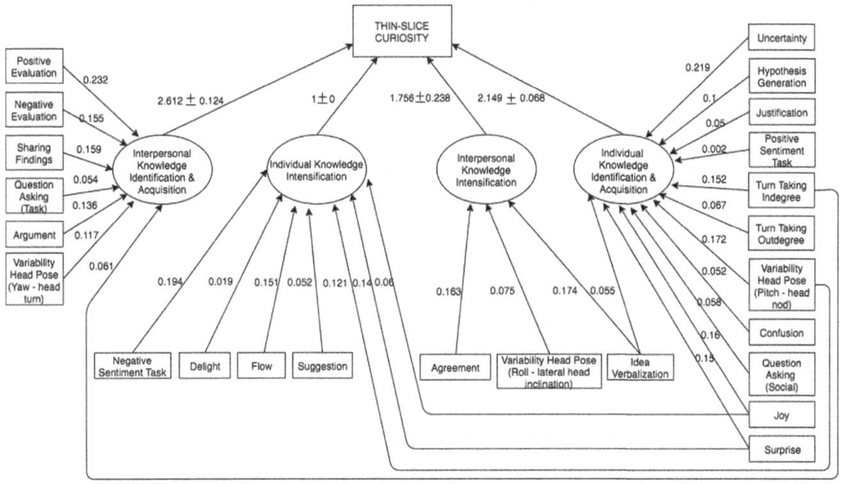

Fig. 1. Continuous time SEM factor analysis results. Direction and degree of predictive influences are represented by edges between multimodal behaviors and latent variables

Second, "Individual Knowledge Identification and Acquisition" shows a strong influence to curiosity (2.149 ± 0.066). Similar to the interpersonal level function, knowledge identification and acquisition merge into one coherent function, as knowledge-seeking behaviors can sparkle new unknown or conflicting information within the same individual. Behaviors from cluster 2 (*hypothesis generation, justification, idea verbalization*) and cluster 4 (*confusion, joy, surprise, uncertain, positive sentiment towards task*) mainly contribute to this function. *Head nod*, as indicative of positive feelings towards the stimulus due to its compatibility with the response [14], maps to this function as well. Finally, we find that *turn taking (indegree and outdegree)* and *social question asking* contribute positively to individual knowledge identification and acquisition. Interest in other people reflects a general level of trait curiosity and influences inquisitive behavior [37].

Third, we find that a relatively small group of behaviors including *agreement, idea verbalization* and *lateral head inclination* have predictive influence on the latent function of "Interpersonal Knowledge Intensification", which in turn has a high positive influence on curiosity (1.756 ± 0.238). Agreement may contribute to information seeking by promoting acceptance and cohesion. Working in social contexts broadcasts idea verbalization done by an individual to other group members, which might in turn increase their willingness to get involved. Lateral head inclination during the RGM activity is associated with intensive investigation of the RGM solution offered by both oneself and other group members. Overall, engagement in cooperative effort to overcome common blocking points in the group work may result in intensifying knowledge seeking.

Finally, the latent function of "Individual Knowledge Intensification" has the least comparative influence on curiosity. It is associated with non-verbal behaviors such as *head nod* and emotional expressions of positive affect (*flow, joy* and *delight*), which function towards increasing pleasurable arousal. In addition, *surprise* and *suggestion* also positively influence this latent function, and signal an increased anticipation to discover novelty, conceptual conflict, and correctness of one's own idea. Interestingly, results also show that *negative sentiment about the task* positively influences an individual's knowledge seeking behaviors. A qualitative examination of the corpus reveals that such verbal expressions often co-occur with evaluation made by a group member within the same 10 s thin-slice that signals a desire for cooperation. Thus, a potential explanation of this association is that expressing negative sentiment about task may signal hardship, which draws group members' attention and increases chances of receiving assistance, thus increasing engagement in knowledge seeking.

5 Implications and Conclusion

In this work, we articulated key social factors that appear to account for curiosity in learning in social contexts, proposed and empirically validated a novel theoretical framework that disentangles individual and interpersonal functions linked to curiosity and behaviors that fulfill these functions. We found strong positive predictive relationships of the interpersonal functions of knowledge identification, acquisition and intensification on curiosity, which reinforces our original hypotheses about the social nature of curiosity and the need to disentangle its interpersonal precursors from its individual precursors. The current analyses are part of a larger research effort to understand and implement the social scaffolding of curiosity [41] through an ECA [7]. The theoretical framework lays foundation of a computational model of curiosity that can enable an ECA to sense real-time curiosity level of each member in small group interaction. Despite acknowledging importance of the metacognitive in collaborative learning, prior work seems to be inadequately equipped with theoretical formalisms to capture intricate factors such as curiosity, and lacks operational ways to embed this theoretical understanding into computational models by mapping between behaviors and their underlying mechanisms to offer scaffolding strategies. The research presented in this work therefore goes beyond prior work that has worked on inferring curiosity directly from visual and vocal cues [3,10,32], without adequate consideration of underlying mechanisms that link these low-level cues to curiosity, as well how these cues interact with group dynamic behaviors and other discourse-level verbal cues. Knowing what forms of multimodal behaviors and their corresponding functions are good indicators of curiosity in human-human interaction allows us to design better learning technologies that can sense these behaviors, and intentionally look for opportunities to use strategies to scaffold curiosity in real-time by triggering such productive individual and interpersonal behaviors.

References

1. Ambady, N., Rosenthal, R.: Thin slices of expressive behavior as predictors of interpersonal consequences: A meta-analysis (1992)
2. Baltrušaitis, T., Robinson, P., Morency, L.P.: Openface: an open source facial behavior analysis toolkit. In: 2016 IEEE Winter Conference on Applications of Computer Vision (WACV), pp. 1–10. IEEE (2016)
3. Baranes, A., Oudeyer, P.Y., Gottlieb, J.: Eye movements reveal epistemic curiosity in human observers. Vis. Res. **117**, 81–90 (2015)
4. Berlyne, D.E.: Conflict, Arousal, and Curiosity. McGraw-Hill, New York (1960)
5. Van den Bossche, P., Gijselaers, W.H., Segers, M., Kirschner, P.A.: Social and cognitive factors driving teamwork in collaborative learning environments: team learning beliefs and behaviors. Small Group Res. **37**(5), 490–521 (2006)
6. Cartwright, D.E., Zander, A.E.: Group Dynamics Research and Theory. Harper & Row, New York (1953)
7. Cassell, J., Ananny, M., Basu, A., Bickmore, T., Chong, P., Mellis, D., Ryokai, K., Smith, J., Vilhjálmsson, H., Yan, H.: Shared reality: physical collaboration with a virtual peer. In: CHI 2000 Extended Abstracts on Human Factors in Computing systems, pp. 259–260. ACM (2000)
8. Chi, M.T., Wylie, R.: The ICAP framework: linking cognitive engagement to active learning outcomes. Educ. Psychol. **49**(4), 219–243 (2014)
9. Costikyan, G.: Uncertainty in Games. MIT Press, Cambridge (2013)
10. Craig, S.D., D'Mello, S., Witherspoon, A., Graesser, A.: Emote aloud during learning with autotutor: applying the facial action coding system to cognitive-affective states during learning. Cogn. Emot. **22**(5), 777–788 (2008)
11. Dörnyei, Z., Murphey, T.: Group dynamics in the language classroom. Ernst Klett Sprachen, Munich (2003)
12. Driver, C.C., Oud, J.H., Voelkle, M.C.: Continuous time structural equation modelling with R package ctsem. J. Stat. Softw. **77**(5) (2017)

13. Engel, S.: Children's need to know: curiosity in schools. Harv. Educ. Rev. **81**(4), 625–645 (2011)
14. Förster, J., Strack, F.: Influence of overt head movements on memory for valenced words: a case of conceptual-motor compatibility. J. Pers. Soc. Psychol. **71**(3), 421 (1996)
15. Gatica-Perez, D., McCowan, L., Zhang, D., Bengio, S.: Detecting group interest-level in meetings. In: IEEE International Conference on Acoustics, Speech, and Signal Processing, Proceedings (ICASSP 2005), vol. 1, pp. I-489. IEEE (2005)
16. Gordon, G., Breazeal, C., Engel, S.: Can children catch curiosity from a social robot?. In: Proceedings of the Tenth Annual ACM/IEEE International Conference on Human-Robot Interaction, pp. 91–98. ACM (2015)
17. Grafsgaard, J.F., Boyer, K.E., Phillips, R., Lester, J.C.: Modeling confusion: facial expression, task, and discourse in task-oriented tutorial dialogue. In: Biswas, G., Bull, S., Kay, J., Mitrovic, A. (eds.) AIED 2011. LNCS, vol. 6738, pp. 98–105. Springer, Heidelberg (2011). doi:10.1007/978-3-642-21869-9_15
18. Jirout, J., Klahr, D.: Children's scientific curiosity: in search of an operational definition of an elusive concept. Dev. Rev. **32**(2), 125–160 (2012)
19. Johnson, D.W., Johnson, R.T.: Energizing learning: the instructional power of conflict. Educ. Res. **38**(1), 37–51 (2009)
20. Jordan, M.E., McDaniel Jr., R.R.: Managing uncertainty during collaborative problem solving in elementary school teams: the role of peer influence in robotics engineering activity. J. Learn. Sci. **23**(4), 490–536 (2014)
21. Kapur, M., Toh, L.: Learning from productive failure. In: Cho, Y., Caleon, I., Kapur, M. (eds.) Authentic Problem Solving and Learning in the 21st Century. Education Innovation Series, pp. 213–227. Springer, Singapore (2015). doi:10.1007/978-981-287-521-1_12
22. Kashdan, T.B., Fincham, F.D.: Facilitating curiosity: a social and self-regulatory perspective for scientifically based interventions. In: Linley, P.A., Joseph, S. (eds.) Positive Psychology in Practice, pp. 482–503. Wiley, Hoboken (2004)
23. Keller, J.M.: Strategies for stimulating the motivation to learn. Perform. Improv. **26**(8), 1–7 (1987)
24. Kidd, C., Hayden, B.Y.: The psychology and neuroscience of curiosity. Neuron **88**(3), 449–460 (2015)
25. Kruger, J., Endriss, U., Fernández, R., Qing, C.: Axiomatic analysis of aggregation methods for collective annotation. In: Proceedings of the 2014 International Conference on Autonomous Agents and Multi-Agent Systems, pp. 1185–1192. International Foundation for Autonomous Agents and Multiagent Systems (2014)
26. Lai, C., Carletta, J., Renals, S., Evanini, K., Zechner, K.: Detecting summarization hot spots in meetings using group level involvement and turn-taking features. In: INTERSPEECH, pp. 2723–2727 (2013)
27. Law, E., Yin, M., Goh, J., Chen, K., Terry, M.A., Gajos, K.Z.: Curiosity killed the cat, but makes crowdwork better. In: Proceedings of the 2016 CHI Conference on Human Factors in Computing Systems, pp. 4098–4110. ACM (2016)
28. Le, Q.V., Mikolov, T.: Distributed representations of sentences and documents. ICML **14**, 1188–1196 (2014)
29. Loewenstein, G.: The psychology of curiosity: a review and reinterpretation. Psychol. Bull. **116**(1), 75 (1994)
30. Luce, M.R., Hsi, S.: Science-relevant curiosity expression and interest in science: an exploratory study. Sci. Educ. **99**(1), 70–97 (2015)

31. McDaniel, B., D'Mello, S., King, B., Chipman, P., Tapp, K., Graesser, A.: Facial features for affective state detection in learning environments. In: Proceedings of the Cognitive Science Society, vol. 29 (2007)
32. Nojavanasghari, B., Baltrušaitis, T., Hughes, C.E., Morency, L.P.: Emoreact: a multimodal approach and dataset for recognizing emotional responses in children. In: Proceedings of the 18th ACM International Conference on Multimodal Interaction, pp. 137–144. ACM (2016)
33. Ogata, H., Yano, Y.: Combining knowledge awareness and information filtering in an open-ended collaborative learning environment. Int. J. Artif. Intell. Educ. (IJAIED) **11**, 33–46 (2000)
34. Oudeyer, P.Y.: Intelligent adaptive curiosity: a source of self-development (2004)
35. Parr, J.M., Townsend, M.A.: Environments, processes, and mechanisms in peer learning. Int. J. Educ. Res. **37**(5), 403–423 (2002)
36. Piaget, J.: The Language and Thought of the Child. Psychology Press, Chicago (1959)
37. Renner, B.: Curiosity about people: the development of a social curiosity measure in adults. J. Pers. Assess. **87**(3), 305–316 (2006)
38. Schuller, B., Müller, R., Eyben, F., Gast, J., Hörnler, B., Wöllmer, M., Rigoll, G., Höthker, A., Konosu, H.: Being bored? recognising natural interest by extensive audiovisual integration for real-life application. Image Vis. Comput. **27**(12), 1760–1774 (2009)
39. Schwartz, D.L., Martin, T.: Inventing to prepare for future learning: the hidden efficiency of encouraging original student production in statistics instruction. Cogn. Instr. **22**(2), 129–184 (2004)
40. Shum, S.B., Crick, R.D.: Learning dispositions and transferable competencies: pedagogy, modelling and learning analytics. In: Proceedings of the 2nd International Conference on Learning Analytics and Knowledge, pp. 92–101. ACM (2012)
41. Sinha, T., Bai, Z., Cassell, J.: Curious minds wonder alike: studying multimodal behavioral dynamics to design social scaffolding of curiosity. In: Lavoué, É., et al. (eds.) EC-TEL 2017. LNCS, vol. 10474, pp. 270–285. Springer, Cham (2017). doi:10.1007/978-3-319-66610-5_20
42. Von Stumm, S., Hell, B., Chamorro-Premuzic, T.: The hungry mind: intellectual curiosity is the third pillar of academic performance. Perspect. Psychol. Sci. **6**(6), 574–588 (2011)
43. Wu, Q., Miao, C.: Modeling curiosity-related emotions for virtual peer learners. IEEE Comput. Intell. Mag. **8**(2), 50–62 (2013)

Curious Minds Wonder Alike: Studying Multimodal Behavioral Dynamics to Design Social Scaffolding of Curiosity

Tanmay Sinha(✉), Zhen Bai, and Justine Cassell

School of Computer Science, Carnegie Mellon University, Pittsburgh, USA
{tanmays,zhenb,justine}@cs.cmu.edu

Abstract. Curiosity is the strong desire to learn or know more about something or someone. Since learning is often a social endeavor, social dynamics in collaborative learning may inevitably influence curiosity. There is a scarcity of research, however, focusing on how curiosity can be evoked in group learning contexts. Inspired by a recently proposed theoretical framework [30] that articulates an integrated socio-cognitive infrastructure of curiosity, in this work, we use data-driven approaches to identify fine-grained social scaffolding of curiosity in child-child interaction, and propose how they can be used to elicit and maintain curiosity in technology-enhanced learning environments. For example, we discovered sequential patterns of multimodal behaviors across group members and we describe those that maximize an individual's utility, or likelihood, of demonstrating curiosity during open-ended problem-solving in group work. We also discovered, and describe here, behaviors that directly or in a mediated manner cause curiosity related conversational behaviors in the interaction, with twice as many interpersonal causal influences compared to intrapersonal ones. We explain how these findings form a solid foundation for developing curiosity-increasing learning technologies or even assisting a human coach to induce curiosity among learners.

1 Introduction and Motivation

Curiosity is an important metacognitive skill that arises from a strong desire for learning [2] and leads to knowledge acquisition through coming to one's own understanding, rather than "being told" or "instructed". While there is an increasing emphasis on the educational benefits of learning in groups, as co-constructivism and collaborative learning theories argue that knowledge is jointly constructed through social interactions [5], existing research on curiosity mainly focuses on investigating its cognitive mechanisms at an individual level, and often conceives curiosity as an inherently individual and stable disposition toward seeking novelty and approaching unfamiliar stimuli [15]. Ignoring social factors in evoking curiosity may prevent us from designing effective forms of support in learning environments (technological or not), because in group work the behaviors of each member (both what they say and what they do) affect the curiosity of others [12]. Prior learning sciences literature on the social and

É. Lavoué et al. (Eds.): EC-TEL 2017, LNCS 10474, pp. 270–285, 2017.
DOI: 10.1007/978-3-319-66610-5_20

technological dimensions of scaffolding emphasizes that "scaffolds are not found in software but are functions of processes that relate people to performances in activity systems over time" [27]. It is therefore important to investigate the dynamics of these fine-grained processes as they happen spontaneously.

The theoretical motivation for studying these "multimodal behavioral dynamics" (as we will call them) in order to better understand how to design for social scaffolding of curiosity stems from a fundamental psychological question - what causes variations in the curiosity level of children as they engage in open-ended collaborative problem-solving activities? Patterns of verbal and nonverbal behaviors comprise salient cues, and can provide valuable insights into how an individual's curiosity changes as they progress through the task. However, looking at summative measures (e.g. - frequency of productive versus unproductive learning behaviors) alone will not suffice in understanding how curiosity arises and disappears over time. We believe that studying the social scaffolding of curiosity therefore requires examining sequential behavioral patterns that co-occur with – or just before – high curiosity moments, and then explicitly modeling the precise nature of causal relationships among these interpersonal patterns. Prior work on studying curiosity has not adequately addressed these behavioral dynamics. Even research that has looked at the effect of peers on curiosity has looked into mostly dyadic contexts rather than small group, used a limited strategy repertoire for eliciting curiosity-related behavior based on theory rather than empirical data, and subjectively assessed success of those strategies post-hoc using questionnaires [13,14,34].

In this paper, then, we look at the social scaffolding of curiosity in detail, based on audio and video data of groups of elementary and middle school students engaged in informal learning. A subset have been coded for ground truth curiosity (see below for an explanation of what we mean) and a wide range of multimodal behaviors, using a mix of manual and semi-automated procedures. These behaviors are specified in the theoretical framework of curiosity, which we proposed and empirically validated in other work [30] by articulating the underlying functions of these behaviors in contributing to curiosity in group learning. Building on this theoretical framework, we here address the research question of how to elicit these behaviors. To that end, we first look into sequential patterns of behaviors across group members that maximize an individual's curiosity within every one minute time frame. These sequential patterns inform *what* behaviors to elicit in increasing or maintaining curiosity level of the target subject, based on the behavior trajectories recognized so far. We then study causal relationship between these behaviors to establish strategies of *how* to elicit certain behaviors. The main contribution of this work is novel data-driven behavioral heuristics that we discover for enabling the design of supportive and responsive learning environments that can foster curiosity. In remainder of this paper, we first describe methods including data collection, annotation and analyses in Sect. 2, followed by discussion of results in Sect. 3. We end with implications for designing learning technologies and conclusion in Sects. 4 and 5.

2 Method

In preparation for analyses of sequential behavioral patterns, we used the same annotated dataset annotated described in [30], which we summarize here as well. We then describe the detailed rationale behind our multimodal data analyses.

2.1 Data Collection

Audio and video data was collected for 12 groups of children (aged 10–12, 3–4 children per group, 44 in total) engaged in a hands-on activity commonly used in informal learning contexts - collaboratively build a Rube Goldberg machine (RGM). A RGM includes building chain reactions that are to be triggered automatically for trapping a ball in a cage. This paper describes fine-grained analyses of the first 30 min (out of 35–40 min given each group) of the RGM task for half of the sample; that is, 22 children across 6 groups.

2.2 Data Annotation

Ground Truth Curiosity: Person perception research has demonstrated that judgments of others based on brief exposure to their behaviors is an accurate assessment of interpersonal dynamics [1]. We used the Amazon MTurk to obtain ground truth for curiosity via such a thin-slice approach, using the definition "curiosity is a strong desire to learn or know more about something or someone", and a rating scale comprising 0 (not curious), 1 (curious) and 2 (extremely curious). Amazon MTurk is a crowdsourcing platform that allows online workers to complete tasks that computers are currently unable to do, for a monetary payment. Our previous research has successfully deployed thin-slice coding for other social phenomena like rapport using this platform [31]. Four naive raters annotated every 10 s slice of videos of the interaction for each child presented to them in randomized order. We post-processed the ratings by removing those raters who used less than 1.5 standard deviation time compared to the mean time taken for all rating units (HITs). We then computed a single measure of Intraclass correlation coefficient (ICC) for each possible subset of raters for a particular HIT, and then picked ratings from the rater subset that had the best reliability for further processing. Finally, inverse-based bias correction [19] was used to account for label overuse and underuse, and to pick one single rating of curiosity for each 10 s thin-slice. The average ICC was 0.46.

Verbal and Non-verbal Behaviors: We used semi-automatic (machine learning + human judgment) and manual (human judgment) annotation procedures to code 11 verbal behaviors of interest in our corpus that came from our review of prior research in psychology and learning sciences, and our hypotheses about how these behaviors fulfill putative functions of curiosity. In other work, we have described details of the coding procedure, empirical validation of these hypotheses, and confirmation of positive predictive relationships between these behaviors, functions (that, because they cannot be directly observed, were our latent variables) and thin-slice curiosity [30]. Here, in Table 1, we provide a summarized description of the verbal behaviors of uncertainty, argument, justification, suggestion, question asking (on-task, social), idea verbalization, sharing findings, hypothesis generation, attitude/sentiment towards task (positive, negative) and evaluation (positive, negative) that were coded at the clause level, and agreement that was coded at the turn level. A clause contains a subject (a noun or pronoun) and a predicate (conjugated verb – that says something about what the subject is or does). During a full turn, a speaker holds the floor and expresses one or more interpretable clauses (propositions). Inter rater reliability (Krippendorf's alpha) for each of these annotations was above 0.7. It is important to note that the above annotation categories are not mutually exclusive, and can co-occur. In addition to these verbal behaviors, we also used automated visual analysis to construct five facial-landmark feature groups corresponding to emotional expressions that provide evidence for the presence of affective states of joy, delight, surprise, confusion and flow. More details are described in [30].

2.3 Multimodal Data Analyses

We now describe our data-driven approach for discovering behavioral sequences that maximize curiosity and causal relationships between these behaviors.

Temporal Behavioral Relationships that Maximize Curiosity: To discover the temporal relationships among multimodal behaviors that maximize curiosity, we needed to specify how these behavioral states change over time. We therefore used sequential pattern mining approaches to find productive high-curiosity conversational episodes in the group interaction. Traditionally, the selection of such interesting sequences is based on the frequency/support framework, where sequences of high frequency are treated as significant. However, this often leads to many patterns being identified, most of which are may not be informative enough for choosing precise forms of scaffolding. Some sequential patterns, despite occurring rarely (having frequencies lower than the given minimum support), might still be useful since they co-occur with episodes of high individual curiosity. On the contrary, there might be other sequential behavioral patterns that occur frequently, but mostly co-occur with episodes of low individual curiosity. This motivated our current approach of incorporating utility in the classical sequential pattern mining framework. Our objective was to find what sequence of group member's behaviors maximize an individual's curiosity.

Towards this end, we leveraged the USpan algorithm [35], which uses lexicographic quantitative sequence tree to extract the complete set of high utility sequences, and includes efficient concatenation mechanisms and pruning strategies for calculating the utility of a node and its children. Formally, in our work, we represented an input behavioral sequence using 6 itemsets $X_1, X_2, ...X_6$, where each itemset represented an unordered set of distinct co-occurring behaviors from group members within a 10 s span, and therefore each input sequence spanned

Table 1. Definition & Examples of Curiosity-related verbal behavior coded. Detailed coding scheme can be found at http://tinyurl.com/codingschemecuriosity

Verbal behavior	Definition and Corpus examples
1. Uncertainty	Lack of certainty about ones choices or beliefs, and is verbally expressed by language that creates an impression that something important has been said, but what is communicated is vague, misleading, evasive or ambiguous. e.g. - *"well maybe we should use rubberbands on the foam pieces"*, *"wait do we need this thing to funnel it through?"*
2. Argument	A coherent series of reasons, statements, or facts intended to support or establish a point of view. e.g. - *"no we got to first find out the chain reactions that it can do"*, *"wait, but anything that goes through is gonna be stuck at the bottom"*
3. Justification	The action of showing something to be right or reasonable by making it clear. e.g. - *"oh we need more weight to like push it down"*, *"wait with the momentum of going downhill it will go straight into the trap"*
4. Suggestion	An idea or plan put forward for consideration. e.g. - *"you could kick a ball to kick something"*, *"you are adding more weight there which would make it fall down"*
5. Question asking	Asking any kind of questions related to the task (e.g. - *"so what's gonnna..what will happen like after the balls gets into the cup?"*, *"why do we need to make it that high?"*, *"do you want to build something like a chain reaction or something like that?"*) or non-task relevant (e.g. - *"do you two go to the same school?"*, *"who else watched the finale of gravity falls?"*) aspects of the social interaction
6. Idea verbalization	Explicitly saying out an idea, which can be just triggered by an individual's own actions or something that builds off of other peer's actions. e.g. - *"yeah that ball isn't heavy enough"*, *"so it's like tilted a bit up so it catches it instead of tilted down"*
7. Sharing findings	An explicit verbalization of communicating results, findings and discoveries to group members during any stage of a scientific inquiry process. e.g. - *"look how I'm gonna see I'm gonna trap it"*, *"look I made my pillar perfect"*
8. Hypothesis generation	Expressing one or more different possibilities or theories to explain a phenomenon by giving relation between two or more variables. e.g. - *"we could use scissors to cut off the baby's head which would cause enough friction"*, *"okay we need to make it straight so that the force of hitting it makes it big"*
9. Task sentiment	A view of or attitude (emotional valence) toward a situation or event; an overall opinion towards a subject matter. We were interested in looking at positive (e.g. - *"oh it's the coolest cage I've ever seen, I'd want to be trapped in this cage"*, *"ok so I'm gonna try to find out a way for the end to make this one go and fall"*) or negative attitude (e.g. - *"I'm getting very mad at this cage"*, *"but I don't know how to make it better"*) towards the task that students were working on
10. Evaluation	Characterization of how a person assesses a previous speaker's action and problem-solving approach. It can be positive (e.g. - *"oh that's a pretty good idea - that was a good idea"*, *"let's make this thing elevated and make it go down"*) or negative (e.g. - *"oh wait this doesn't- you're not pushing anything over here"*, *"no it can't go like that otherwise it will be stuck"*)
11. Agreement	Harmony or accordance in opinion or feeling; a position or result of agreeing. e.g. - *"But we need to have like power, and weight too"* (Quote)—*"Yeah we need more weight on this side"* (Response), *"And we put the ball in here..I hope it still works, and it goes..so it starts like that, and then we hit it"* (Quote)—*"Ok that works"* (Response)

one minute. Every behavior displayed by a group member in each itemset was associated with an additional utility value, which we defined as the ground truth thin-slice curiosity for that particular group member for the corresponding 10 s slice. For each group, we ran multiple passes of the USpan algorithm, varying the objective function each time to be the overall curiosity of each individual group member within the minute span. The overall utility O of curiosity of a sequential behavioral pattern S was the sum of utilities associated with S in each of the input sequences where it appeared. The final output of USpan algorithm in each pass therefore comprised all high utility sequential patterns above an overall threshold utility value of O.

Social Influence of Curiosity-Related Behaviors: To examine how social interaction evoked curiosity, we needed to find the interdependence among behavioral signals at a fine-grained level. In many situations of interest, symmetric measures of behavioral coordination aren't satisfactory to tear apart which signal is coordinating towards which. In our work, we therefore leveraged the notion of causal influence proposed by Granger [9], which states that if the prediction of one time series could be improved by incorporating the knowledge of a second one, or, if variance of the autoregressive prediction error of the first time series at the present time is reduced by inclusion of past measurements from the second time series, then the second series is said to have a causal influence on the first. For three or more simultaneous time series, a pairwise analysis can be performed to reduce the problem to a bivariate problem, the limitation however being that the causal relation between any two of the series may be direct, mediated by a third one, be a combination of both. This situation can be addressed by the technique of conditional Granger causality.

Formally, to determine whether causal influence of behavioral time series Y on X was mediated by Z, we created two ordinary least square auto-regressive models - (i) Restricted (RR), where we predicted X using past values of X and Z, (ii) UnRestricted (UR), where we predicted X using past values of X, Y and Z. The conditional granger causality magnitude (G-ratio) of Y influencing X, given Z (Y→X|Z) = log (variance(Residual$_{RR}$)/variance(Residual$_{UR}$)), which is essentially ratio of the log of variance of errors in the restricted and unrestricted regression. If G-ratio $<=$ 0, no further improvement of X can be expected by including past measurements of Y (full mediation). If G-ratio is $>$ 0, there is still a direct causal influence component from Y to X, and the inclusion of past measurements of Y in addition to that of X and Z results in better predictions of X (partial mediation). Maximum lag length was set to 6 (we looked back at most $6 * 10 = 60$ s in the behavioral time series X, Y and Z), and the optimal lag length M was the one that minimized the Bayesian Information Criterion (BIC) obtained by fitting the restricted and unrestricted regression models to the data. Statistical significance was computed using an F-test under the null hypothesis that one time series does not granger cause the other, where $F(M, n-k-1) =$ ((Sum of Square Residual$_{RR}$ − Sum of Square Residual$_{UR}$) $*(n-k-1)$) / ((Sum of Square Residual$_{UR}$) $* M$), where n is the number of observations, k is the number of explanatory variables in the unrestricted regression, and $n-k-1$ refers to the residual degrees of freedom. We acknowledge that our notion of influence is based on cause-effect relations with constant conjunctions and is only a limited view of causation, and we invite future work to build upon this approach.

3 Results and Discussion

This section discusses representative behavioral patterns and causal relationships that resulted from our described analyses in Sect. 2.3. To reiterate, our goal behind running these analyses was to inform the social scaffolding of curiosity by discovering *what* behaviors to elicit in increasing or maintaining curiosity level of the target subject based on the behavior trajectories recognized so far, and then discovering strategies of *how* to elicit these particular behaviors.

3.1 Temporal Behavioral Relationships that Maximize Curiosity

We synthesized representative sequential behavioral patterns across group members with high utility of individual curiosity by selecting those patterns that had a curiosity utility higher than 35 (where 35 was the average utility across all patterns discovered). For clarity, we explain these patterns along 5 themes based on the behaviors involved (Table 2). Each pattern spans a total of 60 s, and comprises multiple co-occurring behavioral itemsets. Each of these individual itemsets, although unordered, is linked sequentially across time with a subsequently occurring itemset. For e.g., a pattern $B_a(other), B_b(other) \twoheadrightarrow B_c(own)$ means that a behavioral itemset comprising behaviors A and B done by a different group member within a 10 s span are followed by a behavioral itemset comprising behavior C done by the target individual within the one minute span, and the pattern maximizes curiosity of this target individual.

Group 1 comprises patterns following the general theme of **ideation** that are linked to high curiosity. In this group, *justification* comes up as a frequently co-occurring and contingent behavior with *idea verbalization* and together maximizes the utility of curiosity. *Justification* attempts to establish an idea's validity by linking it to evidence. This in turn helps identify errors in group problem solving, and clarifies relationships among task subcomponents to trigger creation of new ideas [4]. For example, in the RGM task, group members often initially start working on different parts needed to assemble a complete RGM, and subsequently engage in justifying why and how their solution sub-pieces can be integrated. We also see that contingent occurrences of *idea verbalization* done by group members maximizes curiosity. Prior work [26] has posited that group members may build on one another's diverse perspectives to create new ideas via underlying mechanisms such as activation of related concepts (sparked ideas), engagement into putting together pieces of a solution (jigsaws) and creative misinterpretations of incorrect ideas.

Table 2. Salient sequential behavioral pattern groups that maximize the utility of individual (own) curiosity for the pattern. Each pattern spans 60 s. Flow of time between subsequent behavioral itemsets within the pattern is depicted by ↠

Corpus Examples of Sequential Behavioral Patterns [Utility of Curiosity]
Theme 1: involving Justification (J), Idea verbalization (IV)
1. IV(own) ↠ J(own), IV(own) ↠ J(own), IV(own) ↠ J(own) [**129**]
2. J(own) ↠ J(own), IV(own) ↠ IV(own) ↠ Confusion (other) [**120**]
3. J(other) ↠ J(own), IV(own) ↠ J(own) [**108**]
4. J(own), J(other) ↠ J(own) ↠ J(own) [**94**]
5. J(own), IV(own) ↠ J(own) ↠ J(other) [**92**]
6. J(other) ↠ J(other) ↠ J(own) [**67**]
Theme 2: involving Neg/Pos Evaluation (NE/PE), Justification (J), Idea verbalization (IV)
1. PE (own), J(own) ↠ J(own) [**80**]
2. Confusion(other) ↠ NE(other) [**59**]
3. NE(other) ↠ PE(own), J(own), IV(own) ↠ J(own), Confusion (own) ↠ PE(own), J(own) ↠ J(own) [**55**]
Theme 3: involving Question asking Task (QAT), Justification (J), Idea verbalization (IV)
1. Confusion(other), QAT(own) ↠ Confusion(other) ↠ Confusion(other) [**53**]
2. J(other), IV(other) ↠ QAT(other) [**52**]
3. Confusion(own) ↠ QAT(other) [**45**]
Theme 4: involving Suggestion (S), Idea verbalization (IV)
1. Confusion(other), S(own), IV(own), Confusion(own) ↠ Confusion(other), IV(own), Confusion(own) ↠ Confusion(other) ↠ IV(own) [**67**]
Theme 5: involving Positive Emotional states, Positive Task Sentiment (PTS)
1. Joy(own) ↠ Joy(own) [**80**]
2. Joy(own), Delight(other) ↠ Joy(own) [**55**]
3. Confusion (other) ↠ PTS(other) [**44**]
4. Joy(other) ↠ Flow(own) [**42**]

Group 2 comprises patterns following the general theme of **evaluation** that are linked to high curiosity. *Positive evaluations* support correct information by showing solidarity, a desire for cooperation and expressing positive emotions. On the other hand, *negative evaluation* is often an expression of disagreement, where flaws are identified in a peer's problem-solving approach by being critical of or even dismissing the peer's idea. It results in conflict, and group members are motivated to reduce that conflict via discussion (increased involvement or commitment), by getting others to change (attempting an influence), seeking additional social support for the opinion held (adding new ideas that are consonant with one's own opinions) or by changing their own opinion. All these tactics for reducing opposing beliefs will involve sequential behaviors of *justification, idea verbalization* and further *evaluation* [6], as we see in Table 2. In addition, even if inaccurate, *negative evaluation* often stimulates the attention of group members, and therefore might help them consider more aspects of the task from different perspectives to aid in creation of new ideas indirectly [24]. The group dynamics literature provides complementary insights to explain the relationships between *evaluation* and the subsequent discussion trajectory - it suggests that *negative evaluations* made by some group members might be comparatively more tolerable than if they are made by others. Such *evaluations* are likely to be taken seriously (rather than being dismissed or overruled), and there will be a high motivation to consider and resolve the obstacle by engaging in reasoning together, which can trigger curiosity. This can happen, for instance, because of positive impressions of a group member held by others that accumulate as members contribute to progress of the group towards desired goals, or, if certain group members possess valuable personal characteristics [3].

Group 3 comprises patterns following the general theme of **closing knowledge gaps** [21] and that are linked to high curiosity. These comprise *question asking* behaviors that co-occur or are contingent with *confusion-related facial expressions*. Prior literature in socio-emotional learning [11] has found *confusion* to be a key signature of cognitive disequilibrium, or, a state of uncertainty, and occurs when an individual faces contradictions or comes across novel stimuli, both of which are precursors of curiosity [2]. In our work, we coded for questions belonging to specific task aspects such as how and why things work, what-if something affects or will affect something else, underlying mechanisms or causal factors of a process or observation in detail, and other general knowledge (e.g. fact, terms, classification, or other general information) as on-task questions [22]. Such *on-task question asking* in group work, which reflects lacunae in understanding, reveals uncertainties in front of group members, and can be part of a think-aloud about the subject matter/specific scientific phenomenon/task that students are working on themselves. Think aloud in scientific inquiry helps monitor one's own thinking and understanding, and initiates meta-cognitive reflection to trigger awareness of knowledge gaps for engaging in further exploration. When tackling complex tasks in open-ended collaborative learning environments, thinking aloud together has been empirically shown to regulate co-construction of knowledge and lead to improvement in the ability to articulate collaborative reasoning processes [16,23]. *On-task question* asking can also be part of a question asked to another group member regarding what they are working on, how they act and think, their opinions or requesting suggestions relating to the task. We find in our RGM corpus that when group members recognize problematic ideas or flaws in the chain-reaction sub-components made by a peer, they often ask questions to express these knowledge gaps and elicit more information. These questions invite further *idea verbalization*.

Group 4 comprises patterns involving **making suggestion** to other group members, where an idea, possible plan or action for others to consider is mentioned, or, an opinion about what other people should do and how they should act in a particular situation is offered. Making *suggestions* is an evidence that a shared conception of the problem has very likely been developed, and therefore the *suggestion* is geared towards engaging in cooperative effort to overcome the obstacle, and joint creation of new interpretations. Thus, at a fundamental level, it not only signals interest in other's work, but also a child's anticipation to know whether the proposed idea will work or not (impact of the suggestion) and therefore find out the uncertain/unknown result. Engaging in these socio-cognitive processes of knowledge acquisition will spur an individual's curiosity, as is evident from the high utility sequential pattern shown in Table 2.

Group 5 comprises the dynamics of **positive emotional states** [11] that maximize the utility of curiosity. *Delight* and *joy* denote the pleasure associated with discovering new ideas by oneself or other group members. Emotional expressions of *flow* point to spending time and effort in acquiring a solution. It is indicative of persistence in engaging in knowledge acquisition processes.

3.2 Social Influence of Curiosity-Related Behaviors

To investigate social influence, we first ran the conditional granger causality algorithm separately for each group. We then synthesized similar causal behavioral influences across groups that were significant at 0.001 level of significance and averaged their G-ratios for presentation (Tables 3 and 4). Overall, we found ~2x higher number of significant interpersonal causal influence involving 2 or more group members (325) compared to intrapersonal causal influence (154). This strongly points towards why social scaffolding in group work is necessary, which corroborates with other work [30], as well as the precise way to provide it. We describe these significant causal influences at the interpersonal level along 4 themes and explain our interpretation of these results below (see Tables 3 and 4).

Group 1 reflects the theme of **behavioral contagion**, or the propensity for certain behavior exhibited by a group member to be repeated in close temporal proximity by others. The putative mechanism underlying this social phenomena might be entrainment, which in previous work we found had an impact on rapport and learning [31,32], or alternately, can also involve careful evaluation of conditions under which group members would be willing to be influenced. These conditions can involve looking at the motivational consequences of accepting or rejecting the influencing peer's behavior, such as the desire to receive reward or avoid punishment, desire to be like an admired person in the group (normative social influence), desire to abide by one's values (establishing self-identity), desire to be correct (informational social influence), other group oriented desires (such as welfare of the group), or intrinsically rewarding consequences [3].

In particular, in Table 3, we can see a significant causal influence of *uncertainty* expressed by one child on *uncertainty* of another child. Looking through the lens of group dynamics [10], closely contingent expressions of *uncertainty* from group members about similar (or related) aspects of the task is a signal of "joint hardship", or the experience of common blocking points for the group to proceed in its task. This causal relationship has been posited to positively influence the social interaction, since individuals expressing uncertainty will subsequently engage in cooperative effort to overcome the cause of uncertainty, often enhancing acceptance and group attraction because of having coped with the hardship situation. Moreover, the hope of resolving uncertainty under joint effort will make children more eager to explore, in turn increasing their curiosity. In addition, we also see significant interpersonal causal influences along behavioral constructs such as *sharing findings*, *argument* and *social question asking* (see Table 3). Such social questions reflect a general interest in gaining new social information about non-task relevant personal information and feelings, likes, dislikes, preferences from other group members [20]. They are a motivator for joint exploratory behaviors since they increase group member familiarity, build interpersonal closeness and promote an unconditional positive regard towards group members [10,29].

Table 3. Salient examples of direct social influence (⇝) along with corresponding conditional granger causality magnitudes (significant at 0.001 LOS)

Social influence (Direct)	G-ratio
Theme 1: Contagion	
1. Uncertainty (other) ⇝ Uncertainty (own)	0.687
2. Sharing Findings (other) ⇝ Sharing Findings (own)	0.223
3. Question Asking Social (other) ⇝ Question Asking Social (own)	0.379
4. Argument (other) ⇝ Argument (own)	0.177
Theme 2: Constructive controversy	
1. Suggestion (other) ⇝ Argument (own)	0.176
2. Argument (other) ⇝ Idea Verbalization (own)	0.160
3. Argument (other) ⇝ Negative Evaluation (own)	0.138
4. Argument (other) ⇝ Justification (own)	0.131
Theme 3: Idea/View refinement	
1. Hypothesis generation (other) ⇝ Suggestion (own)	0.256
2. Question Asking Task (other) ⇝ Hypothesis generation (own)	0.248
3. Suggestion (other) ⇝ Negative Evaluation (own)	0.109
4. Sharing Findings (other) ⇝ Negative Evaluation (own)	0.086
Theme 4: Supportive responses	
1. Uncertainty (other) ⇝ Agreement (own)	0.171
2. Uncertainty (other) ⇝ Suggestion (own)	0.111
3. Idea Verbalization (other) ⇝ Positive evaluation (own)	0.098
4. Uncertainty (other) ⇝ Hypothesis generation (own)	0.086

Group 2 reflects the theme of **constructive controversy** [17], or group members' involvement in seeking out to reach an agreement when their ideas, conclusions and theories are incompatible with those of one another. Such constructive controversy, as instantiated in interpersonal behaviors such as *argument*, *negative evaluation* etc. leads to an active search for additional perspectives to support correctness of one's own view. This is likely to improve the quality of group decision making by providing a medium through which problems can be aired and tensions released. This environment of self-evaluation and change will in turn encourage interest and curiosity among group members [25]. For our corpus, some salient direct interpersonal causal influences from this group include those of *suggestion* on *argument*, *argument* on *idea verbalization*, *argument* on *negative evaluation* and *argument* on *justification* (see Table 3). Additional fully mediated causal influences among behaviors in this group are shown

Table 4. Salient examples of fully mediated social influence ($\rightsquigarrow$) along with corresponding conditional granger causality magnitudes (significant at 0.001 LOS)

Social influence (Fully mediated)	G-ratio
Theme 1: Constructive controversy	
Argument (p1) $\rightsquigarrow$ Surprise (p2) $\rightsquigarrow$ Justification (p3)	0.251
Theme 2: Idea/View refinement	
1. Hypothesis Generation (p1) $\rightsquigarrow$ Sharing Findings (p2) $\rightsquigarrow$ Suggestion (p3)	0.399
2. Hypothesis Generation (p1) $\rightsquigarrow$ Sharing Findings (p2) $\rightsquigarrow$ Negative Evaluation (p3)	0.250
3. Sharing Findings (p1) $\rightsquigarrow$ Hypothesis Generation (p2) $\rightsquigarrow$ Idea Verbalization (p2)	0.233
4. Sharing Findings (p1) $\rightsquigarrow$ Hypothesis Generation (p2) $\rightsquigarrow$ Justification (p2)	0.167
Theme 3: Supportive responses	
Sharing Findings (p1) $\rightsquigarrow$ Hypothesis Generation (p2) $\rightsquigarrow$ Positive Evaluation (p2)	0.148

in Table 4, where we find *sharing findings* fully mediates the causal influence of *hypothesis generation* on *suggestion/negative evaluation*. In addition, *hypothesis generation* fully mediates the causal influence of *sharing findings* on *idea verbalization/justification*.

Group 3 reflects the theme of **refining a group member's ideas or views**. This can be seen via direct interpersonal causal influences of *hypothesis generation* on *suggestion*, *task question asking* on *hypothesis generation*, *suggestion* on *negative evaluation* and *sharing findings* on *negative evaluation* in Table 3. Prior work has posited that such *negative evaluation*, as a common expression of disagreement referring to epistemic (task) content, will enhance an individual's curiosity because of enhancement of perceived contribution of the peer [8]. Additional fully mediated causal influences among behaviors in this group are shown in Table 4, where we find that the causal influence of *argument* made by person A on *justification* done by person B is fully mediated by an emotional expression of *surprise* from a third group member person C.

Group 4 reflects the theme of **supportive responses to uncertainty**, which are more likely when one's peers either share the uncertainty or at least consider it warranted, reasonable, or legitimate [18]. In particular, for our corpus, some salient direct interpersonal causal influences include those of *uncertainty* on *agreement/suggestion/hypothesis generation*, and *idea verbalization* on *positive evaluation* (see Table 3). Additional fully mediated causal influence among behaviors in this group are shown in Table 4, where we find that the causal influence of *sharing findings* by person A on *positive evaluation* made by person B is fully mediated by *hypothesis* generated by person B.

4 Implications for Designing Learning Technologies

In spite of its critical link with learning, curiosity is often found to decrease with age and schooling, partially because of prevalence of test-oriented education strategies that follow from educational policies such as the "common core" [28]. This effect is even more pronounced in inner city classrooms with limited teaching resources that are constantly under great pressure to adhere to academic standards. Understanding how to design computer support to raise and sustain curiosity will make this important metacognitive skill more accessible to students from diverse socioeconomic backgrounds. In this paper then, we claim that such forms of computer support should be equipped with fine-grained understanding of the unfolding behavioral trajectory, to allow for detection of behaviors belonging to a larger sequential pattern that maximizes the utility of curiosity for a target learner. Our work in the first part of this paper can aid in development of data-driven heuristics for providing a principled way of choosing the kind of support to be provided (given the observed behavior trajectories). However, since not all productive conversational behaviors that maximize the utility of curiosity in human-human interaction might occur naturally in interactions between human and a learning technology, it might be worthwhile to make some arrangements for the appearance of such behaviors. We can then leverage insights gained from second part of the work presented in this paper to decide an action (behavior) to be performed by a learning technology that will cause/trigger a particular behavioral change in a peer.

Investigation of social influence of curiosity-related behaviors provides a simple, yet elegant solution to an important and fundamental research question in human perception and reasoning - given a desired mental state change (curiosity), how can a learning technology (for example, in the form of a pedagogical agent) act to cause that mental state change in a human. For example - let's suppose we have the sequential behavioral pattern of: Task Question Asking(person 2) $\twoheadrightarrow$ Uncertainty(person1) that maximizes the utility of curiosity of person 1. On perceiving that person 2 has asked a task-related question, and person 1 is passive in subsequent time steps, the social influence knowledge database can be consulted and the specific causal influence rule of: Uncertainty (other) $\rightsquigarrow$ Uncertainty (own) can be picked by a pedagogical agent to verbalize an expression of uncertainty about some aspect of the task that was related to the question asked by person 2, along with (maybe) asking person 1's opinion about the same. This is likely to capture person 1's attention, who might express uncertainty about similar aspects of the task. Such shared uncertainty might make person 1 eager to reduce their knowledge gap by engaging in joint exploration, in turn maximizing their curiosity. Furthermore, since data-driven approaches cannot capture the exhaustive set of productive social interaction practices that educators have been using for raising children's curiosity in different learning settings (e.g. - promoting risk taking by rewarding exploration of diverse solutions, helping group members find causal relationships between processes by asking them to make an explicit link between learning representations) [7,33], we must acknowledge that results derived from this research can be augmented with those top-down strategies to provide complementary benefits to a learner.

5 Conclusion

In this work, we looked at sequential patterns of multimodal behaviors across group members that maximize an individual's utility of curiosity when learning in social contexts. To provide rich forms of social scaffolding for fostering curiosity, we further investigated direct and mediated interpersonal causal influences that can be used to trigger particular productive conversational behaviors in the interaction. These results draw on various theoretical lenses in learning sciences and the social psychology of group dynamics, as well as results from our analyses of small group informal learning. We believe that such a fine-grained theoretical understanding of the construct of curiosity holds the key to combating its absence in collaborative learning settings by leveraging simple, yet powerful insights that we gain from analytical approaches outlined in this work. The underlying rationale is applicable more generally for developing computer support for other metacognitive skills as well. Our larger vision is to develop socially-aware learning technologies [36] that can bring back an individual's curiosity, maintain the momentum ignited by it, and help individuals engage in task-completion by pooling interpersonal resources when working in a group, motivated by their intrinsic interest. Through the design of such learning technologies and confirming their effectiveness, we also hope to provide additional pedagogical instructions for school teachers to help children with diverse socio-economical background develop knowledge-seeking skills driven by intrinsic curiosity.

References

1. Ambady, N., Rosenthal, R.: Thin slices of expressive behavior as predictors of interpersonal consequences: A meta-analysis (1992)
2. Berlyne, D.E.: Conflict, Arousal, and Curiosity. McGraw-Hill, New York (1960)
3. Cartwright, D.E., Zander, A.E.: Group Dynamics Research and Theory. Harper and Row, New York (1953)
4. Chen, G., Chiu, M.M., Wang, Z.: Social metacognition and the creation of correct, new ideas: a statistical discourse analysis of online mathematics discussions. Comput. Hum. Behav. **28**(3), 868–880 (2012)
5. Chi, M.T., Wylie, R.: The ICAP framework: linking cognitive engagement to active learning outcomes. Educ. Psychol. **49**(4), 219–243 (2014)
6. Chiu, M.M.: Flowing toward correct contributions during group problem solving: a statistical discourse analysis. J. Learn. Sci. **17**(3), 415–463 (2008)
7. Correnti, R., Stein, M.K., Smith, M.S., Scherrer, J., McKeown, M., Greeno, J., Ashley, K.: Improving teaching at scale: design for the scientific measurement and learning of discourse practice. In: Socializing Intelligence Through Academic Talk and Dialogue. AERA (2015)

8. Darnon, C., Doll, S., Butera, F.: Dealing with a disagreeing partner: relational and epistemic conflict elaboration. Eur. J. Psychol. Educ. **22**(3), 227–242 (2007)
9. Ding, M., Chen, Y., Bressler, S.L.: Granger causality: basic theory and application to neuroscience. In: Schelter, B., Winterhalder, M., Timmer, J. (eds.) Handbook of Time Series Analysis: Recent Theoretical Developments and Applications, p. 437. Wiley, Weinheim (2006)
10. Dörnyei, Z., Murphey, T.: Group Dynamics in the Language Classroom. Ernst Klett Sprachen, Stuttgart (2003)
11. D'Mello, S., Graesser, A.: Dynamics of affective states during complex learning. Learn. Instr. **22**(2), 145–157 (2012)
12. Forsyth, D.R.: Group Dynamics. Cengage Learning, Belmont (2009)
13. Gordon, G., Breazeal, C., Engel, S.: Can children catch curiosity from a social robot? In: Proceedings of the Tenth Annual ACM/IEEE International Conference on Human-Robot Interaction, pp. 91–98. ACM (2015)
14. Graesser, A.C., Person, N.K., Magliano, J.P.: Collaborative dialogue patterns in naturalistic one-to-one tutoring. Appl. Cogn. Psychol. **9**(6), 495–522 (1995)
15. Grossnickle, E.M.: Disentangling curiosity: dimensionality, definitions, and distinctions from interest in educational contexts. Educ. Psychol. Rev. **28**(1), 23–60 (2016)
16. Hogan, K.: Thinking aloud together: a test of an intervention to foster students' collaborative scientific reasoning. J. Res. Sci. Teach. **36**(10), 1085–1109 (1999)
17. Johnson, D.W., Johnson, R.T.: Energizing learning: the instructional power of conflict. Educ. Res. **38**(1), 37–51 (2009)
18. Jordan, M.E., McDaniel, R.R.: Managing uncertainty during collaborative problem solving in elementary school teams: the role of peer influence in robotics engineering activity. J. Learn. Sci. **23**(4), 490–536 (2014)
19. Kruger, J., Endriss, U., Fernández, R., Qing, C.: Axiomatic analysis of aggregation methods for collective annotation. In: Proceedings of the 2014 International Conference on Autonomous Agents and Multi-agent Systems, pp. 1185–1192. International Foundation for Autonomous Agents and Multiagent Systems (2014)
20. Litman, J.A., Pezzo, M.V.: Dimensionality of interpersonal curiosity. Personality Individ. Differ. **43**(6), 1448–1459 (2007)
21. Loewenstein, G.: The psychology of curiosity: a review and reinterpretation. Psychol. Bull. **116**(1), 75 (1994)
22. Luce, M.R., Hsi, S.: Science-relevant curiosity expression and interest in science: an exploratory study. Sci. Educ. **99**(1), 70–97 (2015)
23. Mockel, L.J.: Thinking aloud in the science classroom: Can a literacy strategy increase student learning in science? (2013)
24. Orlitzky, M., Hirokawa, R.Y.: To err is human, to correct for it divine a meta-analysis of research testing the functional theory of group decision-making effectiveness. Small Group Res. **32**(3), 313–341 (2001)
25. Paletz, S.B., Schunn, C.D., Kim, K.H.: Intragroup conflict under the microscope: micro-conflicts in naturalistic team discussions. Negot. Confl. Manage. Res. **4**(4), 314–351 (2011)
26. Paulus, P.B., Brown, V.R.: Enhancing ideational creativity in groups. In: Paulus, P.B., Nijstad, B.A. (eds.) Group Creativity: Innovation Through Collaboration, pp. 110–136. Oxford University Press, New York (2003)
27. Pea, R.D.: The social and technological dimensions of scaffolding and related theoretical concepts for learning, education, and human activity. J. Learn. Sci. **13**(3), 423–451 (2004)
28. Porter, A., McMaken, J., Hwang, J., Yang, R.: Common core standards the new us intended curriculum. Educ. Res. **40**(3), 103–116 (2011)

29. Rogers, C.R.: Freedom to Learn for the 80's. No. 371.39 R724f. Merrill Publishing, Ohio (1983)
30. Sinha, T., Bai, Z., Cassell, J.: A new theoretical framework for curiosity for learning in social contexts. In: Lavoué, É., et al. (eds.) EC-TEL 2017. LNCS, vol. 10474, pp. 254–269. Springer, Cham (2017). doi:10.1007/978-3-319-66610-5_19
31. Sinha, T., Cassell, J.: We click, we align, we learn: impact of influence and convergence processes on student learning and rapport building. In: Proceedings of the 1st Workshop on Modeling INTERPERsonal SynchrONy And infLuence, pp. 13–20. ACM (2015)
32. Sinha, T., Zhao, R., Cassell, J.: Exploring socio-cognitive effects of conversational strategy congruence in peer tutoring. In: Proceedings of the 1st Workshop on Modeling INTERPERsonal SynchrONy And infLuence, pp. 5–12. ACM (2015)
33. Spektor-Levy, O., Baruch, Y.K., Mevarech, Z.: Science and scientific curiosity in pre-school–the teacher's point of view. Int. J. Sci. Educ. **35**(13), 2226–2253 (2013)
34. Wu, Q., Miao, C.: Modeling curiosity-related emotions for virtual peer learners. IEEE Comput. Intell. Mag. **8**(2), 50–62 (2013)
35. Yin, J., Zheng, Z., Cao, L.: USpan: an efficient algorithm for mining high utility sequential patterns. In: Proceedings of the 18th ACM SIGKDD International Conference on Knowledge Discovery and Data Mining, pp. 660–668. ACM (2012)
36. Zhao, R., Sinha, T., Black, A.W., Cassell, J.: Socially-aware virtual agents: automatically assessing dyadic rapport from temporal patterns of behavior. In: Traum, D., Swartout, W., Khooshabeh, P., Kopp, S., Scherer, S., Leuski, A. (eds.) IVA 2016. LNCS, vol. 10011, pp. 218–233. Springer, Cham (2016). doi:10.1007/978-3-319-47665-0_20

Using Sequential Pattern Mining to Explore Learners' Behaviors and Evaluate Their Correlation with Performance in Inquiry-Based Learning

Rémi Venant[1(✉)], Kshitij Sharma[2], Philippe Vidal[1], Pierre Dillenbourg[2], and Julien Broisin[1]

[1] Université de Toulouse, IRIT, 31062 Toulouse Cedex 9, France
{remi.venant,philippe.vidal,julien.broisin}@irit.fr
[2] Computer-Human Interaction in Learning and Instruction (CHILI), Ecole Polytechnique Fédérale de Lausanne (EPFL), Station 20, 1015 Lausanne, Switzerland
{kshitij.sharma,pierre.dillenbour}@epfl.ch

Abstract. This study analyzes students' behaviors in a remote laboratory environment in order to identify new factors of prediction of academic success. It investigates relations between learners' activities during practical sessions, and their performance at the final assessment test. Based on learning analytics applied to data collected from an experimentation conducted with our remote lab dedicated to computer education, we discover recurrent sequential patterns of actions that lead us to the definition of learning strategies as indicators of higher level of abstraction. Results show that some of the strategies are correlated to learners' performance. For instance, the construction of a complex action step by step, or the reflection before submitting an action, are two strategies applied more often by learners of a higher level of performance than by other students. While our proposals are domain-independent and can thus apply to other learning contexts, the results of this study led us to instrument for both students and instructors new visualization and guiding tools in our remote lab environment.

1 Introduction

Research on predictors of success in learning has been a hot topic for decades [1–4]. Many studies in that field focused on finding predictors of performance, which is commonly measured through academical assessment. Predictors are traditionally based on information about learners collected through past academic results, pre-course tests or questionnaires that include, among others, work style preference, self-efficacy [5], background or expectations [6]. However, the development of Technology Enhanced Learning (TEL), combined with the emergence of Educational Data Mining (EDM) and Learning Analytics (LA), provide new capabilities to explore learners' behaviors during specific learning situations and to study their influence on students' performance.

É. Lavoué et al. (Eds.): EC-TEL 2017, LNCS 10474, pp. 286–299, 2017.
DOI: 10.1007/978-3-319-66610-5_21

Remote or virtual laboratories (VRL) are learning environments designed to support inquiry learning through practical activities with the mediation of computers. Within these environments, learners develop inquiry and self-regulated skills through interactions with remote or simulated apparatus, but also collaborative skills through interactions with peers and instructors. With the tracking of these interactions, VRL may provide an insight of learners' behaviors at a high resolution that could lead to a better understanding of the learning process. While studying these actions through independent measures can be a first approach, the analysis of sequential patterns may provide another understanding of how learners act [7]. Sequential pattern mining, as a method to identify relevant patterns of actions within a set of sequences [8], is then to be considered.

In order to explore the potential links between learners' behaviors and their performance, we conducted an experiment in a real class environment, with 85 students enrolled in a Computer Science program. We explore in this article the interactions between learners and the remote apparatus to study the potential correlations between their performance score at the final assessment test, and both quantitative indicators and sequential action patterns. Our objective is to identify behavioural patterns for a practical session that lead to better learning outcomes, in order to predict learners' performance and to automatically guide students who might need more support to complete their tasks.

The next section presents the computational settings (i.e., our learning environment, with a focus on its tracking framework), and exposes the experimentation protocol together with the resulting dataset. While a first analysis exposed in Sect. 3 covers engagement indicators such as the number of actions achieved by a student, or the time between two actions, Sect. 4 proposes a methodology based on sequential pattern mining to discover sequences of actions that are representative of the learners' level of performance. These patterns allow for specification of abstract indicators, viewed as learning strategies and correlated with students' success. We then situate our research work among existing studies in the field of computer education and dedicated laboratories, and discuss about the impact of our study on new artificial intelligence features integrated into our remote lab environment.

2 Experimental Settings

The experimentation was conducted at the Computer Science Institute of Technology (CSIT) of the University of Toulouse (France). For the whole experimentation, learners used our web-based virtual laboratory environment dedicated to computer education, and especially to system and network administration, to complete the whole set of practical tasks they were asked to.

2.1 The Learning Environment: Lab4CE

Lab4CE (Laboratory for Computer Education) is a web-based platform that relies on a cloud manager to offer on-demand remote laboratories made of virtual computers and networks, and that features advanced learning capabilities [9]. Lab4CE has been designed to overcome the spatial limitations and restrictions of access to physical resources: it provides, for example, each learner with a set of virtual machines, routers and switches accessible from anywhere and without any limitation of use (i.e., students are granted with the administrator role).

Within this environment, instructors can create a practical activity by designing the topology of machines and networks needed by learners to achieve the pedagogical objectives; the activities achieved within that environment are up to the teacher, as the environment does not enforce any form of learning scenario. When a learner accesses a particular activity, the system automatically creates and sets the different virtual resources up. Learners can then manipulate the machines (i.e., start them up, put them to sleep, etc.) and interact with them through a web-based terminal similar to a traditional computer terminal.

At the time of the experimentation, the learning features accessible to learners (and instructors as well) included real-time communication (i.e., an instant messaging system), collaborative work (i.e., several learners can work together on the same machine and see what others are doing), awareness tools (i.e., learners can compare actions they are carrying out against the actions being carried out by their peers), as well as tools for replay and deep analysis of working sessions. Let us note that the system makes it possible for teachers to deactivate a given learning feature for a particular practical activity.

In addition to the above pedagogical facilities, our virtual lab environment integrates a learning analytics framework able to collect in the xAPI format [10] most of users interactions with the system. In this study, we focus on interactions between learners and the remote virtual resources they had to administrate, as this kind of activity can be considered as almost fully representative of the learning tasks completed by learners.

Such interactions rely on the Shell commands executed within the web terminal. These commands include a name and, sometimes, one or more arguments (e.g., *ls -a -l* is the command name *ls* with the arguments *-a* and *-l*). Also, once a command is executed, the machine may return a textual answer (e.g., the execution of the command *ls -a -l* returns the list of all files and folders stored in the current directory). Thus, the xAPI statements at the basis of the pattern analysis suggested further in this paper consists of the 8 following elements: (i) the timestamp, (ii) the id of the laboratory, (iii) the learner's username, (iv) the id of the machine, (v) the name of the command, (vi) its arguments, (vii) the output the machine produced, and (viii) the technical rightness of the command. That last element is a boolean value inferred on the basis of the elements (v), (vi) and (vii) to indicate whether the command was executed successfully [11].

2.2 Experimentation Protocol and Learning Scenario

The experiment took place for an introductory course on Shell commands and programming; it involved 107 first year students, with a gender repartition that reflects the distribution of CSIT students.

We conducted the experiment at the beginning of the course, which implies that all students were beginners in Computer Sciences. The experimentation lasted for three weeks, during which students had a 24–7 access to their own virtual machine deployed within our remote lab environment. Each week, one face-to-face practical session of 90 min was given. For that three weeks, the course targeted three main learning outcomes: understanding of a Shell command, Linux file system management using Shell commands, and understanding of several basic concepts of Shell programming. For each session, learners had to achieve a list of tasks involving a set of Shell commands. They first had to understand what the commands do, how they work (i.e., what arguments must/may be used), and then to execute them to achieve the given tasks. The last session required learners to reuse the commands they discovered during the first two sessions to build simple Shell scripts made of conditional statements or loops. To achieve this latter outcome, learners reused some skills acquired previously through an introductory course on algorithmic.

Finally, the pedagogical material provided to students only comprised, as PDF files, a textual description of the tasks to achieve and the name of the commands to use, along with few simple examples. For a full understanding of a certain command, learners had to consult the matching manual available in the Shell of their virtual machine.

2.3 The Resulting Dataset

Once outliers have been removed, the dataset comprises 85 students which submitted a total of 9183 commands. Then the mean number of commands by learner is 108.00 with a standard deviation $\sigma = 66.62$. The minimum of command submitted for a learner is 22 while the maximum is 288.

2.4 Measure of Academic Performance

We defined in this study the assessment score (AS) as a continuous variable between 0 and 20 that denotes the score learners got when they took the test at the end of the course. The distribution of AS in the experiment presents qualitative cutpoints that make clearly appear three categories of AS (AScat): low (named L; number of students (N) within this category = 22), medium (M, with N = 27) and high (H, with N = 36).

In the next two sections, the dataset resulting from the experimentation is analyzed against the AS and/or the categories of AS. The following section defines some quantitative indicators as independent variables and investigates their correlation with the two above mentioned dependent variables, before we go into deeper pattern mining analysis in Sect. 4.

3 Study of Quantitative Indicators

Starting from the records of the dataset, we first studied the four following quantitative indicators: (1) the number of commands submitted by a learner

(*#submissions*); (2) the percent of commands executed successfully (*%success*); (3) the average time spent between two submissions of commands of the same working session ($\Delta Time$); and (4) the number of commands submitted by a learner referring to help seeking (*#help*). The first three indicators can be found in other research works [4,12] and allow quantifying learners' production. The last indicator identifies help access. While it can be difficult to compute in other contexts (i.e., when help resources reside outside the learning environment), remote or virtual labs often come with their own assistance material, whose access can be easily tracked [13].

In order to identify working sessions, we applied a time series clustering algorithm and checked for each learner that their class schedule was consistent with the algorithm (i.e., the list of working sessions for a given learner includes at least the sessions she attended in class). The *#help* indicator is based on well-known patterns such as the command *man* that provides a complete manual of a certain command, or the arguments *-help* and *-h* that give a lightweight manual. Table 1 shows the Pearson correlation analysis between the four indicators defined above and the assessment score.

The indicators *#submissions* and $\Delta Time$ do not appear to be correlated with the assessment score, as the p-value for both indicators is greater than 0.05. Also, even if *%success* and *#help* present a weak significant correlation with AS, they only roughly reflect how students behaved during practical learning: *%success* is an indicator of production that does not take into account learners' progress, so as *#help* which does not reflect the way students sought for help (i.e., after a command failure, before testing a new command, etc.).

In order to go further in the analysis of learners' behaviors, we explore in the next section how they carried out their activities in terms of sequences of commands; let us note that the word *instructions* may also be used in the remaining of the paper to designate such Shell commands.

Table 1. Pearson correlation between quantitative indicators and AS

	r	p-value
#submissions	0.193	0.076
%success	0.248	0.022
ΔTime	−0.127	0.247
#help	0.226	0.037

4 Pattern Mining Analysis

A pattern mining analysis was applied on the experimentation dataset to identify the significant sequences of actions carried out by learners during practical activities, and to analyze whether these sequences are related to the two dependent variables AS and AScat.

4.1 Nature of Actions

First, we propose to go further the restriction of the learning context by applying a pattern mining analysis not on commands themselves, but on their nature, their relationships, and the result of their execution. Hence, we define a generic *action* submitted by a learner on a resource in the context of a practical session as a structure of three components: its *type*, its *parameters* and its *nature*. The type and the parameters depend on the learning domain; for instance, *to supply a RLC electrical circuit* with a nominal tension of *12 V* represent a type and a parameter of an action carried out for a practical work in Electronic. In our context, the *type* is the *command name*, whereas the *parameters* represent its *arguments* (see end of Sect. 2.1). The *nature* provides semantic about the relation between an action and the action that has been submitted just before.

According to the above definition, we specified eight exclusive natures of actions: *Sub_S*, *Sub_F*, *ReSub_S*, *ReSub_F*, *VarSub_S*, *VarSub_F*, *Help* and *NewHelp*. The natures *Sub_** refer to an action whose type is different from the type of the previous action, and which has been executed successfuly (*Sub_S*) or not (*Sub_F*) by the resource. The natures *ReSub_** address an action that is identical to the previous one (i.e., same type and parameters), while the natures *VarSub_** represent an action of the same type than the previous one, but with different parameters. Finally, *Help* depicts an action of help seeking about the type of the previous action, while *NewHelp* indicates a help access without relations with the previous action. For instance, if the previous command is *ls -al*, the next command *rm* will belong to *Sub_F* (as *rm* has a different command name, and is technically wrong because that command requires at least one argument), *ls -al* to *ReSub_S*, *ls -alRU* to *VarSub_S*, while *man ls* will be classified with the nature *Help* and *man rm* with the nature *NewHelp*.

4.2 Patterns of Actions

To discover which sequences of actions were statistically significant, we analyzed two-length and three-length sequences only, as no sequences of length four or more were used by enough learners to be significant. The statistical tests applied for each sequence were a Pearson correlation test for AS, and an analysis of variance (i.e., one-way ANOVA) for AScat. The patterns appearing in Table 2 are those whose p-value is lower than 0.05 for at least one of the two tests. Also, the column "Trend of use" of Table 2 depicts the order of use of a pattern among the categories of AS, with its significance given in the column "ANOVA p-value". For instance, high-level students used the pattern #2 more often than the low-level students, and medium level students also used this pattern more often than the low level students; however, no ordered relation is given between high- and medium-level students for this pattern.

As shown in Table 2, 13 patterns appeared to be statistically significant. Most of them present both a significant trend of use between performance levels, and a significant weak (i.e., $0.1 < |r| < 0.3$) or medium (i.e., $0.3 < |r| < 0.5$) correlation with AS. It appears that most of these patterns are used by

Table 2. Analysis of action patterns

#	Pattern	Test with AScat		Test with AS	
		Trend of use	ANOVA p-value	r	cor. p-value
1	Sub_S, VarSub_S	$H, M > L$	< 0.001	0.335	0.002
2	Help, ReSub_S	$H, M > L$	0.003	0.293	0.006
3	VarSub_S, NewHelp	$H, M > L$	0.007	0.210	0.053
4	VarSub_S, Sub_S	$H, M > L$	0.021	0.264	0.014
5	ReSub_S, NewHelp	$H, M > L$	0.026	0.361	< 0.001
6	VarSub_S, VarSub_S	$H, M > L$	0.031	0.203	0.062
7	Sub_S, VarSub_S, VarSub_S	$H, M > L$	0.002	0.286	0.008
8	VarSub_S, VarSub_S, Sub_S	$H, M > L$	0.003	0.294	0.006
9	Sub_S, VarSub_S, NewHelp	$H, M > L$	0.007	0.250	0.020
10	NewHelp, Sub_S, VarSub_S	$H, M > L$	0.009	0.243	0.025
11	Sub_S, ReSub_S, NewHelp	$H, M > L$	0.020	0.335	0.002
12	Sub_F, VarSub_F, VarSub_S	$L > H, M$	0.021	−0.217	0.046
13	Sub_S, NewHelp, ReSub_S	$H, M > L$	0.047	0.244	0.024

high- and medium-level students at a higher frequency than by low-level students, and positively correlated with the performance at the academic test; only one pattern of actions (i.e., pattern #12) is used more often by low-level students than by others, where students unsuccessfully submit a particular action by modifying its parameters until the submission succeeds. Nonetheless, no patterns make it possible to clearly distinguish high- and medium-level students.

Also, the patterns reveal common semantics depicting the students' behaviors. For instance, the patterns 1, 6, 7, 8 and 9 show a sequence of a successful action (i.e., *Sub_S*, *ReSub_S* or *VarSub_S*) followed by another successful action characterized by the same type (i.e., *VarSub_S*). We make here the hypothesis that these patterns illustrate learners building a complex action progressively.

The set of patterns we identified can thus be viewed as approaches applied by learners to carry out a task or solve a problem. Some of them refer to a common methodology we define as *learning strategy*. In the next section, we identify these strategies from the patterns of Table 2, and analyze their relation with the academic performance.

4.3 Learning Strategies

The 13 patterns highlight eight strategies: *confirmation*, *progression*, *success-then-reflexion*, *reflexion-then-success*, *fail-then-reflexion*, *trial-and-error*, and *withdrawal*. *Confirmation* is the successful resubmission of the same action (i.e., command and arguments remain unchanged), while *progression* depicts a sequence of successfully executed actions of the same type, but whose parameters get more complex from one to another. *Success-then-reflexion* expresses a successful action, followed by access to the help related to the matching type.

Conversely, *reflexion-then-success* appears when students first access the help of a certain type of action, and then submit the matching action successfully. *Fail-then-reflexion* shows an access to the help related to an action that failed. *Trial-and-error* expresses a sequence of trial of the same action with a variation of its parameters until the submission succeeds. Finally, *withdrawal* matches with an action of a different type than the previous one whose submission failed.

Table 3. Regular expressions used for detection of learning strategies

Strategy	Regular expression
Confirmation	(?:Sub|ReSub|VarSub)_S,(?:Sub_S,) * (?:Sub_S)
Progression	(?:Sub|ReSub|VarSub)_S,(?:Help,)?VarSub_S
Success-then-reflexion	(?:Sub|ReSub|VarSub)_S,(?:Help|NewHelp)
Reflexion-then-success	(?:Help|NewHelp),(?:Sub|ReSub|VarSub)_S
Fail-then-reflexion	(?:Sub|ReSub|VarSub)_F,(?:Help|NewHelp)
Trial-and-error	(?:Sub|ReSub|VarSub)_F,
	(?:(?:ReSub|VarSub)_F,) * (?:ReSub|VarSub)_F
Withdrawal	(?:Sub|ReSub|VarSub)_F,(?:Help,) * (?:NewHelp,Sub_)

Table 3 shows the regular expressions we used to detect the above strategies within the learning paths followed by learners (i.e., within the sequences of natures of actions carried out by learners). For instance, the regular expression related to the *progression* strategy matches with patterns of successfully executed actions of the same type but with different parameters, while help accesses to this type of action may appear between submissions.

4.4 Results

We studied the relationships between each of these strategies and the academic performance with the same tests than in Sect. 4.2 (i.e., an ANOVA for AScat, and a Pearson correlation test for AS). Table 4 shows the results for that study. The significant values are highlighted in bold, while the strategies whose at least one result is significant appear in italic.

Progression, *success-then-reflexion*, *reflexion-then-success* and *fail-then-reflexion* are the strategies that present significant results. The first three ones allow to cluster students in a category of performance and seem to be traits of behavior of students of high- and medium-levels of performance.

Also, significant strategies are all positively correlated to the AS: the results do not reveal any particular behaviors of learners of low-level performance. The trial-and-error strategy does not present any significant results in this experimentation. This may be explained by the experimental settings mentioned before (see Sect. 2): students were beginners in Computer Science, and the learning tasks they were assigned to relied on exploratory learning where learners had

Table 4. Analysis of learning strategies

Strategies	Test with AScat		Test with AS	
	Trend of use	ANOVA p-value	r	cor. p-value
Confirmation	∅	0.745	0.108	0.321
Progression	***H,M > L***	**0.001**	**0.294**	**0.006**
Success-then-reflexion	***H,M > L***	**0.010**	**0.282**	**0.008**
Reflexion-then-success	***H,M > L***	**0.015**	**0.242**	**0.026**
Fail-then-reflexion	∅	0.020	**0.273**	**0.011**
Trial-and-error	∅	0.341	−0.050	0.670
Withdrawal	∅	0.457	−0.004	0.968

to discover by themselves the Shell commands. In this form of learning, doing multiple trials to discover and understand how the machine reacts is an expected behavior [14], no matter the performance level of the student is.

Another interesting result is the *withdrawal* strategy which does not seem to be related with the assessment score. This strategy, applied homogeneously by all students, whatever their performance level is, does not express that students fail at achieving a particular task. Different hypothesis can explain the fact that a learner suspends the completion of an action, such as the curiosity or the discovery of new actions. This strategy thus does not seem to be relevant to predict performance or to make a decision.

This analysis of learning strategies mainly reveals behaviors of high- and medium-level students that are positively correlated to the assessment score. With the *progression* strategy, high-level students seem to decompose their problem in steps of increasing complexity. The three others strategies used by high-level students are related to reflexion through the use of help; this result is in line with the findings of Sect. 3, where the indicator *#help* (i.e., the number of help accesses) is weakly and positively correlated with the academic performance.

5 Discussion

5.1 Results Exploitation

The outcomes of this study gave us the opportunity to enrich our remote lab environment with new analytics providing insights of learners' behaviors to teachers and students as well. Figure 1 represents a set of visualizations illustrating the occurrences of both the success-then-reflexion (in green) and the reflexion-then-success (in purple) strategies followed by four different learners, for the whole duration of the experiment; each graph comes with the academic score and category of the matching student. The different visualizations strengthen the findings of the previous section: the more these strategies are used, the better score the student obtained at the assessment.

Fig. 1. Visualization of success-then-reflexion and reflexion-then-success strategies adopted by learners

While these visualizations are of interest to understand how learners act, the results of our analysis allow for on-the-fly detection of their behaviors and open the door for new opportunities. Indeed, the continuous improvement of TEL-based systems, according to experimental findings resulting from their usage, is a critical part of the re-engineering process [15]. Applied to learning analytics, this enhancement cycle makes it possible to discover new design patterns and to generate new data for research about and improvement of TEL [16].

Thus, with respect to this methodology, we integrated into our remote lab environment two new features built on two distinct design patterns. The first feature relies on an intelligent tutoring system (ITS) able to guide learners during their practical sessions according to the learning strategies they are currently engaged in. For instance, when a learner fails several times to execute a command, the ITS suggests the learner to read the matching manual or to seek help from a peer that has successfully used that command, so that the learner becomes engaged in the reflexion-then-success strategy leading to better performance. The second design pattern we implemented is an awareness system intended for teachers and highlighting, based on the learning strategies followed by learners, students that seem to present weaknesses. For instance, if several learners follow the withdrawal strategy on the same command, the system notifies the teacher so she can make a collective intervention. These new features are already implanted into our system and will be evaluated in the near future through different axis: their usability, their reliability to guide learners and notify teachers, and the impact they may have on both learners' and teachers' behaviors.

5.2 Related Work

In computer education, several studies have been conducted to find out what characteristics of learners' profile may predict their success or failure in a given learning activity; such characteristics include pre-activity properties like personality traits and past academic achievement [5,17], or demographic factors and learners' expectations [6]. To take into account such indicators is useful, for example, to identify learners that may require more attention and for which a personalized tutoring would be beneficial. However, this approach restrict learners' data to information that cannot evolve during the activity: the learning activity is seen as an object that does not impact learning outcomes. Instead, the approach we adopted, based on learning analytics about learners' interactions occurring all along the practical activity, tends to overcome this issue since it considers learners' interactions as a potential variable of performance prediction.

In Computer Science, other research works also adopt a learning analytics approach to predict performance. For instance, Blikstein [3] and Watson & al. [12] rely on the source codes produced by learners to analyze various indicators such as the code size, the number of compilations, the time between two compilations, or the score students got at the post-experimental test. In another way, Vihavainen [4] presents a quantitative study in an introductory programming course where snapshots of students' code are regularly logged during practical sessions to detect good practices (i.e., code indentation or variables shadowing) or compilation results (i.e., success or failure). In these works, indicators are tightly coupled to the programming activity. In the LaboRem [18] or Ironmaking [19] systems dedicated to physics education, students have to input values of several parameters of different devices before launching a simulation whose output is used to analyze different physical phenomenons. The notions of actions and variation of parameters we introduced in our study apply here as well, and allow to analyze learners' behaviors by reusing both the nature of actions and learning strategies we defined. Our learning strategies thus allow to monitor learners' behaviors in a homogeneous way across different disciplines, and thus to strengthen and generalize the results we found out in our specific context.

With the constant increase of traces a system is able to collect at a higher resolution, data mining methods become salient. In particular, the sequential pattern mining we adopted, and which is used to determine the most frequent action patterns occurring among a set of action sequences [8], is becoming a common approach to better understand learners' behaviors, especially in the MOOC domain. Very closed to our works, [20] suggests a topical N-gram Model applied to two Coursera MOOCs to extract common session topics (e.g., "Browse Course", "Assignment and Forum"), to cluster learners according to these topics, and eventually to study the difference of apparition of the topics between high- and low-grade students. Still on the dataset of Coursera MOOCs, [21] studied patterns of actions at a higher level of abstraction to distinguish between high- and low-achieving users. The authors proposed a taxonomy of exclusive MOOC behaviors (i.e., viewer or collector, solver, all-rounder, and bystander) based on the observation of the number of assignments and lectures users completed, and explored their distribution through different dimensions such as engagement, time of interaction, or grades. In this research, the sequential pattern mining allowed the authors to conclude, for instance, that the population of high-achievers was mainly composed of two subgroups: solvers, that primarily hand in assignments for a grade without or poorly watching lectures, and all-rounders who diligently watch the lectures, finish the quizzes and do assignments.

Also closed to our methodology, [22] suggests an algorithm based on a combination of sequence mining techniques to identify differentially frequent patterns between two groups of students. The authors aimed at identifying and comparing high- and low-achievers' behaviors during productive and counter-productive learning phases. Their methodology includes (i) an algorithm based on Pex-SPAM [23] to find out a set of patterns, and (ii) the use of a piecewise linear representation algorithm to identify productive and counter-productive phases. They identified differentially frequent sequential patterns of actions that are more used by one group of learner than by the other, according to the performance learning phase. While an abstract representation of actions composing the patterns is proposed, the dedicated vocabulary is specific to MOOCs and cannot apply to remote or virtual laboratory, as in [20]. However, the abstraction approach is comparable to ours, since we used regular expressions to define learning strategy as they add specific suffix to their alphabet to express multiplicity of occurrence and relevance/irrelevance to express the relation between an action and the previous one. Also, their proposal aims at finding out patterns that tend to be significantly used by one group of students more than the other, while in our methodology, we filtered patterns based on their direct correlation with the learners' performance. Their study of relation between patterns and performance, achieved afterwards, is only applicable for performance or progress that is measured as a scalar metric and periodically assessed by the environment.

6 Conclusion

The study presented in this paper, based on data collected from an experimentation conducted in an authentic learning context, aimed at revealing relationships between learners' behaviors during practical learning situations, and their academic performance. We adopted a sequential pattern mining approach to identify correlations between several learning strategies and performance, the most significant strategies being: (i) the *progression*, when learners successfully perform actions of the same nature but more and more complex; the *reflexion* (through the consultation of help manuals) before (ii) or after (iii) the execution of a related action. These strategies seem to be representative of students of high- and medium-level performance. The data analyzed in this study only relate to interactions between learners and the resources required to achieve the practical activities; some works are in progress to extend our analysis model to other data collected by the system in order to deeper investigate learners' behaviors.

While we focused here on the relations between learners' behaviors and their performance, we must now deal with these links in depth, in order to analyze their causal nature, but also to compute a predictive model to help reducing failing rate. Moreover, the learning strategies depicting learners' behaviors have been defined based on analysis, but a lack of formal representation is obvious. Thus, consistent taxonomy and definitions of these strategies have to be investigated, especially by educational sciences experts, in order to provide a solid basis for behavioral studies within different learning situations. While the ITS we developed may be used to study causal relationship between learning strategy and performance, we first have to analyze its impact on learners' behaviors, as much as we have to validate the visualization tool dedicated to teachers.

Finally, our remote laboratory environment also includes features dedicated to cooperative and collaborative learning [9]. Activities based on collective tasks would allow to study new research questions about learners' behaviors in practical work situation, in a socio-constructivism context. The influence of learning strategies on interactions between learners, or the evolution of the strategies learners apply as they go along the learning path, are some of the research questions we plan to address in a near future.

References

1. Bunderson, E.D., Christensen, M.E.: An analysis of retention problems for female students in university computer science programs. J. Res. Comput. Edu. **28**(1), 1–18 (1995)
2. Workman, M.: Performance and perceived effectiveness in computer-based and computer-aided education: do cognitive styles make a difference? Comput. Hum. Behav. **20**(4), 517–534 (2004)
3. Blikstein, P.: Using learning analytics to assess students' behavior in open-ended programming tasks. In: 1st International Conference on Learning Analytics and Knowledge, pp. 110–116. ACM, Banff (2011)
4. Vihavainen, A.: Predicting Students' Performance in an Introductory Programming Course Using Data from Students' Own Programming Process. In: 13th International Conference on Advanced Learning Technologies, pp. 498–499. IEEE, Beijing (2013)
5. Wilson, B.C., Shrock, S.: Contributing to success in an introductory computer science course - a study of twelve factors. ACM SIGCSE Bullet. **33**(1), 184–188 (2001)
6. Rountree, N., Rountree, J., Robins, A., Hannah, R.: Interacting factors that predict success and failure in a CS1 course. ACM SIGCSE Bullet. **36**(4), 101–104 (2004)
7. Aleven, V., Mclaren, B., Roll, I., Koedinger, K.: Toward meta-cognitive tutoring: A model of help seeking with a cognitive tutor. Int. J. Artif. Intell. Edu. **16**(2), 101–128 (2006)
8. Agrawal, R., Srikant, R.: Mining sequential patterns. In: 11th International Conference on Data Engineering, pp. 3–14. IEEE, Taipei (1995)
9. Broisin, J., Venant, R., Vidal, P.: Lab4ce: a remote laboratory for computer education. Int. J. Artif. Intell. Edu. **27**(1), 154–180 (2017)
10. Taamallah, A., Khemaja, M.: Designing and eXperiencing smart objects based learning scenarios: an approach combining IMS LD, XAPI and IoT. In: 2nd International Conference on Technological Ecosystems for Enhancing Multiculturality, pp. 373–379. ACM, New York (2014)
11. Venant, R., Vidal, P., Broisin, J.: Evaluation of learner performance during practical activities: An experimentation in computer education. In: 16th International Conference on Advanced Learning Technologies, pp. 237–241. IEEE, Austin (2016)

12. Watson, C., Li, F.W.B., Godwin, J.L.: Predicting Performance in an Introductory Programming Course by Logging and Analyzing Student Programming Behavior. In: 13th International Conference on Advanced Learning Technologies, pp. 319–323. IEEE, Beijing (2013)
13. Orduna, P., Almeida, A., Lopez-de Ipina, D., Garcia-Zubia, J.: Learning analytics on federated remote laboratories: Tips and techniques. In: Global Engineering Education Conference, pp. 299–305. IEEE, Istanbul (2014)
14. de Jong, T., Linn, M.C., Zacharia, Z.C.: Physical and Virtual Laboratories in Science and Engineering Education. Science **340**(6130), 305–308 (2013)
15. Corbière, A., Choquet, C.: Re-engineering method for multimedia system in education. In: 6th International Symposium on Multimedia Software Engineering, pp. 80–87. IEEE, Miami (2004)
16. Inventado, P.S., Scupelli, P.: Data-driven design pattern production: a case study on the ASSISTments online learning system. In: 20th European Conference on Pattern Languages of Programs, pp. 1–14. ACM, Pittsburg (2015)
17. Hostetler, T.R.: Predicting student success in an introductory programming course. ACM SIGCSE Bullet. **15**(3), 40–43 (1983)
18. Luthon, F., Larroque, B.: LaboREM—A remote laboratory for game-like training in electronics. IEEE Trans. Learn. Technol. **8**(3), 311–321 (2015)
19. Babich, A., Mavrommatis, K.T.: Teaching of complex technological processes using simulations. Int. J. Eng. Edu. **25**(2), 209–220 (2009)
20. Wen, M., Rosé, C.P.: Identifying latent study habits by mining learner behavior patterns in massive open online courses. In: 23rd ACM International Conference on Information and Knowledge Management, pp. 1983–1986. ACM, Shanghai (2014)
21. Anderson, A., Huttenlocher, D., Kleinberg, J., Leskovec, J.: Engaging with massive online courses. In: 23rd International Conference on World Wide Web, pp. 687–698. ACM, Seoul (2014)
22. Kinnebrew, J.S., Loretz, K.M., Biswas, G.: A contextualized, differential sequence mining method to derive students' learning behavior patterns. J. Edu. Data Mining **5**(1), 190–219 (2013)
23. Ho, J., Lukov, L., Chawla, S.: Sequential pattern mining with constraints on large protein databases. In: 12th International Conference on Management of Data, pp. 89–100. Computer Society of India, Hyderabad (2005)

MOOC Dropouts: A Multi-system Classifier

Massimo Vitiello[1(✉)], Simon Walk[2], Vanessa Chang[3], Rocael Hernandez[4], Denis Helic[1], and Christian Guetl[1]

[1] Graz University of Technology, Graz, Austria
massimo.vitiello@student.tugraz.at, dhelic@tugraz.at, cguetl@iicm.edu
[2] Stanford University, Stanford, USA
walk@stanford.edu
[3] Curtin University of Technology, Perth, Australia
vanessa.chang@curtin.edu.au
[4] Universidad Galileo, Guatemala City, Guatemala
roc@galileo.edu

Abstract. In recent years, technology enhanced learning platforms became widely accessible. In particular, the number of Massive Open Online Courses (MOOCs) has—and still is—constantly growing. This widespread adoption of MOOCs triggered the development of specialized solutions, that emphasize or enhance various aspects of traditional MOOCs. Despite this significant diversity in approaches to implementing MOOCs, many of the solutions share a plethora of common problems. For example, high dropout rate is an on-going problem that still needs to be tackled in the majority of MOOCs. In this paper, we set out to analyze dropout problem for a number of different systems with the goal of contributing to a better understanding of rules that govern how MOOCs in general and dropouts in particular evolve. To that end, we report on and analyze MOOCs from Universidad Galileo and Curtin University. First, we analyze the MOOCs of each system independently and then build a model and predict dropouts across the two systems. Finally, we identify and discuss features that best predict if users will drop out or continue and complete a MOOC using Boosted Decision Trees. The main contribution of this paper is a unified model, which allows for an early prediction of at-risk or dropout users across different systems. Furthermore, we also identify and discuss the most indicative features of our model. Our results indicate that users' behaviors during the initial phase of MOOCs relate to their final results.

1 Dropouts and At-Risk Users in MOOCs

With a widespread access to the Internet, education has evolved remarkably. Massive Online Open Courses (MOOCs), which can potentially reach audience at a global scale emerged as an option to acquire knowledge, as they also exhibit significant advantages for both users and content creators. The majority of MOOCs on the Web are freely available and have no entry requirements, which further

É. Lavoué et al. (Eds.): EC-TEL 2017, LNCS 10474, pp. 300–314, 2017.
DOI: 10.1007/978-3-319-66610-5_22

encourage enrollments [17,21]. Over time, platforms such as edX[1], Coursera[2] and Udacity[3], developed a monetisation model around this emerging ecosystem. The idea of obtaining a certificate after completing a MOOC in exchange for a small fee has already proven to be an appealing option for users, acknowledging their time, efforts and achievement.

Issue. Despite their massive appeal, MOOCs are known to suffer from high dropout rates. This is a particularly pressing issue, as on average about 90% of all enrolled users do not complete their classes [14]. Early detection of at-risk users, who are nevertheless eager to successfully complete a course, is very important. This would allow operators of MOOCs to devise strategies to intervene and mitigate the number of *dropouts*, those at-risk users who eventually abandon a course. Moreover, studies on MOOCs dropouts generally focus on very specific domains, with well-structured courses, characterized by assignment deadlines and fixed course lengths. What has been missing up to now is a study or a baseline that compares factors that influence the dropout rates across different MOOC systems and layout of MOOCs.

Motivation. Hence, it is important to identify features that are best suited to predict potential dropouts at an early stage. This would give MOOCs' providers actionable information, allowing them to adapt their courses accordingly. Additionally, comparing features that best distinguish completers and dropouts across different systems will yield new insights into general behavioral patterns that dictate individual outcomes of MOOCs for online learners. Specifically, the identification of such features, common to MOOCs across different systems, can reveal useful information to devise new strategies to mitigate the high dropout rates and keep users engaged and motivated when participating in MOOCs.

Approach. First, we conduct and evaluate prediction experiments to detect at-risk users in early stages of MOOCs from two different systems. Second, we train a model based on features present in all our datasets, to identify the best predictors of dropouts across different systems. Third, we conduct all of our experiments with a varying number of interactions, allowing us to measure if the ranking and importance of the features change over time. Finally, we discuss the implications of our findings in the context of the different experiments.

2 Related Work

Analyzing MOOCs and Features. Traditionally, analyses involving MOOCs are carried out by first identifying groups of users based on the similarity of their expectations and goals at the point of enrollment. A foundation for all of these studies is the *Funnel of Participation* [5]. In this study, the process towards completion of a course is composed of 4 phases: awareness, registration, activity

[1] https://www.edx.org/.
[2] https://www.coursera.org/.
[3] https://www.udacity.com/.

and progress. Each of these phases is characterized by a certain *attrition* of the number of active users. Further studies analyzed users' surveys to understand reasons for drop out, detailing the attrition as either *healthy* or *unhealthy* [8,11]. Server logs were also analyzed for users classification by means of clustering approach [15,16] and linear regression model [6]. Features' importance and their mutual interactions, were studied in relation to machine learning algorithms, such as Support Vector Machines (SVM) [3,4] and Decision Trees [10].

Detecting Dropouts. Many researchers dealt with dropout classification by means of log analysis and machine learning. Jiang et al. [13] applied a logistic regression model on a four weeks MOOC offered on Coursera. They tried to predict if users would obtain a certificate and if it would be a normal or a distinction one. Their findings indicated that the first-week assignment scores were a strong indicator of users' performance at the end of the course. In Xing et al. [20] the authors proposed a model to predict whether a user will drop out in the following week. Their results indicated that weekly features were more effective than the cumulative ones. Boyer and Veeramachaneni [2] experimented with dropout prediction in a real-time scenario. They used a rolling window, whose size represented the number of past weeks which they considered to construct features. Their results suggested that using a lower amount of past information could yield results comparable to the ones from a full window size.

Balakrishnan and Coetzee [1] used Hidden Markov Models (HMM) to predict if users will drop out in the following week. The dataset consisted of a MOOC from Berkeley University, offered on edX. Their results can be used to suggest changes in the engagement style to those students who are more likely to drop out in the close future. Vitiello et al. [19] attempted dropout predictions over a set of 5 MOOCs. Their results indicated that certain combinations of features could significantly improve prediction scores. In Sinharay [18], the author presented a detailed review of different data mining techniques and compared their performance with real-data examples. Particularly, the author predicted dropouts on a dataset including students from various high schools in Florida. The obtained results indicated that methods such as Random Forests and Boosting can improve performance in regard to linear and logistic regression approaches.

The work presented in this paper further extends the state-of-the-art by analyzing MOOCs from two different sources: Universidad Galileo and Curtin University. We initially analyze and perform a dropout prediction experiment on each of these individually. Then, we excerpt a multi-systems model for MOOC evaluation and classification of users likely to drop out. In order to do so, we rank our features according to their importance and compare the obtained results.

3 Materials and Methods

3.1 Dataset

Table 1 shows the characteristics of the MOOCs from Universidad Galileo and Curtin University. Logs of Curtin University include interactions of each enrolled

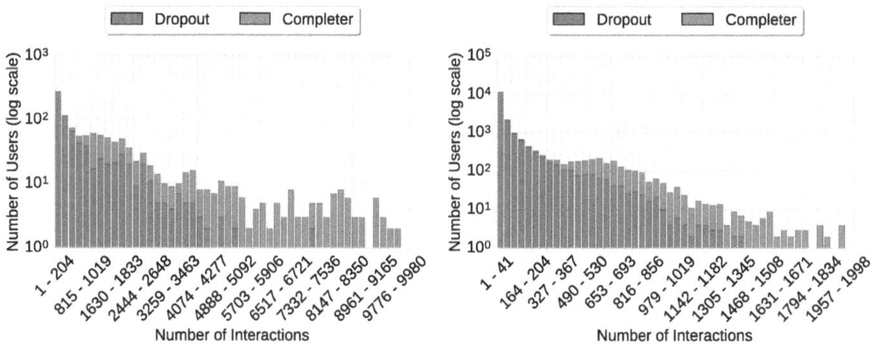

(a) Universidad Galileo (b) Curtin University

Fig. 1. Number of interactions for each class (dropout vs. completer). (a) refers to Universidad Galileo and (b) to Curtin University. The number of interactions are grouped in bins and reported on the x-axis, while the y-axis represents the amount of users (in log scale). Completers are plotted in green and Dropouts in red. For both systems, Dropouts are present in higher number and are less active than the Completers. (Color figure online)

person, while those of Universidad Galileo only report interactions of active users (or learners). In our setting, interactions coincide with clicks of users in the MOOCs' environment. In particular, a total of 3,157 active users in our datasets are from Universidad Galileo, and 35,473 enrolled users are from Curtin University. We will use the more general term *users* to refer to these groups for each system. The average number of interactions for MOOCs of Curtin University is significantly lower than the ones of Universidad Galileo (see Fig. 1). We can see that Completers interact more often with the MOOCs in both systems, while the percentage of Dropouts is higher for the datasets from Curtin University.

MOOC Systems. It is important to understand that the MOOCs are hosted and implemented on two different systems, and, therefore, the structure and organization radically differ. In particular, Universidad Galileo's courses are organized with a predetermined schedule and calendar, where each MOOC lasts 8 weeks, including assignments. In contrast, the courses from Curtin University are organized in a self-paced mode; after a MOOC's official start, all the materials would be available online to the enrolled users, who would then participate and engage at their own pace. Moreover, there are no deadlines for the assignments and the duration of the MOOCs is generally flexible. Universidad Galileo's MOOCs are implemented for experts with a technical background in a particular field, who want to further develop their knowledge. The ones from Curtin University, however, are intended for a more general audience, not necessarily with experience on the topic of the course.

Feature Comparison. Additional differences include the tools that each system deployed/implemented and the level of granularity of the logged interactions for

Table 1. Characteristics of all MOOCs. The analyzed MOOCs belong to 2 different systems, Universidad Galileo and Curtin University. MOOCs of Universidad Galileo have a fixed schedule and are characterized by lower number of active users and restrained dropout rates. In contrast, MOOCs of Curtin University are self-paced and account for a higher number of enrolled users and dropout rates. The average number of interactions of Curtin University's MOOCs is lower than the ones from Universidad Galileo's MOOCs.

System	MOOC title	Users	Completers	Dropouts	Dropout rate	Average interactions		
						Global	Completers	Dropouts
Universidad Galileo	Android (AND)	583	77	506	87%	433	1597	260
	Authoring tools for E-Learning (AEL)	255	101	154	60%	722	1401	279
	Client Attention (CA)	89	60	29	33%	394	510	154
	Cloud Based Learning (CBL)	274	121	153	56%	2353	4423	747
	Community Manager (CM)	811	320	491	60%	850	1760	268
	Digital Interactive TV (DITV)	117	63	54	46%	999	1582	319
	Introduction to E-learning (EL)	239	81	158	66%	1623	3804	545
	Medical Emergencies (ME)	118	49	69	59%	1671	3172	606
	User Experience (UE)	182	62	120	66%	499	1137	170
	Web Tools and Educational Applications (WTEA)	176	99	77	44%	265	369	131
	Web Tools in the Classroom (WTC)	313	131	182	58%	1044	2078	299
Curtin University	MOOCC1	21948	1500	20448	93%	93	683	49
	MOOCC2	10368	208	10160	98%	58	760	44

later analysis. Aside from common information, such as *Timestamp* and *User id*, interactions in Universidad Galileo's logs would fall into one of 20 categories: *Assessment*, *Assignment*, *Evaluation*, *File Storage*, *Forum*, *Learning Content*, *Peer Evaluation*, *Calendar*, *Course Members* among others. On the other hand, the MOOCs offered on edX by Curtin University provide more detailed logs of interactions[4]. In particular, requests are divided into 7 different macro-groups (as shown in Table 2). EdX logs from Curtin University also include *Enrollment* interactions, which indicate enrollments for both users and course instructors. We use these interactions to identify the total amount of enrolled users, but we do not consider such interactions when constructing the features.

Multisystem Dataset. We create three additional datasets; the first one combines users of all MOOCs of Universidad Galileo, the second one includes users of all MOOCs of Curtin University and the third one combines users of all MOOCs from both systems. We reference them as *Galileo*, *Curtin* and *MIX* respectively.

[4] A complete description of edX logs can be found at http://edx.readthedocs.io.

Table 2. Feature Description. We consider 3 kind of features, one is common to both systems and the other two are system dependent. *Temporal* features are derived from users' sessions and are used with both systems. *Tool* from Universidad Galileo includes 20 different features that map to the tools available for this system. *Tool* from Curtin University accounts for 7 different groups (MOOCs' components), each of these comprising a wide range of interactions, for a total of around 100. For both systems, we calculate these features counting the number of interactions that belong to each tool.

Type	Feature	Domain	Description
Temporal	Sessions & Requests	Both	Total number of sessions and of requests
	Active Time & Days	Both	Total amount of active time and of active days
	Timespan Clicks	Both	Average timespan between two consecutive clicks (within same session)
	Session Length & Session Requests	Both	Average session lengthh and requests per session
	Active Days Requests	Both	Total number of requests for each active day
Tool	Requests per Tool	Universidad Galileo	Total requests per each tool (ex. *Evaluation*, *Assignment*, *Forum*)
	Course Navigation	Curtin University	Interactions within the course content page (ex. *Link Clicked*, *Tab Selected*)
	Video	Curtin University	Interactions with video components (eg. *Play Video*, *Show/Hide Transcript*)
	Problem	Curtin University	Interactions with the problem module (eg. *Problem Grade*, *Show Hint*)
	Poll & Survey	Curtin University	Interactions with the Poll and Survey block (eg. *Submit*, *Show Results*)
	Bookmark	Curtin University	Interactions with the Bookmark component (eg. *Add/Remove Bookmark*)
	Discussion Forum	Curtin University	Interactions happening within the Forum (eg. *Search*, *Comment*, *Vote*)
	Main Page Links	Curtin University	Clicks on main page links (ex. *Progress*, *Instructor*, *Study at Curtin*)

We use these datasets to predict dropouts on a system-to-system and multisystem level. Moreover, we use these to analyze the importance of the features.

Feature Extraction. A *feature* is a characterization of users' engagement in a MOOC that we regard indicative and helpful to identify dropouts. We describe each user in terms of a set of features, which is input to the classifier and summarize these in Table 2. These features can be split into two groups. The features within the first group consist of time-related information, obtainable for both systems. These features build up the concept of user' sessions, which are defined as a set of actions, where the timespan between each action is less or equal than 30 min. The second group of features is system dependent.

3.2 Prediction Model

We first outline the steps for the proposed experiments and then describe each of these in detail.

Feature Extraction. The sooner we can predict if a user is likely to drop out, the earlier we can develop strategies to intervene and engage with the user. Hence, we focus on users' initial interactions and construct the features described in Sect. 3.1, following two different strategies. First, we focus on the initial per-user absolute interactions. We set up our experiments ranging from 1 to 100 per-user absolute initial interactions, on which we calculate the features. Secondly, we consider the number of interactions taking place in the first week after users' first interaction with the MOOC. In this case, we determine the timestamp of a users' first interaction and consider all interactions that take place within a certain timespan (1 to 7 days).

Class Balancing. For both systems, the number of Dropouts is significantly higher than the number of Completers. We addressed this class imbalance problem by oversampling [9,12]. This means that new samples are randomly picked and added to the class with fewer examples until its dimension equals to the one of the larger class.

Training. Once classes are balanced, we split the examples into a training set, used to train the classifier, and a test set, which we use for evaluation. We use a ratio of 80:20 between training and test datasets, using a Stratified Shuffle Split with 10 folds. With this approach, each fold will also be balanced in the number of examples from each class. Furthermore, the shuffle assures that each fold will consist of different examples.

Evaluation. Finally, we use accuracy to evaluate the prediction error of the experiments. Accuracy is defined as the fraction of correctly predicted examples and is therefore bounded between 0 and 1. An accuracy of 0 means that every example has been misclassified, while an accuracy of 1 indicates that every example has been correctly classified. Furthermore, we run the experiments for each fold until the mean prediction error converges.

3.3 Dropout Classification

We are interested in understanding the reasons that lead users to drop out at a certain point and to assess the number of interactions that are necessary to identify potential dropouts and if different features yield equivalent results. Furthermore, we want to compare different MOOCs and systems to check for similarities and differences. Initially we run prediction experiments on each MOOC independently (see Fig. 2) before comparing the results between systems (see Fig. 2(c) and (d)). For the individual prediction experiments we use Support Vector Machines (SVM), which try to find the optimal hyperplane (in higher dimension spaces) to separate data points. For the system-to-system and multi-system experiments, we predict dropouts using Boosted Decision Trees [7]. This ensemble classifier combines the outputs from a set of single decision tree in a sequential way. For each learned model, the examples are re-weighted; the misclassified ones receive a higher weight, while the correctly classified ones get a lower weight. This way, the next decision tree will focus more on the misclassified examples. Overall, we propose three experiments. First, we conduct two system-to-system dropout prediction experiments. We use the *Curtin* dataset for training and the *Galileo* dataset to test our classifier. Second, we switch the datasets and train on *Galileo* to predict dropouts on *Curtin*. We denote these experiments as *Curtin on Galileo* and *Galileo on Curtin* respectively. Third, we use the *MIX* dataset, in which the training and test sets include examples from both systems. Finally, we determine the importance scores for our features from the Boosted Decision Trees to identify the predictive power of each feature for the detection of dropouts.

4 Results

4.1 Dropout Classification

Figure 2 depicts the mean (over the 10 folds) accuracy for each MOOC. The y-axes reports the accuracy and the x-axes indicates the number of absolute interactions (Fig. 2(a) and (c)) and the considered number of days from the users' first interaction (Fig. 2(b) and (d)).

Universidad Galileo. As shown in Fig. 2(a) and (b), for MOOCs of Universidad Galileo, we see that not always increasing the number of considered interactions and days guarantee higher accuracy. Firstly, there is a set of MOOCs plotted in green, for which the accuracy increases over time or, after an initial growth, stabilizes. The second group is plotted in red and consists of MOOCs for which the accuracy trend is less steady. For the Absolute Experiment, except for the *AND* MOOC, the first 100 users' absolute interactions are too few for a correct classification of the users. For the First 7 Days Experiment, the increase in accuracy is less significant in respect of the Absolute Experiments. In some cases, as for the *CA* and *AEL* MOOCs, considering more days can lead to a worsening of the accuracy. With the exception of *AND*, these two approaches do not guarantee a precise detection of dropouts over the MOOCs in this system.

Curtin University. Figure 2(c) and (d) report the results for Curtin University's MOOCs. For the Absolute Experiment, we obtain for both MOOCs an accuracy always higher than 0.8 already with only 5 absolute interactions. We investigate further these situations and find out that the most used tools with 5 interactions belong to *Video* and *Main Page Links* components. The higher the amount of absolute considered interactions is, the more the users

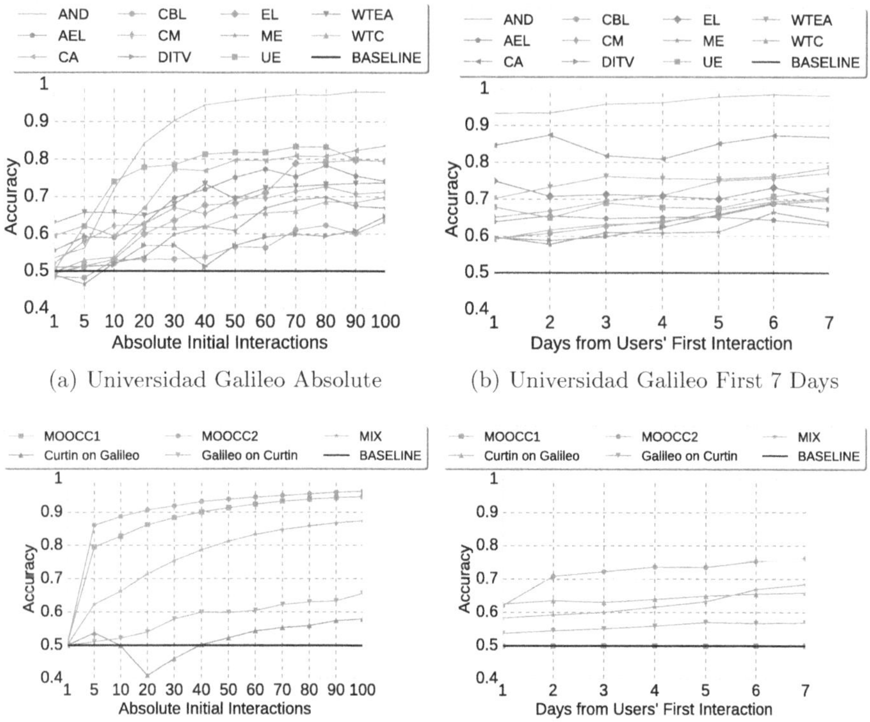

(a) Universidad Galileo Absolute

(b) Universidad Galileo First 7 Days

(c) Curtin & Multi-System Absolute

(d) Curtin University & Multi-System First 7 Days

Fig. 2. Single SVM and multi-system boosted decision tree results. (a) and (b) report the accuracy results for Universidad Galileo in relation to the absolute number of interactions and the first 7 days from users' first interaction metrics (for MOOCs label explanation see Table 1). The results for these metrics for Curtin University and the multi-system experiments are depicted in (c) and (d) respectively. Accuracy of the MOOCs plotted in green is increasing or becoming stable after a certain point. MOOCs plotted in red are not characterized by such trend. (Color figure online)

engage with *Video*, *Course Navigation* and *Problem. Discussion Forum* is only rarely used, mostly for visualization purposes. Therefore, we conclude that there is a particular set of components that strongly catalyze users' attention. Results for the First 7 Days Experiment have a generally low accuracy. The accuracy for *MOOCC2* has a slightly increase the more days are considered, while for *MOOCC1* the accuracy is steady at 0.5. These low accuracy values can be due to the Course Enrollment interactions (see Sect. 3.1) that introduce a certain noise in this setting.

Multi-system. Figure 2(c) and (d) also report the accuracy for the three multi-system experiments. For the Absolute Experiment, the accuracy of *Curtin on Galileo* increases steadily when the interactions considered are more than 20.

The accuracy for *Galileo on Curtin* and *MIX* instead, is always increasing. Particularly, the accuracy for *MIX* resembles the ones of *MOOCC1* and *MOOCC2*. For the First 7 Days Experiment, we notice a slight increase in the accuracy the more days are considered for all the experiments. The accuracy profile for *MIX*, is the one with the broader increase the more days are taken into consideration, while *Galileo on Curtin* is the setting that yields the higher accuracy. For *Curtin on Galileo* the accuracy remains almost unaltered. Generally, we obtain better results with the absolute number of interactions approach. The difference in the accuracy is particularly marked for the *MIX* dataset.

Findings. For self-paced MOOCs, such as those from Curtin University, a small number of initial interactions contains already valuable information for a correct classification of the users. Particularly, given the high details of the logs, the number of interactions with each tool is a strong indicator whether users will drop out or not. Due to users' enrollment actions, the first 7 days from users initial interaction reveals to be a less effective approach for self-paced MOOCs. For fixed schedule MOOCs, such as those from Universidad Galileo, both metrics are less accurate. This may be partly due to the structure of the courses.

4.2 Features Analyses

Considering the results for the absolute interactions experiment, we can split the features into 2 groups; a group of high scoring features, consisting of *Session Length*, *Timespan Clicks*, *Requests* and *Active Time*, and a group of low scoring ones, including *Days*, *Active Days Requests* and *Sessions*. We note that, for the high-scoring group, there is no feature that always outperforms the others. Moreover, this group division is present across all 3 experiments despite the considered number of interactions. We conclude that using the initial 100 users' interactions as a metric, we can clearly identify the features that best split the users between Completers and Dropouts. Also for the first 7 days from users' first interaction experiment, we can still split the features in high and low scoring ones. For *Curtin on Galileo* and *MIX* experiments, the high scoring features group consists of *Timespan Clicks*, *Requests* and *Active Time*. These remain unmodified in respect to the considered days. For *Galileo on Curtin* the scoring seems to be less definite, with only *Session Length* always belonging to the high scoring ones. From this metric, we are able to identify a set of most valuable features.

Findings. Among the different multi-system experiments and the considered metrics, we identify two classes of features; high-scoring and low-scoring. Beside small variations, features always belong to only one of these classes. This implies that, despite the differences between the two systems, when they are analyzed together, there are strong similarities regarding the importance of the features. Moreover, *Days*, *Sessions* and *Active Days Requests* are always the features with lowest weights. The remaining features represent a set with high weights for both metrics and across the systems.

5 Discussion

5.1 Dropout Classification

Curtin University's MOOCs are characterized by a steady increase in accuracy the more interactions or days are considered and by an accuracy higher than 0.8 for 5 absolute interactions. Such an increase in accuracy is not always present for MOOCs from Universidad Galileo. Except for *AND*, which has an accuracy profile similar to the MOOCs from Curtin University, MOOCs from Universidad Galileo rarely have an accuracy of 0.8 or higher. Reasons of this discrepancy in the accuracy could be due to differences in the didactic settings, including the structure of the course and type of activities between the systems. First, Universidad Galileo's MOOCs, although having a defined 8 week duration, are sometimes subjected to a later start. This happens, for example, when a MOOC is accessible to the users but the material is not yet available on the platform. In this situation, there is an initial phase characterized by few interactions (see Fig. 3(a)), followed by a burst of activity of Completers and Dropouts, once either the material has become available or the MOOC officially started (see Fig. 3(b)). The lower accuracy values for some of the MOOCs from this system, can be a consequence of these particular situations. On the other hand, Curtin University's MOOCs are organized in a self-paced manner, with the entire material and resources available to users from the start. Furthermore, *MOOCC1* and *MOOCC2* have an average number of interactions of 93 and 58 respectively (see Table 1). This means that the first 5 interactions of each user represent, on average, 5.38% and 8.62% of their total interactions for *MOOCC1* and *MOOCC2* respectively. These percentages are much higher than those from Universidad Galileo's MOOCs; the highest for this system comes from *WTEA*, for which 5 interactions represent on average only 1.89% of a users' total interactions. Therefore, the considered number of absolute interactions is too low for Universidad Galileo.

Similarly, these situations can be also observed when considering the first 7 days after a users first interaction. As previously mentioned, the lack of interactions in the initial phase of Universidad Galileo's MOOCs, could be due to delays with uploading of materials and the official start. In the first case, it is possible that users do not interact with the MOOC in the successive days. It is more likely that only when a MOOC's material becomes available, users will again engage with the MOOC. Thus, it is possible that considering only the first 7 days from a users first interaction will only add a few extra interactions. The results for the MOOCs from Curtin University are presented in Fig. 2(d). These are generally worse than those from the absolute experiment, particularly for *MOOCC1*, where the accuracy is constant at 0.5. We believe that users who only sign up for a MOOC, but never interact with it, or potentially interact with it at very late stages of the course could potentially influence the prediction. From Curtin University's logs we can extract a total of 8,552 Dropouts with only one interaction for the MOOC *MOOCC1*, and a total of 4,436 for *MOOCC2*. Furthermore, if we consider only the active users, by completely dropping the

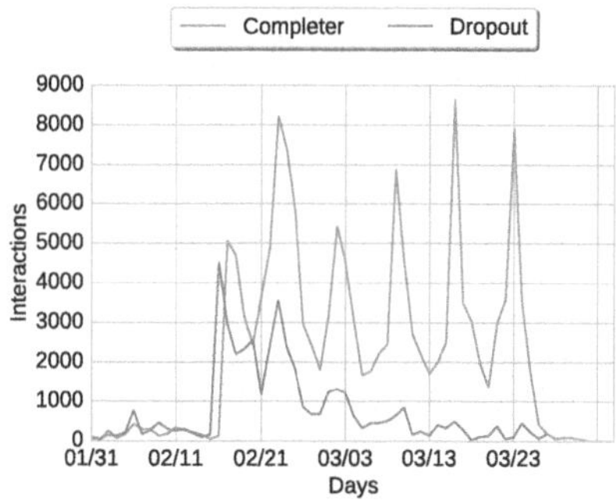

(a) Interactions per Class

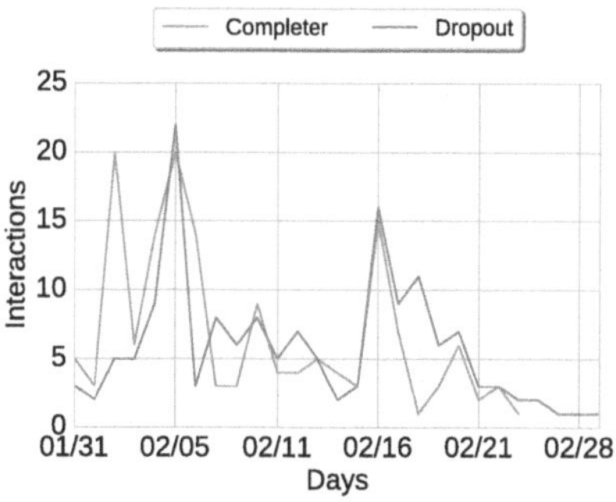

(b) Users' First Interaction per Class

Fig. 3. MOOC AEL interaction per class. (a) reports distribution of all interactions per class. Interactions antecedent 02/16 took place during a phase where probably course's material was not available or the MOOC did not start yet. The distribution for Completers and Dropouts is similar during this time. (b) shows users' first interaction for each class. Most first interaction happened before 02/16, date in which there is an increase for both classes. Some Dropouts firstly interacts with the MOOC more than one week after the 02/16.

Course Enrollment actions together with these Dropouts and re-run the experiments we obtain the results as shown in Fig. 4. These results are much more in line with those obtained for the absolute number of interaction experiments. For *MOOCC1* and *MOOCC2*, users' first day of interactions, is sufficient to achieve an accuracy of 0.9, which steadily increases when more days are considered. The multi-system experiments, using Boosted Decision Trees, also benefit of the removal of Course Enrollment actions. *Galileo on Curtin* and *Curtin on Galileo* have values for the accuracy higher than the ones in the absolute interaction experiments. For *Curtin on Galileo* the accuracy increases when more days are considered, while for *Galileo on Curtin* it lowers slightly for 6 and 7 days. This may be caused by an initial phase with a low number of interactions in Universidad Galileo's MOOCs (see Fig. 3(a)), which introduces noise for the classifier. However, the accuracy increases for the prediction experiment using the *MIX* dataset. Already the first day of interactions is sufficient for an accuracy of 0.7.

5.2 Feature Analyses

For the Absolute Experiment the group of high scoring features includes *Session Length*, *Timespan Clicks*, *Requests* and *Active Time*. From these, the weights for *Requests* are the highest when 100 absolute interactions are considered. This is reasonable for MOOCs with predefined schedule as those from Universidad Galileo, in which users are forced to keep up with a certain pace according to deadlines, exams and assignments. The high score of this feature for all multi-system experiments, seems to imply that this is true also for self-paced MOOCs from Curtin University. Although *Sessions* is one of the less valuable features,

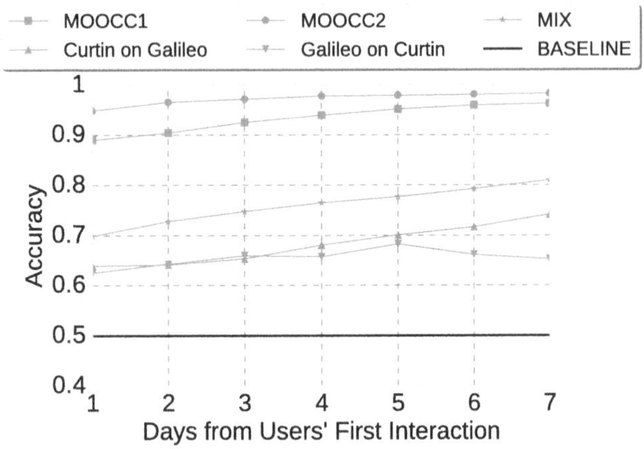

Fig. 4. Single SVM and multi-system boosted decision tree results without enrollments. Discarding the enrollment actions, yields better results. This is due to Curtin University's MOOCs schedule, for which an enrollment phase of up to a couple of months precede the official start of the MOOCs.

the (average) session characteristics, such as *Session Length*, *Timespan Clicks* and *Active Time*, have higher scores. This suggests that users' behavior during a session relates stronger to whether users are Completers or Dropouts, than the number of sessions they have. For the First 7 Days Experiment, the rankings of *Curtin on Galileo* and *MIX* are similar to those obtained in the Absolute Experiment, with *Timespan Clicks*, *Requests* and *Active Time* always being the features with highest weights. For *Galileo on Curtin*, *Session Length* and *Requests* are almost always the highest scoring features. This mixed ranking could be due to the smaller dimension of Universidad Galileo's dataset, in respect to Curtin University's one. However, this aspect does not seem to be relevant for the Absolute Experiment. We can conclude that, features constructed considering up to the first 7 days after users' first interaction, do not relate to users dropping out, as much as those obtained from users' initial absolute interaction. This claim is supported by the results of Fig. 2, where for Universidad Galileo's MOOCs the increase in accuracy for the First 7 Days Experiment, is more moderate than the one from the Absolute Experiment. The features *Active Days*, *Sessions* and (with one exception) *Requests Active Days* are always the lowest scoring for all experiments in the multi-system scenario.

6 Conclusion

With this work, we faced the problem of early classification of at-risk users in MOOCs. To address this shared problem, we analyzed MOOCs from two different systems in a homogeneous way, using Support Vector Machine and Boosted Decision Tree. We investigated two aspects, the initial absolute number of users interaction and the first 7 days after users' first interaction with the system. We obtained the best results when up to the first 100 absolute interactions were considered. For Curtin University's MOOCs we identified a set of components mostly used by the users, that strongly indicates whether users will drop out or not. Particularly, we verified that interactions with *Video* and *Course Navigation* components are representative of user engagement even during the very initial phase of the course. We also discovered that other components (*Discussion Forum* primarily) are only marginally important and scarcely used. Furthermore, we proposed a model for early dropouts detection in a multi-system setting. Despite the differences in the systems' structure (self-paced vs fixed schedule), topic, intended audience and conceptualization, we constructed a set of features shared by both systems.

In our future work, we will extend our model by enlarging the number of common features between the various systems. Further, we will conduct analyses with alternative approaches, which will also help to grasp and discover further aspects of the systems that we did not consider in this work. Moreover, we aim at further characterizing Completers and Dropouts by verifying if subgroups of users exist and experiment with users classification in a multi-class scenario.

Acknowledgments. The authors would like to thank the MOOC Maker Project (http://www.moocmaker.org/), Universidad Galileo and Curtin University for providing the datasets for the analysis and the Graz University of Technology and Curtin University for supporting the research visits of Massimo Vitiello and Christian Guetl.

References

1. Balakrishnan, G., Coetzee, D.: Predicting student retention in massive open online courses using hidden Markov models. Electrical Engineering and Computer Sciences, University of California at Berkeley (2013)
2. Boyer, S., Veeramachaneni, K.: Transfer learning for predictive models in massive open online courses. In: Conati, C., Heffernan, N., Mitrovic, A., Verdejo, M.F. (eds.) AIED 2015. LNCS, vol. 9112, pp. 54–63. Springer, Cham (2015). doi:10.1007/978-3-319-19773-9_6
3. Chapelle, O., Vapnik, V., Bousquet, O., Mukherjee, S.: Choosing multiple parameters for support vector machines. Mach. Learn. **46**(1–3), 131–159 (2002)
4. Chen, Y.W., Lin, C.J.: Combining SVMs with various feature selection strategies. In: Guyon, I., Nikravesh, M., Gunn, S., Zadeh, L.A. (eds.) Feature Extraction, pp. 315–324. Springer, Heidelberg (2006). doi:10.1007/978-3-540-35488-8_13
5. Clow, D.: MOOCs and the funnel of participation. In: Proceedings of the Third International Conference on Learning Analytics and Knowledge, pp. 185–189. ACM (2013)
6. Coffrin, C., Corrin, L., de Barba, P., Kennedy, G.: Visualizing patterns of student engagement and performance in MOOCs. In: Proceedings of the Fourth International Conference on Learning Analytics and Knowledge, pp. 83–92. ACM (2014)
7. Friedman, J.H.: Greedy function approximation: a gradient boosting machine. Ann. Stat. **29**, 1189–1232 (2001)

8. Guetl, C., Chang, V., Hernández Rizzardini, R., Morales, M.: Must we be concerned with the massive drop-outs in MOOC? An attrition analysis of open courses. In: Proceedings of the International Conference Interactive Collaborative Learning, ICL 2014 (2014)
9. Guo, X., Yin, Y., Dong, C., Yang, G., Zhou, G.: On the class imbalance problem. In: Fourth International Conference on Natural Computation, ICNC 2008, vol. 4, pp. 192–201. IEEE (2008)
10. Guruler, H., Istanbullu, A., Karahasan, M.: A new student performance analysing system using knowledge discovery in higher educational databases. Comput. Educ. **55**(1), 247–254 (2010)
11. Gütl, C., Rizzardini, R.H., Chang, V., Morales, M.: Attrition in MOOC: lessons learned from drop-out students. In: Uden, L., Sinclair, J., Tao, Y.-H., Liberona, D. (eds.) LTEC 2014. CCIS, vol. 446, pp. 37–48. Springer, Cham (2014). doi:10.1007/978-3-319-10671-7_4
12. Japkowicz, N., et al.: Learning from imbalanced data sets: a comparison of various strategies. In: AAAI Workshop on Learning from Imbalanced Data Sets, Menlo Park, CA, vol. 68, pp. 10–15 (2000)
13. Jiang, S., Williams, A., Schenke, K., Warschauer, M., O'dowd, D.: Predicting MOOC performance with week 1 behavior. In: Educational Data Mining 2014 (2014)
14. Jordan, K.: Initial trends in enrolment and completion of massive open online courses. Int. Rev. Res. Open Distrib. Learn. **15**(1), 133–160 (2014)
15. Kizilcec, R.F., Piech, C., Schneider, E.: Deconstructing disengagement: analyzing learner subpopulations in massive open online courses. In: Proceedings of the Third International Conference on Learning Analytics and Knowledge, pp. 170–179. ACM (2013)
16. Li, N., Kidziński, Ł., Jermann, P., Dillenbourg, P.: MOOC video interaction patterns: what do they tell us? In: Conole, G., Klobučar, T., Rensing, C., Konert, J., Lavoué, É. (eds.) EC-TEL 2015. LNCS, vol. 9307, pp. 197–210. Springer, Cham (2015). doi:10.1007/978-3-319-24258-3_15
17. Liyanagunawardena, T.R., Adams, A.A., Williams, S.A.: MOOCs: a systematic study of the published literature 2008–2012. Int. Rev. Res. Open Distrib. Learn. **14**(3), 202–227 (2013)
18. Sinharay, S.: An ncme instructional module on data mining methods for classification and regression. Educ. Meas. Issues Pract. **35**(3), 38–54 (2016)
19. Vitiello, M., Walk, S., Hernández, R., Helic, D., Gütl, C.: Classifying students to improve MOOC dropout rates. In: Research Track, p. 501 (2016)
20. Xing, W., Chen, X., Stein, J., Marcinkowski, M.: Temporal predication of dropouts in MOOCs: reaching the low hanging fruit through stacking generalization. Comput. Hum. Behav. **58**, 119–129 (2016)
21. Yousef, A.M.F., Chatti, M.A., Wosnitza, M., Schroeder, U.: A cluster analysis of MOOC stakeholder perspectives. RUSC Univ. Knowl. Soc. J. **12**(1), 74–90 (2015)

Effects of a Teacher Dashboard for an Intelligent Tutoring System on Teacher Knowledge, Lesson Planning, Lessons and Student Learning

Françeska Xhakaj(✉), Vincent Aleven(✉), and Bruce M. McLaren(✉)

Human-Computer Interaction Institute, Carnegie Mellon University, Pittsburgh, PA, USA
{francesx, aleven, bmclaren}@cs.cmu.edu

Abstract. Intelligent Tutoring Systems (ITSs) help students learn but often are not designed to support teachers and their practices. A dashboard with analytics about students' learning processes might help in this regard. However, little research has investigated how dashboards influence teacher practices in the classroom and whether they can help improve student learning. In this paper, we explore how Luna, a dashboard prototype designed for an ITS and used with real data, affects teachers and students. Results from a quasi-experimental classroom study with 5 middle school teachers and 17 classes show that Luna influences what teachers know about their students' learning in the ITS and that the teachers' updated knowledge affects the lesson plan they prepare, which in turn guides what they cover in a class session. Results did not confirm that Luna increased student learning. In summary, even though teachers generally know their classes well, a dashboard with analytics from an ITS can still enhance their knowledge about their students and support their classroom practices. The teachers tended to focus primarily on dashboard information about the challenges their students were experiencing. To the best of our knowledge, this is the first study that demonstrates that a dashboard for an ITS can affect teacher knowledge, decision-making and actions in the classroom.

Keywords: Intelligent Tutoring Systems · Dashboard · Data-driven instruction · Teachers' use of data · Learning analytics

1 Introduction

Intelligent Tutoring Systems (ITSs) are a type of advanced learning technology that provides detailed guidance to students during complex problem-solving practice, while also being adaptive to student differences [3, 21, 24]. ITSs have been shown to enhance student learning [8, 11, 19]. However, ITSs are rarely designed to support teachers, who might greatly influence student learning with an ITS. The addition of a teacher dashboard might help them do so. For instance, when many students in a class are learning a particular skill as they are working with the ITS, a dashboard could let the teacher know about this situation, and the teacher could include, in their lesson plan

É. Lavoué et al. (Eds.): EC-TEL 2017, LNCS 10474, pp. 315–329, 2017.
DOI: 10.1007/978-3-319-66610-5_23

and actual lesson, specific steps to address the challenge. More generally, a dashboard could help make "the invisible visible" for teachers by displaying aggregated, up-to-date information about their students. Based on this information, teachers could provide help to their students beyond what the ITS can provide.

By now, researchers have developed many dashboards with analytics from educational technologies. Much research focuses on evaluating whether such dashboards are useful to teachers and what visualizations or information is most used by them. Some studies found that a dashboard can help teachers determine in real-time when to intervene and help students work more collaboratively in a multi-tabletop learning environment [13], or can help them single out problems concerning participation in digital discussion environments and intervene as needed [20]. Other studies have shown that a dashboard's information can help teachers manage web-based distance courses [15], support teachers in moderating discussions in digital learning environments [16] or support their awareness of the classroom state, student progress, and students in need of immediate help in an exploratory learning environment [14].

In the current work, we focus on creating a teacher dashboard for an ITS, in contrast to much other research on dashboards. Given the somewhat unique characteristics of ITSs, it seems reasonable to assume that a dashboard for ITSs would be different compared to dashboards for other learning technologies. ITSs generate and collect data related to self-paced learning with step-level support for problem solving, adaptive mastery learning based on a detailed skill model, characteristics not widely shared with other educational technologies. In addition, ITSs typically generate and maintain a student model, which might create some interesting opportunities for dashboards. Exceptions are work by Lovett et al. (2008) who report on instructors using reports from an ITS in an online course [10], by Arroyo et al. (2014) who describe teacher reports generated by an ITS [4], and by Kelly et al. (2013) who study how a teacher used a report from a web-based homework system to decide what parts of the homework to review in class [7].

Further, while much work has focused on real-time dashboards (dashboards that teachers use while students are working with a learning software in class), few have looked at other scenarios in which a dashboard might be helpful. In the current work, we look at a scenario in which a teacher uses a dashboard when preparing for a class session; a dashboard might help in focusing the class discussion on the topics most in need of discussion (e.g., problems or specific error types that are currently challenging for the students). One study that comes close to this scenario is Kelly et al. (2013) who found positive effects of in-class review of reports from a web-based homework system [7]. In another study, Mavrikis et al. (2015) report that information from a dashboard about difficulties students are facing in an exploratory learning environment may help teachers decide what to focus on in the following lesson [14].

Finally, although many evaluation studies involving dashboards have been conducted, few studies have looked at the influence a dashboard might have on student learning, in spite of a growing realization in the field that effects on student learning should be studied [18, 22]. In the current paper, we present results from a quasi-experimental classroom study investigating effects of a dashboard prototype, Luna, with analytics from an ITS, used for lesson planning. Our study looks at effects on teacher knowledge, teacher decision-making, and student learning. It looks at realistic decision making, namely, planning and executing a classroom lesson following sessions during which the students used the ITS.

2 A Causal Chain that Captures Dashboard Influences

We defined a hypothesized causal chain that represents how information in a dashboard may affect teachers and, through them, student learning (Fig. 1). It focuses on scenarios in which a teacher uses a dashboard to prepare for a class session, in blended courses that use some form of educational technology. The dashboard, it is assumed, displays up-to-date information about students' performance, progress, and learning, with some technology. The causal chain may apply to any dashboard, learning analytic tool, teacher awareness tool, or report on student learning in blended courses, where teachers use it to create a lesson plan and prepare for a class session.

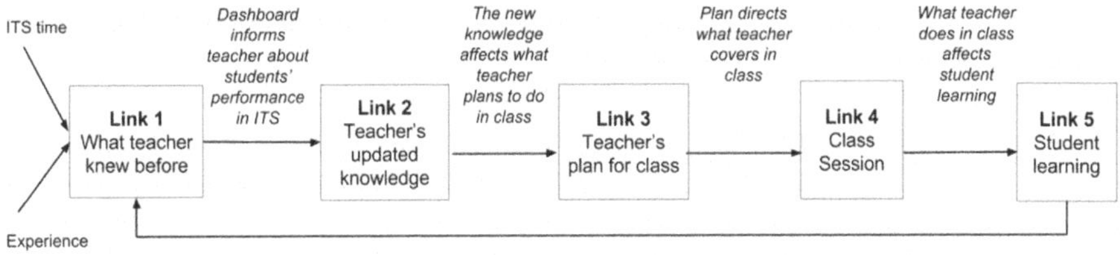

Fig. 1. A causal chain that represents a dashboard's effects on teacher practices.

From their experience with a particular class, teachers have knowledge about what their students generally can and cannot do well, at any given point in time (link 1, Fig. 1). As they work with a dashboard, they may learn new information about the performance and knowledge of their students (link 2 in Fig. 1). When teachers plan for a class session, their updated knowledge may affect the lesson plan (link 3 in Fig. 1), which then guides what they cover in class (link 4 in Fig. 1). Ultimately, what teachers do in the class session is what students get exposed to and what affects their learning (link 5 in Fig. 1). Thus, the dashboard information needs to "travel" through many links; it must be embraced by teachers, incorporated in the lesson plan and used in the class session, for it to reach students and impact their learning. In our analysis, we investigate the dashboard's influence along each of the links in the chain.

This causal chain differs from the LATUX [12] framework, which describes ways to design, develop, evaluate and deploy learning analytics tools for teachers. By contrast, the causal chain captures potential effects of a dashboard from proximal influences on teacher classroom practices and to distal influences on student learning.

3 Methodology

In this work, we focus on the following research questions: (RQ1) How does a dashboard with analytics from an ITS affect teachers' lesson planning and (subsequent) classroom sessions? and (RQ2) Does the teacher's use of the dashboard help students learn better? This early, preliminary evaluation is a formative evaluation. A key goal is to gather information that helps us in the redesign of the dashboard.

3.1 The Dashboard: Luna

Our study focused on Luna, a high-fidelity dashboard prototype (Fig. 2). We created Luna employing a user-centered design approach [2, 6, 25]. We involved teachers in the design process through a variety of design methods including Contextual Inquiry, Speed Dating, Storyboarding and Prototyping [5]. Luna is powered with data from Lynnette, an ITS for middle school mathematics (grades 6–8) created with CTAT [1] and with an evidence-based record of helping students learn to solve linear equations [9, 23]. We used Tableau, a data visualization tool (http://www.tableau.com/), to create Luna's interface. In our study, we populated Luna with student data logged by Lynnette from the participating teachers' own classes. Luna displays data about students' learning, both at the class and individual level. At the class level, Luna shows (1) the number of students who have mastered each skill in Lynnette (as a horizontal bar chart), (2) the number of students who made certain errors (as a horizontal bar chart), and (3) a comparison of the level of mastery versus the amount of practice per skill averaged across students (as a scatter plot). At the individual level (Fig. 2), Luna shows per student (1) if they mastered each skill in Lynnette and the percent mastery, (2) if they had errors and the number of times they made each error, and (3) time versus progress in the ITS (as a scatter plot). Luna is interactive, for example hovering over a skill or error shows a definition and an example exercise of the skill being applied or the error manifesting. The Cognitive Mastery algorithm in Lynnette generates skill mastery information (essentially, the tutor's student model), while an extended cognitive model generates error types.

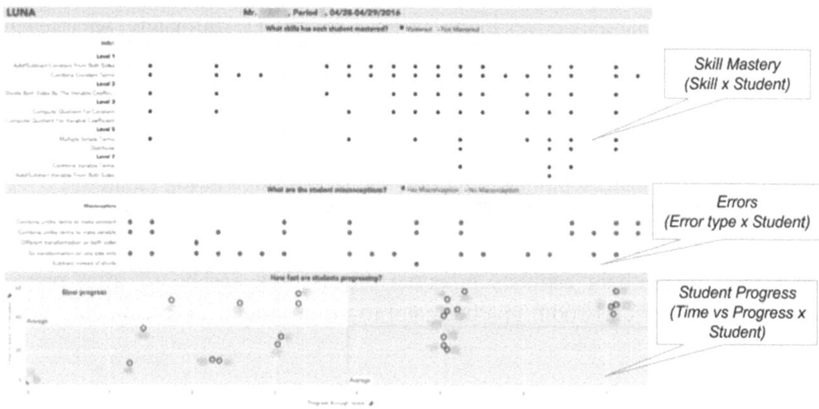

Fig. 2. Individual level dashboard prototype (Luna). Student names are obfuscated.

3.2 Experimental Design

Five teachers from two suburban schools took part in the study (17 classes, 300 students total). All classes were 7th grade (medium achieving or honors) except for a 6th grade honors class and an 8th grade low-achieving class. Two out of the five teachers had participated in previous iterations of Luna's design. The experiment had two conditions, an experimental condition, in which teachers used Luna while preparing a lesson plan, and a control condition, in which there was no dashboard. Classes were assigned to conditions such that each teacher had classes in both conditions. Conditions were balanced per teacher and school in terms of the level of achievement (high or low achieving class) and the order in which they happened during the school day. There were 9 classes in the control condition and 8 in the experimental condition.

We first provided teachers with 10–20 min of instruction on the analytics and visualizations that Luna displays (see Fig. 3). For this instruction session, Luna displayed student data collected in previous studies. Students then worked for 60 min with Lynnette, completing problem sets dealing with basic equation solving. Next, they took a 20-minute pre-test. In both conditions, teachers were asked to prepare for 20 min for a class session and think out loud during the process; during these sessions, the researcher occasionally asked teachers to explain what they were doing. The sessions were video-recorded. For the experimental condition classes, teachers were asked to prepare for the class session using Luna, which provides information about their students' performance during the session with Lynnette. For the control condition classes, teachers were asked to prepare without a dashboard, based on their experience, their knowledge of their students, and on what they noticed when students were working with Lynnette in the lab. (The only difference between the two conditions therefore was whether or not the dashboard was available during the preparatory sessions.) Teachers then conducted the class sessions they prepared for. (The students did not use Lynnette during these sessions.) During these sessions, each 40 min, 2–4 coders (undergraduate students and staff from our institution) took observational notes using a tool with predefined categories of observations that also allowed for free-form note taking. After the class session, students took a 20-minute post-test. Both pre- and post-tests contained 9 exercises based on 9 problem sets in Lynnette, covered the same equation types, with different numbers, and were assigned in counterbalanced manner. The pre- and post-tests allow us to assess student learning gains due to the class session teachers conducted based on their preparation with or without the dashboard. (Learning gains due to the ITS would have happened prior to the pre-test.)

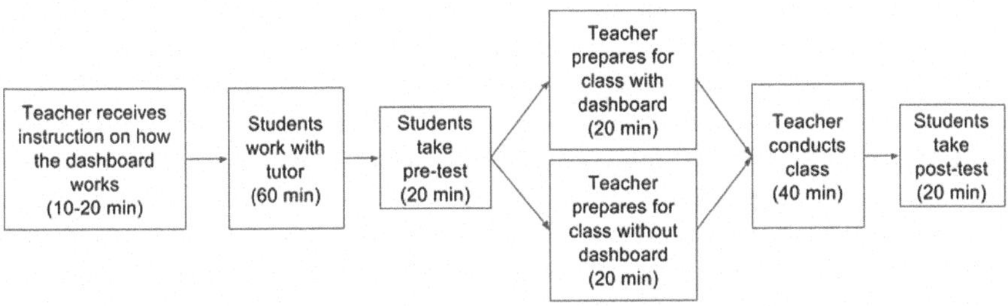

Fig. 3. Experimental set up for an individual teacher and an individual class.

3.3 RQ1: How Does the Dashboard Affect Teachers?

We study how the dashboard affects teachers in each of the links of the causal chain.

Table 1. Table of a teacher's updated knowledge at the class and individual level.

Row		Code	Statement
1	Teacher's knowledge or expectations for class	--	KC1- Expect students are good at because they have done this already: Add/Subtract Constant From Both Sides
		--	KC2- Expect students are good at because they have done this already: Combine Like [Constant] Terms
		--	KC3- Expect students are good at because they have done this already: Divide Both Sides By Variable Coefficient
		--	KC4- The Distributive Property, I thought they would struggle with
2	Learned from dashboard for class	(✓)G	LC1- Add/Subtract Constant From Both Sides
		(✓)G	LC2- Combine Like [Constant] Terms
		(✓)G	LC3- Divide Both Sides By Variable Coefficient
		(+)G	LC4- Compute Quotient For Constant (8 did not get to Level 3, 16 who got there mastered it), ok that's good
		(+)N	LC5- 8 students did not get to Level 3
		(+)N	LC6- Combine Like [Variable] Terms (who got there mastered it, it's just that not everybody got there)
		(+)N	LC7- Add/Subtract Variables On Both Sides, the same kids who got to that [Combine Variable Terms] got this
		(✓)B	LC8- Distribute Property, ok that is where they are starting to fall of
		(+)N	LC9- A couple of kids did not grab this [gesturing Level 1 Add/Subtract Constant From Both Sides and Combine Constant Terms]
		(+)N	LC10- A couple of kids did not grab this [gesturing Level 2 Divide By Variable Coefficient]
3	Teacher's knowledge or expectations for individual students	--	KS1- Student 1 would be in one of the higher levels if she was here the first day
		--	KS2- Student 2 wasn't here at all
		--	KS3- Student 3 was here only the second day
		--	KS4- Student 4 and Student 5 would goof around if they work together
		--	KS5- Student 6 would be ok working with Student 7
		--	KS6- Student 4 is pretty strong
4	Learned from dashboard for individual students	(+)N	LS1- I have a high [level 7], medium [level 5], and low group [level 3]
		(!)N	LS2- Student 8 is kind of surprising
		(+)B	LS3- Student 1 is behind
		(+)B	LS4- Student 2 is at (0:0) (wasn't here?)
		(+)B	LS5- Student 3 is at (0:0) (thought was here the second day?)

Teacher's updated knowledge. Targeting the first link in the causal chain, we analyzed the video-recordings of the teachers' preparation sessions to assess how Luna affected their knowledge. From these video-recordings, the first author distilled and paraphrased the main ideas teachers expressed (which we will call statements) as they were thinking out loud during the preparation sessions. A second coder verified the segmentation of the recording into statements by time-tagging each of them. As shown in Table 1, we distinguished four categories of teacher knowledge, characterized by whether they knew it *before* inspecting Luna or became aware of it *while* inspecting it, and whether the focused-on information pertains to the class overall or to individual students. We created such tables with teachers' statements for each of the 8 experimental condition classes.

The statements that represent what teachers learned from the dashboard (rows 2 and 4 in Table 1) were coded based on two coding schemas. The first set of codes aims to classify how Luna's information relates to the teacher's prior knowledge, using the following codes: (1) "✓" means that Luna's information confirms what teachers knew about their students (e.g.,"*Yeah, [student name] is not surprising…*"), (2) "!" means that teachers were surprised by Luna's information, or it was inconsistent with what teachers knew (e.g.,*"The only thing that stands out for me is this [pointing at combine like terms make constant and make variable]…)*, and (3) "+" means that teachers learned from Luna, but it did not confirm or reject what they already knew, (e.g., "*… looking at it, [the]distributive property they have all pretty much mastered…*"). The second set of codes aims to classify whether the teacher's comment was about students doing well or not in Lynnette, based on data from Luna. It has the following codes: (1) "**G**" means that the teacher's comment is about information from Luna that showed students did well in Lynnette (e.g., "*I am actually kind of surprised that [student name] made it that far, that's good!*"), (2) "**B**" means that the teacher's comment is about students not doing well (e.g., "*… I see that that's what students have most trouble in, combine unlike terms to make a variable…*"), and (3) "**N**" means that the teacher's comment is ambiguous (e.g., if the teacher says, "*Only one hasn't mastered the distributive property,*" it is not clear whether he/she views that as positive or negative). The codes were assigned based only on what teachers explicitly said in the video-recordings of the preparation sessions. The first author and a trained coder first

Table 2. Lesson plan, with information attributable to Luna coded in the first column.

<table>
<tr><th>Code</th><th></th><th colspan="4">Concepts teacher will cover/review in class (WHAT?)</th><th>Exercises teacher will do in class (HOW?)</th></tr>
<tr><td>--</td><td></td><td colspan="4">(Revise concepts through equation solving + students working in groups)</td><td></td></tr>
<tr><td>LC9</td><td>1</td><td colspan="4">Add/Subtract Constant From Both Sides</td><td>x+8=-15</td></tr>
<tr><td>LC10</td><td>2</td><td colspan="4">Divide Both Sides By The Variable Coefficient</td><td>3x = 24</td></tr>
<tr><td>--</td><td>3</td><td colspan="4">Distributive Property/Combining Like Terms</td><td></td></tr>
<tr><td>LC8</td><td></td><td>a</td><td colspan="3">(Stus started to fall of at the Distributive Property)</td><td>5(x+4)=40
3=7(4-2u)-6u</td></tr>
<tr><td>LC6</td><td></td><td>b</td><td colspan="3">(This has that combine in it)</td><td>3(1+4n)-2(5n-3)=25</td></tr>
<tr><td rowspan="5">(From other class)</td><td>4</td><td colspan="4">Variables On Both Sides</td><td></td></tr>
<tr><td></td><td>a</td><td colspan="3">Variables On Both Sides</td><td>5x+6=2x+15</td></tr>
<tr><td></td><td>b</td><td colspan="3">With Negative Numbers</td><td>-7x-2=24-9x</td></tr>
<tr><td></td><td>c</td><td colspan="3">Distributive Property + Variables On Both Sides</td><td>4(5n-7)=10n+2</td></tr>
<tr><td></td><td>d</td><td colspan="3">Distributive Property + Variables On Both Sides</td><td>2(6d+3)=18-3(16-3d)</td></tr>
<tr><td>LS1,
LS2,
LS3,
LS4,
LS5</td><td>5</td><td colspan="2">Students work in groups of 3 with worksheet with exercises on Distributive Property + Variables On Both Sides (same worksheet as previous class)</td><td>Level 7
1 Student 6
2 Student 9
3 Student 10
4 Student 11
5 Student 12
6 Student 13
7 Student 14
8 Student 4</td><td>Level 5
6 Student 15
3 Student 16
2 Student 17
1 Student 18
~~5 Student 19~~
7 Student 20
4 Student 21</td><td>Level 3
3. ~~Student 8~~ Student 24
1 Student 7
2 Student 22
5 Student 1
6 Student 23
7 Student 5
8 ~~x Student 3~~ x Student 2
(with Student 4 who is pretty strong and they were not here)</td></tr>
<tr><td>--</td><td>6</td><td colspan="2">Give worksheet from previous class</td><td colspan="3"></td></tr>
</table>

coded all statements independently. They then met and resolved all disagreements in coding through discussion and mutual consensus. The results reported here are based on this consensus coding.

Lesson Plan. Moving to the next link in the causal chain (link 3 in Fig. 1), we analyzed how the knowledge gained from the dashboard may have influenced teachers' lesson plans. We focused on the lesson plans for the 8 classes in the experimental condition, which teachers created with help from Luna. To represent the lesson plans, we created tables (Table 2) based on the distilled and paraphrased main ideas teachers mentioned or wrote down during the preparation sessions. These tables show the topics along with the exercises (if any) that teachers planned to cover during the class session, as well as their plans about individual students, when applicable. To study how the information learned from Luna affected the teacher's lesson plan, each of the items in the lesson plan (rows in Table 2) was matched with what teachers learned from Luna (rows 2, 4 in Table 1). For example, if the teacher stated, "... *that is where they are starting to fall off, at the distributive property"* (LC8 in Table 1) and then said *"... we are back into distributive property... so I can steal some examples from my other... [the plan for my other class] (writes down some exercises with the distributive property used in the previous class they prepared for),"* we would put the code LC8 under the respective row in the lesson plan table. This coding procedure was applied only to statements for which teachers explicitly stated that the reason they were going to cover it in class because was information from Luna.

Table 3. Part of a lesson plan compared with what happened during the class session.

Code			Concepts teacher will cover/review in class (WHAT?)	Exercises teacher will do in class (HOW?)	Covered?	Concept/Misconceptions	Who?
--			(Revise concepts through equation solving + students working in groups)		Yes	-Focus on what they will do today -Focus on what teacher saw in dashboard: weaknesses and strengths -Focus on Distribute Property and Combine Like Terms where most did not get to -Most reached Level 5 but not all -Focus on working with things they have never done before (Part B)	
LC9	1		Add/Subtract Constant From Both Sides	x+8=-15	No		
LC10	2		Divide Both Sides By The Variable Coefficient	3x = 24	No		
--	3		Distributive Property/Combine Like Terms		Yes		
LC8		a	(Stus started to fall of at the Distributive Property)	5(x+4)=40	Yes	-Focus on Distribution -Focus on two step equations: do add/subtract -Focus on canceling and simplification -Focus on checking answer	Teacher discusses with students, Student 7, 2, 5, 24
				3=7(4-2u)-6u	Yes	-Focus on Distributive Property and Combine Like Terms -Focus on distributing the 7 -Focus on divide and the other steps	Teacher discusses with students, Student 14, 11, 4, 16
					Not planned	-Focus on not distributing to the other side -Focus not distributing to the 6u term	
LC6		b	(This has that combine in it)	3(1+4n)-2(5n-3)=25	Yes	-Focus on splitting stus in groups -Focus on distribution of both parenthesis -Focus on Combine Like Terms, add/subtract, divide -Focus on checking solution	Teacher discusses with students, students work in groups, Student 11
					Not planned	-Focus on distributing the negative -2 with the other negative -3 as it is tricky	

Class Session. Moving to the next link in the causal chain (link 4 in Fig. 1), we counted how many of the statements in the lesson plan that were based on information from Luna, actually made it into the class session. For each class session, we analyzed the joint set of all notes taken during the sessions by all coders. We created tables to compare the lesson plan with the class session (Table 3). Next to each statement of the lesson plan, columns were added to show (1) whether teachers covered the planned statement in class, (2) a summarized description of what they discussed, and (3) who was involved in the discussion during the class session. The categories under the column Covered indicate whether teachers covered that statement in class (*Yes/No/Not planned*, with the latter code meaning the teacher did something they did not plan for or did not say they were planning for).

3.4 RQ2: Does Teacher's Use of the Dashboard Help Students Learn Better?

We studied whether students in the experimental condition, where teachers used Luna to prepare for the class session, had higher learning gains attributable to the class session, compared to the control condition. We consider the learning gains from pre- to post-test. (These gains can be attributed to the class session led by the teacher, since there were no other learning activities in between the pre-test and post-test.) We had analyzable data for 242 students (students who missed the pre-test, class session or post-test were removed from the analysis). Seven independent graders and the first author graded the tests. Fleiss's Kappa was 0.98. The grading schema gave full credit for correct statements and no credit for incorrect statements.

4 Results

4.1 RQ1: How Does the Dashboard Affect Teachers?

Teacher's updated knowledge. Across 5 teachers in 8 experimental condition classes, we recorded on average 12.6 statements per class that were evidence of the dashboard affecting what teachers knew about their students (Updated Knowledge in Table 4). (We will refer to the statements learned from Luna as "learned statements.") There were slightly more such statements at the class level compared to the individual level (7.1 statements per class at the class level versus 5.5 statements per class at the individual level). Teachers seemed surprised more often by information at the individual level (on average 1.4 statements per class) than at the class level (on average 0.38 statements per class). Further, out of the 12.6 statements on average that provide evidence that teachers learn from Luna, 34.7% relate to things that students are not doing well (19.8% at the class and 14.9% at the individual level), while 29.7% relate to things they are doing well (19.8% at the class and 9.9% at the individual level). Thus, Luna's information affected the teacher's knowledge about the class overall and individual students. Furthermore, these learned statements are about students doing well and not doing well with roughly equal frequency.

Lesson plan. Moving to the next link in the causal chain (Lesson Plan in Table 4), 44.6% of the learned statements get incorporated in the lesson plans (5.6 out of 12.6 statements per class learned from Luna). At the class level, teachers include in the lesson plans 33.3% of the learned statements, compared to 59% at the individual level. This finding suggests that Luna prompted change in teachers' lesson plans, both with respect to the class as a whole and to individual students, though more so with respect to the latter. In addition, teachers include an average of 3.1 statements per lesson plan pertaining to students not doing well (24.7% of all learned statements), namely, 1.9 (14.9%) at the class level and 1.3 (9.9%) at the individual level. By contrast, they include only 0.75 statements per class (5.9% of the learned statements) pertaining to students doing well (Fig. 4)! As a different way of looking at this contrast, teachers include in their lesson plans 20% of the learned statements regarding students doing well, whereas they include 71.4% of the learned statements regarding students not doing well. Thus, the knowledge that teachers gain from Luna is accounted for in various ways in their lesson plans, in particular knowledge about where students are struggling.

Table 4. Effect of the dashboard measured as average number of statements per class.

	Class Overall			Individual Students		
	Updated Knowledge	Lesson Plan	Class Session	Updated Knowledge	Lesson Plan	Class Session
(✓)	1	0.13	0.13	0.5	0.13	0.13
(+)	5.8	2	1.4	3.6	2.6	1
(!)	0.38	0.25	0.25	1.4	0.5	0.5
G	2.5	0.13	0	1.3	0.63	0.5
B	2.5	1.9	1.6	1.9	1.3	0.63
N	2.1	0.38	0.13	2.4	1.4	0.5
Total	**7.1**	**2.4**	**1.8**	**5.5**	**3.3**	**1.6**

We also made informal observations as to how the information teachers learned from Luna made it into their lesson plans. At the class level, in 6/8 classes where teachers prepared the control before the experimental classes, they used as a basis for the experimental classes the plan they prepared for the control ones, but changed and adapted it based on Luna's information. For example, they planned to discuss specific topics students were having trouble with, or added and removed exercises or topics from the plan based on Luna's information. One teacher, who prepared for the experimental before the control class, based the lesson plan for the former entirely on the dashboard, focusing on discussing errors the class was having with example exercises Luna provided for each error. In addition, based on Luna's information, in 1/8 classes the teacher decided not to cover a topic because the class had mastered it, while another teacher planned what topics to cover for the rest of the week, after the class session. At the individual level, in 3/8 classes teachers planned to work one-to-one, during or after class, with students who were not doing well as shown by Luna, while in 2/8 classes one teacher decided they did not need to spend time with individual students, who despite initially not doing well according to Luna, had fixed the problems they had, also according to Luna. In 2/8 classes, teachers adapted a worksheet they planned to give students based on the information in Luna. And lastly, somewhat to our surprise, in 2/8 classes one teacher assigned students to work in groups during the class session, with group composition based on students' progress as shown by Luna. In conclusion, there is a variety of ways in which teachers incorporate in their lesson plans knowledge they gain from Luna both at the class and individual level.

Class session. Moving down the causal chain, teachers implement in the class session 60% of those planned statements (Fig. 4), which is 26.7% of the ones they learned from Luna (13.9% at the class and 12.9% at the individual level). Furthermore, 17.8% of the learned statements about students not doing well make it to the class session (12.9% at the class and 5% at the student level), as opposed to 4% of the ones about students doing well. Thus, the knowledge teachers gain from Luna that makes it to the lesson plan also gets accounted for and reaches students in the class session.

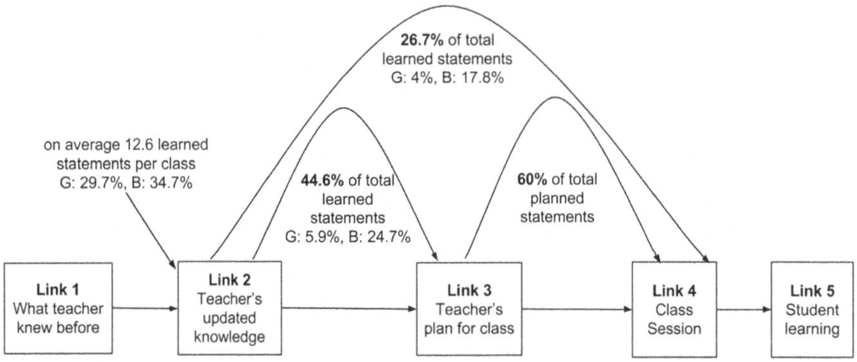

Fig. 4. How the information from the dashboard traveled down the causal chain. The percentages on the arrows are percentages of the total number of statements teachers learned from Luna. "G" and "B" refer to statements about students doing well and not so well, respectively.

4.2 RQ2: Does Teacher's Use of the Dashboard Help Students Learn Better?

To test for knowledge differences between the conditions right before the class session, we ran a Welch Two Sample t-test on the pre-test data to compare the means of the control condition (M = 5.48, SD = 2.89) and experimental conditions (M = 4.53, SD = 3.23). We found that, in spite of our efforts to create balanced conditions, students in the control condition had a significantly higher pre-test mean than those in the experimental condition (t = 2.3908, df = 236.31, p = 0.0176). We used a hierarchical linear model (HLM [17]) with three nested levels to compare the gains from pre- to post-test (which can be attributed to the class session, with condition differences attributable to the dashboard). In the model, students (level 1) were nested within classes (level 2) which were nested within teachers (level 3). We included the condition as a fixed effect, and the difference between post- and pre-test as the dependent variable. There was no significant difference between the conditions in learning gains ($t = -1.620$, $df = 240$, $p = 0.1065$).

5 Discussion and Conclusions

We examine and trace the influence of a dashboard on teachers' knowledge of their students, their lesson plans and execution of these plans, and ultimately on student learning; these influences are summarized in a "causal chain" that guides our analysis. To the best of our knowledge, the use of this causal chain, to trace the effects of a dashboard for an ITS on teacher practices and student learning, is a methodological innovation in dashboard research. We note that this causal chain is not specific to ITSs or to the particular dashboard used. Further, to the best of our knowledge, the current study is one of the first that tries to measure *student learning gains* due to the teacher's use of a dashboard in a classroom setting [18, 22], with the exception of [7].

Our results show that the dashboard affects teachers at all the links in the causal chain. First, teachers update their knowledge with an average 12.6 statements per class (Fig. 4). In turn, the teachers' updated knowledge helps them to adapt or change their lesson plan. Teachers incorporate 44.6% of the statements they learned from the dashboard in their lesson plans, which suggests that Luna provided useful information to teachers on their students' performance in the ITS. Furthermore, teachers implement in the class session 60% of the planned statements, which is 26.7% of the statements they learned from the dashboard (Fig. 4). This is a substantial portion, even if as we move down the causal chain, the number of statements that can be attributed to the dashboard decreases at every link. Perhaps that kind of "dilution" of influence, as we look at causal effects further removed from what teachers gleaned directly from the dashboard, is not surprising, although we believe our study is the first to document this phenomenon regarding dashboards.

In addition, we found teachers attend mostly to information from Luna that shows their students are not doing well in certain aspects of equation solving, as opposed to information about doing well. This perhaps is not surprising in and of itself but it suggests that the dashboard presents information that teachers do not have. Furthermore, although teachers learn almost the same number of statements for both the class overall and individual students who are not doing well, more statements related to the class, rather then individuals, get accounted for in the class session. Lastly, contrary to our expectation, we did not find that Luna influenced student learning. Generally, we can conclude that the dashboard's information, about skill mastery, occurrence of errors and student progress in an ITS, at the class and individual level, is helpful to teachers as they prepare for a class session, even if more is needed to demonstrate an improvement in student learning.

There are reasons to think that a fully designed dashboard, used over an extended period of time, could be even more influential than we found in the current study. First, as mentioned, at the time of the study, Luna was a high-fidelity dashboard prototype with some interactivity. A complete dashboard might provide more opportunities for teachers to look at more detailed information about their students' learning or might provide an option to project the dashboard in front of the class (cf. [7]). Second, the planning sessions were only 20 min total (for creating two or three lesson plans), which in retrospect was not enough time for teachers to fully digest Luna's information and plan what to cover in class. The class session was only 40-minutes, which restricted how much teachers planned for and covered. These time limitations could explain why teachers only planned for part of the information they learned from Luna and why fewer statements made it into the class session. Third, students took the post-test either right after the class session or the day after. Thus, they had no time to practice what teachers covered in the class session. Fourth, the dashboard was a new technology for teachers; the study gave them only limited time to become familiar with it, not enough to integrate it into their daily routines. In addition, only 2 out of the 5 teachers had previously worked with an ITS. When Luna is fully developed, with more opportunities for teachers to look at detailed information, and when used for longer periods of time, it could potentially help teachers bring more information from the dashboard into the class session, and ultimately help their students achieve higher learning gains.

In sum, the results of our study indicate that a dashboard with analytics from an ITS, based primarily on its student modeling methods, can be helpful to teachers. We found that the dashboard's information affects the teacher's knowledge, lesson plans, and what they cover in the class session. In particular, the teachers paid much attention to their students' struggles. In our previous work [25] we found that teachers can have surprisingly detailed knowledge about their students; it was therefore not obvious that the dashboard would tell them much that they didn't already know. However, our study shows that even though teachers generally know their classes well, a dashboard with analytics from an ITS can still help them know more about their students, and can influence their lesson plans and lesson.

Acknowledgments. We thank all the teachers, schools and students who took part in our study, Gail Kusbit, Kenneth Holstein, the coders and graders for the project. This work is supported by NSF Award # 1530726.

References

1. Aleven, V., McLaren, B.M., Sewall, J., van Velsen, M., et al.: Example-tracing tutors: intelligent tutor development for non-programmers. Int. J. Artif. Intell. Educ. **26**, 224–269 (2016)
2. Aleven, V., Xhakaj, F., Holstein, K., McLaren, B.M.: Developing a teacher dashboard for use with intelligent tutoring systems. In: The Proceedings of the 4th International Workshop on Teaching Analytics, IWTA 2016 at the 11th European Conference On Technology Enhanced Learning, EC-TEL 2016, 13–16 September 2016, Lyon, France (2016)
3. Anderson, J.R., Corbett, A.T., Koedinger, K.R., Pelletier, R.: Cognitive tutors: lessons learned. J. Learn. Sci. **4**(2), 167–207 (1995)
4. Arroyo, I., Woolf, B.P., Burleson, W., Muldner, K., Rai, D., Tai, M.: A multimedia adaptive tutoring system for mathematics that addresses cognition, metacognition and affect. Int. J. Artif. Intell. Educ. **24**(4), 387–426 (2014)

5. Hanington, B., Martin, B.: Universal Methods of Design: 100 Ways to Research Complex Problems, Develop Innovative Ideas, and Design Effective Solutions. Rockport Publishers, Beverly (2012)
6. Holstein, K., Xhakaj, F., Aleven, V., McLaren, B.M.: Luna: A Dashboard for Teachers Using Intelligent Tutoring Systems. In: Proceedings of the 4th International Workshop on Teaching Analytics, IWTA 2016 at the 11th European Conference On Technology Enhanced Learning, EC-TEL 2016, 13–16 September 2016, Lyon, France (2016)
7. Kelly, K., Heffernan, N., Heffernan, C., Goldman, S., Pellegrino, J., Goldstein, D.S.: Estimating the Effect of Web-Based Homework. In: Lane, H.C., Yacef, K., Mostow, J., Pavlik, P. (eds.) AIED 2013. LNCS, vol. 7926, pp. 824–827. Springer, Heidelberg (2013). doi:10.1007/978-3-642-39112-5_122
8. Kulik, J.A., Fletcher, J.D.: Effectiveness of Intelligent Tutoring Systems: a meta-analytic review. Rev. Educ. Res. **86**(1), 42–78 (2016)
9. Long, Y., Aleven, V.: Mastery-oriented shared student/system control over problem selection in a linear equation tutor. In: Micarelli, A., Stamper, J., Panourgia, K. (eds.) ITS 2016. LNCS, vol. 9684, pp. 90–100. Springer, Cham (2016). doi:10.1007/978-3-319-39583-8_9
10. Lovett, M., Meyer, O., Thille, C.: The open learning initiative: Measuring the effectiveness of the OLI statistics course in accelerating student learning. J. Interact. Media Edu. **1**, 1–16 (2008). doi:10.5334/2008-14
11. Ma, W., Adesope, O.O., Nesbit, J.C., Liu, Q.: Intelligent Tutoring Systems and learning outcomes: A meta-analysis. J. Educ. Psychol. **106**(4), 901 (2014)
12. Martinez-Maldonado, R., Pardo, A., Mirriahi, N., Yacef, K., Kay, J., Clayphan, A.: The LATUX workflow: designing and deploying awareness tools in technology-enabled learning settings. In: Proceedings of the Fifth International Conference on Learning Analytics And Knowledge, LAK 2015, pp. 1–10 (2015)
13. Martinez Maldonado, R., Kay, J., Yacef, K., Schwendimann, B.: An interactive teacher's dashboard for monitoring groups in a multi-tabletop learning environment. In: Cerri, S.A., Clancey, W.J., Papadourakis, G., Panourgia, K. (eds.) ITS 2012. LNCS, vol. 7315, pp. 482–492. Springer, Heidelberg (2012). doi:10.1007/978-3-642-30950-2_62
14. Mavrikis, M., Gutierrez-Santos, S., Poulovassilis, A.: Design and evaluation of teacher assistance tools for exploratory learning environments. In: Proceedings of the Sixth International Conference on Learning Analytics & Knowledge, LAK 2016, pp. 168–172. ACM, New York (2016)
15. Mazza, R., Dimitrova, V.: CourseVis: a graphical student monitoring tool for supporting instructors in web-based distance courses. Int. J. Hum. Compu. Stud. **65**(2), 125–139 (2007)
16. McLaren, B.M., Scheuer, O., Miksatko, J.: Supporting collaborative learning and eDiscussions using artificial intelligence techniques. Int. J. Artif. Intell. Educ. **20**(1), 1–46 (2010)
17. Raudenbush, S.W., Bryk, A.S.: Hierarchical Linear Models: Applications and Data Analysis Methods. Sage Publications, Newbury Park (2002)
18. Schwendimann, B.A., Rodríguez-Triana, M.J., Vozniuk, A., Prieto, L.P., Boroujeni, M.S., Holzer, A., Gillet, D., Dillenbourg, P.: Understanding learning at a glance: An overview of learning dashboard studies. In: Gasevic, D., Lynch, G., Dawson, S., Drachsler, H., Rose, C. P. (eds.), Proceedings of the Sixth International Conference on Learning Analytics & Knowledge, LAK 2016, pp. 532–533. ACM, New York (2016)
19. Steenbergen-Hu, S., Cooper, H.: A meta-analysis of the effectiveness of Intelligent Tutoring Systems on college students' academic learning. J. Educ. Psychol. **106**(2), 331–347 (2014)

20. van Leeuwen, A., Janssen, J., Erkens, G., Brekelmans, M.: Supporting teachers in guiding collaborating students: effects of learning analytics in CSCL. Comput. Educ. **79**, 28–39 (2014)
21. VanLehn, K.: The behavior of tutoring systems. Int. J. Artif. Intell. Educ. **16**(3), 227–265 (2006)
22. Verbert, K., Govaerts, S., Duval, E., Santos, J.L., Van Assche, F., Parra, G., Klerkx, J.: Learning dashboards: an overview and future research opportunities. Pers. Ubiquit. Comput. **18**(6), 1499–1514 (2014)
23. Waalkens, M., Aleven, V., Taatgen, N.: Does supporting multiple student strategies lead to greater learning and motivation? Investigating a source of complexity in the architecture of Intelligent Tutoring Systems. Comput. Educ. **60**, 159–171 (2013)
24. Woolf, B.P.: Building Intelligent Interactive Tutors: Student-Centered Strategies for Revolutionizing E-learning. Morgan Kauffman, Burlington (2009)
25. Xhakaj, F., Aleven, V., McLaren, B.M.: How teachers use data to help students learn: contextual inquiry for the design of a dashboard. In: Verbert, K., Sharples, M., Klobučar, T. (eds.) EC-TEL 2016. LNCS, vol. 9891, pp. 340–354. Springer, Cham (2016). doi:10.1007/978-3-319-45153-4_26

Scalable Mind-Wandering Detection for MOOCs: A Webcam-Based Approach

Yue Zhao(✉), Christoph Lofi, and Claudia Hauff

Web Information Systems, Delft University of Technology, Delft, The Netherlands
{y.zhao-1,c.lofi,c.hauff}@tudelft.nl

Abstract. Mind-wandering or loss of focus is a frequently occurring experience for many learners and negatively impacts learning outcomes. While in a classroom setting, a skilled teacher may be able to react to students' loss of focus, in Massive Open Online Courses (MOOCs) no such intervention is possible (yet). Previous studies suggest a strong relationship between learners' mind-wandering and their gaze, making it possible to detect mind-wandering in real-time using eye-tracking devices. Existing research in this area though has made use of *specialized* (and expensive) hardware, and thus cannot be employed in MOOC scenarios due to the inability to scale beyond lab settings. In order to make a step towards *scalable* mind-wandering detection among online learners, we propose the use of ubiquitously available consumer grade webcams. In a controlled study, we compare the accuracy of mind-wandering detection from gaze data recorded through a standard webcam and recorded through a specialized and high-quality eye tracker. Our results suggest that a large-scale application of webcam-based mind-wandering detection in MOOCs is indeed possible.

Keywords: Learning analytics · MOOCs · Mind-wandering · Eye tracking

1 Introduction

Mind-wandering is an essential part of human behavior consuming up to 50% of everyday thoughts [8], and can be described as "thoughts and images that arise when attention drifts away from external tasks and perceptual input toward a more private, internal stream of consciousness" [12]. While mind-wandering can also have positive effects (such as fostering creativity [23]), many educational tasks including following a lecture or solving an assignment require active attention and focus to reach the desired learning outcomes. For these tasks, excessive mind-wandering has disastrous effects on learning efficiency [19].

In the traditional classroom setting, mind-wandering and attention lapses have been studied for a long time, e.g. [3,24]. Although researchers do not yet

C. Hauff—This work is partially supported by the *Leiden-Delft-Erasmus Centre for Education and Learning*.

É. Lavoué et al. (Eds.): EC-TEL 2017, LNCS 10474, pp. 330–344, 2017.
DOI: 10.1007/978-3-319-66610-5_24

agree on the actual attention span of learners, several past works have found attention among students during lecture time to vary in a cyclic manner.

For online courses and MOOCs, this problem is even more severe as they are consumed using digital display devices. This mode of consumption is particularly prone to mind-wandering. Likely due to the ubiquity of smartphones and digital content, a significant subgroup of online users adopt a "heavy media multitasking" behavior [10], making it challenging for them to focus on a single multimedia content unit. This finding is also supported by our work, where learners frequently lose focus even in short video clips of around seven minutes.

In order to detect mind-wandering among online learners during their consumption of digital materials, we require an approach that is *scalable* (it can be deployed to thousands of learners), *near real-time* (mind-wandering is detected as soon as it occurs), *unobtrusive* (learners are not distracted by the detection procedure) and *autonomous*. In addition to providing insights into learners' behaviors, such a method would also enable real-time interventions that lower the amount of mind-wandering taking place. As a concrete example we envision an intelligent MOOC video player: the player (via the webcam feed) monitors a learner's attention state and when a loss of focus is detected, the player pauses the video automatically in order to avoid skipping over relevant content. In order to ensure learners' privacy, all necessary processing will be client-side (i.e. executed within the browser).

To this end, previous research showed that by analyzing people's gaze data, mind-wandering can be detected, e.g. whilst reading texts on screen [1], or watching (non-educational) films [2]. These results can be attributed to the eye-mind link effect [15], which states that "there is no appreciable lag between what is fixated and what is processed." Existing works usually rely on expensive and specialized eye-tracking hardware (e.g. a Tobii eye tracker) to obtain gaze data, which is not available to the average MOOC learner. It is therefore still an open question whether eye-tracking based mind-wandering detection can be performed in a scalable manner.

Our goal in this paper is to develop a fully automatic method for detecting mind-wandering and loss of focus in near real-time using only low-end webcams ubiquitously found on laptop computers. To this end, we conducted a laboratory study with 13 participants, collecting a dataset of gaze features (i.e. features extracted from gaze data) and self-reported mind-wandering. To motivate this approach, refer to Fig. 1 which visualizes the gaze of two of our study participants through heatmaps. The MOOC video shown has several relevant visual areas, including the lecture slides, the subtitles, and the speaker's face. In the depicted scene, a changing set of examples is shown on the slides which are important to grasp the lecture content. The participant who reported mind-wandering in the 30 s interval intently gazed on a spot on the speaker's face, ignoring the slides and the shown examples, while the second participant who reported no mind-wandering focused on all relevant areas of the video. Our proposed approach employs supervised machine learning to automatically learn such mind-wandering patterns based on gaze features.

(a) reported mind-wandering (b) no mind-wandering

Fig. 1. Gaze heatmaps of two study participants over a 30 s interval

Our contributions in this work are as follows:

1. We create an elaborate gold dataset to foster eye-tracking based mind-wandering research, featuring 13 participants watching two MOOC videos each in a controlled laboratory setting, reporting feedback on mind-wandering in brief intervals. In addition to these mind-wandering reports, we provide video and gaze data as recorded and analyzed by a professional eye tracker as well as gaze data recorded by a webcam and processed by an open-source gaze library. We make this data available on our companion Web page [25].
2. We implement and evaluate an approach to automatically detect mind-wandering based on gaze data (i) collected with a specialized eye-tracking device (`Tobii X2-30`), relying on the results and best practices published in [2], and (ii) collected with a standard webcam.
3. We extensively discuss and evaluate both approaches, and argue that our webcam-based method is indeed suitable for large-scale deployment outside a controlled laboratory setting.

2 Background: Mind-Wandering

Different data collection methods have been used to study mind-wandering of students in traditional classrooms since the 1960s, such as the observation of inattention behaviors [7], the retention of course content [11], using direct probes in class [9,21] and relying on self-reports from students [3]. A common belief was that learners' attention may decrease considerably after 10–15 min of the lecture, which was supported by [21]. However, Wilson and Korn [24] later challenged this claim and argued that more research is needed. In a recent study, Bunce et al. [3] asked learners to report their mind-wandering voluntarily during 9–12 min course segments. Three buttons were placed in front of each learner, representing attention lapses of 1 min or less, of 2–3 min and of 5 min or more. During the lectures, the learners were asked to report their mind-wandering by pressing one of three buttons once they *noticed* their mind-wandering. This setup led Bunce et al. [3] to conclude that learners start losing their attention early on in the lecture and may cycle through several attention states within the 9–12 min course segments.

In online learning environments, mind-wandering may be even more frequent. Risko et al. [16] used three one hour video-recorded lectures with different topics (psychology, economics, and classics) in their experiments. While watching the videos, participants were probed four times throughout each video. The mind-wandering frequency among the participants was found to be 43%. Additionally, Risko et al. [16] found a significant negative correlation between test performance and mind-wandering. Szpunar et al. [22] investigated the impact of interpolated tests on learners' mind-wandering within online lectures. The study participants were asked to watch a 21-minute video lecture (4 segments with 5.5 min per segment) and report their mind-wandering in response to random probes (one probe per segment). In their experiments, the mind-wandering frequency was about 40%. Loh et al. [10] also employed mind-wandering probes to measure learners' mind-wandering and found a positive correlation between media multitasking activity and learners' mind-wandering (average frequency of 32%) whilst watching video lectures. Based on these considerably high mind-wandering frequencies we conclude that reducing mind-wandering in online learning is an important approach to improve learning outcomes.

Inspired by the eye-mind link effect [15], a number of previous studies [1,2,13] focused on the automatic detection of learners' mind-wandering by means of gaze data. In [1,2], Bixler and D'Mello investigated the detection of learners' mind-wandering during computerized reading. To generate the ground truth, the study participants were asked to manually report their mind-wandering when an auditory probe (i.e. a beep) was triggered. Based on those reports, the mind-wandering frequency ranged from 24.3% to 30.1%. During the experiment, gaze data was collected using a dedicated eye tracker. In [13], Mills et al. asked the study participants to watch a 32 min, non-educational movie and self-report their mind-wandering throughout. In order to detect mind-wandering automatically, statistical features and the relationship between gaze and video content were considered. In contrast to [1,2], the authors mainly focused on the relationship between a participant's gaze and areas of interest (AOIs), specific areas in the video a participant should be interested (like the speaker or slides).

3 Methodology

In our study, we focus on the automatic detection of learners' mind-wandering through webcam-based eye tracking. The scenario we consider is video lecture watching, which is the most common manner of conveying lecture content in MOOCs [16]. We collect data through a lab study with 13 participants who were asked to watch two lecture videos and regularly report their mind-wandering during this time. We recorded their gaze data with a dedicated high-quality eye tracker and a standard webcam. In our paper, gaze data refers to both gaze points (the points on the screen a participant is actively looking at) and gaze events (i.e. fixations and saccades). Fixation refers to the action that concentrates the gaze points on a single area, and saccade refers to the quick and simultaneous movement of both eyes between two or more phases of fixations.

Compared to previous works [10,13,16,22], the two MOOC lecture videos in our study are considerably shorter - they are between six and eight minutes in length, in line with standard MOOC practices today. To collect the ground-truth (did mind-wandering occur in the last n seconds?) we rely on mind-wandering probes which have proven to be effective in the traditional classroom setting [4, 9,21] and online learning [1,2]. Probes (regularly and actively seeking input from the study participants) are more reliable than self-caught reports which require study participants to think about their loss of focus and about reporting it [20]. In response to our probes (in the form of an auditory signal—a bell) during video lecture playback, participants were asked to press a key to indicate that they experienced mind-wandering in the past 30 s. Participants who did not experience mind-wandering were asked to ignore the bell and continue watching.

Having collected the ground truth data, we next turned to the extraction of features from gaze data, following [13]. In line with previous works, we extracted features from gaze events. These gaze events are generated by gaze points. Note that gaze points are not measured directly - they are estimated from the recorded eye and iris movements; we used the existing software libraries of our dedicated high-quality eye tracker and our open-source webcam-based framework to turn eye and iris movements into gaze points.

Finally we used employed the ground truth data and extracted features in a supervised machine learning task to explore to what extent the automatic detection of mind-wandering in this setting is possible.

The overview of the processing pipeline is shown in Fig. 2. In the following sections, we first describe in more detail the experimental design of our study, and then elaborate on the features we extracted.

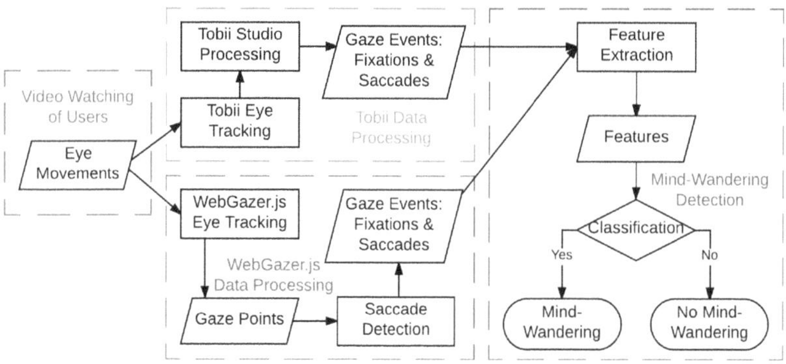

Fig. 2. Overview of the processing pipeline

3.1 Study Setup

Our study is built around two introductory videos taken from two different x-MOOCs [17] professionally produced and offered by the Delft University of Technology on the edX[1] platform. One video, (taken from the *Understanding Nuclear Energy* MOOC), covers the basics of the atomic model with a length of 6:41 min; the second one (part of the *Solar Energy* MOOC and 7:49 min long) introduces the concept of energy conversion. We selected those videos specifically as they contain rich visual lectures slides overlayed with the speaker (see Fig. 1). They cover topics we consider interesting to a wider audience and do not require extensive prior knowledge due to their introductory nature. All study participants watched both videos; their order was randomized to avoid order effects.

We used two eye-tracking devices in the study, a high-quality one as a reference and a low-quality webcam. Concretely, we made use of the professional `Tobii X2-30` eye tracker and its corresponding software Tobii Studio to estimate participants' gaze points. Our webcam is the built-in camera of our experimental laptop, a Dell Inspiron 5759 with a 17-inch screen and a 1920 × 1080 resolution. To estimate the gaze points based on a live webcam feed, we relied on `WebGazer.js` [14], an open source eye-tracking library written in JavaScript. We built a Web application closely resembling existing MOOC lecture video players with additional logging capabilities. In order to alert our participants to each mind-wandering probe, we included a medium-volume acoustic bell signal played by the Web application. After the bell, participants reported their mind-wandering in the past 30 seconds by pressing a feedback button. The next bell signal occurred after another 30–60 s. The actual time was randomized within those boundaries, as previous research [1,10] suggests that participants perceive interruptions which are not perfectly periodic as less interrupting. In order to further limit the mental annoyance of this process, participants were only asked to actively report in case they had indeed experienced mind-wandering. This process resulted in mind-wandering reports for each participant, including the bell signals and participant responses with respect to mind-wandering as shown in Fig. 3.

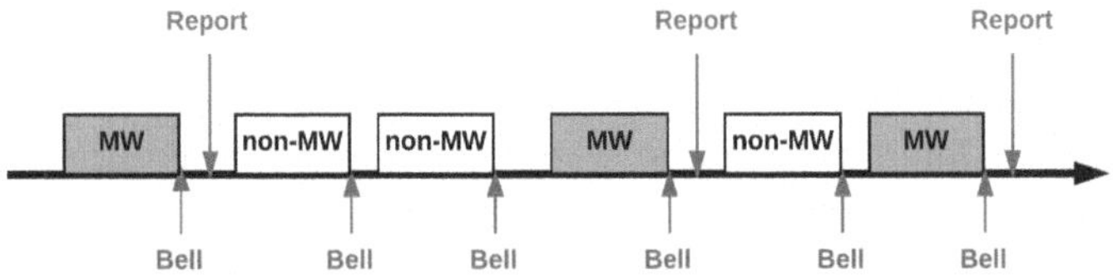

Fig. 3. An example of mind-wandering reports

We recruited our study participants (six females, seven males, all with a computer science background) through an internal mailing list and did not pay

[1] http://edx.org/.

them. After a pre-study briefing, we asked our participants, six of whom wore glasses or contact lenses, to sit stable and comfortably in front of the laptop (with a distance of 52–68 cm between eyes and screen). The study consisted of pre- and post-study questionnaires, an instruction phase by the experimenter, a calibration phase (to calibrate the eye trackers) and the watching of the two lecture videos; overall, participants spent about 35 min in the experiment. We conducted all experiments during daylight hours with both office lights and natural daylight contributing to our lighting.

The data generated by Tobii Studio during the study includes (among others) the estimated 2D coordinates of gaze points for each eye, the duration and coordinates of gaze events (i.e. fixations and saccades), the eye and pupil positions of the participant as well as the distance between the participant and the camera with a sample rate of 30 samples/second. In contrast, the data extracted from our webcam-based eye-tracking solution only includes the estimated 2D coordinates of gaze points of both eyes sampled at a rate of 5 samples/second.

3.2 Mind-Wandering Detection Using Gaze Features

To realize eye-tracking based mind-wandering detection using the professional eye tracker and our webcam-based solution, we turn the task into a standard supervised machine learning task. Our classifiers are trained using the aforementioned mind-wandering reports as reference labels, and extracted gaze features for each time span between two bell signals as collected by either technique as input.

Given Tobii Studio's gaze data and inspired by [1,2] we extracted 58 features in total. These features can be classified into two groups, global features and local features. The global features refer to features which are independent of the current content of the MOOC video, and are as shown in Table 1 based on fixations and saccades. The feature vector of a given bell time span covers statistical aggregates of fixation and saccade data such as maximum, minimum, mean, median, standard deviation, range, kurtosis and skew of fixation durations, saccade durations, saccade distance and saccade angles.

Local features are mainly based on the relationship between fixations/saccades and the areas of interest (AOIs) in the MOOC video, i.e. local features correlate gaze data with the current video content. There are certain areas of a video where a focused learner should focus her attention (e.g. the slides) in order to follow the content, while others are less interesting. While this opens a complex design space for engineering features, we opted for a simple implementation in which we manually defined three fixed areas of interest: the instructor's face, subtitles, and the lecture slides. The resulting local features include then the number and length of saccades and fixations which focus on different areas of interest for a given time span. Recall once more that all saccade and fixation data are computed by Tobii Studio with high precision for each bell time span based on a raw sample rate of 30 Hz.

Table 1. Features leveraged in the detection of participants' mind-wandering

Feature name	Explanation
Global features	
Fixation duration	The durations (ms) of fixations
Saccade duration	The durations (ms) of saccades
Saccade distance	The distances (pixel) of saccades
Saccade angle	The angles (degree) between saccades and the horizon
Number of saccade	Total number of saccades
Horizontal saccade ratio	The proportion of the number of saccades which have saccade angles less than 30°
Fixation saccade ration	The ratio of the durations of fixations to the duration of saccades
Local features	
Saccade landing	The proportion of the number of saccades landing in different areas
Fixation duration AOI	The durations (ms) of fixations located in different areas

Due to limitations of the `WebGazer.js` framework[2], we only achieve a sample rate of 5 Hz for our webcam-based experiments. As changes of fixations and saccades usually happen within the range of 200 ms to 400 ms [18], reliable gaze data comparable to the one provided by the high-speed Tobii tracker is impossible to obtain using such a low sample rate and thus needs to be estimated algorithmically. For this purpose we implement micro-saccade detection as discussed in [6]: we first determine whether the movement between two consecutive gaze points is a saccade based on the movements' velocity. Then we treat gaze points between two saccades as a fixation. If there is only a single gaze point between two saccades, we assume this gaze point is a fixation with a duration between this gaze point and the previous gaze point. After the detection of saccades and fixations, we can generate the same 58 features as already shown in Table 1. Intuitively, the feature vectors from the webcam-based solution are less precise (as the sampling rate is much lower), however, we will show later that they still show comparable classification performance as we aggregate features over the time spans between consecutive bells, thus this imprecision carries little weight.

To train our classifiers, we adopt leave-one-participant-out cross-validation [13]. In each run, the data of one participant is selected as test data and the data of all other participants is used for training. Based on the results reported in previous works [1,2,13], the collected data on learners' mind-wandering is usually unbalanced with considerably less than 50% of probes resulting in reported mind-wandering. We counter the effects of this imbalance

[2] It is based on an iterative algorithm that each detection runs after the previous detection is finished.

by applying the oversampling method Synthetic Minority Over-sampling Technique (SMOTE) [5].

We have two requirements for our choice of classifiers as follows:

1. The selected models trained with our data can be used effectively to infer mind-wandering in data of unseen participants.
2. The selected models trained with our data can be used in *real-time* mind-wandering detection.

For the first requirement, we consider the bias-variance trade-off of machine learning models and the data size in our experiments. We select Logistic Regression, Linear SVM and Naive Bayes classifiers in our experiments as they have a low variance on small datasets like ours. These classifiers are also suitable for our second requirement. Since the trained models are small and require few inference steps, they can easily be integrated into Web applications within MOOC platforms.

In order to determine the effect of different feature types, we evaluate different subsets of features in our experiments: (i) global features only (G), (ii) local features only (L) and (iii) the combination of global and local features (G+L). Since we also include SMOTE as a pre-processing step to deal with the unbalanced nature of our data, overall we report results on six different setups.

4 Results

In this section, we focus on the experimental results of our study and described mind-wandering detection methods. We address two main research questions:

RQ1: How many mind-wandering reports are collected from participants across each video, and what can be learned from them?

RQ2: How well does our webcam-based mind-wandering detection method perform, and how does it compare to detection based on data collected from a professional eye tracker?

For **RQ2**, we first compare the overall effectiveness of our three selected classifiers with different sets of gaze features. Then, we delve deeper into the mind-wandering detection results. Considering that the mind-wandering reports are not evenly distributed among participants nor across the entire length of the lecture videos, we address two sub-questions **RQ2.1** and **RQ2.2**. A final sub-question is dedicated to the generalizability of our trained models.

RQ2.1: Does mind-wandering detection perform equally well across all participants?

RQ2.2: Does mind-wandering detection perform equally well across the entire length of a lecture video?

RQ2.3: Does a mind-wandering detection model trained on one video perform well to detect mind-wandering on a different video?

4.1 Exploratory Analysis of Mind-Wandering Reports

In order to answer **RQ1**, we now analyze our participants' mind-wandering behaviour while watching the two MOOC lecture videos.

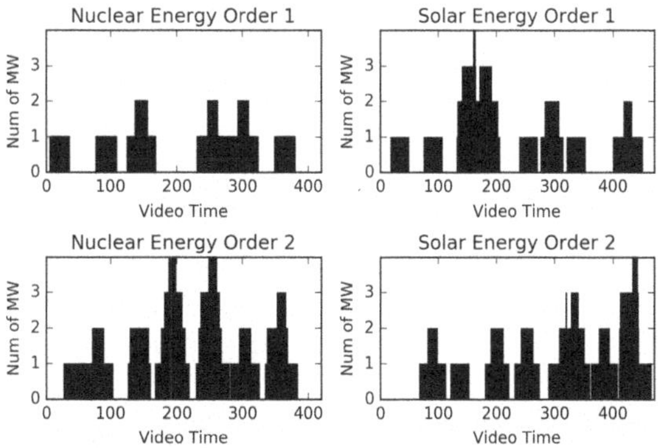

Fig. 4. Overview of the reported mind-wandering (MW) reports across the MOOC videos. Due to the randomized video order in the experiment, we partitioned the results according to whether the video was shown first ("order 1") or last ("order 2"). The video time displays the number of seconds since the start of the video.

In Fig. 4, the distributions of participants' reported mind-wandering events over the course of each of the two videos are shown. As discussed in the last section, participants were shown both videos in a random order, which is also reflected in the diagram. As the number of participants in each of the experimental groups is very small, no statistically significant conclusions can be drawn. However, it is visible that mind-wandering is indeed a rather frequent occurrence even for very short video lectures of roughly 7 min: our measured mind-wandering rate is 29%; i.e. in 71% of all bell time spans, our subjects actually stayed focused. In addition, it appears that our participants tire considerably during the second video when the experiment draws to its conclusion. This feedback was pro-actively provided by several of our participants in a post-experiment questionnaire, and seems to be at least anecdotally confirmed by the presented mind-wandering reports.

4.2 Mind-Wandering Detection

In order to answer **RQ2**, we investigate how accurately we can detect participants' mind-wandering based on gaze data extracted by `WebGazer.js` compared to Tobii's `X2-30`. The results are shown in Table 2. The results are based on the nested leave-one-participant-out cross-validation, which means that a leave-one-participant-out cross-validation is used as the inner cross-validation for model selection and a leave-one-participant-out cross-validation is used as the outer

Table 2. Mind-wandering detection results based on gaze data (*G* means global features and *L* means local features)

Data	Feature	SMOTE	Precision	Recall	F1	Classifier
Baseline	–	–	0.290	0.291	0.290	–
Tobii data	G	–	0.316	0.515	0.350	Logistic Regression
	G	✓	**0.358**	0.487	0.336	Logistic Regression
	L	–	0.263	0.625	0.309	Logistic Regression
	L	✓	0.294	**0.682**	**0.364**	Naive Bayes
	G+L	–	0.342	0.486	0.335	Naive Bayes
	G+L	✓	0.346	0.502	0.330	Linear SVM
WebGazer data	G	–	0.309	0.671	0.395	Naive Bayes
	G	✓	0.306	**0.744**	**0.405**	Naive Bayes
	L	–	0.313	0.650	0.394	Naive Bayes
	L	✓	**0.320**	0.691	0.403	Naive Bayes
	G+L	–	0.289	0.696	0.378	Naive Bayes
	G+L	✓	0.286	0.674	0.378	Naive Bayes

cross-validation for measuring performance of the selected model. For the sake of brevity[3], we only list the best performing classifier for each feature set. As a *baseline method*, we used a random classifier which includes the knowledge that the mind-wandering rate is 0.29 and thus each feature vector is labeled as mind-wandering with a probability of 0.29. Since accuracy is not a suitable metric for unbalanced data, precision, recall, and F1-measure are reported.

Based on our results in Table 2, all our methods are significantly better than the random baseline according to all three metrics. We do not observe a large impact of SMOTE: applying the SMOTE pre-processing method on Tobii data slightly increases *Precision*, however it has no effect on the detection results on `Webgazer.js` data. The combination of local and global features does not benefit the detection on Tobii data nor the detection on `Webgazer.js` data.

All our reported F1 scores are slightly lower than reported by previous research [2] which relied on similar features and classifiers. We believe the difference (0.1 in F1 score) to be due to the slightly different data collection setup: Bixler et al. [2] utilized a short movie instead of MOOC lectures and free self-reporting instead of periodic self-reporting to obtain mind-wandering reports. With respect to the evaluated classification methods, we find that the Gaussian Naive Bayes models outperform the other approaches on `WebGazer.js` data in every feature set combination.

The most surprising finding in this experiment is that compared to the Tobii data we achieve higher *Recall* and *F1* scores based on the gaze features extracted

[3] The full results, as well as all hyperparameter settings of the classifiers can be found online [25].

from `WebGazer.js` data. Based on our intuition, features extracted from the data which is generated from the high-quality eye tracker `X2-30` should lead to a more accurate detection of mind-wandering, than features extracted from the data which is generated by a standard webcam. A possible reason for this experimental artifact is the small number of participants in our study; in future work we plan increase our participant pool to at least 100 participants.

Based on Table 2, we now delve deeper into our mind-wandering detection results. In order to answer **RQ2.1**, we investigate the detection results on each participant separately. For this step, we select the best-performing models for each data source (Table 2). For the detection on Tobii data, we use Gaussian Naive Bayes with local features and the SMOTE method. For the detection on `Webgazer.js` data, we use Gaussian Naive Bayes with global features and the SMOTE method. The results are shown in Table 3. We observe that across all metrics, the minimum observed accuracy is zero (for both Tobii and Webgazer data), which implies that there are participants for whom our prediction is not working at all. At the same time, we observe that at best a participant's mind-wandering can be detected with high accuracy with an F1 of 0.7 (Tobii data) and 0.8 (Webgazer data) respectively. The large standard deviations across the three metrics - 0.2 to 0.35 - further show that the accuracy of our detector varies widely between participants. Therefore, we conclude that *the detection does not work equally well for all participants in our experiments.*

Table 3. Statistics of detection results on individual participants ($P_{highest}$ shows the detection results of the participant with highest F1-measure, P_{lowest} with lowest)

Data	Metrics	Max	Min	Mean	Std	$P_{highest}$	P_{lowest}
Tobii data	Precision	0.714	0	0.294	0.198	0.600	0
	Recall	1.000	0	0.682	0.357	0.857	0
	F1	0.706	0	0.364	0.200	0.706	0
WebGazer data	Precision	0.700	0	0.306	0.209	0.700	0
	Recall	1.000	0	0.744	0.354	1.000	0
	F1	0.824	0	0.405	0.244	0.824	0

Based on the analysis in Sect. 4.1, we find that mind-wandering is not evenly distributed throughout a video. This leads to our **RQ2.2**. We split each video into two parts with the same length. Then, for each part of the video, we use the data of the other part and the data of the other video to train the model and to detect the mind-wandering in this specific left-out part of the video. The models, feature sets and the SMOTE method used in this experiments are same as in **RQ2.1**. The results are shown in Table 4. We conclude that *the detection of mind-wandering cannot be made equally well across the entire length of the lecture videos in our experiments.* For `X2-30` data, we find the results of the mind-wandering detection in the second part of the same video to be much better

Table 4. Detection across the entire length of the video (*Part 1* means the first half part of the video, and *Part 2* means the second half part of the video)

Data	Metrics	Solar Energy		Nuclear Energy	
		Part 1	Part 2	Part 1	Part 2
Tobii data	Precision	0.147	0.410	0.276	0.321
	Recall	0.308	0.763	0.397	0.462
	F1	0.195	0.474	0.285	0.369
WebGazer data	Precision	0.365	0.240	0.295	0.327
	Recall	0.615	0.500	0.462	0.615
	F1	0.438	0.285	0.344	0.416

than the first part. For `WebGazer.js` data, we observe no trend, the results vary depending on the lecture video. We hypothesize this result to be connected to the fact that different participants were shown the videos in different orders.

Our last experiment answers **RQ2.3**. So far we have shown that our method can detect a participant's mind-wandering based on a model trained on the gaze data and mind-wandering reports of other participants. To scale out, we need to determine to what extent we can detect learners' mind-wandering in video lectures of one course with a model trained in lecture videos of other courses. If we were to obtain good detection results for such scenarios, there may be a general model which can be used in different lecture videos at scale (i.e., "train once, deploy everywhere"). In this experiment, the experimental settings for classifiers, feature sets and the SMOTE method on different kinds of data are same as in our previous experiments (**RQ2.1** and **RQ2.2**). We evaluate the cross-video performance by training our model on one video, and test the performance of the model using the other video. The results of all video combinations are shown in Table 5. For reference, this table also includes training and testing using the same video, using leave-one-participant-out cross-validation.

Table 5. Detection with model translation (i.e. using a model on a different video than it was trained on)

Data	Metrics	Trained on solar		Trained on nuclear	
		Used in solar	Used in nuclear	Used in nuclear	Used in solar
Tobii data	Precision	0.267	0.171	0.294	0.149
	Recall	0.705	0.372	0.410	0.205
	F1	0.355	0.229	0.296	0.150
WebGazer data	Precision	0.240	0.298	0.346	0.344
	Recall	0.679	0.692	0.596	0.667
	F1	0.317	0.401	0.392	0.423

Based on the results in Table 5, we find the model trained on `WebGazer.js` data to be more robust to a change of video context than the model trained on `X2-30` data. We also observe that it does matter whether we train on video A and test on B or vice versa as results are comparable. Overall, we believe that *a model trained on the `WebGazer.js` data collected on one video can lead to good predictions in other videos*, at least if the videos share similarities with respect to style and type as in our scenario.

5 Conclusions

In this paper, we presented a study on the automatic and scalable detection of mind-wandering during lecture video watching collected by a standard consumer-grade webcam. In a lab study we compared the effectiveness of a webcam plus the open-source library `WebGazer.js` to the effectiveness of the specialized (and expensive) `Tobii X2-30` for the task of mind-wandering detection. In our experiments, we could show that the accuracy of our webcam-based approach is on par with the specialized eye-tracking device. This opens the way for large-scale experiments in real-world MOOCs, allowing for both investigating learners' mind-wandering behavior and investigating the effectiveness of interventions based on mind-wandering detection in future research under realistic conditions.

Our work is in a preliminary stage and has a number of limitations including the small pool of participants all sharing similar educational backgrounds. Similarly, the number of evaluated MOOC videos is very limited and both videos have a comparable (but very common) style. Thus, it is unclear how well our approach can be applied to completely different types of videos or user groups. In addition, we relied on a number of established and straightforward-to-implement features; we expect a further boost in detection accuracy when more sophisticated features are introduced.

A core contribution provided by our work is the published repository of data collected during our controlled lab study. In addition to including the mind-wandering reports of our experiment's participants, we also provide the full set of gaze data obtained by the `X2-30` and our webcam as well as the complete results of our data analysis.

References

1. Bixler, R., D'Mello, S.: Toward fully automated person-independent detection of mind wandering. In: Dimitrova, V., Kuflik, T., Chin, D., Ricci, F., Dolog, P., Houben, G.-J. (eds.) UMAP 2014. LNCS, vol. 8538, pp. 37–48. Springer, Cham (2014). doi:10.1007/978-3-319-08786-3_4
2. Bixler, R., D'Mello, S.: Automatic gaze-based user-independent detection of mind wandering during computerized reading. User Model. User Adapt. Interact. **26**(1), 33–68 (2016)
3. Bunce, D.M., Flens, E.A., Neiles, K.Y.: How long can students pay attention in class? A study of student attention decline using clickers. J. Chem. Educ. **87**(12), 1438–1443 (2010)

4. Cameron, P., Giuntoli, D.: Consciousness sampling in the college classroom or is anybody listening? Intellect **101**(2343), 63–64 (1972)
5. Chawla, N.V., Bowyer, K.W., Hall, L.O., Kegelmeyer, W.P.: SMOTE: synthetic minority over-sampling technique. J. Artif. Intell. Res. **16**, 321–357 (2002)
6. Engbert, R., Kliegl, R.: Microsaccades uncover the orientation of covert attention. Vision. Res. **43**(9), 1035–1045 (2003)
7. Johnstone, A.H., Percival, F.: Attention breaks in lectures. Educ. Chem. **13**(2), 49–50 (1976)
8. Killingsworth, M.A., Gilbert, D.T.: A wandering mind is an unhappy mind. Science **330**(6006), 932 (2010)
9. Lindquist, S.I., McLean, J.P.: Daydreaming and its correlates in an educational environment. Learn. Individ. Differ. **21**(2), 158–167 (2011)
10. Loh, K.K., Tan, B.Z.H., Lim, S.W.H.: Media multitasking predicts video-recorded lecture learning performance through mind wandering tendencies. Comput. Hum. Behav. **63**, 943–947 (2016)
11. McLeish, J.: The Lecture Method. Cambridge Institute of Education, Cambridge (1968)
12. McMillan, R., Kaufman, S.B., Singer, J.L.: Ode to positive constructive daydreaming. Front. Psychol. **4**, 626 (2013)
13. Mills, C., Bixler, R., Wang, X., D'Mello, S.K.: Automatic gaze-based detection of mind wandering during narrative film comprehension. In: EDM 2016, pp. 30–37 (2016)
14. Papoutsaki, A., Daskalova, N., Sangkloy, P., Huang, J., Laskey, J., Hays, J.: Webgazer: scalable webcam eye tracking using user interactions. In: IJCAI 2016, pp. 3839–3845 (2016)
15. Rayner, K.: Eye movements in reading and information processing: 20 years of research. Psychol. Bull. **124**(3), 372–422 (1998)
16. Risko, E.F., Anderson, N., Sarwal, A., Engelhardt, M., Kingstone, A.: Everyday attention: variation in mind wandering and memory in a lecture. Appl. Cogn. Psychol. **26**(2), 234–242 (2012)
17. Rodriguez, O.: The concept of openness behind c and x-MOOCs (Massive Open Online Courses). Open Praxis **5**(1), 67–73 (2013)
18. Salvucci, D.D., Goldberg, J.H.: Identifying fixations and saccades in eye-tracking protocols. In: Proceedings of the 2000 Symposium on Eye Tracking Research & Applications, pp. 71–78. ACM (2000)
19. Smallwood, J., Fishman, D.J., Schooler, J.W.: Counting the cost of an absent mind: mind wandering as an underrecognized influence on educational performance. Psychon. Bull. Rev. **14**(2), 230–236 (2007)
20. Smallwood, J., Schooler, J.W.: The restless mind. Psychol. Bull. **132**(6), 946–958 (2006)
21. Stuart, J., Rutherford, R.: Medical student concentration during lectures. Lancet **312**(8088), 514–516 (1978)
22. Szpunar, K.K., Khan, N.Y., Schacter, D.L.: Interpolated memory tests reduce mind wandering and improve learning of online lectures. Proc. Natl. Acad. Sci. **110**(16), 6313–6317 (2013)
23. Tan, T., Zou, H., Chen, C., Luo, J.: Mind wandering and the incubation effect in insight problem solving. Creat. Res. J. **27**(4), 375–382 (2015)
24. Wilson, K., Korn, J.H.: Attention during lectures: beyond ten minutes. Teach. Psychol. **34**(2), 85–89 (2007)
25. Zhao, Y., Lofi, C., Hauff, C.: EC-TEL 2017 companion webpage (2017). https://yue-zhao.github.io/MWDET_Project/

Short Papers

From MOOCs to SPOCs... and from SPOCs to Flipped Classroom

Carlos Alario-Hoyos(✉), Iria Estévez-Ayres, Carlos Delgado Kloos, and Julio Villena-Román

Department of Telematic Engineering, Universidad Carlos III de Madrid, Av. Universidad, 30, 28911 Leganés (Madrid), Spain
{calario,ayres,cdk,jvillena}@it.uc3m.es

Abstract. The concept of SPOCs (Small Private Online Courses) emerged as a way of describing the reuse of MOOCs (Massive Open Online Courses) for complementing traditional on-campus teaching. But SPOCs can also drive an entire methodological change to make a better use of face-to-face time between students and teachers in the classroom. This paper presents the redesign and evaluation of a first-year programming course in several engineering degrees, with over 400 students overall, through the reuse of MOOCs as SPOCs on campus, combined with a flipped classroom strategy aimed at promoting active learning. Results from a students' self-reported questionnaire show a very positive acceptance of the SPOC, which includes both videos and complementary formative activities, and an increase of motivation through the combination of the SPOC and activities implemented in lectures to flip the classroom.

Keywords: MOOCs · SPOCs · Flipped classroom · Programming course

1 Introduction

MOOCs (Massive Open Online Courses) have brought major changes to traditional education. On one side, they provide access to quality courses from top Universities to any learner worldwide [1]. On the other side, they can be reused [2] to complement residential courses [3] under the name SPOC (Small Private Online Course) [4].

In addition to serving as a complement to face-to-face classes, it is possible to reuse MOOCs in a more integrated way to support flipped classroom strategies [5], where students work in the theoretical concepts (mainly watching videos and doing basic exercises) before going to the classroom, and then class time is used to work in practical and applied activities with the objective to promote a more active learning.

This paper presents a successful case of reusing MOOCs as SPOCs, this being the core for a flipped classroom strategy in which lecture time is reallocated to do hands-on activities that promote active learning. The case refers to a first-year programming course taught in several engineering degrees, with more than 400 students enrolled per year average. Both SPOC and flipped classroom strategy are evaluated through a questionnaire filled out by students in the middle of the semester to know their opinions on the usefulness of these innovations and their effect on students' motivation.

É. Lavoué et al. (Eds.): EC-TEL 2017, LNCS 10474, pp. 347–354, 2017.
DOI: 10.1007/978-3-319-66610-5_25

2 Case Study: Systems Programming

Systems Programming is a first-year second-semester programming course of four bachelor's engineering degrees at Universidad Carlos III de Madrid (UC3M) (Spain); it is taught in both English and Spanish. Typically, more than 400 students enrol this 15-week course, which has two sessions per week: a 100-minute lecture in large groups (up to 120 students) and a 100-minute laboratory session in small groups (up to 40 students). This is the second programming course students take after a basic programming course in the first semester. Java is the programming language used, as it is also the language used in the first semester programming course, so students are supposed to already have the background on the syntax and basic control flow instructions. One of the main problems encountered by Systems Programming teachers is that, even though the theoretical explanations are important, this is an eminently practical subject, and there is little time for practical activities (100 min per week). Furthermore, it is difficult to get more time for practicing as theoretical sessions follow a strict schedule, and take place in large classrooms of up to 120 students. Before starting the course 2016/2017 teachers decided to redesign the structure of large group classes reusing MOOCs as a SPOC, this being the core of a flipped classroom strategy focused on hands-on activities and the promotion of active learning.

2.1 First Phase: MOOCs

In 2015, teachers from the Departments of Telematics Engineering and Computer Sciences at UC3M began the development of three five-week MOOCs on "Introduction to Programming with Java." These three MOOCs cover the syllabus of the first basic programming course (first semester), and of Systems Programming (second semester). The three MOOCs are deployed in edX and form an XSeries (sequence of interrelated courses) (https://www.edx.org/xseries/introduction-programming-java).

- "Part 1, Starting to Code with Java," focuses on the programming basics and goes from imperative programming to object orientation; Part 1 was developed in 2015 and has run thrice so far.
- "Part 2, Writing Good Code," focuses on error detection and correction, going from low-level development to high-level design, including, among other topics, debugging, testing, complexity, software engineering and ethical issues; Part 2 was developed in 2016 and has run twice so far.
- "Part 3, Fundamental Data Structures and Algorithms," focuses on linear and non-linear data structures, as well as on basic and advanced algorithms applied on them; Part 3 was developed in 2017 and has run once so far.

These three MOOCs are offered in English (videos also include subtitles in both English and Spanish) and together add up more than 300,000 enrollees in the several runs, with Part 1 the most successful MOOC. Although videos are an important part, a special emphasis was put on having many interactive activities supported by edX built-in tools, external tools integrated in edX (e.g. Blockly or Codeboard), animations and simulations [6]. The quality of the educational materials in these MOOCs has been improved through learners' contributions, who act as critical reviewers.

2.2 Second Phase: SPOCs

The three MOOCs were used to create dedicated SPOCs for Systems Programming, one in English and another one in Spanish. The SPOC in English has entirely reused contents from the MOOCs. The SPOC in Spanish has partially reused contents from the MOOCs, but some videos were re-recorded in Spanish, and some assignments were translated to Spanish. Both SPOCs are equivalent and share the same structure. With the contents of the three MOOCs it was possible to create SPOCs that cover 100% of the Systems Programming syllabus. The SPOCs are deployed in an Open edX instance, hosted at UC3M servers. Only students enrolled in Systems Programming can access this SPOC and there is no relationship between the students who use the SPOCs and the learners enrolled in the MOOCs.

2.3 Third Phase: Flipped Classroom

The SPOCs made it possible the restructuring of large groups classes to put into practice a flipped classroom strategy. Students were told to watch videos and do some assignments before coming to class. This way, they got sufficient knowledge to quickly review the main concepts at the beginning of the class, and then, have time to do practical activities. Large group classes were redesigned as follows:

- First, there is a brief presentation of the highlights of the session with time for questions (about 20–25 min). This part has a twofold purpose: students who watched the videos and did the assignments at home some days ago refresh them, while student who did not watch the videos nor did the activities at home have at least a basic background to continue with the following parts.
- Next, students are presented a set of exercises in which they must code small programs (about 40–45 min). They can do this activity alone or in small groups. Solutions to the exercises are later provided and briefly explained.
- Finally, a questionnaire is presented to learners using the quiz-based platform Kahoot! (https://kahoot.it/) (about 30–40 min). The questionnaire has 10–20 questions, and has a twofold purpose: it serves as a formative evaluation for students; and teachers can detect the main conceptual gaps students have. Questions and answers are projected in a big screen and students can answer from their mobile devices or laptops, through the browser, and without installing anything. Each question is timed (e.g. 30/60 s) and the whole class moves forward to the following question together. Students pick a nickname and receive points to answer correctly and quickly; a leaderboard is shown between questions to encourage students' motivation through competition.

This design is usually replicated in each large group class with minor variations, such as including a basic, short Kahoot! at the beginning of the class (5–10 min) so that the teacher can know if students watched the videos and did the activities at home, and otherwise dedicate a little more time to the highlights explanation.

Finally, those students who come to Systems Programming without having passed the first semester basic programming course are actively encouraged by teachers to enroll the XSeries on edX and start with the first MOOC ("Part 1: Starting to Code with Java,") to catch up.

3 Results

An anonymous voluntary questionnaire filled out by students in the middle of the course was used to evaluate the SPOC and the redesign of the course through a flipped classroom strategy. The questionnaire included closed-ended questions (to be assessed using a Likert scale), and open-ended questions (in which students could provide more elaborated answers). The data analysis followed a mixed methodology in which closed-ended questions served to gain insights and detect tendencies, which were afterwards confirmed or discarded through the open-ended questions. 104 students of the four bachelor's degrees answered this questionnaire. (25.6% of enrolees).

3.1 Results About the SPOC

63 students (60.6%) said that they used the SPOC weekly to prepare the following large group classes, 37 students (35.6%) said that they used the SPOC occasionally to review some concepts, and 4 students (3.8%) said that they did not use the SPOC. Students who used the SPOC could assess statements about the usefulness and effect of its materials (mainly videos and interactive activities) (see Table 1). 91 students (90.1%) agreed or strongly agreed that the videos were useful for better understanding the main concepts, 63 students (62.4%) agreed or strongly agreed that the videos increased their motivation to keep working at home, 84 students (84%) agreed or strongly agreed that the activities were useful for practicing the main concepts, and 68 students (67.3%) agreed or strongly agreed that the activities increased their motivation to keep working at home. Overall, 91 students (90.1%) agreed or strongly agreed that including a SPOC in future editions of the course would be useful. These results are reinforced by positive comments from students, such as "*I am doing the course for a second time and with this kind of teaching I have the motivation I did not find last year,*" "*it [the SPOC] is well organized to have a previous background of what we will see in the class,*" "*I am very satisfied and motivated thanks to this format. (…) I would like all courses to be taught in this way.*" Critical comments mainly refer to the use of the SPOC for passing the course: "*I believe that for passing the course we need to do more exercises and coding instead of watching videos,*" "*Great videos, maybe doing all the exercises should be considered towards the grade.*"

Table 1. Statements to be assessed by students about the SPOC.

Assertion	Strongly agree	Agree	Neither agree nor disagree	Disagree	Strongly disagree	*Total answers*
Videos in the SPOC are useful for my learning to better understand the main concepts of the course	38	53	4	5	1	101
Exercises in the SPOC are useful for my learning to practice the main concepts of the course	25	59	13	2	1	100
Videos in the SPOC increase my motivation to keep working in the course at home	22	41	33	2	3	101
Exercises in the SPOC increase my motivation to keep working in the course at home	18	50	29	2	2	101
I believe that including a SPOC like this in future editions of this course would be useful	54	37	6	2	2	101

3.2 Results About the Redesign of Large Group Classes Using Flipped Classroom

The novelties with respect to traditional lectures are problem solving in small groups, and Kahoots, and these two elements were the ones assessed (see Table 2). 93 students (89.4%) agreed or strongly agreed that practical exercises helped them to understand better the concepts, 65 students (62.5%) agreed or strongly agreed that these exercises motivated them to keep working at home, 76 students (73.1%) agreed or strongly agreed that the exercises had an appropriate level of difficulty, and 97 students (93.3%) agreed or strongly agreed that including practical exercises in future editions of the course would be useful. These results are reinforced by positive comments from students such as: "*They [The videos] help me to connect concepts, remember them, and sometimes learn from errors*," "*since we have been working with the same [Java] Class as we advanced with new contents, and these contents are applied to the same Class, everything is more structured*." However, there are students who pointed out some of the external constraints to carry out practical activities in large group classes, such as time and facilities: "*There is not enough time, and in the end, everything is done very fast*," "*there are not enough power sockets in the classroom, and it is difficult that everyone can use his own laptop*."

90 students (86.5%) agreed or strongly agreed that Kahoots help them to better understand the concepts, 84 students (80.8%) agreed or strongly agreed that Kahoots motivated them to keep working at home, 87 students (83.7%) agreed or strongly agreed that Kahoots had an appropriate level of difficulty, 82 students (78.8%) agreed or strongly agreed that the competition with the classmates in the Kahoots increased their motivation, and 90 students (86.5%) agreed or strongly agreed that including Kahoots in future

editions of the course would be useful. These results are reinforced by positive comments from students, such as: "*If Java is my religion, Kahoots are its prophets. Keep them,*" "*they motivate me a lot and I am having fun. I wish there were more of this in other courses.*" There were also a few students which criticized the use of this tool in class, and demanded more time to better prepare them for exams: "*I do not think this is useful, it would be better to include more exercises from exams.*"

Table 2. Statements to be assessed by students about practical exercises and Kahoots.

Assertion	Strongly agree	Agree	Neither agree nor disagree	Disagree	Strongly disagree	*Total answers*
The practical exercises done during large group classes help me understand better the theoretical concepts explained	54	39	7	2	2	104
The practical exercises done during large group classes motivate me to keep working in the course at home	33	32	32	5	2	104
The practical exercises done during large group classes have an appropriate level of difficulty according to the concepts explained	41	35	18	7	3	104
I believe that including practical exercises like these in future editions of this course would be useful	55	42	6	0	1	104
Kahoots done during large group classes help me understand better the theoretical concepts explained	44	46	6	4	4	104
Kahoots done during large group classes motivate me to keep working in the course at home	52	32	10	6	4	104
Kahoots done during large group classes have an appropriate level of difficulty according to the concepts explained	46	41	9	5	3	104
The fact that there is a competition with my classmates in the Kahoots increases my motivation	63	19	13	5	4	104
I believe that including Kahoots like these in future editions of this course would be useful	61	29	8	3	3	104

4 Conclusions and Future Work

This paper has presented a successful case of reusing MOOCs as a SPOC, this SPOC being the core for redesigning large group classes in an engineering course using flipped classroom. This experience is intended as example of how to reuse MOOCs, once tested in the open world, to improve the quality of on-campus courses by rethinking traditional lectures. Results are very positive in terms of the usefulness of the SPOC, practical activities and Kahoots, and moderately positive in terms of the effect they all have on increasing students' motivation to work beyond class time.

These results were obtained with a sample that represents approximately a quarter of the students enrolled in the course, and approximately half of those who attend regularly to class. Despite possible bias it is noteworthy that voluntary questionnaires tend to be answered more frequently by those students who had very positive or very negative experiences. Answers to open-ended questions allow deepening in students' opinions, and iterate in the redesign of the course for its improvement in future editions. Most of the few negative comments point out the use of class time for better preparing students for exams; some of these comments may come from repeaters.

The implementation of a flipped classroom strategy supported by a SPOC is not without risks. First, the number of students attending to class may decrease, as theoretical concepts are explained in the videos. Here, teachers detected a slight decrease in the number of students attending to class (compared to previous years). For this, teachers need to make good use of class time to carry out activities which add value to what is already available in the SPOC, as it was intended with the redesign of large group classes in this course. Second, there is a well-known risk in flipped classroom strategies, which is that students do not complete their homework before coming to class. To alleviate this problem, teachers used motivation strategies based on gamification, such as the use of Kahoot! in class, which promotes competition through interactive questions about knowledge students should have acquired at home.

Acknowledgements. This work has been co-funded by the Erasmus + projects MOOC-Maker (561533-EPP-1-2015-1-ES-EPPKA2-CBHE-JP), SHEILA (562080-EPP-1-2015-BE-EPPKA3-PI-FORWARD), and COMPETEN-SEA (574212-EPP-1-2016-1- NL-EPPKA2-CBHE-JP), by the eMadrid Network (S2013/ICE-2715), and by project RESET (TIN2014-53199-C3-1-R).

References

1. Pappano, L.: The year of the MOOC. In: The New York Times, **2**(12), 1–7 (2012)
2. Pérez-Sanagustín, M., et al.: H-MOOC framework: reusing MOOCs for hybrid education. J. Comput. High. Educ. **29**(1), 47–64 (2017)
3. de la Croix, J.P., Egerstedt, M.: Flipping the controls classroom around a MOOC. In: Proceedings of the American Control Conference 2014, ACC, pp. 2557–2562. IEEE (2014)
4. Fox, A.: From MOOCs to SPOCs. Commun. ACM **56**(12), 38–40 (2013)

5. Li, Y., Zhang, M., Bonk, C.J., Guo, N.: Integrating MOOC and flipped classroom practice in a traditional undergraduate course: students' experience and perceptions. Int. J. Emerg. Technol. Learn. (iJET) **10**(6), 4–10 (2015)
6. Alario-Hoyos, C., et al.: Interactive activities: the key to learning programming with MOOCs. In: Proceedings of EMOOCS 2016, pp. 319–328. Graz, Austria 2016

Identifying Game Elements Suitable for MOOCs

Alessandra Antonaci(✉), Roland Klemke, Christian M. Stracke, and Marcus Specht

Welten Institute – Research Centre for Learning, Teaching and Technology, Open University of the Netherlands, P.O. Box 2960 6401 DL Heerlen, The Netherlands
{alessandra.antonaci,roland.klemke,christian.stracke, marcus.specht}@ou.nl

Abstract. Massive Online Open Courses (MOOCs) have increasingly become objects of research interest and studies in recent years. While MOOCs could be a means to address massive audiences, they suffer from high drop-out rates and low user engagement. Gamification is known as the application of game design elements in non-gaming scenarios to solve problems or to influence a user's behaviour change. By applying gamification to MOOCs, we aim to enhance users' engagement and goal achievement within a MOOC environment. To define our gamification strategy, we asked 42 experts in the fields of game design, learning science and technology-enhanced learning to rate 21 selected game design patterns according to their suitability within a MOOC environment application. The data collected allowed us to identify a set of nine game design patterns as promising candidates to be tested in MOOC environments.

Keywords: Gamification · Game design patterns · MOOCs · Quantitative · Qualitative · Data · Analysis

1 Introduction

Despite their recent success in reaching mass audiences [1] and their potential to deliver education to the majority of world inhabitants [2], Massive Online Open Courses (MOOCs) in their current form also suffer from several drawbacks, including low completion rates [3] and lack of participants' engagement [4].

Gamification is a well-known phenomenon in Technology-Enhanced Learning (TEL) [5]. However, examples of gamified MOOCs that aim at overcoming the lack of user engagement as well as increasing completion rates via the design of paths that allow users to pursue and achieve their goals are currently sparse [6]. One of the first empirical studies aiming at investigating gamification in MOOCs can be found in [7]. It identifies 40 suitable game mechanics to engage students in MOOCs, of which 10 game mechanics with the highest level of engagement (virtual goods; three different types of points; leader boards; trophies and badges; peer grading and emoticon feedback; two types of games) where selected in an online survey with 5,020 participants [7]. The study did, however, not consider the game designer's perspective and furthermore the level of engagement of these game mechanics was defined based on users' self-perception, not on an empirical basis.

É. Lavoué et al. (Eds.): EC-TEL 2017, LNCS 10474, pp. 355–360, 2017.
DOI: 10.1007/978-3-319-66610-5_26

The purpose of this paper is to present a study aiming at identifying a suitable set of Game Design Patterns (GDPs)[1] to be applied to and tested in a MOOC environment to enhance learners' engagement, goal achievement, and learning performance. We first study the literature related to the type of game elements generally used to design and implement gamification [8]. Particularly, nine elements are most used and often aim at stimulating users' behaviour change playing on external rewards [9]. We complemented these findings by consulting the game design pattern collection of Björk and Holopainen [10]. This collection represents a resource of 200 GDPs designers, each of them described by name, description, consequences, implication in using the pattern and relations with others GDPs.

To pre-select candidates for gamification in MOOCs the collection of GDPs compiled from literature and the pattern collection in [10] was scrutinised based on the following inclusion criteria: (1) the frequent use of a GDP in literature, (2) the applicability of a GDP in a multi-user environment, and (3) our hypothesised impact of the selected pattern on learners' engagement, goal achievement, or learning performance. As a result, the following 21 GDPs were selected from these collections and presented to 42 experts to be validated: (1) *Avatars/Characters*; (2) *Time Limits*; (3) *Levels*; (4) *Communication Channels*; (5) *High Score Lists*; (6) *Score*; (7) *Status Indicators*; (8) *Public Information*; (9) *Story Telling*; (10) *Rewards*; (11) *Goal Indicators*; (12) *Stimulated Planning*; (13) *Clues*; (14) *Cooperation*; (15) *Limited Planning Ability*; (16) *Competition*; (17) *Team Play*; (18) *Replayability*; (19) *Smooth Learning Curves*; (20) *Handicaps*; (21) *Empowerment*.

The experts involved in this study are game designers, learning scientists and TEL experts. The game designers were included for their expected ability to evaluate effects of specific GDPs in a given scenario; the learning scientists to judge the GDPs from a didactic and educational perspective; and the TEL experts to evaluate both perspectives and rate applicability and feasibility of the GDPs chosen.

The remainder of this paper is organised as follows: first the methods used are explained; secondly the participants and the procedures are presented; thirdly a summary of the quantitative and qualitative data are detailed and our conclusions drawn.

2 Game Design Pattern Evaluation Study

Methods. Two methods were used to assess the GDPs selected for designing a gamified MOOC: a survey and a focus group. The survey was designed to validate our GDPs selection and to collect feedback from our target population. The GDPs proposed to our audience population were rated according to designing a MOOC with one of the three following gamification purposes (*gp*s) in mind: *gp*1. Enhancing learning performance; *gp*2. Enhancing goal achievement; *gp*3. Enhancing engagement. Secondly, the focus group was conducted for game designers to conceptualize a gamified MOOC using the GDPs deemed most relevant for the selected gamification purpose.

[1] In this paper the terms game elements, game mechanics and game design patterns are used as synonymous even if the authors are aware of their differences.

Participants. Atotal of 42 subjects took part in our study: 17 game designers; 9 learning science experts and 16 TEL experts. The subjects decided individually on which of the three gamification purposes (*gp*1-*gp*3) they wanted to focus. Six of the game designers worked on *gp*1; six on *gp*2 and five on *gp*3. Four learning scientists, worked on *gp*1; three on *gp*2 and two on *gp*3. Five TEL experts focused on *gp*1; four on *gp*2 and seven on the *gp*3.

Procedures. Participants were introduced to "MOOCs" and "Gamification". The game designers were invited to take part in the focus group as part of a game design workshop and were divided into six groups assigned to the three intervention purposes *gp*1-*gp*3 (two groups for each purpose). The topic of the MOOC was predefined as cyber-security. Each group elaborated a concept that was presented to the other colleagues. The data of the focus group are detailed in the results paragraph under the qualitative section. All participants filled out the survey, comprising 2 questions for each of the 21 GDPs selected: a closed question, rating the GDPs in relation to the purpose selected (*gp*1-*gp*3) using a scale from 0 ("strongly negative effect") to 4 ("strongly positive effect"). The second question for each GDP was optional and open; here participants could detail the advantages and/or disadvantages of using the given GDP for the specific purpose.

3 Results

The experts' evaluation. Table 1 shows the results related to the quantitative data collected with the questionnaires according to the three gamification purposes *gp*1-*gp*3.

Hints from Game Design Experts' Focus Group. Each group of game designers was invited to conceptualise the design of a gamified MOOC selecting, based on their experience, the most suitable game elements according to *gp*1, *gp*2, or *gp*3.

The game elements proposed by the two groups that worked on *gp*1 were: *collaboration* via wiki and *forum*, aiming at developing a *sense of community* and information sharing, track of *personal progress*, *levels* and *different levels of tasks*, with a *rewarding system* for their completion and an *inventory for personal notes*, in which to save helpful posts from the community forum, plus they thought of implementing a *game* itself within the MOOC. *Autonomous path*, as well as a *collaborative path*, that could be enabled by the creation of *alliance*, *asymmetrical information* distribution for the solution of *boss tests*. A *skills tree,* a game element often present in roleplaying games, (the Diablo[2] series made it famous) enables custom configurations of a character's abilities. Once the basic skills are gained by the users, it opens several branches and the user can choose the path to follow.

[2] Blizzard production, 1998. http://eu.blizzard.com/en-gb/games/.

Table 1. Sample GDP selection based on the average score (x)

Purposes	Experts					
	Game designers' GDP selection	x	Learning scientists' GDP selection	x	TEL experts' GDP selection	x
*gp*1 - enhancing MOOC users' learning performance	*Communication Channels*	*3.83*	*Levels*	*4*	*Levels, Smooth Learning Curve*	*3*
			Empowerment	3.75		
	Cooperation, Replayability and *Smooth Learning Curves*	3.5	*Avatar/ Characters, Storytelling* and *Clues*	3.5	*Storytelling, Replayability* and *Empowerment*	*2.8*
*gp*2 – enhancing MOOC users' goal achievement	*Goal Indicators*	*3.67*	*Smooth Learning Curve*	*4*	*Goal Indicators*	*4*
	Empowerment	*3.6*				
			Clues and *Empowerment*	*3.67*	*Levels*	*3.5*
	Communication Channels	*3.5*			*Replayability* and *Smooth Learning Curves*	*3.25*
*gp*3 – enhancing MOOC users' engagement	*Smooth Learning Curves*	*4*	*Storytelling, Clues* and *Empowerment*	*4*	*Communication Channels, Score, Goal Indicators, Cooperation* and *Smooth Learning Curves*	*3.43*
	Communication Channels and *Rewards*	*3.8*				

The two groups focussing on *gp*2 suggested the following game elements: "*personal profiles* that can be shared with others, badges as *reward, progress bar* and *autonomy*". As well as to transfer MMORPG (Massive Multiplayers Online Role Play Games) elements into MOOC, such as: *Skill tree,* "*Knowledge inventory* (completed tasks for the course); *Overview* (whole offer, progress per Skill tree) *Co-op* (Cooperation with "Classes"); *PVP* (Player vs Player "Knowledge Battle"); *Reward inside of System* (Skill tree, Knowledge Inventory, Succeeded Students as mentor for newbies); *Reward: outside of Systems* (Achievements, Link to LinkedIn)".

Finally, two groups considered the following game elements for *gp*3: *competition, collaboration* and *immediate feedback* as, as well as online quizzes for two players, stimulating *social comparison* and students' engagement, by sending the same question to both and the one who replies faster and correctly wins. Other game elements proposed were: *Quests, Narrative, Player/Character, Enemy/Boss, Community (Guild)/ Community Experience* and *Status Parameter.* In particular, the narrative concept consists of "some sort of opposing power that threatens the participants' characters and their private information". "The player needs to use what s/he learns in the modules of the course to contribute to the success of this resistance". Being part of this resistance could help in developing "a *sense of community* similar to MMORPG -communities such as guilds". Therefore "even if participants are working alone, they should feel like they are contributing to the cause of the resistance/ the community".

Hints from Learning Scientists and TEL experts. Learning Scientists (LS), as the TEL experts, were not involved in a focus groups, however they could express their point of view through the use of the open questions contained in the survey that asked them to detail the advantages and disadvantages of using a specific GDP for the purpose selected. Chosen comments are reported here to give a better overview of the LS and TEL experts' perception on gamification applied to MOOC.

As it is possible to derive from data, the LS indicate with a high score the GDP *Clues* for the three purposes, as well as *Empowerment*. While *Storytelling* was ranked high for *gp*2 and *gp*3. Among others *Empowerment* was appreciated because "people like to have autonomy" and "it can help users to positively achieve their learning goals. While *Clues* to stimulate the *gp*1 given only at request ("hints button") "could be useful". For *gp*2, LS said that *Clues*, can work as "scaffolding for learners who need a little more support, through clues everybody can achieve their goals", as disadvantages foreseen: "If it is too easy to attain clues, the students might not try to figure things out themselves". While for the *gp*3 *Clues* expert commented: "It helps to have clues, especially for complex goals. However, having them pop up can also be distractive" for users and be a disadvantage.

The TEL experts ranked with a high score the GDPs: *Smooth Learning Curves (SLC)* for all 3 purposes; *Goal Indicators* for *gp*2 and *gp*3. SLC received the following comments: "If a learner is an international learner who struggles with language or novice learner, it may help them through the course; it could "avoiding discouragement" among users. SLC could have as an advantage the decrease of users' "frustration and boredom" but as a disadvantage the TEL expert raises the problem that it is "hard to design". The game element *Goal Indicators* was perceived in relation to *gp*2 as to "provide useful insight about a learner's performance and may set the pace of the learning progress", it could especially be useful "as goals might change over time", while for *gp*3 considering that "the success is not defined in MOOCs. One might want to finish only the two weeks that they are interested in. So, if that person puts those goals beforehand, and completing them makes that person successful in the course. I think this is very much suitable for the nature of MOOCs".

Comparing LS and TEL experts for GP1 they both highly rated the GDPs: *Levels*, *Empowerment* and *Storytelling*. For *gp*2 TEL and LS experts ranked highly the GDP: *Smooth Learning Curves*. For *gp*3 there are no common GDPs with high score.

Considering the similarity among the groups in ranking the GDPs, game designers and LS experts have the GDP *Empowerment* chosen for *gp*2 and none for *gp*1 and *gp*3. Game designers and TEL experts issued high ratings GDP for *gp*1 was *Smooth Learning Curves*; while for *gp*2 *Goal Indicators;* and for *gp*3 *Communication Channels* and *Smooth Learning Curves.*

4 Discussion, Conclusion and Future Work

With the aim of identifying suitable GDPs to design our gamification strategy to be applied in a MOOC to enhance users' goal achievement and engagement, we analysed the literature and other sources, in particular Björk and Holopainen's GDPs collection [10]. Our selection was evaluated by experts in several domains: game design, learning science and technology enhanced learning.

Investigating the point of view of game designers, learning scientists and TEL experts on the selection made, allows us to understand that despite the different backgrounds of our study participants, there are several points of agreement. Table 1 represents in synthesis the most ranked GDPs by purpose and group of experts.

From our quantitative and qualitative data analysed we can deduce that the following game elements are eligible for further testing within MOOCs:

- For *gp*1: *Empowerment*, *Smooth Learning Curves* and *Communication Channels;*
- For *gp*2: *Levels, Clues, Communication Channels*, *Smooth Learning Curves, Goal Indicators* and *Skills tree;*
- For *gp*3: *Guild*, *Skills tree*, *Storytelling.*

We plan to test with formative and summative studies the above-mentioned GDPs, analyse the effects of gamification on MOOC users' behaviour and evaluate whether our assumptions were correct.

Acknowledgments. This study is partly funded by the I SECURE - Empowering education systems in information security project (n. 2015-1-IT02-KA201-015005) under the Erasmus+ programme of the European Commission. We would like to thank the participants that voluntarily took part in this study.

References

1. Yousef, A.M.F., Chatti, M.A., Schroeder, U., Wosnitza, M.: What drives a successful MOOC? An empirical examination of criteria to assure design quality of MOOCs. In: 14th IEEE International Conference on Advanced Learning Technologies ICALT 2014, pp. 44–48 (2014)
2. OECD: Students, Computers and Learning: Making the Connection, PISA (2015)
3. Reich, J.: Learner Intention Recasts "Low" MOOC Completion Rates | HarvardX. http://harvardx.harvard.edu/news/learner-intention
4. Cook, S., Bingham, T., Reid, S., Wang, L.: Going massive: learner engagement in a MOOC environment (2015)
5. Nah, F.F.-H., Zeng, Q., Telaprolu, V.R., Ayyappa, A.P., Eschenbrenner, B.: Gamification of education: a review of literature. In: Nah, F.F.-H. (ed.) HCIB 2014. LNCS, vol. 8527, pp. 401–409. Springer, Cham (2014). doi:10.1007/978-3-319-07293-7_39
6. Antonaci, A., Klemke, R., Stracke, C.M., Specht, M.: Gamification in MOOCs to enhance users' goal achievement. In: Proceedings of IEEE Global Engineering Education Conference (EDUCON 2017), 25–28 April, Athens Greece. IEEE Xplore (2017)
7. Chang, J.W., Wei, H.Y.: Exploring engaging gamification mechanics in massive online open courses. Educ. Technol. Soc. **19**, 177–203 (2016)
8. Dicheva, D., Dichev, C.: Gamification in education: where are we in 2015? In: E-Learn 2015, Kona, Hawaii, USA. pp. 1445–1454 (2015)
9. Dicheva, D., Dichev, C., Agre, G., Angelova, G.: Gamification in education: a systematic mapping study gamification in education: a systematic mapping study. Educ. Technol. Soc. **18**, 75–88 (2015)
10. Björk, S., Holopainen, J.: Patterns in Game Design. Charles River Media, Newton (2005)

Targeting At-risk Students Using Engagement and Effort Predictors in an Introductory Computer Programming Course

David Azcona[1,2](✉) and Alan F. Smeaton[1,2](✉)

[1] Insight Centre for Data Analytics, Dublin, Ireland
David.Azcona@insight-centre.org, alan.smeaton@dcu.ie
[2] School of Computing, Dublin City University, Glasnevin, Dublin 9, Ireland

Abstract. This paper presents a new approach to automatically detecting lower-performing or "at-risk" students on computer programming modules in an undergraduate University degree course. Using historical data from previous student cohorts we built a predictive model using logged interactions between students and online resources, as well as students' progress in programming laboratory work. Predictions were calculated each week during a 12-week semester. Course lecturers received student lists ranked by their probability of failing the next computer-based laboratory exam. At-risk students were targeted and offered assistance during laboratory sessions by the lecturer and laboratory tutors. When we group students into two cohorts depending on whether they failed or passed their first laboratory exam, the average margin of improvement on the second laboratory exam between the higher and lower-performing students was four times higher when our predictions were run and subsequent laboratory support targeted at these students, compared to students from the year our model was trained on.

Keywords: Computer science education · Learning Analytics · Prediction

1 Introduction

Programming is challenging and few students find it easy at first. The mean worldwide pass rate for the first introductory programming course, denoted CS1, has been estimated at 67% [2]. In research, there has been significant interest in looking for factors that motivate students to succeed in CS1 and master a programming skill set. Particularly, researchers have been identifying weak students by looking at their characteristics, behaviour and performance. More recently, researchers have shifted to a more data-driven approach by analysing programming behaviour, including patterns in compilations and programming states. These parameters are substantially more effective at reflecting the students' effort and learning progress throughout their course.

É. Lavoué et al. (Eds.): EC-TEL 2017, LNCS 10474, pp. 361–366, 2017.
DOI: 10.1007/978-3-319-66610-5_27

In addition, students at universities usually interact with a Virtual Learning Environment (VLE) and leave a digital trace that has previously been leveraged to predict student performance in exams. The most popular online educational systems are Moodle and Blackboard. Purdue University's Course Signals project was a pioneer in this area [1]. Learning Analytics have proven to provide a good indicator of how students are doing by looking at how online resources are being consumed. In programming classes and blended classrooms, students leave a far greater digital footprint we can leverage to improve their experience and help to identify those in need [4].

This paper presents a system that uses machine learning techniques by combining engagement and effort predictors to classify students in an introductory programming module at an earlier stage. A retrospective analysis was carried out to verify the viability of our project after gathering data for a year and pseudo real-time predictions were run every week the year on a new cohort of students. Our two research questions were firstly to determine how accurately could predictive models using engagement and progress features, perform in identifying students in need of support and secondly whether identifying such weaker students for subsequent laboratory mentoring have any impact on the gap between higher and lower-performing students?

2 Data Collection

Dublin City University's Computer Programming I module, is a core and fundamental subject taught during the first semester of the first year of the honours Bachelors degree in Computer Applications. Students learn the fundamentals of computer programming. The course combines four hours of taught lectures with four more hours of supervised laboratory work using the Python language. A previous version of CS1 was taught using Java before it was redesigned. The current version with Python has been taught for two academic years, 2015/2016 and 2016/2017. Students are assessed by taking a number of laboratory computer-based programming exams, typically two or three during the semester. Each laboratory exam contributes equally to their continuous assessment mark which is 60% of the overall grade for the module. 138 students registered for CS1 during 2015/2016 and 128 students in 2016/2017. The CS1 Lecturer developed a custom Virtual Learning Environment (VLE) for the teaching of computer programming. This platform is used in a variety of courses in CS, including CS1. Like a conventional VLE, students can go online and browse course material and can also submit and verify their laboratory work. On every programming submission for the laboratory exercises, a set of unit tests are run.

3 Predictive Modelling

We developed a predictive model that uses interaction logs from student programming work to predict their performance in laboratory computer-based programming exams.

3.1 Students' Digital Footprints in CS1

The data sources we leverage in order to model student behaviour in CS1 are:

- **Programming submissions**: The custom platform allows students to submit their laboratory programs and provides instant feedback for each submission based on a suite of unit tests.
- **Interaction logs**: Students interact online with the course's custom VLE and every instance of student access to a page of any kind is recorded and stored.

Figure 1 shows student activity on the course VLE and the programming submissions during 2015/2016. The laboratory sessions for the 12-week semester are ticked on the X-axis, Tuesdays and Thursdays. The submission platform is introduced at a later stage as students get familiar with Python and learn first how to run and debug their programs locally.

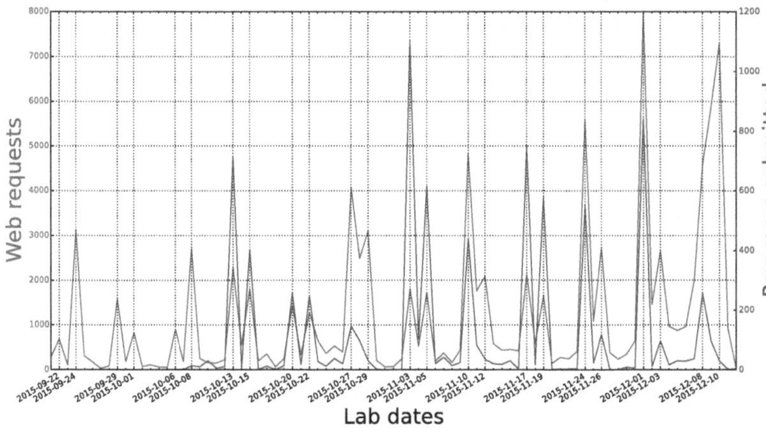

Fig. 1. Activity levels and programs submitted for CS1 during 2015/2016

3.2 Training a Predictive Model

We developed a classification model trained with student activity data from 2015/2016 in order to predict student performance. The target was to predict whether each student would pass or fail their next laboratory exam. Shortly, we will assess whether we can find patters of programming work and engagement predictors. A set of features were generated for each student based on raw log data, interaction events for students accessing material and corresponding programming submissions.

A set of binary classifiers, one per week, were built to predict a student's likelihood of passing or failing the next computer-based laboratory exam. In 2015/2016, there was a mid-semester exam and an end-of-semester exam.

On that case, to clarify, classifiers from week 1 to 6 were trained to predict the mid-semester outcome (pass or fail for each student) and from 7 to 12 the end-of-semester's outcome. At a given week, the features mentioned above were extracted from that week's activity and programming submissions. A classifier was built by concatenating all the features from previous weeks' classifiers and appending the new ones in order to account for each student's progression and engagement throughout the course. The empirical error minimization approach was employed to determine the learning algorithm with the fewest empirical errors from a bag of classifiers C [3]. The misclassification error, also known as empirical error or empirical risk, was calculated for each learning algorithm for each week of the semester. For consistency, we picked the learning algorithm which minimized the empirical risk on average for the 12 weeks which was then used for each weekly classifier.

3.3 Retrospective Analysis

Following the Empirical Error Minimization approach, we selected the Logistic Regression classification algorithm which gave lowest empirical risk on average for the 12 weeks, 29.84%, based on our training data using 10-fold CV. The bag of classifiers C also contained SVMs with linear and Gaussian kernels, a decision tree, a K-neighbours classifier and a Random Forest. The retrospective analysis carried out on CS1 using 2015/2016's data shows we can successfully gather student data about their learning progress and leverage that information for predictions, reaching a usable accuracy. We then progressed to run pseudo real-time predictions every week on the incoming 2016/2017's dataset.

4 Results

Predictions were calculated on a pseudo real-time basis every week for students during 2016/2017 based on a model trained with data from 2015/2016. Individual reports were sent to the CS1 Lecturer every week. An anonymised snapshot of class predictions can be found in Fig. 2. At-risk students were targeted and offered assistance and mentoring during laboratory sessions. We will now examine how the results impact the two specific research questions we set out to ask.

Student	Fail / Pass Prediction	Fail Prediction Confidence
John Doe	Pass	26.95%
Jane Roe	Fail	69.27%
Johnny Smith	Pass	27.03%

Fig. 2. Anonymised snapshot of predictions with associated probabilities

4.1 Automatic Classification of At-risk Students

In order to evaluate how our predictions performed, we compared the corresponding weeks' predictions with the actual results of the three laboratory exams that took place in weeks 4, 8 and 12 in 2016/2017. As the semester progressed, our early alert system gathered more information about students' progression and, hence, our classifiers learned more as shown by the increased F1-score metric reaching 64.38% on week 12. In short, we could automatically distinguish in a better way who is going to pass or fail the next laboratory exam. In addition, the prediction passing probabilities associated with each student for the last laboratory exam was highly correlated with their performance. Pearson's linear correlation ($r = 0.57$; p-value < 0.0001) and Spearman's non-linear ($r = 0.62$, p-value < 0.0001) were very confident on that relationship.

4.2 Higher and Lower Performing Students

If we cluster students into higher and lower-performing groups based on their results in the first laboratory assessment and whether they failed or passed that exam, the differential learning improvement was four times more the year the predictions were generated and the reports were sent than the year our model is trained with, see Table 1.

Table 1. Differential learning improvement between academic years

Academic year	Cohort	Number students	1-exam average	2-exam average	Improvement	Differential	Learning differential
2015/16	Passing 1-exam	80	67.38%	79.50%	+12.12%	+11.52%	4.36
	Failing 1-exam	58	13.47%	37.12%	+23.64%		
2016/17	Passing 1-exam	101	86.63%	47.57%	-39.06%	+50.26%	
	Failing 1-exam	28	10.00%	21.20%	+11.20%		

It is important to note higher-performing students do not have the same room for improvement than lower-performing students so for higher-performing students, maintaining their grade is an accomplishment. However, we are trying to measure learning and whether lower-performing students tend to learn more in our blended classrooms and complete more programs with mentoring and further assistance.

5 Conclusion and Future Work

Predictive models using engagement and programming effort as drivers have proven to contain useful information about the student's learning progress and behaviour. Automatically classifying students and notifying the lecturer and tutors along with offering assistance to weak students, helps those at-risk to learn more and reduce the gap between higher-performing students and them. We believe this approach could be applicable to other courses not only in introductory programming but CS2 or even Mathematics and other courses with significant amount of laboratory material or programming work which students need to check and complete in a weekly basis.

Lastly, we are excited to automatically identify students having difficulties on CS1, offer them assistance and measure how that aids their learning. We believe computer programming is an ability but also a skill that needs work to help it develop. Our contribution is in providing a set of tools that help and encourage the student's learning and interest in programming.

Acknowledgements. This research was supported by the Irish Research Council in association with the National Forum for the Enhancement of Teaching and Learning in Ireland under project number GOIPG/2015/3497, and by Science Foundation Ireland under grant number 12/RC/2289. The authors are indebted to Dr. Stephen Blott, Lecturer on the module which is the subject of this work, for his help.

References

1. Arnold, K.E., Pistilli, M.D.: Course signals at purdue: using learning analytics to increase student success. In: Proceedings of the 2nd International Conference on Learning Analytics and Knowledge, pp. 267–270. ACM (2012)
2. Bennedsen, J., Caspersen, M.E.: Failure rates in introductory programming. ACM SIGCSE Bull. **39**(2), 32–36 (2007)
3. Gyorfi, L., Devroye, L., Lugosi, G.: A probabilistic theory of pattern recognition (1996)
4. Ihantola, P., et al.: Educational data mining and learning analytics in programming: literature review and case studies. In: Proceedings of the 2015 ITiCSE on Working Group Reports, pp. 41–63. ACM (2015)

Prompting to Support Reflection: A Workplace Study

Oliver Blunk(✉) and Michael Prilla

Clausthal University of Technology, Clausthal-Zellerfeld, Germany
{oliver.blunk,michael.prilla}@tu-clausthal.de

Abstract. Reflection is an activity which needs facilitation in order to motivate users to engage in it regularly. In a study we analyzed how prompts can support reflection in a workplace setting. Results show that prompts might be beneficial to stimulate users to write new topics. Our results show that if user generate own prompts, user reply more often in comparison to our generic prompts.

Keywords: Reflection · Collaborative reflection · Prompting · Informal learning · Community of practice

1 Introduction

Reflection can be understood as returning to experiences, re-assessing them and deriving insights for future behavior [1], making it a mechanism that transforms experiences into learning. While reflection has long been understood as a purely individual activity, research shows that reflective learning benefits from social influence and support such as sharing experiences, making sense of them together and drawing conclusions for the future together [2]. While such collaborative reflection is desirable to create among employees, it often does not happen as ideally planned: many people have no practice in systematically reflecting together (and using tools for it), urgent tasks and other constraints interrupt reflection and create a need for reflection over a longer period of time [2, 3]. Thus, there is a need to support collaborative reflection.

This paper describes work done in a field study of supporting collaborative reflection in a community support tool used in a medium sized (about 900 employees) public administration in Europe in order to facilitate experience exchange. To support reflection in the tool, we used prompts to stimulate reflective interaction.

2 Collaborative Reflection, Communities and Prompts

Communities are a good place for collaborative reflection to happen [4, 5], as they provide opportunities for people to meet and support each other emotionally [6] and professionally, and to learn from each other [7]: It has been shown that activities like relating own experiences to other statements and experiences, and proposing solutions based on what was discussed significantly increase the occurrence of learning outcomes in discussion threads [2], and it is exactly this reflective interaction that is supposed to amplify learning in communities [8]. In practice, however, this potential is often not

É. Lavoué et al. (Eds.): EC-TEL 2017, LNCS 10474, pp. 367–372, 2017.
DOI: 10.1007/978-3-319-66610-5_28

used, as reflective interactions do not occur to an extent needed [9]. Facilitation has been shown to be beneficial to initiate and sustain interaction in communities [10], and may therefore also foster activities that increase reflection.

Work on human facilitation of reflection in face-to-face settings shows that asking good questions and adapting questions to different phases of reflection such as problem elicitation, discussion and deriving resolutions facilitates and amplifies face-to-face reflection [3, 11]. While this shows the possibility to positively influence reflection, human facilitation is strongly dependent on the availability of facilitators when reflection happens. Therefore, on the level needed for reflection, it is hard to scale in larger groups, and prompting was suggested as a technical complement (e.g., [12]).

The term prompt usually refers (often) to text-based queues, which are presented to a user to stimulate certain behavior. This can be done by presenting sentence starters to be completed [13], or by using questions as prompts [12]. A key aspect of all types of prompts is that they do not force the user to act in a specific way and leave it to the recipient whether or how to respond [14]. Prompts have been used to guide learners in applying learning techniques [15] or to support individual reflection [16].

Besides the potential of prompts, there is no work available on the effect of prompting for reflection in professional communities.

3 The Case Study

To support the needs mentioned above, we created a reflective community platform for peer exchange and informal learning. In the platform, prompts are used to facilitate reflection. Each prompt was focused on a different aspect of reflection like recommending the user to write about personal experiences, which we identified from literature and our own work (e.g., [2]). We implemented the prompts, based on our earlier work

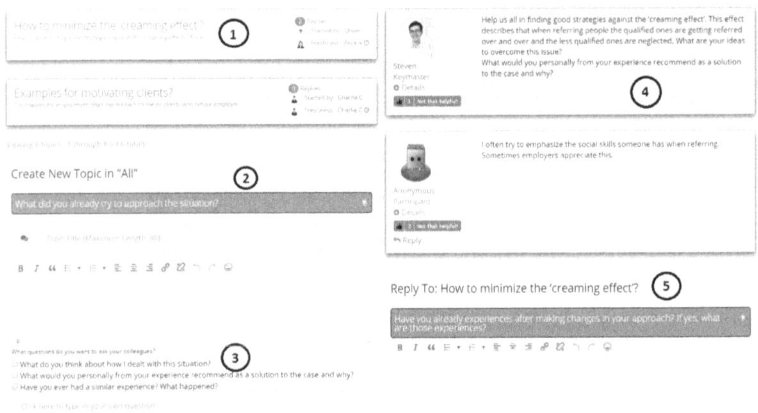

Fig. 1. Prompts (2, 5) are located below the list of discussions (left, 1) and within a thread (right, 4). Prompts are visually highlighted above the editor box (2, 5) where users create new topics. Upon creating new topics, users can choose different questions (3), and type in own questions, which in turn override the generic prompts within threads (5).

on prompting for reflection [17]. Prompts helped users to phrase an initial discussion entry (topic prompts, see Fig. 1, No. 1 and 2). We differentiate between *topics*, which are used to start a new discussion and *replies* which are answers to an existing topic or reply. Both topics and replies are summarized as *posts*. Within a discussion different prompts (reply prompts) are aimed at helping users to phrase a reply (see Fig. 1, No. 4 and 5). Prompts were shown directly above the text input box with the aim to be visible while the user phrases her post.

In addition to system generated prompts, users were able to select questions after writing down a new topic to ask others for specific reactions (prompts replaced by users, see Fig. 1, No. 3). We created this feature based on existing research showing that asking personal questions is beneficial to reflection [3]. When selecting a custom question at the end of their post, our generic prompt was overridden by the user prompt so that the custom question of the user was graphically highlighted (see Fig. 1, No. 5). In addition, the selected prompt was integrated into the post as its last sentence, creating the impression that the user wrote it as a personal question.

To be able to evaluate whether prompts actually helped facilitating reflection, we conducted a quantitative analysis to check whether the prompts lead to a difference in behavior. For this, we first needed to operationalize whether a prompt was recognized by a user.

Therefore, we differentiate between whether the system displayed (that is, *rendered*) a prompt somewhere on the community website and whether the prompt was actually in the viewing area of a user (prompt *visible*). Being able to see a prompt on the website and having actually read and understood the prompt are two very different things, and we recognize this. As there is no way to automatically verify that the user read the prompt, we interpret it as read if it was visible to the user.

In this study users were randomly experienced a phase in which they received prompts and also a phase in which they did not receive prompts. The starting phase varied for each user. As new users registered every day, each user found a different environment as the community and the amount of content increased. Thus, in this paper, we compare the results of the data from the phase in which users were receiving prompts to the phase in which they did not.

As this was a study conducted during day to day activity within a public organization and we had to control for larger external interventions. In order to remove influences which highly skewed the data, we removed users who contributed exceedingly often, and we removed data from special events which gained a lot of attention.

4 Results

We analyzed the activity of users in both conditions (see Table 1) in terms of reading or writing. Table 1 lists how often the list of threads (Forum-Reads) has been read and how often an individual thread has been read. This way we can differentiate between users who had a look at the list of topics and users who went further and had a look at the actual content of a discussion. Additionally, the table contains the number of how many topics (the start of a new discussion) and replies (an answer in a discussion) have been written. Comparing the quote of how many topics respectively replies were written per read event, we can see that for both topics (see Table 1) and replies, while prompts are being displayed, the rate of posts per read event is higher. This might indicate that prompts have a positive influence on the amount of posts written in the community platform, although the difference in the quote is rather small. The higher difference in the forum read-write quote between the *No Prompts* and *Prompts* condition might indicate that prompts worked better at facilitating new topics.

Table 1. Activity during the time of February 2016 to January 2017 of all users. The quote represents a read-write quote for both the forum (F) and the threads (T).

Condition	#Forum-reads	#Thread-reads	#Topics	#Replies	Forum-quote F	Thread-quote T
No prompts	427	616	7	28	1.64%	4.55%
Prompts	657	996	18	47	2.74%	4.72%

Furthermore, we analyzed how often each prompt was being picked up. We differentiated in our data between the cases in which a prompt was just rendered on the website and cases in which the prompt was actually visible to the user. As can be seen in Table 2 prompts were visible in 62–76% of all page views.

Table 2. Distribution per prompt type showing how often a prompt was answered.

	%	% Prompt visible
Topic prompt visible to user	58.79%	61.96%
User wrote a topic	3.17%	
Reply prompt visible to user	62.38%	65.56%
User wrote a reply	3.17%	
Replaced prompt visible to user	71.91%	76.40%
User wrote a reply	4.49%	

When users overwrote the generic prompts with custom questions, we could observe that users wrote more replies than when generic prompts were visible (see Table 2).

5 Discussion

The results of the study show that reactions of users on our prompts differed between the types of prompts. As Table 1 shows, prompts worked most when users were browsing the list of discussion topics in the community platform, resulting in more topics created per view in the prompting condition. For the number of written replies per read event, we only found a minor difference, which means that these prompts were not (as) successful in terms of increasing user activity. We may attribute this to different reasons. First, there may be a threshold perceived by users of a community platform, which inhibits the creation of initial topics compared to commenting on topics may be higher. Second, the prompts for replies were shown at the bottom of the page (see Fig. 1), so it is difficult to see prompt and topic simultaneously.

As our results indicate, user who generate prompts might receive more replies than the generic prompts (see Table 2). This may be attributed to the prompts being phrased differently. More likely, this happened because prompts were added both to the content of a topic and to the prompting area rather than shown in the promoting area only. It also seems likely that because it users chose the prompts, these prompts fitted a little bit better to the content of their posts. This makes user generated prompts seem worth pursuing further in the future, as they may help to create more activity.

The study was conducted in the regular day to day work of a public administration, and there were some variables influencing our results as previously mentioned, like new users finding different environments than users who registered previously, highly active moderators and the issue that it is difficult to measure whether a prompt was actually read. Despite this, our data is still likely to be polluted, and therefore further work with our platform in different places needs to approve our results to make them generalizable.

In addition, our paper focused on quantitative analysis of reactions on prompts rather than looking into these reactions. Further work needs to include content analysis to evaluate whether the intention of the prompt is reflected in its content.

6 Conclusion and Outlook

The present paper used prompts in a community of practice platform to facilitate reflection efforts of user. The study was conducted during a time span of almost one year in the day to day work of a public administration. Our results indicate that our prompts have worked to stimulate users to start new topics, and that this worked better for new topics than for stimulating replies in threads. We also saw an increase in replies per read event in cases where the person who created the thread overwrote our generic prompt. To our knowledge, there is no work looking at these effects in community systems so far, and therefore we regard these insights as contributions to the TEL community and as work to build on – we also recognize that these are initial insights that need to be built on rather than standing alone.

We plan to further analyze how user generated prompts can work in a community of practice setting. Additionally, we plan to conduct an analysis on content coding to evaluate, whether the text of the prompt really influenced the written discussion posts.

Acknowledgements. This work is part of the EmployID (http://employid.eu) project on "Scalable & cost-effective facilitation of professional identity transformation in public employment services" supported by the EC in FP 7 (project no. 619619). We thank all colleagues and associated partners for their cooperation and our fruitful discussions. Special thanks to our colleagues Urša and Barbara.

References

1. Boud, D.: Reflection: Turning Experience into Learning. Kogan Page, London (1985)
2. Prilla, M., Nolte, A., Blunk, O., Liedtke, D., Renner, B.: Analyzing collaborative reflection support: a content analysis approach. In: Boulus-Rødje, N., Ellingsen, G., Bratteteig, T., Aanestad, M., Bjørn, P. (eds.) ECSCW 2015, pp. 123–142. Springer, Cham (2015). doi: 10.1007/978-3-319-20499-4_7
3. Wood Daudelin, M.: Learning from experience through reflection. Organ. Dyn. **24**, 36–48 (1996)
4. Prilla, M.: Supporting collaborative reflection at work: a socio-technical analysis. AIS Trans. Hum.-Comput. Interact. **7**, 1–17 (2015)
5. Nyhan, B.: Collective reflection for excellence in work organizations. In: Cressey, P., Boud, D., Docherty, P. (eds.) Productive Reflection at Work: Learning for Changing Organizations. Routledge, Abingdon (2005). p. 133
6. Introne, J., Semaan, B., Goggins, S.: A sociotechnical mechanism for online support provision. In: Proceedings of the 2016 CHI Conference on Human Factors in Computing Systems, pp. 3559–3571. ACM, New York, NY, USA (2016)
7. Wenger, E.: Communities of Practice: Learning, Meaning, and Identity. Cambridge University Press, Cambridge (1998)
8. Mercer, N.: Talk and the development of reasoning and understanding. Hum. Dev. **51**, 90–100 (2008)
9. de Groot, E., Endedijk, M.D., Jaarsma, A.D.C., Simons, P.R.-J., van Beukelen, P.: Critically reflective dialogues in learning communities of professionals. Stud. Contin. Educ. 1–23 (2013)
10. Bliss, C.A., Lawrence, B.: From posts to patterns: a metric to characterize discussion board activity in online courses. J. Asynchronous Learn. Netw. **13**, 15–32 (2009)
11. Vince, R.: Organizing reflection. Manag. Learn. **33**, 63–78 (2002)
12. Davis, E.A.: Scaffolding students' knowledge integration: prompts for reflection in KIE. Int. J. Sci. Educ. **22**, 819–837 (2000)
13. King, A.: Guiding knowledge construction in the classroom: effects of teaching children how to question and how to explain. Am. Educ. Res. J. **31**, 338–368 (1994)
14. Davis, E.A.: Prompting middle school science students for productive reflection: generic and directed prompts. J. Learn. Sci. **12**, 91–142 (2003)
15. Deitz, S.M., Malone, L.W.: Stimulus control terminology. Behav. Anal. **8**, 259–264 (1985)
16. Isaacs, E., Konrad, A., Walendowski, A., Lennig, T., Hollis, V., Whittaker, S.: Echoes from the past: how technology mediated reflection improves well-being. In: Proceedings of the SIGCHI Conference on Human Factors in Computing Systems, pp. 1071–1080. ACM, Paris, France (2013)
17. Blunk, O., Prilla, M.: Prompting users to facilitate support needs in collaborative reflection. In: Kravcik, M., Mikroyannidis, A., Pammer, V., Prilla, M., Ullmann, T.D. (eds.) Proceedings of the 5th International Workshop on Awareness and Reflection in Technology Enhanced Learning (ARTEL 2015) in Conjunction with the ECTEL 2015 Conference, pp. 43–57. CEUR-WS (2015)

An Approach for the Analysis of Perceptual and Gestural Performance During Critical Situations

Yannick Bourrier[1,2(✉)], Francis Jambon[1], Catherine Garbay[1], and Vanda Luengo[2]

[1] Univ. Grenoble Alpes, LIG, Grenoble, France
{yannick.bourrier,francis.jambon,catherine.garbay}@imag.fr
[2] Univ. Pierre et Marie Curie, LIP6, Paris, France
{yannick.bourrier,vanda.luengo}@lip6.fr

Abstract. Our objective is the design of a Virtual Learning Environment to train a person performing a work activity, to acquire non-technical skills during the experience of a critical situation. While the person's performance level is due to carefully acquired technical skills, how it is maintained in front of criticality depends on non-technical skills, such as decision-making, situation awareness or stress management. Following previous break downs of the domains ill-defined aspects, we focus in this paper on the design of an approach to evaluate the variation of a learner's performance in front of learning situations showing varying degrees of criticality, in the domains of driving and midwifery.

Keywords: Ill-defined domains · Non-technical skills · Critical situations · Neural networks

1 Background

In most technical domains, non-technical skills (NTS) complement work activity. However, these skills are mostly mobilized during critical situations [1], and play a role in whether situations become catastrophic or not. There is a strong interest in teaching NTS in an Intelligent Learning Environment (ILE) as criticality is controlled in these environments. Our objective is to design an ILE able to improve the learner's abilities to handle critical situations thanks to their NTS, by confronting them with a wide range of different scenarios. Doing so requires diagnosing their NTS to provide scenarios of adapted difficulty. However, since NTS can only be observed in an individual's perceptions and gestures, they overlap with the learners' technical skills: two different kinds of skills are blended into the same activity [2]. Thus, the teaching of NTS in an ILE is an ill-defined domain [3]. The central issue is how to differentiate which part of a learner's performance is due to technical proficiency, and which part to their appropriate use of NTS. We first present the conceptual choices made in response to the problematic of technical and non-technical skills intertwining. These choices lead to the adoption of a hybrid approach [4] combining expert knowledge and data-mining techniques for the analysis of perceptual and

This research is funded by the French National Research Agency (ANR) via the MacCoy-Critical Project (ANR-14-CE24-0021).

É. Lavoué et al. (Eds.): EC-TEL 2017, LNCS 10474, pp. 373–378, 2017.
DOI: 10.1007/978-3-319-66610-5_29

gestural performance separately in non-critical and critical situations, as the gap in performance between them is a strong marker of NTS influence. We then detail the reasoning behind the construction of an indicator layer from the learner's activity in critical and non-critical situations, and highlight the benefits of using a neural network (NN) trained only during non-critical situations, for performance evaluation both in non-critical and critical situations. Finally, we present a first proof of concept. We conclude by presenting how this performance evaluation could lead to non-technical skills diagnosis.

2 General Approach

To evaluate NTS influence on general performance, we assume that a learner has a constant technical-skill level throughout a learning session, which is an acceptable hypothesis since our ILE focuses on non-novice learners. If this is true, then the variations in a learner's performance between two situations who require the same technical skills, and whose main varying factor is the presence of a critical element in one of them, must be a marker of the influence of NTS. Evaluating the variations in performance requires to identify couples of non-critical and critical situations satisfying this criterion, and to evaluate performance in both independently from criticality, as a learner's ability to handle criticality is the marker of NTS influence we aim to extract.

2.1 Identification of Similar Situations and Indicators Generation

In addition to a specific dimension such as ambiguity, danger and so on, criticality can be identified through the presence of a precursor, which [5] describe as "an element foreshadowing a hazard". To provide non-critical situations which are as close as it is possible to critical situations, we generate situations having the same precursors states, but without the criticality dimension associated. Similar precursors being identified by domain experts in critical and non-critical situations, allow us to hypothesize that during the learning situation, a learner's perceptions and gestures are made in reaction to the problematic induced by the precursor's current state. The learning situation here is the succession of interactions between the virtual world (whose focal point is the pre-cursor) and the learner. This succession of interactions is the root of our phase separation process. A phase is a discretization of a learning situation through a semantic criterion, which is the different states the precursor can take. The separation of a learning situation into phases provides a solution to the problematic of time handling which is crucial for the evaluation of a learner's activity inside a real-time VE. Moreover, phases provide the contextual grounding for interpretation of a learner's activity inside the VE, allowing to extract high level indicators from the learner's activity traces.

Once a situation has been split into several phases, we added an indicator layer to the performance analysis architecture, whose objective is to reduce data dimensionality and to facilitate the NN-based performance evaluation process, by selecting the most relevant features about the learner's perceptual-gestural activity produced during a phase in response to a precursor's state. To generate this higher level of interpretation, with applied domain-specific expert rules to the learner's traces. Three kinds of indicators are generated: action-based and perception-based indicators provide a snapshot of the perceptual-gestural activity produced within a phase; they are coupled with criticality-based indicators who situate this human activity within a particular context, and the situation's current degree of criticality.

2.2 The Use of Neural Networks for Performance Evaluation

Since a major objective is to provide relevant feedback in relation to NTS diagnosis, there is an interest in evaluating both perceptual performance and gestural performance to improve the precision of feedback. However, it is still necessary to consider that some relevant indicators for perceptual evaluation will be found in gestural-based indicators and vice-versa. Moreover, as NTS can only be trained through the experience of many different situations, applying symbolic modelling techniques to identify experts' solution paths would be required for every critical situation provided to the learner, increasing the risk of error, e.g. the omission of possible solution paths. A symbolic approach would also struggle to provide insights into the separate influence of perceptions and actions on the general learner's performance or take into account elements implicitly considered by the expert, such as driving style for example. Thus, we focus upon supervised learning regression techniques to train a NN to rate a learner's performance in non-critical situations, from the evaluation of an expert. We hold that for similar situations where the main variation is the addition of a criticality factor, the structure learnt by the network can be used for performance evaluation in the corresponding critical situation, thanks to transfer learning mechanisms [6]. This allows performance evaluation independently from criticality and compensates for the low number of critical situations in comparison to non-critical ones (Fig. 1).

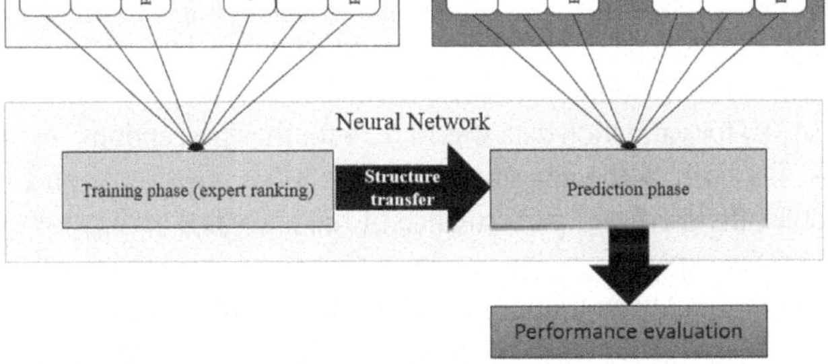

Fig. 1. Training and validation phase of the NN during a non-critical situation. The approximated structure is transferred for performance evaluation in the associated critical situation.

3 Proof of Concept in a Driving Situation

We artificially generated data simulating drivers' behaviour in the form of high level indicators of perceptions, actions, and criticality. This data was created to provide relevant information in accordance to experts' analysis, about two driving situations, one of them being critical. In the non-critical situation, the driver proceeds on a straight road, with a crossroad which can be seen at the beginning of the situation, and a pedestrian about to commit herself to the crosswalk. In the critical situation, the driver drives on a similar straight road, with no crossroad and a group of children playing close to the road. One of the children will cross without giving any clear indication of wanting to do so. Both situations can be separated into two phases as proposed in part 2, namely a first phase where the precursor (the pedestrian or the child) has not started to cross the road, and a second phase starting when crossing begins. Both require the learner to assess the situation and to stop the car before impacting the pedestrian. We generated perception-based, action-based, and criticality based indicators for the two phases, such as, for example, the timing of the early perception during a phase (a perception-based indicator), the average intensity of brakes (an action-based indicator), and the worst Time to Collision reached during a phase (a criticality-based indicator). We gave them a discrete value ranging from 0 to 5. 1000 runs were generated representing the full spectrum of driver's actions for the handling of the non-critical situation. We identified, using k-means clustering, a set of 30 clusters representing different kinds of driver behaviours.

The input layer of the NN used for training was comprised of the data generated by our simulator. An expert rated each cluster, separately for perceptions and for actions under a scale ranging from 0 to 5, to provide the two NN a target value during training phase, representing the learner's performance. To facilitate the rating task, a textual description was provided to the expert as well as the average numerical values for each indicator and for each cluster. To rate the clusters, the expert first analysed the perceptions and actions of the learner phase by phase, before regrouping the complete information to provide his rating. The NN input layer was constituted 9 values for each phase, each corresponding to one of the generated indicators. Therefore, the input layer was comprised of 18 nodes. Each run was labelled by the performance value furnished by the expert. The network was composed of two fully connected hidden layers of 9 and 5 units respectively. For both layers, a rectified linear unit activation function [7] was used. The network was trained to predict a continuous value corresponding to a learner's performance. The output layer was comprised of a single node with a linear activation function as is standard for regression learning. We randomly selected 90% of the runs for training, and 10% for validation. The network was trained for 50 iterations, which was when loss stopped improving. The mean squared error (MSE) for validation data was of 0.24 for the "perceptions" network, and 0.14 for the "actions" network, both values being like the MSE observed during training. After 50 training epochs, the predicted performance of both NN fell very close to the performance evaluated by the expert.

Once the network had been trained, we observed the network's ability to transfer the approximated structure to the critical situation. To do so, we asked the expert to describe a set of driver's behaviours in the critical situation. Seven behaviours were described. We provided to a different expert a set of indicators and a textual description matching each of these behaviours, similarly to what had been done with the behaviours during the non-critical situation. In the critical scenario, criticality is due to the unexpected character of the precursor's behaviour, but to rate the seven behaviours, we asked the expert to consider that the child's intention was explicit. This was done because we aim at testing the ability of the NN to transfer their performance analysis from a non-critical situation to a critical one, and we expect this transfer to be efficient because the only difference between the situations is the presence of a criticality element in one of them. Asking the expert to rate the previous behaviours disregarding criticality is asking him to realize the same task the NN will perform. The set of indicators generated for each of the critical behaviours were fed as input to both networks. This operation was repeated 50 times, for both perceptions and actions ranking. The NN analysed the behaviours as follows (Table 1):

Table 1. NN output values for the 7 behaviours during critical situations, in comparison to the expert ranking.

Behaviour	Actions				Perceptions			
	Avg. NN value	Expert rating	MSE	MSE during training	Avg. NN value	Expert rating	MSE	MSE during training
B1	0.93	1.5	0.17	0.14	4.01	3.25	0.62	0.24
B2	1.17	1.5			1.54	3.00		
B3	0.32	1			0.59	1.25		
B4	1.84	2			1.28	2.00		
B5	2.00	2.25			1.72	2.00		
B6	2.80	2.5			2.99	3.75		
B7	4.09	3.75			3.99	3.75		

For the "actions" network, the MSE is very close to the MSE observed during validation phase, which confirms the ability of the network to transfer the approximated structure. For the "perceptions" network, the MSE was higher than the "actions" network. This was mostly due to a single behaviour, B2, which can be explained by the fact that the expert created this behaviour to model a tunnel vision phenomenon ending up with the driver not stopping to the child. In B2, the driver perceived the children early, but did not change his behaviour. While the expert rated highly the learner's perceptions, the network was faced with a completely new pattern, as during training phase, there was no run where early and frequent perceptions were followed by an impact. Facing a completely new pattern, the network fell back to the criticality indicator to provide a rating for B2. Since during training, most "bad" criticality indicators generated bad rankings both in perceptions and actions, B2 was heavily penalized by the network. While the ability of the NN to fall back to criticality indicators when faced with some completely different patterns strikes us as acceptable, this suggests that adding to the NN training the observed behaviours during the critical situation, when the ranking of an expert is available, will further improve the NN overall performance.

4 Conclusion, Limits, and Perspectives

We presented the main challenges of NTS evaluation from the point of view an ill-defined problem, specifically the blending of non-technical and technical skills in a learner's perceptual-gestural activity. We have identified the variation in criticality between two contextually similar situations to differentiate the two kinds of skills, assuming a hypothesis of stability in the learner's technical skills. We proposed an approach to analyse a learner's performance in both non-critical and critical situations. We decided to use a neural network trained on a non-critical situation, for performance evaluation during a critical situation. This was done firstly, because this process permits the evaluation of a learner's ability to maintain their usual performance when facing different degrees of criticality, which is a marker of NTS. Secondly, because a critical situation should only be experienced once by a learner, which is problematic to the structure approximation process. We then detailed the construction of the different analysis layers of our model. The first experimental results suggested that transfer learning was efficient given our conceptual hypothesis. In the future, we will compare performance in non-critical situations and critical situations for specific learners, a task which will be done with real data produced from learner's activity in the VE in driving and midwifery. We expect this comparison to be the basis of NTS diagnosis, given other factors such as the learner's technical knowledge, the situation's criticality, or physiological markers such as heart rate variation (HRV).

References

1. Fletcher, G., Flin, R., McGeorge, P., Glavin, R., Maran, N., Patey, R.: Anaesthetists' non-technical skills (ANTS): evaluation of a behavioural marker system. Br. J. Anaesth. **90**(5), 580–588 (2003)
2. Bourrier, Y., Jambon, F., Garbay, C., Luengo, V.: An approach to the TEL teaching of non-technical skills from the perspective of an ill-defined problem. In: Verbert, K., Sharples, M., Klobučar, T. (eds.) EC-TEL 2016. LNCS, vol. 9891, pp. 555–558. Springer, Cham (2016). doi:10.1007/978-3-319-45153-4_62
3. Lynch, C., Ashley, K., Aleven, V., Pinkwart, N.: Defining Ill-defined domains; a litera- ture survey. In: Proceedings of the Intelligent Tutoring Systems for Ill-Defined Domains Workshop, ITS 2006, pp. 1–10 (2006)
4. Fournier-Viger, P., Nkambou, R., Nguifo, E.M.: Building intelligent tutoring systems for ill-defined domains. In: Nkambou, R., Bourdeau, J., Mizoguchi, R. (eds.) Advances in Intelligent Tutoring Systems. Studies in Computational Intelligence, vol. 308, pp. 81–101. Springer, Heidelberg (2010). doi:10.1007/978-3-642-14363-2_5
5. Crundall, D., Chapman, P., Trawley, S., Collins, L., Van Loon, E., Andrews, B., Underwood, G.: Some hazards are more attractive than others: drivers of varying experience respond differently to different types of hazard. Accid. Anal. Prev. **45**, 600–609 (2012)
6. Pan, S.J., Yang, Q.: A survey on transfer learning. IEEE Trans. Knowl. Data Eng. **22**(10), 1345–1359 (2010)
7. Nair, V., Hinton, G.E.: Rectified linear units improve restricted boltzmann machines. In: Proceedings of the 27th International Conference on Machine Learning (ICML 2010), pp. 807–814 (2010)

One Tablet, Multiple Epistemic Instruments in the Everyday Classroom

Teresa Cerratto Pargman(✉) and Jalal Nouri

Stockholm University, Stockholm, Sweden
{tessy,jalal}@dsv.su.se

Abstract. Grounded in the analyses of 23 semi-structured interviews and 31 field notes from classroom observations, this study scrutinizes the relationships that teachers and learners entertain with/through the tablet in their process of technology appropriation in the classroom. The results reveal that, on the one hand, the learners elaborate a variety of instruments from their interactions with the tablet and, on the other hand, that the teachers' appropriation plays a central role in configuring a creative, critical and participatory pedagogy in the contemporary classroom.

Keywords: Appropriation · Instrumental genesis · Tablets · School classrooms · Teaching practices · Learning activities

1 The Study of Technology-Use in Technology-Enhanced Learning (TEL)

Research on the use of tablets in schools shows that studies conducted in the field of TEL have either focused on learning efficiency and learners' performance [2–5], or on the design and evaluation of technologically-driven interventions aimed at integrating mobile devices into the school curriculum [6–8]. As such, we observe a research gap between a majority of studies focused on learning efficiency and learners' performance and, a handful of studies accounting for how the teachers and the learners use and appropriate the tablets in the everyday classroom and for how current school practices are being transformed [9, 10]. This study fills this gap by scrutinizing the use that teachers and learners develop from their interaction with tablets in the everyday school classroom. In particular, this work aims to account for how teachers and learners use and appropriate the tablet as an instrument for achieving their purposes at school. The results obtained contribute the compelling body of research on how learning and teaching practices emerge and how the use of artifacts configures and shapes educational practice [11–17].

2 The Instrumental Genesis Theory

Introduced by [14] into the CSCL community, Rabardel's instrumental genesis theory [18, 19] contributes with a relational lens on the discourse on the agent-artifact connection [13]. Grounded in constructivist epistemologies the instrumental genesis theory is

É. Lavoué et al. (Eds.): EC-TEL 2017, LNCS 10474, pp. 379–384, 2017.
DOI: 10.1007/978-3-319-66610-5_30

built around the concepts of instrument and instrumental genesis [11, 12]. The instrument is considered to be a mixed entity constituted by the artifact, the material or technical part (i.e. its design and affordances) and the subject's utilization schemes or behavioral part (i.e. user's representations, knowledge and practices). Central to this understanding is that an *artifact* becomes an *instrument* through developmental transformations of both the artifact and the user's utilization schemes [15].

For the study of the instrumental genesis, Rabardel (1995) proposes the "Collective Instrument-mediated Activity Situation" (CIAS) model. It provides us with tools for the analysis of artifact appropriation processes. In particular, the CIAS model distinguishes four instrumental mediations [11] of which the *epistemic mediation* is of utmost interest for the understanding of how users appropriate a tool that enable them to comprehend the object of their activity. More precisely, the epistemic mediation is oriented toward *knowing* and *comprehending* the object of study, its properties and its evolution resulting from the subject's actions (e.g., looking at an insect through a microscope is an example of an instrumented activity organized around the epistemic mediations) [11]. The establishment and development of the epistemic mediations depends on how the user deals with and adapts to changes introduced by the tool, and how well the user succeeds to transform or divert the use of the artifact.

2.1 The Study: Context and Participants

We carried out a qualitative study in four elementary schools located in the northwest suburbs of Stockholm and in the city of Växjö in the south of Sweden. The study was part of a project aimed at describing and explaining emergent teaching practices in the tablet-mediated classroom. The schools were selected because they took part in the one-to-one tablet program initiated in 2011 by their respective municipalities. This program consisted of providing schools with tablets computers (i.e. ipads and chromebooks) and wireless Internet connectivity. The school principals selected and introduced us into the teachers we interviewed and observed in the classroom. This is an important piece of information as most of the teachers who participated in the study were familiar with mobile devices and committed to make the tablet work in their classrooms. We started to visit the schools in December 2013 and finished the data collection in December 2015. The qualitative approach adopted was of the ethnographic nature [19].

2.2 Data Collected and Data Analysis

The data collected consisted of 23 interviews we conducted with the teachers and 31 field notes that documented the observations made of the use of the tablet in the everyday classroom. The interviews were semi-structured and lasted between 1 h and 1 h 30 min and were all transcribed. This data constituted a rich semantic corpus that was analyzed following thematic analysis principles [20]. The outcomes from the thematic analysis pointed to a set of emergent teaching practices and learning activities bounded to multimodality, persistence of the digital medium and mobility of the tablet [9]. Of these practices, we already reported in [9], we focused exclusively on multimodal teaching and learning because it is a practice that presents a well-defined material/artifact part, constituted by the semiotic modes afforded by the tablet's apps and, a behavior part, constituted by the users' utilization schemes structuring meaning-making processes in teaching and learning activities [21].

3 Findings

The novelty with our study is that we, the researchers, did not construct the situations observed. In this study the teachers were those driving the integration of the tablets into their school practices. As such, our findings report on actual use and appropriation of tablets in everyday classroom practices. In particular, we report on teachers and learners' tablet-mediated multimodal practice and the epistemic instruments they elaborate.

3.1 One Tablet, Different Epistemic Instruments in the Everyday Classroom

The following examples illustrate that there are different ways in which the learners appropriate the tablet as an epistemic instrument in the classroom. By epistemic instrument we refer to the instrument that enables the learners to comprehend the teacher's lesson and construct knowledge about it. While the first example illustrates a teacher that scaffolds learners' appropriation of the tablet for the design and production of a multimodal presentation, the second example illustrates a teacher scaffolding learners' to use the tablet to reproduce, copy ready-made material from digital sources.

Example 1: Appropriating Selected Generic Apps for the Comprehension of Indicators of the Acidification Process
The teacher asked 7th grade learners (i.e. 13 years old) to conduct an experiment on the process of acidification in nature and use the tablet to document it through photos and short films. The activity entailed that children took photos (i.e. tablet's camera) of the results of their own experiments on acidification and that they used iMovie to document the different steps of the acidification observed. The material once created was sent to the learning management platform used at the school and the learners' material was projected onto the classroom's interactive smartboard. More specifically, the learners watched classmates' films and photos, including children's own explanations of the acidification process experienced whilst the teacher encouraged children to ask classmates about the information sources consulted and to discuss the accuracy of the content shared. The children's photos reporting on the results of their own experiments were also projected onto the smartboard and were analyzed by the whole class. The collaborative analysis activity engaged between the teacher and the learners, who were sharing and reflecting on their own content, constituted the teaching material for a lesson on the acidification phenomenon.

Example 2: Appropriating Selected Generic Apps FOR the Comprehension of Energy Sources and Use in the Home
The teacher asked 5th learners (i.e.11 years old) and use the tablet to create a group presentation about energy use and energy sources in the home. The presentations to be created in Keynote had to be sent by e-mail to the teacher and should contain, according

to the teacher, facts and "images that are most suitable to the topic". Following carefully one of the groups, we observed that the group of three learners initiated the task searching and selecting information in Youtube. Most of the conversation and negotiation observed within the group was related to the choice of the material to copy. Once the group agreed on a film they inserted it in Keynote. The group concluded their presentation copying and pasting images found with Google search engine and adding one more film downloaded from Youtube. The group ended up the task by adding text to the films and images that explained succinctly how energy circulates in the house, how one can save it and how energy in the home is distributed. Once the presentation was finished the learners sent it to the teacher who asked to remain sit and read a book from the digital library available on their tablets.

There are differences among the epistemic instruments the children elaborated in both situations. In the first example, the learners were asked to put in practice activities that structured the creation of own material and challenged them to scrutinize the information sources consulted as well as to discuss and reflect collaboratively on their and classmates' multimodal presentations about the acidification process. The learners' material was projected onto the classroom's smart board and shared, being thus available to everyone in the classroom. As such, the learners' material became a central part of the teaching material on acidification. In the second example, the learners were asked to find digital material already created. Once created, learners' material/presentations were neither shared with the classroom (i.e. they were not displayed onto the smart board) nor discussed in the classroom. They were sent to the teacher.

Reflecting on these examples, one can observe that there are differences in terms of how the teachers' asked the learners to make use of the tablet. Such instructions conditioned the types of epistemic instruments the learners could appropriate from the activities they conducted with the tablets. In the first example, the teacher guided and enticed children to use the tablet as a tool for documenting, discussing and reflecting on the acidification phenomenon as they had observed it and experienced it. The second example shows instead how the learners were encouraged to negotiate the selection of the material to be reproduced from the Internet.

Furthermore, the first example shows that the teacher chose to share the learners' multimodal material about acidification by projecting it onto the smart board; in this way, the teacher allowed everyone in the classroom to get access and work collaboratively on learners' own understandings of the acidification process that was portrayed in their multimodal presentations. By projecting the learners' presentation onto the smart board and by engaging the whole classroom in a collective and analytical activity on such learning material, the teacher grounds his teaching lesson in the learners' presentations (i.e. learners' understanding). In so doing, the teacher recognizes the learners as co-producer of the teaching lesson and participant in the formation of the classroom knowledge.

The second example shows that legitimating the learner as a co-producer of the teaching lesson fails as the teacher encourages, via her task instructions, the learners to be spectators of the information found and selected [23]. Instead of encouraging the learners to be designers and/or co-producers of the teaching material, the teacher creates conditions for the learners to use and appropriate the tablet as an instrument for reproducing information in the classroom.

4 Conclusions

These are exciting times for schools that are already engaged in the process of digitalizing teaching practices. This study shows that in the process of appropriation, the teachers' instrumental geneses are central to the learning conditions they shape and configure for the learners. The study also points to the relevance of a lens on the teachers' instrumental geneses by showing that what is at stake in the integration of tablets into the school classroom, goes beyond a sound and innovative design of didactical apps. Transforming the tablet into a school instrument demands that the teachers appropriate the new artifact whilst they rethink established teaching practices and pedagogical views on power-relationships in the classroom. We wonder if will end up in a critical, creative and participatory pedagogy or if we will go back to pedagogies that have dominating schools until now? It seems that the question is up to the teachers and the educational institutions they belong to. Introducing a new tool without questioning the pedagogy that is in place in the classroom does not really contribute to change learning activities or/and teachers' practices. The introduction of a tablet into the classroom does not make the teaching practice innovative per-se; it is rather how the pedagogy that is in place changes and transforms what makes the tablet-mediated teaching practice innovative.

Acknowledgments. We thank the teachers, learners and school principals who participated in the study and we are grateful to the Swedish Research Council for funding this research.

References

1. Sörensen, E.: The Materiality of Learning: Technology and Knowledge in Educational Practice. Cambridge University Press, New York (2008)
2. Murray, O.T., Olcese, N.R.: Teaching and learning with iPads, ready or not? TechTrends **55**(6), 42–48 (2011)
3. Kucirkova, N., Messer, D., Sheehy, S., Fernández Panadero, C.: Children's engagement with educational iPad apps: insights from a Spanish classroom. Comput. Educ. **71**, 175–184 (2013)
4. Fallon, G.: What's the difference? Learning collaboratively using iPads in conventional classrooms. Comput. Educ. **84**, 62–77 (2015)
5. Sung, T., Chang, K., Liu, T.: The effects of integrating mobile devices with teaching and learning on students' learning performance: a meta-analysis and research synthesis. Comput. Educ. **94**, 252–275 (2016)
6. Outhwaite, L., Gulliford, A., Pitchford, N.: Closing the gap: efficacy of a tablet intervention to support the development of early mathematical skills in UK primary school children. Comput. Educ. **108**, 43–58 (2017)
7. Nordmark, S., Milrad, M.: Influencing everyday teacher practices by applying mobile digital storytelling as a seamless learning approach. In: Brown, T.H., van der Merwe, H.J. (eds.) mLearn 2015. CCIS, vol. 560, pp. 256–272. Springer, Cham (2015). doi: 10.1007/978-3-319-25684-9_19

8. Nouri, J., Cerratto Pargman, T., Eliasson, J., Ramberg, R.: Exploring the challenges of supporting collaborative mobile learning. Int. J. Mob. Blended Learn. **3**(4), 54–69 (2011)
9. Nouri, J., Pargman, T.C.: When teaching practices meet tablets' affordances. Insights on the materiality of learning. In: Verbert, K., Sharples, M., Klobučar, T. (eds.) EC-TEL 2016. LNCS, vol. 9891, pp. 179–192. Springer, Cham (2016). doi:10.1007/978-3-319-45153-4_14
10. Cerratto Pargman, T., Nouri, J.: Tablets in the CSCL classroom: a lens on teachers' instrumental geneses. In: Proceedings of CSCL 2017, Philadelphia. ISLS Press (2017)
11. Lonchamp, J.: An instrumental perspective on CSCL systems. Int. J. CSCL **7**(2), 211–237 (2012)
12. Ritella, G., Hakkarainen, K.: Instrumental genesis in technology-mediated learning: from double stimulation to expansive knowledge practices. Int. J. Comput.-Support. Collab. Learn. **7**(2), 239–258 (2012)
13. Stahl, G., Ludvigsen, S., Law, N., Cress, U.: CSCL artifacts. Int. J. Comput.-Support. Collab. Learn. **9**(3), 237 (2014)
14. Stahl, G.: Cognizing mediating: unpacking the entanglement of artifacts with collective minds. Int. J. CSCL **7**(2), 187–191 (2012)
15. Overdijk, M., van Diggelen, W., Kirschner, P.A., Baker, M.: Connecting agents with artifacts. Towards a rationale of mutual shaping. Int. J. CSCL **7**(2), 193–210 (2012)
16. Cerratto-Pargman, T., Knutsson, O., Karlström, P.: Materiality of online students' peer-review activities in higher education. In: Proceedings of CSCL 2015, Gothenburg, pp. 308–315. ICLS Press (2015)
17. O'Malley, C., Suthers, D., Reimann, P., Dimitracopoulou, A.: Computer-supported collaborative learning practices. In: Conference Proceedings CSCL 2009. ISLS (2009)
18. Rabardel, P.: Les hommes et les technologies: approche cognitive des instruments contemporains. Colin, Paris (1995)
19. Ito, M., Baumer, S., Bittani, M., boyd, d, Cody, R., Stephson, B., Horst, H.: Hanging Out, Messing Around, and Geeking Out: Kids Living AND Learning WITH New Media. MIT Press, Cambridge (2012)
20. Braun, V., Clarke, V.: Using thematic analysis in psychology. Qual. Res. Psychol. **3**(2), 77–101 (2006)
21. Jewitt, C.: Multimodality and literacy in school classrooms. Rev. Res. Educ. **32**(1), 241–267 (2008)
22. Jenkins, H., Clinton, K., Purushtoma, R., Robison, A., Weigel, M.: Confronting the Challenges of a Participatory Culture: Media Education for the 21st Century. McArthur Foundation, Chicago (2007)

Effects of Network Topology on the OpenAnswer's Bayesian Model of Peer Assessment

Maria De Marsico[1], Luca Moschella[1], Andrea Sterbini[1(✉)], and Marco Temperini[2]

[1] Computer Science Department, Sapienza University, Rome, Italy
{demarsico,sterbini}@di.uniroma1.it

[2] Computer, Control, and Management Eng. Department, Sapienza University, Rome, Italy
marte@dis.uniroma1.it

Abstract. The paper investigates if and how the topology of the peer-assessment network can affect the performance of the Bayesian model adopted in OpenAnswer. Performance is evaluated in terms of the comparison of predicted grades with actual teacher's grades. The global network is built by interconnecting smaller subnetworks, one for each student, where intra-subnetwork nodes represent student's characteristics, and peer assessment assignments make up inter-subnetwork connections and determine evidence propagation. A possible subset of teacher graded answers is dynamically determined by suitable selection and stop rules. The research questions addressed are: (RQ1) "does the topology (diameter) of the network negatively influence the precision of predicted grades?"; in the affirmative case, (RQ2) "are we able to reduce the negative effects of high-diameter networks through an appropriate choice of the subset of students to be corrected by the teacher?" We show that (RQ1) OpenAnswer is less effective on higher diameter topologies, (RQ2) this can be avoided if the subset of corrected students is chosen considering the network topology.

Keywords: Peer assessment · Open answers · Bayesian networks · Bayesian model of peer assessment · Network topology

1 Introduction

In Bloom's taxonomy of educational objectives [2] learners need wider and deeper comprehension of topics when passing from pure knowledge (just remembering), to comprehension, application, analysis, evaluation and finally synthesis, as higher meta-cognitive skills. Peer assessment is a possible tool to help students exercise/enforce these abilities [6]. Open answers to questions allow challenging assessment methods, e.g., exercises, free text answers to questions, etc., which are more effective than multiple-choice tests [5], but also harder to handle for teachers. OpenAnswer [7–9] (OA) allows (semi-)automated grading of open answers through peer assessment. During an OA session, each student is assigned a number of peers' answers to grade. To enforce the reliability of the grading results, the system provides the (not mandatory) possibility for teacher grading of a subset of answers, chosen step by step according to some select-next-or-stop strategy.

É. Lavoué et al. (Eds.): EC-TEL 2017, LNCS 10474, pp. 385–390, 2017.
DOI: 10.1007/978-3-319-66610-5_31

In OA, each student's cognitive/metacognitive state is modeled by a fragment of a global Bayesian Network (BN). Assignments of peer answers to grade make up the interconnections among the subnetworks and determine the topology of the global one. Assessments fed by peers (and possibly by the teacher) are propagated within the BN. The system allows providing the students not only with marks, but also with an estimate of their knowledge and ability to judge, that spurs metacognitive awareness.

Earlier works [4, 7–9] analyzed several factors affecting the accuracy of predicted grades. Present research questions are: (RQ1) "does the topology of the network (in particular its diameter) negatively influence the precision of predicted grades?" If the response to RQ1 is positive, (RQ2) "are we able to reduce the negative effects of high-diameter networks through an appropriate choice of the subset of students to be corrected by the teacher?" To answer RQ1 we modified OA: (1) to produce topologic indicators (e.g. diameter of the peer assessment graph, coverage percentage of corrected students plus their immediate neighbors, average distance between inferred and corrected students); (2) to choose the set of corrected students through topological strategies. The available datasets were used to generate also graphs with higher diameter than the original ones. As hypothesized, OA is less effective on higher diameter topologies. While this represents a general result regarding Bayesian models, the response to RQ2 indicates how this can be avoided in the specific case of peer assessment, if the students to be corrected are chosen by considering the network topology. The results provide an educational-specific operational strategy for using OA in a concrete setting, and for designing a suitable peer assessment network for each single session. The topology-based strategies perform even better than the formerly identified best one, as the experiments section shows.

2 Related Work

Peer-assessment entails a higher cognitive level activity [1]. It pursues different goals [10], especially to allow the learner to appreciate the personal cognitive state and progress. A comprehensive study of peer assessment in a prototype application is in [2]. OA evaluates open answers through peer-assessment, by modeling students and assessment by Bayesian Networks. A different machine learning approach to student modeling is in [3], where Bayesian Networks are used within an Intelligent Tutoring System.

3 The Model Underlying OpenAnswer

The OA system models peer-assessment as a Bayesian network composed of interconnected individual sub-networks. Each such subnetwork represents a student, and is made of three discrete nodes/variables, representing respectively: **K** - student's knowledge about the topic; **C** - the correctness of student's answer being evaluated; **J** - student's ability to judge/assess the answer of a peer; one variable **G** for each grade given to a peer (G variables represent the interconnections among subnetworks). K, J and C are updated by information propagation. The final values of C variables represent the estimated answers correctness (grades).

Each variable above has a 6-valued discrete domain ranging from A (best) to F (fail). A-E corresponds to 10–6 (sufficient marks one by one), and F is from 5 below.

For all student's marks of a peer's answer, a corresponding Grade variable (G) and value is injected as evidence into the network, and propagates its effects depending on both the current value of J of the grading student, and on current estimation of C of the answer corrected. Variables C and J are assumed depend from K with conditional probabilities P(C | K) and P(J | K). The C dependence is because writing an essay cannot be easily guessed as it happens in multiple-choice quizzes. As for J, the inspiration is from Bloom's taxonomy of cognitive levels [1] assuming that judging a peer's answer can be considered as a more difficult task than knowing the topic and answering it. The distribution of values for G is conditioned by J and C with distribution P(G | J, C).

When the teacher corrects the essays, OA suggests the next answer to grade and notifies her when no further correction is needed. The possible alternatives for stop condition can be found in [4]. In this work we use a fixed condition, i.e., reaching 30% of answers. The next answer to grade is chosen to maximize the information gain achieved by its teacher correction. Possible criteria are in [4]. Here only the best achieving of past experiments is compared with the new topological selection criteria. Such rule is *maxEntropy*: the next answer to grade is the one with the highest entropy, i.e., the one the system knows less about.

4 Methodology

To show (RQ1) if the propagation of information through the BN drops in quality the more it moves far from the set of corrected nodes, we need networks with higher diameter (the maximum of minimal distances between any two nodes). In our datasets we have two groups of real assessments (datasets I and M, respectively with 2 and 6 peer-assessment sessions) where each student graded the 3 next peers in order from the group (modulo the size of the group). This produced "ring-shaped" networks with a diameter proportional to the number of nodes and inversely proportional to the number of corrected peers (Fig. 1, left).

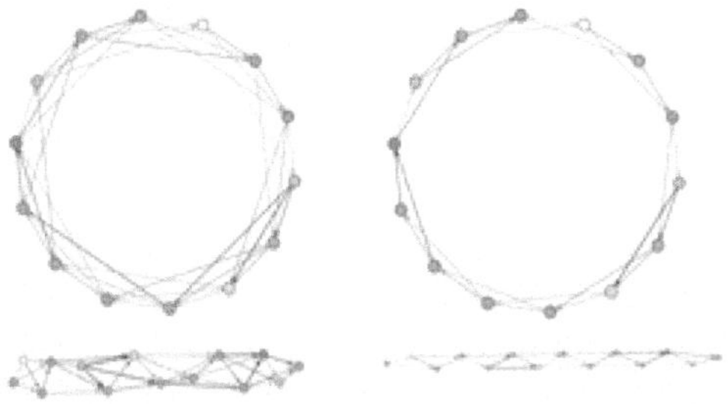

Fig. 1. Peer-assessment from dataset I - left: 3 peers - right: 2 peers – top: ring, bottom: broken - node color intensity: teacher's grade - edge color intensity: peer's grades, (darker = better)

To get even higher diameters we can either cut the ring (Fig. 1, bottom, "broken" network) or reduce the number of assessments by each student (Fig. 1, right, "2-peers" network), or both (Fig. 1, bottom right). The figure shows also the teacher grades for each student (node color, darker = better) and the grades given by each peer (edge color, darker = better). When a new teacher grade is asserted for a student C variable (new evidence), two information propagations happen in two directions: from the corrected student towards her "judging" peers, and towards her "judges" peers. Because the information flows both directions the edges are considered as undirected (propagation has same weight in both directions).

Table 1 shows for each assessment in datasets I and M the diameter for the graphs depending on the transformations: 3 peers or 2 peers, and ring shaped or broken.

Table 1. Diameter of original and modified peer-assessments for datasets I and M

Dataset	Assessment Id	Num. Peers	2 peers		Original (3 peers)	
		Type	Ring	Broken	Ring	Broken
		Num. Students	Diameter			
I High School, physics	3	14	4	7	3	5
	4	12	3	6	2	4
M University, C programming	3	13	3	6	2	4
	4	13	3	6	2	4
	6	11	3	5	2	4
	7	11	3	5	2	4
	8	9	2	4	2	3
	9	11	3	5	2	4

The aim of the experiments is to show that the distance traversed by the information in the model has an adverse effect. This requires: (1) topological indicators that describe the network with respect to both static properties (diameter) and to dynamic ones (e.g. the current average distance between corrected students and inferred ones); (2) a new group of selection strategies which takes into account the static and dynamic topological measures of the network when selecting the next student to be corrected.

To this aim three new "good" strategies for the OA greedy selection algorithm are introduced here, to counteract the (expected) negative outcomes of higher distances: **maxCoverage**: chooses the next student so to maximize the network coverage (the number of corrected students union their immediate neighbors); **maxAvgDistCorrected**: chooses the next student so to maximize the average distance among corrected students (to distribute them better through the network); **minAvgDistInferredCorrected**: chooses the next student so to minimize the average distance among the inferred students and their nearest corrected peer (to reduce the average distance the information should traverse). For further verification, three corresponding "bad" strategies are tested that try to keep higher the distance among inferred and corrected students: **minCoverage**, **minAvgDistCorrected**, **maxAvgDistInferredCorrected**.

The available ground truth (complete teacher grades) allows us to simulate different settings and strategies for teacher's correction. The experiments presented here adopt and compare the above strategies to select the next answer to grade, together with the former *maxEntropy*, and stop teacher's grading when 30% of the students have been corrected. The remaining grades are inferred. To compare the prediction performances we examine the percentage of exact inferred grades (OK/INFERRED), and the average distance in the graph between inferred students and their nearest corrected peer (AVG_PEER_DISTANCE). The simulations have been run with these different sets of parameters: **Selection strategy:** *maxEntropy* or the above topology based ones; **Initialization of the P(K) distribution:** *flat* or *TgradeDist*; **Number of peers corrected by each student:** 3 or 2; **Shape of the network:** ring or broken.

5 Experimental Results

Table 2 shows the OK/INFERRED percentage and the maximum AVG_PEER_DISTANCE at the end of the correction. Because of space limits we show only one of the topology-based "good" and "bad" strategies. As a first observation, the maximum AVG_PEER_DISTANCE is very low (1) for the "good" topology-based selection strategies, and also maxEntropy shows a low value for this outcome (near 1.4). Conversely, the "bad" topology-based strategies show higher AVG_PEER_DISTANCE, as expected (in particular, 2-peers-based networks and broken networks show the highest distances). Yet, the max AVG_PEER_DISTANCE when 30% of students have been corrected is not too high (max 2.9).

Table 2. OK/INFERRED vs NUM. PEERS, STRATEGY, RING/BROKEN, P(K) initialization averaged over all assessments in the I and M datasets (green = best values, red = worst values)

			Average of OK/INFERRED		Max of Avg Peer Distance	
		SHAPE	ring	broken	ring	broken
NUM. PEERS	P(K) init.	STRATEGY				
2	flat	maxEntropy	33%	35%	1.5	1.5
		maxCoperture	38%	38%	1	1
		minCoperture	29%	29%	1.9	2.9
	TgradeDist	maxEntropy	38%	39%	1.5	1.5
		maxCoperture	47%	49%	1	1
		minCoperture	34%	39%	1.9	2.9
3	flat	maxEntropy	32%	33%	1.4	1.4
		maxCoperture	37%	36%	1	1
		minCoperture	34%	32%	1.5	2
	TgradeDist	maxEntropy	39%	38%	1.5	1.5
		maxCoperture	45%	42%	1	1
		minCoperture	43%	35%	1.5	2

When we examine the OK/INFERRED results we see that the "good" topology-based selection strategy outperforms the "bad" one and the maxEntropy strategy. In this we affirmatively answer to both our research questions RQ1 and RQ2, regarding the accuracy of correctly inferred marks: network diameter seems to have a negative effect on prediction accuracy, but this can be addressed by suitable topology-oriented strategies for selecting the answers to grade by the teacher.

Other observations can be drawn from the table. The P(K) initialization affects the outcome with better results for TgradeDist, i.e. OA, as expected, works better with some global knowledge about the class. Cutting the ring to increase the diameter ("broken" shape) reduces the OA performances for almost all selection strategies. Reducing the number of peers from 3 to 2 reduces the performances as expected. More investigation is due on the "perfect" number of corrected peers per student.

6 Conclusions

Higher-diameter networks induced by assignments of peer grading tasks to students, reduce the prediction precision of OpenAnswer. However, an appropriate choice of the selection strategy for teacher graded answers can counteract this negative effect and perform even better than the earlier best selection strategy, *maxEntropy*.

References

1. Bloom, B.S., Engelhart, M.D., Furst, E.J., Hill, W.H., Krathwohl, D.R.: Taxonomy of Educational Objectives: The Classification of Educational Goals. Handbook I. McKay, New York (1956)
2. Lan, C.H., Graf, S., Lai, R., Kinshuk, K.: Enrichment of peer assessment with agent negotiation. IEEE TLT Learn. Technol. **4**(1), 35–46 (2011)
3. Conati, C., Gartner, A., Vanlehn, K.: Using Bayesian networks to manage uncertainty in student modeling. User Model. User-Adap. Inter. **12**, 371–417 (2002)
4. De Marsico, M., Sterbini, A., Temperini, M.: Towards a quantitative evaluation of the relationship between the domain knowledge and the ability to assess peer work. In: Proceeding of ITHET 2015, pp. 1–6. IEEE (2015)
5. Palmer, K., Richardson, P.: On-line assessment and free-response input-a pedagogic and technical model for squaring the circle. In: Proceeding of 7th CAA Conference, pp. 289–300 (2003)
6. Sadler, P.M., Good, E.: The impact of self- and peer-grading on student learning. Ed. Ass. **11**(1), 1–31 (2006)
7. Sterbini, A., Temperini, M.: Dealing with open-answer questions in a peer-assessment environment. In: Popescu, E., Li, Q., Klamma, R., Leung, H., Specht, M. (eds.) ICWL 2012. LNCS, vol. 7558, pp. 240–248. Springer, Heidelberg (2012). doi: 10.1007/978-3-642-33642-3_26
8. Sterbini, A., Temperini, M.: OpenAnswer, a framework to support teacher's management of open answers through peer assessment. In: Proceeding FIE 2013 (2013a)
9. Sterbini, A., Temperini, M.: Analysis of OpenAnswers via mediated peer-assessment. In: Proceeding 17th IEEE International Conference on System Theory, Control and Computing (ICSTCC 2013) (2013b)
10. Topping, K.: Peer assessment between students in colleges and universities. Rev. Ed. Res. **68**, 249–276 (1998)

Fostering Interdisciplinary Knowledge Construction in Computer-Assisted Collaborative Concept Mapping

Jacco de Weerd[1], Esther Tan[2], and Slavi Stoyanov[2(✉)]

[1] NHL University of Applied Science, Leeuwarden, The Netherlands
jaccodw@yahoo.com

[2] Open University of the Netherlands, Heerlen, The Netherlands
{esther.tan,slavi.stoyanov}@ou.nl

Abstract. Research has argued that the way learning activities are sequenced over different social levels has an effect on learning effectiveness. This study investigates the effect of embedding an individual preparation phase prior to collaborative concept mapping (CCM) on the epistemic and social dimension of the CCM process. Using a quasi-experimental design, a multi-disciplinary group of 24 3rd year bachelor students were put into two different conditions: one with individual preparation phase (WIP) and one without individual preparation phase (WOIP). The students worked on a collaborative assignment about macro trends analysis using computer-assisted CCM. For the epistemic dimension, students in the WIP condition showed more occurrences of utterances seeking clarification and positioning one's perspectives. In the social mode of knowledge construction, students in the WIP condition displayed more conflict-oriented and integrated consensus building statements to negotiate shared knowledge.

Keywords: Collaborative concept mapping · Interdisciplinary knowledge integration · Social modes of knowledge co-construction · Epistemic dimension of knowledge co-construction

1 Introduction

Contemporary problems are often transcending the boundaries of a single discipline. This implies a need to integrate knowledge from different professional fields [1]. According to Songer and Linn [2] knowledge integration could be perceived as synthesizing concepts and ideas from different disciplines into a coherent whole. To this end, collaborative knowledge construction (CKC) could play an instrumental role [3]. However, coordination, communication and interaction challenges ensue when individuals from various disciplines construct shared meaning and knowledge [4]. In this regard Novak and Cañas's [5] study showed the pivotal role of collaborative concept mapping (CCM). CCM enhances coordination and communication within groups, which in turn, facilitates a more integrated conceptual framework [6]. Notwithstanding the plethora of research on CKC and the use of CCM to facilitate this process, there remains paucity of empirical works on interdisciplinary knowledge constructing using CCM. Hence, this study investigates how the sequencing of learning activities, i.e., embedding

É. Lavoué et al. (Eds.): EC-TEL 2017, LNCS 10474, pp. 391–396, 2017.
DOI: 10.1007/978-3-319-66610-5_32

an individual preparation phase prior to collaborative work, could have an effect on the interdisciplinary knowledge co-construction process during collaborative concept mapping.

1.1 Challenges of Collaborative Knowledge Construction

Learning is a social process and knowledge is a negotiated product of a collaborative discourse [7, 8]. Hewitt and Scardamalia [9] liken the CKC process to "distributed cognition" where "each person's individual cognitions are continually reorganized in an effort to construct meaning out of the other person's speech acts" (p. 79). Beers et al. [1] captured the challenges of CKC in four main stages: knowledge externalization, internalization, negotiation and integration (see Fig. 1).

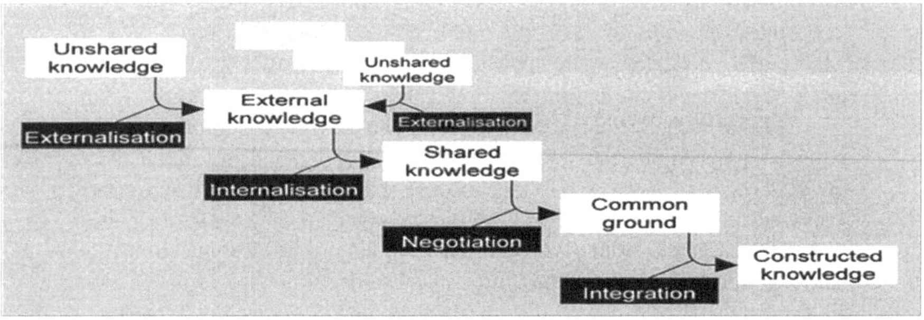

Fig. 1. From unshared knowledge to constructed knowledge (Beers et al. 2006)

1.2 Facilitating Interdisciplinary Knowledge Construction with Concept Maps

Concept mapping scaffolds knowledge externalization and internalization more effectively than text [6, 10]. The explicit representation of mental models facilitates the grounding process where concepts and relationships can be more effectively negotiated [11, 12]. Research showed that concept maps structure the collaborative discourse and fosters more in-depth and productive interaction [13]. The three main theoretical arguments for an individual concept mapping preparatory phase are: (1) more room for personal reflection and development of an individual mental model; (2) better preparation for knowledge negotiation; and (3) more openness to the contributions of group members [14–16]. The theoretical arguments for CCM without an individual concept mapping preparation phase are: (1) peer scaffolding; (2) preventing fragmented thinking; and (3) preventing defensive reasoning [17, 18]. This study addresses the following research questions:

RQ 1. To what extent does with- or without-individual preparation phase (WIP & WOIP) affect the epistemic dimension of interdisciplinary knowledge construction in computer-assisted collaborative concept mapping?

RQ 2. To what extent does with- or without-individual preparation phase (WIP & WOIP) affect the social dimension of interdisciplinary knowledge construction in computer-assisted collaborative concept mapping?

2 Methodology

2.1 Sample and Design

A total of N = 24 third year bachelor students, distributed among four groups of six participated in a quasi-experimental field study. Four of the participants were female and twenty - male. The groups were randomly assigned to one of the two experimental conditions (WIP - with individual preparation phase and WOIP - without individual preparation phase), that is 12 for each condition. In each group students from different disciplines such as marketing, industrial engineering, multimedia design, Business IT and management, and computer science were represented.

2.2 Learning Environment

Students worked on a collaborative assignment about macro trends using CCM. They first got a plenary lecture about macro trends, concept mapping and the opportunity to practice concept mapping with CmapTools [19]. Subsequently the WIP groups got 30 min to prepare an individual concept map before proceeding to CCM for 45 min. The WOIP groups started directly to create CCM for an hour and 15 min. Students in both conditions observed the same duration and undertook a similar task.

2.3 Data Analysis

To investigate the effects of the two experimental conditions on the epistemic and social dimension in the CCM process, data for the analysis was derived from audio recordings of the collaborative discourse. Each unit may contain one or more statements depending on the discussion threads, ideas and turn of talks. For the epistemic dimension, there was a total of 580 units of analysis for the WIP groups and 318 for the WOIP groups. For the social dimension, there was a total of 490 units of analysis for the WIP groups and 359 for the WOIP groups. The coding scheme for the epistemic dimension is adapted from Beers et al. [1] and includes the following categories: contribution, verification, clarification, elaboration, and positioning.

Of equal significance is the analysis of the social dimension of the collaborative discourse during the CCM process. The five coding categories of the social dimension are: externalisation, elicitation, quick-consensus building, integrated consensus building and conflict-oriented consensus building [16].

3 Findings

Figure 2 shows the means of the frequency of the occurrences of statements for both experimental conditions in regard to RQ1.

Overall, the findings indicate that the WIP groups showed higher occurrences of statements for all categories in the epistemic dimension than the WOIP groups. Two distinguished differences lie in the occurrences of clarification and positioning

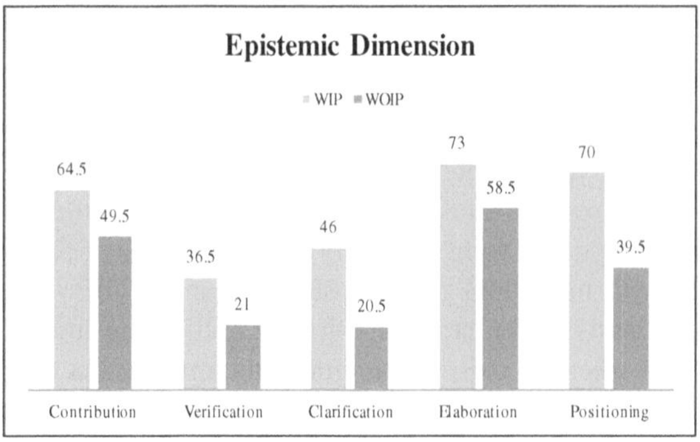

Fig. 2. Means of the five categories in the Epistemic mode of knowledge co-construction.

statements. The WIP groups generated almost twice as many statements on clarification and positioning than the WOIP groups. These statements are instrumental in CKC and negotiation of shared meaning and understanding. The findings are best understood when examined against the effects of WIP and WOIP on the social modes of CKC in the succeeding segment (RQ2).

Figure 3 shows the means of the frequency of the occurrences of statements in the social mode of knowledge co-construction for the two experimental conditions (Note: Consensus = quick-consensus building, Integration = integration-oriented consensus building, Conflict = conflict-oriented consensus building).

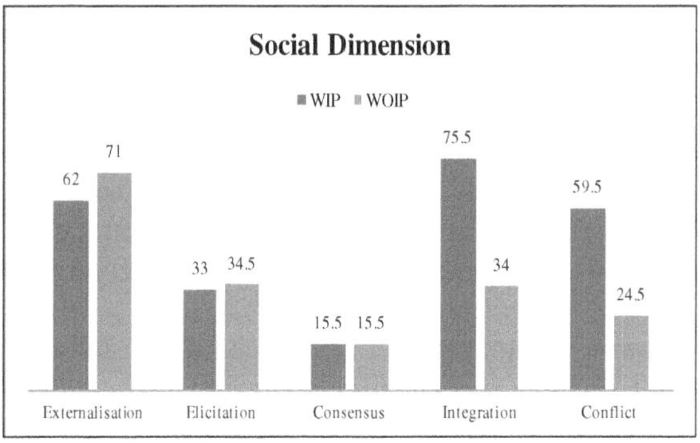

Fig. 3. Means of the five categories in the social mode of knowledge co-construction.

The two groups in both conditions displayed almost similar tendency in eliciting contributions and ideas from peers, as well as in seeking quick-consensus building. However, it is evident that there were more integrated- and conflict-oriented consensus building statements for the WIP groups, as compared to the WOIP groups. The findings on the social modes of the knowledge co-construction also illustrate the quality of the collaborative discourse. Higher occurrences of the integrated- and conflict-oriented consensus building indicate that there was more in-depth discourse for the two groups in the WIP condition.

4 Discussion and Conclusions

This study investigated the effect of the WIP and WOIP conditions on the epistemic and social dimension of CKC during the CCM process. The overall findings suggest that an individual preparation phase prior to CCM led to better interdisciplinary knowledge co-construction because it facilitates the grounding process where new knowledge is questioned, contended and verified. The WIP groups were more engaged and more forthcoming with ideas: resulting in more in-depth discourse as exemplified by the higher occurrences of clarification, positioning statements in the epistemic dimension, as well as more integrated- and conflict-oriented building statements in the social modes of CKC. As evident in the findings, there was higher occurrences of externalization and elicitation of contributions and ideas in the WOIP condition, as compared to the groups in WIP condition. Peer scaffolding accentuated the element of interdependency to achieve shared goals and provided individuals transitory support during the CKC process. In the epistemic dimension, students in the WOIP condition were also less forthcoming with statements to seek clarification and to question positioning of peer's perspectives and ideas.

Although we witnessed some interesting patterns in the epistemic and social dimension of the knowledge co-construction during the CCM process, we acknowledge that there are certainly inherent limitations in the attribution of effects to the two conditions (WIP & WOIP). However, we believe that the interesting findings from this research study have been insightful on how the sequencing of activities at different social levels might have an effect on the type and depth of collaborative discourse, the collaborative knowledge construction and interdisciplinary knowledge integration process.

References

1. Beers, P.J., Boshuizen, H.P., Kirschner, P.A., Gijselaers, W.H.: Common ground, complex problems and decision making. Group Decis. Negot. **15**(6), 529–556 (2006)
2. Songer, N.B., Linn, M.C.: How do students' views of science influence knowledge integration? J. Res. Sci. Teach. **28**(9), 761–784 (1991)
3. Roschelle, J., Teasley, S.D.: The construction of shared knowledge in collaborative problem solving. In: O'Malley, C. (ed.) Computer Supported Collaborative Learning, pp. 69–97. Springer, Heidelberg (1995)
4. Roschelle, J., Clancey, W.J.: Learning as social and neural. Educ. Psychol. **27**(4), 435–453 (1992)
5. Novak, J.D., Cañas, A.J.: The origins of the concept mapping tool and the continuing evolution of the tool. Inform. Visual. **5**(3), 175–184 (2006)
6. Engelmann, T., Hesse, F.W.: How digital concept maps about the collaborators' knowledge and information influence computer-supported collaborative problem solving. Int. J. Comput.-Supported Collaborative Learn. **5**(3), 299–319 (2010)

7. Palincsar, A.S.: Social constructivist perspectives on teaching and learning. Annu. Rev. Psychol. **49**(1), 345–375 (1998)
8. Scardamalia, M., Bereiter, C.: Knowledge Building. The Cambridge (2006)
9. Hewitt, J., Scardamalia, M.: Design principles for distributed knowledge building processes. Educ. Psychol. Rev. **10**(1), 75–96 (1998)
10. Basque, J., Lavoie, M.C.: Collaborative concept mapping in education: major research trends. In: Proceedings of the Second International Conference on Concept Mapping, Costa Rica, pp. 79–86 (2006)
11. Stoyanova, N., Kommers, P.: Concept mapping as a medium of shared cognition in computer-supported collaborative problem solving. J. Interact. Learn. Res. **13**(1), 111–133 (2002)
12. Schmid, R.F., McEwen, L.A., Locke, J., De Simone, C.: Use of electronic concept mapping in organizing, analyzing and representing complex knowledge-based information. In: American Educational Research Association Annual Meeting, New Orleans (2002)
13. Sizmur, S., Osborne, J.: Learning processes and collaborative concept mapping. Int. J. Sci. Educ. **19**(10), 1117–1135 (1997)
14. van Boxtel, C., van der Linden, J., Roelofs, E., Erkens, G.: Collaborative concept mapping: provoking and supporting meaningful discourse. Theory Pract. **41**(1), 40–46 (2002)
15. Gao, H.: The Effects of Key Concepts Availability and Individual Preparation in the Form of Proposition Formation in Collaborative Concept Mapping on Learning Problem Solving and Learner Attitudes. ProQuest Dissertations Publishing, Florida (2007)
16. Weinberger, A., Fischer, F.: A framework to analyze argumentative knowledge construction in computer-supported collaborative learning. Comput. Educ. **46**(1), 71–95 (2006)
17. Collins, A., Brown, J.S., Newman, S.E.: Cognitive apprenticeship: teaching the crafts of reading, writing, and mathematics. In: Resnick, L.B. (ed.) Knowing, Learning, and Instruction: Essays in Honor of Robert Glaser, pp. 453–494. Lawrence Erlbaum Associates, Hillsdale (1989)
18. Rogoff, B.: Apprenticeship in Thinking. Oxford, New York (1990)
19. Cmap [Computer software] (2017). http://cmap.ihmc.us/cmaptools

"We're Seeking Relevance": Qualitative Perspectives on the Impact of Learning Analytics on Teaching and Learning

Tracie Farrell(✉), Alexander Mikroyannidis, and Harith Alani

Open University, Milton Keynes, UK
{tracie.farrell-frey,alexander.mikroyannidis,h.alani}@open.ac.uk

Abstract. Whilst a significant body of learning analytics research tends to focus on impact from the perspective of usability or improved learning outcomes, this paper proposes an approach based on Affordance Theory to describe *awareness and intention* as a bridge between usability and impact. 10 educators at 3 European institutions participated in detailed interviews on the affordances they perceive in using learning analytics to support practice in education. Evidence illuminates connections between an educator's epistemic beliefs about learning and the purpose of education, their perception of threats or resources in delivering a successful learning experience, and the types of data they would consider as evidence in recognizing or regulating learning. This evidence can support the learning analytics community in considering the proximity to the student, the role of the educator, and their personal belief structure in developing robust analytics tools that educators may be more likely to utilize.

1 Introduction and Motivation

Learning analytics intends to leverage the "collection, measurement, analysis and reporting of data" to "understand and optimize learning" [7]. However, the real impact of learning analytics has been difficult to determine, in particular with respect to the effects of personal agency and a lack of standardization in how tools are used [5].

The study presented in this paper adopted a qualitative approach to this problem, based on Affordances, the "actionable properties" that an individual can perceive about a given object [9]. Educators' perceptions of the "actionable properties" of learning analytics were derived from how they spoke about using them, now or in the future. The aim of this study was to probe the ideological and practical assumptions of educators, to determine how this relates to their understanding and intention to use learning analytics to support practice (personal agency). This knowledge can assist the learning analytics research community and other key stakeholders in making more accurate estimations of software engineering requirements, more effective measurements and evaluations of impact, and targeted approaches for deploying learning analytics tools.

É. Lavoué et al. (Eds.): EC-TEL 2017, LNCS 10474, pp. 397–402, 2017.
DOI: 10.1007/978-3-319-66610-5_33

2 Related Work

2.1 The Problem of Relevance

Institutions and educators are currently burdened with an abundance of data about their educational contexts [5]. For example, technology is used to gather and present trace data about learners' activities on the web [15] or within virtual learning environments (VLE) [1,8], to collect data about learners' physiological responses [2], and even to highlight social interactions in learning processes [13]. However, researchers have illustrated that educators are likely to be most interested in using analytics data to interrogate the efficacy of *specific interventions* that they implement in their classrooms, whereas most of the tools with which they are presented are complex and overshoot their requirements [6]. These results indicate a necessity for deeper investigation into what kinds of data matter, to whom they matter and why they matter to support the search for relevance in this vast landscape of information.

2.2 Evaluating Impact

Challenges of relevance are also manifested in how real impact on practice is evaluated. If the data is overwhelming, evaluations are likely to be either too broad or too narrow to get an accurate picture of an educator's *intentions* to use a given tool, their understanding of its utility and their *actual* use of the tool in an authentic environment. For example, research on disparities in how Learning Management System (LMS) tools are used showed that most disparities can be related to *specific* tool, task and interface combinations [12]. At the other end of the spectrum, a 2013 survey of 15 learning analytics dashboard applications for educators and learners found that evaluations of tools were primarily organized around usability studies and efficacy in controlled environments [14]. In a usability study, the perceived utility of the object at the time of evaluation is already provided to the user. This makes it difficult to ascertain how likely an educator is to incorporate the tool into their practice, even if the educator expresses confidence in the tool's utility. The knock-on effect of this tendency is that the research community knows much more about how tools could and should work, than how they *do* work [11].

3 Research Design

To prompt educators to articulate affordances, they were asked to reflect on their perceptions of challenges unique to their practice, their understanding of the "desired state" of successful learning and the steps they believe are necessary to achieve it.

1. *To which extent are educators able to perceive specific affordances of learning analytics? Will those affordances be linked to the educator's domain?*
2. *What recommendations can be made to learning analytics researchers and developers?*

To probe these questions, we deployed a multi-stage, purposive sampling strategy to gain access to educators from various types of institutions (formal and non-formal), who embodied different roles within the institution (staff tutors, associate lecturers, facilitators, module chairs, tutors, etc.). The term "educator" was defined as any individual involved directly in the process of working with learners or developing their curriculum. We conducted 10, 60-min interviews, concluding sampling through saturation and constant comparison among the transcripts. An inductive, qualitative analysis exposed and connected the research participants' perspectives [3]. We coded 1225 participant statements. A second rater coded a random subset of 150 participant statements from 6 of the 10 interviews. We calculated interrater reliability (IRR) using the Cohen's Kappa statistical test [4]. For the first coding procedure, kappa was .76, which rose to .87 after the two individuals coding the data negotiated some of the wording for descriptions of general themes. While this study cannot generalize across a large number of educators and institutions, it did provide a rich description of educators' perceptions and intentions with regard to using learning analytics.

4 Findings

Participants consistently framed their arguments about the challenges they perceive, their ideas of the"desired state", and the ways in which they monitor their progress in terms of their *personal* beliefs about learning and the *goal* of education. Goals tended to cluster around one of three general categories: *to develop strong minds, to prepare learners for practice and to satisfy the learner.* Domain differences were noted in that the goal to develop strong minds was exclusively found among educators working in the social sciences, arts and humanities. STEM [1] educators primarily described preparing learners for practice. Educators with the goal of satisfying learners all had class sizes of 1000+ students (regardless of platform or domain). The domain differences prompted us to conduct an analysis of the modules in which the educators were involved, using the learning design taxonomy provided by the Open University Learning Design Initiative [10] and comparing this to how educators described the classroom experience in the interview evidence. There was consistency between goals and activities for all of the educators' interviews, indicating a conscious learning design, on behalf of the educator, and an expression of their educational epistemology. Interview data suggested that educators with different educational epistemology have significantly different priorities and viewpoints on challenges and success in education. To triangulate these findings, we conducted a frequency analysis of the open codes and discovered that educators with a shared epistemology also tend to share a similar perspective on challenges and desired states. For example, learner background and agency is of particular concern to educators preparing learners for practice, whereas communication and interaction are consistently mentioned as challenges by educators from the social sciences, arts and humanities, who aim to develop strong minds. Analysis of educators' statements

[1] Science, Technology, Engineering and Mathematics.

of the "desired state" also mirrored educators' goals. For example, educators who are preparing students for practice tended to connect performance with having a strong motivation for learning and identification with a specific career objective. Educators who felt they were responsible for developing strong minds tended to determine their success through energy and euphoria in the classroom, particularly in the presence of lively, rich discussion.

4.1 Sources of Data and Affordances of Learning Analytics

An analysis of the kinds of data educators use or need also showed continuity from personal belief structure, through to the affordances that educators perceived in learning analytics. For example, educators preparing their learners for practice appear to focus on the hard evidence that they can see, e.g. if the learner is able to demonstrate skill, if the learner is active in the VLE. While they did show interest in the personal lives of learners, in terms of stress and time management, educators did not see many opportunities for gathering data about learner emotions, unless the student provided it directly. Thus, educators preparing for practice relied more on institutional analytics that predict learner performance or activity. Educators that wished to develop strong minds focused much more on their intuitions about learners and what they can observe in the class. Educators in this category had sincere and significant reservations about how their learners are assessed and whether or not it is a meaningful measure of what they have learned. For this reason, educators with this goal wondered if institutional analytics could collect enough relevant data to support their practice. Figure 1 shows the breakdown of mentions of learning analytics by educational goal. 7 major themes were identified in the transcripts regarding how educators use learning analytics: to understand learner engagement, learner performance, learner motivation and use of resources, to uncover more about the social interactions between learners, to interrogate and modify learning design, and to predict performance.

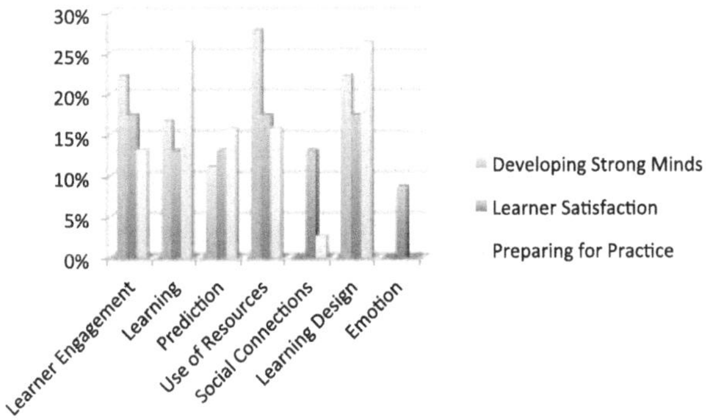

Fig. 1. Affordances by educational goal

One unexpected finding was that only educators in senior roles or with class sizes of 1000+ provided *unprompted* affordances of learning analytics for understanding or improving their practice. This included predictive analytics, which was surprising because tutors and assistant lecturers are responsible for making interventions on the basis of the predictions. Instead, participants described having access to this data as overwhelming and they were unsure of how to interpret it or develop a response. A preference for having the management of this data lie in outside of their own remit was evident.

5 Recommendations for Learning Analytics Research

The tension between having too much and too little data, as described in the previous section on related work, was reflected in our findings. Educators are looking for *relevant data* that is *appropriate for their role* within the institution, makes sense within the context of their *domain* and their *learning design*, and meets their *specific needs* with regard to those contexts. To help educators reduce cognitive load in dealing with analytics data, we recommend that developers and institutions begin to filter educator requirements according to epistemology and learning design. With a clear line from goal to outcome, the path to understanding the impact of learning analytics tools (as a source of actionable information) would be much clearer. It would also provide a mechanism for refining specific analytics that interrogate certain types of learning designs and classroom orchestrations. Finally, it would also make it easier for institutions and developers to build stakeholder buy-in for learning analytics initiatives, by targeting tools toward the most appropriate academic communities.

At the time of writing, the authors are concluding a more in-depth case study of the Open University UK (OU), in which several learning analytics initiatives have already been launched and evaluated.[2] This case study involves both educators and students, connecting affordances of learning analytics with personal educational goals to gather more information for specific software engineering requirements within the OU.

6 Conclusion

The research study described in this paper was designed to explore connections between educators' beliefs about their work and how they perceive and utilize learning analytics. Applying Affordance Theory to the evidence highlighted how the participants in the study currently use learning analytics and their specific reasons for doing so. The findings indicate that an educator's personal, background and belief structure, professional domain, and role within an institution all play a part in their willingness and ability to use learning analytics as a resource for understanding and optimizing learning. The learning analytics community can use this research to help filter requirements and provide more targeted tools that assist educators in fulfilling the responsibilities of their role.

[2] http://www.open.ac.uk/iet/main/research-innovation/learning-analytics.

References

1. Arnold, K.E., Pistilli, M.D.: Course signals at Purdue: using learning analytics to increase student success. In: Proceedings of the 2nd International Conference on Learning Analytics and Knowledge, pp. 267–270. ACM (2012)
2. Blikstein, P.: Multimodal learning analytics. In: Proceedings of the Third International Conference on Learning Analytics and Knowledge, pp. 102–106. ACM (2013)
3. Charmaz, K.: Grounded theory methods in social justice research. Sage Handb. Qual. Res. **4**, 359–380 (2011)
4. Cohen, J.: A coefficient of agreement for nominal scales. Educ. Psychol. Measur. **20**(1), 37–46 (1960)
5. Dawson, S., Gašević, D., Siemens, G., Joksimovic, S.: Current state and future trends: a citation network analysis of the learning analytics field. In: Proceedings of the Fourth International Conference on Learning Analytics and Knowledge, pp. 231–240. ACM (2014)
6. Dyckhoff, A.L., Zielke, D., Bültmann, M., Chatti, M.A., Schroeder, U.: Design and implementation of a learning analytics toolkit for teachers. Educ. Technol. Soc. **15**(3), 58–76 (2012)
7. Ferguson, R.: Learning analytics: drivers, developments and challenges. Int. J. Technol. Enhanc. Learn. **4**(5–6), 304–317 (2012)
8. Kuzilek, J., Hlosta, M., Herrmannova, D., Zdrahal, Z., Wolff, A.: OU analyse: analysing at-risk students at the open university. Learn. Anal. Rev. 1–16 (2015)
9. Norman, D.A.: Affordance, conventions, and design. Interactions **6**(3), 38–43 (1999)
10. Rienties, B., Toetenel, L., Bryan, A.: Scaling up learning design: impact of learning design activities on LMS behavior and performance. In: Proceedings of the Fifth International Conference on Learning Analytics And Knowledge, pp. 315–319. ACM (2015)
11. Rodriguez Triana, M.J., Prieto Santos, L.P., Vozniuk, A., Shirvani Boroujeni, M., Schwendimann, B.A., Holzer, A.C., Gillet, D.: Monitoring, awareness and reflection in blended technology enhanced learning: a systematic review. Technical report (2016)
12. Schoonenboom, J.: Using an adapted, task-level technology acceptance model to explain why instructors in higher education intend to use some learning management system tools more than others. Comput. Educ. **71**, 247–256 (2014)
13. Shum, S.B., Ferguson, R.: Social learning analytics. Educ. Technol. Soc. **15**(3), 3–26 (2012)
14. Verbert, K., Duval, E., Klerkx, J., Govaerts, S., Santos, J.L.: Learning analytics dashboard applications. Am. Behav. Sci. **57**(10), 1500–1509 (2013)
15. Winne, P.H., Hadwin, A.F.: nStudy: tracing and supporting self-regulated learning in the internet. In: Azevedo, R., Aleven, V. (eds.) International Handbook of Metacognition and Learning Technologies. SIHE, vol. 28, pp. 293–308. Springer, New York (2013). doi:10.1007/978-1-4419-5546-3_20

Affordances for Capturing and Re-enacting Expert Performance with Wearables

Will Guest[1], Fridolin Wild[1], Alla Vovk[1(✉)], Mikhail Fominykh[2], Bibeg Limbu[3], Roland Klemke[3], Puneet Sharma[4], Jaakko Karjalainen[5], Carl Smith[6], Jazz Rasool[6], Soyeb Aswat[7], Kaj Helin[5], Daniele Di Mitri[3], and Jan Schneider[3]

[1] Oxford Brookes University, Oxford, UK
{16102434, wild, 16022839}@brookes.ac.uk
[2] Europlan UK Ltd., London, UK
mikhail.fominykh@europlan-uk.eu
[3] Open University of the Netherlands, Heerlen, Netherlands
{bibeg.limbu, Roland.Klemke, Daniele.Dimitri, jan.schneider}@ou.nl
[4] University of Tromsø, Tromsø, Norway
puneet.sharma@uit.no
[5] VTT, Espoo, Finland
{Jaakko.karjalainen, Kaj.Helin}@vtt.fi
[6] Ravensbourne, London, UK
{c.smith, j.rasool}@rave.ac.uk
[7] Myndplay, London, UK
soyeb@myndplay.com

Abstract. The WEKIT.one prototype is a platform for immersive procedural training with wearable sensors and Augmented Reality. Focusing on capture and re-enactment of human expertise, this work looks at the unique affordances of suitable hard- and software technologies. The practical challenges of interpreting expertise, using suitable sensors for its capture and specifying the means to describe and display to the novice are of central significance here. We link affordances with hardware devices, discussing their alternatives, including Microsoft Hololens, Thalmic Labs MYO, Alex Posture sensor, MyndPlay EEG headband, and a heart rate sensor. Following the selection of sensors, we describe integration and communication requirements for the prototype. We close with thoughts on the wider possibilities for implementation and next steps.

Keywords: Affordances · Augmented reality · Wearable technologies · Capturing expertise

1 Introduction

In recent years, delivery devices and sensor technology evolved significantly, while costs of hard- and software and development kits decreased rapidly, bringing about novel opportunities for the development of multi-sensor, augmented reality systems that will be investigated here for their ability to contribute to the much needed

É. Lavoué et al. (Eds.): EC-TEL 2017, LNCS 10474, pp. 403–409, 2017.
DOI: 10.1007/978-3-319-66610-5_34

continuous up-skilling of already skilled workers (to support product innovation), as they usually do not get enough vocational training in Europe: According to the Eurostat's lifelong learning statistics, e.g., the EU-27 show only a participation rate of 10.7%, instead of the 2020 target of 15% [1].

In this paper, we elaborate which affordances are both possible and needed for capturing of expert experience and its guided re-enactment by trainees. Our understanding of 'affordance', beginning with Gibson's notion of a subject finding usefulness in their environment [2], finds interesting application with the inclusion of virtual elements into the environment, specifically those with which the user can interact. Affordances are opportunities for action and belong neither to the environment nor to the individual directly, but rather to the relationships between them [3].

Capturing and re-enactment of expert performance is a form of Performance Augmentation, serving, for example, as scaffold in training procedural tasks, possibly increasing training efficiency (reduced time to competence, increased number of iterations at same cost, with less constraints on trainer involvement) and training effectiveness (error proofing with more active learning under direct guidance).

In this paper, we unravel affordances that are conducive to capturing and re-enactment of experience. We outline recent work in this domain (Sect. 2), those affordances of particular interest and the hardware selection that offers them (Sect. 3), and, finally, concluding remarks with next steps and current limitations (Sect. 4).

2 Background and Related Work

Ericsson and Smith define expert performance as consistently-superior, effective behaviour on a specified set of representative tasks [4]. Expert performance can be attained in a particular domain through collecting experience in a deliberate manner, differing from everyday skills in the level of proficiency as well as in the level of conscious and continuous planning invested into updating and upgrading.

Apprentices often collect experience in their craft through hands-on practice under supervision of an expert, rather than from written manuals or textbooks. As Newell and Simon propose, the outstanding performance of the expert is the result of incremental increase in knowledge and skill due to continuous exposure to experience [5]. Enabling experts to share their experience with apprentices in a perceptible way is an essential aspect of expertise development.

Wearable sensors and AR bear potential to capture expert performance and knowledge contained in a training activity. If knowledge is stored in such learning activity, it can be re-experienced many times over, analysed, and reflected upon, individually or collaboratively [6, 7]. AR then provides a rich multimodal and multisensory medium for apprentices to observe captured expert performance. Such medium enriches the apprentice's experience, augmenting their perception through visual, audio, and haptic modes. AR overlays virtual content on the real environment to create an immersive platform [8, 9], placing the apprentice in a real-world context, engaging all senses. Augmented perception allows better interaction with the environment [10], equipping apprentices with better tools to mimic expert performance and build knowledge. Fominykh et al. provide an overview on existing approaches for capturing performance in the real world [6], with consideration also given to the tacit knowledge and the its role in learning new tasks.

3 Affordances for Capturing and Re-enactment

The WEKIT framework guides the sensor selection process [7] identifying affordances that allow the capture of specific key aspects of expert performance and provision of affordances to the trainees in re-enactment (Table 1). For each affordance, suitable technological solutions are considered together with the type of sensor that would need to be used.

Table 1. Affordances in capturing and re-enactment of expert performance using sensors

Affordance	Applications for prototype	Sensor types	Related work
Virtual/tangible manipulation, object enrichment	Record of inertial data	Wireless inertial sensor, depth camera	[10–15]
Contextualisation, In situ real time feedback, haptic hints	Record of force applied	Pressure sensor	[16, 17]
Directed focus, Contextualisation	Record of eye tracking data or gaze direction	Eye tracker, gyroscope	[18, 19]
Self-awareness of physical state	Monitor and record physiological data	EEG, EMG, ECG, gyroscope, accelerometer, VHR	[17, 20–22]
Virtual post it (annotation), Contextualisation	Record annotations and display in AR	AR and spatial environment	[12, 23]
Think aloud	Record audio	Microphone	[24]
Remote symmetrical tele-assistance, zoom	Record video	Camera	[24]

The proposed hardware framework for capturing expertise and re-enactment is depicted in Fig. 1, accommodating for comfort, wearability and accessibility.

This hardware platform uses panels incorporated into the garment to encase both the Myo Armband and the heart rate sensor at the wrist, with wire casing running up the outer sleeve. Sensors sit flat against the body and do not move about with wear. The hardware prototype integrates sensors in total a wearable item of clothing, connecting a Microsoft Hololens, a Thalmic Labs MYO, an Alex Posture sensor, an EEG headband, and a heart rate sensor [25]. The garment provides an inclusion for wires of posture sensor and armband connecting them with the smart glasses. Additional, adjustable casings for Leap Motion sensors were designed for use on the arms and torso.

Choosing AR glasses was based on a requirements analysis report [25]. After taking into consideration features such as built-in microphone array, environment capture, gesture tracking, mixed reality capture, Wi-Fi 802.11ac, and fully untethered holographic computing, Microsoft Hololens was selected. Furthermore, the built in components of Hololens enable us to capture several different attributes of the user and her environment. For EEG, the MyndBand and Neurosky chipset were favoured due to the availability of the processed data and real time feedback. For detecting hand, arm movements and gestures: Leap Motion and Myo armband were chosen. To track the position and angle of the neck, Alex posture tracker was suggested.

In Table 2, we look at the requirements associated with capturing, re-enactment, and data bandwidth. We can clearly see that different sensors require different bandwidths. It is particularly high for video signals (e.g., AR display, Point of view) and low for Myo, Myndband, and Alex posture tracker.

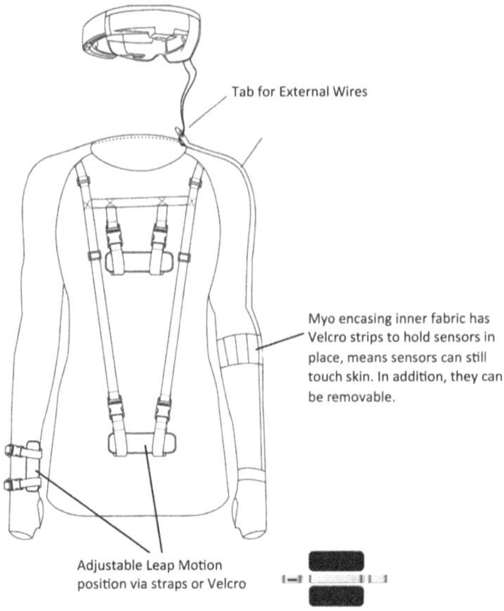

Fig. 1. WEKIT wearable solution

4 Concluding Remarks

Understanding that both expert and learner advance from the affordances provided by wearable technology, we make begin to weave together the requirements for maximising the benefit at each stage of knowledge transfer. This paper summarises the integration of new knowledge on the pedagogical level (by creating the WEKIT learning framework), technological level (by designing a hard- and software for

Table 2. Selected sensors and requirements for capturing, and re-enactment

Sensors	Requirements for capturing affordances	Requirements for re-enactment affordances	Requirements for bandwidth
AR glasses (Hololens)	Track location of user and objects in the environment	View instructions, activity, videos, and virtual post-its, application	High (60 fps, maximum resolution 1268 by 720 per eye)
Point of view camera (Hololens)	Start/stop video recording, take digital pictures, enable/disable camera, capturing current view	Capturing current point of view, enable/disable point of view camera	High (2.4-megapixel resolution)

(*continued*)

Table 2. (*continued*)

Sensors	Requirements for capturing affordances	Requirements for re-enactment affordances	Requirements for bandwidth
Built-in microphone (Hololens)	Start/stop the microphone, enable/disable microphone	Start/stop the microphone, enable/disable microphone	Moderate (4 audio streams)
Gaze (Hololens)	Estimate gaze direction, select objects in the environment, place virtual post-its	Estimate gaze direction, select objects in the environment, place virtual post-its	Low (XYZ coordinates)
MyndBand and Neurosky chipset	Estimate attention, focus eye blinks, and other metrics, enable/disable EEG	Estimate attention, focus eye blinks, and other metrics, enable/disable EEG	Low (Attention and stress levels, range [0,100])
Leap Motion	Recognize hand movements and gestures	Recognize hand movements and gestures	Moderate (3D model, skeleton data)
Position tracker (Myo)	Recognize gestures and location of user	Recognize gestures, use vibrations as feedback on some activities	Low (XYZ coordinates and gestures)
Electromyogram (Myo)	Recognise hand movements	Recognise hand movements	Low (gestures)
Alex posture tracker	Recognize posture	Vibration feedback	Low (XYZ coordinates)

capturing and re-enactment of expertise), and on the semantic level (by describing a process model for sharing and dissemination of task performance).

As a training method, expertise capturing needs to complement existing/new technical documentation. It has to be done at the right level of abstraction and enabling comparison of performances using the recorded data. Both knowledge capture and representation should strive to blend with the user's actions, considering the manner in which information is conveyed and ensuring that it is realistic, believable and correct. With the right hardware and a software platform, this method will provide trainees with a useful approximation to the full experience of becoming the expert, enabling immersive, in-situ, and intuitive learning just as a traditional apprentice would, following in the footsteps of the master and fitted with the specialist knowledge of technical communicators.

References

1. Eurostat: Lifelong learning statistics (2016). http://ec.europa.eu/eurostat/statistics-explained/index.php/Lifelong_learning_statistics
2. Gibson, J.J.: The theory of affordances. In: Shaw, R., Bransford, J. (eds.) Perceiving, Acting, and Knowing: Toward an Ecological Psychology, pp. 67–82 (1977)
3. Rizzo, A.: The origin and design of intentional affordances. In: Proceedings 6th Conference Designing Interactive Systems, University Park, PA, USA, pp. 239–240. ACM, New York (2006)
4. Ericsson, K.A., Smith, J.: Prospects and limits of the empirical study of expertise: an introduction. In: Ericsson, K.A., Smith, J. (eds.) Toward a General Theory of Expertise: Prospects and Limits, pp. 1–39. Cambridge University Press, Cambridge (1991)
5. Newell, A., Simon, H.A.: Human Problem Solving. Prentice Hall, Englewood Cliffs (1972)
6. Fominykh, M., Wild, F., Smith, C., Alvarez, V., Morozov, M.: An overview of capturing live experience with virtual and augmented reality. In: Preuveneers, D. (ed.) Workshop Proceedings of the 11th International Conference on Intelligent Environments, pp. 298–305. IOS Press, Amsterdam (2015)
7. Limbu, B., Fominykh, M., Klemke, R., Specht, M., Wild, F.: Supporting training of expertise with wearable technologies: the WEKIT reference framework. In: The International Handbook of Mobile and Ubiquitous Learning. Springer, New York (2017)
8. Bacca, J., Baldiris, S., Fabregat, R., Graf, S.: Kinshuk: augmented reality trends in education: a systematic review of research and applications. Educ. Technol. Soc. **17**(4), 133–149 (2014)
9. Bower, M., Sturman, D.: What are the educational affordances of wearable technologies? Comput. Educ. **88**, 343–353 (2015)
10. Wagner, R.K., Sternberg, R.J.: Practical intelligence in real-world pursuits: the role of tacit knowledge. J. Pers. Soc. Psychol. **49**(2), 436–458 (1985)
11. Wei, Y., Yan, H., Bie, R., Wang, S., Sun, L.: Performance monitoring and evaluation in dance teaching with mobile sensing technology. Pers. Ubiquit. Comput. **18**(8), 1929–1939 (2014)
12. Li, H., Lu, M., Chan, G., Skitmore, M.: Proactive training system for safe and efficient precast installation. Autom. Constr. **49**(Part A), 163–174 (2015)
13. Prabhu, V.A., Elkington, M., Crowley, D., Tiwari, A., Ward, C.: Digitisation of manual composite layup task knowledge using gaming technology. Compos. Part B: Eng. **112**, 314–326 (2017)
14. Jang, S.-A., Kim, H.-i., Woo, W., Wakefield, G.: AiRSculpt: a wearable augmented reality 3D sculpting system. In: Streitz, N., Markopoulos, P. (eds.) DAPI 2014. LNCS, vol. 8530, pp. 130–141. Springer, Cham (2014). doi:10.1007/978-3-319-07788-8_13
15. Meleiro, P., Rodrigues, R., Jacob, J., Marques, T.: Natural user interfaces in the motor development of disabled children. Procedia Technol. **13**, 66–75 (2014)
16. Araki, A., Makiyama, K., Yamanaka, H., Ueno, D., Osaka, K., Nagasaka, M., Yamada, T., Yao, M.: Comparison of the performance of experienced and novice surgeons. Surg. Endosc. **31**(4), 1999–2005 (2017)
17. Asadipour, A., Debattista, K., Chalmers, A.: Visuohaptic augmented feedback for enhancing motor skills acquisition. Vis. Comput. **33**(4), 401–411 (2017)
18. Kim, S., Dey, A.K.: Augmenting human senses to improve the user experience in cars. Multimed. Tools Appl. **75**(16), 9587–9607 (2016)
19. Ke, F., Lee, S., Xu, X.: Teaching training in a mixed-reality integrated learning environment. Comput. Hum. Behav. **62**, 212–220 (2016)

20. Duente, T., Pfeiffer, M., Rohs, M.: On-skin technologies for muscle sensing and actuation. In: Proceedings of UbiComp 2016, pp. 933–936. ACM, New York (2016)
21. Kwon, Y., Lee, S., Jeong, J., Kim, W.: HeartiSense: a novel approach to enable effective basic life support training without an instructor. In: CHI 2014 Extended Abstracts on Human Factors in Computing Systems, pp. 431–434. ACM, New York (2014)
22. Benedetti, F., Catenacci Volpi, N., Parisi, L., Sartori, G.: Attention training with an easy–to–use brain computer interface. In: Shumaker, R., Lackey, S. (eds.) VAMR 2014. LNCS, vol. 8526, pp. 236–247. Springer, Cham (2014). doi:10.1007/978-3-319-07464-1_22
23. Kowalewski, K.-F., Hendrie, J.D., Schmidt, M.W., Garrow, C.R., Bruckner, T., Proctor, T., Paul, S., Adigüzel, D., Bodenstedt, S., Erben, A., Kenngott, H., Erben, Y., Speidel, S., Müller-Stich, B.P., Nickel, F.: Development and validation of a sensor-and expert model-based training system for laparoscopic surgery: the iSurgeon. Surg. Endosc. **31**, 1–11 (2016)
24. Sanfilippo, F.: A multi-sensor fusion framework for improving situational awareness in demanding maritime training. Reliabil. Eng. Syst. Saf. **161**, 12–24 (2017)
25. Sharma, P., Wild, F., Klemke, R., Helin, K., Azam, T.: Requirement analysis and sensor specifications: First version. WEKIT, D3.1 (2016)

An Ontology for Describing Scenarios of Multi-players Learning Games: Toward an Automatic Detection of Group Interactions

Mathieu Guinebert[1(✉)], Amel Yessad[1], Mathieu Muratet[1,2], and Vanda Luengo[1]

[1] Sorbonnes Universités, UPMC Univ Paris 06, CNRS, LIP6 UMR 7606, 4 place Jussieu, 75005 Paris, France
mathieu.guinebert@lip6.fr

[2] INS HEA, 58-60 Avenue des Landes, 92150 Suresnes, France

Abstract. Multi-players learning games (MPLG) tend to foster learners' engagement and immersion in learning games' activities. They are an interesting way to organize learning situations in which learners interact with each other and solve challenges.

In this context, teachers need to orchestrate MPLGs' scenarios to arouse desired interactions such as cooperation, collaboration or competition. Do the intended interactions by the teachers occur when learners really play the scenario?

Developing an automatic system to help teachers to detect interactions between learners in a MPLG's scenario or to help them to build a multi-players scenario according to their objectives in term of interactions is a challenging task. This is largely due to the lack of formal and shared model that describes MPLG's scenario accurately.

In this paper, we present an ontology that formalizes MPLG's scenarios and their identified requirements: the modularity, the multiple roles, the resource management and the final state. The ontology was built iteratively by using the methodology METHONTOLOGY and used to model the knowledge of four different MPLGs' scenario. A study was carried out in order to check the completeness of the ontology and the effectiveness of the knowledge modeling process.

Keywords: Multi-player learning games · Scenarios · Group interactions · Ontology · Knowledge modeling

1 Introduction

A number of research shows that learners' engagement and learning are better when they interact with each other [1, 2]. Multi-player Learning Games (MPLG) are learning environments that foster interactions between learners, namely group interactions, such as cooperation, collaboration and competition. Thanks to their immersive and multiuser potential, they hold strong potential for learning as they can support the acquisition of higher order skills in an effective, efficient, and attractive way [3]. Thus, MPLGs offer to learner's virtual worlds in which they can actively participate, where what they know

É. Lavoué et al. (Eds.): EC-TEL 2017, LNCS 10474, pp. 410–415, 2017.
DOI: 10.1007/978-3-319-66610-5_35

is directly related to what they are able to do [3]. Their deployment enables social interaction and role play, personalized and experiential learning, and learner empowerment through increased interactivity [3]. However, only fewer research address the analysis and the automatic detection of interactions between learners in MPLG scenarios. It could bring a useful feedback to teachers and learning game designers to improve scenarios according to their needs.

Indeed, many research questions are related: Which types of group interactions do the teachers arouse in their MPLG scenarios? Which interactions' types emerge from players' behaviors in a MPLG scenario? Do the targeted goals by the teacher's influence players' interactions and so the MPLG's scenario progression?

The objective of our research is to analyze MPLG scenarios orchestrated by teachers in order to identify group interactions statically (offline) and thus to help them to improve modify the scenarios to match better to their needs/goals.

In this paper, we present a formal language to model MPLG scenarios (this is the first step to achieve the automatic analysis of scenarios). This formal language has to be well adapted to model MPLGs' scenarios and their features such as: multiple roles, activities, player inventories, game resources, knowledge and competencies. We choose to model scenarios with an ontology: MPLGO (Multi-Player Learning Game Ontology). The ontological language is a pivot language that should provide a formal and a shared interface, allowing the interaction's detection system to interact with quite different MPLG's scenarios. To evaluate MPLGO, a study was carried out in order to check its completeness and the effectiveness of knowledge modeling process of MPLG scenarios.

In the next section, we present a brief overview of related works. In the Sect. 2, we describe the proposed model of MPLG's scenarios and the ontology we created to formalize it. Finally, we describe the evaluation of MPLGO and the obtained results.

2 Related Work

A number of online platforms (Emergo[1] [4], Fablusi[2], Cyberdam[3], etc.) enable teachers to develop their own learning game scenarios efficiently. These platforms allow the development of multi-role-playing games where learners take on roles of specific characters. However, these platforms do not provide the teachers with information about the matching degree between the created scenarios and their needs, especially if the scenarios are multiplayer, nonlinear and arouse interactions such as cooperation, collaboration or competition.

Several research works address the issue of describing learning scenarios. An interesting framework is the Learning Design (IMS LD) specification. Many initiatives have been undertaken to build authoring tools in order to use IMS Learning Design (IMS LD) specification that are simple enough to be used by teachers and non-technical pedagogical engineers [5]. McAndrew et al. [6] point out that even at the simplest level (the level A of IMS LD), IMS LD (itself draws on the Educational Modelling Language developed

[1] https://sourceforge.net/projects/emergo/, acceded last 23/04/17.
[2] http://www.fablusi.com/, acceded last 23/04/17.
[3] http://www.cyberdam.nl/, acceded last 23/04/17.

at the Open University of the Netherlands [7]) has the power to describe complex collaborative learning tasks with multiple roles and tools. Although the specification was conceived as very powerful considering its pedagogical expressiveness [8], it didn't reach a high level of adoption, due to its perceived complexity [5]. In addition, IMS LD lacks of flexibility because the activity sequences and learning resources are rigidly defined during authoring and the instructors cannot give "their personal touch" to courses [9].

Another interesting research is the model MoPPLiq [10]. MoPPLiq is a formal design model allowing teachers to build learning game scenarios by linking learning game activities between them, based on prerequisite relationships that exist between activities' competence inputs. However, MoPPLiq is well-adapted to quite linear mono-player learning games and not at all adapted to multi-player learning games. In addition, MoPPLiq is described by a XML model with limited inference capabilities.

The model proposed here to describe MPLG scenarios takes into account four requirements to be met by the scenarios: the modularity, the multiple roles, the resource management and the goal state. Above all, in our work, we aim to describe MPLG scenarios formally in order to allow interoperation between applications such as the interactions' detection system or the learners' traces analyzer.

3 Scenarios and Activities of MPLG

3.1 Scenarios in MPLG and Requirements

Inspired by the definition of [11], scenario-based MPLGs that interested us are games where learners are placed in complex problem spaces. They are confronted with problems, often allowing multiple solutions and requiring application of necessary methodologies or tools and various types of interactions with fellow learners.

Based on this definition and the analysis of 17 games with different genres, gameplays and goals (Sciences en Jeu, Taiga Park, Hiragana battle, Refraction, Battlefield, Europa Universalis, classic MMORPGs, etc.), we extracted key concepts and properties that allowed us to build the ontology describing MPLG scenarios. The development process of the ontology was driven by four requirements of the MPLG's scenarios which emerged from the analysis of these 17 games and the interviews with learning game experts and experienced gamers.

First, MPLGO has to allow a modular description of scenarios in order to increase their flexibility thereby enabling the description of a large panel of games. In our case, the modularity means that each MPLG's scenario can be decomposed into elementary scenarios that are themselves decomposed into game activities. An elementary scenario ES is a couple (A, a) composed of a set "A" of MPLG activities and the activity "a" which represents the final activity of the elementary scenario ES, enabling players to switch to another elementary scenario.

Second, the ontology has to allow the description of multiple roles that players can take in MPLG's activities, an important feature of a MPLG.

Third, MPLGO has to formalize the resource management in MPLGs. It consists on describing the game objects that are consumed and these produced by players who take on roles in an activity. This concern also the competences the players have to perform in an activity and those that the players could acquire at the end of the activity. Each player owns his/her inventory composed of his/her resources (game objects and competences). The player's inventory is updated at the end of an activity. Thus, performing an activity allows player to use and acquire resources according to consuming and producing rules, associated to the role that the player takes on in the activity. Of course, these rules constrain the sequencing of activities in the scenario. Thus, according to the resource consuming and producing in activities, we may have a wide range of scenarios, from very linear scenarios to very open scenarios without sequencing constraints. Furthermore, to be able to represent more complex rules for consummation and production of resources, we created a formal grammar. This grammar uses Variable and Resources to express more efficiently multi-outcomes Activities.

Finally, the ontology has to allow the description of the goal state of the scenario which expresses the teacher's objective. This requirement is a significant difference with some multi-players video games where achieving a goal is not always necessary. The goal state is given by the teacher and could express victory conditions of the scenario like the acquiring of competences by the players or other specific states of the players' inventories.

The Fig. 1 is a conceptual model that shows MPLGO's classes and properties. The colors are used to denote the link between the ontology components and the four requirements of the MPLG's scenario.

3.2 Activities in the MPLGs' Scenarios

The need to formalize an activity has prompted us to define this concept accurately. We consider an activity in a MPLG's scenario as a challenge for players allowing them to reach objectives (win a medal, acquire a competence, etc.). It is the indivisible unit belonging to a MPLG's scenario. It is composed of various roles consuming and producing game resources. In addition, the roles may be dependent on the players' competences and the success in an activity allows the players to acquire the competences associated to their roles. A resource belongs either to the player inventory or to the world inventory. The world inventory contains resources that are available for all players and not owned by only one player.

The ontology concepts must be able to correctly and easily represent the objects of the MPLGs' scenarios related to the four requirements described above. For this, we have used the methodology METHONTOLOGY [12] that gave us a set of guidelines to build MPLGO from scratch. We instantiated MPLGO to model 4 different MPLG scenarios. The models are available at:

https://cloud.lip6.fr/index.php/s/A8y4w1aEXp42Vz5.

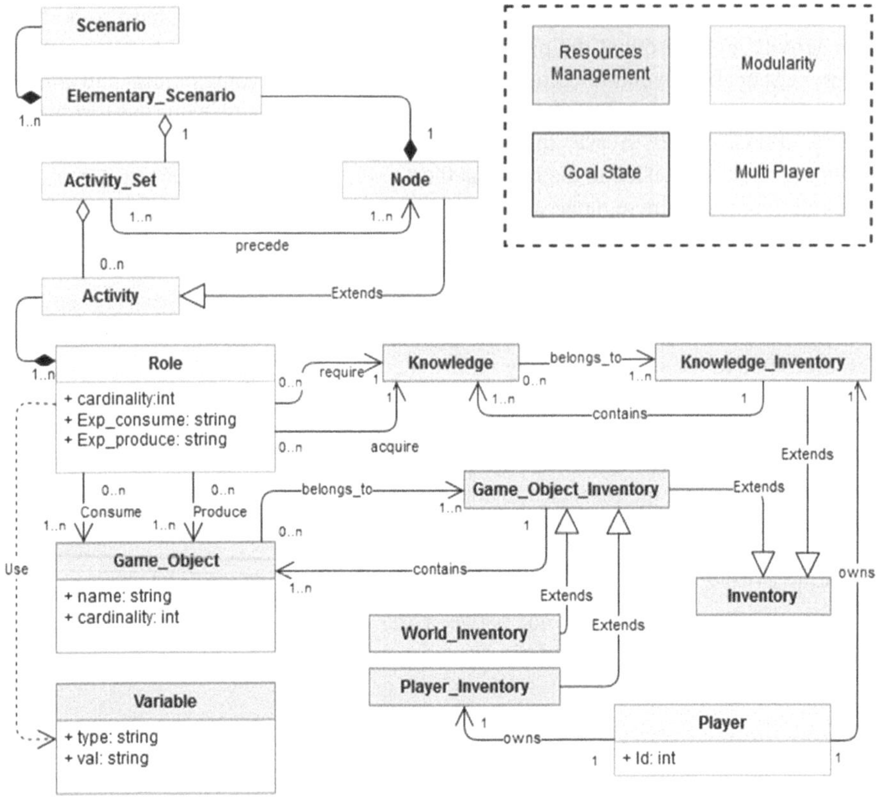

Fig. 1. Conceptual model of MLPGO.

4 Conclusion

Detecting automatically interactions between players in MPLG scenarios is a challenging task. In order to do so, we must first have a formal model to represent scenarios. In this paper, we presented the ontology MPLGO, built to describe the main features the scenario should have: modularity, multiple roles, resource management and a goal state. These features emerged from the analysis of 17 games and interviews with learning game experts and experienced gamers. The methodology METHONTOLOGY was used to give us a set of guidelines to build MPLGO.

This model is the first step of our work and deeper studies should be carried out on various MPLGs to ensure both its usability and efficiency. Afterwards, the next step consists on querying the knowledge model of MPLG's scenario to analyze and detect automatically group interactions.

Acknowledgements. We would like to thank the EIAH Chair of Sorbonne-Universités for financing this work.

References

1. Eseryel, D., Law, V., Ifenthaler, D., Ge, X., Miller, R.: An investigation of the interrelationships between motivation, engagement, and complex problem solving in game-based learning. Educ. Technol. Soc. **17**(1), 42–53 (2014)
2. Bell, B.S., Kozlowski, S.W.: Advances in technology-based training. In: Managing Human Resources in North America, pp. 27–42 (2007)
3. Nadolski, R.J., Hummel, H.G., Slootmaker, A., Van der Vegt, W.: Architectures for developing multiuser, immersive learning scenarios. Simul. Gaming **43**(6), 825–852 (2012)
4. Slootmaker, A., Kurvers, H., Hummel, H.G., Koper, R.: Developing scenario-based serious games for complex cognitive skills acquisition: design, development and evaluation of the EMERGO platform. J. UCS **20**(4), 561–582 (2014)
5. Hermans, H., Janssen, J., Koper, R.: Flexible authoring and delivery of online courses using IMS learning design. Interact. Learn. Environ. **24**(6), 1265–1279 (2016)
6. McAndrew, P., Goodyear, P., Dalziel, J.: Patterns, designs and activities: unifying descriptions of learning structures. Int. J. Learn. Technol. **2**(2), 216–242 (2006)
7. Hummel, H.G.K., Manderveld, J.M., Tattersall, C., Koper, E.J.R.: Educational modelling language and learning design: new opportunities for instructional reusability and personalised learning. Int. J. Learn. Technol. **1**(1), 111–126 (2004)
8. Derntl, M., Neumann, S., Griffiths, D., Oberhuemer, P.: The conceptual structure of IMS learning design does not impede its use for authoring. IEEE Trans. Learn. Technol. **5**(1), 74–86 (2012)
9. de-la-Fuente-Valentín, L., Leony, D., Pardo, A., Kloos, C.D.: Towards flexibility on IMS learning design scripts. In: Frontiers in Education Conference, FIE 2011, p. T1E-1. IEEE, October 2011
10. Marne, B., Labat, J.M.: Model and authoring tool to help teachers adapt serious games to their educational contexts. Int. J. Learn. Technol. **9**(2), 161–180 (2014)
11. Westera, W., Nadolski, R.J., Hummel, H.G., Wopereis, I.G.: Serious games for higher education: a framework for reducing design complexity. J. Comput. Assist. Learn. **24**(5), 420–432 (2008)
12. Fernández-López, M., Gómez-Pérez, A., Juristo, N.: Methontology: from ontological art towards ontological engineering (1997)

Identifying Misconceptions with Active Recall in a Blended Learning System

Matthias Hauswirth(✉) and Andrea Adamoli

Università della Svizzera italiana, Via Giuseppe Buffi 13, 6904 Lugano, Switzerland
{Matthias.Hauswirth,Andrea.Adamoli}@usi.ch

Abstract. Active recall is a pedagogical technique that improves learning. In this paper we investigate a second benefit of active recall: its use to identify student misconceptions, early on, even before students first solve quizzes, assignments, or exams. We describe our approach to collect recall statements in a blended learning system and perform a small pilot study which shows that using active recall in a programming course can uncover rich sets of student misconceptions about programming.

1 Introduction

In many university courses, especially when using blended or flipped classroom approaches, students first get exposed to new concepts through a textbook section or a video. Reading texts and watching videos are *passive* forms of direct instruction. They are helpful for introducing a concept, but they are not very effective for learning. *Active* recall, the practice of information retrieval by students as a study technique, has been shown to significantly increase the effectiveness of learning [5]. A comparative study by Karpicke and Blunt [4] further found that active recall can be superior to an alternative study technique, concept mapping, even if students were asked to ultimately draw concept maps of their newly learned concepts.

A student using an active recall approach will spend considerable time recalling what they just learned. This can be done in various ways, for example by writing down in free form text whatever they can recall. The point of active recall is the *production* of such statements; once a student has created them, they are not really needed anymore. We believe that such recall statements actually might contain valuable information about students' conceptual understanding, and we wondered whether we could use them to identify student misconceptions. For this reason we conducted a small pilot study, on which we report in this short paper.

The remainder of this paper is structured as follows. Section 2 describes the methodology of our pilot study; Sect. 3 presents and discusses our results; and Sect. 4 concludes.

2 Methodology

To determine whether it is reasonable to use recall statements for the identification of misconceptions, we extended a learning management system to allow us

É. Lavoué et al. (Eds.): EC-TEL 2017, LNCS 10474, pp. 416–421, 2017.
DOI: 10.1007/978-3-319-66610-5_36

to collect recall statements, we used that system in an undergraduate programming course, and we manually analyzed the collected recall statements.

2.1 System

We implemented the active recall approach in the Informa blended learning system.[1] Informa is a mix between a traditional learning management system and a MOOC platform. It organizes course material into a hierarchy of themes and topics. For each topic, it lists a set of skills students are expected to acquire, and it provides study tasks that help students in their studies. A central kind of study task is a reading assignment, which directs students to work through a set of textbook sections related to the topic. We extended Informa to collect recall statements from students for the textbook sections they read (Fig. 1). For each textbook section, a student goes through 4 stages: They have not yet started to read ("Prepare" stage), they are reading the section ("Read"), they are recalling what they just learned ("Recall"), and they can view and optionally revise their recall statement ("Review").

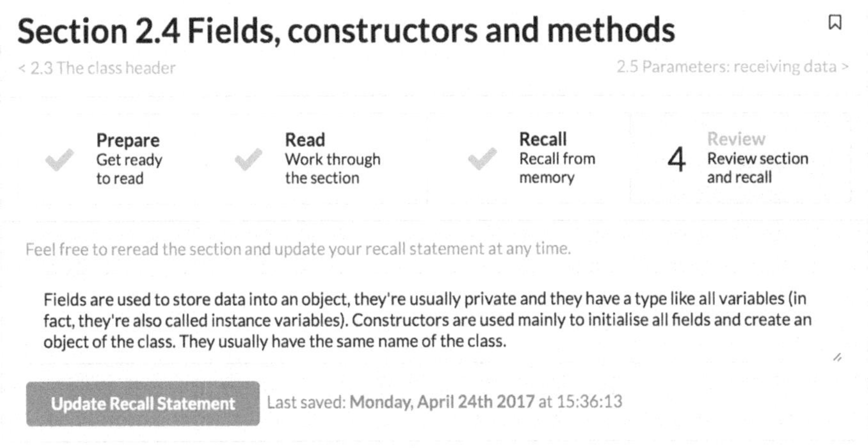

Fig. 1. Recall statement involving the concepts of *field* and *constructor*

2.2 Course

We conducted this study in a second-semester undergraduate programming course. The course taught object-oriented programming in Java using the fifth edition of *Objects First with Java* [1] as a textbook. Students were asked to read the corresponding textbook sections as a preparation for lectures, quizzes, and homework assignments. They received 10% of their grade for submitting high quality recall statements, and they were told that the teaching team would read all of their recalls to assess them.

[1] https://informa.inf.usi.ch/, https://bitbucket.org/hauswirth/informamastery.

2.3 Analysis Approach

A textbook section rarely discusses an individual concept in isolation. This means that the analysis of a textbook recall statement may bring out student conceptions about multiple concepts. Moreover, a recall statement usually includes multiple propositions about a concept. Thus it often reflects more than one conception for any given concept.

Our analysis followed a three step process: (1) We selected three *recall statements* from the first three chapters of the book, which focus on the key concepts covered by prior misconception research [2,3,6]. We picked the statements based on a manual assessment of all recall statements, and we focused on statements that were assessed with a lower score, and which thus had a higher chance of involving misconceptions. (2) We manually broke down each selected recall statement into a set of *propositions*. We did this by reading the student-provided statement and breaking it into phrases. We ignored the correctness of the resulting propositions. (3) We then used the conceptions represented by these propositions, and our understanding of the underying concepts, to formulate *conceptual questions* that would help to confirm potential misconceptions.

Our analysis is inspired by the Socratic way of teaching, where an instructor takes a students' statement as a basis for asking follow-up questions. Thus, the set of propositions in a given student recall caused us to formulate several questions, each question probing about a potential misconception.

3 Results

The 54 students in the course submitted a total of 5358 recall statements for the 181 sections in the 14 main chapters of the book. This is an average of 99 statements per student.

On average we collected 29 recall statements per textbook section, starting with 42 statements per section in Chapters 1 and declining to 8 statements per section in Chapters 14. The section with the largest number of recall statements got 50 statements, which means that 4 of the 54 students never submitted any recalls. Nevertheless, the overall number of recall statements is surprisingly high and provides a rich source of information to mine for misconceptions.

Missing Conceptions. We found that many textbook recalls do not cover *all* the concepts discussed in the corresponding textbook section. A student might just have omitted the concept because they did not recall it, or they found it to be less important in the given section. Alternatively, a student's conception also simply might not have been clear enough for the student to be able to express it. Nevertheless, note that even a recall statement that does not cover all the concepts of a section is valuable for misconception identification.

Non-conceptual Content. Book sections discuss concepts, but not exclusively. Much of the text in the book provides *context* surrounding the concepts (e.g., motivating the concepts or providing meta-information). Recall statements often include such non-conceptual content (e.g., "Summary of chapters 1" or "just talks about a new project 'lab-classes' which will help us understand new concepts."). We ignore these parts of the recall statements in our analysis.

3.1 Analysis of Recall Statements

We now present the selected recall statements, their breakdown into the underlying propositions, and the conceptual questions we derived.

Recall Statement: *"A class is a set of objects having the same proprieties. An instance is an object from a class."* (Section 1.1. Objects and classes.)

Propositions:

- A class is a **set** of objects.
- An instance is an object **from** a class.
- A class is a **set of objects having the same properties**.
- Objects in a class have the **same properties**.

Conceptual Questions: Does this student understand...

- a class as a blueprint for objects, where, given a class, one can create an arbitrary number of objects of that class?
- that two objects with the *same* set of fields might be in *different* classes (i.e., Java does not use structural typing, but it uses nominal typing)?
- that instances of a class have more in common (e.g., the methods defined in that class) than just the set of fields?
- that two objects of a class, while they have an identical set of fields, can have different values in those fields? [the use of the term 'the same properties' is slightly ambiguous; e.g., it might mean both have a field called 'int age', or both have a field 'int age' with the value 20.]

Recall Statement: *"The creation of an object is defined in the class source code, the class provide the fields of the objects, the constructor create the object with default values written on the source code."* (Section 2.4. Fields, constructors and methods)

Propositions:

- creation of an object is defined in the class **source code**
- the **class provides fields** of objects
- **the constructor** create the object
- the constructor create the object **with default values written on the source code**

Conceptual Questions: Does this student understand...

- the difference between design time (when source code is written) and run time?
- the difference between definition of a class and an invocation of its constructor?

- that constructors can have arguments?
- the difference between constructor arguments and instance variables?
- that a class could have multiple constructors? [not covered yet at this point of the course]
- default values of instance variables?
- that classes also define the methods?

Recall statement: *"We can use a class as type for a variable in another class. This is called Class Define Types."* (Section 3.5 Implementing the clock display)

Propositions:

- use a **class as type**
- type **for a variable**
- use... **in another class**
- this is called **Class Define Types**

Conceptual Questions: Does this student understand...

- that classes define types?
- that classes can be used as types of method arguments and return values?
- that you may use a class as a type also in the class itself (e.g., recursive types)?
- that "Class[es] define Types" is just a statement to explain this concept and not a standard term?

3.2 Discussion

The above analysis shows that student conceptions (and thus also misconceptions) extracted from recall statements can be fine-grained and involve intricate details. Moreover, conceptions are context-specific: they are affected by the specific terminology used in a textbook, and, in our situation, they are affected by the programming language taught in our course. Furthermore, recall statements are influenced by students' natural language skills: if students are not native speakers, it can be difficult to distinguish between misconceptions and weak language skills. Nevertheless, our pilot study also shows that even a small number of relatively short recall statements, when throughly analyzed, are a rich source of information for learning about student conceptions of programming concepts. Moreover, our study opens up a couple of follow-up questions:

Analysis Scalability. While instructors can manually analyze recall statements to find misconceptions, is there a way to reduce instructor effort? Our exercise in extracting propositions from the statements and in formulating conceptual questions showed that a deep understanding of the concepts was useful in extracting potential misconceptions. An automated natural language processing approach thus might have to be guided by information about the concepts. Similarly, an approach that uses peer learners to assess recall statements will need to ensure that the peers themselves have a deep enough understanding of the concepts.

Deep Recalls. While the recall statements we analyzed seemed to be genuinely produced by students, there is a risk that students literally copy statements from the readings. To reduce the risk for such shallow recalls, a platform could explicitly ask students to produce recall statements in their own words, to identify and describe the covered concepts, or to provide analogies or metaphors, and it could compare recall statements with the textbook to detect copies.

4 Conclusions

The recall statements students produce in an active recall pedagogy enable the identification of student misconceptions early on. Identifying misconceptions this way has several advantages: (1) It allows instructors to focus in-class activities on areas of weak understanding. This is especially beneficial in flipped-classroom pedagogies, where students do the assigned reading ahead of class. (2) It can enable textbook authors to identify sections in their book that might need to be clarified or improved. This could be especially beneficial if such reading recalls were collected in a centralized fashion, e.g., via an e-book reader or a companion web site for the textbook. (3) It can enable the construction of concept inventories, multiple choice assessments useful for assessing conceptual understanding at low cost. Our work has shown that recall statements are rich enough for misconception identification, thereby motivating research into scaling the approach using peer assessment or automatic natural language processing.

References

1. Barnes, D.J., Kölling, M.: Objects First with Java: A Practical Introduction Using BlueJ, 5th edn. Pearson, Upper Saddle River (2011)
2. Eckerdal, A., Thuné, M.: Novice java programmers' conceptions of "object" and "class", and variation theory. In: Proceedings of the 10th Annual SIGCSE Conference on Innovation and Technology in Computer Science Education, ITiCSE 2005, NY, USA, pp. 89–93 (2005). http://doi.acm.org/10.1145/1067445.1067473
3. Kaczmarczyk, L.C., Petrick, E.R., East, J.P., Herman, G.L.: Identifying student misconceptions of programming. In: Proceedings of the 41st ACM Technical Symposium on Computer Science Education, SIGCSE 2010, NY, USA, pp. 107–111 (2010). http://doi.acm.org/10.1145/1734263.1734299
4. Karpicke, J.D., Blunt, J.R.: Retrieval practice produces more learning than elaborative studying with concept mapping. Science **331**(6018), 772–775 (2011). http://science.sciencemag.org/content/331/6018/772
5. Karpicke, J.D., Roediger, H.L.: The critical importance of retrieval for learning. Science **319**(5865), 966–968 (2008). http://science.sciencemag.org/content/319/5865/966
6. Sanders, K., Boustedt, J., Eckerdal, A., McCartney, R., Moström, J.E., Thomas, L., Zander, C.: Student understanding of object-oriented programming as expressed in concept maps. In: Proceedings of the 39th SIGCSE Technical Symposium on Computer Science Education, SIGCSE 2008, NY, USA, pp. 332–336 (2008). http://doi.acm.org/10.1145/1352135.1352251

Let Voices of Both Teachers and Students on the Development of Educational Technologies Be Heard

Effie Lai-Chong Law(✉), Robert Edlin-White, and Matthias Heintz

Department of Informatics, University of Leicester, Leicester, LE1 7RH, UK
{lcl9,rew25,mmh21}@leicester.ac.uk

Abstract. The aim of adopting the Participatory Design (PD) approach in the development of educational technologies is to enhance their usefulness and usability. Nonetheless, many of the related PD activities only employ students as end-users to elicit requirements and feedback. Based on the empirical data of two workshops conducted with teachers and students, who were asked to provide feedback on the design of online lab-based lessons, we tend to conclude that involving teachers as well as students in such PD work can lead to a richer and more valuable source of information than students alone.

Keywords: Online labs · Participatory Design · Usability · Evaluation · Feedback

1 Introduction and Background

Usability is an important factor in the acceptance or abandonment of technology. This is particularly relevant to educational technologies which have low take-up and high abandon rates but significant societal values. Participatory Design (PD) involving end-users can lead to considerable improvements and are regarded as important for the development of interactive technology.

For educational technologies, usability studies tend to involve students rather than teachers. However, literature suggests that in other technological areas, the inclusion of experts of various sorts in PD can add valuable extra perspectives. It is therefore worth investigating how contributions derived from teachers differ from contributions arising from students, and to what extent, if any.

According to the Technology Acceptance Model ("TAM") (Davis 1993), the main factors influencing technology acceptance are perceived usefulness and perceived ease of use. Educational technology is no exception (Holden and Rada 2011). Much of the educational technology research literature focuses on the educational effectiveness of technology in (partly) controlled field studies. There is a little discussion on processes by which users (teachers, students) can contribute to or influence the design of a technology. Nonetheless, there are strong arguments for including users in the design of technology, in accordance with User-Centred Design (UCD) (e.g. Mao et al. 2005) and PD (e.g. Muller and Druin 2010; Heintz 2017). UCD methods often involve an iterative process of design, development and user testing providing a regular flow of user input and ongoing refinement of prototypes. End-users may be involved in some or all of the

É. Lavoué et al. (Eds.): EC-TEL 2017, LNCS 10474, pp. 422–427, 2017.
DOI: 10.1007/978-3-319-66610-5_37

following: establishing requirements, providing/critiquing/refining design ideas, formative evaluations of prototypes in increasing levels of fidelity, and summative evaluations of the final system, leading to improvements in both usefulness and ease of use. The involvement of users in design can also be applied to children as users (Read et al. 2014).

When involving users in PD, some researchers (e.g. Marti and Bannon 2009) have recognised that end-users are experts in their own needs, but also argued for the benefits of engaging other parties, who can provide relevant supplementary insights. Yet in the education literature we find that teachers are rarely if ever involved in the evaluation of software which are used by their students. But there are some precedents. For instance, Pardo et al. (2006) involved both teachers and students in the evaluation of a commercial educational software. Large et al. (2006) used inter-generational teams for designing a web portal for use in an elementary school. However, they did not compare inputs from teachers and students in a systematic manner.

2 Methodology

2.1 Participants and Procedure

Thirteen science teachers participated in the teacher workshop that was aimed to introduce to them the resources and facilities offered in the portal Golabz and to gather their feedback on a specific learning resource. For the student workshop, 24 science students aged 15 to 16 years old were involved. None of the teachers or students had ever worked with Golabz before attending the workshop.

The student workshop was conducted in the morning lasting ~2 h whereas the teacher workshop was held in the afternoon lasting ~3 h. Both took place in the computer lab of the school. Each participant worked individually on a desktop. The workflow of the two workshops is illustrated in Fig. 1. Both workshops shared Steps 3–6: Interacting with a specific learning resource called ILS on Electrical Circuit Lab. The acronym ILS stands for *inquiry learning space* (Pedaste et al. 2015), a web-based lesson grounded in the inquiry learning cycle. The longer duration of the teacher workshop was due to the additional Steps 1, 2 and 7. Step 8 – summary and conclusion – varied with the activities undertaken by the teachers and students in the workshop.

2.2 Instruments

Electrical Circuit Lab was developed by a Go-Lab project partner and is accessible in the GoLabz portal[1]. Specifically, students can build virtual electrical circuits with the basic components given: resistors, light bulbs, switches, capacitors, coils, batteries, ammeter, voltmeter, wattmeter, and ohmmeter (Step 5 in Fig. 1). They can take measurement on a circuit and analyse the data by plotting graphs.

PDot (Participatory Design online tool) was developed by the third author to support web-based PD activities to enable participants to give feedback (Step 3 in Fig. 1). When participants interact with the system under evaluation and want to

[1] (a) http://www.golabz.eu; (b) http://www.golabz.eu/lab/electrical-circuit-lab.

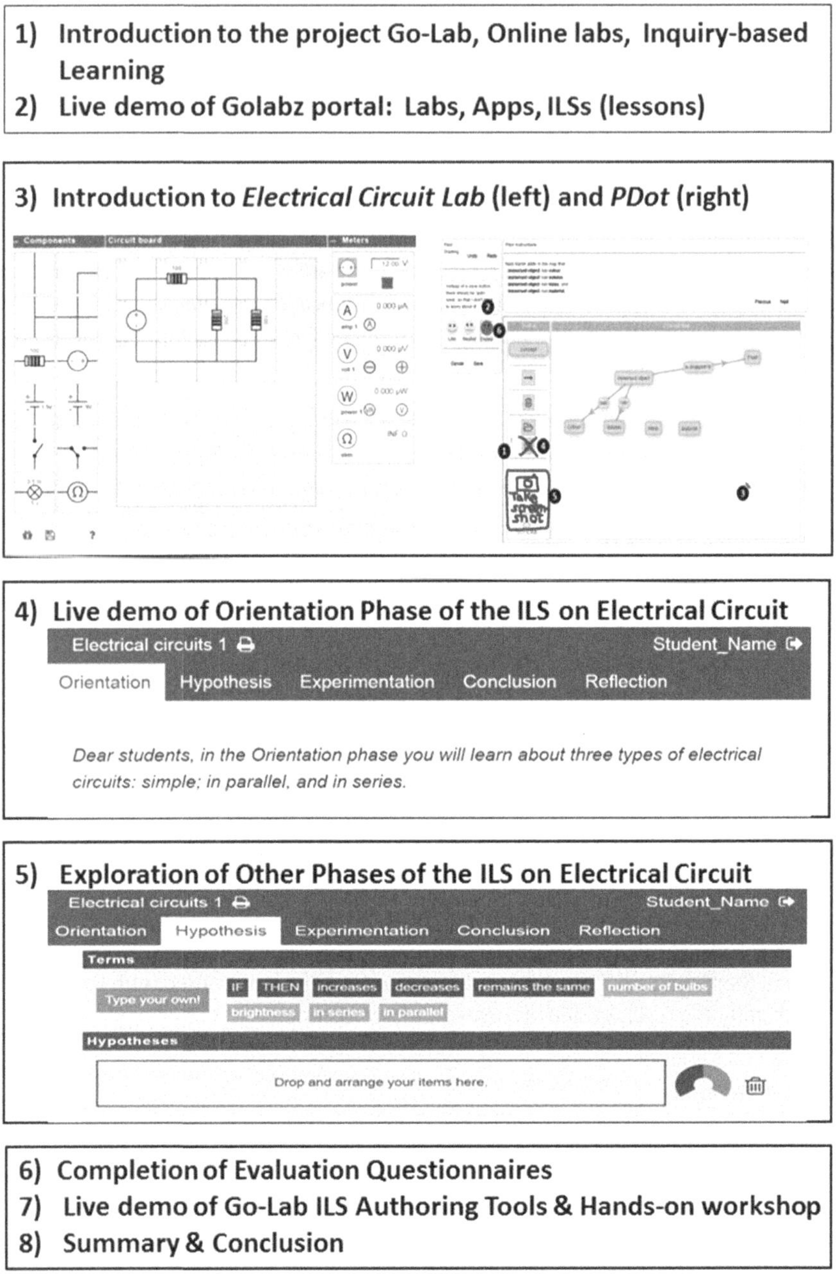

Fig. 1. The workshop workflow. Steps 1, 2 & 7 were for the teacher workshop only. Due to the space limit, only parts of the ILS were shown: in Step 4, the top lines of the Orientation phase; in Step 5, the app called Hypothesis Scratchpad used in the Hypothesis phase. The content of the three other phases – Experimentation, Conclusion and Reflection – was not shown.

comment on a certain feature, they click on the "Give feedback" button in the tool box; the system under evaluation then becomes non-interactive and is covered by a transparent layer on which one can give feedback. The participant can freely draw on the system. PDot also allows the participant to provide detailed comments in a text box and indicate her current mood by selecting one of the three smiley faces given (Heintz 2017).

3 Results and Discussion

With the use of PDot, the 13 teachers and 24 students generated 50 and 57 items of feedback, respectively. Altogether 107 units of feedback data were obtained from the two workshops. On average the teachers produced roughly 60% more items of feedback than students per head. The data were categorised by the second and third authors, who are experienced Human-Computer Interaction (HCI) researchers, along several dimensions using the CAt+ rating scheme (Heintz et al. 2015). CAt+ is designed to categorise user feedback with the primary purpose of creating a prioritised list of actions for system changes. The main categorisations in CAt+ are:

(i) Tone of feedback (negative, neutral or positive)
(ii) Type of change requested (e.g. content, functionality)
(iii) The scale of change requested (i.e. the scale of impact on the user interface)
(iv) The clarity of feedback/usability problem/suggested solution

Correspondingly, the major findings with regard to the CAt+ categorisations are: (i) The "tone" of the comments (positive, neutral or negative/constructive) was *not* significantly different between the teachers and students. (ii) The feedback provided by teachers was in general more constructive than that by students, which was often vague. For both groups, the type of change requested was somewhat balanced in terms of content and functionality. (iii) Student feedback tended to be focused on a small isolated part of the user interaction, whereas teachers made more high-impact feedback comments. (iv) There were no significant differences in how clearly the two groups specified the part of the interaction. Nor in how well they specified a recommended solution. In addition, teachers more often provided a clear rationale (in term of user impact) for their recommendations than students.

The two researchers achieved a good inter-rater reliability for all nine major categories and associated items (details omitted due to the space limit) with Cohen's kappa ranging from 0.73 to 0.85.

Apart from applying CAt+, a more open thematic analysis was used to make sense of the feedback. The major themes identified include:

- *Empathy (self- vs. other-referencing).* Student feedback is nearly always based on personal experiences they have had, whereas teacher feedback more often considers how other users might experience the system. Occasionally teachers made specific mentions of particular groups of users, e.g. by age or ability level or vocational/academic streaming, or special needs. No such comments were found in the student data.

- *Usability and User Experience*. Students more often than teachers made comments about the hedonic aspects of the software (e.g. fun vs. boredom) whereas teachers more often than students made comments about the educational and scientific aspects of the software. Similarly, teachers appear to be more concerned than students about issues of lesson productivity and effectiveness. Students were more concerned for interactivity and aesthetics.
- *Scope*: Teachers' feedback was more often holistic, with a broader vision and thus a wider impact of the software.

Interestingly, the contrasts between teacher and student feedback somewhat coincide with the major differences between the usability and user experience (UX) perspectives (Law et al. 2009). The teachers tended to adopt a more usability-oriented pragmatic view of the educational technology under evaluation whereas their students reflected a more UX-oriented hedonic view.

The distinctive teacher perspectives which we discovered in the data and observed in practice can be a natural derivation from their different role in pedagogy (e.g. their concern for educational outcomes, for scientific accuracy, and for efficient use of time), their maturity and consequent reflective ability (e.g. their concern for different types of users and different contexts of use) and their longer (median 12 years) classroom experience (e.g. their concern for the effect of the interaction on the whole class).

There is a suggestion from our observations that teachers may be more prone to providing speculative feedback (e.g. about how others may experience the interaction) whereas student feedback tends to be based on personal experience. Students, even more than teachers, wanted an interaction to be enjoyable.

Participatory design literature (Muller and Druin 2010) makes a strong and unequivocal case for involving users in design. For educational software for use in classrooms, the primary user is the student. We have shown (and observed) that students bring important and distinctive perspectives, particularly in areas such as interactivity and engagement.

4 Conclusion

For evaluating the usability of teaching technology for use in classrooms, we find that the use of teachers to evaluate a student experience can add considerable value to a study programme compared to a programme involving only students. The inclusion of teachers can provide:

- high quality and actionable feedback, with more rationales
- a much better focus on educational and pedagogical perspective
- a greater breadth of vision and maturity of insight
- a useful understanding of the needs and preferences of a wide range of students, and an awareness of different contexts of use

In the HCI literature, usability is recognised as depending on the user, task, tools and context and it is interesting to notice that teachers tended to have a greater awareness of some of these factors than students. It may be worth considering the use of this model for future rating schemes and feedback gathering tools. On the basis of the literature and our findings, we recognise that the authentic voice of the user (i.e. students) is indispensable in user-centred and participatory design of educational technology, but we commend the use of feedback from teachers also, to supplement student feedback.

Acknowledgements. This work was partially funded by the European Union in the context of the Go-Lab project (Grant Agreement no. 317601) under the Information and Communication Technologies (ICT) theme of the 7th Framework Programme for R&D (FP7). This document does not represent the opinion of the European Union, and the European Union is not responsible for any use that might be made of its content.

References

Davis, F.D.: User acceptance of information technology: system characteristics, user perceptions and behavioral impacts. Int'l. J. Man-Mach. Stud. **38**(3), 475–487 (1993)

Heintz, M.: Software-supported Participatory Design and Evaluation of the Tool PDot, Ph.D. thesis. University of Leicester (2017). Unpublished manuscript

Heintz, M., Law, E.L.-C., Soleimani, S.: Paper or pixel? comparing paper- and tool-based participatory design approaches. In: Abascal, J., Barbosa, S., Fetter, M., Gross, T., Palanque, P., Winckler, M. (eds.) INTERACT 2015. LNCS, vol. 9298, pp. 501–517. Springer, Cham (2015). doi:10.1007/978-3-319-22698-9_34

Holden, H., Rada, R.: Understanding the influence of perceived usability and technology self-efficacy on teachers' technology acceptance. J. Res. Technol. Educ. **43**(4), 343–367 (2011)

Kopcha, T.J.: Teachers' perceptions of the barriers to technology integration and practices with technology under situated professional development. Comput. Educ. **59**(4), 1109–1121 (2012)

Large, A., Nesset, V., Beheshti, J., Bowler, L.: "Bonded design": a novel approach to intergenerational information technology design. Libr. Inf. Sci. Res. **28**(1), 64–82 (2006)

Law, E.L.-C., Roto, V., Hassenzahl, M., Vermeeren, A., Kort, J.: Understanding, scoping and defining user experience: a survey approach. In: Proceedings of Conference on Human Factors in Computing Systems (CHI 2009). ACM (2009)

Mao, J.Y., Vredenburg, K., Smith, P.W., Carey, T.: The state of user-centered design practice. Commun. ACM **48**(3), 105–109 (2005)

Marti, P., Bannon, L.J.: Exploring user-centred design in practice: Some caveats. Knowl. Technol. Policy **22**(1), 7–15 (2009)

Muller, M., Druin, A.: Participatory design as third space in HCI. In: Sears, A., Jacko, J. (eds.) The Human-Computer Interaction Handbook. Taylor and Francis (2010)

Pardo, S., Vetere, F., Howard, S.: Teachers' involvement in usability testing with children. In: Proceedings of Interaction Design and Children (IDC 2006), pp. 89–92. ACM (2006)

Pedaste, M., Mäeots, M., Siiman, L.A., De Jong, T., et al.: Phases of inquiry-based learning: definitions and the inquiry cycle. Educ. Res. Rev. **14**, 47–61 (2015)

Read, J.C., Fitton, D., Horton, M.: Giving ideas an equal chance: inclusion and representation in participatory design with children. In: Proceedings of Interaction Design and Children (IDC 2004), pp. 105–114. ACM (2014)

Learning Analytics for Learning Design: Towards Evidence-Driven Decisions to Enhance Learning

Katerina Mangaroska(✉) and Michail Giannakos

Norwegian University of Science and Technology (NTNU), Trondheim, Norway
{katerina.mangaroska,michailg}@ntnu.no

Abstract. As the fields of learning analytics and learning design mature, the convergence and synergies between them become an important area for research. Collecting and combining learning analytics coming from different channels can clearly provide valuable information in designing learning. Hence, this paper intends to summarize the main outcomes of a systematic literature review of empirical evidence on learning analytics for learning design. The search was performed in seven academic databases, resulting in 38 papers included in the main analysis. The review demonstrates ongoing design patterns and learning phenomena that improve learning, by providing more comprehensive background of the current landscape of learning analytics for learning design and its impact on the current status of learning technologies. Consequently, future research should consider how to capture and systematize learning design data. Moreover, it should evaluate and document what learning design choices made by educators using what learning analytics techniques influence learning experiences and learning performances over time.

Keywords: Learning analytics · Learning design · Empirical studies

1 Introduction

Due to the pervasion of learning technologies, the use of learning analytics to discover important learning phenomena (e.g., moment of learning or misconception) and portray learners' experiences and behaviors, becomes evident and commonly accepted. At present, there are various analytic methods and e-learning tools that can be used to improve the learning experience [8]. However, without contextual interpretation of the data collected with e-learning tools, learning analytics capabilities are limited. From this perspective, learning design is utterly important as it provides the framework for analyzing and interpreting learner's behavior and data. Learning design defines the educational objectives and the pedagogical approaches that educators can reflect upon, take decisions and make improvements. Moreover, learning design "document the sequence of learning tasks, the resources, and the sequence of teaching methods" as main premises for reusability and transferability of good practices across educational contexts [5]. Yet, past research was focused on "conceptualizing learning design principles, without evaluating what happens after the design process" [9]. In addition, several studies have tried to understand and improve the learning design experiences by utilizing

É. Lavoué et al. (Eds.): EC-TEL 2017, LNCS 10474, pp. 428–433, 2017.
DOI: 10.1007/978-3-319-66610-5_38

learning analytics, but only few of them tried empirically to show that learning analytics and learning design are complementary research areas that together have significant impact on the learning process [8]. Consequently, a research work is missing to measure what learning design decisions affect learning behavior and stimulate productive learning environment.

To bridge the gap, this paper centers in a systematic literature review with aim to examine the intersection between learning analytics and learning design, and provide important insights beyond the specific research findings within the individual discipline. The study addresses the following research questions:

RQ1: *What is the current status of learning analytics for learning design research*, seen through the lens of educational contexts (i.e. users and rational for use), distribution of pedagogical practices, and methodologies (i.e. types of data and data analysis techniques employed).

RQ2: *What learning analytics have been used to inform learning design decisions*, and explore the extent to which learning analytics can support dynamic and data-driven learning design decisions.

2 Methodology

To answer the research questions, the authors decided to follow the guidelines for systematic literature review in software engineering [4]. In fact, before conducting the review, the authors developed a review protocol to reduce researcher bias and to keep a clear scope of the study. The search was performed in iterations in five main academic electronic databases in Technology Enhanced Learning (TEL): ACM DL, IEEE Xplore, SpringerLink, Science Direct, and Wiley, and two additional databases, SAGE and ERIC. The second cycle, included an independent search in the top ten educational and technology journals listed in the Google metrics sub-category: Educational Technology. The third and final cycle included search in the reference section for each selected paper in order to find additional relevant papers (i.e. the snowball technique). For the search, a research string was generated using combination of three terms: "*analytics*" AND "*design*" AND "*learning*". The literature search was performed from mid-October 2016 till mid-December 2016.

The process of evaluation and selection of papers consisted of several stages and followed inclusion/exclusion criteria defined by the authors. As a result, 288 papers were selected for the second stage of the systematic review. After the second stage and following the CAPS checklist, a total of 38 papers were retrieved, read it entirely, coded, and critically assessed by two researchers (see the list of papers here: https://figshare.com/articles/Bibliography_for_systematic_review_on_learning_analytics_and_learning_design_docx/4871690).

3 Findings

Regarding RQ1, the authors established the following parameters:

Sample population. The predominant sample population consists of undergraduates (n = 14) and educators (n = 14) including teachers and instructors, followed by high school (n = 6), graduates (n = 5), and middle school (n = 3) students.

Learning setting. Majority of the studies (n = 16) were conducted within VLEs and/or LMSs, followed by web-based environments (n = 6), MOOCs (n = 4), and multimodality (n = 4), computer-based environments (n = 3), video-based environment (n = 2), cognitive tutors (n = 1), and mobile learning environment (n = 1). The selected studies were conducted in purely digital (n = 19) and blended (n = 11) learning settings.

Learning scenarios. Formal learning was addresses in most of the studies (n = 27) rather than informal and non-formal learning.

Pedagogical approach. Majority of the papers (n = 19) did not refer to a specific pedagogical approach, but those that reported, includes: problem-based learning (n = 4), project-based learning (n = 4), game-based learning (n = 3), and CSCL (n = 3).

Technology and tools. Most used are applications specifically developed to test types of learning analytics, and web 2.0 social media tools (e.g. wiki, chat, google apps). Some studies reported use of devices for multimodal human-computer interaction such as tabletops, kinetic sensors, EEG, and eye tracking.

Type of methodology. Majority of the studies used quantitative analysis (n = 23), mixed methods (n = 8), and qualitative analysis (n = 7).

Data collection methods. Most practiced data collection methods are user activity LMS logs (n = 14) or logs coming from web 2.0 social media tools (n = 14), followed by analytics coming from questionnaires (n = 12), interviews (n = 6), observations (n = 4), and multimodal analytics (n = 3).

Data analysis techniques. Most popular techniques used are inferential statistics (n = 20) especially regression and clustering, followed by descriptive statistics (n = 9), content analysis (n = 6), and correlation (n = 5). Other used techniques included data mining (n = 3), social network analysis (n = 3), discourse analysis (n = 3), thematic (n = 2), and text analysis (n = 2). Reported only once are grounded theory, phenomenology, semantic analysis, sentiment analysis, and heuristic mining.

Research objectives. Student learning behavior (n = 8), collaboration and interaction (n = 7), and student assessment (n = 7) are the primary research objectives. Next are design and management of learning scenarios (n = 5), student retention (n = 5), learning performance (n = 5 studies), predictive modelling (n = 5), and student monitoring and engagement (n = 5).

Regarding RQ2, the authors analyzed the learning analytics used in the studies, and the learning design challenges/decisions that have been proposed.

One of the most known practices in learning analytics is collecting and analyzing historical and current LMS user activity data to study students' learning paths (i.e. trajectories) [3]. Another type of analytics often used in the selected studies are ready to be visualized learning analytics that emphasize informed and real-time feedback [6]. Next, the authors observed analytics coming from student's digital artifacts, such as artifacts from project-work or video-based learning settings. Furthermore, a very interesting finding was the expanded use of combined learning analytics coming from different data sources [14]. Finally, few studies reported the importance and use of multimodal sensor data like kinetics, EEG, eye-movement, speech and body-movement [7, 13].

When it comes to learning design, one of the main challenges found in the analyzed studies is the seamless integration of design tools and strategies for lessons planning with tools for monitoring and analysis [10]. Moreover, the results also demonstrated the need for seamless integration of multimodal data (e.g. integrating physiological measures for better understanding learners' actions and experience) and the need to differentiate what can truly be designed in the learning environment [7, 13]. However, the current landscape of learning design depicts the visual representations of the outcomes from learning analytic, especially dashboards, as an easy to understand and concise way of presenting valuable information [1, 11].

4 Discussion and Conclusion

From the results described above, we can extract several main findings and propose directions for future research studies. The results show that quantitative methodology still takes precedence over mixed methods and qualitative methodology due to the abundance of user activity data from LMSs. However, simple clicking behavior in a LMS is a poor proxy for the actual learning behavior students have [12]. *This heavy reliance on log analysis, often using a single platform as a source of data is one of the primary issues that needs to be address in near future.* Furthermore, learning is becoming more blended and distributed across different learning environments and contexts, making it impossible to holistically understand the process of learning if integration is neglected. Therefore, the authors want to highlight *the importance of learning analytics integration and aggregation of learning-related data across multiple sources for designing informed and optimal learning strategies.*

Although most of the studies follow the traditional paradigm in which the teacher is the main user monitoring students, more and more studies are reporting results from using visualization analytics to increase awareness among students for self-monitoring and self-reflection [2]. The main idea is to help learners improve self-diagnostic of their own performance and seek solutions accordingly. In fact, for this issue there is a limited research on how students interpret and use learning analytics to follow their own learning performance. Another important finding is that there is no accepted framework or agreed method for research which learning analytics are used for what learning design challenges, nor examples of sharing and reuse of current methods and practices across various educational contexts. *This is one of the hallmarks of young fields, as well as the lack of longitudinal and comparative studies.*

On the other side, one of the most striking findings of this review is the lack of studies which directly consider and measure student learning gains, or any other learning-related constructs. Another unexpected finding is the shortage of studies on how educators are planning, designing, implementing, and evaluating learning design decisions [9]. Furthermore, there is an insufficient number of studies that consider using learning analytics to intentionally design learning activities that support collaboration and cooperation among students, rather than just following learner performance over time [3]. Finally, what is often overlooked and underestimated but immensely important to educators, is the need for explicit guidance on how to use, interpret and reflect on the learning analytics findings to adequately refine and re-design learning activities. *A direction towards closing this gap is to consider establishing a participatory culture of design, and a habit among educators to see learning design as an inquiry process and learning analytics as a part of the teaching culture* [8].

Based on the reviewed papers, the authors want to offer the following checklist for future work on learning analytics for learning design:

- provide details about the learning environment and the used pedagogical approaches, where improvements in learning design experiences based on learning analytics outcomes will be measured;
- evaluate and compare what learning design patterns and learning phenomena make learning effective;
- evaluate and denote student learning gains, or any other learning-related constructs;
- evaluate and denote the impact of learning analytics outcomes on learning design decisions and experiences;
- evaluate and denote how educators are planning, designing, implementing, and evaluating learning design decisions;
- provide common guidance on how to use, interpret and reflect on the learning analytics to adequately refine and redesign learning activities.

This review has shown that future research should consider developing a framework on how to capture and systematize learning design data, and follow what learning design choices made by educators influence subsequent learning activities and performances over time. Addressing these elements could help in further maturation of the fields of learning analytics and learning design, and provide foundation for longitudinal and comparative studies among various educational contexts. Finally, educators and researchers need to leverage the use of learning analytics and focus on developing students' skills and natural predispositions by designing personalized feedback and tailored learning while decreasing assimilative activities as traditional lecturing, reading or watching videos.

Acknowledgments. This work was supported by the Research Council of Norway under the project FUTURE LEARNING (255129/H20).

References

1. Berland, M., Davis, D., Smith, C.P.: AMOEBA: Designing for collaboration in computer science classrooms through live learning analytics. Int. J. Comput. Supported Collaborative Learn. **10**(4), 425–447 (2015)
2. Gašević, D., Mirriahi, N., Dawson, S., Joksimović, S.: Effects of instructional conditions and experience on the adoption of a learning tool. Comput. Hum. Behav. **67**, 207–220 (2017)

3. Joksimović, S., Gašević, D., Loughin, T.M., Kovanović, V., Hatala, M.: Learning at distance: effects of interaction traces on academic achievement. Comput. Educ. **87**, 204–217 (2015)
4. Kitchenham, B., Charters, S.: Guidelines for performing systematic literature reviews in software engineering. EBSE Technical report, Ver. 2.3 edn. Keele University, United Kingdom (2007)
5. Lockyer, L., Heathcote, E., Dawson, S.: Informing pedagogical action: aligning learning analytics with learning design. Am. Behav. Sci. **57**(10), 1439–1459 (2013)
6. Melero, J., Hernández-Leo, D., Sun, J., Santos, P., Blat, J.: How was the activity? A visualization support for a case of location-based learning design. Br. J. Educ. Technol. **46**(2), 317–329 (2015)
7. Pantazos, K., Vatrapu, R.: Enhancing the professional vision of teachers: a physiological study of teaching analytics dashboards of students' repertory grid exercises in business education. In: 49th Hawaii International Conference on System Sciences (HICSS) 2016. IEEE, pp. 41–50 (2016)
8. Persico, D., Pozzi, F.: Informing learning design with learning analytics to improve teacher inquiry. Br. J. Educ. Technol. **46**(2), 230–248 (2015)
9. Rienties, B., Toetenel, L.: The impact of learning design on student behaviour, satisfaction and performance: A cross-institutional comparison across 151 modules. Comput. Hum. Behav. **60**, 331–341 (2016)
10. Rodríguez-Triana, M.J., Martínez-Monés, A., Asensio-Pérez, J.I., Dimitriadis, Y.: Scripting and monitoring meet each other: aligning learning analytics and learning design to support teachers in orchestrating CSCL situations. Br. J. Educ. Technol. **46**(2), 330–343 (2015)
11. Schwendimann, B., Rodriguez-Triana, M., Vozniuk, A., Prieto, L., Boroujeni, M., Holzer, A., Gillet, D., Dillenbourg, P.: Perceiving learning at a glance: a systematic literature review of learning dashboard research. IEEE Trans. Learn. Technol. 30–41 (2016)
12. Tempelaar, D.T., Rienties, B., Giesbers, B.: Verifying the stability and sensitivity of learning analytics based prediction models: an extended case study. In: Zvacek, S., Restivo, M.T., Uhomoibhi, J., Helfert, M. (eds.) CSEDU 2015. CCIS, vol. 583, pp. 256–273. Springer, Cham (2016). doi:10.1007/978-3-319-29585-5_15
13. Worsley, M., Blikstein, P.: Leveraging multimodal learning analytics to differentiate student learning strategies. In: 5th International Conference on Learning Analytics and Knowledge, pp. 360–367. ACM (2015)
14. Zacharis, N.Z.: A multivariate approach to predicting student outcomes in web-enabled blended learning courses. Internet High. Educ. **27**, 44–53 (2015)

Search of the Emotional Design Effect in Programming Revised

Mikko Nurminen[1(✉)], Leo Leppänen[2], Heli Väätäjä[1], and Petri Ihantola[1]

[1] Laborotory of Pervasive Computing, Tampere University of Technology, Korkeakoulunkatu 3, 33720 Tampere, Finland
{mikko.nurminen,heli.vaataja,petri.ihantola}@tut.fi
[2] Department of Computer Science, University of Helsinki, Yliopistonkatu 4, 00014 Helsinki, Finland
leo.leppanen@helsinki.fi

Abstract. In this paper, we validate and extend previous findings on using emotional design in online learning materials by using a randomized controlled trial in the context of a partially-online university level programming course. For students who did not master the content beforehand, our results echo previous observations: emotional design material was not perceived more favourably, while materials' perceived quality was correlated with learning outcomes. Emotionally designed material lead to better learning outcomes per unit of time, but it didn't affect students navigation in the material.

Keywords: Emotional design · Electronic learning material

1 Emotional Design in Online Learning

With the increasing distribution – both spatial and temporal – of learning that is both allowed for and caused by online learning, the role of the lecturer is largely overtaken by the online learning material. In the light of the effect of emotions on learning outcomes [9], it seems reasonable to expect that eliciting an emotional response from the students with the online learning material would be similarly beneficial. Indeed, this can been achieved by what is known as emotional design of (online) learning materials, often defined as "redesigning the graphics [...] to enhance the level of personification and visual appeal of the essential elements in the lesson" [6]. The use of emotional design in on-line learning has gained wide attraction in the recent years [4,5,7,8,10,11].

The effect of text-accompanying images on learning has been studied for decades, with a multitude of results that are somewhat hard to interpret as a whole. However the general trend seems to be that properly chosen text-accompanying images can result in better learning outcomes for students [3]. At the same time, even subject matter experts have trouble identifying problems students might have with certain text-image combinations [2]. This indicates that the interactions between the text and the accompanying visuals are

É. Lavoué et al. (Eds.): EC-TEL 2017, LNCS 10474, pp. 434–440, 2017.
DOI: 10.1007/978-3-319-66610-5_39

complex and hard to understand. As Haaranen et al. after applying emotional design to enhance online study material in programming state: "if there is an emotional design effect, it is likely to depend in a complex way on the use of different colors, metaphors, and visualization types, and will not work equally well for all content and all kinds of learners" [4].

Inspired by both Haaranen et al. challenging the generalizability of their own results, and the recent discussions on the need for replication in relation to computer science education studies [1], we decided to replicate the previous experiment in a different context. We adopted the learning material used by Haaranen et al. into our CS1 programming course and conducted a randomized controlled trial seeking to understand how well students learn from the different versions of the material and how much time they spend with it. In addition, we seek to observe whether emotional design affects student navigation through the web pages in an online learning material.

The rest of this article is organized as follows: Sect. 2 details the research questions, the context of the study and the methodology. Section 3 details the answers to the research questions. Finally, Sects. 4 discuss our results in the larger context of the previous work, and draw some final conclusions.

2 Research Design

2.1 Research Questions

Our research questions extended from the previous work are:

RQ1: How is emotional design related to learning outcomes?
RQ2: How is emotional design correlated with student perceptions of material and visualization quality and helpfulness?
RQ3: How are student perceptions of material and visualization quality and helpfulness correlated with learning outcomes?
RQ4: Is emotional design correlated with material usage statistics?

2.2 Data and Context

The experiment was conducted as part of the introductory programming course held at the Tampere University of Technology in 2015. The course participants were divided into two groups. One group acted as the control group and was shown a learning material with "traditional" visualizations. The treatment group was shown a learning material with "emotionally designed" visualizations. Both versions of the study material were the same as in the study we replicated with the exception that emotionally designed images were coloured as described in the future work section of the said article. The participants were free to take part in the experiment from any location.

The material consisted of 21 short pages of content with text and visualization, followed by a short questionnaire. The questionnaire consisted of the following questions, each answered on a Likert-scale from 1 to 5, with 5 indicating the most "positive" response:

Q1: How focused were you while reading the material?
Q2: How pleasant was the material to read?
Q3: How understandable was the material?
Q4: How well did the visualizations help you to learn?
Q5: How pleasant were the visualizations?

Participants were also to answer two questions regarding the material they had just completed reading, as well whether they would have been able to successfully answer said questions before reading the material. These questions were used to assess how well the participants had learned the material. The two questions used to assess student's comprehension and transfer of information were:

1. Weekly exercise 10.1: Based on what you read, describe what is meant by object-oriented programming.
2. Weekly exercise 10.2: What kind of objects would you use in a program, that keeps the records of a hotel's room bookings? Give an example of how these objects would communicate?

2.3 Methodology

As the students browsed the online learning material, their page visits were recorded. For each page view, we collected: student ID, the page, the time at the beginning of the page visit and the time at the end of the page visit.

All those participants that indicated in the questionnaire that they already knew the content beforehand and would have been able to answer the questions correctly even before reading the material were excluded, as they wouldn't need to study the material and were likely to just rapidly click through the material to get through it. These eliminations reduced the study to population of $n = 206$ participants. In this filtered population, the control and treatment groups had $n = 107$ and $n = 99$ participants, respectively. Based on the survey in the beginning, there were no significant differences between the groups.

The participant answers to the two material related questions were graded on a binary scale: if the participant demonstrated that he or she had understood the material well enough to correctly answer a question, a score of 1 was given for that question. If the participant failed to demonstrate sufficient understanding of the material, a score of 0 was given.

3 Results

3.1 RQ1: Emotional Design and Learning Outcomes

Subjecting the learning outcomes of the treatment and the control group to a Kruskal-Wallis analysis produced the following result: The treatment group (Mean = 1.58, St. Dev = 0.54) and the control group (Mean = 1.38, St. Dev = 0.56) have different mean ranks with $p = 0.009$. Thus, emotionally designed visualizations led to better learning outcomes but the effect is rather small: both groups are within one standard deviation of each other.

3.2 RQ2: Emotional Design and Participant Perceptions of Quality

No statistically significant difference was found between the control group and the treatment group for any of the questionnaire questions, once a Holm correction for multiple comparisons was applied. While minor differences in means were observed, the means of the groups are always within half of a standard deviation of each other. Thus, the results related to RQ2 are inconclusive. The statistics are tabulated in Table 1.

3.3 RQ3: Participant Perceptions of Quality and Learning Outcomes

In order to answer our third research question, we searched for correlations between learning outcomes and student perceptions of learning material quality as reported in the final questionnaire. The results are tabulated in Table 2.

All questionnaire factors exhibited a statistically significant correlation with learning outcomes. Perceiving the material as pleasant to read, easy to understand, the visualizations as helpful and pleasant, as well as feeling focused are all as factors positively correlated with learning outcomes.

3.4 RQ4: Emotional Design and Material Usage

In order to answer our fourth research question, we observed two key material usage statistics: time spent on material and amount of backtracking. We defined backtracking as user moving to a material page they had already opened.

Both groups exhibited very few backtracking events. A Kruskal-Wallis test failed ($H = 0.40$, $p = 0.51$) to show any statistical difference in the mean ranks between these two groups in the amount of backtracking events.

Table 1. Answers to a questionnaire on material and visualization quality and helpfulness. "p" is the uncorrected p-value produced by a Kruskal-Wallis analysis. * indicates statistical significance at $p < 0.05$ before a correction for multiple comparisons is applied, ** indicate that the result is significant at $p < 0.05$ after the correction is applied.

	Control		Treatment		p
	Mean	S.Dev	Mean	S.Dev	
How focused were you while reading the material?	3.38	0.86	3.42	0.79	0.94
How pleasant was the material to read?	3.57	0.87	3.66	0.95	0.37
How understandable was the material?	3.82	0.86	3.85	1.01	0.52
How well did the visualizations help you learn?	4.22	1.35	4.02	1.06	0.05*
How pleasant were the visualizations?	3.74	0.98	4.01	1.03	0.03*

Table 2. Correlations of participant answers to learning outcomes. "r" and "p" are the Pearson's correlation coefficient and its accompanying (uncorrected) p-value. ** indicate that the result is significant at $p < 0.05$ after the correction is applied.

	r	p
How focused were you while reading the material?	0.15	0.03**
How pleasant was the material to read?	0.18	<0.01**
How understandable was the material?	0.26	<0.01**
How well did the visualizations help you learn?	0.21	<0.01**
How pleasant were the visualizations?	0.21	<0.01**

Next, we defined time-on-material as the time difference (in seconds) between the start time of the first material visit and the time when the user closed a non-questionnaire material page for the last time. Kruskal-Wallis failed to show any statistically significant difference between the treatment and the control group for time-on-material, with $H = 2.07$ and $p = 0.15$.

4 Discussion and Conclusions

The results presented in Sect. 3 show that the treatment group that was shown emotionally designed visualizations had slightly better learning outcomes than the control group. At the same time, the results fail to show any statistically significant difference in the time used to read the material between the treatment and the control groups. When looking at individual results, our findings seem to be opposite to those reported in Haaranen et al. [4], where it was found that the treatment group and the control group had similar learning outcomes but that the treatment group spent less time in the material. Yet when the combinatorial effect of the findings is considered for both this research and Haaranen et al. [4], a similarity is found: In both studies, the treatment group "learned more per unit of time", so to speak. This result is also in line with the work of such authors as Heidig et al. [5], including in that the observed effect is rather small.

Our results pertaining to RQ 3 – whether perceptions of material quality and pleasantness are related to learning outcomes – further corroborate the overall result presented above: participant perceptions of material and visualization quality, pleasantness and understandability were all positively correlated with learning outcomes. This result, too, is in line with previous studies [5].

In this light, our answer to RQ 2 – whether participant perceptions of material quality were different between the treatment and the control group – are curious. While the treatment group displayed marginally better learning outcomes and student perceptions of material quality and pleasantness were correlated with learning outcomes, no statistically significant differences were observed in the groups' answers to the questionnaire on material quality and pleasantness.

Despite the failure to detect any difference in the backtracking behaviours of the groups, our view is that these findings indicate that emotional design helps the students assimilate knowledge, at least insofar as measured by our metrics of learning outcomes. Furthermore, our results seem to indicate that student perceptions of material quality and pleasantness are related to learning outcomes. Yet surprisingly, said perceptions seem to not be affected by emotional design. This somewhat counter-intuitive result warrants further study.

The generalizability of the results presented here is mostly limited by two factors: the homogeneousness of the participant population and the context of the study. The participants largely come from a socially homogeneous population and from a relatively narrow spread of economic and educational backgrounds. Similarly, as the study was conducted only in the context of one course of a single subject, whether the results generalize to other subjects is as of now unknown. At the same time, authors are unaware of any reasons why these results would fail to generalize within the context of higher education.

A further limitation is that students' learning was assessed by their answers to two questions that were graded on a binary scale. This rather narrow spectrum could have hidden some smaller trends in learning outcomes. Similarly, as the learning outcomes were only assessed immediately after the students had completed reading the material, any possible effects of emotional design on long-term retention are unknown within this study.

References

1. Ahadi, A., Hellas, A., Ihantola, P., Korhonen, A., Petersen, A.: Replication in computing education research: researcher attitudes and experiences. In: Proceedings of the 16th Koli Calling International Conference on Computing Education Research, pp. 2–11. ACM (2016)
2. Benson, P.J.: Problems in picturing text: a study of visua/verbal problem solving. Techn. Commun. Q. **6**(2), 141–160 (1997)
3. Carney, R.N., Levin, J.R.: Pictorial illustrations still improve students' learning from text. Educ. Psychol. Rev. **14**(1), 5–26 (2002)
4. Haaranen, L., Ihantola, P., Sorva, J., Vihavainen, A.: In search of the emotional design effect in programming. In: Proceedings of the 37th International Conference on Software Engineering, ICSE 2015, vol. 2. pp. 428–434. IEEE Press, Piscataway (2015)
5. Heidig, S., Müller, J., Reichelt, M.: Emotional design in multimedia learning: differentiation on relevant design features and their effects on emotions and learning. Comput. Hum. Behav. **44**, 81–95 (2015)
6. Mayer, R.E., Estrella, G.: Benefits of emotional design in multimedia instruction. Learn. Instr. **33**, 12–18 (2014)
7. Navarro, O., Molina, A.I., Lacruz, M., Ortega, M.: Evaluation of multimedia educational materials using eye tracking. Procedia - Soc. Behav. Sci. **197**, 2236–2243 (2015). 7th World Conference on Educational Sciences
8. Park, B., Knörzer, L., Plass, J.L., Brünken, R.: Emotional design and positive emotions in multimedia learning: an eyetracking study on the use of anthropomorphisms. Comput. Educ. **86**, 30–42 (2015)
9. Pekrun, R., Goetz, T., Titz, W., Perry, R.P.: Academic emotions in students' self-regulated learning and achievement: a program of qualitative and quantitative research. Educ. Psychol. **37**(2), 91–105 (2002)

10. Plass, J.L., Heidig, S., Hayward, E.O., Homer, B.D., Um, E.: Emotional design in multimedia learning: effects of shape and color on affect and learning. Learn. Instr. **29**, 128–140 (2014)
11. Um, E.R., Plass, J.L., Hayward, E.O., Homer, B.D.: Emotional design in multimedia learning. J. Educ. Psychol. **104**(2), 485–498 (2012)

How Gamification Is Being Implemented in MOOCs? A Systematic Literature Review

Alejandro Ortega-Arranz(✉), Juan A. Muñoz-Cristóbal, Alejandra Martínez-Monés, Miguel L. Bote-Lorenzo, and Juan I. Asensio-Pérez

GSIC-EMIC Research Group, Universidad de Valladolid, Valladolid, Spain
{alex,juanmunoz}@gsic.uva.es, amartine@infor.uva.es, {migbot,juaase}@tel.uva.es

Abstract. Although MOOCs are being established as a very popular technology to support learning, they are often criticized for their lack of support to active pedagogies and the high drop-out rates. One approach to face this problem is gamification, due to the promising benefits already shown at small-scale environments. Attending to the current and growing use of game elements in MOOCs, this paper presents a systematic literature review of the usage of gamification in MOOCs, aimed at analyzing how gamification is being implemented in MOOCs, and to identify unexplored research opportunities in this field. The results show that gamification is still at an early stage in MOOCs, and it is being implemented in similar ways to those at small scale contexts.

Keywords: Gamification · MOOCs · Literature review · Game elements

1 Introduction

Massive open online courses (MOOCs) are a form of global education that is increasing their popularity over the last years. As a consequence, there is a growing research interest around the MOOC phenomenon, its consequences, and potential benefits [17]. However, the research community also perceives important shortcomings in MOOCs such as the high students' drop-out rates [11], the lack of students' motivation, engagement, and interaction [12] or the lack of active learning [17]. One of the approaches followed to address the aforementioned problems is gamification.

Gamification is defined as the inclusion of elements and structures that frequently appear in games (*e.g.*, narrative, badges, missions) in non-game contexts [5]. Specifically, the gamification in education (gamification from now on) has shown potential benefits in non-massive contexts (*e.g.*, increase students' motivation and engagement) to overcome such current MOOCs' issues (*e.g.*, high drop-out rates) [4,7,8]. However, MOOCs present some peculiarities that

É. Lavoué et al. (Eds.): EC-TEL 2017, LNCS 10474, pp. 441–447, 2017.
DOI: 10.1007/978-3-319-66610-5_40

may affect the outcomes shown by gamification in other educational contexts and scales; as well as the ways in which these gamifications are designed, implemented and enacted. For example, the different students' background, motivation and intentions can make the design of rewarding criteria more difficult; the high probability of many online students connected at the same time open new possibilities of collaborative and competitive online gamifications; the high drop-out rates forces teachers in many cases to design and implement individual gamifications; or the necessity of intelligent and automated gamification, since MOOC instructors cannot draw the attention of each student independently.

Attending to the current and growing interest in the use of gamification in MOOCs, a systematic literature review can be useful for researchers, instructional designers and teachers, to be aware of the work done so far, and to identify issues that need further work. There are already several literature reviews regarding the current state of MOOCs [10,12,14,16]. However, these reviews do not focus on the use of game elements or gamification in such contexts. There are also literature reviews about gamification, focused on small scale and which cover a very limited number of studies about the use of gamification in MOOCs [1,4,6–8].

This document presents a systematic literature review (*SLR*) aiming to explore which is the current state of the implementation of gamification in MOOCs. The next section describes the methodology and protocol followed, including the search strategy, the inclusion/exclusion criteria and the data extraction procedure. Section 3 discusses the results obtained. Finally, the conclusions and future research lines are outlined in Sect. 4.

2 Review Methodology

The review methodology followed to carry out this SLR is described in Kitchenham and Charters (2007) [13] which has been already employed in previous surveys in technology-enhanced learning. This methodology structures the SLR in three phases (*i.e.*, planning, conducting, reporting) providing guidelines for key issues such as the definition of the search strategy and study selection. In our case, the selected databases were ACM Digital Library, IEEE Xplore Digital Library, Science Direct, Scopus and Springer Link, since the authors consider that these databases are the most relevant databases in the topic field. Moreover, other articles not stored in these databases but cited in the retrieved publications have been also included in the review. The search includes journal publications, conference proceedings, books, book chapters, technical reports and thesis, trying to avoid possible bias.

The search string used was <gamif*> AND <*MOOC*> to be found in the title, abstracts or keywords without any time restrictions. Therefore, publications with derivations of the gamification term such as *gamified* or *gamify* and with derivations of the MOOC term such as *cMOOC* or *MOOCs* are also included in the search. The inclusion criterion was publications where **the use of gamification in MOOCs is a central topic**, *i.e.*, gamification is discussed or studied

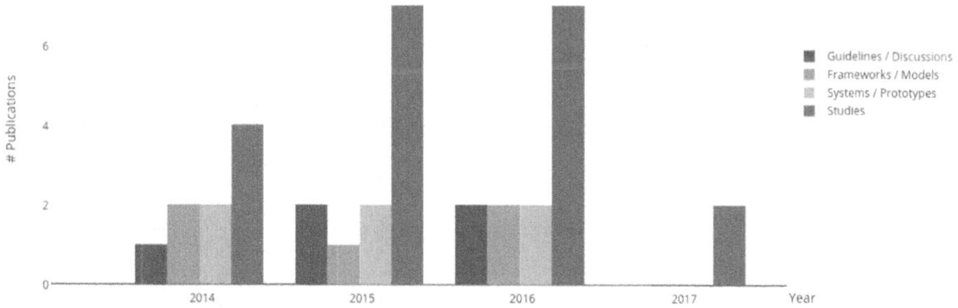

Fig. 1. Distribution of publications attending to the year and type of proposal.

in the work. The retrieved publications were reviewed based on the title first, abstract second, and finally, the whole document to check if the publications meet the inclusion criteria.

Thirty six publications were finally selected. As it is shown in Fig. 1, from 2014 the number of publications regarding gamification in MOOCs has slightly been increasing. However, the low number of publications in scientific journals (4) and the high number of publications in conferences and symposia (24), book chapters (3) and workshops (3) suggest that gamification in MOOCs is still at an early stage. The remaining documents are (1) technical report, and (1) master thesis. Two of the thirty six selected publications extend the work of previous publications also considered for the literature review. Therefore, the resulting number of works analyzed in this paper is thirty four[1].

3 Results

The analysis of the implementation of gamification in MOOCs has been subdivided into: (a) the MOOC platforms used, (b) the proposed game elements, and (c) the students' actions associated to such elements.

Currently, many **MOOC platforms** do not allow the implementation of game elements into their courses by default. In that sense, Hansch et al. (2015) made an empirical analysis of the gamification capabilities of several massive online platforms, including some MOOC platforms such as FutureLearn, NovoEd, or OpenHPI [9]. In the reviewed works, most of the models/frameworks, prototypes/systems and studies are proposed to be evaluated or are finally evaluated in educational platforms. On the one hand, in the works that use Moodle (3), OpenHPI (2), OpenLearn (1), Claroline Connect (1), iMOOX (1), and Quizlet (1), the gamification was either not evaluated in real environments or evaluated in non massive-scale contexts (*i.e.*, with less than 500 enrolled students). On the other hand, there are several works evaluated in real contexts involving the educational platforms: Telescopio (2), ECO platform (1), Canvas Network

[1] The selected publications and the extracted data is accessible at: https://owncloud.gsic.uva.es/index.php/s/YRje3C1UHghvmG8.

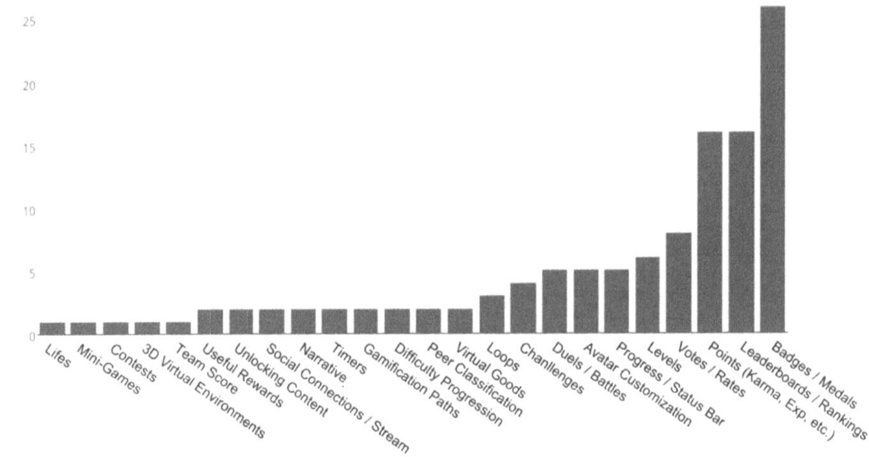

Fig. 2. Game mechanics proposed for the usage of gamification in MOOCs.

(1), Coorpacademy (1), Coursera (1) and MiríadaX (1). Therefore, although there are some educational platforms with gamification capabilities, the effects of gamification in real MOOC contexts have not been thoroughly explored yet.

The decision of which **game elements** to use and how they are going to interact with the students are important considerations during the design and enactment phases of MOOCs. Figure 2 shows the game elements implemented or proposed to be employed in MOOCs. The top used game elements in MOOCs are points, badges and leaderboards (PBL), similarly to what is shown by other gamification reviews focused on small scale [6,7]. Also, we can see that some game elements that are not frequently implemented in small-scale contexts are gaining importance in MOOCs such as duels, ratings, status bars and avatar customizations. In this sense, Chang and Wei (2016) [2] classify the game elements used in MOOCs regarding their engagement level based on the results of a survey to more than 5.000 MOOC students. Points, badges and team leaderboards are in the top 5 of the most engaging game elements in MOOCs. Nevertheless, there are some other top engagement game elements such as virtual goods and memory-game interactions that have not been highly explored in MOOCs. Further work is needed to understand why PBL are the most used elements even when they have been criticized by some researchers [15], and how can other top engaging game elements be implemented in MOOCs.

While some game elements can be independent of the students' performance such as narrative or 3D graphics, other elements are associated with the **actions performed by the students** in the learning environments (*e.g.*, the requirements behind the rewards). Figure 3 shows the students' rewarded actions found in the reviewed works. The most frequent students' actions related to gamification are individual actions that can involve interaction with other students: contributing to forums, completing assignments and modules, and rating other

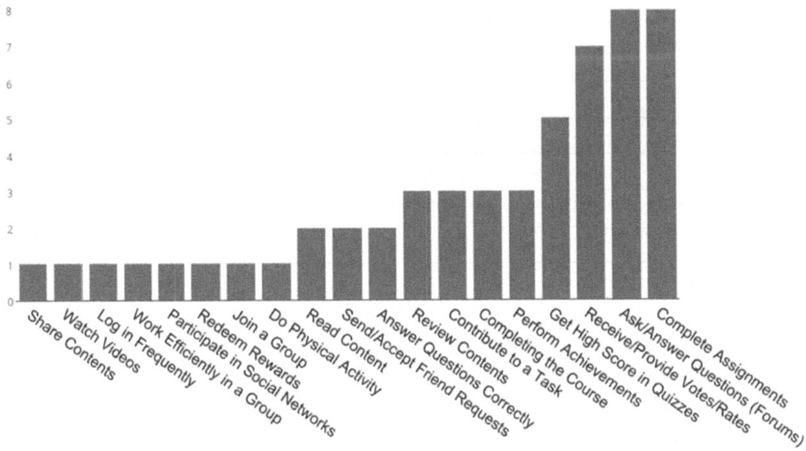

Fig. 3. Students' actions associated to game elements in MOOCs.

students' comments and content. Most of the students' actions in MOOCs that are related to game elements are automatically analyzed and processed to check if the rewards have to be issued. Few works such as Cross et al. (2014) do the rewarding process manually. In this work, students are rewarded with a badge when other members of the team manually assess the positive contribution to the teamwork [3].

4 Conclusions and Future Work

This literature review has analyzed the most relevant contributions on the use of gamification in MOOCs, identifying the current state of the art on how gamification is being implemented in MOOCs. Gamification has been proposed and tested in few MOOC platforms, mainly by means of points, badges and leaderboards. These game elements are frequently related to individual student actions such as contributing to forums, completing assignments and modules, and rating other students' comments and content. Further work is needed to analyze the relationship among the gamification design purposes, the game elements and the students' actions since most existing works focus on the analysis of the gamification effects instead of understanding their correlation with the design and implementation decisions.

The review carried out shows that the game elements implemented in MOOCs and rewarded actions are similar to those used in small-scale educational contexts (*e.g.*, PBL, completing assignments). However, there exists some game elements that are gaining presence in MOOCs such as rates, duels or avatar customizations. Another important difference with the small scale is the scarcity of empirical studies exploring the effects of gamification in authentic MOOC-like learning situations. Further work and empirical studies are necessary to understand the effectiveness of different gamification purposes, game elements, and the students' actions on which they are based.

Acknowledgements. This research has been partially supported by the Junta de Castilla y León (VA082U16) and Ministerio de Economía y Competitividad (TIN2014-53199-C3-2-R). The authors thank the GSIC-EMIC research team for their ideas and support and the "Movilidad Doctorandos UVa 2017" grant program.

References

1. Caponetto, I., Earp, J., Ott, M.: Gamification and education: a literature review. In: Proceedings of the 8th European Conference on Games Based Learning, pp. 50–57 (2014)
2. Chang, J.W., Wei, H.Y.: Exploring engaging gamification mechanics in massive online open courses. Educ. Technol. Soc. **19**(2), 177–203 (2016)
3. Cross, S., Whitelock, D., Galley, R.: The use, role and reception of open badges as a method for formative and summative reward in two Massive Open Online Courses. Int. J. e-Assess. **4**(1) (2014)
4. De Sousa Borges, S., Durelli, V., Reis, H., Isotani, S.: A systematic mapping on gamification applied to education. In: Proceedings of the 29th Annual ACM Symposium on Applied Computing, pp. 216–222. ACM (2014)
5. Deterding, S., Dixon, D., Khaled, R., Nacke, L.: From game design elements to gamefulness: defining gamification. In: Proceedings of the 15th ACM International Academic MindTrek Conference on Envisioning Future Media Environments, pp. 9–15 (2011)
6. Dichev, C., Dicheva, D.: Gamifying education: what is known, what is believed and what remains uncertain: a critical review. Int. J. Educ. Technol. High. Educ. **14**(1), 9 (2017)
7. Dicheva, D., Dichev, C., Agre, G., Angelova, G.: Gamification in education: a systematic mapping study. Educ. Technol. Soc. **18**(3), 75–88 (2015)
8. Hamari, J., Koivisto, J., Sarsa, H.: Does gamification work?-a literature review of empirical studies on gamification. In: Proceedings of 47th Hawaii International Conference on System Sciences, pp. 3025–3034. IEEE (2014)
9. Hansch, A., Newman, C., Schildhauer, T.: Fostering engagement with gamification: review of current practices on online learning platforms. HIIG Discussion Paper Series (2015)
10. Jacoby, J.: The disruptive potential of the massive open online course: a literature review. J. Open Flex. Distance Learn. **18**(1), 73–85 (2014)
11. Jordan, K.: Initial trends in enrolment and completion of massive open online courses. Int. Rev. Res. Open Distrib. Learn. **15**(1) (2014)
12. Khalil, H., Ebner, M.: MOOCs completion rates and possible methods to improve retention-a literature review. In: Proceedings of the World Conference on Educational Multimedia, Hypermedia and Telecommunications, vol. 1, pp. 1305–1313 (2014)
13. Kitchenham, B., Charters, S.: Guidelines for performing systematic literature reviews in software engineering. Technical report, Ver. 2.3 EBSE (2007)
14. Liyanagunawardena, T.R., Adams, A.A., Williams, S.A.: MOOCs: a systematic study of the published literature 2008–2012. Int. Rev. Res. Open Distrib. Learn. **14**(3), 202–227 (2013)

15. Robertson, M.: Can't play, won't play. Hide & Seek 6 (2010). http://kotaku.com/5686393/cant-play-wont-play. Accessed June 2017
16. Veletsianos, G., Shepherdson, P.: A systematic analysis and synthesis of the empirical MOOC literature published in 2013–2015. Int. Rev. Res. Open Distrib. Learn. **17**(2) (2016)
17. Yuan, L., Powell, S.: MOOCs and open education: implications for higher education (2013). http://publications.cetis.org.uk/wp-content/uploads/2013/03/MOOCs-and-Open-Education.pdf. Accessed Jan 2017

Using a Mixed Analysis Process to Identify the Students' Digital Practices

Laëtitia Pierrot(✉), Jean-François Cerisier, Hassina El-Kechaï, Sergio Ramirez, and Lucie Pottier

Université de Poitiers, TECHNÉ - EA 6316, 86000 Poitiers, France
{laetitia.pierrot,cerisier,hassina.el.kechai,sergio.ramirez, lucie.pottier}@univ-poitiers.fr

Abstract. Our work is focused on young users' digital behaviors, specifically during instrumented learning activities. Social sciences researchers mostly consider these behaviors through a central yet polysemic concept, the "digital practices".

In this paper, we introduce a new definition of the "digital practices" based on a literature review that led us to formalize it through a model. To identify and analyze the young users' practices, we use a data-driven approach. We propose an analysis model, which uses a prescriptive observation method. The model includes two different kind of data to identify the digital practices and its components: usage tracking logs and students' interviews.

The two goals we pursue from the data analysis are, on the one hand, to provide indications on the students' practices to adjust digital educational policies carried out. On the other hand, we aim to identify the generic characteristics of our analysis model and use it on other contexts.

Our approach has been validated by a first experimentation involving students enrolled in a French high school. In this paper, we focus on the general analysis process, from its definition to its operationalization.

Keywords: Digital practices · Model analysis · Tracking logs · Instrumented activity · Formalization · Data-driven approach

1 Introduction

The work presented in this article is part of the study of the teenagers' behavior in relation to the use of technologies. The study of their digital behaviors allows us to measure the appropriation that they make of technologies. Researchers study these behaviors from different points of view (by focusing on their skills or on their equipment for instance). For our part, we propose to study it from the angle of the central concept of "digital practice" in a specific context that is that of learning. The purpose of this article is to present the analysis process developed to identify the teenagers' digital behaviors. The teenagers' digital practices are mainly described from one-off or recurrent surveys in France [1, 2, 5, 7–9, 19], as in other countries [3, 11, 15, 17]. These works highlight a paradox on their digital practices: despite the widespread access to digital artefacts, the

É. Lavoué et al. (Eds.): EC-TEL 2017, LNCS 10474, pp. 448–453, 2017.
DOI: 10.1007/978-3-319-66610-5_41

teenagers have little diversification and a lack of high-level digital skills. Some authors [14] have demonstrated the homogeneity of the teenagers' digital use, while others [6] have studied their difficulty in developing non-instrumental skills.

From this work, we retain that the notion of "digital practice" is complex and that we can study it through different facets. For our part, we focus on understanding how they can come from the social environment and therefore are interested in the circulation of practices, the way in which the digital practices of one singular subject can become more elaborate by practices arising from the social environment, and how the social environment can benefit from individual practices [18].

In order to understand the digital practices, we could carry out the analysis of practices using interviews, occasional or recurrent observations or questionnaires based on what people declare. However, this type of method can induce biases such as that of social desirability [4]. In order to limit the presence of these biases, we favor a mixed approach, based on digital traces that account for student activity, supplemented by explanatory interviews (individual and collective).

This approach presupposes a specific analysis process, and before that, the formalization of our object of study, the digital practices. It is on these two points that we aim to focus this paper. In Sect. 2, we present the theoretical framework in which we situate this research. Finally, in Sect. 3, we present the analysis approach that we have put in place and how we applied this method.

2 Formalization of the Analysis Approach from the Theoretical Framework: The Digital Practices

In the literature, the "digital practice" is polysemic and regularly invoked, along with the terms "use" and "social usage". We note that, unlike the use that describes an individual and punctual relationship between a user and an instrument, both social usage and practice depict some socialized and instrumented ways of doing things. The "socialized" part refers to the fact that it involve one or more individuals. We mention the "instrumented" part since it include the use of one or more artefacts and action schemes. Depending on the complexity of the instrumentation, we will speak of "social usage" for the elementary yet socialized actions and of "practice" for the socialized and incorporating actions (for example, the social usage of WhatsApp is part of the particular digital practice, which is a communicative practice).

For our part, we define the digital practice as a set of thematic, frequent and usual actions, constructed by some interactions (with an object, with an environment) and aimed at a certain efficiency. Based on a literature study, we retain the four-constitutive dimensions, presented in Table 1, that are characteristics of the practices.

We have formalized these dimensions as a model (see Fig. 1). In this model, we chose to change the "action" dimension into a thematic category, since we consider that the practices are incorporating and thus involve several actions.

Table 1. Constitutive dimensions of the practices identified

Action	What the individual materially does with the technical object for a definite purpose [15]
Context	The practice is inscribed in time because it translates habits [16]
Temporality	Corresponding to the social configuration in which the individual is situated [13]
Intention	The conscious objective of action

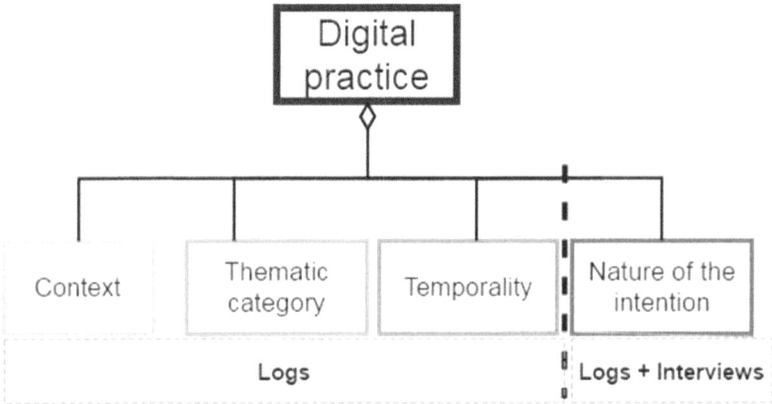

Fig. 1. Formal model for the digital practice

In this model, we have also identified that we can collect the context, the actions, merged into thematic categories and the temporality using the traces. On the other hand, the intention is internal for the subject and hence difficult to capture it using the traces. Instead, we propose therefore to define the nature of the intention (in which context – for academic purposes or personal reasons – the practice takes place), taking into account the three preceding dimensions: if a thematic action group take place in a context A, given a certain temporality, then we assume that it belongs to a school (or non-school) setting.

3 Methodology: General Analysis Process Adopted

3.1 General Principle

The analysis process set up in our study uses a particular approach, originally planned for trace analysis and based on the prescription of observation [12]. It consists in defining beforehand the *needs for observation* and *analysis* (what we wish to observe) and the *indicators* (how and where to observe in the data). The combination of a need for observation, explained in need for analysis and associated with an indicator, constitutes an *analysis scenario* (the complete approach). In our case, each of the concepts that we use (need for observation, need for analysis, indicator, analysis scenario) is described in detail.

We defined the concepts by taking as a guide Engeström's activity system triangle [10]. The activity system model [10] considers that from a systemic view any human activity is constructed and pursued with the interaction of several elements: a "subject" will use an "instrument" to obtain a "result". The subject can interact with several users called "community" through the mediation of "rules". When the community works to achieve the same result, it does so through the "division of labor".

We started from this model to specify our needs for analysis. At this stage, we pursue a single main objective: to identify and characterize practices (isolated or shared practices). Regarding this, we defined four needs for analysis, which are all linked to the Engeström triad "Subject-Rules-Community" and help identify the actions according to the practices' dimensions: according to the context of use [Analysis scenario 1], to the thematic category [Analysis scenario 2], to the temporality [Analysis scenario 3] and to the nature of the intention [Analysis scenario 4]. These four analysis scenarios, along with all the others that we defined have been tested with high school students within the Living Cloud project.

3.2 Context for Our Study

The Living Cloud project aims to transform the learning conditions of students and the pedagogical practices of teachers by and with digital. It takes place in a French high school in the region of New Aquitaine. We contribute to this project by providing scientific support aimed at observing the behaviors of students and teachers in the context of the use of digital technology in learning contexts. One of the facets of this scientific support is the collection and analysis of data (traces, supplemented by interviews) of the high school students. Through this approach, the general objective is to provide the project sponsors with elements to feed the reflection on the digital education policy, while contributing to the other questions related to the scientific support of the Living Cloud project. More specifically, at this stage, the data collection and analysis phase seeks to achieve an objective: to identify and characterize practices (isolated or shared practices).

The high school students we follow were equipped with a tracking software, on their personal digital device.). We also study logs from the high school network (from the proxy). In addition to these two sets of data, we use the students' timetables and transcripts from the explanatory interviews that we conducted with them. For the interviews, we ran a thematic analysis that aim to specify more our analysis process.

3.3 Operationalizing the Practice Model

The analysis scenario 1 corresponds to the identification of the actions of the students according to the context of use. In the context of the study, we distinguish three contexts: when the student is in class, in high school (A), when he/she is in high school but out-of-class (B) and when he/she is outside of the school (C). To obtain these three contexts, we rely on the logs' timestamp and the students' schedules.

The analysis scenario 2 corresponds to the identification of the actions of the students according to the thematic categories. We have listed 11 categories, presented in Table 2.

We elaborate these 11 categories from our literature study and according to what we observe from the data.

Table 2. Thematic Categories for the AS 2

Code	Thematic categories	Examples of applications or sites
BOC	Office or automation tool	Microsoft Word, Kingsoft Office, Geogebra
CAV	Audio or video consultation	Youtube, iTunes, VLC, Audacity
ID	Information-documentation	Chrome, Acrobat reader, iBooks, Aperçu,
Jeux	Games	Dofus, Farm Heroes Saga, OverWatch
MegaP	Web portals	Google.fr, bing.com, msn.com, qq.com
Orga	Organization	Calendrier, Notes, Skitch
Comm	Communication tools	Mail, Skype, Messages, FaceTime
RSN	Social Networks	Facebook, Twitter, Instagram, vk.com
Stock	Storage	Drive.google.com, Photos, Dropbox, OneDrive
Trans	Transactions	Aliexpress.com, asos.fr, leboncoin.fr, amazon.fr

The analysis scenario 3 corresponds to the identification of students' actions according to the temporality. For temporality, we took into account two dimensions (the recurrence and the duration of the actions) and thus have four variables: the non-frequent actions that have a short duration, as opposed to those that have a long duration, the frequent actions that have a short duration, as opposed to those that have a long duration.

The analysis scenario 4 corresponds to the identification of the actions of the students according to the nature of the intention. Unlike the other three scenarios presented, for this one, we used mainly the students' answers collected during explanatory interviews where one of the questions was to identify which actions were for academic learning and/or for personal reasons.

4 Conclusion

In this paper, we described how, starting from a precise research objective around the digital practices, we formalized this objective and implemented an analysis process using mixed data. The work we have presented in this paper focuses on the complexity of the process, starting from the formalization of our research object, towards the definition of needs for observation and analysis and indicators.

The four scenarios introduced here have been tested. The results obtained by these scenarios contribute to the identification of digital practices. At this stage, we dealt with each dimension separately, taking into account the individual characteristics of the students. The next scenario will consist of combining each of the dimensions to achieve the list of students' digital practices. In addition, it will allow us to realize standard profiles using statistical methods.

Regarding the analysis process, it would be interesting first to reinvest it in other projects and other contexts, in order to confirm its validity. Testing it in different contexts will reveal what is generic of what relates to the context of our study, thus confirming to a fine degree the relevance of this process. The generic dimension of the process can then be capitalized, shared and reused to reduce costs and time. This will constitute an interesting expertise for the working community on the analysis of traces, in particular on themes linked to the appropriation of digital technologies.

References

1. Aillerie, K.: Pratiques informationnelles informelles des adolescents (14–18 ans) sur le Web (Doctoral dissertation, Université Paris-Nord-Paris XIII) (2011)
2. Boubée, N.: Caractériser les pratiques informationnelles des jeunes: Les problèmes laissés ouverts par les deux conceptions. «Natifs» et «naïfs» numériques. Communication Rencontres Savoirs CDI **24**, 1–14 (2011)
3. Boyd, D.: It's Complicated: The Social Lives of Networked Teens. Yale University Press (2014)
4. Butori, R., Parguel, B.: When students give biased responses to researchers: an exploration of traditional paper vs. computerized self-administration. In: EMAC (2010)
5. Cerisier, J.-F.: Acculturation numérique et médiation instrumentale. Le cas des adolescents français. HDR, 375 pages, Université de Poitiers (2011)
6. Cerisier, J.F., Rizza, C., Devauchelle, B., Nguyen, A.: Former des jeunes à l'usage des médias numériques: heurs et malheurs du brevet informatique et internet (B2i) en France. In: Distances et Savoirs. Hors série, Lavoisier, Paris, pp. 1–28 (2008)
7. Dauphin, F.: Culture et pratiques numériques juvéniles: Quels usages pour quelles compétences? Questions vives. Recherches en éducation **7**(17), 37–52 (2012)
8. Devauchelle, B.: Le Brevet Informatique et Internet (B2i) d'un geste institutionnel aux réalités pédagogiques (Doctoral dissertation, Université Paris VIII Vincennes-Saint Denis) (2004)
9. Fluckiger, C.: L'appropriation des TIC par les collégiens dans les sphères familières et scolaires (Doctoral dissertation, École normale supérieure de Cachan-ENS Cachan) (2007)
10. Engeström, Y.: Learning by Expanding: an Activity-Theoretical Approach to Developmental Research. Orienta-Konsultit Oy, Helsinki (1987)
11. Hargittai, E.: Digital Na(t)ives? variation in internet skills and uses among members of the "Net Generation"*. Alpha Kappa Delta **80**(1), 92–113 (2010)
12. Iksal, S.: Ingénierie de l'observation basée sur la prescription en EIAH. HDR, 127 p. Université du Maine (2012)
13. Jauréguiberry, F., Proulx, S.: Usages et enjeux des technologies de communication. Erès (2011)
14. Lardellier, P.: Le pouce et la souris: Enquête sur la culture numérique des ados, Fayard (2006)
15. Livingstone, S.: Digital connections and disconnections. Consulté à l'adresse (2013). http://www.lse.ac.uk/media@lse/WhosWho/AcademicStaff/SoniaLivingstone/pdf/Austintalkwithinserted.PDF
16. Nardi, B.A.: Context and Consciousness: Activity Theory and Human-Computer Interaction. MIT Press (1996)
17. Ólafsson, K., Livingstone, S., Haddon, L.: Children's Use of Online Technologies in Europe A Review of the European Evidence Base, May 2013
18. Rabardel P.: Les hommes et les technologies. Approche cognitive des instruments contemporains, Paris, A. Colin (1995)
19. Solari Landa, M.: L'appropriation collective portée par les représentations et les pratiques: le projet Living Cloud 2016 (2017)

Strong Technology-Enhanced Learning Concepts

Luis P. Prieto[1(✉)], Hamed Alavi[2], and Himanshu Verma[3]

[1] School of Educational Sciences, Tallinn University, 10120 Tallinn, Estonia
lprisan@tlu.ee
[2] CHILI Lab, EPFL, 1015 Lausanne, Switzerland
hamed.alavi@epfl.ch
[3] Human-IST Research Centre, Universtiy of Fribourg, 1700 Fribourg, Switzerland
himanshu.verma@unifr.ch

Abstract. Although not unheard of, there is a scarcity of intermediate-level concepts (not as generalizable as theories, but with an applicability wider than a single technology or intervention) in technology-enhanced learning (TEL) research. In this paper we propose 'strong TEL concepts', as intermediate-level bodies of design knowledge that are both grounded in research evidence from multiple technologies and contexts, and have clear theoretical connections. We describe the main features of this kind of concepts, along with a practical method for developing them as valuable research contributions. We also propose 'purposeful disengagement' as an example of strong TEL concept, to ignite the dialogue in our community about the necessity and benefits of this kind of knowledge to support both TEL design and theory advancement.

Keywords: Learning technology · Design research · Design-based research · Intermediary-level knowledge

1 Introduction

Designing a new learning technology is a challenging task shaped by multiple factors. The ever-changing nature and constraints of the settings we work on; the accelerating pace of technological change; the changes in our own customs, habits and ways of seeing the world. However, a learning technology not only needs to provide nice interaction – it should also *enhance* learning. Although we have theories of how people learn to guide us, the lack of a 'unified theory of learning' and the high level of abstraction of such theories, makes it difficult to apply them to the design of a learning technology fit for a particular context.

This tension between generalizable knowledge and the provision of solutions fit for a context is a well-known problem in design-oriented disciplines like interaction design [11]. In such disciplines, several kinds of 'intermediary forms of knowledge' (more concrete than generalized theories, but more general than a single design instance [3]) have been proposed to bridge this gap. Examples of such knowledge forms include design heuristics [15], annotated portfolios, experiential qualities, or strong concepts [11].

É. Lavoué et al. (Eds.): EC-TEL 2017, LNCS 10474, pp. 454–459, 2017.
DOI: 10.1007/978-3-319-66610-5_42

In the field of TEL research, such tension has led to the proposal and wide application of specific methodologies like design-based research (DBR) [19]. These iterative methodological frameworks have a heavy focus on longer-term contextualized work and ecological validity. However, DBR not only should have an ecologically-valid proposal as an outcome: it should also contribute to a body of more general theory [1]. Developing intermediary forms of knowledge is one clear way in which such theoretical contributions can be made. Indeed, we can find several forms of intermediary knowledge in TEL research literature, such as design patterns and pattern languages [13], or design guidelines [4].

Recent literature reviews on the outputs of TEL design-based research[1] illustrate the scarcity and a lack of variety in the intermediate-level knowledge in our research community. To ameliorate this, we propose 'strong TEL concepts' as a valid and needed form of intermediary knowledge in TEL. These concepts should be both grounded in research evidence about learning benefits from *multiple* design instances or contexts, and should have clear theoretical implications. Below, we also propose a practical method for developing these concepts (based on the one proposed by Höök and Löwgren [11]) along with an initial strong concept example, to seed this discussion within our research community.

2 Strong TEL Concepts

It is our main thesis in this paper that *the TEL community needs a way to abstract knowledge from multiple design-based research processes, in a more explicit and systematic manner.* To aid in this process, we propose here the notion of 'strong TEL concepts'. This notion is not just a direct import of the strong concepts developed by Höök and others in human-computer interaction (HCI) research [11]. Rather, it builds upon the main intrinsic goal of TEL: the enhancement of learning experiences through technology, directly or indirectly by making learning processes more efficient and/or cost-effective (and taking into account the multiple existing conceptions of learning) [8].

Below, the term design *instance* refers to the object of a (design-based) research process. These instances themselves are a socio-technical composite, in which a certain piece(s) of designed *technology* is used in a particular manner (what we will call an *intervention*). Hence, DBR processes are used in TEL research to develop and evaluate design instances fit for certain learning/teaching tasks in a particular *context* (the setting where the DBR process is enacted).

Definition. Strong TEL concepts can be tentatively defined as explicit, cohesive pieces of design knowledge that are at a higher level of abstraction than individual design instances, drawing from multiple such instances to gather evidence of their potential benefits (and limitations) for learning, and connecting to one or more high-level theories of learning and to other intermediate-level knowledge. These concepts can be differentiated from other intermediate knowledge in TEL (like design patterns or guidelines) in that they draw from *multiple* design research instances (something that design patterns often share),

[1] Due to lack of space, these reviews have been made available elsewhere [16].

but also are explicitly *grounded* in learning theory, focusing on the available *evidence of learning benefits* from those individual instances. Furthermore, strong TEL concepts reach beyond pure technology design, defining also aspects of *user interaction with the technology* (i.e., teacher/learner experience).

Benefits. The expected advantages of this conceptual approach to TEL design research are manifold: similar to design patterns, these strong TEL concepts can aid communication among designers/researchers in learning technologies, by creating a common vocabulary; similar to guidelines, strong TEL concepts are generative – they can help TEL designers (especially, newcomers to the field) in generating new design instances for particular tasks and contexts. Furthermore, and in contrast with other intermediate TEL knowledge, strong TEL concepts can more clearly serve to evolve theory, driving and prioritizing our future research agenda (e.g., as researchers explore a concept through different instances of DBR, or try to reproduce existing studies in new contexts).

Method for Development. Strong TEL concepts need to be developed and described for our community's scrutiny. TEL is too multi-disciplinary and heterogeneous a community for us to dare to prescribe a particular order of execution, although we anticipate that the process will be iterative, as we find new design instances and build the groundings and connections needed to support it:

- Provide a *high-level description* of the concept, describing in general terms the gist of the design idea and why it has an impact on learning.
- Perform a *downward grounding*, by collecting multiple design instances that portray this high-level idea in action. This includes publications about the design of the technology, its application in a pedagogical intervention as well as their evaluation (e.g., through DBR processes). It is important not only to gather successful instances of application, but also *failed* ones.
- Perform an *upward grounding* to connect the proposed strong concept to existing, more general learning theories, and specifying what kind of link exists between them (support, contradiction, between two theories, etc.).
- Perform an *horizontal grounding*, to relate this concept to other intermediate TEL knowledge (not only strong TEL concepts, but also existing design patterns, guidelines, etc.).
- Gather and synthesize *available evidence of learning benefits* throughout the different design instances applying the concept. This synthesis will serve to understand what kind of learning this concept seems to be suitable for, and what kind of benefits are expected in an adequate application of the concept.
- Using the synthesis of results above, but very especially the 'failed instances' gathered in step 2, the *scope and limits* of the concept should be outlined, as well as other *design advice* and caveats on its application, synthesizing the experience from the design processes that applied this concept.

These steps can be themselves structured in different ways in research practice or in scientific events. For instance, researcher/designer workshops could be organized to develop and disseminate such concepts, as it has already been done for the development of design patterns in TEL (e.g., [14]).

3 An Example Concept: Purposeful Disengagement

High-level concept. To design a technology or intervention to purposefully 'break the flow' of the current learning activity, to force a pause that enables learning, reflection or interaction at a different social plane.

Downward grounding. Design instances of this concept include the availability of paper cards that interrupt/enable the logistics simulation of Tinkerlamp's augmented tabletops [7]. Teachers can use these cards to ask students to reflect before a simulation round is executed, or to pause all the students' simulations in the classroom for a round of whole-class debriefing. In Kreitmayer et al.'s 4Decades multi-tablet simulation [12], the application's interactivity is purposefully restricted after each interaction and during teacher-defined debriefing/reflection phases of the game. Finally, the in-video questions that interrupt video lectures in many massive online courses (MOOCs) [10] can be seen as another application of this idea.

Upward grounding. This strong TEL concept is at the frontier between several theories. It acts in opposition to the psychological theory of flow, which has been applied to learning, especially by researchers working on increasing the engagement of learning activities [18]. Purposeful disengagement features are however in line with Bloom's seminal work on the need for multiple kinds of learning outcomes [2], and the theories of mastery learning, which argue that much of deliberate practice to achieve mastery cannot really be done in a state of flow [9].

Horizontal grounding. Generally, it can be said to be an educational counterpart of the concept of 'seamfulness' in HCI [11]. Purposeful disengagement can also be related to existing guidelines for TEL design: in pedagogical scripting, the idea that learning activities should occur at multiple social levels [5] (disengagement can serve to mark such transitions among planes); or guidelines on 'designing for orchestration' prescribing control of these transitions by the teacher [4].

Evidence of learning benefits. During Tinkerlamp's DBR process, the evidence from classroom experiments showed a significant difference in problem-solving ability (albeit not in subject understanding) when using purposeful disengagement mechanisms [6]. Kreitmayer et al. [12] do not report direct impact on learning, although they note that participants did not perceive adversely the purposeful restrictions in interactivity.

Scope, limits and application. This kind of concept has been applied mostly on collaborative, simulation-based learning activities – and especially, in authentic classroom conditions. This hints at the concept being especially useful in learning situations that are time-restricted and which need multiplicity of outcomes and activities, and transitions between them. However, the fact that this concept taps into very basic human brain mechanisms like attention and reflection, points to a wider applicability. Further research, including the application of more continuous learning analytics (to understand the diminishing returns of excessive engagement in the current activity), is clearly needed.

4 Discussion

We have sketched 'strong TEL concepts' as an intermediary form of knowledge situated between design *instances* (e.g., the outcome of DBR processes) and more general learning *theories*. This middle-ground position renders them as sustainable, empowering, and coherent channels for knowledge creation, assimilation, and transfer. The overarching ambition behind this article is to methodologically homogenize the (so far, disperse) links between the learning technologies we design and our theoretical frameworks. This will make it easier for design researchers to choose, inherit, replicate or combine different TEL concepts as foundations of their designs.

Strong TEL concepts are inherently different from other intermediary forms of knowledge in TEL. While design patterns, for example, are well established and tend to be static in nature, strong concepts can evolve with the availability of more outcomes and evidence from new design instances, or the apparition of new technology and trends. When compared with design guidelines, strong TEL concepts are explicitly derived from multiple contexts/interventions, therefore increasing the scope of their applicability.

Despite the multiple advantages of pursuing strong TEL concepts as another intermediary form of design knowledge, their development is only now starting within the TEL community [17] (compared to their longer history in other design-oriented research domains). This can be primarily attributed to the lack of a (perceived) straightforward link between them and the learning benefits that might ensue. With our proposed definition of strong TEL concept (which emphasizes learning benefits evidence), we aim at addressing those concerns. In our proposal above we also intend to address tacit problems of this kind of approach (and of other intermediary knowledge forms): that of 'publication bias' which inhibits researchers from reporting failed design instances (and failures in general), or the scarcity of replication studies. Yet, these are deeper problems of our field (and research in general), which we can only start addressing here.

Finally, the notion of strong TEL concepts is presented here without aspirations of completeness. Rather, we present it as a research method which, we believe, needs to be pursued, evaluated, and *collaboratively* developed by (design) researchers in the TEL community, while preserving the core value of "improving learning through technology". This article also sets forth a research agenda that entails the organization of workshops/symposiums, writing handbooks, etc. to elicit and connect more of the existing concepts and knowledge (that remain implicit so far), annotate our large body of design instances with the TEL concepts they endorse, and illustrate the links between such concepts and more general learning theories.

Acknowledgements. This project has received funding from the European Union's Horizon 2020 research and innovation programme under grant agreement No. 669074.

References

1. Barab, S., Squire, K.: Design-based research: putting a stake in the ground. J. Learn. Sci. **13**(1), 1–14 (2004)
2. Bloom, B.S., Engelhart, M.D., Furst, E.J., Hill, W.H., Krathwohl, D.R.: Taxonomy of Educational Objectives, Handbook I: The Cognitive Domain (1956)
3. Dalsgaard, P., Dindler, C.: Between theory and practice: bridging concepts in HCI research. In: Proceedings of the SIGCHI Conference on Human Factors in Computing Systems, pp. 1635–1644. ACM (2014)
4. Dillenbourg, P.: Design for classroom orchestration. Comput. Educ. **69**, 485–492 (2013)
5. Dillenbourg, P., Jermann, P.: Designing integrative scripts. In: Fischer, F., Kollar, I., Mandl, H., Haake, J.M. (eds.) Scripting Computer-supported Collaborative Learning. Computer-Supported Collaborative Learning, vol. 6, pp. 275–301. Springer, Boston (2007). doi:10.1007/978-0-387-36949-5_16
6. Do-Lenh, H.S.: Supporting reflection and classroom orchestration with tangible tabletops. Ph.D. thesis, IC, Lausanne (2012)
7. Do-Lenh, S., Jermann, P., Legge, A., Zufferey, G., Dillenbourg, P.: TinkerLamp 2.0: designing and evaluating orchestration technologies for the classroom. In: Ravenscroft, A., Lindstaedt, S., Kloos, C.D., Hernández-Leo, D. (eds.) EC-TEL 2012. LNCS, vol. 7563, pp. 65–78. Springer, Heidelberg (2012). doi:10.1007/978-3-642-33263-0_6
8. Dror, I.E.: Technology enhanced learning: the good, the bad, and the ugly. Pragm. Cogn. **16**(2), 215–223 (2008)
9. Ericsson, K.A.: The Road to Excellence: The Acquisition of Expert Performance in the Arts and Sciences, Sports, and Games. Psychology Press, Hove (2014)
10. Guo, P.J., Kim, J., Rubin, R.: How video production affects student engagement: an empirical study of MOOC videos. In: Proceedings of the First ACM Conference on Learning@ Scale Conference, pp. 41–50. ACM (2014)
11. Höök, K., Löwgren, J.: Strong concepts: intermediate-level knowledge in interaction design research. ACM Trans. Comput.-Hum. Inter. (TOCHI) **19**(3), 23 (2012)
12. Kreitmayer, S., Rogers, Y., Laney, R., Peake, S.: From participatory to contributory simulations: changing the game in the classroom. In: Proceedings of the SIGCHI Conference on Human Factors in Computing Systems, pp. 49–58. ACM (2012)
13. Mor, Y., Winters, N.: Design approaches in technology-enhanced learning. Inter. Learn. Environ. **15**(1), 61–75 (2007)
14. Mor, Y., Winters, N.: Participatory design in open education: a workshop model for developing a pattern language. J. Inter. Media Educ. (2008)
15. Nielsen, J., Molich, R.: Heuristic evaluation of user interfaces. In: Proceedings of the SIGCHI Conference on Human Factors in Computing Systems, pp. 249–256. ACM (1990)
16. Prieto, L.P., Alavi, H., Verma, H.: From interventions to theories: two literature analyses of knowledge creation in TEL design-based research. Zenodo, June 2017. doi:10.5281/zenodo.816223
17. Sharma, K., Alavi, H.S., Jermann, P., Dillenbourg, P.: Looking THROUGH versus looking AT: a TEL strong concept. In: Proceedings of the 12th European Conference in Technology-Enhanced Learning (EC-TEL) (2017)
18. Shernoff, D.J., Csikszentmihalyi, M., Shneider, B., Shernoff, E.S.: Student engagement in high school classrooms from the perspective of flow theory. Sch. Psychol. Q. **18**(2), 158 (2003)
19. Wang, F., Hannafin, M.J.: Design-based research and technology-enhanced learning environments. Educ. Technol. Res. Develop. **53**(4), 5–23 (2005)

NoteMyProgress: A Tool to Support Learners' Self-Regulated Learning Strategies in MOOC Environments

Ronald Pérez-Álvarez[1,2(✉)], Jorge J. Maldonado-Mahauad[1,3], Diego Sapunar-Opazo[1], and Mar Pérez-Sanagustín[1(✉)]

[1] Department of Computer Science, Pontificia Universidad Católica de Chile, Santiago, Chile
{raperez13,jjmaldonado,dasapunar,mar.perez}@uc.cl
[2] University of Costa Rica, Sede Regional del Pacífico, Puntarenas, Costa Rica
[3] Department of Computer Science, University of Cuenca, Cuenca, Ecuador

Abstract. The lack of self-regulation is one of the main reasons why students find it difficult to complete a MOOC. However, existing learning platforms do not have tools that support student self-regulation strategies and only few have been developed for MOOCs. This study presents NoteMyProgress, a tool designed to support self-regulation in MOOCs. We present the beta version of the tool as "proof of concept" in order to assess its usability and adoption with experts and learners in a MOOC. The results indicate that usability is well evaluated by experts, and students consider the included features to be useful in managing their time and organizing their learning process.

Keywords: Self-Regulated learning · Massive open online courses · Tools

1 Introduction

According to the literature, the lack of self-regulation is one of the main reasons why Massive Open Online Courses (MOOCs) students' find it difficult to complete the course [1]. However, the most popular online learning platforms such as Coursera and edX have very few mechanisms to support the student self-regulation process. Coursera, for example, provides students a visual overview of the estimated time duration for each week, time remaining in videos and readings, and presents a schedule of deadlines of the activities. Otherwise, edX recently included a notes module where students can take notes on texts, and later review and organize those notes. But these mechanisms appear to be insufficient in supporting self-regulation strategies, so new tools are required to complement them [2]. Although several efforts have been made to develop tools that support self-regulated learning (SRL) in traditional online environments [3], only few tools have been proposed for MOOCs [2, 4, 5].

This study presents NoteMyProgress, a tool that allows MOOC learners to take notes and see visuals of their time management within the course. Two research questions: (RQ1) What is the level of usability of the NoteMyProgress tool in a MOOC learning

É. Lavoué et al. (Eds.): EC-TEL 2017, LNCS 10474, pp. 460–466, 2017.
DOI: 10.1007/978-3-319-66610-5_43

environment? (RQ2) What is the perceived implementation of NoteMyProgress as a tool to support students' self-regulation strategies?

2 Self-Regulated Learning (SRL) Strategies and Tools

Self-regulated students are characterized by their ability to initiate cognitive, metacognitive, affective, and motivational processes [6]. Recent studies show that, the students' most common self-regulated problems are related to time management and activity planning [1, 7]. According to Kizilcec et al. [1], goal setting and strategic planning are two of the most effective SRL strategies to predict attainment of personal course goals. A recent study by Veletsianos et al. [7] found that taking notes is a strategy useful for students in MOOCs. Therefore, time management, planning, and note-taking are strategies that require an additional effort from the MOOC students.

In a literature review [8], we identified few tools that support SRL in MOOCs [2, 4, 5, 9]. MyLearningMentor tool, that is either conceptual design proposals [9]. The Serious Game, a tool that allows students, using interactive evaluations, to put their knowledge into practice in realistic industrial problems. Supported self-regulation strategies include self-awareness, self-evaluation, and self-motivation [5]. It was tested with 3,099 students on the Canvas platform. The study's findings indicate that the tool contributes to student motivation and lowers dropout rates. Another tool is Video-Mapper [4], which allow students to take notes on video lessons and promotes collaboration and interaction between students. Video-Mapper supports the self-regulation strategies of organizing and help-seeking and was tested with 50 students in a blended environment where the MOOC was used as a supplement to a traditional course. Only the usage and usability of the tool was evaluated. The most recent proposal is the Learning Tracker tool [2]. It is a widget to support the development of self-regulated learning skills through visual displays in a MOOC. The self-regulation strategies encouraged by this tool are time-management and self-awareness. Learning Tracker was tested in a MOOC environment in edX with around 21,000 students. The results indicate that students who used the tool received higher grades and turned assignments, in earlier in relation to the deadline, than those who did not. Learning Tracker is the only tool that has been implemented and tested in a real MOOC environment. However, its design and evaluation have been limited to the edX platform. Also, its function is limited to a single display that only shows information about activities recorded in the archive logs.

Neither of these tools propose a solution to support the student in a holistic manner; that is to say, to not only assist the student during learning activities, but also allow them to monitor their learning process and review their interaction with the course. Therefore, new tools that complement existing MOOC platforms to support those SRL strategies proven to be the most beneficial for students - goal-setting, strategic planning, organization such as note taking and time management [1, 2, 7] - in an holistic manner are needed.

3 NoteMyProgress

In this section, we describe the architecture and functions of the tool's beta version or "proof of concept". NoteMyProgress is a tool designed to support self-regulated learning strategies for students in MOOCs and promote self-awareness in students about their learning process and their interaction with the course. The tool seeks to help the student not just with monitoring and charting learning activities within the platform, but also with the use of self-regulation strategies outside of it, like taking notes during a study session and tracking the overall learning process.

The tool[1] has two components: (1) a Google Chrome Plugin that permit the integration whit the MOOCs platforms and gathering information about learning activities the students; and (2) a Dashboard that analyzes the data collected and displays it in interactive graphs that help the user take stock of their activity in the course. Figure 1(a) shows the architecture of NoteMyProgress. The plugin, which works independent from the learning platform, collects the URLs the student visits during a learning session (within and beyond the learning platform), the date and time they accessed and exited the URL, the date and time of the notes, the text from the notes, the user, and the course. This data is stored in a *.json* file and sent continuously to the application's core. The data is then processed according to the MOOC platform it came from. The tool currently works to process the activity of students working on Coursera courses in Spanish.

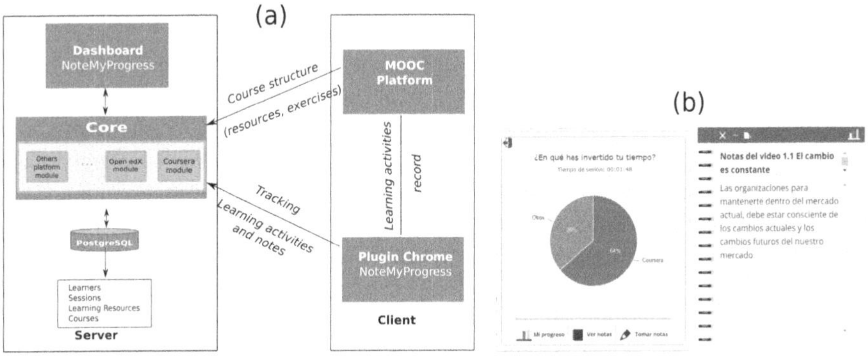

Fig. 1. (a) Architecture of the NoteMyProgress tool. (b) Main interface of the NoteMyProgress plugin and the notebook.

The Beta version of the tool includes features to support three self-regulation strategies: time-management, self-monitoring, and organizing. This version allows students: **(1) Take and download notes,** students can to take notes (Fig. 1b) while completing activities within the MOOC and download them in the dashboard; **(2) Monitor activity on the platform,** allows students to monitor their engagement with learning activities such as videos, forums, exams and complement activities. In this way, the student can

[1] NoteMyProgress beta tool (only available in Spanish): https://drive.google.com/uc?export=download&id=0B1o2CVZQv0Y7ck44eGNSUGd0SmM

relate their interaction with the activities and requirements of the course; **(3) Monitor time spent,** allows students monitoring time spent on the learning activities within the learning platform and other activities outside of the platform during a study session (Fig. 1b). This visualization seeks to raise the student's awareness of distracting activities that can delay the completion of a learning activity.

4 Pilot Study: Context, Participants and Methods

The study was conducted on the MOOC on Coursera, called "Gestión de organizaciones efectivas" from the Pontificia Universidad Católica de Chile. Four experts from three different countries participated in the evaluation of the tool's usability, each with experience in systems development, interface usability and design and MOOC courses. The tool was used by 18 students, 11 of whom were able to install the application. Three of these 11 were personally interviewed. The four experts were invited to participate in the evaluation by email. The evaluators were asked to register as students in the course and follow a guide[2] with a set of activities to complete within the learning platform. The students' participation was voluntary. All students enrolled since the first edition of the course to date received an email inviting them to participate in the research.

A questionnaire[3] was created to collect data on the perception of its usability and implementation. The first section of the questionnaire was created from the usability evaluation heuristics proposed by Nielsen [10] and the second section to assess the implementation of the tool. The questions followed a 5-point Likert scale - 1 "Totally Disagree" and 5 "Totally Agree"-. The average evaluation given by the students and experts for each of the Nielsen principles was calculated for both usability and implementation. Also, the students' interaction with the dashboard collected in the system's logfiles was analyzed. Specifically, the number of student interactions with each type of display and with the notes download page were quantified. Finally, 3 of the students who used NoteMyProgress were also interviewed thoroughly.

5 Results

The average usability evaluation of the tool given by the four experts was above 3.67 and four of the six heuristics of evaluations above 4.08. The experts highlighted certain aspects to be improved: the monitoring of standards and consistency in the use of objects in order to clarify their function. For example, the period selection bar should be better visualized. In terms of the graphic design, they pointed out some aspects to be improved for greater clarity. In the plugin's design, the size of the notebook interface should be reduced and the maximize icon changed. When it comes to the plugin's functionality, there is a delay in updating the time spent.

---

[2] Link to the evaluation guide used by the experts: https://drive.google.com/open?id=0B1o2CVZQv0Y7MjFOcHVPVFZtN28.

[3] Link to usability survey: https://drive.google.com/open?id=0B1o2CVZQv0Y7UTRSWkVuSVFRSFU.

In the majority of the evaluation criteria (Table 1), the average evaluation obtained from the students was greater than 4. Additionally, some features that the learners would like to be included were extracted from the open-ended questions: (1) a display of the time spent on the resolution assessments; (2) a display of the assessment scores; and (3) notifications about the activities planned for each week. In addition, we measured implementation through the activity recorded in the dashboard's logfiles. The analysis of these data shows that students mostly interacted with those pages displaying the time spent and procrastination. The data record a total of 50 interactions and an average time of 271.9 s spent on the page. Additionally, the data show that all users interacted with the notes page, but only three downloaded them.

Table 1. Average implementation evaluations of the tool given by the students.

Evaluation criteria	Avg.
The info. in the displays is relevant to me	4.25
The info. in the displays lets me know what my interaction with the course has been like	3.5
The info. in the displays lets me know what my commitment to the course has been like	4.25
The info. in the displays lets me know how I have spent my time in the course	4.5
The info. in the displays lets me know what my interaction with the course activities has been like	4.25
The displays provide info. that can help me be aware of the time that I spend on the course	4.75
The dialogue boxes (messages that the displays show when the mouse is hovering over them) present relevant information	4
The tool presents info. that lets me draw conclusions about the use of the course	4.5

From the analysis of the interviews, we obtained 4 main results: (1) **The tool's installation process should be improved**. The students pointed out that the installation process is complicated for someone who does not have much experience with computers; (2) **The feature that shows the time spent on the course is very useful and helps them to reflect on the investment of time**. All the interviewees agreed that the time graphics helped them to manage and monitor their time, by giving them a visual idea of the hours spent on each activity and the evolution of how they dedicated their time; (3) **The functionality of note-taking was positively valued**. They pointed out that this feature allowed them to write questions on the subject which they could then share in forums and other platforms to seek help; (4) **Notifications and reminders, as well as expanding the note options (audio, maps…) were two features that interviewees said should be incorporated in the future**.

6 Conclusions and Future Work

The objective of this study was to present the main results of the usability and adoption of a proof of concept of the NoteMyProgress tool to support the self-regulation strategies in MOOCs. The results show that the proof of concept of the tool has a high degree of usability in a MOOC learning environment and mentioned certain aspects to improve on in order to achieve a higher level of usability. In terms of adoption, students consider NoteMyProgress a useful tool that supports them in managing and investing their time throughout the course. The note-taking feature during study sessions and being able to use them later, either in another study session on the platform or outside it, is considered very useful in supporting mental organization and as a means of asking for help within the platform or through other external media. NoteMyProgress includes information about the time spent in the course activities, which was very positively assessed by students in the proof of concept, in terms of awareness and reconsideration of time investment. Similar results were obtained in previous research studies [1, 7]. In addition, the results indicate that students value knowing the time spent on other activities unrelated to the course (procrastination).

This study has several limitations. Firstly, the tool was tested by very few users due to: (1) the short duration of the study (only two weeks from the start of course); or (2) the difficulties that students' found for installing the plugin. Technical issues have been already solved in the current version of the plugin uploaded in web store of google[4]. Secondly, this study only presents the results of a proof of concept evaluation, and does not measure how this intervention is related to students' performance. As future work, we plan to carry out an experiment with a wider group of participants in both a control group and an experimental group to understand if the use of the tool has a positive effect on students' performance and self-regulation strategies.

Acknowledgments. This work was supported by FONDECYT (11150231), University of Costa Rica (UCR), MOOC-Maker (561533-EPP-1-2015-1-ESEPPKA2-CBHE-JP), LALA (586120-EPP-1-2017-1-ES-EPPKA2-CBHE-JP), CONICYT Doctorado Nacional 2017/21170467, CONICYT Doctorado Nacional 2016/21160081.

References

1. Kizilcec, R.F., Pérez-Sanagustín, M., Maldonado, J.J.: Self-regulated learning strategies predict learner behavior and goal attainment in massive open online courses. Comput. Educ. **104**, 18–33 (2017)
2. Jivet, I.: The Learning tracker: a learner dashboard that encourages self-regulation in MOOC learners. Delft University of Technology, Thesis (2016)
3. Nussbaumer, A., Kravcik, M., Renzel, D., Klamma, R., Berthold, M., Albert, D.: A framework for facilitating self-regulation in responsive open learning environments. arXiv Preprint (2014)
4. Chatti, M.: Video - Mapper A video Annotation tool to support collaborative learning. In: Proceeding of the European MOOC Stakehold, pp. 131–140 (2015)
5. Thirouard, M., Bernaert, O., Dhorne, L., Bianchi, S., Pidol, L., Petit, Y.: Learning by doing: integrating a serious game in a MOOC to promote new skills. In: Proceedings of the Second MOOC European Stakeholders Summit, EMOOCs, pp. 92–96 (2015)

[4] Link to plugin in web store: https://chrome.google.com/webstore/detail/extensi%C3%B3n-notemyprogress/aghbcfhpjnmgkgafdbcaljgegcimcmng?authuser=2.

6. Pintrich, P.R.: The role of motivation in promoting and sustaining self-regulated learning. Int. J. Educ. Res. **31**(6), 459–470 (1999)
7. Veletsianos, G., Reich, J., Pasquini, L.A.: The life between big data log events. AERA Open **2**(3), 1–10 (2016)
8. Pérez-Álvarez, R., Pérez-Sanagustín, M., Maldonado, J.J.: How to design tools for supporting self-regulated learning in MOOCs? Lessons learned from a literature review from 2008 and 2016. In: CLEI 2016, pp. 1–12 (2016)
9. Gutiérrez-Rojas, I., Alario-Hoyos, C., Pérez-Sanagustín, M., Leony, D., Delgado-Kloos, C.: Scaffolding self-learning in MOOCs. In: Proceedings of the Second MOOC European Stakeholders Summit EMOOCs, pp. 43–49 (2014)
10. Nielsen, J.: 10 Heuristics for User Interface Design: Article by Jakob Nielsen (1995). http://www.nngroup.com/articles/ten-usability-heuristics/. Accedido 20 Feb 2017

Exploring Competition and Collaboration Behaviors in Game-Based Learning with Playing Analytics

Eric Sanchez[1(✉)] and Nadine Mandran[2]

[1] University of Fribourg, Fribourg, Switzerland
eric.sanchez@unifr.ch
[2] University of Grenoble, Grenoble, France
nadine.mandran@imag.fr

Abstract. This paper draws on an empirical work dedicated to understand how the interplay between competition and collaboration influences play-based learning. We analyze the strategies performed by 242 pre-service teachers trained with Tamagocours, an online multiplayer tamagochi-like game. The study is based on the collection, analysis and reporting of data about players (*playing analytics*). The factorial analysis shows different classes of players. These classes differ in terms of how students perform competition and collaboration. The results also show the evolution of the player's strategies. We conclude on the need for a shift from a game-based to a play-based perspective for conducting research into the use of games for educational purposes.

Keywords: Play-based learning · Playing analytics · Competition · Collaboration · Co-opetition

1 Introduction

In this paper we want to address players' strategies through the analysis of their engagement into competition and collaboration. Our research methodology is based on *playing analytics*, *i.e.* the record and analysis of players' digital traces during a game session. We also want to discuss the extent to which competition and collaboration influence the learning process and learning outcomes. We discuss why games should be considered as *co-opetitive* systems (a neologism formed with the words cooperation and competition) [1]. We present the game used during our study and the methodology adopted. The data collected are discussed and we conclude on the influence of the interplay between competition and collaboration on play-based learning.

2 Games as *Co-Opetitive* Systems

According to Crawford [2], "Conflict arises naturally from the interaction in a game". This conflict results from the obstacles that prevent the player to achieving his/her goals. Thus, conflict is an intrinsic element of all games [3]. Conflict may result from competition with opponents when two or more players compete for the same goal [4]. Conflict

É. Lavoué et al. (Eds.): EC-TEL 2017, LNCS 10474, pp. 467–472, 2017.
DOI: 10.1007/978-3-319-66610-5_44

may also result from a competition with the game system [5]. For a novice player, the resistance of the game to provide positive feedback takes the form of a conflict where the objectives of the player are antagonized by the resistance of this system. The game also plays the role of a formative assessment system. The player can test his way of thinking and behaving. Thus, game-based learning consists of an adaptive process rooted in the recognition of success and failures. By recognizing inappropriate knowledge, the player revises his/her knowledge and learns from his/her reflection on playing.

Cooperation takes place when a player accepts to take on the artificial meaning of the game [3]. In other word, play depends on the *lusory attitude* [6] of an individual who accepts the arbitrary and artificial rules of the game and thus, becomes player. Collaboration is also a core feature for many games. Mutual engagement of participants and coordinated efforts of teammates are needed in order to address the challenge. Players' interactions, through face-to-face or online discussions, enable for the coordination of players' decisions and make the collaboration successful. There is evidence to suggest that collaboration with other players can positively impact learning gains through *epistemic interactions* [7, 8]. *Epistemic interactions* are explanatory and argumentative interactions that play a role in the co-construction of knowledge [9]. Through players' dialogues and according to the experience gained from individual plays, the validity of the strategies and knowledge is collaboratively established. However, these learning gains depend on the quality of players' interactions [8].

Therefore, game-based learning consists of an individual and conflictual play with an antagonist system. Game-based learning also consists of cooperation (taking on the challenge) and collaboration (epistemic interactions with teammates). Learning results both from conflictual interactions (conflict, competition) and epistemic interactions when players collaborate. Game-based learning is *co-opetitive.*

The purpose of our work is to field-testing the *co-opetitive* feature of digital games through a case study. Thus, this paper addresses the following questions:

- What are the strategies performed by the learners/players and to what extend are these strategies linked with the expected learning outcomes?
- How do these strategies evolve among time and does this evolution favor learning?

3 An Empirical Study

The study is based on recording and analyzing the digital traces (*playing analytics*) during a game session with *Tamagocours*. *Tamagocours* is a game implemented as an online and asynchronous teaching program for approximatively 200–300 students each year. The game aims at teaching pre-service teachers the rules (*i.e.* copyright) that comply with the policies for the use of digital educational resources. *Tamagocours* is an online, multiplayer and collaborative Tamagotchi. Each team of 2 to 4 online players 'feeds' a character (*Tamagocours*) with digital educational resources. The challenge consists of selecting appropriate resources for feeding a character and to make it healthy. Each player can see his teammates choosing the resources from a large database and the format with which these resources are used. Each player can see the consequences of using these resources for feeding the character. Teammates can communicate *via* instant messages. The game also provides access to an online documentation about the legal rules that should be followed for using digital educational resources. Feeding the *Tamagocours* provokes feedbacks that depend on the legal characteristics (creative commons, copyrighted…) and the format for the use of a given resource. If the choice made by a player complies with the copyright policies, the character stays healthy and the team earns points. Otherwise, the character gets sick and dies if fed with too many inappropriate resources. Each of the five levels of the game can be replayed indefinitely until the level is completed.

The data discussed in this paper are collected during an experimentation carried out with 242 pre-service teachers in April and May 2015. Different variables are collected or calculated. They provide information about player's engagement (*TotalAction, Duree_sec*) or on his/her successes or failures (*FeedGood vs FeedBad*). The messages sent by the players to their teammates have been coded according to their semantic content, for example, information about the knowledge shared within a team (*Chat_F, Chat_V*). Variables provide information about the strategies followed by the player such as consulting the legal library (*HelpLink*), checking the characteristics of a given resource before feeding the character (*ShowItemCupboard, pattern SBF*) or being involved in a random strategy (*pattern AF*). Other variables provide information about strategies based on repetition (*Title_Max, p_Title, TypeMoU_Max p_TypeMoU*) or collaboration (*ShowItemFridgeOthers*). The data collected are split in two sets. The first set encompasses data from levels 1 to 3, relatively easy to win. The difficulty increases for levels 4 and 5, a second set of data.

We perform a principal component analysis (PCA) and an ascending hierarchical classification (AHC) to identify classes of players' strategies. AHC extracts some classes where players' strategies are similar and where classes are far apart. Then, for each class, the most significant variables (assessed by Student's *t*-test) give indications to build meaning of classes. This analysis sequence is managed with the two datasets, first for levels 1 to 3 and second for levels 4 to 5.

4 Different Strategies, Different Plays

According to the results obtained with the ACH, there are 5 categories of players depending on the actions that they performed. '*Inactive*' players (49%) perform few actions and all the variables are below the average. '*Force Feeders*' (14%) are active and they frequently feed the character without paying attention to the characteristics of the resources that they select (*ShowItemCupboard* is negative). In addition the ratio success/failure (*p_Feedgood*) is below the average. '*Successful Force Feeders*' (8%) are similar to the previous category. However, they develop a strategy based on the repetition of previous successful events and they somehow manage to succeed. *'Industrious' players (14%)* often check the characteristics of the resources that they select to feed the character (*ShowItemCupboard* is positive) and they are often successful (*FeedGood* is positive). Students from class 5 (4%) are named '*Collaborators*'. They send messages to their teammates about the rules that should apply for the selection of digital resources (*Chat_V* and *Chat_F* are positive) and they check the resources selected by their teammates (*ShowItemFridgeOthers* is positive). They also pay attention to the characteristics of the resources and collaborate with their teammates. Indeed, they send many messages and give their opinions about the legal rules that should be followed to succeed.

Though all the players played the same game, there is a diversity of plays. From a learning perspective, these different plays have not the same value. '*Inactive*' students are not able, refuse to play the game or are only spectators. They do not cooperate and play does not take place. It means that this category of students probably does not achieve the learning objectives. '*Force-Feeders*' adopted a random strategy. They accept to cooperate and they are involved in an individual play. However, they do not pay attention to the resources that they use for feeding the character. As a result, there are few chances that they managed to make links between the characteristic of a given resource (numbers of pages, publication date, copyright…) with its legal value. For this second category of players, the learning potential of the game is also low since the strategy followed is not appropriate. However the presence of '*Successful Force-Feeders*' demonstrates that some students (8%) manage to identify successful strategies. These strategies consist of selecting a format for the use of the resources with minimal constrains (*e.g.* oral presentation during a face-to-face course). '*Industrious Players*' are students who try to develop an efficient strategy. They try to face the challenge by carefully selecting the resources that they use to feed the character. They make mistakes but also succeed and there are some chances that they manage to learn from their successes and failures. Their final success demonstrates that they become able to identify the characteristics of the resources that frame their legality. However, they are mainly involved in an individual play for which the knowledge that enables to face the challenge remains implicit. From a learning perspective, players called '*Collaborators*' meet the objectives of the game. They make explicit and share the knowledge that they develop through individual play. Indeed, they formulate and discus the legal rules that should be applied for the selection of appropriate resources and send instant messages to their teammates. Making explicit the knowledge during game-based learning is known as a powerful factor in acquiring knowledge [7, 8]. It is particularly true if the epistemic quality of dialogues is high [8].

The efficiency of the game depends on its capability to motivate students to address the challenge and to shape strategies (cooperation with the game). It is expected that they shape strategies enabling to make links between reasoned decisions and the consequences of these decisions (competition with the game). In this regard, it is important that a random strategy leads to failure. The efficiency of the game also depends on its capability to give students the opportunity to formulate and to discuss the knowledge that is expected to be acquired (collaboration with teammates).

5 Evolution of the Strategies Performed by the Players

Based on the ACH performed for levels 4 and 5, the data shows that a new class of players emerges during levels 4–5. These players, called '*Repeaters*' (29%), are described by 2 main variables: *p_TypeMoU* (over represented) and *p_Title* (under represented). It means that they have a stereotyped strategy that consists of trying to choose the format for the use of the resource with the lowest constrains. They do not pay much attention to the characteristic of the resources that they choose for feeding the character. Others classes of players are present: the number of '*Inactive*' players decreases, '*Force-feeders*' are still present but now, they constitute a unique class. A class of '*Industrious*' players is also present and it is also possible to identify some '*Collaborators*'. The shift of players' strategies from levels 1 to 3 to levels 4–5 is described by percentage shown by Table 1.

Table 1. Percentages of players for levels 1–3 and levels 4–5 (Blue cells indicate the percentage of players who have not changed their strategies. Green cells indicate a significant change of strategy).

Row percent	**Levels 4-5**				
Levels 1-3	Inactive	Force-feeders	Repeaters	Industrious	Collaborators
Inactive	**40.3**	10.9	**32.8**	7.6	8.4
Force-feeders	28.6	**34.3**	28.6	5.7	2.9
Successful force-feeders	15.0	**30.0**	**40.0**	10.0	5.0
Industrious	**51.7**	5.2	22.4	**17.2**	3.4
Collaborators	30.0	0.0	0.0	0.0	**70.0**
Total of players	*38.8*	*14.0*	*28.9*	*9.5*	*8.7*

Many changes occur during the game session. Some are positive in terms of expected learning outcomes: the number of '*Inactive*' students decreases, a minority of '*Force-Feeders*' develop a better strategy and the number of '*Collaborators*' increases. However there is a general tendency for withdrawal ('*Inactive' player*s) or the development of strategies that have few educational potential ('*Force-Feeders*' and '*Repeaters*'). Altogether, the students who are active, are mainly involved in an individual play and do not develop collaborative strategies that we consider important for learning outcomes. Different causes might be stated. One of them is the level of difficulty faced by the students for level 4–5. The difficulty is probably too high and responsible for withdrawal. Another cause might be the quality of the game-play and the subsequent decreasing students' interest. In sum, we do not notice a general and global progress.

6 Discussion and Conclusion

The game *Tamagocours* encompasses a complex combination of conflict, cooperation and collaboration. These two ways of playing are not each other's exclusive. It is expected that the student will address the challenge offered by the game by developing individual (they learn from the recognition of successes and failures) and collaborative strategies (they learn from epistemic interactions with teammates and by making explicit the targeted knowledge). However, our study shows that the strategies developed by students are diverse and different for many of them. In terms of learning outcomes, these strategies have not the same value. Maximum learning gains are expected when players (1) are involved into strategies based on reasoned decisions assessed with the feedbacks provided by the game and (2) when players are involved into epistemic interactions through collaboration with teammates.

We consider that the contribution of this study consists of the development of a methodology adapted to describe players' strategies. This methodology is based on *playing analytics*, *i.e.*, the record and analysis of players' interactions during play. It opens new perspectives for focusing on the player instead on the game. Thus, the results that we obtained from this study advocate for a shift from a game-based to a play-based perspective [1]. Play results from interactions between a player and a game. Play is *performative* and the player matters. Research into game-based learning for educational purposes should take into account how players play. They should not be limited to analyze learning outcomes and too answer to the question "WHAT has been learnt". They should try to answer to the question "HOW and WHY the players learn". In particular we need to know more about how to foster student's ownership of the challenge offered by the game and how to favor epistemic interactions through collaboration. Such research may enable for a better understanding on the relationships between game-design, player's strategies and learning outcomes.

Acknowledgments. The Hubble project (e.Learning Traces Observatory) has been funded by the French National Agency for Research (ANR).

References

1. Sanchez, E.: Competition and Collaboration for Game-Based Learning: A Case Study. In: Wouters, P., van Oostendorp, H. (eds.) Instructional Techniques to Facilitate Learning and Motivation of Serious Games. AGL, pp. 161–184. Springer, Cham (2017). doi: 10.1007/978-3-319-39298-1_9
2. Crawford, C.: The Art of Computer Game Design (1982)
3. Salen, K., Zimmerman, E.: Rules of play, game design fundamentals. MIT Press, Cambridge (2004)
4. Plass, J., O'Keefe, P., Homer, B., Case, J., Hayward, E., Stein, M., et al.: The Impact of Individual, Competitive, and Collaborative Mathematics Game Play on Learning, Performance, and Motivation. J. Educ. Psychol. **15**, 1050–1066 (2013)
5. Alessi, S.M., Trollip, S.R.: Multimedia for learning, 3rd edn. Allyn & Bacon, Inc., Boston (2001)
6. Suits, B.: Grasshopper: Games, Life and Utopia. David R. Godine, Boston (1990)
7. Leemkuil, H., de Jong, T., de Hoog, R., Christoph, N.: Km quest: A collaborativeinternet-based simulation game. Simul. Gaming **34**, 89–111 (2003)
8. ter Vrugte, J., de Jong, T., Vandercruysse, S., Wouters, P., van Oostendorp, H., Elen, J.: How Competition and Heterogeneous Collaboration Interact in Prevocational Game-Based Mathematics Education. Comput. Educ. **89**, 42–52 (2015)
9. Ohlsson, S.: Learning to do and learning to understand: A lesson and a challenge for cognitive modeling. In: Reiman, P., Spade, H. (eds.) Learning in Humans and Machines: Towards an interdisciplinary learning science, pp. 3762. Elsevier Science, Oxford (1995)

Using WiFi Technology to Identify Student Activities Within a Bounded Environment

Philip Scanlon(✉) and Alan F. Smeaton

Insight Centre for Data Analytics, Dublin City University,
Glasnevin, Dublin, 9, Ireland
philip.scanlon@insight-centre.org

Abstract. We use the unique digital footprints created by student interactions with online systems within a University environment to measure student behaviour and correlate it with exam performance. The specific digital footprint we use is student use of the Eduroam WiFi platform within our campus from smartphones, tablets and laptops. The advantage of this data-set is that it captures the personal interactions each student has with the IT systems. Data-sets of this type are usually structured, complete and traceable. We will present findings that illustrate that the behaviour of students can be contextualised within the academic environment by mining this data-set. We achieve this through identifying student location and those who share that location with them and cross-referencing this with the scheduled University timetable.

1 Introduction

The ability of researchers to identify the type of activities and levels of interaction among students on campus is important to research in Learning Analytics and in particular, anthropological studies which explore interactions among students. Historically the collection of base data in such studies has in the main been through observation, questionnaires or a combination of both. In an era where smartphones and WiFi use are widespread, this paper will examine another data source, the use of WiFi-enabled devices within a bounded domain, i.e. within a campus.

Our work uses the digital footprint that WiFi-enabled devices leave to identify student location and thus co-location of students. From this co-location analyses we infer peer groupings and levels of interaction. This can be used for identifying peers in a University community and for the identifying popular locations for different students and their peer groups. This paper examines the data collection process we followed. We use spatio-temporal data derived from WiFi system logs to determine on-campus location as a component of student digital footprints. Once gathered, learning analytics can mine this to produce actionable knowledge for use in the learning process. All data has been anonomised and the work is approved by the University's Research Ethics Committee.

É. Lavoué et al. (Eds.): EC-TEL 2017, LNCS 10474, pp. 473–478, 2017.
DOI: 10.1007/978-3-319-66610-5_45

2 Related Work

Central to research into peer influence is the ability to identify those who spend time with others, and for what purposes. Previous work by Celant [1] asked students directly to recall who they spend time with, socially, academically, jointly working on homework, or as part of formal study groups. Celant found that there was some *blurring* as "different students may have had a different concept of preparing for an exam with a course mate". Other students who, for different reasons, do not interact at a level they would prefer, may say they study with others with whom they have had little interaction with.

In an early example of the use of technology to collect geospatial data from student activities, data was collect over a two year period using a hand-held GPS device as part of Project Lachesis [6]. The aim was *"... extracting stays and destinations from location histories in a pure, data-driven manner"*. Technology has advanced in the intervening years research which have used technologies to collect data on the interaction between parties could be categorised as:

1. Using geospatial data collected through the use of GPS and GMS location data. Examples of this are [7] and [6].
2. Specifically adapted smartphones utilising bespoke data collection applications. Examples of this are [2], [4] and [5].
3. Badges that collect data relevant to the wearer, including [8] and [11].
4. Smartphones used to collect WiFi base station data [9] and [3].

The research data gathered in these papers ranged in scope from 2 users over a 1 year period, to 48 users for a 10-week period and through to 100 users for a period of 9 months. Our research is based on 3 academic years and a cohort of 174 students and we believe that this compares favourably with similar research.

Nathan Eagle's [2] longitudinal research study used data collected over a 9-month period from 100 mobile phones to demonstrate the ability to use Bluetooth technology to log user behaviour and activity information. The intention was to recognize social interaction patterns and to cluster locations, therefore modelling activities and inferring relationships through the monitoring of temporal and geolocation data. This is an approach used in many research projects and will be used in our research. The interaction between WiFi-enabled devices and the WiFi network which we explore here, allows us to identify information previously impossible to gather on both ad-hoc and formal groupings of people.

3 Co-Location Datasets Used

Co-location in the arena of our research can be roughly interpreted as the location of two or more individuals in the same physical place and at the same time. Individual incidence of a co-located pair cannot be interpreted as the individuals as having a relationship and does not infer personal contact between 2 people. Quannan Li [7] having mined subject GPS logs, used an hierarchical clustering algorithm to develop a trajectory model that determines a semantic meaning to stay-points (points where time is spent) and inferred similarity between subjects based on this. In that work, the results could be used as the basis of a recommender system, but in our work we will interpret the *context* of the co-location. In the context of a University campus, meetings can be either formal or informal i.e. they can formally scheduled meetings with others through joint attendance at a class or lab or they can be meetings in locations with their peers with whom they have a social relationship with.

The DCU campus is a modern facility contained on a 50-acre campus in North Dublin city. It compromises 27 separate buildings providing an approximate floor space of 180,000m^2. On-campus facilities include 1,400 residential apartments, 7 restaurants/cafes and numerous shops including convenience, book and a pharmacy. The WiFi coverage for the campus is provided by eduroam (Educational Roaming), a cross-site infrastructure which allows users gain access to the WiFi platforms at other eduroam sites where access is provided following authentication by Radius servers at their home institution. Network access at member sites is via 802.1X protocols and at DCU comprises 1,000 individual Network Access Servers (NAS). These NASs are distributed across the campus ensuring continuous WiFi coverage to users.

Our research cohort is drawn from the Faculty of Engineering and Computing and specifically from the School of Computing. Within this School our research will focus on students in two undergraduate programs namely, Computer Applications (CA) and Enterprise Computing (EC). These two programs have been chosen as they share some modules and a degree format which attracts students with similar interests in the IT domain.

Our research data relates to the academic years 2014/5, 2015/6 and 2016/7 and contains c.220 million log file entries. As with any data, in its raw form it comprises multivariate data requiring pre-processing to ensure usability. To augment our WiFi log access data, we have an additional data-set of basic student demographics and exam performance. Students who first registered in 2015 were identified as the initial cohort whose activities would to be analysed during this research. Using the 2015 intake of students, this paper will illustrate how identifying the use of WiFi access as a part of students' digital footprints, can be used to identify the activities of students on a semester, weekly and daily basis.

Our research relies on the premise that students on campus are there for both formal and informal reasons. They are there to attend classes, scheduled labs, additional study and to interact with friends i.e. they will be engaged in either academic and social activities. Based on the on-campus location of subjects, we will infer activities and therefore infer their purpose. Using a similar approach to that of Rui Wang [10] we sub-divided the campus into academic and social areas. While some locations have a dual purpose for example the on-campus residences which could be considered a social area, some students will also use such locations for study and thus we will classify each area based on the majority use. This means that classrooms, laboratories (labs) and libraries are categorised as *academic* while on-campus residences, cafe, restaurants and bars (hang-out areas) as well as public areas such as transit spaces are classified as *social*.

4 Preliminary Profiling of Student Activity

Using the definition of a "meeting" between students as being two devices from two individual students, both connected to the same eduroam WiFi NAS for an overlapping period of 20 min or longer, we can compare the activities of the cohorts of students from two different degree programmes, Computer Applications (CA) and Enterprise Computing (EC).

Table 1. Student numbers, dyads and meetings

Program	No. students	No. dyads	No. meetings	Avg. meetings per dyad
CA	114	5,523	335,465	60.7
EC	60	1,230	106,500	86.6

Table 1 lists the number of students and dyads who had meetings, i.e. student pairs from the same degree program that interact or "met" during the semester and the number of meetings during the semester among those dyads. To achieve a greater understanding of student activity while on campus we divided each location into two categories and a number of sub-categories. The premise is that *friends* spend a lot of time together in the same location at the same time. It was thus necessary to identify the degree to which students collocate and use this in our analysis. Table 2 outlines the number of meetings in social locations and Table 3 the Academic meetings by sub-category. It can be seen that 70% of the CA students met in *Hang-out* locations compared to 78% of EC students.

Table 2. Student numbers and meeting locations

Program	Social	Hang out	Transit	Residence
CA	36,543	25,386 (70%)	8,409	2,865
EC	16,962	13,268 (78%)	3,282	261

Table 3. Student numbers and meeting location details

Program	Academic	Class	Lab's	Library
CA	298,922	199,968 (67%)	97,803 (33%)	1,027
EC	89,538	32,284 (36%)	55,619 (62%)	1,786

When comparing programs there is a large variance between the percentage of CA student *class* meetings i.e. 67% and EC *class* meetings at 36%. At this time we are not sure why this differential is present. In the Academic domain, Table 3 shows the largest number of meetings took place in the *class*. A large portion of *class* meeting occur within the formal environment of lectures with a smaller amount where students have study groups at class locations. It is common for students to congregate in the Labs to study or work on group projects.

Table 4. Average delta for academic meetings, grouped

	CA		EC	
Academic Meetings	Avg. Delta	Max	Avg Delta	Max
0 : 200	**23.82**	54.84	**6.85**	25.00
200 : 400	11.90	44.59	5.79	19.17
400 : 600	12.22	37.84	7.76	19.00
600 : 800	11.02	32.75	5.58	15.17
800 : 1000	10.72	28.92	5.22	12.17
1000 : 1200	9.79	15.25	3.71	5.09
1200 : 1400	**1.59**	1.59	**0.84**	0.84

Table 5. Average delta for social meetings, grouped

	CA		EC	
Social Meeting	Avg. Delta	Max	Avg Delta	Max
0 : 30	**13.75**	54.84	**6.86**	25
30 : 60	12.39	42.34	6.27	19.17
60 : 90	11.51	32.09	6.67	18.17
90 : 120	9.95	30.42	5.56	11.33
120 : 150	14.56	37.84	5.84	15.17
150 : 180	9.38	15.34	3.02	5.83
180 : 210	6.05	10.25	5.23	10.09
210 : 240	9.38	17.42	5.30	11.84
240 : 270	**10.96**	11.25	**2.39**	4.25

As part of our demographic data we examined student *Precision score*, an aggregated score compiled from the exam marks achieved in all program modules during the year. Our analysis compares the *Precision* score of students and the number of times they met in Academic and Social Locations.

Table 4 groups the number of meetings into groupings of 200 and lists the Average delta between students whose meetings fall into that group and also include the max delta between student pairs in the group. In this, a delta is interpreted as the difference between two student Precision marks for an Academic year. We can interpret from this table that as the number of meetings increases between a dyad in Academic settings, there is a decrease in the Delta score. That is, the more meetings a pair of students have, the closer their exam grades. Whether this is an indication of peer influence or that students of similar ability naturally group together will require further study.

Similarly in Table 5, the Social meetings analysis, the average delta decreases as the number of meetings between pairs increases. However it can be seen that the range of difference in deltas between groups, varies considerably. We see that in the CA (Computer Applications) category there is a wide variance in the Academic deltas.

5 Conclusion

This research has determined that it is possible to identify student locations on a campus through the digital footprint provided by their WiFi activity. We find that, based on co-location data, the degree of each student's activity within the cohort can also be determined. We have illustrated that a longitudinal study of this nature can identify relationships between students and their academic timetables and a difference in group behaviour between students in different programs and variations in their exam performance.

Acknowledgement. This paper is based on research conducted with the support of Science Foundation Ireland under grant SFI/12/RC/2289.

References

1. Hariharan, R., Toyama, K.: Project lachesis: parsing and modeling location histories. In: Egenhofer, M.J., Freksa, C., Miller, H.J. (eds.) GIScience 2004. LNCS, vol. 3234, pp. 106–124. Springer, Heidelberg (2004). doi:10.1007/978-3-540-30231-5_8
2. Eagle, N., Pentland, A.: Reality mining: sensing complex social systems. Pers. Ubiquit. Comput. **10**(4), 255–268 (2006)
3. Gonzalez, M.C., Hidalgo, C.A., Barabasi, A.-L.: Understanding individual human mobility patterns. Nature **453**(7196), 779–782 (2008)
4. Gupta, A., Paul, S., Jones, Q., Borcea, C.: Automatic identification of informal social groups and places for geo-social recommendations. Int. J. Mobile Network Des. Innov. **2**(3–4), 159–171 (2007)
5. Harari, G.M., Gosling, S.D., Wang, R., Chen, F., Chen, Z., Campbell, A.T.: Patterns of behavior change in students over an academic term: A preliminary study of activity and sociability behaviors using smartphone sensing methods. Comput. Hum. Behav. **67**, 129–138 (2017)
6. Hariharan, R., Toyama, K.: Project lachesis: parsing and modeling location histories. In: Egenhofer, M.J., Freksa, C., Miller, H.J. (eds.) GIScience 2004. LNCS, vol. 3234, pp. 106–124. Springer, Heidelberg (2004). doi:10.1007/978-3-540-30231-5_8
7. Li, Q., Zheng, Y., Xie, X., Chen, Y., Liu, W., Ma, W.-Y.: Mining user similarity based on location history. In: Proceedings of the 16th ACM SIGSPATIAL International Conference on Advances in Geographic Information Systems, p. 34. ACM (2008)
8. Pentland, A.: The new science of building great teams. Harvard Bus. Rev. **90**(4), 60–69 (2012)
9. Rekimoto, J., Miyaki, T., Ishizawa, T.: Lifetag: WiFi-based continuous location logging for life pattern analysis. In: Hightower, J., Schiele, B., Strang, T. (eds.) LoCA 2007. LNCS, vol. 4718, pp. 35–49. Springer, Heidelberg (2007). doi:10.1007/978-3-540-75160-1_3
10. Wang, R., Harari, G., Hao, P., Zhou, X., Campbell, A.T.: SmartGPA: how smartphones can assess and predict academic performance of college students. Proceedings 2015 ACM International Joint Conference on Pervasive and Ubiquitous Computing. UbiComp 2015, pp. 295–306. ACM, New York (2015)
11. Watanabe, J.-I., Matsuda, S., Yano, K.: Using wearable sensor badges to improve scholastic performance. In: Proceedings of the 2013 ACM Conference on Pervasive and Ubiquitous Computing Adjunct Publication, pp. 139–142. ACM (2013)

Can Learning by Qualitative Modelling Be Deployed as an Effective Method for Learning Subject-Specific Content?

Erika Schlatter[1], Bert Bredeweg[2(✉)], Jannet van Drie[1], and Peter de Jong[1]

[1] Research Institute of Child Development and Education, University of Amsterdam, Amsterdam, The Netherlands
[2] Informatics Institute, University of Amsterdam, Amsterdam, The Netherlands
B.Bredeweg@uva.nl

Abstract. Modelling can help understanding dynamic systems, but learning how to model is a difficult and time-consuming task. The challenge is to foster modelling skills, while not limiting the learning of regular subject matter, or better, to also improve this learning. We investigate how learning by qualitative modelling can be as successful as a regular classroom setting that uses an active and stimulating approach. 74 students from two high schools participated in two Biology lessons. Particularly, in the school 2 study, students in the modelling condition improved as much as students in the control group.

1 Introduction

One way in which thinking about dynamic systems can be supported is through the use of models [1, 2]. Creating models from scratch is seen as a higher order skill within the larger set of systems thinking skills [3]. Although widely believed, evidence that active modelling can help students develop such understanding is scarce [4]. Moreover, learning how to model takes time. This learning time is especially important: the time spent on learning how to model cannot be spent on learning subject-specific content.

In the studies reported here, the effect of qualitative modelling on subject-specific understanding was investigated. An experiment was developed in which participants were assigned to a modelling or a control condition. The modelling instruction was integrated in the first lesson, which served as a *modelling learning phase (LP)* for students in the modelling condition. In the second lesson, the *modelling application phase (AP)*, these students were expected to be able to apply their modelling knowledge on the second topic. In the control condition, the same topics were treated, making it possible to assess progress of both groups for the LP and for the AP. These control condition also used computers, but created alternative representations (using PowerPoint).

It was expected that in the LP students in the control condition would improve more than students in the modelling condition with regard to subject-specific knowledge. In the control condition, students would only have to concentrate on the subject-specific content, while students in the modelling condition also have to concentrate on modelling.

É. Lavoué et al. (Eds.): EC-TEL 2017, LNCS 10474, pp. 479–485, 2017.
DOI: 10.1007/978-3-319-66610-5_46

In the AP, students in the modelling condition were expected to improve more with regard to subject-specific knowledge than students in the control condition, as the acquired modelling skills were expected to be helpful for understanding this content.

2 Method

Two schools participated in the study with their Biology class (school 1: 44 students, mean age = 16.99, SD = 0.56, 45% girls & school 2: 30 students, mean age = 16.67, SD = 0.72, 83% girls). Students were in their 5th year of pre-university secondary education (grade 11). As the schools made the study part of their program, all students were expected to participate. Each school visited the research location twice within the single week, during which the students followed one lesson. School 2 participated in the study one month after school 1 had done so.

When settled in the room the study was introduced and students took the pre-test (30 min). Next, students worked on the lesson individually (1.5 h, with a short break halfway). The visit event ended with the post-test (10 min). During the second visit, students started immediately with the lesson. After two hours (including a short break) the students took the post-test (25 min). During the school 1 visit, two teachers were present at both days. During the school 2 visit, a different teacher accompanied the students on each of the days. A teacher or a researcher was always present in the room to answer questions. All students were randomly assigned to the conditions.

Students followed two lessons (one on trophic cascades and one on eutrophication). Learning goals were addressed in the same order in both conditions. The lessons were worksheet-based, minimizing the need for instruction by the teachers. Students were instructed to work alone, although they could ask fellow students, their teacher or the researcher for help. In both conditions the lessons were similarly structured: students were given a small amount of information at the beginning of each lesson, on which they were asked to formulate an initial hypothesis. As students gathered more information during the lesson, either through texts provided in the assignment, modelling or looking up information on the internet, students were asked to revise their previous answers or models. As such, a discovery learning element was added and students understanding of the subject matter was built up step-by-step. This was expected to aid students' conceptual understanding of the system they were studying.

In the *modelling condition*, students created as part of the lesson a model from the system that was the principal subject of the lesson. For this, the newly developed software DynaLearn-Web (https://DynaLearn.nl) was used. This instrument is available as an online tool (using web browsers) and implements aspects of the DynaLearn workbench [5] focusing on features which are hypothesized to facilitate effective learning by qualitative modelling. When creating a model with this tool, a student starts by defining entities. These entities can be connected as in a concept map using configurations, but the student can also define any number of quantities for each entity. A quantity is a measurable property of an entity, and can be related to any other quantity. These dependencies can be positive or negative. Furthermore, each quantity has a change rate that can be set to decrease, steady or increase. A simple model is shown in Fig. 1. It depicts part of the eutrophication process in which underwater sunlight is blocked by algae. The entity *waterbody* is connected to three other entities: *algae*, *sunlight* and *water plants*. These all have quantities related to the available amount of the entity. Moreover, the amount of algae is negatively related (P−) to the amount of sunlight, as algae float at the water surface and thus block sunlight under water. The amount of sunlight is positively related (P+) to the amount of water plants, as these plants need sunlight to grow. All three quantities have a change rate, depicted by ∂. Only the change rates at the beginning of a causal chain need to be defined, in this case that of algae. In this example, it is defined as increasing. When the model is simulated, the inferred (green) arrows indicate that sunlight decreases and that because of that the water plants also decrease. This example uses only a few model ingredients. The students were asked to make more elaborate and complex models, such as the one shown in Fig. 2.

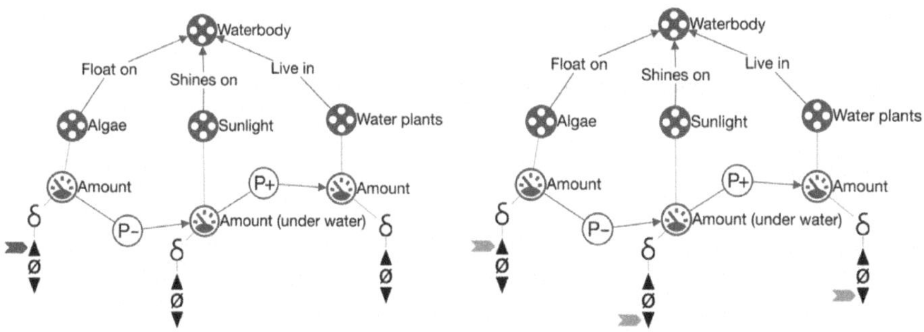

Fig. 1. Example DynaLearn-web model. Right-hand side shows the model in building mode (blue arrow specifies initial changes: Algae increase). Left-hand side shows simulation mode (green arrows denote inferred directions of change). (Color figure online)

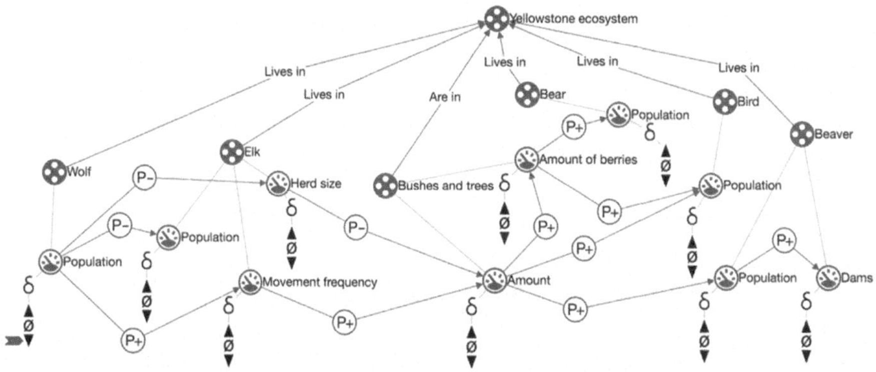

Fig. 2. Model of trophic cascade in the Yellowstone ecosystem.

In the current study, students had to learn how to use 5 out of the 15 possible Dyna-Learn-Web ingredients. As such, the models were relatively simple and without feed-back loops or other complicated causal structures. In the first lesson students were guided through the modelling process. In the second lesson, students were expected to know how to create a model with DynaLearn-Web but were still supported in their decisions as to what ingredients to include. This was done through the assignments.

In the *control condition*, the same texts were presented to the students and similar questions asked regarding the ecosystems: what are the elements in this ecosystem, what properties do they have and how are these properties related? However, students were not asked to show these in a model but in textual answers to questions. Additional computer assignments were added to control for possible effects of computer usage. In the first lesson this consisted of making a PowerPoint on all animals in that lesson. In the second lesson this consisted of looking up information on the internet.

To assess content knowledge pre- and post-tests were developed. For both topics 5 questions were asked: 2 reproduction, 2 comprehension, and 1 application. To allow for comparability, questions were constructed such that for each question on cascade there would be a similar question on eutrophication. Reproduction scored 2.5 and 3 points, comprehension 3 and 4 points, and application 5 points. The pre- and post-test were identical per topic. Test scores thus range from 0 to 17.5 points.

3 Results

Worksheet completion was assessed as a measure of treatment integrity. On average, between 85% and 99% of the worksheet was completed. Students who finished less than 60% of their worksheet were excluded from analyses on content learning, as it was believed that these students did not participate seriously enough.

To assess the acquisition of subject knowledge, pre- and post-tests were administered before and after the lessons. Table 1 shows the school 1 results. Form the 44 participants, 39 could be used to compute results during the LP and 36 to compute results during the AP. During the LP students in the control condition significant improved on their test scores. Students in the modelling condition also obtained a significant change, however, in the opposite direction, as if they unlearned something. During the AP, the students in both conditions improved, with the improvement in the control condition being significant. However, there was a large difference on the pre-test scores, with the students in the control condition scoring significantly lower.

Table 1. Test scores school 1 – Learning & Application phase

Condition	N	Pre-test		Post-test		Average	p
		Mean	SD	Mean	SD	(= *Post* – *Pre*)	
Learning phase (LP)							
Modelling	20	7.18	2.41	5.93	1.59	−1.250 (0.575)	.034*
Control	19	6.37	1.23	7.63	2.29	1.263 (0.590)	.036*
Application phase (AP)							
Modelling	17	8.32	1.83	9.35	2.66	1.03 (0.65)	.120
Control	19	5.70	2.74	7.66	2.66	1.96 (0.62)	.002*

The school 2 study happened a month after the school 1 study. Care was taken to conduct this second study more orderly and homogenous across the two conditions. In addition, because in the school 1 study it appeared that some students lost interest, a situational interest questionnaire was administered at the end of the school 2 study.

Form the 30 participants, 27 could be used to compute results during the LP and 23 to compute results during the AP (Table 2). During the LP, both conditions improved on their average scores. For the modelling condition this increase was statistically significant. During the AP, both conditions increased on their average scores. Both being statistically significant, although the increase in the modelling condition was higher.

Table 2. Test scores school 2 – Learning & Application phase

Condition	N	Pre-test		Post-test		Average	p
		Mean	SD	Mean	SD	(= *Post* – *Pre*)	
Learning phase (LP)							
Modelling	13	6.88	2.22	9.00	2.18	2.12 (0.713)	.004*
Control	14	7.89	2.67	8.89	3.27	1.00 (0.687)	.151
Application phase (AP)							
Modelling	11	6.50	2.47	10.55	2.69	4.05 (0.81)	<.001*
Control	12	6.31	2.09	9.10	3.03	2.79 (0.78)	<.001*

4 Discussion

In the school 1 study, students in the control condition improved on average scores in both phases. However, students in the modelling condition obtained a significant lower average score during the LP on the post-test. This seems to suggest that they had unlearned subject-specific content, which is specifically remarkable because the questions in the pre- and post-test were the same (albeit differently ordered). The students did improve on average during the AP, but not significantly.

Informal observations showed differences as to how orderly the experiment was conducted. In general, the implementation was more orderly the control condition than in the modelling condition. This may have prompted students in the modelling condition to take the experiment less seriously, which may explain the decline in scores for these students during the LP. A few students also left early, and may not have filled out the post-test with sufficient dedication. The poor learning during the LP may also have had an effect on students modelling abilities resulting in less improvement during the AP. A few students in the modelling condition did not show up for the AP. These were some of the less well performing students. This may explain the higher average score on the pre-test in the modelling condition during the AP, and consequently reducing the size of learning effect within this group.

For the school 2 study, care was taken to ensure orderly conduct of the experiment and to have comparable experiences for both conditions. In accordance with the expectations, the results of the second study show that students in all conditions obtained higher average scores. The increase was significant for the students in the modelling condition for both the LP and AP. For the students in the control condition this was only the case in the AP. Consequently, it seems fair to conclude that students in de modelling condition did not fall behind due to the extra cognitive load imposed by the need to model. On the contrary, they even obtained higher average scores than the students in the control condition.

Overall the experiment was demanding for all students. Students were expected to work individually for almost three hours per session. This is considerably longer than the duration of most experimental studies [6] and may have asked a lot of the students' attention span. Although we tried to keep lessons fairly similar in terms of workload, students in the modelling condition did work on a larger number of learning goals and had a larger number of questions on their worksheets. This demand may have affected the scores on the post-test, which was the last activity in the three hours lasting event.

New tests were developed to measure learning. However, the reliability of these tests was found to be low, with Cronbach's α being .074 (pre-test 1), .483 (post-test 1), .409 (pre-test 2), and .435 (post-test 2). It is possible that this imprecision resulted in not finding essential differences between conditions. Another cause of imprecision relates to the pre- and post-test being identical. It appeared to demotivate students, who pointed out that they had already made these questions when filling out the post-test.

5 Conclusion

Learning by modelling is expected to induce better understanding of the subject matter, but deployment in secondary education is hampered by the extra effort it takes for learners to become proficient in modelling. The challenge is to overcome this problem and foster modelling skills, while not limiting the learning of regular subject matter. This paper reports on two studies that investigated whether the newly developed instrument for learning by 'creating qualitative models' (DynaLearn-Web) would be able to address this challenge. Particularly, the results of the school 2 study show that students in the modelling condition performed as well as students in the control condition. This supports the hypothesis that modeling can facilitate subject-specific learning without being hindered by the extra effort needed to acquire modelling skills.

References

1. Clement, J.: Model based learning as a key research area for science education. Int. J. Sci. Educ. **22**(9), 1041–1053 (2000)
2. Rutten, N., van Joolingen, W.R., van der Veen, J.T.: The learning effects of computer simulations in science education. Comput. Educ. **58**(1), 136–153 (2012)
3. Hopper, M., Stave, K.: Assessing the effectiveness of systems thinking interventions in the classroom. In: Proceedings of the 26th International Conference of the System Dynamics Society, pp. 1–26 (2008)
4. VanLehn, K., Wetzel, J., Grover, S., van de Sande, B.: Learning how to construct models of dynamic systems: an initial evaluation of the Dragoon intelligent tutoring system. IEEE Trans. Learn. Technol. **10**(2), 154–167 (2016) doi:10.1109/TLT.2016.2514422. 1939-1382

5. Bredeweg, B., Liem, J., Beek, W., Linnebank, F., Gracia, J., Lozano, E., Wißner, M., Bühling, R., Salles, P., Noble, R., Zitek, A., Borisova, P., Mioduser, D.: DynaLearn an intelligent learning environment for learning conceptual knowledge. AI Mag. **34**(4), 46–65 (2013)
6. Hoyle, R.H., Harris, M.J., Judd, C.M.: Research Methods in Social Relations, 7th edn. Thomson Learning, New York (2002)

Towards 'MOOCs with a Purpose': Crowdsourcing and Analysing Scalable Design Solutions with MOOC Learners

Peter van Rosmalen[1(✉)], Julia Kasch[1], Marco Kalz[2], Olga Firssova[1], and Francis Brouns[1]

[1] Welten Institute, Faculty of Psychology and Educational Sciences, Open University of the Netherlands, Heerlen, The Netherlands
{peter.vanrosmalen,julia.kasch,olga.firssova, francis.brouns}@ou.nl

[2] UNESCO chair of Open Education, Faculty Management, Science and Technology and Welten Institute, Faculty of Psychology and Educational Sciences, Open University of the Netherlands, Heerlen, The Netherlands
marco.kalz@ou.nl

Abstract. In this study we explored the use of a research assignment on instructional design of MOOCs by MOOC students. The use of a research assignment was expected to be of interest for both students and the designer. The assignment is based on a framework to analyse MOOC designs with the objective to identify best practices. It builds on four principles: constructive alignment, task complexity, interaction and formative feedback. The exploration indicates that students positively appreciate this kind of assignments. Moreover, the crowdsourcing alike approach showed to be a valuable way for MOOC designers to get awarded with data gathered by their participants. The participants, be it a small sample, were able to apply the framework to analyse MOOCs and identify best practices. We will discuss the framework and the results of its application. Finally, we will conclude with the experiences of the users.

Keywords: MOOC design · Educational scalability · MOOCs with a purpose · Constructive alignment · Task complexity · Interaction · Formative feedback

1 Introduction

Nowadays there is an increase of demand for the Higher Education Area expected, leading to questions of scalability of the educational system as a whole. "Taking note that 414.2 million students will be enrolled in higher education around the world by 2030 – an increase from 99.4 million in 2000, and that online, open and flexible education is going mainstream, the importance of quality learning outcomes for learners cannot be overestimated" [1]. Delivery at scale has been the essence of the founding missions of the many national Open University systems established from the 70 s onwards. However, at the moment Massive Open Online Courses (MOOCs) seem to have been taken up as a new format of digital learning and teaching for delivery at scale [2]. According to latest statistics from the end of 2016 there are 58 Million learners enrolled

É. Lavoué et al. (Eds.): EC-TEL 2017, LNCS 10474, pp. 486–491, 2017.
DOI: 10.1007/978-3-319-66610-5_47

in more than 7000 courses from more than 1000 institutions [3]. The potential of MOOCs to enable more people around the world with different learner profiles and educational backgrounds to access (higher) education supports the idea of lifelong learning [4]. Moreover, since MOOC designs are open, and therewith can be compared against criteria, they have a potential as a source of less teacher-support-demanding designs in regular education. However, while MOOCs enable large numbers of people to access (higher) education materials, unlike the Open Universities', it is less clear at which level their offerings are supported. A common pattern in MOOCs is the provision of video lectures and multiple choice quizzes [2]. While this approach might have the potential to be a scalable solution, a critical question is which complexity levels of learning and skill acquisition are supported. The design of a final assignment is challenging, in particular, when it has to meet the higher complexity levels of learning. Therefore, in this study we explored how to set-up a final assignment in a MOOC that fits with higher complexity levels of learning and combines the interest of the student and the designer (teacher). For the learner, as in any design, the assignment should correspond with the course and the level of its objectives. However, in particular since most of the time there are no official credits, it also should challenge and motivate them and contribute to their knowledge. For the designer, as an additional constraint, we expect the outcomes of the assignment to contribute to their research. Contributions of the public to research are spread over many domains (www.citizenscience.org). It is common to research behaviour and motivation of MOOC participants, however, also 'MOOCs with a purpose' start emerging [5, 6]. In this study our aims are twofold i.e. to use MOOCs as an instrument to support research. For a designer this is an incentive to develop a MOOC. Since it gives access to a potentially large number of contributors, a relatively simple and convenient way to collect data and, in general, a well-educated audience. For the learner, research based tasks can support deep learning and application of the new knowledge and skills, thus enriching the learning experience.

The research assignment, links to the question of scalability of the educational system introduced above. It was based on a framework [7] developed to analyse the educational scalability of MOOCs *and* to detect best practice. MOOC participants were asked as part of their final assignment to analyse a MOOC of their choice with the help of the framework. This assignment did build on the MOOC's contents and had the objective to give the participants an active insight in MOOC design practice. For the designers the results of the assignment should give insight in the validity of the framework and should yield examples of design practice. The next sections introduces the framework, followed by the study and its results, and a discussion.

2 A Framework to Detect and Analyse Educational Scalability

The literature on quality and design guidelines related to MOOCs is very extensive taking into account many criteria including organizational ones such as institutional organization and a minimal staff student ratio [8, 9]. However, they seem to disregard that MOOCs are another type of educational offering as they also use criteria related to e.g. institutional organisation and to staff size and roles. Moreover, mostly, they serve one of two purposes: either they offer design guidelines or they provide criteria which are used to assess the design. Instead we focussed on just four main criteria commonly agreed upon in the literature as being essential for learning. Our main objective is not to assess or prescribe design guidelines but to use the design criteria to study/identify best practice. In summary, the framework [7] has been based on the following four criteria:

- Constructive alignment: as an overall necessity since it implies coherence and structure [10, 11]. Aligned course design is based on clearly stated learning goals, corresponding learning activities and are assessed by appropriate assessment methods. For students, alignment helps to select the appropriate course and to regulate their learning. Particularly in a MOOC context which lacks the constraints of a curriculum and general academic requirements related to institutional policies and habits.
- Task complexity: courses should offer variation of different learning activities on various complexity levels. They should provide learning activities in the context of real-world problems which ask students to apply their knowledge and skills [12, 13]. Best practice will give insight in task complexity in existing courses, assist development of new courses and give input to further research.
- Interaction promotes learning and therefore should be a part of the learning process [3, 13, 14]. In MOOCs, interaction can take place between students (S-S), student and teacher (S-T) or student and content (S-C). Best practice will help to see how large numbers of students can be supported with different interaction types.
- Formative assessment & feedback: should be part of the learning process, it improves and supports learning [15]. Again, current practices can help us to understand what are the options to provide students with (personalized) feedback [16].

To make the framework fit for use as an assignment, it was translated into a survey. The survey contained a total of 64 questions both open and closed questions, divided over 5 main sections: (1) general information about the MOOC and the unit of learning (UoL) selected; (2) (the degree of) constructive alignment of the UoL.; (3) the type and use of interactions i.e. S-S, S-T and S-C; (4) the use and details of formative assessment and feedback; (5) general demographics of the students and feedback on the assignment. In addition, the survey contained a section on informed consent, in which the learner was asked to confirm they did read the information about the research and that their participation was voluntary. In any case, they could choose to withdraw at any time. Finally, each section was supported by a short introduction explaining the purpose of the section and background to introduce the questions.

3 Method and Materials

The study was situated in the MOOC 'Assessment for learning in practice' focussing on theory and guidelines on the topic of formative assessment. The target audience was teachers and educationalists. Two assignments focused on the use of the above introduced framework. The first assignment was an exercise to train the use of the survey. For this the learners used part of the survey to analyse the third lesson of the MOOC itself. The second assignment was the final assignment of the MOOC. The learners were asked to select a MOOC of their choice and to analyse it with the survey. To limit the size of the assignment, the students only had to analyse one UoL of the MOOC. The UoL had to comply with two constraints: it should contain formative assessment and it should not be the first or last week of the MOOC.

The MOOC was offered on the EMMA platform (platform.europeanmoocs.eu). The level of activity varied strongly, lesson views went from 199 students (lesson 1) to 101 students (lesson 4). The final lesson (lesson 7) that contained the final assignment was viewed by 38 students of which 11 handed in the final assignment.

4 Results and Discussion

Eleven students (9 female, 2 male) completed the survey, with participants from Italy, Germany, the Netherlands and Spain and an age range between 29–58. All did have a professional background in (higher) education and/or research. Five of the participants reported on their prior experience with MOOCs and indicated that they (co) designed one or more MOOCs.

The MOOCs analysed showed to be representative given the variety of designs, the range of topics, durations and platforms supported. In most cases (n = 9) the participants indicated that the learning goals of the MOOCs they analysed were provided and of different levels (5 on the "does"/"shows how" level; 6 on the "knows", "knows how" levels of Miller [12]). Seven of the MOOCs indicated the prior knowledge expected to successfully follow the MOOC. The UoL selected for further analysis was respectively in week 2 (5x), 3 (4x), 5 (1x) and in week 12 (1x).

Constructive alignment was analysed by comparing the level of the learning goals according to Miller's classification and the learning activities in a UoL. Goals and activities are aligned when there was at least one activity at the goal level. According to the participants in 6 of the 11 cases the learning goals of the UoL were aligned with the learning activities. The assignment of the Miller level to learning goals and activities, however, was not always consistent within each survey. The descriptions added, indicated that, in particular, the learning goals were only very superficially defined in the MOOCs making it difficult, if at all possible, to assign a Miller level to them.

For the *learning activity analysis*, the students had to indicate the type and complexity of the provided learning activities and describe them. The activities covered a wide spectrum including reading assignments, video lectures, audio recording, essays, blogposts and design activities, quizzes with open and closed questions, simulations and games, group assignments and brainstorm activities. The designs varied, partly reflecting the level of the learning goal/learning activity, i.e. higher level activities were more connected with activities such as essays, design activities, quizzes with open questions, simulations and games, group assignments and brainstorm activities; lower level activities with reading assignments, video lectures and closed questions. The activities connected to higher level learning activities suggest that MOOCs can contribute to best practice, examples included: collaborating on mind-maps and OER, and sharing examples of soil crusting in students' local neighbourhood.

For *the interactions*, the students had to indicate if an interaction type was used and give a description. S-S interaction (8x) varied between group work, peer feedback, forum exchanges and the use of Facebook. S-T interaction (7x) included questions during live sessions and forum exchanges. In some cases the interaction type was ambiguous e.g. for some students it was unclear whether a pre-designed tutor video is S-T or S-C interaction. While all interactions types were represented, the descriptions indicated that the main focus was on S-C interaction followed by S-S interaction.

Formative feedback was analysed at a relatively high level of detail. In 8 cases the UoL contained activities with formative feedback, partly by the learning material (quizzes, simulations) and partly by peers. In one case selected examples were commented upon by the tutor. While peer feedback was indicated 5 times, other than a worked out example (1x) there was no support or preparation to prime the learner. No practice was reported that could contribute to best practice.

User experiences. The students completed the final assignment within one hour (6x), within two hours (2x), within four hours (2x) and finally 1 student used over six hours. Nine students expressed feedback on the final assignment. Two indicated that it was too long and one student had "no feedback", six of them were clearly positive as is shown by:

- "I appreciate this final assignment; the analysis template is helpful and covers important aspects of formative assessment", and
- "It is an interesting approach: I had never thought about how to analyse a MOOC and since I have done a lot of MOOCs now I realize that some are not well-focussed and need bettering as regards formative and summative feedback".

5 Conclusion

In this paper we explored the use of a research assignment as a final assignment of a MOOC for the benefits of student and designer. Students were positive on the assignment. For the designers, overall, the results were positive, i.e. the crowd-sourced approach showed viable and the framework was applicable and did expose examples of best practice, in particular, for learner activities. The results of the analyses confirmed that MOOCs, in general, are still weak in various aspects of their design. However, unlike the use of existing frameworks [8, 9], it also revealed practices that can be of interest to MOOC or (online) learning designers. With individual respondents participating, the clarity of the survey questions is of utmost importance to assure the validity of the outcome. Some question/answer options showed to be ambiguous, in particular since the information in the MOOC analysed is often ambiguous too. This will require an update of the survey. Another issue was the number of responses. Alike many MOOCs the completion rate was low. However, to establish a representative sample in our case we would like to have had an analysis of at least 50 learners. Finally, depending of the assignment one has to be aware that there is a risk of bias with regard to who participates. Overall, however, the use of the framework showed to be of interest and its focus on best practice an interesting addition to existing frameworks. Finally, at a general level, the use of crowd-sourced research assignments has a clear potential for further exploration both for students and designers.

Acknowledgements. This work is supported by the Dutch National Initiative for Education Research/The Netherlands Organisation for Scientific Research and the Dutch Ministry of Education, Culture and Science under grant 405-15-705 (www.sooner.nu).

References

1. Ossiannilsson, E., Williams, K., Camilleri, A., Brown, M.: Quality Models in Online and Open Education around the Globe: State of the Art and Recommendations (2015)
2. Yuan, L., Powell, S.: MOOCs and Open Education: Implications for Higher Education, pp. 1–21. A white paper, JISC Cetis (2013)
3. Class-Central (2016)
4. Kalz, M.: Lifelong learning and its support with new technologies. In: Wright, J.D. (ed.) International Encyclopedia of the Social & Behavioral Sciences, vol. 14, 2nd edn., pp. 93–99. Elsevier, Oxford (2015)
5. Zimmermann, C., Kopp, M., Ebner, M.: How MOOCs can be used as an instrument of scientific research. In: Khalil, M., Ebner, M., Kopp, M., Lorenz, A., Kalz, M. (Eds.) Proceedings of the EMOOCs 2016, pp. 393–400 (2016)
6. Hodge, R.: Adapting a MOOC for research: lessons learned from the first presentation of literature and mental health: reading for wellbeing. J. Interact. Media Educ. **2016**(1), 1–17 (2016). Article no. 19
7. Kasch, J., Van Rosmalen, P., Kalz, M.: Learning at Scale: Educational Scalability of Open Courses (submitted)
8. Rosewell, J., Jansen, D.: The OpenupEd quality label. Benchmarks for MOOCs. Int. J. Innov. Qual. Learn. **2**(3), 88–100 (2014)
9. Margaryan, A., Bianco, M., Littlejohn, A.: Instructional quality of massive open online courses (MOOCs). Comput. Educ. **80**, 77–83 (2015)
10. Biggs, J.: Aligning teaching for constructing learning. High. Educ. Acad. 1–4 (2003)
11. Blumberg, P.: Maximizing learning through course alignment and experience with different types of knowledge. Innov. High. Educ. **34**, 93–103 (2009)
12. Miller, G.: The assessment of clinical skills/competence/performance. Acad. Med. **65**(9), S63–S67 (1990)
13. Merrill, M.D.: First Principles of Instruction: Identifying and Designing Effective Efficient and Engaging Instruction. Pfeiffer/John Wiley & Sons, Hoboken (2013)
14. Anderson, T.: Toward a theory of online learning. In: Anderson, T., Elloumi, F. (eds.) Theory and Practice of Online Learning, pp. 33–60. Athabasca University, Athabasca, Canada (2004)
15. Floratos, N., Guasch, T., Espasa, A.: Recommendations on formative assessment and feedback practices for stronger engagement in MOOCs. Open Prax. **7**, 141–152 (2015)
16. Dolan, V.: Massive online obsessive compulsion: what are they saying out there about the latest phenomenon in higher education? Int. Rev. Res. Open Distrib. Learn. **15**(2), 268–281 (2014)

Demo Papers

ReaderBench: A Multi-lingual Framework for Analyzing Text Complexity

Mihai Dascalu[1,2(✉)], Gabriel Gutu[1], Stefan Ruseti[1], Ionut Cristian Paraschiv[1], Philippe Dessus[3], Danielle S. McNamara[4], Scott A. Crossley[5], and Stefan Trausan-Matu[1,2]

[1] University Politehnica of Bucharest, Splaiul Independenţei 313, 60042 Bucharest, Romania
{mihai.dascalu,gabriel.gutu,stefan.ruseti,ionut.paraschiv, stefan.trausan}@cs.pub.ro

[2] Academy of Romanian Scientists, Splaiul Independenţei 54, 050094 Bucharest, Romania

[3] Laboratoire des Sciences de l'Éducation, Univ. Grenoble Alpes, F38000 Grenoble, France
philippe.dessus@univ-grenoble-alpes.fr

[4] Institute for the Science of Teaching and Learning, Arizona State University, Tempe, USA
dsmcnama@asu.edu

[5] Department of Applied Linguistics/ESL, Georgia State University, Atlanta 30303, USA
scrossley@gsu.edu

Abstract. Assessing textual complexity is a difficult, but important endeavor, especially for adapting learning materials to students' and readers' levels of understanding. With the continuous growth of information technologies spanning through various research fields, automated assessment tools have become reliable solutions to automatically assessing textual complexity. *ReaderBench* is a text processing framework relying on advanced Natural Language Processing techniques that encompass a wide range of text analysis modules available in a variety of languages, including English, French, Romanian, and Dutch. To our knowledge, *ReaderBench* is the only open-source multilingual textual analysis solution that provides unified access to more than 200 textual complexity indices including: surface, syntactic, morphological, semantic, and discourse specific factors, alongside cohesion metrics derived from specific lexicalized ontologies and semantic models.

Keywords: Multi-lingual text analysis · Textual complexity · Comprehension prediction · Natural Language Processing · Textual cohesion · Writing style

1 Introduction

Two important and cumbersome tasks, which often face many teachers, are selecting reading materials suitable for their students' levels of understanding, and assessing their written productions (e.g., essays, summaries). In order to support both tasks, *ReaderBench* [1], a multilingual, open-source framework centered on discourse analysis, was developed. From an architectural perspective, as shown in Fig. 1, our framework comprises three layers: (a) *linguistic resources* that provide solid language background knowledge and can be used to train the semantic models and compute various measures;

É. Lavoué et al. (Eds.): EC-TEL 2017, LNCS 10474, pp. 495–499, 2017.
DOI: 10.1007/978-3-319-66610-5_48

(b) *linguistic services* used to process and append semantic meta-information to text resources, and (c) *linguistic applications* that rely on machine learning and data mining techniques, and are designed for various educational experiments and visualizations. *ReaderBench* implements various metrics and categories of textual complexity indices that can be used to leverage the automated classification of datasets in multiple languages, such as English [2], French [3], Romanian [4] and Dutch [5].

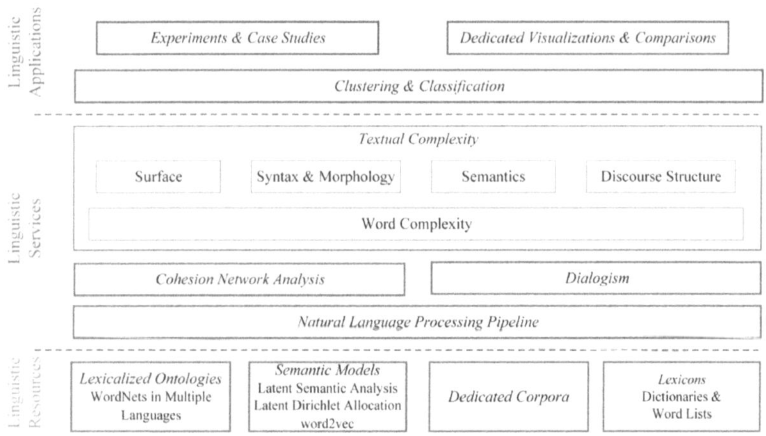

Fig. 1. *ReaderBench* processing architecture.

2 Description of Textual Complexity Indices

More than 200 textual complexity indices computed by the *ReaderBench* platform have been used in a number of experiments. *ReaderBench* integrates a multitude of indices, discussed briefly below, ranging from classic readability formulas, surface indices, morphology and syntax, as well as semantics and discourse structure.

Surface Indices. These are the simplest measures that consider only the form of the text. This category includes indices such as sentence length, word length, the number of unique words used, and word entropy. All these indices rely on the assumption that more complex texts contain more information and, inherently, more diverse concepts.

Word Complexity Indices. This category of indices focuses on the complexity of words, but goes way beyond their form. Thus, the complexity of a word is estimated by the number of syllables and how different the flectional form is from its lemma or stem, considering that adding suffixes and prefixes increases the difficulty of using a given word. Moreover, a word's complexity is measured by considering the number of potential meanings derived from the word's senses available in WordNet, as well as a word's specificity reflected in its depth within the lexicalized ontology.

Syntactic and Morphologic Indices. These indices are computed at the sentence level. The words' corresponding parts of speech and the types of dependencies that appear in each sentence can be used as relevant measures, reflective of a text's complexity. In addition, named entity-based features are tightly correlated with the amount of cognitive resources required to understand the given text.

Semantic Cohesion Indices. Cohesion plays an important role in text comprehension and our framework makes extensive usage of Cohesion Network Analysis. *ReaderBench* estimates both local and global cohesion by considering lexical chains, different semantic models (semantic distances in different multilingual WordNets, LSA – Latent Semantic Analysis, LDA – Latent Dirichlet Allocation, and Word2Vec), as well as co-reference chains.

Discourse Structure Indices. Specific discourse connectives and metrics derived from polyphonic model of discourse [1], which considers the evolution of expressed points of view, provide additional valuable insights in terms of the text's degree of elaboration. Word features and vectors from the integrated linguistic resources are also used to reflect specific discourse traits.

3 Validation Experiments

Multiple experiments have been performed to validate *ReaderBench* as a multi-lingual text analysis software framework. This section focuses on the latest and most representative experiments conducted in English, French, Romanian, and Dutch languages. The *first experiment* [2] was performed on a set of 108 argumentative essays written in English and timed to 25 min. For the analysis, only essays that contained three or more paragraphs were considered in order to use global cohesion measures reflective of inter-paragraph relations. Individual difference measures such as vocabulary knowledge and reading comprehension scores were assessed. The results showed that writers with stronger vocabulary knowledge used longer words with multiple senses and higher entropy, but also created more cohesive essays. Also, students with higher reading comprehension scores created more cohesive and more lexically sophisticated essays, using longer words, and with higher entropy.

The *second experiment* [3] relied on a set of 200 documents collected from primary school French manuals. The documents were pre-classified into five complexity classes mapped onto the first five primary grade levels of the French national education system. A Support Vector Machine (SVM) was used to classify the documents. The pre-trained model was used to determine the complexity for an additional set of 16 documents that were manually classified into three primary grades. Students belonging to the three classes had to read the texts and answer a posttest. Correlations between the textual complexity factors' scores and the students' average scores were computed. This allowed the computation of the impact for each factor in calculating the reliability of prediction of the textual complexity score for a given document.

The *third experiment* [4] was conducted on a set of 137 documents written in Romanian language. The documents were collected from two time periods, 1941–1991 and

1992-present, and two regions, Bessarabia and Romania. The first period altered the Romanian language spoken in the country because of the implementation of the Russian language into the education system of Bessarabia. The aim of the experiment was to determine whether differences between the two regions and the two time periods could be observed in relation to the complexity of written texts. The analysis showed that more elaborated texts were created in the second period for both Bessarabia and Romania, while more unique words have been used in the second period for Bessarabia, but remained the same for Romania. The semantic cohesion of the texts increased over time, but no significant differences were observed between the two regions.

The *fourth experiment* [5] was run on a set of 173 technical reports written in Dutch language belonging to high or low performance students. Due to the length of the documents, a multi-level hierarchical structure was automatically generated based on the section headings. The experiment showed that students who received higher scores had longer reports, but also greater word entropy. They used more pronouns, discourse connectors and unique words, but also had lower inner cohesion scores per paragraph which is indicative of more sophisticated paragraphs.

4 Conclusion

Many pedagogical scenarios can fully integrate the use of *ReaderBench*, thanks to its versatility. The wide range of textual assessment features can support both teachers' assessment and learners' writing self-regulation. Moreover, multiple learning contexts take advantage from *ReaderBench*'s support: either individual textual production and reflection, or collaborative knowledge building.

The presented experiments support the *ReaderBench* framework for determining the textual complexity of texts written in English, French, Romanian, and Dutch languages. Other languages, such as Spanish, Italian, and Latin are also partially supported. To our knowledge, *ReaderBench* is a unique *multilingual* system that provides access to a wide range of textual complexity indices and to various textual cohesion analyses.

Acknowledgments. This research was partially supported by the FP7 2008-212578 LTfLL project, by the 644187 EC H2020 RAGE project, by the ANR-10-blan-1907-01 DEVCOMP project, as well as by University Politehnica of Bucharest through the "Excellence Research Grants" Program UPB–GEX 12/26.09.2016.

References

1. Dascalu, M.: Analyzing Discourse and Text Complexity for Learning and Collaborating. SCI, vol. 534. Springer, Cham (2014)
2. Allen, L.K., Dascalu, M., McNamara, D.S., Crossley, S., Trausan-Matu, S.: Modeling individual differences among writers using ReaderBench. In: EduLearn 2016, Barcelona, Spain, pp. 5269–5279. IATED (2016)

3. Dascalu, M., Stavarache, L.L., Trausan-Matu, S., Dessus, P., Bianco, M.: Reflecting comprehension through French textual complexity factors. In: 26th International Conference on Tools with Artificial Intelligence, ICTAI 2014, Limassol, Cyprus, pp. 615–619. IEEE (2014)
4. Gifu, D., Dascalu, M., Trausan-Matu, S., Allen, L.K.: Time evolution of writing styles in Romanian language. In: ICTAI 2016, San Jose, CA, pp. 1048–1054. IEEE (2016)
5. Dascalu, M., Westera, W., Ruseti, S., Trausan-Matu, S., Kurvers, H.: ReaderBench learns Dutch: building a comprehensive automated essay scoring system for Dutch. In: André, E., Baker, R., Hu, X., Rodrigo, M., du Boulay, B. (eds.) AIED 2017. LNCS, vol. 10331, pp. 52–63. Springer, Cham (2017)

VIRTUS Virtual VET Centre (V3C): A Learning Platform for Virtual Vocational Education and Training

Peter de Lange(✉), Petru Nicolaescu, and Ralf Klamma

Advanced Community Information Systems (ACIS) Group, RWTH Aachen University, Ahornstr. 55, 52056 Aachen, Germany
{lange,nicolaescu,klamma}@dbis.rwth-aachen.de
http://dbis.rwth-aachen.de

Abstract. Given the flexible nature of virtual organizations and the barriers raised by multinational environments, increasing the participation rate of adult learners in vocational training is a difficult task. The latest developments in distant, open and collaborative learning techniques bare the potential to advance knowledge in the field and increase participation rates. In the scope of the European Project VIRTUS, we have developed the Virtual Vocational Educational Training Center, an innovative platform for ECVET standard certified courses that addresses the challenges in vocational training. In this demo, we aim to present the course platform to the TEL community and to gather feedback.

Keywords: Vocational training · Learning unit design · PLE · LMS

1 Introduction

Learning solutions for virtual organizations started to gain large interest, contributing to the development of skills for the labor market and to job growth, for various industries. The "Virtual Vocational Education and Training - VIRTUS" project aims at developing a digital training center platform to provide means for designing modular certified courses for *Vocational Educational Training* (VET). The platform is evaluated in the "Tourism and Hospitality Services" and "Social Entrepreneurship" domains, corresponding to regional growth potential and skill needs in EU countries. It targets at increasing the participation rate of adult learners in continuing VET and providing ECVET standard certified learning.

With the *VIRTUS Virtual VET Center* (V3C), we hereby present the prototypical implementation of the platform. We build upon an integrated combination of established and innovative learning technologies and concepts from latest EU TEL research [1]: *Learning Management Systems* (LMS) and *Personal Learning Environments* (PLE). LMSs are established software applications for the administration, documentation, tracking, reporting and delivery of electronic educational courses or training programs. PLEs are innovative systems helping learners to take control of and manage their own learning, as individuals or in

É. Lavoué et al. (Eds.): EC-TEL 2017, LNCS 10474, pp. 500–503, 2017.
DOI: 10.1007/978-3-319-66610-5_49

groups. They include providing support for learners to set their own learning goals with/without support of tutors, manage their learning, both content and process, communicate with others in the learning process, etc. The integration also features a set of tools for authoring, configuring and deploying modular courses which can be used in formal and informal learning and support both collaborative and self-regulated learning, as well as the assessment of learning outcomes, according to European certification standards.

2 Technological and Functional Background

We realize the V3C platform as a hyper learning environment (consisting of LMS, PLE) using standard, well-established Web development languages and protocols, such as PHP, JavaScript, Java RESTful microservices, HTML5, XMPP and WebRTC. The LMS editor is realized as a stand-alone Website[1] which allows the design of courses and learning units. It features the design (e.g. modeling by drag-and-drop functionality) of course rooms, divided into learning units, via the selection of individual widget components and content which will be part of the personal/collaborative learning environment used for vocational training by learners. Widgets are reusable components running in a Web browser which offer specialized functionality, usually realizing a responsive browser UI to one or more microservices [3]. They support a wide range of devices and can be mashed up into portal containers to create personalized, collaborative or single-usage computing and work environments. The V3C LMS learning units are designed to be extensible with new widget types, such that an extension of the "tool ecosystem" of the V3C is easily possible. This provides a highly customizable solution available for tutors, course designers and certification instructors to design and directly deploy courses/learning units and knowledge assessment elements.

From the PLE perspective, V3C uses the infrastructure developed in the Responsive Open Learning Environments (ROLE) project, consisting of a widget-based PLE [4]. Content widgets such as presentation viewers, document viewers and media players can be orchestrated together with other widgets, e.g., text and video chat, sketching tools, progress tracking and monitoring tools, in order to improve the collaboration and self-monitoring experience. V3C supports learning in so-called "spaces" – i.e. deployed learning environments designed using the LMS component – which are the representation of a course. V3C users can autonomously join these spaces via the respective course unit in their LMS. Each course unit is represented in the learning space as a separate activity. This realizes a separation between the individual units which are part of a course, enables activity and progress tracking for individual units and allows for assessment via quizzes of the respective units' learning outcomes. Each course unit may consist of video lectures, slide presentations, various multimedia content such as audio recordings, videos and images, and self-assessment quizzes. Tutors and other learners can intervene into the learning process at any point via video or text chat, available for each course. Since our target group for both learning designers and learners consists of people from Italy, Austria, Greece and

[1] http://virtus-vet.eu.

Spain, the V3C is developed with extensive translation functionality, providing opportunities to offer and translate learning units into different languages.

Data protection and privacy are ensured for the LMS and PLE components by using the OpenID Connect [2] standard, for secure authentication and authorization in Web applications. It allows a unified Single Sign-On (SSO) login for both course designers and students to be used in the LMS and PLE.

3 Use Case

In the following, we present a scenario for the main use case of our demonstration. As owner of the Gourmet Travel Agency (GTA), Chris (V3C customer) needs to train his employees in using digital technology to book complete packages online. He therefore navigates to the V3C platform and finds a basic travel agent course offered by the V3C provider Traveling Agents Training Services (TATS), including the option of a later ECVET certification. Based on his needs, Tanja, a trainer at TATS, negotiates a customization of the course to his particular business needs. She offers to reuse a basic course by adding GTA-specific metadata to the V3C platform which contains three modules: "flight booking", "hotel booking" and "rental car booking", each of them featuring both synchronous as well as asynchronous elements. Synchronous elements involve real-time communication and collaboration technology and moderation by a designated trainer at TATS. Asynchronous elements involve different kinds of multimedia content delivery elements for knowledge acquisition: a slide presenter, a document viewer, a data upload widget and a video player. The course furthermore offers intermediate assessments after each module, as well as a final assessment at the end of the whole course. The platform provides learners progress awareness. Chris asks for an additional course module for training gourmet restaurant booking, including information on Michelin categories, cuisine styles, etc. and books a full course. Together with the TATS team of professional trainers, Tanja designs this new course module, including curriculum, multimedia contents, custom interactive course elements and the quizzes for each unit. The LMS with the design and the resulting course is shown in Fig. 1. The elements are added by dragging and dropping existing widgets to the course units. Quizzes are developed based on the targeted skills and the requirements of the ECVET certification. For Chris' several international employees, English and German are added as supported languages, with English being selected as the main language. Upon completion of the new custom gourmet module, Tanja creates/exports the course using the V3C platform into the PLE. Each unit is available as a separate activity under the course space address, the widgets under each activity reflecting the design view from the LMS component. Chris employees at GTA navigate to the V3C platform to take the new course over a period of several weeks under Tanjas supervision. Upon course completion, learners are directed to an external certification platform for examination and official certification.

Fig. 1. Course unit/quizz design (above) and resulting PLE (below)

Acknowledgments. This research was funded by the European Research Council under the European Union's Erasmus+ project "VIRTUS" (grant no. 562222).

References

1. Kravčík, M., Neulinger, K., Klamma, R.: Using personal learning environments to support workplace learning in small companies. In: Chiu, D.K.W., Marenzi, I., Nanni, U., Spaniol, M., Temperini, M. (eds.) ICWL 2016. LNCS, vol. 10013, pp. 294–302. Springer, Cham (2016). doi:10.1007/978-3-319-47440-3_33
2. Sakimura, N., Bradley, J., Jones, M., de Medeiros, B.: OpenID Connect Core 1.0 (2014)
3. Newman, S.: Building Microservices: Designing Fine-Grained Systems, 1st edn. O'Reilly, Sebastopol (2015)
4. Soylu, A., Mödritscher, F., Wild, F., De Causmaecker, P., Desmet, P.: Mashups by orchestration and widget-based personal environments: key challenges, solution strategies, and an application. Program: Electron. Libr. Inf. syst. **46**(4), 383–428 (2012)

Lesson Observation Data in Learning Analytics Datasets: Observata

Maka Eradze(✉) and Mart Laanpere

School of Digital Technologies, Tallinn University, Tallinn, Estonia
{maka.eradze,mart.laanpere}@tlu.ee

Abstract. Observational data can be used to illuminate different areas of teaching and learning process and enrich Learning Analytics data. Majority of lesson observation tools provide observational data that is not compliant with LA datasets. The paper presents Observata – a tablet computer application for context-aware semantic annotations of significant events during real time lesson observations. During the demo-session we expect the participants to engage in the discussion and provide feedback on the prototype.

Keywords: Learning Analytics · Classroom observations · Multimodal learning analytics · Learning design · Semantic annotations

1 Introduction and Background

Learning Analytics (LA) is a field that analyzes learners and their contexts mainly utilizing the data coming from digital realms to understand computer-mediated contexts. It has been argued, that multimodal data collection and analysis techniques that go beyond the digital environments can bring novel methods to understand when students solve problems, interact with peers and act in both – digital and physical worlds [1]. In order to analyze learning as a whole and its context, there is additional data needed. This data can be coming from learning scenarios [2, 3] coupled with documenting their enactment [4].

We argue that real-time human semantic labeling can be used to illuminate different areas of teaching and learning process, enrich LA data and be combined into Multimodal LA (MMLA) datasets. To our knowledge, lesson observation tools provide observational data that are not compliant with LA datasets [4]. The proposed solution is the classroom observation application that is able to aggregate semantic annotations and gather context-aware, human-labeled systematic observational data. This approach takes into account pedagogical underpinnings and collects data that is aligned with specific pedagogical intentions and foci.

In this paper we present Observata prototype. The prototype has been validated with design-based research that involved semi-structured focus group interview during a design session with stakeholders.

In order to understand teaching and learning processes, context of the learning experience is highly relevant; for this purpose, data coming from LMS is not

É. Lavoué et al. (Eds.): EC-TEL 2017, LNCS 10474, pp. 504–508, 2017.
DOI: 10.1007/978-3-319-66610-5_50

enough. Moreover, collection and analysis of only digital traces is not sufficient [1] and inclusion of qualitative data into the equation might be beneficial [5]. MMLA data containing observations can offer insights into this issue and help enrich LA with contextual aspects. Aligning Learning Design and LA helps understanding learning behavior and creating actionable feedback loop [6, 7]. Also, linking the generic pedagogical scenarios with contextualized learning scenarios and LA adds more to the evidence [8]. Combining observational data into MMLA datasets has also been proven useful by some studies [9].

As the classroom life is very busy and there can be around 1000 thousand learning interactions (or activities) taking place within a single day, data collection becomes difficult [10, 11]. At the same time, observational data are especially informative [12]. The approaches used in observations may be qualitative or quantitative; quantitative data is criticized for being taken out of context and failing to show the "story of the classroom life" [10]. Systematic classroom observations that are aimed at capturing learning activities need a defined **Unit of Analysis**. It has been suggested that such unit of analysis is an (Learning) *Event* [4] (observable events). Previous study on observations shows that it is possible to annotate lesson events with xAPI statements [13]. Semantically annotated xAPI statements can then be combined with MMLA datasets.

In the next chapter we present observation application Observata that has been validated by scenario-based participatory design-session with participation of 6 persons representing different stakeholder groups, including in-service teachers, their mentors and teacher educators.

2 Observata

The design of the Observata allows for open and axial coding (with pre-defined code-sets). Observata can be used as a stand-alone tool or an extension of learning scenario visualisation tool LePlanner[1]. In latter case, Observata initiates a lesson observation protocol based on a learning scenario from LePlanner, including in lesson annotation of pre-defined tools, artefacts, actors, learning goals and related activities. Even when Observata is used as a stand-alone mode, observer can define beforehand the code sets, classroom settings, devices, actors. Several code sets can be used in parallel during the lesson observation and they can contain different semantics. Each significant *event* in the lesson transcript is documented in a style of a xAPI statement, indicating actor, verb, object, result and context (two latter being optional). Once observer saves the *event*, it is automatically timestamped and represented on a timeline view that creates the story of the lesson. When using pre-defined learning scenario, activities can be marked as delayed by dragging them on the timeline. The transcript of the lesson feeds into the dashboard views. It is possible to connect several data sources and create richer real-time analytics that can be used for reflection and analysis. Below the main use cases of Observata are briefly described.

[1] https://beta.leplanner.net/#/.

Annotating with Open Coding. Classroom map is displayed by the app while annotating the lesson observation. To document a bullying incident between two students (K and L), observer taps first on Student K (*Subject*) on the classroom map, then on Student L (*Object*) and types in the *Verb*: 'bullies'. Optionally, observer may add the photo and also the *Context* for the incident (ongoing whole-class activity). Even in case of open coding, the most typical verbs (e.g. asks, presents, explains) and most typical objects (e.g. question, task, example, solution) can be dragged from the pre-defined code set on the edge of the screen (Fig. 1).

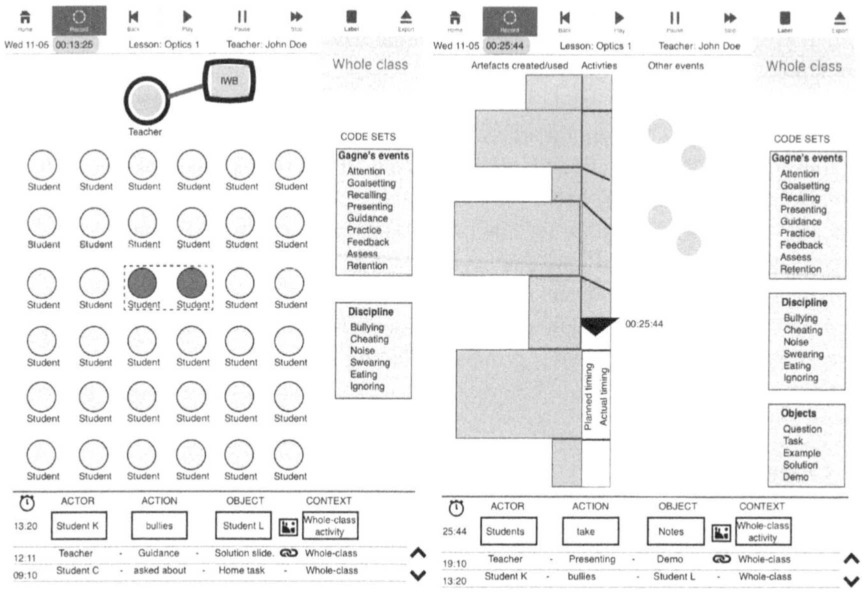

Fig. 1. Classroom (left) and scenario (right) views of the Observata tool

Annotating Using Predefined Code-Sets. To annotate the teacher's response to student C's question, the observer taps on *teacher (Subject)*, then taps on IWB icon and chooses from Code set the *Object* ('solution'). To select pre-defined *Verb*, observer then drags the label 'Guidance' from pre-defined code set based on Gagne's instructional events.

Annotating the Lesson Based on LePlanner Scenario. To validate the pre-designed lesson plan, observer compares the actual progress of lesson with scenario, noting the delays and disruptions of activities if needed. Subjects, Objects and Verbs are transferred automatically to xAPI statements from LePlanner scenario. However, observer may add additional activities (both parallel and sub-activities).

Analyzing the Lesson Transcript. After finishing the lesson annotation and saving the transcript, observer goes through the transcript together with the teacher and may edit it. Lesson transcripts are visualized on a LA dashboard, but Observata also allows exporting LA data sets to LRS or data analysis software for retrospective analytics, to be combined with data from other sources (e.g. log files).

3 Conclusions and Future Plans

Current prototype of Observata is built for demonstrating and validating the approach to xAPI-driven, real-time annotation of classroom events and related reference model that has been described in detail in our upcoming paper. The stable version of Observata will enter piloting in Tallinn University's initial teacher education programme in the end of year 2017. The piloting will focus on improving user experience of the Observata app, but also on increasing the efficiency, error-proneness and speed of annotations.

The future development of Observata is planned to include additional functionalities, such as code set editor, lesson annotation by two coders simultaneously, and calculation of inter-coder reliability. The latter might be interesting for researchers dealing with classroom ethnography.

References

1. Blikstein, P.: Multimodal learning analytics. In: Proceedings of the Third International Conference on Learning Analytics and Knowledge, pp. 102–106. ACM, April 2013
2. Ochoa, X., Worsley, M.: Editorial: augmenting learning analytics with multimodal sensory data. J. Learn. Anal. **3**(2), 213–219 (2016)
3. Rodríguez-Triana, M.J., Prieto Santos, L.P., Vozniuk, A., Shirvani Boroujeni, M., Schwendimann, B.A., Holzer, A.C., Gillet, D.: Monitoring, awareness and reflection in blended technology enhanced learning: a systematic review. Int. J. Technol. Enhanc. Learn. (in press)
4. Eradze, M., Rodríguez-Triana, M.J., Laanpere, M.: How to aggregate lesson observation data into learning analytics datasets? In: MMLA 2017, Vancouver, Canada (2017, in print)
5. Ferguson, R., Clow, D.: Where is the evidence? A call to action for learning analytics. In: Proceedings of the Seventh International Learning Analytics & Knowledge Conference, Vancouver, BC, Canada, 13–17 March 2017 (2017)
6. Lockyer, L., Dawson, S.: Learning designs and learning analytics. In: Proceedings of the 1st International Conference on Learning Analytics and Knowledge, pp. 153–156. ACM, February 2011
7. Lockyer, L., Heathcote, E., Dawson, S.: Informing pedagogical action: aligning learning analytics with learning design. Am. Behav. Sci. **57**(10), 1439–1459 (2013)
8. Kurvits, M., Laanpere, M., Väljataga, T.: Analysis of tools and methods for describing and sharing reusable pedagogical scenarios. In: Li, F., Klamma, R., Laanpere, M., Zhang, J., Manjón, B.F., Lau, R. (eds.) ICWL 2015. LNCS, vol. 9412, pp. 251–257. Springer, Cham (2015). doi:10.1007/978-3-319-25515-6_24
9. Rodríguez-Triana, M.J., Holzer, A., Prieto, L.P., Gillet, D.: Examining the effects of social media in co-located classrooms: a case study based on SpeakUp. In: Verbert, K., Sharples, M., Klobučar, T. (eds.) EC-TEL 2016. LNCS, vol. 9891, pp. 247–262. Springer, Cham (2016). doi:10.1007/978-3-319-45153-4_19
10. Wragg, T.: An Introduction to Classroom Observation (Classic Edition). Routledge, Abingdon (2013)

11. Jackson, P.W.: Life in Classrooms. Holt, Rinehart & Winston, New York (1968)
12. O'Sullivan, M.: Lesson observation and quality in primary education as contextual teaching and learning processes. Int. J. Educ. Dev. **26**(3), 246–260 (2006)
13. Eradze, M., Väljataga, T., Laanpere, M.: Observing the use of e-Textbooks in the classroom: towards "Offline" learning analytics. In: Cao, Y., Väljataga, T., Tang, J., Leung, H., Laanpere, M. (eds.) ICWL 2014. LNCS, vol. 8699, pp. 254–263. Springer, Cham (2014). doi: 10.1007/978-3-319-13296-9_28

Ld-Feedback App: Connecting Learning Designs with Students' and Teachers' Perceived Experiences

Konstantinos Michos(✉), Arnau Fernández, Davinia Hernández-Leo, and Roman Calvo

ICT Department, Universitat Pompeu Fabra, Barcelona, Spain
{kostas.michos,davinia.hernandez-leo}@upf.edu,
{arnau.fernandez01,roman.calvo01}@estudiant.upf.edu

Abstract. This demonstration paper presents the Ld-Feedback mobile application. A variety of learning design tools were developed during the last years. However, there is still lack of substantial understanding on how learning designs are implemented and experienced by students and teachers. Ld-Feedback is connected with the Integrated Learning Design Environment (ILDE) and allows students and teachers to provide feedback during and after the implementation of learning designs. Two interfaces allow teachers to create feedback forms and generate reports for their learning designs' implementations. Students and teachers access feedback forms to evaluate learning designs with ratings and comments. The development of the application aims at facilitating teacher-led inquiry by providing data informed insights for learning designs within communities of educators.

Keywords: Learning design · Student and teacher feedback · Teacher inquiry · Redesign · Communities of educators

1 Introduction

Learning Design (LD) is the field that studies how teachers/designers revise learning activities towards more pedagogically informed decisions to achieve educational objectives [1]. One of the main directions is on how the tacit work of teachers/designers can be represented and shared among educational practitioners [2]. A variety of digital tools were developed to support LD [3] while web-based platforms allow educators to share their learning designs, e.g. LAMS community [4], Learning Designer [5], ILDE [6]. However, limited work so far focuses on "what happens after the design process" [7]. Although LD representations provide a result of the decision making process of the teacher/designer, few information is available for previous particularizations of a learning design, the learners' preferences of the delivery mode and reflection about the teachers' run-time experience [8]. Data-informed learning designs when implemented with learning technologies can take advantage from the digital footprints of students like learning analytics visualizations but teachers/designers often need qualitative data and understanding of how students perceived their learning experience to better inform the redesign of learning activities [9, 10].

É. Lavoué et al. (Eds.): EC-TEL 2017, LNCS 10474, pp. 509–512, 2017.
DOI: 10.1007/978-3-319-66610-5_51

Mobile apps have been increasingly adopted by educators for the facilitation of their teaching and learning. Mobile tools enable teachers to capture real time information from class activities, to move beyond the classroom setting and even author learning activities [11]. In the ecosystem of LD tools few authoring tools connect elements of the design-time with the run-time evaluation of learning designs. An empirical study of a mobile application for location game-based learning presents visualizations of students' activities' enactment to enable teachers revise their learning design [12]. The visualizations supported teacher inquiry with awareness information of students' activity. These studies show the value of learning analytics but they also conclude that students' and teachers' opinion about the implementation of learning activities would also be highly relevant to understand the impact of learning designs. The tool described in this paper aims at facilitating the collection and reporting of this type of feedback information. The approach considered in the design of the tool is generic in that the tool can be applied to multiple types of learning designs, not being specific to particular learning designs tools.

2 Ld-Feedback Mobile App

Ld-Feedback is a mobile application which allows students and teachers to provide feedback regarding the implementation of learning designs created with multiple tools. To achieve that, the application is connected with the Integrated Learning Design Environment (ILDE), a web-based community platform for the creation, co-creation and sharing of learning designs [6]. The application includes two interfaces for supporting teachers and students in providing feedback for learning designs' implementations. Ld-Feedback also runs in non-mobiles devices such as laptops and tablets.

The teacher interface allows teachers to create forms called "Feedback Check". The user selects from a dropdown list one learning design created in ILDE and associates the feedback check to the particular learning design. The feedback is authored by the teacher (e.g. feedback for the whole learning design or partial for a learning activity). The form consists of a default template with items regarding the effectiveness of the whole learning design which can be edited by the teacher. The default template includes three items about students' subjective learning, level of engagement and enjoyment but the teacher can also edit the default items or add other items. Two additional options allow users to enable feedback comments from students and presentation of the results to students. Once the Feedback Check is ready, the teacher can start a feedback session and a code for students is auto generated.

The students can insert the code in the student interface and rate the items in a scale (2 = Awful, 4 = Not very good, 6 = Good, 8 = Very good, 10 = Brilliant) as they were edited by the teacher. Students can write comments about their general experience of the particular learning session. The items of the feedback form depend on the teacher inquiry problem addressed within the particular learning design.

The teacher can stop the feedback session from the professor interface and view the results of the feedback check as a report. Moreover, he/she can enable the presentation of the results to the students so they become aware of their class. The report shows the overall rating between 2-10 and the rating of each item following by all the comments provided by students (Fig. 1). The reports can be visualized in the Ld-Feedback App or in the context of ILDE.

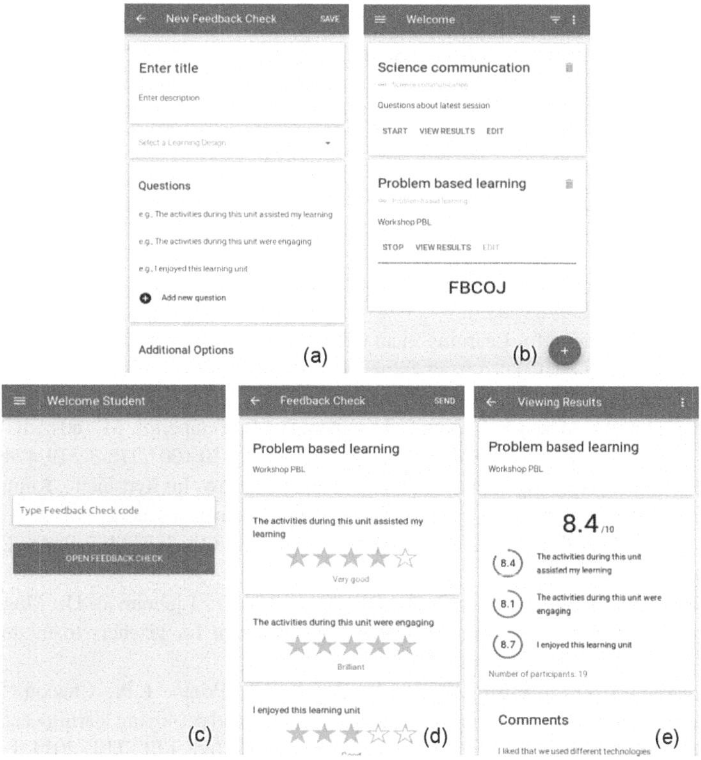

Fig. 1. Screenshots of the Ld-Feedback App. (a) & (b) Teacher interface, (c) & (d) student interface, (e) visualization of students' responses.

A first illustrative case was used in a teacher workshop as part of a project for data informed learning designs within communities of teachers. The Ld-Feedback App was used by the facilitator of the workshop to evaluate elements of the workshops' learning design. Initial teachers' opinion as students in this case was that Ld-Feedback is a useful teacher support tool and its strong point is the intuitive and simple to use interface.

3 Conclusion

This paper presented the Ld-Feedback App, a mobile application which associates learning designs with feedback forms and enables students and teachers to report about their experience. A new generation of data-informed learning design tools aims to support teacher-led inquiry. The experiences of the different stakeholders including teachers and students when using the application will better show how data analytics can inform the quality of learning experiences. Implementations of learning designs from a community of teachers would also reveal effectiveness of different learning-teaching strategies.

Acknowledgments. This research is partly funded by RecerCaixa CoT project and the Spanish Ministry of Economy and Competitiveness under RESET (TIN2014-53199-C3-3-R) and the Maria de Maeztu Units of Excellence Programme (MDM-2015-0502). DHL is a Serra Hunter Fellow. The authors want to sincerely thank Pablo Abenia for the support to the development of this application.

References

1. Mor, Y., Craft, B., Hernández-Leo, D.: The art and science of learning design: editoral. Res. Learn. Technol. **21**, 1–8 (2013)
2. Conole, G.: Designing for Learning in an Open World, vol. 4. Springer Science & Business Media, Heidelberg (2012)
3. Celik, D., Magoulas, G.D.: A review, timeline, and categorization of learning design tools. In: Chiu, D.K.W., Marenzi, I., Nanni, U., Spaniol, M., Temperini, M. (eds.) ICWL 2016. LNCS, vol. 10013, pp. 3–13. Springer, Cham (2016). doi:10.1007/978-3-319-47440-3_1
4. Dalziel, J.: Learning design: sharing pedagogical know-how. In: Iiyoshi, T., Kumar, M.S.V. (eds.) Opening Up Education: The Collective Advancement of Education Through Open Technology, Open Content, and Open Knowledge, pp. 375–387. MIT Press, Cambridge (2008)
5. Laurillard, D., Charlton, P., Craft, B., Dimakopoulos, D., Ljubojevic, D., Magoulas, G., Whittlestone, K.: A constructionist learning environment for teachers to model learning designs. J. Comput. Assist. Learn. **29**(1), 15–30 (2013)
6. Hernández-Leo, D., Asensio-Pérez, J.I., Derntl, M., Prieto, L.P., Chacón, J.: ILDE: community environment for conceptualizing, authoring and deploying learning activities. In: Rensing, C., de Freitas, S., Ley, T., Muñoz-Merino, P.J. (eds.) EC-TEL 2014. LNCS, vol. 8719, pp. 490–493. Springer, Cham (2014). doi:10.1007/978-3-319-11200-8_48
7. Rienties, B., Toetenel, L.: The impact of learning design on student behaviour, satisfaction and performance: a cross-institutional comparison across 151 modules. Comput. Hum. Behav. **60**, 333–341 (2016)
8. Persico, D., Pozzi, F.: Informing learning design with learning analytics to improve teacher inquiry. Br. J. Educ. Technol. **46**(2), 230–248 (2016)
9. Pardo, A., Ellis, R.A., Calvo, R.A.: Combining observational and experiential data to inform the redesign of learning activities. In: Proceedings of the Fifth International Conference on Learning Analytics and Knowledge, pp. 305–309. ACM (2016)
10. Michos, K., Hernández-Leo, D.: Towards understanding the potential of teaching analytics within educational communities. In: CEUR Proceedings of the 4th International Workshop on Teaching Analytics, IWTA 2016, European Conference on Technology Enhanced Learning, Lyon, France, pp. 1–8 (2016)
11. Baran, E.: A review of research on mobile learning in teacher education. Educ. Technol. Soc. **17**(4), 17–32 (2014)
12. Melero, J., Hernández-Leo, D., Sun, J., Santos, P., Blat, J.: How was the activity? A visualization support for a case of location-based learning design. Br. J. Educ. Technol. **46**(2), 317–329 (2014)

SmartZoos: Modular Open Educational Resources for Location-Based Games

Gerti Pishtari(✉), Terje Väljataga, Priit Tammets, Pjotr Savitski, María Jesús Rodríguez-Triana, and Tobias Ley

Tallinn University, Tallinn, Estonia
{gpishtar,terjev,tammets,gnum,mjrt,tley}@tlu.ee

Abstract. Location-based games have the power to transform specific environments into thematic learning experiences. However, their learning content is often managed only by developers and users cannot create their own content, or customize existing ones. This issue affects specific related actors, like teachers, who cannot make use of these technologies to create gaming scenarios for their own purposes. This paper introduces SmartZoos, a location-based game, designed to enhance visitors experience in Zoos. Through it, we present a design mechanism that allow users to generate location-based learning content, as modular Open Educational Resources. These modular contents can be later integrated independently into multiple gaming scenarios by other users. Preliminary results conducted as part of an iterative co-design process, reveal that the prototype is being perceived as effective and easy to use.

Keywords: User-generated content · Open Educational Resources · Location based games · Zoos

1 Introduction

In recent years we have witnessed the explosion of mobile games powered by technologies like geo-localization, augmented reality and QR scanning. Their proliferation is due to the widespread use of smartphones with evermore computational speed. Due to their motivational effect these games have found a successful and large application for educational purposes [3]. They can support the acquisition of skills like critical thinking, collaboration, creativity, responsibility, consideration of multiple perspectives, and social awareness [9].

Various examples exist where similar serious games are applied to specific environments like archeological sites [1], museums [4], or national parks [6]. However, the content provided in these applications, as well as the specific spots of the game scenarios, are static and cannot be customized. This lack of customization causes various problems such as (a) the exclusion of interested users, like teachers, from the process of content creation; (b) outdated application content where no new gaming scenarios are published for a long period of time. Moreover, from an educational perspective it is preferable if tools allow for more dynamic knowledge building activities by students, but also by the teachers. Therefore tools for building game scenarios in teaching should allow continuous updating and upgrading by the users themselves.

É. Lavoué et al. (Eds.): EC-TEL 2017, LNCS 10474, pp. 513–516, 2017.
DOI: 10.1007/978-3-319-66610-5_52

WeQuest is an example that addresses these issues by allowing users to create location-based content [5]. Another example is etiquetAR, which is an authoring tool that enables creating and sharing personalized QR codes [7]. However, these tools do not allow users to adapt and reuse existing content for their own needs, limiting their sustainability in time. Thus, in order to increase the sustainability of these games, it would be necessary not only to offer the content as Open Educational Resources (OER), but also to do it in a modular way that enables partial reusability. An example of the benefits of the modular approach in STEM education are illustrated by projects such as WISE and Go-Lab [8]. In this paper, through the SmartZoos[1] prototype, we present how the idea of modular OER (MOER), could be applied to location-based games.

2 Methodology

The development of SmartZoos is following a design-based research approach [10]. Based on the literature review of location-based games and OER, we extracted the first possible design scenarios. An in-depth contextual inquiry was conducted with 5 zoos' staff, 4 educational experts and 20 pupils. This included observations, interviews, and focus group discussions. All these resulted in user stories and contextual factors that captured the possible usage of the application. Based on an analysis of the transcripts, Personas were created: http://smartzoos.eu/design/.

A co-design process was then initiated with a design team consisting of 4 researchers, 6 developers, 5 professional representatives from the zoos, and 4 teachers. During the co-design process a series of patterns were recognized as important, such as (a) the structure of MOERs; (b) how to make them location based; (c) the inclusion of other technologies into them, like QR codes and augmented reality. The current study reports the preliminary results of the first functional prototype.

3 SmartZoos Prototype

SmartZoos is a location-based augmented reality game that enable users to create gaming scenarios in zoos. The base of the interface is powered by Google Maps (see Fig. 1b). Over it, users can create their own content using location-based MOERs.

The creation of content passes through two different levels, namely activity items, and activities (see Fig. 1a). Activity items are independent and reusable MOERs, which location is freely picked up on the map by users. Together with the location, users can also choose the type of content that they want to insert. In the current prototype there are 7 types of activity item content: one correct answer, multiple correct answers, free-form answer, match pairs, embedded content, information, and photo.

Activities work as containers for activity items, which can be incorporated into them to form a gaming scenario (see Fig. 1c). An activity can contain activity items that were created by other peers before. Users may decide several elements of an activity while creating one: the title; a description of the game that will appear as a popup before starting

[1] https://toolset.smartzoos.eu/.

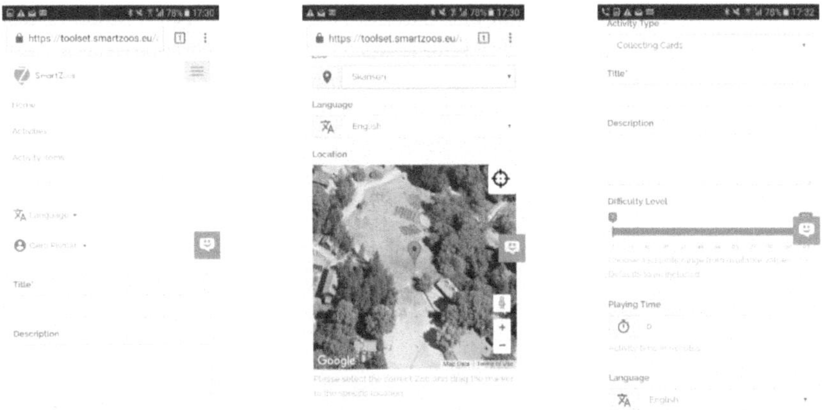

a) b) c)

Fig. 1. (a) Main menu; (b) creating a location based activity item; (c) creating an activity

it; playing time; the zoo, currently among three partner zoos; activity items that will be incorporated on it; proximity, which is the longest distance from which an activity item can be activated. In order to facilitate the process of adding activity items into an activity, the interface has a search option which is based on location, keywords, language, and content type.

4 Preliminary Results

The formative evaluation of the SmartZoos prototype is part of an ongoing co-design process with potential users (teachers, students and zoos' employee). Semi-structured interviews, were conducted after users' interaction with the application. In general, users have been positive about the interaction with interface. They also state to understand and appreciate the underlying idea and purpose of the application, supporting the creation of reusable user-generated leaning content. Preliminary results point that users tend to reuse MOERs created by other peers. At the same time, they prefer to create, or reuse simple modules (e.g.: One/Multiple Correct Answers) rather than the more complex activity items, which are considered as more demanding (requiring more creativity, or further understanding of third party materials that can be incorporated into them). Moreover, a number of usability issues has emerged from these evaluations, e.g., the need to be in the zoo in order to create accurately located activity items, or the necessity of incorporating tips and tutorials in the interface.

5 Conclusion

This paper addresses the problematic of supporting reusable user-generated content in location-based games. We have presented a prototype solution that supports the integration of MOERs into location-based games. Despite positive preliminary results concerning the reusability of content, we have detected that users tended to create simple versions of MOERs that mostly include One/Multiple Correct Answers.

In our future work, we plan to extend the tool by enriching the interface with augmented reality elements and a QR code scanner. With these steps, we hope to extend the possibilities to create interactive and attractive gaming scenarios.

Acknowledgments. This project is partially funded by SmartZoos, CB64, Central Bal- tic Programme 2014–2020; and the European Union's Horizon 2020 Research and Innovation Programme under grant agreement No. 669074.

References

1. Ardito, C., Costabile, M.F., Lanzilotti, R.: Gameplay on a multitouch screen to foster learning about historical sites. In: Proceedings of the International Conference on Advanced Visual Interfaces - AVI 2010, pp. 75–78 (2010)
2. Dennerlein, S., Seitlinger, P., Lex, E., Ley, T.: Take up my tags: exploring benefits of meaning making in a collaborative learning task at the workplace. In: Verbert, K., Sharples, M., Klobučar, T. (eds.) EC-TEL 2016. LNCS, vol. 9891, pp. 377–383. Springer, Cham (2016). doi:10.1007/978-3-319-45153-4_30
3. Gee, J.P.: What video games have to teach us about learning and literacy. Comput. Entertain. **1**, 20 (2003)
4. Klopfer, E., Perry, J., Squire, K., Jan, M.-F., Steinkuehler, C.: Mystery at the museum: a collaborative game for museum education. In: Proceedings of the 2005 Conference n Computer Support for Collaborative Learning: the Next 10 Years, pp. 316–320 (2005)
5. Macvean, A., Hajarnis, S., Headrick, B., Ferguson, A., Barve, C., Karnik, D., Riedl, M.O.: WeQuest: scalable alternate reality games through end-user content authoring. In: Proceedings of the 8th International Conference on Advances in Computer Entertainment Technology - ACE 2011, pp. 22:1–22:8 (2011)
6. Maijala, M.: The stone age trail: a mobile outdoors computer game for nature experience. In: The Virtual: Interaction: A Conference 2007, pp. 30–43 (2010)
7. Pérez-Sanagustín, M., Martínez, A., Delgado-Kloos, C.: etiquetAR: tagging learning experiences. In: Hernández-Leo, D., Ley, T., Klamma, R., Harrer, A. (eds.) EC-TEL 2013. LNCS, vol. 8095, pp. 573–576. Springer, Heidelberg (2013). doi: 10.1007/978-3-642-40814-4_61
8. Rodríguez-Triana, M.J., Govaerts, S., Halimi, W., Holzer, A., Salzmann, C., Vozniuk, A., De Jong, T., Sotirou, S., Gillet, D.: Rich open educational resources for personal and inquiry learning: agile creation, sharing and reuse in educational social media platforms. In: International Conference on Web and Open Access to Learning, ICWOAL, pp. 1–6. IEEE (2014)
9. Schrier, K.: Using augmented reality games to teach 21st century skills. ACM SIGGRAPH 2006 Educators program on - SIGGRAPH 2006, p. 15 (2006)
10. Wang, F., Hannafin, M.J.: Design-based research and technology-enhanced learning environments. ETR&D-Educ. Technol. Res. Dev. **53**, 5–23 (2005)

NoteMyProgress: Supporting Learners' Self-regulated Strategies in MOOCs

Ronald Pérez-Álvarez[1,2(✉)], Mar Pérez-Sanagustín[1(✉)], and Jorge J. Maldonado-Mahauad[1,3]

[1] Department of Computer Science, Pontifical Catholic University of Chile, Santiago, Chile
{raperez13,mar.perez,jjmaldonado}@uc.cl
[2] University of Costa Rica, Sede Regional del Pacífico, Puntarenas, Costa Rica
[3] Department of Computer Science, University of Cuenca, Cuenca, Ecuador

Abstract. NoteMyProgress is a web tool for supporting learners' self-regulation strategies in MOOC environments. NoteMyProgress lets learner take notes, define objectives and goals for their learning, strategically plan their learning activities, and track how they spend their time in the course. This demonstration presents the first prototype of NoteMyProgress, a Google Chrome plugin and web app that includes features for taking notes and managing the time learners spend on the course. Specifically, the article presents: (1) How NoteMyProgress is integrated with the Coursera learning platform to collect information on student learning activities; and (2) how learners can visualize their learning processes on the NoteMyProgress dashboard. This demonstration aims to show how NoteMyProgress, through interactive displays, lets learners monitor how they have spent their time in the course and how to take notes during their study sessions.

Keywords: NoteMyProgress · Self-regulated learning · Massive Open Online Course · Tool · MOOC · SRL

1 Pedagogical Background

NoteMyProgress is a web tool developed to support self-regulation strategies in Massive Open Online Courses (MOOCs). MOOC courses have been considered as one of the main disruptive trends in higher education [1]. One of the main problems that learners face is the lack of self-regulated learning in this type of environment [2]. On the other hand, current learning platforms such as Coursera and open edX lack technological assistance to support the learners' strategies [3]. Likewise, few tools have been developed to support learners in the MOOC learning environment [4].

NoteMyProgress has been specifically designed to support learner self-regulation in MOOCs. This tool is integrated with current MOOC platforms in order to leverage the learning features they offer and support the learner self regulation strategies that have proven to be most effective for learner outcomes in this type of environment. These strategies are: goal-setting and strategy [5]; time management and organization (note-taking) [6]; and social awareness [7].

É. Lavoué et al. (Eds.): EC-TEL 2017, LNCS 10474, pp. 517–520, 2017.
DOI: 10.1007/978-3-319-66610-5_53

2 Technological Background

NoteMyProgress[1] is composed of two parts: (1) a Google Chrome plugin developed in JavaScript; and (2) a dashboard developed in Ruby on Rails. The plugin is the component responsible for integrating the learning platform with the dashboard. Additionally, it collects information on the learning activities that the learner performs from the course URLs that they visit on the learning platform. The dashboard implements the modules that interpret the information collected from the user according to the original learning platform, and stores them in the database defined in PostgreSQL. Once the information is incorporated into the data model, the dashboard generates interactive and personalized displays to help the learner monitor their learning process.

In the bibliography we have identified three tools aimed at supporting learner self-regulation in MOOC environments. However, these tools offer limited assistance: support for taking assessments, watching videos, and time management. The objective of NoteMyProgress is to provide comprehensive support for learner self-regulation strategies in this type of environment. Some of the features that give NoteMyProgress an added value and differentiate it from other tools are:

- **Support for setting learning objectives or goals.** NoteMyProgress allows the learner to set weekly learning goals that they intend to achieve. Subsequently, the learner can view and monitor the achievement of their goals.
- **Support for the strategic planning of activities.** NoteMyProgress provides the learner with past information about certain indicators that may be useful for the implementation of learning activities.
- **Support for monitoring the learners' progress in the course.** NoteMyProgress allows the learner to track their progress in the different learning activities.
- **Support for monitoring time spent on the course.** NoteMyProgress lets the learner know how much time they have spent on course activities, on activities that do not correspond to the course, and on each learning category.
- **Support for the process of taking and downloading notes.** NoteMyProgress, via the Chrome plugin, provides learners with a virtual notebook in which the learner can take notes while they perform learning activities on the learning platform. On the dashboard, the learner is able to download their notes whenever they like.
- **Support for social comparison.** The NoteMyProgress displays allow learners to compare their performance with that of learners who were successful in previous course editions, and who also reported a high level of self-regulation of their learning.
- **Integration with existing platforms.** The NoteMyProgress tool can be integrated with different platforms, just by adding the module for the interpretation of information collected from the learning platform.

[1] Link to the beta version of NoteMyProgress (only available in Spanish): https://es.surveymonkey.com/r/SXMB59R.

3 Results and Outcome

The beta version of the tool, which implements the note-taking feature and the learner time management support feature, was launched and tested in a MOOC on Coursera. The objective of this test was to assess the usability by expert evaluators and the adoption of the tool by learners in a real and uncontrolled MOOC learning environment. The learners had the freedom to choose whether they wanted to download and use the tool. Approximately 200 learners were enrolled in the current edition of the course at the time of the tool's release, and 20 learners used the tool. The expert evaluators judged it to be a usable tool, and the learners evaluated it as a useful tool. The process of downloading and installing the plugin was initially a barrier for the learners to use the tool, but once it was officially added to the Google web store this barrier was overcome. The tool is being continually developed in order to complete pending features and address the comments collected as part of the evaluation of the beta version of NoteMyProgress.

4 Demonstration

The objective of this demonstration is to describe how NoteMyProgress supports and interacts with learners while they perform learning activities in a MOOC on the Coursera platform. A simulation of a learner who performs a series of learning activities in the course "Gestión de organizaciones efectivas" will serve as an illustrative scenario.

This is a learner who is registered for the course on the Coursera platform and wants to use NoteMyProgress as a support tool. The objective of this activity is to make the learner reflect on how they are spending their time during the study sessions carried out on the platform, and also to use the notebook to take notes on the activities they perform. First, the learner downloads and installs the NoteMyProgress plugin. Second, the learner creates their user account and registers for the course that they wish to monitor. Third, the learner performs the learning activities on the Coursera platform and takes notes while doing so. Fourth, the learner logs on to the dashboard to monitor their interaction with the course and how they have spent their time through the interactive displays.

Acknowledgments. This work was supported by FONDECYT (11150231), University of Costa Rica (UCR), MOOC-Maker (561533-EPP-1-2015-1-ESEPPKA2-CBHE-JP), LALA (586120-EPP-1-2017-1-ES-EPPKA2-CBHE-JP), CONICYT Doctorado Nacional 2017/21170467, CONICYT Doctorado Nacional 2016/21160081.

References

1. Cooper, S., Sahami, M.: Reflections on stanford's MOOCs. Commun. ACM **56**(2), 28–30 (2013)
2. Laplante, P.A.: Courses for the Masses? IT Prof. **15**(2), 57–59 (2013)
3. Hew, K.F., Cheung, W.S.: Students' and instructors' use of massive open online courses (moocs): motivations and challenges. Educ. Res. Rev. **12**, 45–58 (2016)

4. Pérez-Álvarez, R., Pérez-Sanagustín, M., Maldonado, J.J.: How to design tools for supporting self-regulated learning in MOOCs? Lessons learned from a literature review from 2008 and 2016. In: Proceedings of 2016 XLII Latin American Computing Conference (CLEI), pp. 1–12 (2016)
5. Kizilcec, R.F., Pérez-Sanagustín, M., Maldonado, J.J.: Self-regulated learning strategies predict learner behavior and goal attainment in Massive Open Online Courses. Comput. Educ. **104**, 18–33 (2017)
6. Veletsianos, G., Shepherdson, P.: A systematic analysis and synthesis of the empirical MOOC literature published in 2013–2015. Int. Rev. Res. Open Distrib. Learn. **17**(2), 198–221 (2016)
7. Chatti, M.: Video - mapper a video annotation tool to support collaborative learning. In Proceeding of European MOOC Stakehold, pp. 131–40 (2015)

Poster Papers

Mapping Employability Attributes onto Facebook: rESSuME: Employability Skills Social Media survEy

Inmaculada Arnedillo-Sánchez(✉), Carlos de Aldama, and Chrysanthi Tseloudi

School of Computer Science and Statistics, Trinity College Dublin, Dublin, Ireland
Macu.Arnedillo@scss.tcd.ie

Abstract. Employability skills comprise soft skills, attitudes and personality traits, and they increase people's chances to be in work. They are generic, non-subject specific, nontechnical, intangible attributes, related to one's personality and professionalism. While there is debate regarding the correlation between these skills and employment, employability skills are perceived as more important than job specific skills. Employers investigate candidates online and their findings affect hiring decisions with rejection, rather than hiring, being the more likely outcome. Studies on graduates highlight a gap between employers and candidates' perspectives on employability skills. A mismatch between skills expected by the employers and those displayed by candidates. This paper presents **rESSuME**: Employability Skills Social Media Survey which was developed to understand how employers screen candidate's social media profiles.

Keywords: Social Media · Employability Skills Survey · Employer perception

1 Introduction

The conceptualization of employability skills has been widely discussed. Frameworks to describe these skills include broader capabilities such as lifelong skills [1]. The definition proposed by the Department of Education, Employment and Workplace Relations of Australia [2] defines them as "*non-technical knowledge, skills and attributes required to effectively participate in the workforce*" (p. 2). The Core Skills for Work Developmental Framework (CSfW) categorizes these skills into three Skill Clusters and ten Skill Areas as follows: Cluster 1- Navigate the world of work: (a) Manage career and work life; (b) Work with roles, rights and protocols. Cluster 2-Interact with others: (a) Communicate for work; (b) Connect and work with others; (c) Recognise and utilise diverse perspectives. Cluster 3-Get the work done: (a) Plan and organize; (b) Make decisions; (c) Identify and solve problems; (d) Create and innovate; (e) Work in a digital world.

In addition to the broad agreement regarding the skills required for effective participation in the workforce, there is also consensus regarding the relevance of identifying attitudes and personal attributes during recruitment. These attitudes are defined as individual's manner or feeling towards something, whilst attributes relate to particular qualities or characteristics of an individual [2]. The role they play in work performance is a topic for ongoing debate. Whereas in the CSfW attitudes and attributes are considered

É. Lavoué et al. (Eds.): EC-TEL 2017, LNCS 10474, pp. 523–527, 2017.
DOI: 10.1007/978-3-319-66610-5_54

Enable Factors, the *Employability Skills Framework* [3] includes them as part of the set of employability skills.

1.1 Social Media Network (SMN) and Employability

Despite ethical issues regarding the privacy of users, SMN such as Facebook, are increasingly being used as tools to gather data about candidates. In fact, at least 60% of employers use SMN to research job candidates [5]. This growing popularity is due to two main reasons: 1. Cost; 2. Access to information. Using SMN and the Internet can reduce the cruitment cost-per-hire from $3,295 to $377 [6]. However, 49% of hiring managers who screen candidates' SM profiles found information that motivated a hiring rejection [5]. For instance, reference to drinking or drug consumption, discriminatory comments regarding race, religion or gender and poor communicational skills. Nonetheless, the information available on SMN did not always cause rejection. In fact, one-third of employers consulted found information available on Facebook or Twitter that encouraged them to hire the candidate. This information mainly concerned evidence of the candidate's background, information supporting job qualifications, professional image, a wide range of interests and great communications skills.

With more than 1.25 billion active daily users in the world [7], Facebook is by far the largest available SMN. It allows its users to communicate with anyone using a myriad of media features such as photos, videos, personal and public messaging, emoticons, and so forth. By examining Facebook hiring decision makers can draw inferences about candidates, determine if they meet the needs of the organization and, asses their employability skills [8]. Aware of this, authors propose guidelines to make Facebook profile's especially appealing for employers. Thus, Chauhan et al. [6] recommend Facebook users begin with the profile picture, since it creates the very first impression on potential employers. They also suggest publishing pictures of the job applicant engaging in professional work-related activities, joining professional groups and associations and including descriptions of their unique talents. However, despite guidelines, the way in which recruiters are using SMN to screen candidates remains unclear [4]. In fact, "*we do not understand if employers have the skills and abilities to assess SNS profiles in a systematic, fair and equitable manner*" [9] (p. 68). In addition according to Smith and Kidder [4], the potential misuse of Facebook to screen candidates can result in biased decisions and ethical and legal issues, such as violation of privacy or discrimination based on gender, race, and age among others. Furthermore, recruiters can develop a misconception of the candidate if they don't gather information from the applicant's profile properly.

Against this background, we present rESSuME: Employability Skills Social Media survey. It aims to illustrate how people how people may display their employability skills personal attributes using the features available on Facebook. Administering rESSuME to recruiters and employers we expect to provide empirical evidence at two levels: (1) Mapping how recruiters and employers are using Facebook to screen job applicants; for instance, what sections and features are they looking at to gather information; and (2) Asserting to what extent recruiters and employers consider the suggestions included in the rESSuME capable of displaying employability skills. These findings will feed into the elaboration of a systematic model for SM recruitment screening.

2 Developing rESSuME

In order to map the employability skills personal attributes onto Facebook we followed the following steps: 1. Identify the Personal Attributes included in the *Employability Skill Framework* [3]; 2. Identify the features available on Facebook; 3. Assess which features available in Facebook allow people to more readily display their employability skills personal attributes.

After identifying the Facebook features that more readily supported people to display their employability skills personal attributes, we cluster the features in two block: Profiling Features and Communication Features. *Profiling Features,* allow the candidates to present themselves in different ways. For instance, in the "About Section" users

Table 1. Sample rESSuME questions mapping Personal Attributes and Facebook's features

Personal Attributes (*Employability Skill Framework, 2002*)				
		Loyalty	*Reliability*	*Honesty and Integrity*
Facebook´s features	"Likes" section	To what extent would you consider someone a "LOYAL" person if you saw s/he "likes" the page of his/her previous company?		
	Predefine Options ("working hard")		To what extent would you consider someone as a "RELIABLE" person if you saw s/he uses the predefine option "working hard"?	
	Hastags (#)			To what extent would you consider someone as an "HONEST person with INTEGRITY" if you saw s/he uses the Hastag #Honesty or similar?

are able to introduce themselves, describe their professional and educational background or highlighted places they've lived. Likewise, there are features to present what kind of things they are interested in ("Likes Section") or who are their friends. *Communication Features*, provide options to communicate in a dynamic way. Thus, users can write posts using emoticons or hastags (#), uploading pictures where they can "tag" their friends or places in which they have been or "like" someone else´s comment. Once we classified Facebook´s features, we generated examples illustrating how users could display employability skills Personal Attributes using the Profiling and Communicantion Features (Table 1). The final Social Media Profile Employability Skills Survey, consists of 63 questions, including the 13 Personal Attributes, 8 Profiling Features, and 9 Communication Features.

3 Conclusion

The cost of not hiring the right person can result in undesirable situations and negative consequences for the company and employee alike: low productivity, training costs, hostile work environment, and so forth. To avoid this, recruiters and employers are encouraged to follow systematic screening procedures in order to effectively assert whether applicants meet the company's needs. Knowing the Personal Attributes and employability skills of candidates is crucial to predict future performance. Although this has been extensively studied in traditional selection procedures, understanding about the role of SMN in this new working scenario is still limited [9].

The current work presents the Social Media Profile Employability Skills Survey that will provide empirical evidence at two levels: (1) Mapping how recruiters and employers are actually using Facebook to screen job applicants; for instance, what sections and features are they looking at to gather information; and (2) Asserting to what extent recruiters and employers consider the suggestions included in the Social Media Profile Employability Skills Survey capable of displaying employability skills. These findings will feed into the elaboration of a systematic model for recruitment screening.

Acknowledgment. This work is supported by the Eduworks Marie Curie Initial Training Network Project (PITN-GA-2013-608311) of the European's Commission 7th Framework programme.

References

1. Recommendations of the European Parliament and of the Council of 18 December 2006 on Key Competences for Lifelong Learning (2006/962/EC). Official Journal of the European Union, 30 December 2006
2. Goodwin, S., McDonald, R., Perkins, K., Wignall, L., Gale, G., O'Callaghan, K., Hopwood, J.: Employability skills framework stage 1, Final report. Brisbane, Australia: Ithaca Group, May 2013
3. ACCI/BCA: Employability Skills for the Future. Department of Education, Science and Training, Canberra (2002)

4. Smith, W.P., Kidder, D.L.: You've been tagged! (then again, maybe not): employers and Facebook. Bus. Horiz. **53**(5), 491–499 (2010)
5. CareerBuilder.com. http://www.careerbuilder.com/share/aboutus/pressreleasesdetail.aspx?ed=12/31/201&id=pr945&sd=4/28/2016. Accessed 24 Apr 2017
6. Chauhan, R.S., Buckley, M.R., Harvey, M.G.: Facebook and personnel selection. Org. Dyn. **2**(42), 126–134 (2013)
7. Statista.com. https://www.statista.com/statistics/346167/facebook-global-dau/. Accessed 24 Apr 2017
8. Brown, V.R., Vaughn, E.D.: The writing on the (Facebook) wall: the use of social networking sites in hiring decisions. J. Bus. Psychol. **26**(2), 219 (2011)
9. Hoek, J., O'Kane, P., McCracken, M.: Publishing personal information online: how employers' access, observe and utilise social networking sites within selection procedures. Pers. Rev. **45**(1), 67–83 (2016)

ESCORT: Employability Skills COntent cuRation Tool for Social Media Profiles

Inmaculada Arnedillo-Sánchez(✉) and Chrysanthi Tseloudi

School of Computer Science and Statistics, Trinity College Dublin, Dublin, Ireland
Macu.Arnedillo@scss.tcd.ie

Abstract. Social media profiles (SMPs) are defined as people's digital DNA. They provide information about the social characteristics of individuals such as interests, activities, affiliations, location and so forth. They're also a rich source of subtle information that may help understand the type of person one is. Employers screen candidates' SMPs during the recruiting process and reconsider their decision in light of what they find. Occasionally the information in SMPs leads to employment but often, it has a negative effect on hiring decisions leading to rejection. While no employability criteria appears to be used for social media screening, employers are negatively affected by profanity, reference to drugs, alcohol, or posts of sexual nature. However, positively impressed by references to voluntarism or charitable activities. Employability skills comprise soft skills, attitudes and personality traits. They are generic, non-subject domain specific, nontechnical, intangible attributes, related to one's personality and professionalism. The current work investigates how people can curate their SMPs to display employability skills. To do so, it presents ESCORT: Employability Skills COntent cuRation Tool which was designed and developed to support the assessment of SMPs and guide the curation of the same.

Keywords: Social media · Employability skills · Social media curation tool

1 Introduction

Employability skills, also referred to as "personal attributes" [1, 2], comprise soft skills, attitudes and personality traits that increase one's chances of being employed and successful in their job [3]. They are generic, not subject domain specific, nontechnical, intangible and related to one's personality [4] and professionalism. Efforts to identify employability skills and create frameworks exist [1, 5, 6]. The Employability Skills Framework [1] incorporates Key Skills and Personal Attributes as follows: a) Key Skills: Communication; Team work; Problem solving; Initiative and enterprise; Planning and organising; Self-management; Learning skills; and Technology. b) Personal attributes: Loyalty; Commitment; Honesty and integrity; Enthusiasm; Reliability; Personal presentation; Common sense; Positive self-esteem; sense of humor; balanced attitude to work and home life; Ability to deal with pressure; Motivation; and Adaptability.

É. Lavoué et al. (Eds.): EC-TEL 2017, LNCS 10474, pp. 528–531, 2017.
DOI: 10.1007/978-3-319-66610-5_55

1.1 Social Media: A Recruitment Screening Tool

Social media networks (SMN) are web-based applications where people create profiles, generate or upload content and develop networks by connecting to people and groups [7]. They are a rich source of information that may help onlookers understand the type of person one is. To this end, employers and recruiters examine candidates online during the recruitment process and the information they find influences hiring decisions [8, 9]. Occasionally, the information found encourages hiring but more often candidates are disqualified based on content found online [8].

Tools recruiters use to research candidates include search engines, social networking sites and personal information aggregators [9]. Content leading to hiring rejection includes: inappropriate pictures, videos or information; indications of drinking, drugs use, speaking negatively about work or colleagues, discriminating, profanity or having lied about qualifications [8]. Employers want candidates not to hide too much information [8], have a mainstream personality and shared values with the employer and company [10]. Candidates are expected to be visibly passionate about their work outside of work hours. Their interests should show they are mature, well-rounded and spending their free time in ways an employer considers worthwhile [8]. Employers assume jobseekers create an online image that is similar to their personality and that they will behave at work as they do outside it [10]. Hence, they prefer candidates that portray a professional image [8, 10] at all times.

1.2 Social Media Management Tools

The importance of managing one's SMPs is reflected by the proliferation of tools to teach people how to do so. There are tips on the Do's and Don'ts of social media, books, papers and online articles [11]. Materials include exercises to find your brand [12], institutional policies [13], training, and online guides. Applications that help people manage their online reputation also exist. BrandYourself (brandyourself.com) helps improve one's Google results by selecting the SMPs or websites one wants others to find, analysing one's profiles, and providing advice on how to promote specific search results. Hootsuite (hootsuite.com) aids managing accounts in multiple social media and scheduling posts to keep profiles updated more effectively [12]. RepnUp (repnup.com) automatically identifies problematic content, such as profanity, and displays it to the profile owner.

Jobseekers are aware of the potential of social media as "professional/self-promotion" tools [14]. They understood how to use the platforms for their own benefit gradually transforming them from casual places for "self-expression" and keeping in touch with friends, to stages for presenting and promoting their brand [14]. Facebook's interface, with the narrative-focused, chronologically ordered Timeline, image-focused layout, pictures, likes, music sections and so forth, is a tool for individuals to shape their online identity by finding a balance between self-expression and self-promotion [14]. Nonetheless, the fact that employers find information on candidates' profiles that leads to hiring rejection implies not all candidates promote themselves effectively. Furthermore since employability skills are paramount to gain employment, jobseekers have to portray and communicate their employability skills to employers who search them online.

2 ESCORT: Employability Skills COntent cuRation Tool

Though social media is used for recruitment screening, its role will significantly increase. For instance, Facebook recently expanded its functionality allowing people to post and apply for jobs within the platform. Although there are tools to support jobseekers clean their profiles, promote their best content or manage multiple social media accounts, there are no tools to curate SMP to portray and display employability skills jobseekers possess. ESCORT: Employability Skills COntent cuRation Tool was designed and developed to meet this need.

ESCORT is informed by the Employability Skills Framework [1] and incorporates the Key Skills and Personal attributes (presented in Sect. 1). It is also 'conceptually mapped' onto Facebook's interface to avail of the features it provides to support people shaping their online identity [14]. ESCORT is designed as a three-phase process (Fig. 1):

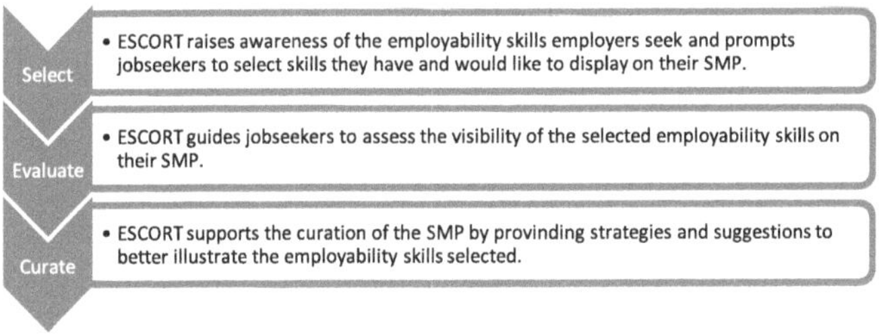

Fig. 1. ESCORT's phases

Phase 1: Select - jobseekers are presented with the list of Key Skills and Personal attributes. They select those they possess, relevant to the target position, and which they would like to display to prospective employers.

Phase 2: Evaluate - jobseekers view their public profile to understand what employers see. They examine the following Facebook sections: 1. Timeline, including their cover and profile photos, the first 25 posts and any information such as photos or the introduction section; 2. About, which may include information about their education, the places they have lived in, life events etc.; 3. Photos, Likes, Reviews, etc. After screening their profiles, they assess whether the skills selected in the phase 1 are visible on their public Facebook profile.

Phase 3: Curate - Once the evaluation is completed, jobseekers see the mismatches between the employability skills they selected and the information found on their profile and are provided with suggestions to curate it and better portray the skills.

The 'conceptual mapping' onto Facebook involved identifying the interface features, and related content, that could be used to display evidence of a jobseeker having a skill. The features taken into account are: 1. Profile and cover photos; 2. Name; 3. Intro; 4. About (e.g.: Overview, work and education, etc.); 5. Likes; 6. Friends; 7. Check-ins,

Groups, Events; 8. Posts; 9. Comments; 10. Pictures; 11. Videos; 12. Hashtags; 13. Emojis; 14. Feeling/Activity; 15. Location tags; and 16. People tags.

3 Conclusion

While SMPs' use as a recruitment screen tool is well reported and tools exist to help jobseekers manage their SMPs, no tool supports curating SMPs in terms of employability skills. This paper presented ESCORT: Employability Skills COntent cuRation Tool. To the best of our knowledge the first tool specifically designed to support jobseekers to evaluate and curate their SMPs to displaying their employability skills.

Acknowledgment. This work is supported by the Eduworks Marie Curie Initial Training Network Project (PITN-GA-2013-608311) of the European Commission's 7th Framework programme. We thank Stéphanie Gauttier for her contribution in the first steps of this endeavor and the employability skills review.

References

1. ACCI/BCA: Employability Skills for the Future. Department of Education, Science and Training, Canberra (2002)
2. Pellegrino, J.W., Hilton, M.L.: Education for Life and work: developing transferable knowledge and skills in the 21st century. National Academies Press, Washington, DC (2012)
3. Nathan, S.K., Rajamanoharane, S.: A study on the various employability skills required for different levels of employees. Int. J. Econ. Res. **12**(2), 537–545 (2015)
4. Robles, M.M.: Executive perceptions of the top 10 soft skills needed in today's workplace. Bus. Commun. Q. **75**, 453–465 (2012)
5. Organisation for Economic Cooperation and Development (OECD): The Definition and Selection of Key Competencies: Executive Summary. OECD, Paris (2005)
6. Partnership for 21st Century Skills (P21CS): P21 Framework Definitions. P21CS, Washington, DC (2009)
7. Obar, J.A., Wildman, S.: Social media definition and the governance challenge: an introduction to the special issue. Telecommun. Policy **39**(9), 745–750 (2015)
8. CareerBuilder: Number of Employers Using Social Media to Screen Candidates Has Increased 500 Percent over the Last Decade (2016)
9. Cross-Tab: Online reputation in a connected world (2010)
10. de la Llama, V.A., Trueba, I., Voges, C., Barreto, C., Park, D.J.: At face (book) value: uses of Facebook in hiring processes and the role of identity in social networks. Int. J. Work Innov. **1**(1), 114–136 (2012)
11. Osborn, D., Miller, A., McCain, S., Belle, J.G.: Using social media for personal online reputation management. Career Plan. Adult Dev. J. **32**(2), 136–145 (2016)
12. Kelly, M.: Social Media for Your Student and Graduate Job Search, 1st edn. Palgrave Macmillan, Basingstoke (2015)
13. Williams, J., Feild, C., James, K.: The effects of a social media policy on pharmacy students' Facebook security settings. Am. J. Pharm. Educ. **75**(9), 177 (2011)
14. van Dijck, J.: 'You have one identity': performing the self on Facebook and LinkedIn. Media Cult. Soc. **35**(2), 199–215 (2013). doi:10.1177/0163443712468605

A Tool for Developing Design-Based Learning Activities for Primary School Teachers

Tilde Bekker[1(✉)], Saskia Bakker[1], Ruurd Taconis[2], and Anika van der Sanden[1]

[1] Industrial Design, Eindhoven University of Technology, Eindhoven, The Netherlands
{m.m.bekker,s.bakker}@tue.nl, anikavandersanden@gmail.com
[2] Eindhoven School of Education, Eindhoven University of Technology, Eindhoven, The Netherlands
r.taconis@tue.nl

Abstract. The paper describes the iterative design process of a tool to support primary school teachers in creating Design-Based Learning (DBL) activities. DBL is a promising approach for teaching 21st Century skills. In developing DBL activities teachers face challenges such as determining the right level of openness of the challenge and mapping appropriate learning goals to activities. The DBL tool is being developed in collaboration with three primary schools. The process has led to user requirements for such a tool, and an understanding of how to map curriculum/learning design decisions on a design process.

Keywords: Design-based learning · Learning design · Teachers · Properties of design-based learning

1 Introduction

To prepare adequately for future work life, children are more and more encouraged to learn '21st century skills' such as collaboration and problem solving. Teachers face the challenge to incorporate these skills in their lessons while also reaching classical learning goals. A suitable approach to teach 21st century skills is *Design-Based Learning* (DBL) [1, 2]: a teaching approach in which students learn by collaboratively creating solutions to open (societal) challenges by means of design. DBL allows students to work on authentic challenges, which often leads to intrinsic motivation, and increased insights into how the learned knowledge and skills can be applied in practice.

DBL has been identified as an innovation with the potential to provoke a major shift in educational practice and constitute a new pedagogy, which might transform education [4]. Although teachers are key to successful implementation of DBL, there are practical obstacles, which often prevent them from (successfully) applying DBL in their classrooms. The teacher needs to adopt a coaching-role rather than a traditional teaching role and the teaching materials usually need to be developed by the teachers themselves [3]. The development of appropriate DBL teaching materials, however, is challenging and time-consuming; teachers often are unacquainted with the concept of DBL, unable to pinpoint the appropriate level of openness of the challenge given to students, and experience difficulties matching the activities to the development of crucial basic skills (such

É. Lavoué et al. (Eds.): EC-TEL 2017, LNCS 10474, pp. 532–536, 2017.
DOI: 10.1007/978-3-319-66610-5_56

as mathematics or language skills). Hence, teachers need tools, exemplars and professional development opportunities [5].

This paper presents a web-based tool which supports primary school teachers in creating DBL learning activities. This DBL creation tool particularly focuses on supporting the integration of particular learning outcomes in DBL activities, and aims to achieve this by encouraging teachers to frequently and critically reflect on the DBL activities they are developing.

2 Background and Related Work

A variety of educational frameworks for developing learning materials is available, such as the curricular spider web [8]. Such frameworks can help structuring educational processes and their design. In this study, it was used for developing the practical tool for teachers to design DBL learning activities. Combining 21st century skills and traditional learning goals is a main aim of DBL. The DBL creation tool presented in this paper is grounded in a theoretical framework to lead to successful learning activities which also take into account the appropriate educational context including the student, the school, and the social and economic ecosystem in which learning activity is situated.

In order to develop a tool to support the creation of DBL learning activities in primary education it is important to ensure that the crucial components of DBL are considered. A starting point for determining the properties of DBL, was the empirical work by Gomez and colleagues who first determined properties of DBL through an extensive literature review and subsequently conducted an empirical validation of DBL characteristics in higher education [7]. We examined how the framework could be adjusted and extended for use in primary and secondary education [1].

3 Development of the DBL-Creation Tool

To develop a successful DBL-creation tool, we adopted a design research approach [8], an educational methodology which comprises cycles in which – after an initial start design – 'experimental teaching and evaluation' and 'redesign' alternate.

At the start of the development of the tool we examined how to link the structure of a design process to topics and practices normally occurring in a primary school class. We **collaborated with three schools of the PlatOOlab organization** in the design process. The second phase consisted of the following activities:

- Two design workshops with teachers and directors to examine how a DBL activity would be organised in practice and requirements for a DBL creation tool.
- An expert review by educational experts to determine the support for the teacher's reflection process.
- Observations of three teachers using the tool and observations of children engaging in the DBL activity created by the teacher.

The web-based DBL creation tool supports teachers in mapping learning design decisions to a design process. The tool provides support for (see Fig. 1): (1) handling the openness of design activities, (2) linking a design problem/challenge to a theme and learning goals, (3) building up a set of learning activities linked to concrete learning goals, (4) selecting design methods related to design phases, (5) selecting collaboration forms for the different learning activities.

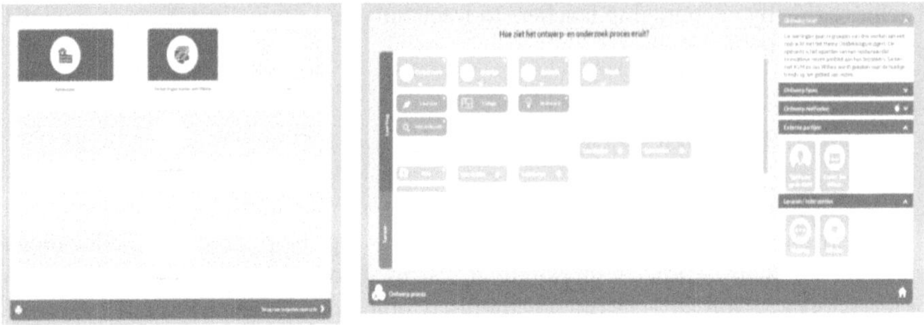

Fig. 1. The topics to be considered in the web-based tool (left). Clicking on the main blocks gives access to more detailed decisions: e.g. deciding on design phases and activities (right).

4 Conclusion and Discussion

The DBL creation tool was developed with input from practitioners and experts. We conclude with the main insights of our design process.

The importance of a good structure for a DBL creation tool. While in early explorations teachers liked a structure that followed the design process, later observations of the web-based tool showed this structure did not work well for considering the basic learning design components. A re-design has been made where a mapping is provided between the learning design components and a design process (see Fig. 2).

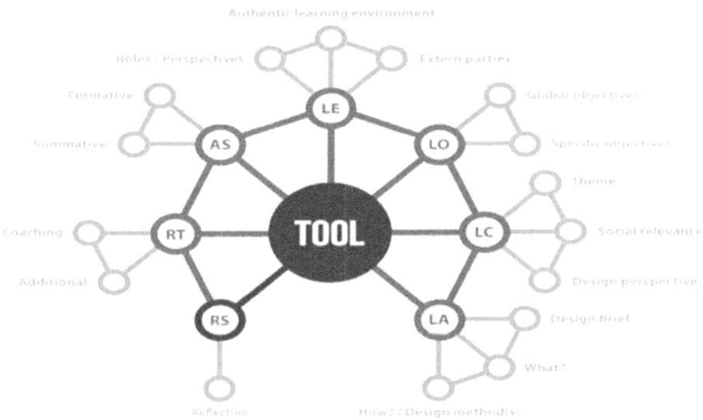

Fig. 2. The curricular spider web (according to [6], extended with components related to design-based learning activities (RS = Role Student, RT = Role Teacher, AS = Assessment, LE = Learning Environment, LO = Learning Objectives, LC = Learning Content, LA = Learning Activity).

DBL related properties that need special attention in the tool. From the evaluation of the tool, we learned that teachers frame a design brief in terms of a specific domain and related themes. To result in a design challenge with the correct level of openness, it is important to provide a balance between open design challenges with enough guidance to ensure pupils reaching learning goals. Other support by the tool supports translating a design brief to detailed learning design decisions: such as working from a global domain, to more detailed themes, with roles and perspectives to be taken by children, and defining possible involvement of experts and other people from the school network.

How the tool supports teachers in developing DBL activities. The tool provides good support for teachers to develop a learning activity integrated in a design process. The observations of the tool's use showed that improvements can be made to the outcome of using the tool in terms of the presentation of the learning activities: so that they are readily usable in class.

The collaboration with the three schools has been very valuable in developing an understanding of the challenges of getting DBL activities embedded in school contexts. More research is needed to determine how to adjust the amount of explanation teachers to develop high quality learning activities to the experience and affinity they have with design-based learning.

Acknowledgements. The work is financed by the Netherlands Organization for Scientific Research (NWO), project number 405-16-5010. Thanks to the PlatOOlab schools, and Eduventure for their input to the project.

References

1. Bekker, T., Bakker, S., Douma, I., van der Poel, J., Scheltenaar, K.: Teaching children digital literacy through design-based learning with digital toolkits in schools. Int. J. Child Comput. Interact. **5**, 29–38 (2015)
2. Thijs, A., Fisser, P., van der Hoeven, M.: Digital Literacy and 21st century skills in primary education: a conceptual framework (in Dutch), Enschede (2014). Accessed http://www.slo.nl/nieuws/dig-gelett/
3. van Cuijk, L., van Keulen, H., Jochems, W.: Are primary school teachers ready for inquiry and design based technology education? In: Proceedings of the PATT-22 Conference, pp. 108–121 (2009)
4. Sharples, M., de Roock, R., Ferguson, R., Gaved, M., Herodotou, C., Koh, E., Weller, M.: Innovating Pedagogy 2016: Open University Innovation Report 5 (2016)
5. Bocconi, S., Kampylis, P.G., Punie, Y.: Innovating learning: key elements for developing creative classrooms in Europe. Joint Research Centre–Institute for Prospective Technological Studies. EC. Publications Office of the EU, Luxembourg (2012)
6. van den Akker, J.: Curriculum perspectives: an introduction. In: Curriculum Landscapes and Trends, pp. 1–10. Springer, Dordrecht (2004). doi:10.1007/978-94-017-1205-7_1

7. Gómez Puente, S.M., van Eijck, M.W., Jochems, W.M.G.: Empirical validation of characteristics of design-based learning in higher education. Int. J. Eng. Educ. **29**(2), 491–503 (2013)
8. Van den Akker, J., Gravemeijer, K., McKenney, S., Nieveen, N.: Educational design research. Routledge, London (2006)

An Empirical Study Comparing Two Automatic Graders for Programming. MOOCs Context

Anis Bey[1,2(✉)], Patrick Jermann[3], and Pierre Dillenbourg[4]

[1] LRI, University of Badji Mokhtar-Annaba, Annaba, Algeria
anis.bey@univ-annaba.org
[2] Ecole Supérieure des Sciences de Gestion-Annaba, Annaba, Algeria
[3] Center for Digital Education, Lausanne, Switzerland
patrick.jermann@epfl.ch
[4] Computer Human Interaction in Learning and Instruction, École Polytechnique Fédérale de Lausanne, Lausanne, Switzerland
pierre.dillenbourg@epfl.ch

Abstract. The present paper compares Algo+, an assessment tool for computer programs, to an automatic grader used in a MOOC course at EPFL. This empirical study explores the practicability and the behaviour of Algo+ and analyses whether Algo+ can be used to evaluate a large scale of programs. Algo+ is a prototype based on a static analysis approach for automated assessment of algorithms where programs are not executed but analysed by looking at their instructions. The second tool, EPFL grader, is used to grade programs submitted by students in MOOCs of Introductory programming with C++ at EPFL and is based on a compiler approach. In this technique submissions are assessed via a battery of unit tests where the student program is run with standard input and assessed on whether they produced the correct output.

Keywords: Computer education · MOOCs · Assessment · Automated grading · Programming education

1 Introduction

Computer based assessment is useful for handling very large numbers of students. Apart from giving a score, these tools may also offer an environment to practice programming, which is useful for students to develop programming skills. Since programming cannot be learned solely from books as in other subjects, students have to learn programming by developing algorithms themselves to deepen their understanding [1].

In this paper, we study the effectiveness of Algo+, a prototype system developed to assess algorithmic competencies [2,3] compared to EPFL grader, an automated grader developed at EPFL (Ecole Polytechnique Fédérale de Lausanne, Switzerland) and used to grade students' assignment in MOOCs courses [4]. In the EPFL grader, the solutions submitted by the students are compiled and unit-tested over a set of inputs, and the students receive a score and an

É. Lavoué et al. (Eds.): EC-TEL 2017, LNCS 10474, pp. 537–540, 2017.
DOI: 10.1007/978-3-319-66610-5_57

automatic feedback on how their code performed in the tests. The EPFL Programming MOOCs Automated Grader is based on two main components for assigning grades: a battery of unit tests where student programs are run with standard input and assessed on whether they produced the correct output, and style checker which may deduct points for bad style in working programs.

In Algo+, a submitted program is assessed by comparing it to a set of predefined solutions previously assessed by the instructor called *referent* solutions. A referent solution is a common and frequent submission that has been detected among students submissions and assessed by the instructor. In each submission, the incoming programs are recognized automatically by Algo+. Programs are scored according to referent solutions that are correct. Correct referent solutions are used for awarding scores while erroneous solutions are used to give feedback.

The question that guided this study was: Could Algo+ tool also be used to automatically assess the submissions of students in the context of MOOCs?

2 Evaluation

The comparison was performed with large samples of programs collected from a MOOC course in Introduction to programming with C++ at EPFL.

Two different exercises were selected for this study. The first exercise (Exercise 1, n = 3130) was about swapping values. Students were required to write a C++ program that swap three values. For example, for these input data $a = 51, b = 876$ and $c = 235$ we obtain $a = 235, b = 51$ and $c = 876$. The second exercise (Exercise 2, n = 4914) was to write a C++ program that guesses which character (among a list known in advance) the user has in mind. The purpose of this exercise is the ability to use conditional structure.

Scores assigned by the two tools, Algo+ and EPFL grader, rated on 0–30 and 0–50 for the first and the second exercise respectively.

2.1 Results

The main summary descriptive statistics are presented in Table 1. Both measures of centre that is mean and median marks are almost similar in the first exercise but they differ in the second exercise. The measure of variation that is standard deviation is also similar in the first exercise but different in the second. The results of correlational analyses, using the nonparametric Spearman Rank Correlation Coefficient tests, indicated that a statistically significant correlations were present between Algo+ and EPFL grader in both exercise 1 ($rs = 0.92, p < .001$) and exercise 2 ($rs = 0.59, p < .001$). These results show excellent correspondence between the two sets of marks for both the direct comparison with EPFL grader and with the ranked order of student programs in the two exercises.

The inter-rater agreement between Algo+ and EPFL grader was calculated with the Intraclass Correlation Coefficient (ICC) [5] with a two-way mixed model. The intra-class correlation (ICC) is a measure of agreement and it is

Table 1. Descriptive statistics

	Exercise 1		Exercise 2	
	Algo+	EPFL grader	Algo+	EPFL grader
Min	0.00	0.00	0.00	0.00
1st Qu	0.00	10	0.00	16.35
Median	30.00	30.00	30	29.81
Mean	20.26	21.6	24.76	28.96
3rd Qu	30.00	30.00	50	50
Max	30.00	30.00	50	50
SD	14.03	12.06	22.20	17.02
Mode	30	30	0	50

useful when ratings are made along a continuous scale such as in this study (e.g., one that allows ratings of rational numbers such as 2.3, 2.4, 2.5, etc.). The "agreement" ICC is the ratio of the subject variance by the sum of the subject variance, the rater variance and the residual. The inter-rater agreement between Algo+ and EPFL grader was substantial in the first exercise (ICC = 0.88, 95% CI 0.86–0.89, $p < 0.001$) but it was a moderate agreement in the second exercise (ICC = 0.51, 95% CI 0.48–0.55, $p < 0.001$) based on the cut-off value for acceptability level [6].

To further investigate scores assigned by the two tools and to understand differences, frequencies were performed to examine the distribution of scores. For ease of comparison and discussion, we presented the frequency table by three score ranges, namely, by *erroneous* programs ($scores = 0$), *somewhat* correct programs ($scores_{Exerc.1} \in]0, 30[$, $scores_{Exerc.2} \in]0, 50[$) and *correct* programs ($scores_{Exerc.1} = 30$, $scores_{Exerc.2} = 50$).

Table 2. Agreement and Disagreement between Algo+ and EPFL grader

		Algo+							
		Correct		Somewhat		Erroneous		*Total*	
		Exerc.1	*Exerc.2*	Exerc.1	*Exerc.2*	Exerc.1	*Exerc.2*	Exerc.1	*Exerc.2*
EPFL grader	Correct	2022	*1242*	38	*49*	39	*362*	**2099**	***1653***
	Somewhat	0	*0*	14	*209*	5	*1696*	**19**	***1905***
	Erroneous	0	*0*	557	*136*	455	*1220*	**1012**	***1356***
	Total	**2022**	***1242***	**609**	***394***	**499**	***3278***	**3130**	***4914***

Table 2 presents data on differences and similarities in scores among EPFL grader and Algo+. The two graders agree on scores for 2491 (79%) cases in the first exercise and 2671 (54%) in the second exercise but differ for the others (21% and 46% Exercise 1 and Exercise 2 respectively). EPFL grader awards high scores than Algo+ when the submitted program is not frequent, and so Algo+ does not recognise it among referent solutions. In other case, where Algo+ awards high scores than EPFL grader is due to the fact that Algo+ awards scores even if the program does not give a correct output, it looks at the existence of the correct part in the submitted program whereas EPFL grader assigns scores only if the program gives correct output. We can deduce that the most important limit of Algo+ is when it underestimates *correct* programs that are not popular and so awarding low scores.

3 Conclusion and Future Work

In this work it has been attempted to examine the assessment behaviour of Algo+ when placed in the context of a MOOC based on the EPFL grader experience. In the light of these study, we believe that Algo+ can provide a useful assessment to students learning and it can be used to complement tools based on output correctness as EPFL grader.

The ability to find and to capitalise common submissions by Algo+, can be used for assessment in the other session with new subscriber or another new MOOC that use the same exercise battery. For future work, we still need to assess how much Algo+ can improve student achievement in programming and to analyse the mechanism of Algo+ in reaching performance and hence to determine how much time instructor is solicited in each exercise to annotate frequent submissions.

Acknowledgment. We thank Ian Anthony Flitman and Jean-Cédric Chappelier from EPFL for their support and for providing us the EPFL grader data.

References

1. Lahtinen, E., Ala-Mutka, K., Jrvinen, H.-M.: A study of the difficulties of novice programmers. In: Proceedings of the 10th Annual SIGCSE Conference on Innovation and Technology in Computer Science Education, Monte de Caparice, 27–29 June 2005, pp. 14–18 (2005)
2. Bey, A., Bensebaa, T.: Algo+, an assessment tool for algorithmic competencies. In: IEEE Engineering Education 2011 Learning Environments and Ecosystems in Engineering Education, EDUCON 2011, Amman, Jordan, pp. 941–946 (2011)
3. Bey, A., Bensebaa, T.: Assessment makes perfect: improving student's algorithmic problem solving skills using plan-based programme understanding approach. Int. J. Innovat. Learn. **14**(2), 162–176 (2013)
4. MOOC: Sam, J., Chappelier, J.,-C., Lepetit, V.: Introduction à la programmation orientée objet (en Java). Coursera
5. Graham, M., Milnowski, A., Miller, J.: Measuring and Promoting Inter-Rater Agreement of Teacher and Principal Performance Ratings. Center for Educator Compensation Reform, US Department of Education (2012)
6. McGraw, K.O., Wong, S.P.: Forming inferences about some intraclass correlation coefficients. Psychol. Methods **1**(1), 30–46 (1996)

ASR in Classroom Today: Automatic Visualization of Conceptual Network in Science Classrooms

Daniela Caballero[1(✉)], Roberto Araya[1], Hanna Kronholm[2], Jouni Viiri[2], André Mansikkaniemi[3], Sami Lehesvuori[2], Tuomas Virtanen[4], and Mikko Kurimo[3]

[1] CIAE, Universidad de Chile, Periodista José Carrasco Tapia 75, Santiago, Chile
daniela.caballero@ciae.uchile.cl
[2] University of Jyväskyla, Alvar Aallon katu 9, 40014 Jyväskylä, Finland
[3] Aalto University, 00076 Aalto, Finland
[4] Tampere University of Technology, Korkeakoulunkatu 10, 33101 Tampere, Finland

Abstract. Automatic Speech Recognition (ASR) field has improved substantially in the last years. We are in a point never saw before, where we can apply such algorithms in non-ideal conditions such as real classrooms. In these scenarios it is still not possible to reach perfect recognition rates, however we can already take advantage of these improvements. This paper shows preliminary results using ASR in Chilean and Finnish middle and high school to automatically provide teachers a visualization of the structure of concepts present in their discourse in science classrooms. These visualizations are conceptual networks that relate key concepts used by the teacher. This is an interesting tool that gives feedback to the teacher about his/her pedagogical practice in classes. The result of initial comparisons shows great similarity between conceptual networks generated in a manual way with those generated automatically.

Keywords: Automatic Speech Recognition · Conceptual network · Classroom dialogue · Teacher discourse

1 Introduction

A single teacher can teach hundreds of hours of classes per year. In most of the times he/she doesn't get automatic and quick feedback regarding his/her class. Moreover, the ubiquity of smartphones makes them an easy to find and economic tool to collect data, like teachers' class audio. In previous work the structure of the classroom speech was analyzed [1], considering that the content of the lesson has an impact on the conceptual structure of students, and specifically, the connections of the lesson's content relate to students' learning and in the quality of the lesson [2].

Automatic Speech Recognition (ASR) has many applications such as automatically detection of teachers' questions [3], identify keywords to captioning systems [4], indicate difficulties in second language learners [5], and several others [6]. This paper aims to provide another application of ASR in learning by showing preliminary results using this technology in Chilean and Finnish middle school to automatically provide teachers a visualization of the structure of concepts present in their speech in physics classrooms,

É. Lavoué et al. (Eds.): EC-TEL 2017, LNCS 10474, pp. 541–544, 2017.
DOI: 10.1007/978-3-319-66610-5_58

which, as shown in previous work [1] could be related with students' learning gains, specifically measuring different concepts and the number of pairs of related concepts. The research question presented here is: what is the correspondence between automatic and manual concept network, in other words whether the ASR technology allows us to present a suitable feedback for teachers.

2 Method

2.1 Participants

Two teachers participated in our pilot study: one teacher from Chile and other from Finland. Both recorded themselves in a regular physics class. The classes were about cinematic in Chile (11th grade) and electricity for the Finnish classroom (9th grade).

2.2 Procedure and Equipment

During their classes the Chilean teacher wore a SmartLav+ microphone and the Finnish teacher wore two microphones, AKG C520 and DPA IMK-SC4060, and a dictator ZOOM H4N. Both teachers recorded a single lesson of 43 and 36 min for the Chilean and Finnish class respectively.

2.3 Automatic Speech Recognition Systems

To run the ASR experiments on Spanish, the Google Cloud Speech API [6] was used. It supports over 80 languages including Spanish from Latin America. It showed higher levels of recognition in Spanish than in Finnish in our early experiments. For that reason, ASR experiments on Finnish were run using the Kaldi toolkit [7]. The recognition system was based on time-delay neural networks (TDNNs) combined with long short-term memory (LSTM) layers.

3 Data Analysis

Each of the audio file is split into small slices of audio (5–10 s). A person transcribed the audio and also did, automatically, the ASR systems. With both transcriptions (manual and ASR) and a keyword list based on curricular directions, we build a connectivity matrix which relates the frequency of two pairs of concepts that appear together within a 10 s window (it is the same process shown in previous work [1]). Finally, with this matrix the conceptual network is automatically generated with R's library *igraph*.

4 Preliminary Results

For both classrooms, the ASR has shown to be quite trustful. The resume of the results are shown in Table 1, where the recognition rates for the keywords are calculated.

Table 1. Recognition rates for Chilean and Finnish classrooms.

Classroom	Number of keywords	Number of total keywords appearance	Number of keywords recognized	Recognition rate
Chilean	12	146	109	74.7%
Finnish	17	324	212	65.4%

The Figs. 1 and 2 shows the conceptual network for the Chilean and Finnish class. Each of the keyword is located in one vertex of a polygon. Two pairs of concepts are related (i.e. there is a line connecting them) if they were mentioned in a 10 s slot. The width of the line is related to the amount of time those two concepts were mentioned in the whole class. For instance, in both concept map of Fig. 2 *"distancia"* (distance) and *"tiempo"* (time) are the two concepts which were highly mentioned together.

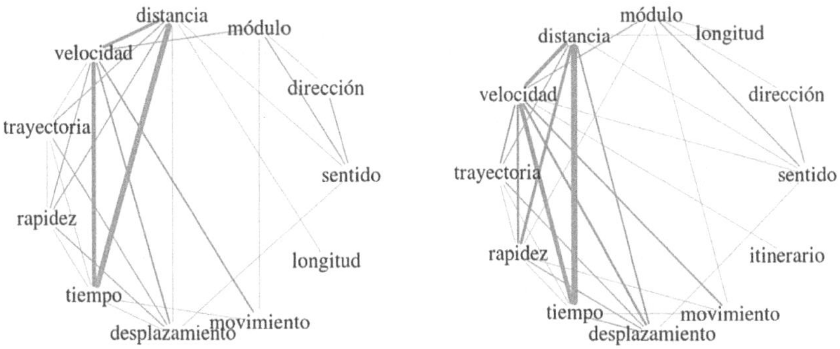

Fig. 1. Conceptual network from Automatic (left) and Manual (right) Transcription for Chilean class.

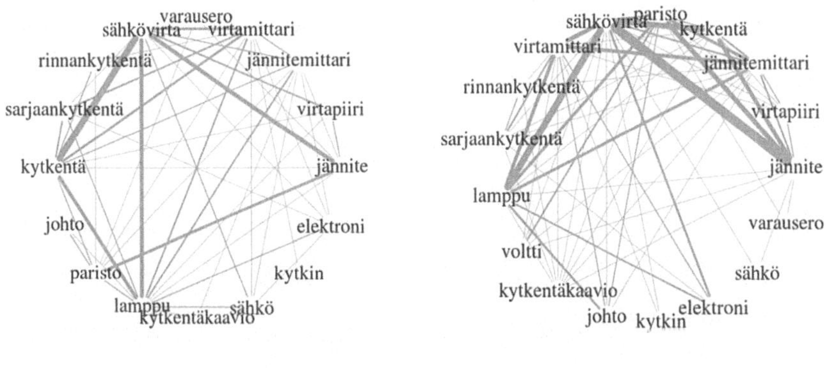

Fig. 2. Conceptual network from Automatic (left) and Manual (right) Transcription for Finnish class.

5 Conclusions and Future Work

The analysis and results shown in this paper could help teachers to have a better understanding of his/her class without much effort which, without the technology could be extremely high time consuming and expensive. We do not expect replacing other ways of feedback and training, but we think this information can enhance teaching analysis. We neither want to have a tool that evaluates the quality of teaching of teachers.

Regarding the future work, we still need to improve the automatic analysis and collect feedback from teachers to get new visualizations like names of the students for instance or appearance of content in each section of the class (start, middle and end). Finally, we have to propose metrics to compare the different networks as for instance in [1].

Acknowledgements. Funding from PIA-CONICYT Basal Funds for Centers of Excellence Project FB0003 is gratefully acknowledged and to the AKA-EDU-01 grant from CONICYT. The authors are also thankful for the funding provided to project No. 294218 by the Academy of Finland

References

1. Helaakoski, J., Viiri, J.: Content and content structure of physics lessons and students' learning gains. In: Fischer, H.E., Labudde, P., Neumann, K., Viiri, J. (eds.) Quality of Instruction in Physics. Comparing Finland, Germany and Switzerland, pp. 93–110. Waxmann, Münster (2014)
2. Klieme, E., Pauli, C., Reusser, K.: The pythagoras study. Investigating effects of teaching and learning in Swiss and German mathematics classrooms. In: Janík, T., Seidel, T. (eds.) The Power of Video Studies in Investigating Teaching and Learning in the Classroom, pp 137–160. Waxmann, Münster (2009)
3. Donnelly, P., Blanchard, N., Olney, A., Kelly, S., Nystrand, M., D'Mello, S.: Words matter: automatic detection of teacher questions in live classroom discourse using linguistics, acoustics, and context. In: Proceedings of the Seventh International Learning Analytics and Knowledge Conference, pp. 218–227. ACM (2017)
4. Ikeda, N., Takeuchi, Y., Matsumoto, T., Kudo, H., Ohnishi, N.: Support system for lecture captioning using keyword detection by automatic speech recognition. In: Miesenberger, K., Bühler, C., Penaz, P. (eds.) ICCHP 2016. LNCS, vol. 9759, pp. 377–383. Springer, Cham (2016). doi:10.1007/978-3-319-41267-2_53
5. Mirzaei, M.S., Meshgi, K., Kawahara, T.: Automatic speech recognition errors as a predictor of L2 listening difficulties. In: CL4LC 2016, pp. 92–201 (2016)
6. Shadiev, R., Hwang, W.-Y., Chen, N.-S., Huang, Y.-M.: Review of speech-to-text recognition technology for enhancing learning. J. Educ. Technol. Soc. **17**(4), 65–84 (2014)
7. Google: Google Cloud Speech API. https://cloud.google.com/speech/

A Course Agnostic Approach to Predicting Student Success from VLE Log Data Using Recurrent Neural Networks

Owen Corrigan(✉) and Alan F. Smeaton

Insight Centre for Data Analytics, Dublin City University,
Glasnevin, Dublin 9, Ireland
owen.corrigan@insight-centre.org

Abstract. We describe a method of improving the accuracy of a learning analytics system through the application of a Recurrent Neural Network over all students in a University, regardless of course. Our target is to discover how well a student will do in a class given their interaction with a virtual learning environment. We show how this method performs well when we want to predict how well students will do, even if we do not have a model trained based on their specific course.

Keywords: Learning analytics · Student intervention · Machine learning

1 Introduction

Our goal is to improve student outcomes by predicting how well they will do in exams, by the middle of a semester. One approach to this is to take student data from systems they interact with, and feed it into a machine learning algorithm to identify students who are struggling [4]. We examine students interactions with a Virtual Learning Environment (VLE).

We faced two major difficulties when we designed our system. The first was a lack of data to build the models with. Typically when training a machine learning we need a large amount of training samples. Our data set included over 255,659 exam sittings, where we had both the student who took the exam and associated Moodle logs with that person. However we discovered that class sizes were not that large, with the largest one containing 2,879 students across 5 years and the average amount of students per module was 127. Classifiers trained on individual classes had poor results, particularly those where we had few examples of failures. We dealt with this issue by only keeping courses in our intervention program if they met some heuristics. For example, the classification accuracy was sufficiently high (e.g. 0.6 minimum ROC), the class size must have at least 100 students per year, and a maximum of 85% pass rate. However, this only left us with a handful of the largest classes for which we could run our intervention system on.

É. Lavoué et al. (Eds.): EC-TEL 2017, LNCS 10474, pp. 545–548, 2017.
DOI: 10.1007/978-3-319-66610-5_59

The second was that it is impossible to build a model for a new course, due to a lack of training data. If a new course starts, we cannot include it in our alerting system, until one year of data has been collected.

In this paper we propose method of getting a larger data set for training, by training our classifier over all students in all 255,659 modules. This solves the first problem by building a model which can serve as a baseline model, across all students, which can be applied to offset the poor performance of a model trained on a small class. This also approach also allows us to predict student success for modules where we do not even have any training data for the course that they are in.

As a side effect of this, we are able to model the data using a recurrent neural network. This is useful, as they can perform very well on time series data, but can only be trained on a large corpus of data. We show they easily outperform random forests, which is what we found previously to perform the best on the data.

2 Related Work

The signals project [2] was an early pioneer of the concept of predicting student success, and feeding that information back to students and faculty in order to improve student outcomes. In their project they divided how well a student was doing in three tiers - red, amber and green. This is a very broad range of values to give and our project aims to improve the granularity of these predictions, making them more useful for staff and administrators.

There are many other examples of systems which make predictions and use them to make [3,5,7,8]. In [1] Agudo et al. examine whether it is possible to predict student performance in VLE environments, face to face environments and online only environments. In [6] Okubo et al. use a Recurrent Neural Network to predict student grades. However, this is over a single course with 108 students, and so suffers from the same generalizability issues that we encountered earlier.

In a novel paper [9] Zorrilla et al. attempt to solve a similar problem by training many ready-made models. They then train a meta-classifier to take a new dataset and classify it based on which model is most similar to it. We believe that our method improves on this, as it does not require extracting meta-features from sets of data.

3 Regression Analysis

In our solution we extract very simple features from our data namely the number of times a user accessed Moodle in a given week.

Since these data points come in a stream, one natural solution to this algorithm is to use Recurrent Neural Networks, in it's most popular architecture variation — Long Short Term Memory (LSTM). A RNN is a type of Artificial Neural Network in which neurons can also connect back to themselves. This allows them to be trained on sequences, and to learn to remember important features of the series. They have been applied successfully to time series predictions, as well as a wide variety of other tasks such as handwriting simulation and speech synthesis. Because our problem involves predictions based on time series and making predictions at multiple steps in time, we used RNN's as we believed they would be a natural fit. We also evaluate our results using a Random Forest, as this was what we found worked best previously.

4 Experiment Details

In Table 1 we see the results of running our regressor across several regression algorithms and parameters.

Table 1. Regression Results

Classifier	Mean squared error	r-squared	p-value
Dummy regressor	203.81967	0	0.99999
LSTM	200.64860	0.13382	5.36e−238
Random forest regressor	210.50645	0.08072	2.30e−87
LSTM - Dropout 0.2	201.0785	0.13547	6.81e−244
LSTM - Dropout 0.5	200.1333	0.13360	3.08e−237

The models we ran in our experiments were:

- A "Dummy" Regressor which always returns the mean exam results. Our classifiers should be at least as good as the Dummy Regressor;
- An Random Forest regressor. This had 1,000 estimators as a hyper parameter;
- A simple LSTM. All of the LSTM's were run for 300 epochs over the whole data set;
- 2 Versions of an LSTM with different values for "Dropout". This is a technique to reduce over-fitting. During training, this will set a random set of hidden nodes to be ignored. This forces the system to build in redundancy, which reduces the ability of the network to learn features based on noise.

From the table we can see that LSTM far outperforms the Random Forest regressor, explaining 13.3% of the variance of the model, as opposed to 8.1%. This result is particularly good, as when we tried to fit a regressor to course-level features, the results were not significant at the $p < 0.05$ level. We can also see that setting dropout to 0.2 improves the performance of the LSTM marginally.

5 Conclusions and Future Work

In this paper we have shown that it is possible to build accurate models for predicting student exam outcomes over all courses. Doing so provides surprisingly good results which can be used as part of a student intervention system. We have shown that RNN's perform very well at this task.

In future work we will explore combining this information with more complex features such as activity types, times of day accessed, etc. We also believe there is scope for a method which gets the best of both worlds — using a course-agnostic approach when there is isn't a lot of information available about a course, and adapting the predictions to a particular course when there is more data.

Acknowledgements. This research was supported by Science Foundation Ireland under grant number SFI/12/RC/2289, and by Dublin City University.

References

1. Agudo-Peregrina, Á.F., et al.: Can we predict success from log data in VLEs? Classification of interactions for learning analytics and their relation with performance in VLE-supported F2F and online learning. Comput. Hum. Behav. **31**, 542–550 (2014)
2. Arnold, K.E., Pistilli, M.D.: Course signals at Purdue: using learning analytics to increase student success. In: Proceedings of the 2nd International Conference on Learning Analytics and Knowledge, pp. 267–270. ACM (2012)
3. Cai, Q.V., Lewis, C.L., Higdon, J.: Developing an early- alert system to promote student visits to tutor center. Learn. Assist. Rev. **20**(1), 61 (2015)
4. Corrigan, O., Smeaton, A.F., Glynn, M., Smyth, S.: Using educational analytics to improve test performance. In: Conole, G., Klobučar, T., Rensing, C., Konert, J., Lavoué, É. (eds.) EC-TEL 2015. LNCS, vol. 9307, pp. 42–55. Springer, Cham (2015). doi:10.1007/978-3-319-24258-3_4
5. Howard, E., Meehan, M., Parnell, A.: Analytics, Developing Accurate Early Warning Systems Via Data Analytics (2016). eprint: arXiv:1612
6. Okubo, F., et al.: A neural network approach for students' performance prediction. In: Proceedings of the Seventh International Learning Analytics & Knowledge Conference, LAK 2017, Vancouver, British Columbia, Canada, pp. 598–599. ACM (2017). ISBN: 978-1-4503-4870-6. doi:10.1145/3027385.3029479
7. Park, Y., Jo, I.-H.: Development of the learning analytics dashboard to support students' learning performance. J. UCS **21**(1), 110–133 (2015)
8. Saqr, M., Fors, U., Tedre, M.: How learning analytics can early predict under-achieving students in a blended medical education course. Med. Teach. **39**(7), 757–767 (2017). doi:10.1080/0142159X.2017.1309376
9. Zorrilla, M., García-Saiz, D.: Meta-learning: can it be suitable to automatise the KDD process for the educational domain? In: Kryszkiewicz, M., Cornelis, C., Ciucci, D., Medina-Moreno, J., Motoda, H., Raś, Z.W. (eds.) RSEISP 2014. LNCS (LNAI), vol. 8537, pp. 285–292. Springer, Cham (2014). doi:10.1007/978-3-319-08729-0_28

Transferring a Question-Based Dialog Framework to a Distributed Architecture

Peter de Lange[1(✉)], Tracie Farell-Frey[2], Bernhard Göschlberger[3,4], and Ralf Klamma[1]

[1] RWTH Aachen University, Aachen, Germany
[2] Open University, Milton Keynes, UK
lange@dbis.rwth-aachen.de
[3] Research Studios Austria FG, Vienna, Austria
[4] Johannes Kepler University Linz, Linz, Austria

Abstract. Inquiry skills are an essential tool for assessing and integrating knowledge. In facilitated face-to-face settings, inquiry skills were improved successfully by using a "question-based dialog" and its resulting visual representation. However, groups that work without a facilitator, or in which members collaborate asynchronously or in different geographical regions, such as Communities of Practice (CoP), cannot schedule face-to-face inquiry meetings. This paper summarizes the unmet requirements of CoPs for a collaborative inquiry tool found by previous research on the *Noracle* model and proposes a distributed Web architecture as a solution. It mitigates the need for a common infrastructure, central coordination or facilitation, addresses the evolutionary nature of communities of practice and reduces the cognitive load for the individual by filtering and organizing the representational artifacts with respect to the social network of the community. The implementation we envision in this paper aims at applying the concept to a much broader audience, ultimately replacing the need for local meetings.

Keywords: Question-based dialog · Social collaboration · Inquiry-based learning

1 Introduction

Learners often have difficulties formulating meaningful, higher-order questions that allow them to trigger deeper metacognitive processes [1,3] *Noracle* [2], the pedagogical method referenced in this paper, was developed to promote "question-based dialog" for improving inquiry skills and representing group knowledge. Digitizing this method could have benefits for groups that work without a facilitator, or in which the members collaborate asynchronously or in different geographical regions, such as a *Community of Practice* (CoP) [6], by bringing structure to typically unstructured and informal collaborative environments. However, existing software does not achieve the same quality of social or representational insight as the face-to-face method. It also does not resolve

É. Lavoué et al. (Eds.): EC-TEL 2017, LNCS 10474, pp. 549–552, 2017.
DOI: 10.1007/978-3-319-66610-5_60

the problem of growing communities, which require a stronger network overview to decrease cognitive load as the network evolves. Experiments with existing argumentation software demonstrated the feasibility and value of *Noracle* for predetermined small groups, but also revealed the limitations of a centralized approach in terms of scalability and cognitive load. The proposed distributed approach addresses both limitations by mimicking real world social network structures. It allows growth, networked organization of knowledge and provides a personalized view on mapped knowledge using social network based information filtering.

2 Background and Related Work

Noracle was originally a face-to-face method for collaborative "question-based dialog". A group of learners typically works on a problem relevant for the whole group, for which no answer is currently available. Salient questions are generated and exchanged among the group members in quick succession, similar to speed-dating. However, rather than offering an *answer*, the other group members are limited to offering only related or follow-up *questions*, that allow the initial questioner to further explore their own thinking on the subject.

The group, with the help of a facilitator, gathers insights about the types of questions they heard and found useful by visually documenting and clustering contributions according to shared characteristics such as how the question was asked, who asked it and why the question was helpful. This creates a representational artifact of what the group does not understand about a given theme that can offer an avenue for improving overall coherence and collaboration within the group [5]. Additionally, it provides the group with some orientation on the characteristics of good question-asking and interpersonal dynamics within the group context [2]. This implementation is inappropriate for professional CoPs of the long-tail, which do not possess the shared skills, resources, structures or geographical location for such a meeting. Digitizing *Noracle*, and particularly the process of clustering and analyzing responses, would make it possible to provide some of the benefits of the face-to-face method to CoPs without the necessity of a facilitator. However, initial trials with the argumentation software LiteMap showed that while it is possible to track users and their contributions, as well as some social aspects of collaborative processes, such software does not offer a mechanism for reducing the cognitive load, for automatically weighting individual contributions, and for positioning their representational artifacts relative to others. They also do not remove the function of a facilitator for introducing and monitoring the process [2].

3 A Distributed Question-Based Dialog Framework

Rather than a facilitated group activity with a determined, synchronized starting and end point, our vision is a *continuous community activity*, where community membership is not necessarily stable. New or existing community members with

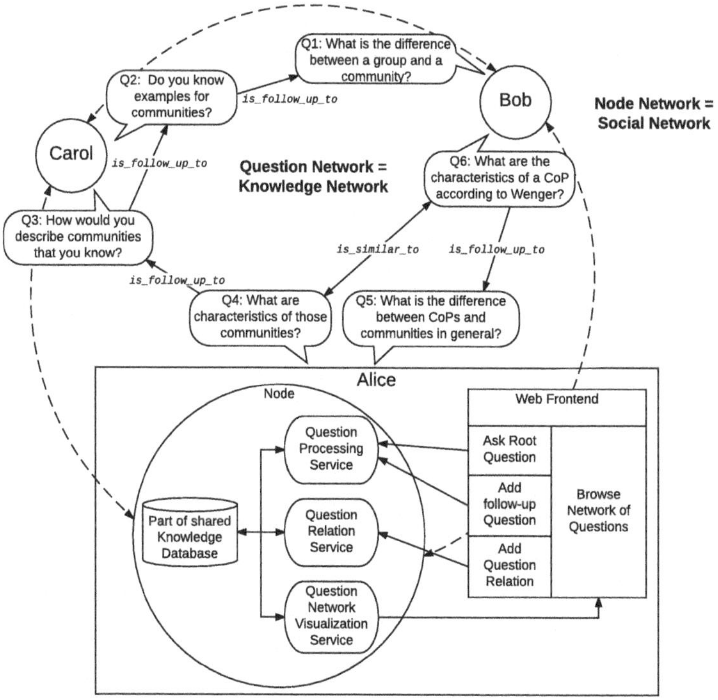

Fig. 1. Distributed question-based dialog framework

difficult queries can trigger a thought exchange with a knowledgeable community using the digitized *Noracle* space. The community's existing social network structure can be used to push requests for follow-up questions, all of which are quickly situated in an existing network of questions that represent the community's knowledge on the issue. Similarities or duplicates in questions represent the weight of certain contributed questions and their linkages. Reflection on different points of view, concepts and ideas related to question are triggered by exploring the question network that has been built around the question. The communities' knowledge is explored, potential gaps are identified ultimately reaching a deeper, more complete understanding of the underlying issue.

As the underlying technological basis, we chose the las2peer [4] framework, an open source implementation for distributing community services in a peer-to-peer infrastructure, featuring easy scalability and workload distribution with self-replicating services and shared, secure data control that avoids a single point of failure. A las2peer network consists of interconnected nodes, which share their workload between each other. Either communities create a new network within their community, or they connect their nodes to an already existing network to share their experiences with other communities. It is also conceivable for small communities to rely on externally hosted networks without the need to provide own hardware. With an eye on our target group – small, long-tail CoPs –, this flexibility in terms of deployment is important, since especially smaller communities cannot afford a complete setup of a full-featured client-server approach. On the other hand, relying on externally deployed solutions, like cloud-based approaches, shifts the control of the application and data away from the community to the service provider, generating a "black-box" view on the used applications.

Taking together this distributed architecture of las2peer and the theoretical underpinning of the question-based dialog framework of Noracle, we propose a *Distributed Question-Based Dialog Framework*, which is depicted conceptually in Fig. 1. Each participant is represented by her own *Node*, containing a full-featured set of services needed to realize a complete question-based dialog framework. By connecting their node to other participants nodes, users form a *Network of Knowledge-Sharing Nodes*, with already existing information on each node being distributed across all participants. This way, new communities can form dynamically, with members connecting and leaving at any time. This flexibility in terms of participation is especially important in the domain of CoPs, since they often do not have fixed schedules and rely on dynamic tool support that eases their collaboration scenarios. Additionally, the connection to our proposed solution does not rely on external infrastructure, with each member of the CoP being able to either start a new network or join an existing one, having all the tooling needed included in her *Node Package*.

4 Summary and Outlook

In this paper we described our vision of transferring a question-based dialog framework named *Noracle* to a distributed architecture. By this, we hope to render the concept for otherwise not supported long-tail CoPs usable. We are currently in the process of implementing and evaluating our approach. Ultimately, we want to compare, if the digitized *Noracle* framework produces similar results than its face-to-face equivalent.

References

1. Edelson, D., Gordin, D., Pea, R.: Addressing the challenges of inquiry-based learning through technology and curriculum design. J. Learn. Sci. **8**(3–4), 391–450 (1999)
2. Farrell-Frey, T., Gkotsis, G., Mikroyannidis, A.: Are you thinking what I'm thinking? representing metacognition with question-based dialogue. In: 6th Workshop on Awareness and Reflection in Technology Enhanced Learning. vol. 1736, pp. 51–58 (2016). http://ceur-ws.org/Vol-1736/
3. Graesser, A., Person, N.: Question asking during tutoring. Am. Educ. Res. J. **31**(1), 104–137 (1994)
4. Klamma, R., Renzel, D., de Lange, P., Janßen, H.: las2peer - A Primer. ResearchGate (2016). https://dx.doi.org/10.13140/RG.2.2.31456.48645
5. Suthers, D., Hundhausen, C.: An experimental study of the effects of representational guidance on collaborative learning processes. J. Learn. Sci. **12**(2), 183–218 (2003)
6. Wenger, E.: Communities of Practice: Learning, Meaning, and Identity. Learning in doing. Cambridge University Press, Cambridge (1998)

Collaborative Knowledge Building Through Simultaneous Private and Public Workspaces

Carolina Gracia-Moreno[1(✉)], Jean-François Cerisier[1], Bruno Devauchelle[1], Fernando Gamboa[2], and Laëtitia Pierrot[1]

[1] Université de Poitiers, TECHNE, EA6316, 86073 Poitiers, France
{carolina.gracia.moreno, cerisier, bruno.devauchelle, laetitia.pierrot}@univ-poitiers.fr

[2] UNAM, CCADET, Mexico DF, Mexico
fernando.gamboa@ccadet.unam.mx

Abstract. Socioconstructivism postulates that learning is both a personal and a social process. The specific needs of diverse student audiences' forces educators and pedagogical engineers to redesign digital environments to foster collaborative and personal learning. As collaborative platforms evolve, rethinking their activity settings (task, artefact, scenario) becomes critical. The aim of this research is to assess whether the use of simultaneous private and public digital workspaces promotes collaborative knowledge building through the analysis of students' performance and interactions in a collaborative concept map. The focus is on an experimentation carried out with 5 groups of tenth-grade history classes in two different high schools in France. The results show a tendency of the techno-pedagogical device to foster the collaborative knowledge building.

Keywords: Private workspace · Concept mapping · Collaborative knowledge building · Social learning · Digital environments · Sociocognitive conflicts

1 Introduction

Collaborative knowledge building theory highlights the importance of cognitive conflicts [1], which are the cognitive changes provoked in individuals after they found differences among them in interaction with the group. Sociocognitive learning processes happen while individuals interact with each other through speech and therefore create a shared knowledge within the group. Digital environments have a potential to organize tasks in a cooperative and collaborative way [2] allowing students' interactions and knowledge building. When students are asked to work together, they collaborate when they mutualize their knowledge in the same task, they cooperate when they work individually in every subdivided task. The analogy of these concepts can be found in a "private workspace", which correspond to cooperative moments, and a "public workspace", where students collaborate on the same workplace: "the private space is the one built by every individual, on their own way, on their device" [3]. Empirical studies have tested the effects of private and public views in knowledge building [4]. Our hypothesis is that the synchronic use of an individual and public workspace can facilitate thinking together, negotiating and causing cognitive changes

É. Lavoué et al. (Eds.): EC-TEL 2017, LNCS 10474, pp. 553–556, 2017.
DOI: 10.1007/978-3-319-66610-5_61

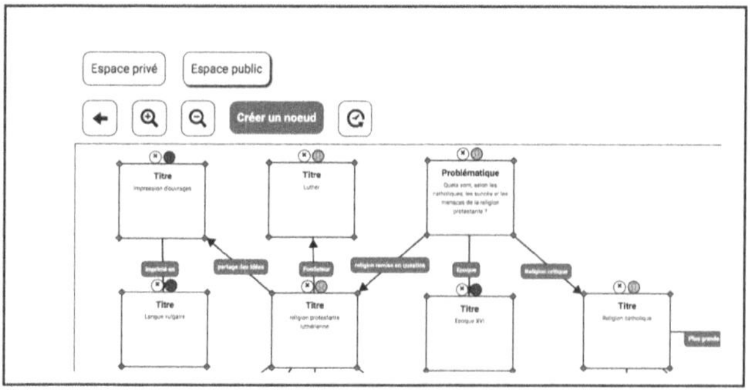

Fig. 1. INCA concept map

on others. We have conceived and developed a digital concept map where a private and a public workspace coexist (Fig. 1).

To understand students' cognitive processes, we have created a grid adapted to our study, where three categories allow us to evaluate sociocognitive processes in the students' knowledge building: Explaining; Refusing; Proposing. To ensure the reliability of the coding system, we applied a Cronbach Alpha test to a sample coded by 3 researchers and obtained a 0.842 (a = 1) degree of reliability, which indicates a high reliability between the three coders using our coding system. We have completed our analysis by the identification of students' interactions on the collaborative concept map: Adding a node/link, Modifying a node/link and Deleting a node/link. In our research, these three actions are equivalent to the three oral interactions.

2 Experimental Plan

5 groups of students passed different modalities of collaboration in two different French high schools [5]. Students followed the same pedagogical scenario to realize a collaborative concept mapping activity composed of 4 tasks (Table 1):

Table 1. Activity and experimental plan description

	With private workspace	Without private workspace
Task n°1–10 min	Reading a text	
Task n°2–10 min	Choosing keywords (personal computer)	Choosing keywords (personal computer + videoprojector for public workspace)
Task n°3–10 min	Keywords relationship (personal computer)	Keywords relationship (personal computer + videoprojector for public workspace)
Task n°4–20 min	Concept-map final construction (personal computer + videoprojector for public workspace)	Concept -map final construction (personal computer + videoprojector for public workspace)

To neutralize the learning or the appropriation effects in the different modalities, we randomly altered the order of the sessions for all groups. The independent variable (IV) is the presence or absence of a private workspace. The dependent variable (DV) measures the collaborative knowledge dimension through the analysis of their oral and digital interactions, and their written productions in the concept-maps. Only interactions collected from task n°4 have been analysed for this research. Students could see the public workspace both in their computer and from the public workspace projection on the wall. However, they were not allowed to see others' private workspaces.

3 Results on Collaborative Knowledge Building in a Public Workspace from a Previous Private Workspace

The table below shows the mean results of oral interactions and digital actions (left), as well as groups' productions (right) in the concept map tool. We have calculated the standard deviation of private nodes in the private workspace (s = 5,87) and in the public workspace (s = 2,56). The deviation is closer to the mean in the public workspace than in the private workspace, which means that some students have proposed a broader quantity of ideas in their private workspace than in the public workspace.

Table 2. Mean oral and digital interactions (left), and groups' productions (right)

	Modality	PROPOSE (Add)	EXPLAIN (Modify)	OPPOSE (Delete)
Oral interactions (interventions)	**WPW**	11,50	22,25	11,85
	W/O PW	7,75	15,90	14,85
Digital interactions (nodes)	**WPW**	6,4	13,85	2,45
	W/O PW	5,45	21,6	2,35
Digital interactions (links)	**WPW**	6	2,7	0,65
	W/O PW	6,2	5,8	1,3
	Total	**43,3**	**82,1**	**33,45**

	PRIVATE WORKSPACE (20 min, individual)	**PUBLIC WORKSPACE (20 min, collective)**	
Group ID	Total n° private nodes	N° private nodes in public	Total n° public nodes
lp2iG2	73	13	19
alG4	49	17	21
alG2	50	21	25
alG3	58	26	30
lp2iG1	69	16	29
Total	**299**	**93**	**124**

The results on the left table show that students tend to better verbalize their knowledge ("explain" and "propose") after having worked with a personal workspace (WPW), than when they work directly in groups without having used a personal workspace (W/O PW). Students also tend to "add" more digital nodes after having used a private workspace. The rise of oral "explanations" and "propositions", and "added" nodes in the WPW modality can be understood by the need of students to propose, explain and negotiate their thoughts after having developed their ideas in a private workspace. When students have worked with a personal workspace, they prefer refusing others' ideas through digital interactions ("delete") rather than oral interactions ("oppose"). We can also notice that, after having worked in a private workspace, students "modify" fewer nodes. We can say that the private workspace allows students to better explain their ideas in the collaborative concept map so they don't need to modify as many nodes. At the same time, students find more difficult to create relationships between concepts when they have created their own relationships and knowledge in their private workspace, than when they work with the group by creating, explaining, accepting and refusing knowledge together. We can observe this difficulty in the results obtained in the "links" task and the Table 2 (right), which show that students "add", "modify" and "delete" more links when they work directly in group, as they build knowledge together. Students tend to write more than half of their ideas (nodes) in their private workspace than in the public workspace. This shows that students may have more sociocognitive conflicts when they have first overcome a reflective thinking process in a personal workspace.

4 Conclusion

The results indicate that the presence of a simultaneous private and public workspace fosters sociocognitive conflicts in small groups of students. The private workspace allows students to develop their own ideas which are difficult to integrate to the group's ideas. When some students are negotiating in the public workspace, others are creating and thinking by themselves to propose to the group or to complete from the group's propositions. Next steps consist on a semantic analysis of the students propositions in both workspaces to evaluate the contagion effect [6] in the group.

References

1. Cress, U., Kimmerle, J.: A systemic and cognitive view on collaborative knowledge building with wikis. Int. J. CSCL **3**(2), 105–122 (2008)
2. Fischer, F., Kollar, I., Mandl, H., Haake, J.M. (eds.): Scripting CSCL: Cognitive, Computational and Educational Perspectives. Springer, Berlin (2007). doi:10.1007/978-0-387-36949-5
3. Henri, F., Basque, J.: Conception d'activités d'apprentissage collaboratif en mode virtuel. In: Deaudelin, C., Nault, T. (dir.) Collaborer pour apprendre et faire apprendre. La place des outils technologiques, pp. 29–53. Québec, Presses de l'université du Québec (2008)
4. Dennerlein, S.M., Seitlinger, P., Ley, T.: Adaptive and Adaptable Learning (2016)
5. Gracia-Moreno, C., Cerisier, J.-F.: Le rôle de l'espace privé numérique dans les environnements collaboratifs d'apprentissage. In: EIAH 2017, Strasbourg (2017)
6. Pentland, A.: Social Physics: How Good Ideas Spread. Lessons from a New Science. Penguin Press, London (2014)

An Ethical Waiver for Learning Analytics?

Dai Griffiths(✉)

University of Bolton, Deane Road, Bolton BL3 5AB, UK
d.e.griffiths@bolton.ac.uk

Abstract. The discourse and practice of data governance in learning analytics, and the ethics which inform it, are confused and contradictory. This can be elucidated by considering the coming together of two contrasting research traditions: academic research and operations research.

Keywords: Learning analytics · Ethics · Nuremberg · Operations research

1 Two Research Traditions

Following the trials of the Nazis after the Second World War, the Nuremberg Code [17] was agreed, to ensure that research would never again establish an abusive or exploitative relationship with its subjects. Article 1 states:

> The voluntary consent of the human subject is absolutely essential ...the person involved should ... be able to exercise free power of choice, there should be made known to him the nature, duration, and purpose of the experiment; the method and means by which it is to be conducted .... [17]

The Code was originally conceived in the context of medical research, but became extended to all research involving human subjects. This is the case in all major policies and codes on ethics in the social sciences, including the Common Rule [18] in the USA. For example, the International Sociological Association code of ethics states that "The consent of research subjects and informants should be obtained in advance" [4], while the British Educational Research Association Ethical Guidelines for Educational Research affirms that "The securing of participants voluntary informed consent, before the research gets underway, is considered the norm or the conduct of research" and stipulates "the right of any participant to withdraw from the research for any or no reason" [3] p. 6.

In parallel with the expanding influence of the Nuremberg Code in the academic research community, investigations were carried out in businesses and the state sector, with the aim of establishing effective strategies. This work is often referred to as operations or operational research (OR). Pocock states:

> Operations Research is a scientific methodology — analytical, experimental, quantitative — which, by assessing the overall implications of various alternative courses of action in a management system provides an improved basis for management decisions [9].

É. Lavoué et al. (Eds.): EC-TEL 2017, LNCS 10474, pp. 557–560, 2017.
DOI: 10.1007/978-3-319-66610-5_62

OR applies scientific methodologies to understand the world, and is therefore 'research', but it has not been governed by research ethics procedures equivalent to those of the academic research community. As Picavet (p. 1122) indicates "in operational research, efficiency is not usually viewed as something which conflicts with ethics. Quite simply, it does not refer to the same category of problems [8]". There has been ongoing discussion of ethics within the OR community over a number of years, see, for example, [5]. However, where ethical codes for OR exist, they make no mention of informed consent or a right to withdraw, for example the code of the OR Society [16].

2 Blurring Between OR and Academic Social Science

Computer networks generate huge quantities of information about their users, and vastly increased volumes of data are becoming available to OR researchers. As a result the range of contexts in which OR researchers can offer their services has also expanded dramatically. Consequently "Businesses now possess more social-science data than academics do" [13], for example through loyalty cards [11]. Indeed McFarland et al. state that employment of social scientists "may hinge on their ability to adopt a computer science approach and utilize social science merely as an afterthought..." [7]. The 'big data' collection strategy that dominates this research was summarised pithily by Bill Schmarzo, chief technical officer of EMC Global Services: "I'm a hoarder, I want it all And even if I don't yet know how I'll use that data, I want it ... My data science team might find a use for it" [1]. Informed consent for a specified purpose, required in academic research, is incompatible with such a strategy.

Educational research has followed the same trajectory as the social sciences in general. Educational institutions have always collected and used data about students, but were constrained by the available technology. The analysis which could be conducted on these small data sets was limited, carried out by academic researchers, and published in academic journals or commissioned reports. Rich data is now available from both teaching applications and student information systems, library systems, etc. Analytics on this data informs the decision making of teachers and educational managers, addressing questions which have long been the preserve of academic educational research. For example, the LACE Evidence Hub [6] holds 34 learning analytics papers about learning outcomes. LA also provides new ways to support traditional educational practice, for example by identifying students at risk of dropping out [19]. From this perspective LA is an extension of existing educational practice, and the research community might expect established ethical processes to be applicable. However, LA methods have more in common with OR, and with 'big data' analytics. Data is often not gathered for a particular purpose, but rather is accumulated and then interrogated to identify possible correlations. The people who carry out this work may not identify themselves as working within the OR tradition, perhaps preferring to refer to themselves as data scientists, or learning analytics practitioners, but the parallels remain strong. From the perspective of OR, the ethical processes of academic research seem a straitjacket which prevents them from applying their methods. The universally accepted principle in academic research that consent should be gathered from users before their data is collected, and that this is only valid for specified uses of the data, is particularly remote from OR practice.

3 Is There a Learning Analytics Waiver?

The ethics of LA is in a tangle. Let us take as an example the Open University (OU), because of the praiseworthy clarity of its policies on ethics and LA. The OU FAQs on LA inform students that "it is not possible, at present, to have your data excluded" because the OU wishes to use the dataset as a whole [14]. On the other hand the OU's Ethics Principles for Research Involving Human Participants state that "Except in exceptional circumstances, where the nature of the research design requires it, no research shall be conducted without the opt-in valid consent of participants." and that "Participants ... have a right to withdraw their consent at any time up to a specified date" [15]. LA at the OU are intended to "identify interventions which aim to support students in achieving their study goals" [14]. One may suppose that a PhD student addressing this aim with data from an external organisation would need to obtain consent, while the OU itself carries out research on its own students without this constraint. In effect, the University grants itself an ethical review waiver that it does not offer to its students. The OU is not unique in viewing very similar research activities through two different lenses, and many institutions are currently developing LA policies, following the OU's example. This will aid transparency, but there is no evidence that these policies will defuse the contradiction identified above.

Two questions arise. Firstly, should LA be considered an OR intervention, with all that implies for the organisation, its members, and the research which they carry out? Secondly, if the answer is 'yes', what does this imply for the ethics of LA, and for educational research in general? Brans and Gallo [2] describe an ethical split in OR. Some view ethical issues as restricted to effective results and lack of bias. Others focus on the effects on society and the nature of the decisions derived from their analyses and models, the values and objectives of clients, and the choice of problems on which to work. If we choose to see LA as a variety of OR, then it is necessary to take a position in this debate, and to be ready to address ethical issues which are perhaps unfamiliar. To take three examples:

Bridge International schools in the Third World enforce detailed teaching scripts, based on analytics carried out in Massachusetts [10]. *What process could determine the ethics of these relationships, and this use of LA to facilitate them?*

The rationale for ethical waivers in medicine is that data generated in the course of normal practice can improve quality of service. A similar argument applies in education. *Can such a waiver apply in education if the data analysed is not incidental, but rather the educational service is itself based on the generation of data, perhaps to the point that it is the main medium of contact with learners?*

Managers, and the regulatory environment exercise "outside social pressure on educational institutions to make substantive reforms and prove their success with data" [12]. Use of OR methods, in combination with methods such as key performance indicators, are a manifestation of this pressure. *By what process can learning technologists take ethical decisions on consent and withdrawal in LA while exposed to the managerial and economic pressures on education?*

References

1. Bertolucci, J.: When Data Hoarding Makes Sense. InformationWeek (2014). http://www.informationweek.com/big-data/big-data-analytics/when-data-hoarding-makes-sense/d/d-id/1297474
2. Brans, J.P., Gallo, G.: Ethics in OR/MS: past, present and future. Ann. Oper. Res. **153**(1), 165–178 (2007)
3. British Educational Research Association: Ethical guidelines for educational research (2014). https://www.bera.ac.uk/researchers-resources/publications/ethical-guidelines-for-educational-research-2011
4. International Sociological Association: Code of ethics (2001). http://www.isa-sociology.org/en/about-isa/code-of-ethics/
5. Le Menestrel, M., Van Wassenhove, L.N.: Ethics in operations research and management sciences: a never-ending effort to combine rigor and passion. Omega **37**(6), 1039–1043 (2009). 12, Special Issue on Ethics and Operations Research
6. Learning Analytics Community Exchange: Evidence hub (2017). http://evidence.laceproject.eu/
7. McFarland, D.A., Lewis, K., Goldberg, A.: Sociology in the era of big data: the ascent of forensic social science. Am. Sociologist **47**(1), 12–35 (2016)
8. Picavet, E.: Opportunities and pitfalls for ethical analysis in operations research and the management sciences. Omega **37**(6), 1121–1131 (2009)
9. Pocock, J.W.: Operations Research', Special Report No. 13, chap. Operations Research: Challenges to Management. American Management Association (1956)
10. Ross, T.F.: Is It Ever Okay to Make Teachers Read Scripted Lessons? The Atlantic, 10 October 2014
11. Rowley, J.: Reconceptualising the strategic role of loyalty schemes. J. Consum. Mark. **24**(6), 366–374 (2007)
12. Rubel, A., Jones, K.M.: Student privacy in learning analytics: an information ethics perspective. Inf. Soc. **32**(2), 143–159 (2014)
13. Shaw, J.: Big data is a big deal. Harvard Mag. **3**, 30–35 (2014)
14. The Open University: Policy on Ethical use of Student Data for Learning Analytics (2014). http://www.open.ac.uk/students/charter/essential-documents/ethical-use-student-data-learning-analytics-policy
15. The Open University Human Research Ethics Committee: Ethics principles for research involving human participants. Open University (2014). http://www.open.ac.uk/research/ethics/
16. The Operational Research Society: Ethical guidelines for educational research (2017). https://www.theorsociety.com/Media/Documents/Users/CaraQuinton01011978/OriginalDocument/24_06_2011-13_13_17.pdf
17. U.S. Government: Trials of War Criminals before the Nuremberg Military Tribunals under Control Council, law No. 10, vol. 2 (1949)
18. U.S. Government: Federal policy for the protection of human subjects. Federal Register, 01/19/2017 (2017)
19. West, D.: Learning analytics: Assisting universities with student retention, final report. Australian Government Office for Learning and Teaching (2015)

Better Later Than Ever: Comparative Analysis of Feedback Strategies in a Dynamic Intelligent Virtual Reality Training Environment for Child Pedestrians

Yecheng Gu[1] and Sergey Sosnovsky[2(✉)]

[1] Saarland University, Campus, 66123 Saarbrücken, Germany
s9guyech@stud.cs.uni-saarland.de
[2] Utrecht University, Princetonplein 5, 3584 CC Utrecht, The Netherlands
s.a.sosnovsky@uu.nl

Abstract. Children require practical roadside training to learn safe pedestrian behaviour. However, problems associated with exercising on real roads greatly restrict the opportunities to provide such training. This paper presents the results of a study on an alternative approach for practical safety training using a combination of Intelligent Tutoring and Virtual Reality. In a classroom experiment, children of second and third grades worked on virtual road crossing exercises. They received instructions and feedback according to several different strategies. We have observed a high general acceptance for this form of training and compared effects of different feedback strategies on children's' performance. The delayed feedback strategy has been the most successful; its impact has been especially notable on more advanced pedestrian safety skills that are the most challenging for the children of the target age.

Keywords: Virtual Reality · Intelligent tutoring systems · Pedestrian safety · Feedback strategies

1 Introduction

Children in urban environment are often exposed to the dangers of traffic from an early age. According to worldwide statistics [1] and academic studies (e.g. [2]), children between five and nine constitute the largest at-risk group of traffic participants. Therefore, repeated practical safety training is required as preventive measure, which is difficult to provide due to the dangerous nature of traffic. A promising approach is to use Virtual Reality (VR) environments simulating real traffic. Several studies have successfully employed VR in this context (e.g. [3, 4]). However, in all those experiments, a presence of a human expert performing the teaching task was still necessary. This paper evaluates the SafeChild[1] system [5] that enables children to train pedestrian skills on their own with minimum supervision by adding Intelligent Tutoring System (ITS) features. In particular, we have been interested to study the effectiveness of the adaptive feedback provided by SafeChild on the acquisition of several difficult to train (advanced)

[1] This research was funded by BMBF (grant 01IS12050) under the Software Campus program.

É. Lavoué et al. (Eds.): EC-TEL 2017, LNCS 10474, pp. 561–565, 2017.
DOI: 10.1007/978-3-319-66610-5_63

pedestrian skills. Such skills require cognitive and perceptual-motor abilities that are typically underdeveloped in young children. Two different adaptive feedback methods (the immediate and the delayed feedback) have been examined. While, human tutors tend to favour immediate feedback [6], the dynamic nature of the SafeChild environment in which pedestrian skills should be applied, accompanied by a dynamic feedback could result in demanding to much cognitive effort from a learner.

2 Experiment Design

The experiment investigates whether targeted adaptive support can help children improve advanced skills in a constantly changing environment. Two strategies varying the time of feedback presentation are examined. The model "I" (immediate) has provided learners with instructions about what to do next and with the direct feedback in the form of popping-up color-coded and icon-annotated messages (Fig. 1 left). The other model "D" (Delayed) has presented the same set of instructions but have not presented any feedback until the completion of an exercise (Fig. 1 right). An additional model "N" (None) was used for the control group that does not show any instructions or feedback.

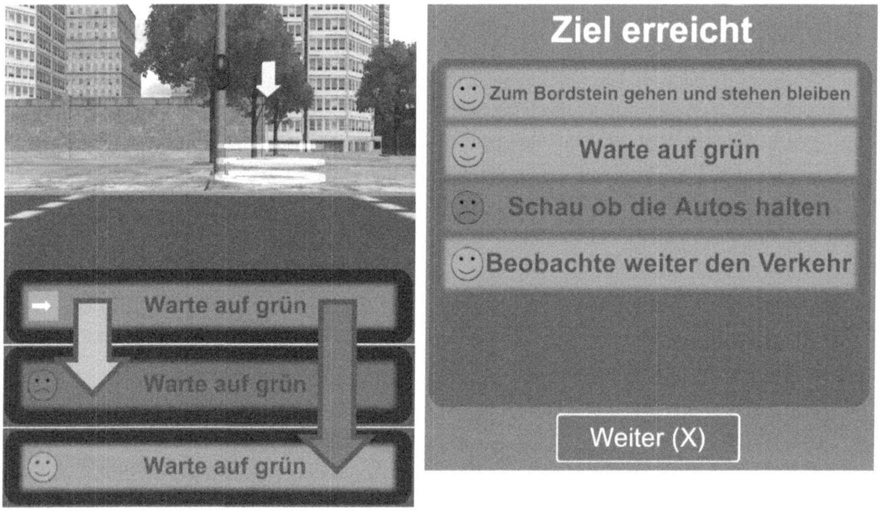

Fig. 1. Two feedback strategies

The participants of the study were 58 children (males = 31, females = 27; 2nd-graders = 29, 3rd-graders = 29). The software was installed on ten 15" notebooks equipped with gamepads. Six sessions of 45 min were completed. The participants of each session were from the same class and were balanced across different instructional models. The work with the system consisted of one familiarization exercise, three practical pre-test exercises (1 traffic light (TL), 1 zebra crossing (ZC), 1 unregulated crossing (UC)), seven training exercise (2 TL, 2 ZC, 3 UC) and 3 post-test exercises (1 TL, 1 ZC, 1 UC). The goal of each exercise is to cross a virtual road to reach a target location, while following safety rules and avoiding traffic. Variations include change of starting and goal positions and the addition of sight obstacles. The pre- and post-test exercises were nearly identical with slight cosmetic changes. The main hypothesis of the experiment has been that adaptive support can help children improve in advanced skills while "D" is expected to outperform "I" in dynamic (timing relevant) skills due to the tight timing constraints to process feedback in near real time.

3 Experiment Results

Four advanced skills were relevant in the experiment: "*Observe cars while crossing*", "*Find a good unregulated area to cross*", "*Find a good time gap to cross*", and "*Make sure that cars have stopped*". "*Observe cars while crossing*" requires a child to look right and left while s/he walks across the road. To evaluate this skill, we computed the number of right and left looks during road crossings The paired t-test on this data indicates that children in the "D" group improved significantly on "*observing cars while crossing*" both, zebra crossings (from ($M = 0.11$, $SD = 0.32$) to ($M = 0.74$, $SD = 1.10$), $t(18) = 2.59$, $p = .009$) and unregulated crossings (from ($M = 0.21$, $SD = 0.54$) to ($M = 0.74$, $SD = 1.00$), $t(18) = 2.14$, $p = .02$). The group improved in the traffic light scenario as well, but not significantly. The other groups ("N" and "I") did not improve significantly in any crossing scenario. To "*Find a good unregulated area to cross*", a learner needed to walk to a place with sufficient vision in both directions. In the test scenario, a curve and a parking car were present as sight obstacles and the task of a learner was to walk a short distance until s/he could see far enough (to detect an oncoming a car with 40 km/h). Although no participant walked far enough, a significant increase in the effort to avoid the obstacles has been observed for all groups. The comparison of the per-group improvements (i.e. gains in distance walked toward the safe crossing area between the pre- and post-test measured in meters) across the groups showed that the "N" group ($M = 2.29$, $SD = 2.73$) was significantly outperformed by both, the "I" group ($M = 4.60$, $SD = 5.12$), $t(36) = 1.76$, $p = .043$, and the "D" group ($M = 5.38$, $SD = 5.79$), $t(37) = 2.14$, $p = .019$. Between the "I" and "D" groups, there was no significant difference $t(35) = 0.43$, $p = .34$. The correct behaviour of the skill "*Find a good time gap to cross*" consists of looking in both directions while having sufficient vision and starting to cross when cars are sufficiently far away or not present at all. The last right and left looks need to be within a few seconds from the moment of starting to cross. This is one of the most challenging but also one of the most important skills. We could observe partial improvement children have made on this skill. For this, we counted the number of left and right looks before starting to cross as a measure of attention. A paired t-tests on all three groups indicates that the "D" group had a significant increase from pre- ($M = 0.18$, $SD = 0.40$) to post-test ($M = 0.74$, $SD = 1.10$), $t(18) = 2.58$, $p = .009$, while the other two groups improved, but not significantly ("I": from ($M = 0.61$, $SD = 1.14$) to ($M = 0.83$, $SD = 1.69$), $t(17) = 0.61$, $p = .28$; "N": from ($M = 0.25$, $SD = 0.72$) to ($M = 0.30$, $SD = 0.66$), $t(19) = 0.21$, $p = .42$). Finally, neither group significantly improved in "*making sure that cars have stopped*". This skill requires children to visually inspect whether cars have really stopped at a regulated crossing.

This could be due to the misconception that drivers will always obey traffic rules acquired through observation of others and/or insufficient details during theoretical traffic safety education. The current design of SafeChild did not target this misconception specifically.

4 Conclusion

The results of the experiment demonstrate that adaptive feedback functionality of the SafeChild system is beneficial for the training of the three out of four advanced pedestrian safety skills "*Find a good unregulated area to cross*", "*Observe cars while crossing*" and "*Find a good time gap to cross*". Except for the first one (where timing is irrelevant), the delayed feedback group has outperformed the immediate one, which confirms suggestions of previous studies for dynamic skills in VR context (e.g. [7]). Despite the overall promising outcomes, some limitations of the study need to be mentioned. Most notably, the text-based presentation of information seemed to be a problem for some participants as children of the target age can differ considerably in reading abilities. Second, the sample size and the duration of the study were rather small. Further, although children showed significant progress on most skills, the exhibited behaviour was often far from safe. SafeChild does allow children to reach the goal of an exercise even if the crossing has not been 100% safe. The incorrect applications of skills are registered and the feedback is given; yet, it is up to a learner to act upon it. The emphasis of our future work should be on the psychological and pedagogical aspects of the system. The research challenges are to find an appropriate way to present feedback and instructions in a non-distracting and easy-to-understand manner, appropriate for a highly dynamic nature of the SafeChild domain. Other feedback modalities including audio or symbolic elements could be evaluated in combination with more elaborate introduction or tutorial exercises.

References

1. Toroyan, T., Peden, M.: Youth and Road Safety. World Health Organization, Geneva (2007)
2. Schwebel, D.-C., Davis, A.-L., O'Neal, E.-E.: Child pedestrian injury a review of behavioral risks and preventive strategies. Am. J. Lifestyle Med. **6**(4), 292–302 (2012)
3. McComas, J., MacKay, M., Pivik, J.: Effectiveness of virtual reality for teaching pedestrian safety. Cyberpsychol. Behav. **5**(3), 185–190 (2002)
4. Thomson, J.-A., Tolmie, A.-K., Foot, H.-C., Whelan, K.-M., Sarvary, P., Morrison, S.: Influence of virtual reality training on the roadside crossing judgments of child pedestrians. J. Exp. Psychol. Appl. **11**(3), 175–186 (2005)
5. Gu, Y., Sosnovsky, S., Ullrich, C.: SafeChild: an intelligent virtual reality environment for training pedestrian safety skills. In: Conole, G., Klobučar, T., Rensing, C., Konert, J., Lavoué, É. (eds.) EC-TEL 2015. LNCS, vol. 9307, pp. 141–154. Springer, Cham (2015). doi: 10.1007/978-3-319-24258-3_11

6. Merrill, D., Reiser, B., Ranney, M., Trafton, J.: Effective tutoring techniques: a comparison of human tutors and intelligent tutoring systems. J. Learn. Sci. **2**(3), 277–305 (1992)
7. Lane, H.-C., Johnson, W.-L.: Intelligent tutoring and pedagogical experience manipulation in virtual learning environments. The PSI Handbook of Virtual Environments for Training and Education (2008)

Child-Friendly Programming Interfaces to AI Cloud Services

Ken Kahn(✉) and Niall Winters

Department of Education, University of Oxford, 15 Norham Gardens, Oxford, OX2 6PY, UK
toontalk@gmail.com

Abstract. AI cloud services are available for speech synthesis, speech recognition, image and video recognition, text analysis, and machine learning. School students could use these services in a wide variety of programming projects including voice commands to robots, chatbots, audio games, and vision-based robotics. In doing so they may learn about perception, language, psychology, and the latest empowering technologies. A major obstacle to using these services in schools is that they are technically complex APIs beyond the ability of most school students. The challenge addressed in this paper is how to provide interfaces that are much easier to use and yet still supports most of the functionality of these AI services. We describe the addition of new programming blocks to the Snap! visual programming language [1] that provide easy-to-use interfaces to these services. We have developed new blocks for speech input and output and image recognition. Learning materials have been developed and preliminarily trialed with a small number of children.

Keywords: Visual programming · Block languages · Snap! · AI services · Cloud services

1 AI Cloud Services for Student Programmers

1.1 AI Cloud Services

Several companies are offering AI cloud services via a web connection. These include Google's machine learning services, IBM Watson cloud services, Microsoft cognitive services, and Amazon AI services. Many of these services are recognition services for providing descriptions of what is being spoken or seen. Others analyze text for content, tone, and sentiment. They all include machine learning services that find patterns in data. These are commercial services that cost a few dollars for a thousand queries. Fortunately for schools with limited budgets, free quotas are provided which allow a few hundred queries per day.

The service providers support accessing these services from many programming languages. Unfortunately, these are complex interfaces designed for use by professional programmers. In this paper, we show how to provide easy-to-use interfaces to these services, opening up their potential to children who are learning to program.

É. Lavoué et al. (Eds.): EC-TEL 2017, LNCS 10474, pp. 566–570, 2017.
DOI: 10.1007/978-3-319-66610-5_64

1.2 Toward Student Projects Relying upon AI Cloud Services

Students today are often doing physical computing projects involving micro-controllers such as Raspberry Pi, Arduinos, or Micro:bits or they are programming pre-built robots. In many cases these projects could benefit significantly from the ability to recognize what is being spoken or what is in front of a camera. For example, a student could build a robot that when it hears "push the red ball" will move to the ball and push it. This could be accomplished by sending the output from a microphone to an AI cloud service, picking out the keywords in the response, then repeatedly turning and sending images from a camera to a service until the response is that a red ball is in the image and then heading in the direction the camera is facing.

There is a long tradition of children programming language-oriented programs. In the early days of Logo children programmed poetry generators, silly sentence makers, chatbots, and more [2, 3]. The appeal of these kinds of projects increases when speech input and output replaces typing and reading, an area of research that has been neglected but can now be revisited to use the analytical power of cloud-based AI services. In addition, student projects can use other AI services including sentiment analysis of what is spoken to respond in appropriate or amusing ways. This opens up the potential of AI to children in a simple and interactive manner, an emerging area of research we are exploring. Our first efforts are described below.

2 Creating Child-Friendly Programming Interfaces

Our goal is not to create a new programming environment for children, but instead to enhance existing ones. We have added speech input and output to ToonTalk Reborn [4] and to Snap! [1]. We have also added image recognition to Snap!. This paper reports on our Snap! efforts.

2.1 Why Was Snap! Chosen?

Snap! is a superset of the very popular children's blocks-based programming language Scratch [5]. It is well-suited to our efforts because (1) it is a powerful language that supports first-class data structures and functions; (2) it is easy to define new blocks using JavaScript without touching the source code; (3) it runs in every modern browser; (4) and there are versions that connect to Arduinos and the Raspberry Pi.

2.2 Speech Synthesis

All the popular browsers except for Internet Explorer support the Speech Synthesis API. The API utters the provided text with control for the pitch, rate, volume, language, and voice. The first version of the speak command took a text argument and an optional function called when the speaking finishes while the second version exposed nearly all the functionality of the Speech Synthesis API:

While this looks more difficult to use, all but the first parameter is optional and can be ignored. As discussed later students were clearly amused by entering different values for the pitch, rate, and voice.

2.3 Speech Recognition

While speech recognition is part of the Web Speech API, as of this writing only Chrome and Opera support it. However, an AI cloud service for speech recognition is available from Google, Microsoft, and IBM. The Snap! speech recognition block we designed has a success continuation and an optional error continuation.

The asynchronous nature of recognition services forces a reliance upon continuations. Continuations are ideal from a technical point of view; however we are concerned that student programmers may find them difficult. To address this, we implemented a block using the 'listen' block that supports event broadcasting and a global variable. This complexity is hidden (but available for the ambitious students) so that one needs only to call 'listen' and then receive broadcasts when something was heard and read a global variable containing the last thing spoken. For example, this program repeats what was spoken, prefaced with "I think I heard you say":

2.4 Image Recognition

There are no standard APIs for image recognition so the block we implemented supports the Google, IBM, and Microsoft APIs. A block is also needed to setup the camera. The image recognition block has a parameter specifying which cloud provider, a continuation that will receive a description of the image, and a flag as to whether the image should be displayed.

3 User Testing

As of this writing the speech input and output blocks have been tested with about 25 undergraduate students and 6 children (aged 7 to 13). This preliminary testing has been very encouraging. The new Snap! blocks were easily understood and the users indicated that they enjoyed adding speech to their programming projects. One student asked for a way to respond to nothing being said. A good suggestion we are exploring. Some students discovered that it is best to program a final ‘else’ clause for speech recognition to provide user feedback instead of ignoring those utterances that aren’t understood.

4 Discussion and Future Directions

From the early days of Logo research [2, 3] there was interest in supporting children in creating artificial intelligence programs. The decision making, perception, learning, and natural language understanding in these programs was necessarily very simple. In the process of programming AI system one is forced to reflect on one’s own thinking processes. This provided a very good fit for the constructionist ideas of learning through construction and reflection.

Today’s AI cloud services provide a new opportunity to support a new class of student AI projects – those that rely upon a state-of-the-art AI “subroutines”. Children can design and build impressive intelligent artefacts by composing and customizing components provided by world-class AI teams. Among the reasons for doing this are that students (1) may become better motivated and empowered to produce very capable artefacts; (2) may learn about perception, reasoning, psychology, and animal behavior in the process of building perceptive robots and apps; (3) may learn about cloud services, artificial intelligence, and other advanced technologies; and (4) may reflect more deeply upon their own abilities to hear, see, and respond appropriately.

There are many open issues that need further research: (1) How to incorporate recognition confidence scores provided by the AI services? (2) How to provide user control over the kinds of image recognition desired and the format of the responses? (3) Should broadcasting alternatives of all the continuation-based blocks be provided? (4) How to make the blocks multi-lingual? (5) What additional AI services should be added to the current collection? (6) How different would child-friendly interfaces to AI cloud services be when integrated with other programming systems such as ToonTalk [4]. These future developments will proceed iteratively with user testing to provide insights into the children’s perception of AI. With much discussion today focused how AI will “put people out of a job”, ways in which children can be supported to program AI services promotes learning and understanding of AI’s potential and the skills by which to use it in new, creative and effective ways.

Acknowledgement. These programs are available at tinyurl.com/ai-snap-demos. This research was supported by the eCraft2Learn project [6] funded by the European Union’s Horizon 2020 Coordination & Research and Innovation Action under Grant Agreement No 731345.

References

1. Harvey, B., Mönig, J.: Bringing “No Ceiling” to scratch: can one language serve kids and computer scientists? In: Constructionism, Paris, France (2010)
2. Papert, S., Solomon, C.: Twenty Things to Do with a Computer, MIT AI Lab (1971). http://hdl.handle.net/1721.1/5836
3. Kahn, K.: A Logo natural language system. Technical report, MIT AI Lab, LOGO Working Paper 46 (1975)
4. Kahn, K.: TOONTALK REBORN - Re-implementing and re-conceptualising ToonTalk for the Web. In: Constructionism, Vienna, Austria (2014)
5. Resnick, M., Maloney, J., Monroy-Hernández, A., Rusk, N., Eastmond, E., Brennan, K., Millner, A., Rosenbaum, E., Silver, J., Silverman, B., Kafai, Y.: Scratch: programming for all. Commun. ACM **52**(11), 60–67 (2009). doi:10.1145/1592761.1592779
6. http://www.project.ecraft2learn.eu/

A Case of Career Consultancy in STEM for Youths

Anna Mavroudi(✉) and Monica Divitini

Norwegian University of Science and Technology, Trondheim, Norway
{anna.mavroudi,divitini}@ntnu.no

Abstract. Career consultancy is an important but often downplayed aspect in technology-enhanced learning systems designed for youths although there is much learning in the career decision-making process. This case study focuses on identifying career consultancy services for STEM that can be useful and relevant to them. It involves participatory design for the school of the future in conjunction with workplace learning with a small group of adolescents. The paper provides an overview of existing online career consultancy services in STEM focusing on their unique characteristics, reports the findings of a group interview with participant STEM students about career consultancy, and presents future recommendations derived from the students themselves. The final student product involves a low-fidelity prototype of the envisioned career consultancy system. The case study can potentially inform practice on the topic of career consultancy in STEM education among youngsters.

Keywords: Career consultancy · STEM · Youth · Technology-enhanced learning

1 Introduction

There is much learning associated with career orientation in terms of knowledge, skills and attitude. According to [1], knowledge might involve actions like retrieval of occupational information and self-appraisal; also, learning in the attitude level might involve beliefs associated to a career decision. The concern herein is how we can design technology enhanced learning systems that incorporate CC services for STEM targeted to high-school pupils. It involves three high school students (aged 15–16 years old) that live in Norway and a three-hour workshop on the topic.

2 Process and Instruments

First, the facilitator conducted a semi-structured group interview about the topic of CC for STEM with the participant students. The dimensions of the interview were: (1) students' choices about career paths and existing CC services, (2) kind and type of information needed, and (3) CC events taking place in their (school) environment. The purpose of the interview was to understand students' practices and prior experiences about CC in STEM. Next, the workshop facilitator demonstrated twelve existing online

É. Lavoué et al. (Eds.): EC-TEL 2017, LNCS 10474, pp. 571–575, 2017.
DOI: 10.1007/978-3-319-66610-5_65

Table 1. Existing online career consultancy services for students

Short description and URL of the online service	Special characteristic/functionality that helps students to….
This is a website about women in STEM jobs, https://goo.gl/20qRpO	Reflect by presenting professionals sharing careers perspectives
Information about live events, such as a summer camp on Careers in STEM through Interactive Workshops and Game-Based Learning, https://goo.gl/o6Oy1b	Receive information by notifying them automatically about such events and discuss their perceived usefulness
This website provides a simulation or game that lets you explore STEM careers, http://ionfuture.org/ in a playful way	Receive basic information about each STEM career profile, organized in four sections Each career profile is associated with a game
This website provides a STEM career glossary and informative videos, http://stemstudy.com/stem-careers-glossary/	With terminology and accessibility: STEM CC Glossary and mobile –friendly version (mobile app)
The Reality Check Tool will tell whether you can achieve your desired lifestyle based on your career of interest, http://www.careerwise.mnscu.edu/careers/realitytool.html	Determine whether their career goals are realistic using an interactive resource
This webpage references other industry websites in the area, http://www.careerwise.mnscu.edu/jobs/industry.html	Explore the job market by providing connections to relevant industry websites in their region
This webpage has self-assessment quizzes for the students, http://www.careerwise.mnscu.edu/careers/assessmentsuite.html	Self-assess and reflect on relevant or interesting career paths in STEM using quizzes
It enables selecting types of Open Educational Resources (OER) using various selection criteria, http://www.discovere.org/our-activities	Access a portal that contains relevant OERs; in our case, to the online repository that will contain STEM educational material
Live chat between students and experts or counsellors, https://goo.gl/At4kEi	Live chat with experts or counsellors on career orientation
Request information via an online form, https://goo.gl/LnGurq	Complete a request online in order to receive informative material
Email career consultancy questions or ask a counselor, https://goo.gl/J4M6OY and https://goo.gl/Xdcny7	Submit their questions to experts or counsellors on career orientation via an online form

services on CC about STEM. In doing that, she placed special focus on a few functional characteristics for each of the twelve services. Table 1 presents details about these.

Perceived usefulness is critical for technology adoption [3]. The questionnaire also included an open-ended question where students could write any additional critical feature that they considered important. This process lead to requirements' prioritisation by the students for the envisioned system. The final phase of the workshop included two main design activities concerning the envisioned CC system for STEM. The first activity followed a scenario-based requirements elicitation process of the system [2].

Having seen, explored, rated (and suggested) characteristics of the various STEM CC online systems, students described a scenario of use concerning a STEM CC system of ideal for them characteristics and functionality. The scenario-based approach was the basis for co-operative design. Before the beginning of the activity, in order to familiarize students with the paradigms of scenarios of use and the persona concept, the facilitator provided a written example. In addition, she explained the basics about paper prototyping and showed some examples. Next, the students created the scenarios and the low-fidelity prototype taking into account the requirements prioritisation that took place in the previous phase. That is, the prototype had to be in line with the requirements mentioned in the previous phase and the scenarios of use that the students had already created. The students worked together towards the creation of a mock-up user interface (UI) of the envisioned CC for STEM system. The facilitator created the digital version of the mock-up UI replicating the students' sketches while using a dedicated software.

3 Results

The group interview: the students had already chosen a career orientation. They think that students in Norway select what they want to study at the age of 15–16 years old. Regarding the kind of information that they need for CC purposes: (a) companies active in their domains of interest and their profile, (b) relevant positions and internships available in Norway and in Europe, (c) salary information, (d) (online) communities to get inspiration and feedback. To find such information, they used a website created by the Norwegian government, namely utdanning.no (https://utdanning.no/). There they find useful information, such as information about careers and main tasks, studies associated with a certain career path, and so on. One student was also using two other services specialised on his domain of interest (namely, gnist.no and elskolen.no). The students stressed the importance of finding updated information in such services. Regarding CC activities taking place in school, the students believe that counsellors can give useful advice; yet a few times, they gave bad (i.e. irrelevant) advice because they were not as well-informed as a professional/practitioner (e.g. an engineer). The students consult their parents, peers, teachers, and university students.

The student questionnaire: Table 2 presents the ratings on the perceived importance of the demonstrated functionalities. At the open-ended question, students answered that they would appreciate: postings with updated information coming from the industry sector about the profile of the people hired, and tracking the user activity in order to get an overview of the platform activity and possibly orientate themselves better.

The student scenarios: the scenarios of use created by the students were short and incomplete. Yet, they nicely incorporated the persona concept as well as the functional characteristics discussed, including their relative usefulness.

Table 2. Perceived importance of the system characteristics

Characteristic/functionality	Importance (mean, st. dev.)
General information about the career path	M = 5, S.D. = 0
Online discussion forum	M = 4.7, S.D. = 0.6
Video interviews with the experts	M = 4.7, S.D. = 0.6
Connection to relevant industry websites	M = 4.3, S.D. = 0.6
Information about live events in your area	M = 4, S.D. = 0
Connection to relevant OERs in an organised way	M = 3.7, S.D. = 0.6
Glossary of relevant terms	M = 3.7, S.D. = 0.6
Live chat with experts or counsellors	M = 3.7, S.D. = 0.6
Self-assessments for students	M = 2.7, S.D. = 1.5
Email questions on career consultancy	M = 2, S.D. = 1
Request information about a career path via an online form	M = 1.7, S.D = 0.6

The prototype: it was in line with the requirements prioritization that took place in the first phase of the workshop and with the scenarios of use. Figure 1 shows the main (low fidelity) UI mockup of the students' proposed system.

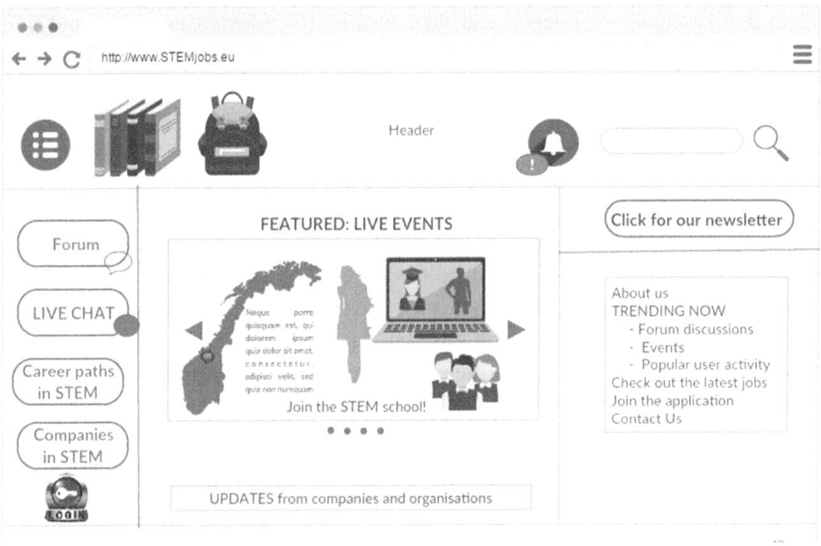

Fig. 1. The students' prototype of the envisioned system

Acknowledgement. This work is supported by the European's Union Horizon 2020 research and innovation programme under grant agreement No. 710583.

References

1. Cantrell, P., Ewing-Taylor, J.: Exploring STEM career options through collaborative high school seminars. J. Eng. Educ. **98**(3), 295–303 (2009)
2. Carroll, J.M., Rosson, M.B., Chin, G., Koenemann, J.: Requirements development in scenario-based design. IEEE Trans. Softw. Eng. **24**(12), 1156–1170 (1998)
3. Davis, F., Bagozzi, R., Warshaw, R.: User acceptance of computer technology: a comparison of two theoretical models. Manag. Sci. **35**, 982–1003 (1989)

Mass Customization in Continuing Medical Education: Automated Extraction of E-Learning Topics

Nicolae Nistor[1,2(✉)], Mihai Dascălu[3], Gabriel Guţu[3], Ştefan Trăuşan-Matu[3], Sunhea Choi[4], Ashley Haberman-Lawson[5], Brigitte Angela Brands[5], Christian Körner[5], and Berthold Koletzko[5]

[1] Faculty of Psychology and Educational Sciences, Ludwig-Maximilians-Universität, Leopoldstr. 13, 80802 Munich, Germany
nic.nistor@uni-muenchen.de

[2] Richard W. Riley College of Education and Leadership, Walden University, 100 Washington Avenue South, Suite 900, Minneapolis, MN 55401, USA

[3] Faculty of Automatic Control and Computer Science, University "Politehnica" Bucharest, Splaiul Independenţei 313, 60042 Bucharest, Romania
{mihai.dascalu,gabriel.gutu,stefan.trausan}@cs.pub.ro

[4] Faculty of Medicine, University of Southampton, University Rd, Southampton, SO17 1BJ, UK
s.choi@soton.ac.uk

[5] Faculty of Medicine, Ludwig-Maximilians-Universität, Bavaria Ring 10, 80336 Munich, Germany
{ashley.habermanlawson,brigitte.brands,christian.koerner, de office.koletzko}@med.uni-muenchen.de

Abstract. To satisfy the individual learning needs of the high number of the Early Nutrition (EN) eAcademy participants, and to reduce development costs, the mass customization (MC) approach was applied. Key concepts of the learning needs, and corresponding learner subgroups with similar needs were extracted from learner-generated text using the natural language processing tool ReaderBench. Two collections of key concepts where built, which enabled EN experts to formulate topics for e-learning modules to be developed. Ongoing work will assess learner satisfaction and e-learning development costs, in order to evaluate the MC application in continuing medical education.

Keywords: Continuing medical education · Mass customization · Natural language processing · Massive open online courses · Online courses

1 Introduction

In recent years, Early Nutrition has emerged as an important subdomain of medical research and practice, due to the huge impact of nutrition in early life, as well as on immediate and long-term health [1]. The related continuing medical education (CME) faces particular challenges in this domain. Qualified personnel are ill-equipped for effective dissemination of research findings. As a first attempt to bridge the CME gap, the open distance learning program Early Nutrition eAcademy (ENeA) was established at the Medical Center of the Ludwig-Maximilians-Universität München, Germany, in

É. Lavoué et al. (Eds.): EC-TEL 2017, LNCS 10474, pp. 576–579, 2017.
DOI: 10.1007/978-3-319-66610-5_66

2011. However, ENeA is challenged by the high diversity of participants who are faced with regionally diverse problems. Such challenges call for a customized CME that, at the same time, should be available at affordable costs. To achieve this, the approach of mass customization (MC) [2] has been chosen for further ENeA development, and extended to continuing education [3]. Due to the high number of participants, the implementation of MC in ENeA requires automated methods of needs analysis and topic extraction for e-learning modules to be developed.

MC was originally established in Operations Management and related to the design and mass production of customized products or services [2], including educational products such as learning environments built on traditional delivery [4] or e-learning [3]. Understanding MC applications in education requires delimitations from related concepts. Adaptive and personalized learning environments, for instance, include a learner model describing individual cognitive features, whereas MC is mainly based on task models. For example, Nistor, Dehne and Drews [3] designed a mass-customized learning environment accompanying an office software migration. The needs assessment started from a product analysis of the artifacts (e.g. electronic forms) used in the customer organization (i.e. local residents' registration office), selecting from all software functions only those actually used by the members of the customer organization. Subsequently, e-learning modules were produced and delivered in individual combinations, which resulted in more efficient learning.

In the case of ENeA, MC aims to satisfy diverse learning needs of a large and heterogeneous CME participant group in an emerging domain lacking an established curriculum. ENeA providers need to know which e-learning modules to develop, on which topics, and for which knowledge needs. This decision is based on automated content analysis of the communication between ENeA providers and participants, initiated by an open question participant survey, to be further discussed in online discussion forums. Key concepts are automatically extracted from the learner-generated text, then classified by semantic similarity, finally indicating a reduced number of e-learning topics and participant groups – as described in the following.

2 The Automated Topics Extraction

Employed Tools. Key concepts were extracted using *ReaderBench* version 2.3, a multilingual, Natural Language Processing (NLP) framework described in detail in [5–7]. Prior to performing topics extraction, *ReaderBench* was trained on a text corpus consisting of 1,700 EN documents related to pregnancy, nutrition, epigenetics, and nutrients, and combined with the TASA corpus (http://lsa.colorado.edu/spaces.html).

Topics Extraction. In an online survey, the ENeA project partners from Malaysia and Thailand were asked the question "What would you like to learn and be continually educated for in the field of Early Nutrition & Lifestyle?" The sample of N = 100 respondents included 30 pediatricians, 26 nutritionists, 13 doctors in practice, 10 dieticians, 10 lecturers, 2 nurses, 2 PhD students, and single occupations such as child psychiatrist, coach, diabetologist, food science technologist, gynecologist, medical sales representative, and oncologist. From the free text responses, a total of 290 keywords were extracted, from which the most relevant three keywords were: early (relevance score 3.97), feed (2.41), and late (2.31). Additionally, the most relevant three combinations of keywords extracted were: (1) early, late, infancy, childhood, life, period, development, time, affect, pregnancy, (2) feed, breast, complement, formula, infant, breastfeed, milk, month, (3) late, early, life, time, infancy, childhood, start, consequence.

In order to find a minimal number of profession groups related to the extracted scores, the initially indicated profession groups were considered as cases described by the extracted keywords. A principal component analysis with varimax rotation and Kaiser normalization was performed, indicating a two factor solution. Factor 1 loaded 0.79, 0.94, 0.88 for the professions: lecturer, nutritionist and pediatrician, and under 0.3 for the others; factor 2 loaded 0.96, 0.92 for the professions: doctor in practice and dietician, respectively.

For the profession subgroup lecturer/nutritionist/pediatrician, a total of 237 keywords were extracted, from which the most relevant keywords were: early (3.69), feed (2.34), infant (2.16), in the combinations: (1) early, infancy, childhood, life, period, development, adulthood, affect, stage, pregnancy, (2) feed, breast, complement, formula, infant, breastfeed, milk, infancy, (3) infant, formula, feed, premature, preterm, newborn, infancy, neonate, milk, birth, breast, enteral complement, mother, growth. For the profession group dietician/doctor-in-practice, a total of 82 keywords were extracted, from which the most relevant keywords were: early (relevance score 1.71), infant (1.49), feed (1.34), occurring in the combinations: (a) early, infancy, childhood, life, development, time, affect, pregnancy, (b) infant, feed, preterm, newborn, breast, complement, (c) feed, complement, formula, infant, breastfeed, infancy. From the extracted keywords, 192 designated topics of interest were found for the lecturer/nutritionist/pediatrician subgroup only, 37 only for the dieticians/doctors in practice subgroup, and 45 were common for both subgroups.

3 Discussion and Conclusions

This study aimed to provide the basis for MC of e-learning in the ENeA project by extracting from learner-generated text, key concepts that reflect the participant learning needs. Pediatricians dominated the participant sample, as compared to only one gynecologist. Accordingly, topics like infant, child feeding, newborn, breastfeed etc. frequently occurred, while pregnancy and pre-conception seldom arose. The automated topics extraction resulted in two concept maps, corresponding to the subgroups lecturer/nutritionist/pediatrician (i.e. EN experts, scholars, researchers) and dietician/doctor-in-practice (i.e., EN practitionists). The vocabulary differences between these were evident and reflected specific concepts of interest from each area. For the lecturer/nutritionist/pediatrician subgroup, the topics included general aspects of pre- and postnatal nutritional programming of long-term health. For the dieticians/doctors in practice subgroup, the recommended topics focused on infant feeding. As a direct, practical consequence for ENeA mass-customized e-learning development, e-learning modules should be developed on topics described by the extracted key concepts. Thus, the topics will not cover the entire EN domain following a "one-size-fits-all" approach, but correspond to specific learning needs of participant subgroups, which in turn may reduce e-learning development costs and increase learner satisfaction. Future content development should no longer be limited to relying on brief survey responses of the small sample of under 100 (from over 6000) participants. The topics can be better extracted from ongoing online discussions accessible to all ENeA participants and facilitated to elicit the description of cases from participants' everyday practice, and the knowledge deficits they perceive in this context. Additionally, participant satisfaction and development costs should be evaluated to assess the efficiency of the MC approach applied to e-learning.

Acknowledgements. This research was partially supported by the FP7 2008-212578 LTfLL project, and by European Union's Seventh Framework Programme (FP7/2007-2013), project EarlyNutrition under grant agreement n°[289346]. This work has received an unrestricted educational grant by Wyeth Nutrition.

References

1. Koletzko, B., Brands, B., Chourdakis, M., Cramer, S., Grote, V., Hellmuth, C., Kirchberg, F., Prell, C., Rzehak, P., Uhl, O., Weber, M.: The power of programming and the EarlyNutrition project: opportunities for health promotion by nutrition during the first thousand days of life and beyond. Ann. Nutr. Metab. **64**(3–4), 187–196 (2014)
2. Pine, B.J.: Mass Customization: The New Frontier in Business Competition. Harvard Business Press, Boston (1993)
3. Nistor, N., Dehne, A., Drews, F.T.: Mass customization of teaching and training in organizations. Design principles and prototype evaluation. Stud. Continuing Educ. **32**(3), 251–267 (2010)
4. Waslander, S.: Mass customization in schools: strategies Dutch secondary schools pursue to cope with the diversity–efficiency dilemma. J. Educ. Policy **22**(4), 363–382 (2007)
5. Gutu, G., Dascalu, M., Trausan-Matu, S., Dessus, P.: ReaderBench goes online: a comprehension-centered framework for educational purposes. In: Romanian Conference on Human-Computer Interaction (RoCHI 2016), pp. 95–102. MATRIX ROM, Iasi, Romania (2016)
6. Dascalu, M.: Analyzing Discourse and Text Complexity for Learning and Collaborating, Studies in Computational Intelligence, vol. 534. Springer, Cham (2014)
7. Dessus, P., Gutu, G., Dascalu, M., Diouf, J. B., Trausan-Matu, S.: Vers des manuels de cours universitaires ouverts et interactifs promouvant l'apprentissage auto-régulé. In: Atelier "Evaluation formative pratiquée en classe ou en amphithéâtre" joint à l'ORPHEE, Font-Romeu, France (2017)

Using CollAnnotator to Analyze a Community of Inquiry Supported by Educational Blogs - Preliminary Results

Elvira Popescu(✉) and Gabriel Badea

Computers and Information Technology Department, University of Craiova, Craiova, Romania
popescu_elvira@software.ucv.ro, gabriel.badea@yahoo.com

Abstract. Community of Inquiry (CoI) model can be used to describe an online learning community (supported by various communication channels between students) on three interdependent components: cognitive, social and teaching presence. In this paper, we use CoI for investigating the online community formed in a social learning environment, focusing especially on the affordances of blogs. The novelty of our approach consists in the use of a dedicated content analysis tool, specifically built for CoI, called CollAnnotator. The paper provides a preliminary experimental validation of the tool, which was successfully applied in practice for analyzing the content of 479 blog posts, created by 75 students. The context of study, content analysis procedure and a brief overview of the results are reported in the paper.

Keywords: Community of Inquiry · Content analysis · Educational blogging

1 Introduction

The *Community of Inquiry (CoI)* model, proposed in [3], addresses the development of online learning communities in terms of three components: (i) *Cognitive presence* (learners' construction of meaning through sustained reflection and discourse); (ii) *Social presence* (learners' identification with the community and development of interpersonal relationships); (iii) *Teaching presence* (design, facilitation, and direction of cognitive and social processes to support learning)[1]. While initially introduced for computer conferencing, the model has been recently applied for other online communication spaces between students, including blog [1], Twitter [7] or Facebook [4].

Despite its widespread use, to the best of our knowledge, there is no support tool available for content analysis according to CoI framework. Therefore, we decided to develop an in-house solution, called CollAnnotator, which was specifically designed to work in conjunction with our eMUSE social learning environment [5] and provide support for tweets and blog posts content analysis [2].

The goal of this paper is to provide a preliminary experimental validation of the tool, illustrating its practical use for investigating a Community of Inquiry supported by educational blogs. The rest of the paper is structured as follows: Sect. 2 describes the context of study, briefly introducing the CollAnnotator tool, the study settings and the

[1] Community of Inquiry Model: https://coi.athabascau.ca/coi-model.

É. Lavoué et al. (Eds.): EC-TEL 2017, LNCS 10474, pp. 580–583, 2017.
DOI: 10.1007/978-3-319-66610-5_67

content analysis procedure. Section 3 presents and discusses the results of the content analysis process. Section 4 draws some conclusions and future research directions.

2 Context of Study

2.1 CollAnnotator Tool and Study Settings

Given the popularity of the Community of Inquiry model [6], a dedicated platform for supporting content annotation based on CoI would prove useful to the researchers. We therefore developed such a content analysis tool, called *CollAnnotator,* which provides the following functionalities: rich annotation support, possibility to attach more than one code to a message, support for multiple coders and suggestive comparisons between them, support for the negotiation phase, detailed statistics and reports of the coding results, all in an intuitive and easy to use interface. Furthermore, CollAnnotator is adapted to our goal of using CoI for investigating the online community formed in our social learning environment, eMUSE [5]; it directly retrieves student content (blog posts and tweets) from eMUSE database and generates reports and statistics specific to our instructional scenario. More details regarding the tool rationale, functionalities and implementation details can be found in [2].

As an initial experimental validation, we applied CollAnnotator to investigate the affordances of blogs to create and support a community of inquiry. The blog posts of 75 students enrolled in a Web Applications Design course were analyzed. The course took place during the first semester of the 2015-2016 academic year and was taught to 4th year undergraduate students in Computer Science from the University of Craiova, Romania. A project-based learning scenario was implemented, in which students collaborated in teams of 3–4 peers in order to build a relatively complex web application. Students could use three social media tools (blog, wiki and Twitter) for communication and collaboration tasks. All students' contributions on these tools were retrieved and stored in a local database by means of the eMUSE platform [5].

In particular, every team had a blog where each member could contribute and report the progress of the project, share interesting resources, describe problems encountered and potential solutions, ask questions to peers, provide feedback etc. A total of 479 contributions were recorded on students' blogs: 399 posts and 80 comments. These were subsequently analyzed using CollAnnotator, according to the procedure described in the next subsection.

2.2 Content Analysis Procedure

Two researchers performed the content analysis of the 479 student blog posts, using CollAnnotator tool and the coding scheme proposed in [6]. The use of two coders was aimed to increase the reliability and validity of the results [6]. The unit of analysis was the blog post, according to the recommendations in [1]; however, coders were encouraged to use the highlight feature included in CollAnnotator in order to provide annotations at finer levels of granularity. Due to the richness of the blog posts, both a primary (mandatory) and a secondary (optional) category were assigned to each post. In addition, the coders were asked to add a comment in order to justify or explain their choice (e.g., specify the *indicator* used for the particular category).

Coding took place in two phases: first, the researchers annotated and classified all the posts independently, obtaining an agreement percentage of around 80%. Secondly, they met in order to compare the codes, discuss the disagreements and try to reach a consensus; after negotiation, the agreement between the coders reached 98.33% when considering only the primary category and 96.19% when considering also the secondary category.

3 Results and Discussion

Figure 1 presents the frequency counts for blog posts, at category level, as shown by CollAnnotator (including both primary and secondary categories); a brief discussion of the results is provided next.

Blog Statistics (based on both categories)

Agreement percentage between coders: 96.19 %

Classification Table for Blog Posts & Comments

Presence	Category	Count (for coder Gabriel)	Count (for coder Elvira)
Cognitive	Triggering event	19	18
	Exploration	101	104
	Integration	247	246
	Resolution	0	0
Social	Affective	38	39
	Open communication	97	89
	Group cohesion	202	210

Fig. 1. Summary report provided by CollAnnotator - frequency count for blog post categories

First of all, it should be noted that the *teaching presence* was not considered in our analysis; this is due to the fact that the instructor's blog and contributions were not taken into account. While students could also initiate teaching components (e.g., peer instruction), related studies show that most of them originate from the instructor [1].

We could also notice that the largest number of posts belong to the *integration* phase of learning (*cognitive presence*), since students regularly reported on the progress of their project, pointing towards the creation of solutions. The *exploration* phase is also relatively well represented, with many students sharing interesting resources and ideas (information exchange) or providing suggestions for consideration. The *resolution* phase is not documented on the blog, since complete solutions were generally presented and defended on the wiki. The *triggering* phase is also scarcely represented, as students tend to post not when they encounter a problem or puzzlement, but rather when they have a solution to share.

As far as the *social presence* is concerned, most posts account for *group cohesion*, with many students addressing or referring to the group in their posts. *Open communication* is also well represented, including answers to peers' posts, asking questions, complimenting and expressing appreciation. Only few posts express emotions or use humor (*affective* category), as students preferred to use the blog in a slightly more formal manner.

4 Conclusion

CollAnnotator tool was successfully applied in practice for analyzing the blog posts of 75 students who used the blog in the context of a project-based learning scenario. A total of 479 posts were annotated and classified by two coders, who found the tool easy to use, effective and efficient; a high level of agreement was obtained after the negotiation phase, leading to a valid and reliable classification. Results indicate blog's support for cognitive and social presences, especially for exploration and integration, group cohesion and open communication.

More in-depth analyses are planned to be performed, relying on the support offered by CollAnnotator. First, students' tweets could be included in the investigation, to give a more comprehensive perspective on the created community of inquiry. Second, team-level and student-level analyses could be conducted, to explore their contribution to the community. Third, comparisons between different student cohorts could be performed, given that the instructional scenario has been running for several years.

Acknowledgements. This work was supported by a grant of the Romanian National Authority for Scientific Research and Innovation, CNCS – UEFISCDI, project number PN-II-RU-TE-2014-4-2604.

References

1. Angelaina, S., Jimoyiannis, A.: Educational blogging: developing and investigating a students' community of inquiry. In: Jimoyiannis, A. (ed.) Research on e-Learning and ICT in education, pp. 169–182. Springer, New York (2012)
2. Badea, G., Popescu, E.: CollAnnotator - a support tool for content analysis according to Community of Inquiry framework. In: Proceedings ICALT 2017, pp. 212–214 (2017)
3. Garrison, D.R., Anderson, T., Archer, W.: Critical inquiry in a text-based environment: computer conferencing in higher education. Internet High. Educ. **2**(2–3), 87–105 (2000)
4. Lim, J., Richardson, J.C.: Exploring the effects of students' social networking experience on social presence and perceptions of using SNSs for educational purposes. Internet High. Educ. **29**, 31–39 (2016)
5. Popescu, E.: Providing collaborative learning support with social media in an integrated environment. World Wide Web **17**(2), 199–212 (2014)
6. Shea, P., Hayes, S., Vickers, J., et al.: A re-examination of the community of inquiry framework: social network and content analysis. Internet High. Educ. **13**, 10–21 (2010)
7. Sinnappan, S., Zutshi, S.: Using microblogging to facilitate community of inquiry: an Australian tertiary experience. In: Proceedings of ASCILITE 2011, pp. 1123–1135 (2011)

The Implicit Pedagogy of Teachers' Design Patterns

Elisabeth Rolf(✉), Ola Knutsson, and Robert Ramberg

Department of Computer and Systems Science, Stockholm University, 16407 Kista, Sweden
elisabeth@dsv.su.se

Abstract. This paper presents an analysis of upper secondary teachers' design patterns portraying their technology use in teaching by answering the question: What pedagogy is implicit in technology supported learning activities designed by teachers? Building on a framework defining key characteristics of contemporary learning theories, seventeen design patterns describing technology use in teaching were analyzed. The analysis reveals that individual activities are dominating the patterns. In addition, there is a trend towards activities favoring students' non-reflection, but also activities being more informative than experiential.

Keywords: Learning design · Designs for learning · Design patterns · Pattern analysis

1 Introduction

Teachers are in their practice engaged in designs for learning. In their planning and carrying out teaching they make choices that are grounded in their teaching experience. These designs could be labelled design solutions, counting as examples of designs for learning [1]. Design patterns have been used to support the representation of design solutions, and it is reported how these can support the use of technology in schools [2–4].

Design patterns are currently used in several different domains and have been analyzed to some extent in computer science [5]. Within TEL, there is however still a lack of analytical studies of patterns although exceptions do exist [6, 7]. In [7] patterns are compared with much more detailed solutions to learning design such as IMS Learning design (IMS LD) and Learning Activity Management System (LAMS). In contrast to IMS LD and LAMS, the patterns have less elaborated technical and pedagogical solutions, thus putting a higher demand on pedagogically adept teachers to put the patterns to use in teaching. In spite of this, the patterns did support teachers' reflection and commitment to design components. Our research digs deeper into the use of patterns in processes of communication and transformation, by departing from an understanding of what kinds of learning activities that are designed in the patterns. Hence, our research question is: What pedagogical characteristics are implicit in technology supported learning activities designed by teachers?

É. Lavoué et al. (Eds.): EC-TEL 2017, LNCS 10474, pp. 584–587, 2017.
DOI: 10.1007/978-3-319-66610-5_68

2 Method

The analysis presented is based on seventeen design patterns created by a group of upper secondary teachers in Stockholm municipality in Sweden, participating in five two-hour long workshops. Teachers with an interest of technology use in education were invited to the workshop series, and a total of fourteen teachers from ten upper secondary schools participated. They represent a variety of school subjects.

Our approach to analyzing the patterns is qualitative, but some descriptive statistics is used to present an overview of the design patterns and their characteristics. We utilized a structure for design patterns based on a template created by Alexander, Ishikawa and Silverstein [8] and Finlay et al. [9]. The format is also inspired from previous use of design pattern template formats in participatory design processes [10]. An aim is to develop a suitable template that facilitates documentation and communication while also constituting a reflective tool in teachers design of learning activities. The template, available for the teachers in a wiki, contains twelve sections: Pattern name, Problem, Context, Solution, Miscellaneous, Creator, Status, Reference to larger patterns, Reference to minor patterns, Recipient, and Sketch. A model by Conole et al. [11] is deployed for analyzing the pedagogics of learning activities identified in the patterns. The model builds on six components depicting continua of key pedagogical aspects having their origin in different learning theories. The six components are paired in three clusters: individual - social, non-reflective - reflective, information - experience, and introduce more complexity than simple binary distinctions. The model thus aids in grasping and characterizing the learning activities and the key pedagogical aspects described by the teachers in their patterns of technology use in teaching. In the model, students' learning activities are described as mini-learning activities [11]. Several such activities are described and examples are: brainstorming a concept, self-assessment of level of competence, sharing ideas and coming up with a combined list, discussion, presentation, receiving information, and carrying out a task [11].

3 Results

To answer the research question, mini-learning activities had to be identified and analyzed. In the 17 design patterns, 26 mini-learning activities were identified. Single activities were centered around the following: Migration to Microsoft Office365, flipped classroom, video production, and brainstorming online. Four mini-learning activities concerned the use of response apps. Digital literacy training was by far the largest category including fifteen activities of various kinds, for instance email handling, information search on the web, source criticism, learning of reference systems, and managing a specific application.

Secondly, to understand the pedagogical character of those mini-learning activities, they were interpreted in relation to the three clusters of defined key components in the model by Conole et al. [11]. The original model is represented by 7 intermediate positions, enabling to more precisely define and theoretically position a planned learning activity. However, to enable an analysis and characterization of the mini-learning activities, a decision was made to create one intermediate position to each pair of components (Fig. 1). The intermediate positions describe the pedagogies of a mini-learning activity where the actual redesign and use of a pattern will determine if the activity will traverse towards one or the other end of the continuum.

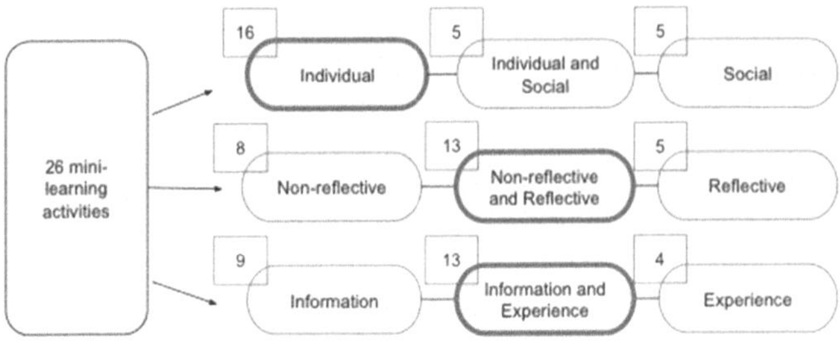

Fig. 1. Pedagogical characteristics of 26 mini-learning activities. Identified numbers of mini-learning activities are given in the adjacent squares.

The analysis demonstrated a majority, 16 of 26 mini-learning activities, to be performed by individual students. 13 of the activities, are interpreted as Non-reflective and Reflective, and 13 activities are interpreted as Information and Experience. Furthermore, a trend towards activities promoting students' non-reflection is identified, as well as students' activities being more informative than experiential.

4 Discussion

Pedagogics favoring individual learning activities dominate the mini-learning activities. An explanation is found in the plentitude of digital literacy activities for students, pointing at teachers' perceived need for students to be able to manage applications and systems relevant to education. More precisely, an increased competence of students specialized digital literacy [12] for managing technology useful in education is identified as a need expressed by the teachers.

For many mini-learning activities it is a challenge to understand whether or not students are to reflect or not since teachers do not advance the issue in the patterns. If the activity is to be realized in a school setting, then teachers will have to redesign the activity with an option of designing the activity's mode of reflection according to their preferences. Hence, we have therefore categorized many solutions as being both non-reflective and reflective. The third cluster of components of pedagogies are about students' knowledge acquisition, displaying an option for teachers to design learning activities that either inform students or ask them to learn by experience. Half of the activities are identified as both informative and experiential since the technology resources to be used invites the students only to limited experiential experiences. Despite of a quite extensive supply of tools available for students' learning, technology use is limited to few technology tools that are mainly not complicated to use: Response apps are very easy-to-use for both teachers and students; Lucidchart and Twine is mildly more complicated; Information on Wikipedia is very easy to access. The advantage of those applications is precisely their simplicity and accessibility, requiring little time to comprehend for teachers and students. Time spent on developing the students' specialized digital literacy is thus shortened.

The overall picture given by analyzing the design patterns expose the need for students to develop a specialized digital literacy, that is, to be able to effectively use technology for educational purposes. In use however, the patterns need to be redesigned and none of the mini-learning activities offer quick fixes to teachers' dilemmas, and neither do they present a ready to use instruction for teachers to put into practice. On the contrary, the redesign of design patterns will take the teacher into a process of deciding of how to implement the design pattern into the actual context, and thus create specific learning environments or 'learnplaces' for the students. This highlight both the potentials and dilemmas of design patterns as compared to other approaches.

References

1. Kress, G., Selander, S.: Multimodal design, learning and cultures of recognition. Internet High. Educ. **15**(4), 265–268 (2012)
2. Goodyear, P., Retalis, S.: Learning, technology and design. In: Goodyear, P., Retalis, S. (eds.) Technology-Enhanced Learning: Design Patterns and Pattern Languages, pp. 1–28. Sense, Rotterdam (2010)
3. Mor, Y., Winters, N.: Participatory design in open education: a workshop model for developing a pattern language. J. Interact. Media Educ. **2008**(1) (2008)
4. Laurillard, D.: Teaching as a Design Science. Building Pedagogical Patterns for Learning and Technology. Routledge, New York (2012)
5. Hsueh, N.L., Chu, P.H., Chu, W.: A quantitative approach for evaluating the quality of design patterns. J. Syst. Softw. **81**(8), 1430–1439 (2008)
6. Kohls, C., Köppe, C.: Evaluating the applicability of alexander's fundamental properties to non-architecture domains. In: Baumgartner, P., Sickinger, S. (eds.) PURPLSOC, The Workshop 2014. Department for Interactive Media and Educational Technologies, Danube University Krems (2015)
7. McAndrew, P., Goodyear, P., Dalziel, J.: Patterns, designs and activities: unifying descriptions of learning structures. Int. J. Learn. Technol. **2**(2–3), 216–242 (2006)
8. Alexander, C., Ishikawa, S., Silverstein, M.: A Pattern Language: Towns, Buildings, Construction. Oxford University Press, New York (1977)
9. Finlay, J., Gray, J., Falconer, I., Hensman, J., Mor, Y., Warburton, S.: Planet: pattern language network for web 2.0 in learning. Final project report submitted to JISC (2009)
10. Knutsson, O., Ramberg, R.: Collaborative pattern language representation of designs for learning. In: Proceedings of the 5th International Conference on Designs for Learning, Copenhagen, Denmark (2016)
11. Conole, G., Dyke, M., Oliver, M., Seale, J.: Mapping pedagogy and tools for effective learning design. Comput. Educ. **43**(1), 17–33 (2004)
12. Knutsson, O., Blåsjö, M., Hållsten, S., Karlström, P.: Identifying different registers of digital literacy in virtual learning environments. Internet High. Educ. **15**(4), 237–246 (2012)

Cyberlearning Community Report: Emerging Design Themes in US TEL

Jeremy Roschelle[1], Wendy Martin[2], and Patricia Schank[1(✉)]

[1] SRI International, Center for Technology in Learning, Menlo Park, CA 94025, USA
roschelle@acm.org, patricia.schank@sri.com
[2] EDC, Center for Children and Technology, New York, NY 10014, USA

Abstract. The cyberlearning community in the United States parallels EC-TEL in Europe; both research communities bring computer scientists and learning scientists together to design and study innovative learning technologies. We report on six design themes emerging across multiple US-based, NSF-funded cyberlearning projects, based on the analysis of a team of over a dozen researchers who worked together in 2016 and 2017 to create a more extensive "Cyberlearning Community Report". This work is driving the need for new learning sciences in areas such as embodied cognition, identity, and affect, and requires advances in methods, such as multimodal analytics, and in computer science, such as in context-sensitive computing. By sharing this overview of US-based work with European colleagues at EC-TEL, we aim to foster international connections and stimulate mutual thinking about next steps in research as well as the potential to strengthen positive societal impacts.

Keywords: Cyberlearning · Design · Context

1 Introduction

1.1 What is Cyberlearning?

In the United States, the National Science Foundation (NSF) adopted the name "cyber-learning" to describe research projects that combine advances in emerging technologies with advances in the learning sciences [1]. NSF has funded approximately 220 projects that are tackling different aspects of learning with different technologies, and in different settings, concerned with similar issues, such as: What advances in computation and technology are needed to support complex human endeavors such as learning? How can learning with technology increase access, equity, and the intensity of learning across a range of institutions and settings?

The usage of the term "cyberlearning" parallels how "technology-enhanced learning" has been used to describe European projects with similar aims. At the 2016 EC-TEL conference, our community presented a poster aimed at bridging the EC-TEL and cyberlearning research communities [2]. Following the 2016 conference, The Center for Innovative Research in Cyberlearning (CIRCL), which has a role that is similar to a "knowledge network" in European research communities, organized an extensive

É. Lavoué et al. (Eds.): EC-TEL 2017, LNCS 10474, pp. 588–592, 2017.
DOI: 10.1007/978-3-319-66610-5_69

"Cyberlearning Community Report" to share design themes emerging in cyberlearning research. This poster highlights some of these core themes; readers can download the full report from the CIRCL web site (circlcenter.org) for more details.

2 Six "Genres" of Design

The aspirational goal for cyberlearning research is to understand the implications of a class of designs to inform a range of specific products in the future. To signal this focus on the general and generative, cyberlearning research has adopted the word *genre*. Below we highlight six types of general designs created by cyberlearning researchers that draw upon innovations in learning science and computer science.

2.1 Community Mapping for Learning

Mobile City Science [3] is a curriculum that provides youth innovative mapping and tracking tools to document and share their own lived experiences. MCS occurs "on-the-move," in the city, as well as in classroom and museum spaces. MCS helps young people collect, analyze, and argue from spatial and digital data they collect within different communities, using location-aware and mobile technologies. Youth participating in MCS are generating first person and collaborative accounts of not just living in these communities, but imagining what these places could become from a youth perspective. Designed activities such as historic neighborhood geocaches, mobile augmented reality walking tours, and counter-mapping are not merely novel learning experiences for youth themselves, but "expand[s] adult-centric notions of civic agency and develop[s] participatory mapping practices that elicit young people's knowledge on their own terms" [4]. This genre drives research that connects learning with civic engagement, and has the potential to inform "smart cities" research and technologies to better engage the potential of youth. Methodologically, research about this genre is challenging because it occurs beyond the walls of institutions.

2.2 Playful Learning with Expressive Representations

Projects in this genre focus on developing new forms of play that provide expressive representations. In the Makescape project [5], visitors to the New York Hall of Science play a game-exhibit ("Oztoc") on a digital tabletop. To play the game, visitors must create working electronic circuits which "lure" fish to be cataloged by biologists. The experience emphasizes collaborative play for learning, and a great deal of the exhibit's value is in the discussion that visitors have explaining to each other how to play the game. Another unique aspect of Oztoc is that the project leverages physical blocks on a virtual tabletop so that visitors can see each others' work; by enabling learners to bridge representations, they can engage in deeper scientific and engineering practices while learning to communicate and represent the ideas in ways that feel authentic to them and to the game. Playful learning and expressive representations have long traditions in the learning sciences, but bringing these experiences to less-controlled settings is challenging. The projects press on issues of how interfaces can be designed to support easy entry into playful group engagement while also supporting learning conversations about the play. Using streaming data and AI agents to shape productive play brings forth important technical challenges.

2.3 Classrooms as Digital Performance Spaces

Projects in this genre seek to strongly link play to the process of scientific investigation of phenomena scaled to the size of a typical classroom, where learners adopt roles as collaborative investigators of a shared, public phenomenon [6]. In WallCology, for example, students observe and manipulate biotic and abiotic variables within ecosystems presented as animated habitats occupying the walls of their classroom. The class collectively builds a population relationship web, which they then use as a tool to predict effects of invasive species and environmental change and design sustainable habitats. The investigators showed how embedded phenomena simulations could be integrated with community knowledge construction tools to support multi-week inquiry units. Related work is occuring in informal settings too, for example, with wall sized displays that museum visitors can interact with. This genre re-thinks the role of the spatial context for learning, and puts an emphasis on how multiple people and multiple devices can work smoothly together in the same activity and experience. It pushes HCI research to tackle how combinations of people and machines do productive work together, and learning science research about participation, agency, and the role of spatial context in collaborative learning.

2.4 Virtual Peers and Coaches

Virtual tutors and coaches draw upon sophisticated AI functionalities to create social and pedagogical interactions that support student learning, particularly among youth who may not always be successful in typical classrooms. For example, Justine Cassell and her colleagues have developed artificial agents that help a child tell a story or develop a scientific explanation. The virtual peer can listen and respond to a child in a natural manner and its behavior can be adjusted to explore the effect of peer interaction on learning. Virtual peer technology has been used to explore ways of helping children with autism, engaging children in creating stories, and developing students' language skills in science. This genre drives learning and technology research forward through examination of what it takes for a virtual peer to build *rapport* with a child. Building rapport is technically demanding, requiring multimodal sensing that builds on recent advances in computer vision, signal processing, and machine learn-ing. It also pushes better socio-technical models of how people attend to emotional and social cues while supporting learning [7].

2.5 Remote Scientific Labs

In common with many EC-TEL projects, cyberlearning researchers are exploring the genre of remote scientific labs. Research themes of note include how to support collaboration in remote labs, how to leverage a mix of remote and local labs, and how to support learners with disabilities. See the community report for details.

2.6 Multiuser Touch Interfaces and Collaborative Sketching

Another genre concerns how touch surfaces can be used to support groups of learners in creating informal representations to support knowledge building. This is crucial in engineering education, for example, where developing sketching skills is important for conceptualizing and communicating. See the community report for details.

3 Discussion

To inform greater sharing between US and EC technology-enhanced learning projects, we have reported on six genres of designs that are under investigation by the cyberlearning community. For each genre, there are many individual investigators, projects, and designs; in the interest of space, we have shared one illustrative example for each. With regard to the learning sciences, these designs foster our investigation of affect, embodied learning, identity, and learning across settings and within communities. With regard to technological research, we have found that exploring these genres is fertile with regard to how to design for playful interaction that also has a serious purpose, how to design for multiple people and machine-based agents who work together, and how to leverage multimodal data streams for research. Moving forward, we hope to engage with EC-TEL colleagues to identify research questions that can be answered together in the context of mutual research interests.

Acknowledgements. We thank the authors of the Cyberlearning Community Report: June Ahn, Jodi Asbell-Clarke, Matthew Berland, Catherine Chase, Judith Fusco, Erica Halverson, Kemi Jona, Chad Lane, Emma Mercier, Tom Moher, Amy Ogan, Nichole Pinkard, Joseph Polman, Katie Headrick Taylor, Michelle Wilkerson, and Marcelo Worsley. This material is based in part upon work supported by the National Science Foundation under Grant No. IIS-1233722. Any opinions, findings, and conclusions or recommendations expressed in this material are those of the author(s) and do not necessarily reflect the views of the National Science Foundation.

References

1. National Science Foundation (2008): Fostering Learning in the Networked World: The Cyberlearning Opportunity and Challenge. https://www.nsf.gov/pubs/2008/nsf08204/nsf08204.pdf. Accessed 22 Apr 2017
2. Roschelle, J., Grover, S., Bakia, M.: Introducing the U.S. cyberlearning community. In: Verbert, K., Sharples, M., Klobučar, T. (eds.) EC-TEL 2016. LNCS, vol. 9891, pp. 644–647. Springer, Cham (2016). doi:10.1007/978-3-319-45153-4_82
3. Mobile City Science. http://www.education.uw.edu/mcs/. Last accessed 22 April 2017
4. Gordon, E., Elwood, S., Mitchell, K.: Critical spatial learning: participatory mapping, spatial histories, and youth civic engagement. Children's Geographies **14**, 558–572 (2016)
5. OZTOC. http://nysci.org/tag/oztoc/.Accessed 22 Apr 2017

6. WallCology. https://www.evl.uic.edu/entry.php?id=1944.Accessed 22 Apr 2017
7. Zhao, R., Papangelis, A., Cassell, J.: Towards a dyadic computational model of rapport management for human-virtual agent interaction. In: Bickmore, T., Marsella, S., Sidner, C. (eds.) IVA 2014. LNCS, vol. 8637, pp. 514–527. Springer, Cham (2014). doi: 10.1007/978-3-319-09767-1_62

Towards Personalized Vibrotactile Support for Learning Aikido

Olga C. Santos(✉)

aDeNu Research Group, Artificial Intelligence Department, Computer Science School, UNED, Madrid, Spain
ocsantos@dia.uned.es

Abstract. Aikido is a defensive martial art that involves the acquisition of specific motor skills by practicing the techniques over and over with another learner. Most of existing technological support to learn martial arts track learner's postures or gestures with optical caption techniques and deliver non-personalized visual support about the performance. This paper proposes a sensor-based learning environment that aims to track body and mind interactions when learning Aikido techniques and deliver personalized vibrotactile support when learners' movements differ from the expected performance.

Keywords: Personalization · Adaptation · Psychomotor learning · Motor skills · Martial arts · Aikido · User centered design · TORMES methodology

1 Introduction

Sensor technology can support learning in the three domains proposed by Bloom: cognitive, affective and psychomotor [1]. Efforts have been made to personalize the learning systems in terms of cognitive [2, 3] and affective [4] aspects, but hardly regarding the acquisition of motor skills [5]. The increasing progress in ubiquitous technology makes it possible to track learners' motions in an unobtrusive way [6]. As a result, this technology can potentially serve to build personalized procedural learning systems that sense learners' corporal behavior as they learn specific skilled movements and guide them on how body and limbs should move to achieve the learning goal [5]. For this guidance, vibrotactile support has been proposed elsewhere [7].

2 Background

Aikido is more than just a psychomotor learning domain task [8]. It is a defensive martial art that trains both body and mind and requires learning skilled movements that redirect the momentum of an opponent's attack, so that the attacker is either thrown to the floor or immobilized. Thus, it can help learners "feel" the angular motion and improve their learning of Physics while performing a corporal activity [9].

The learning of Aikido is traditionally developed by watching the execution of the movement by experts and trying to replicate it with a peer. In addition to live sessions

É. Lavoué et al. (Eds.): EC-TEL 2017, LNCS 10474, pp. 593–597, 2017.
DOI: 10.1007/978-3-319-66610-5_70

in the gym (dojo) and recorded videos available on YouTube, there is an interactive tool called Aikido3D [10] that allows the learner to select the angle to visualize the proper execution of Aikido techniques by two virtual characters (built by recording with motion capture the execution of the techniques by real high-degree Aikido practitioners). However, no technological solution has been found that monitors how learners are actually performing the movement, compares it with the expert's execution and suggests corrective feedback that can be felt by the learner herself while performing the movement and thus, guides her towards mastery. Most existing systems for learning martial arts only track -with optical caption techniques- learner's postures or gestures replicated by facing the instructor who performs them, and deliver non-personalized visual support about the performance [11]. However, other kinds of sensorial support such as haptic may be more effective [12]. For instance, vibrotactile cues can reduce motion errors while learning simple arm motion [13].

3 A Proposal for Personalized Vibrotactile Support in Aikido

Vibrotactile feedback can be used to deliver information on how to perform a particular task (e.g., which muscles to contract, what joints to rotate and at what instance, etc.) comparing the difference between the target and the current movement, and it is especially appropriate for dynamic situations [14]. It is aimed to reduce workload of the visual and auditory system and the vibration can be meant either to pull the body part toward the signal or to push it away (polarity preferences are individual) [12].

Vibrotactile feedback needs to be communicated to the learner that is training her motor skills through the user interface of the learning system. Thus, the user interface should involve the haptic sense. A haptic input could collect users' movement information from sensors in devices worn by users on their bodies and the output could be 3D and deliver vibrations on learners' body. In addition, an approximation to the state of the mind while learning Aikido could be obtained with affective computing techniques that, among others, can consider diverse physiological signals [4].

Figure 1 proposes a high level architecture for a sensor-based learning system for Aikido that collects inertial and physiological data to deliver personalized vibrotactile support both for attacker (uke) and defender (tori), taking into account the modeling required for the personalization issues, as discussed in [7].

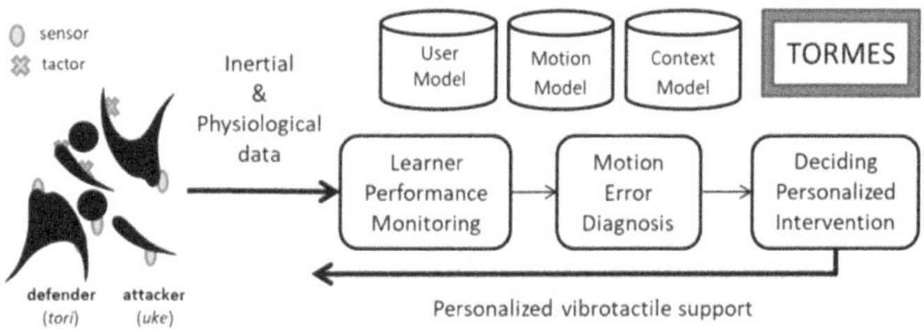

Fig. 1. Processing and modeling steps for a sensor-based learning system for Aikido

As discussed in [11], inertial sensors to monitor motion in martial arts systems have been considered in [15–18], while vibrotactile support has been provided in [19, 20] to correct body pose. However, no martial arts system has been found that both collects motion information with inertial and physiological sensors and delivers vibrotactile support. Furthermore, the personalization issues required have not been investigated yet. For this, the first stage of the TORMES user-centered design elicitation methodology [21] (i.e., context of use) has been run to contextualize the users' needs, one of the seven Garret's classical elements of user experience [22]. In particular, both a questionnaire and a focus group were used to gather information.

The questionnaire was sent online to Aikido practitioners in 3 dojos of Madrid (Spain) and asked, among other issues, if they would like to receive meaningful vibrations on their body when performing techniques well or bad. 20 responses were anonymously received (85% men, age range 14-63, 70% +3 years of practice). Only about half of the responses considered that vibrotactile feedback seemed appropriate for them, while most of them preferred to visually watch their performance on a video compared to the correct one. Although the sample was small for statistical purposes, it served to question if this findings were leading to a similar situation as the "faster horse" innovation paradox (i.e., users were not being properly asked to be able to elicit their real needs).

To clarify what the situation was, a focus group was set up with 4 participants that had previously answered the questionnaire (2 men and 2 women, age range 34-39, +7 years of practice). First, they were explained in detail about the proposed approach (as described in Fig. 1). After that, they were asked their opinions about the vibrotactile support. Benefits for the delivery of vibrotactile support were identified, such as: i) it does not force to be looking at a specific direction but users can concentrate on the movements to perform, ii) it does not disturb other users that may be practicing together, and iii) it helps to physically engage in the learning process. The discussion also served to identify different kinds of support that might be useful during Aikido practice: 1) feedback during (of after) the execution of the movement that shows performance and can serve either for error awareness or consolidating accurate movements, and 2) guidance on what to do next (i.e., feed forward).

4 Conclusions

This paper outlines a proposal for a personalized psychomotor learning environment for Aikido martial art. It relies on both inertial and physiological information to support the training of body and mind and delivers personalized vibrations to improve the movements' execution. User, motion and context models account for adapted individual support. In this way the system can support learning the correct performance of the movements (in terms of physical variables, such as speed, force, direction, duration, etc. as well as affective state) depending on learners' specific features and goals.

References

1. Schneider, J., Börner, D., van Rosmalen, P., Specht, M.: Augmenting the senses: a review on sensor-based learning support. Sensors **15**, 4097–4133 (2015)
2. Kulik, J.A., Fletcher, J.D.: Effectiveness of intelligent tutoring systems. a meta-analytic review. Rev. Educ. Res. **86**(1), 42–78 (2016)
3. Drachsler, H., Verbert, K., Santos, O.C., Manouselis, N.: Panorama of recommender systems to support learning. In: Ricci, F., Rokach, L., Shapira, B. (eds.) Recommender Systems Handbook, pp. 421–451. Springer, Boston, MA (2015). doi:10.1007/978-1-4899-7637-6_12
4. Santos, O.C.: Emotions and personality in adaptive e-learning systems: an affective computing perspective. In: Tkalčič, M., De Carolis, B., de Gemmis, M., Odić, A., Košir, A. (eds.) Emotions and Personality in Personalized Services. HIS, pp. 263–285. Springer, Cham (2016). doi:10.1007/978-3-319-31413-6_13
5. Santos, O.C.: Training the body: the potential of aied to support personalized motor skills learning. Int. J. Artif. Intell. Educ. **26**(2), 730–755 (2016)
6. Martinez-Maldonado, R., Yacef, K., Dias Pereira Dos Santos, A., Shum, S.B., Echeverria, V., Santos, O.C., Pechenizkiy, M.: Towards Proximity Tracking and Sensemaking for Supporting Teamwork and Learning. In: ICALT 2017. IEEE Proceedings (2017, accepted)
7. Santos, O.C.: Toward personalized vibrotactile support when learning motor skills. Algorithms **10**(1), 15 (2017)
8. Santos, O.C.: Education still needs artificial intelligence to support motor skill learning. a case study with Aikido. In: AIED 2015 workshops, CEUR, vol. 1432, no. 4, pp. 72–81 (2015)
9. Mroczkowski, A.: Using the knowledge of biomechanics in teaching Aikido. In: Goswami, T. (ed.) Injury and Skeletal Biomechanics. Intech, Osaka (2012)
10. Aikido3D: http://www.aikido3d.com/
11. Santos, O.C.: Psychomotor learning in martial arts: an opportunity for user modelling, adaptation and personalization. In: UMAP 2017 Adjunct proceedings. ACM (2017, accepted)
12. Sigrist, R., Rauter, G., Riener, R., Wolf, P.: Augmented visual, auditory, haptic, and multimodal support in motor learning: a review. Psychon. Bull. Rev. **20**, 21–53 (2013)
13. Bark, K., Hyman, E., Tan, F., Cha, E., Jax, S.A., Buxbaum, L.J., Kuchenbecker, K.J.: Effects of Vibrotactile Feedback on Human Learning of Arm Motions. IEEE Trans. Neural Syst. Rehabil. Eng. **23**, 51–63 (2015)
14. Alahakone, A.U., Senanayake, S.M.N.A.: Vibrotactile feedback systems: Current trends in rehabilitation, sports and information display. In: Proceedings of IEEE/ASME International Conference on Advanced Intelligent Mechatronics, Singapore, pp. 1148–1153, 14–17 July 2009
15. Heinz, E.A., Kunze, K.S., Gruber, M., Bannach, D., Lukowicz, P.: Using wearable sensors for real-time recognition tasks in games of martial arts - an initial experiment. In: IEEE Symposium on Computational Intelligence and Games, 2016, pp. 98–102 (2016)
16. Kunze, K., Barry, M., Heinz, E.A., Lukowicz, P., Majoe, D., Gutknecht, J.: Towards recognizing Tai Chi - an initial experiment using wearable sensors. In: 3rd International Forum on Applied Wearable Computing 2006, pp. 1–6 (2006)
17. Kwon, D.Y., Gross, M.: Combining body sensors and visual sensors for motion training. In: Proceedings of Advances in Computer Entertainment Technology 2005, pp. 94–101 (2005)
18. Takahata, M., Shiraki, K., Sakane, Y., Takebayashi, Y.: Sound feedback for powerful karate training. In: Conference on New interfaces for musical expression (NIME 2004), pp. 13–18 (2004)

19. Portillo-Rodriguez, O., Sandoval-Gonzalez, O.O., Ruffaldi, E., Leonardi, R., Avizzano, C.A., Bergamasco, M.: Real-time gesture recognition, evaluation and feed-forward correction of a multimodal tai-chi platform. In: Pirhonen, A., Brewster, S. (eds.) HAID 2008. LNCS, vol. 5270, pp. 30–39. Springer, Heidelberg (2008). doi:10.1007/978-3-540-87883-4_4
20. Bloomfield, A., Badler, N.: Virtual training via vibrotactile arrays. Teleoper. Virtual Environ. **17**, 103–120 (2008)
21. Santos, O.C., Boticario, J.G.: Practical guidelines for designing and evaluating educationally oriented recommendations. Comput. Educ. **81**, 354–374 (2015)
22. Garrett, J.J.: The Elements of User Experience: User-Centered Design for the Web and Beyond. New Riders, Berkeley (2002)

Interoperable Adaptivity and Learning Analytics for Serious Games in Image Interpretation

Alexander Streicher(✉) and Wolfgang Roller

Fraunhofer IOSB, Karlsruhe, Germany
{Alexander.streicher,Wolfgang.roller}@iosb.fraunhofer.de

Abstract. Personalization and adaptivity in computer simulations and serious games are being used to achieve positive long term effects on the users' engagement, motivation and ultimately on the learning outcome. Interoperability regarding the collection of usage data allows for an effective analysis of the interaction and learning progress data. This paper presents an interoperable adaptivity framework combined with a web-based tutoring interface which gives learning analytics insights. The developed framework "E-Learning A.I." (ELAI) acts as an intelligent tutoring agent for simulations and serious games and uses the Experience API (xAPI) protocol. The application of the ELAI has been demonstrated in an adaptive map-based learning game for aerial image interpretation. The scientific research questions affect the possible usages of the collected interaction data, how to manifest adaptivity in games, how to realize interoperable adaptivity mechanisms for simulations and serious games, and how to make use of collected usage data.

Keywords: E-learning · Adaptivity · Interoperability · Serious games · Image interpretation

1 Introduction

This paper describes an adaptivity framework for serious games and simulations. Adaptivity in this paper means the continuous adaptation of serious games and computer simulations to the needs of the learners, i.e., interaction mechanisms, content or recommendations are episodically personalized by an automatic intelligent tutoring component. Adaptive serious games and computer simulations for training should keep the users motivated to ultimately increase the learning or training outcome. The users should be kept in an immersive state. For simulations and games user engagement can be achieved by adapting the simulations and games to the needs of the users and by keeping them immersed, e.g., by balancing the adaptivity inside the *Flow Channel* [1,2].

The contribution of this paper is the description of the further developed ELAI concept [9] with focus on the adaptivity technologies, its application and the tutor interface for learning analytics. The problem statement is that in current computer simulations and digital game based learning systems little or no

É. Lavoué et al. (Eds.): EC-TEL 2017, LNCS 10474, pp. 598–601, 2017.
DOI: 10.1007/978-3-319-66610-5_71

concepts for didactic adaptivity exist [10]. Which interaction usage data can be used for adaptivity and how to manifest that adaptivity in real games? How to realize interoperable adaptivity mechanisms for simulations and serious games? The proposed ELAI framework is designed to enable interoperable adaptivity to the attached game engines and games or computer simulations, and to enable tutors to monitor the users' progress. The application domain of this research is e-learning for aerial image interpretation for reconnaissance, i.e., the identification and analysis of structures and objects by experts (image interpreters) according to a given task on basis of imagery data [8].

Similar to our approach is the ISAT architecture [4], which provides trainees with a story-wise individualized training environment. Another similar examples for decentralized adaptive architectures are the ALIGN architecture [7], the test and training architecture TENA [5] or the CIGA middleware [6]. A similar architecture also using the xAPI but mainly for learning or gaming analytics (and not directly for adaptivity) can be found in the RAGE EU project [11]. Though multiple overlaps exist between the aforementioned architectures and our ELAI framework, our approach focuses on a holistic interoperability architecture for both learning analytics and adaptivity.

2 Interoperable Adaptivity - E-Learning A.I. (ELAI)

Our interoperable adaptive framework "E-Learning A.I." (ELAI) provides adaptivity to attached simulations or serious games [9]. Its characteristic features are its interoperability aspects and the externalization of the tutoring agent (Fig. 1). The software architecture decouples a game engine from the adaptivity component which typically is built into (adaptive) simulations or serious games in a monolithic fashion. It consists of a game engine adapter to capture usage data and to present the adapted content. At its core it has an intelligent tutoring controller which interprets the collected data to adjust the simulations or games [10]. A web-based interface provides tutors with learning analysis insights, e.g., diagrams on the task and learning progress, learning profiles classifications, or features to control the level of adaption for specific users.

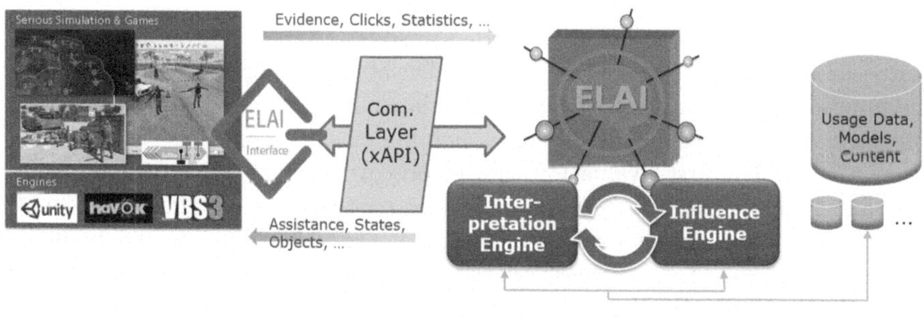

Fig. 1. ELAI framework

The game engine adapter is specific to each engine, genre and game. Its main purpose is to bidirectionally communicate with the ELAI controller, i.e., it collects data on the users' interaction, on the game, on the scene and on the game objects. On the way back it modifies the game, e.g., it "injects" a virtual agent which gives recommendations, or it makes in-game modification to game objects or of the game flow, i.e., modification of the underlying state machines. The communication layer mediates the data between the game (game engine) and the ELAI controller, and it uses the e-learning interoperability protocol *Experience API* (xAPI). The tutoring component, the ELAI controller, is the central "intelligent" element of the ELAI framework. It has an interpretation engine (for usage data analysis) and an influence engine (to select adequate reactions). Both can make use of artificial intelligence technologies. In our prototype we implemented rule-based heuristics and k-means clustering. The rule-based heuristics are used to determine the learners' state to get a performance score which is used by the adaptation (influence) component. Clustering is used to dynamically find difficulty levels (i.e., the borders) and classify new learners according to that levels. In contrast to other e-learning systems we propose to use a flat user model which basically is a collection of all user interaction data in the xAPI/Activity Stream format. Additional extracted "higher information" from the *Didactic Factors* [3] is stored in that collection as special xAPI statements as well.

We implemented a software prototype in a serious game for image interpretation. The game's objective has the serious background to train image interpreters to correctly differentiate various vehicle types which could differ by very subtle differences, e.g., by just an additional antenna. The implemented didactic factors to analyze the player's state are the overall task duration, the task difficulty and the task helping count. The weighted linear combination of these factors yields an index value which is used as helping level and adaptivity trigger. Techniques for dynamic difficulty adaptation for image interpretation have been realized, e.g., blurring, noise, partial occlusion, deterioration by compression artifacts, etc. The helping level controls how often and in which quality the virtual agent offers context-relevant textual hints, i.e., at the lowest level the agent is passive, whereas at the highest level the agent pro-actively offers navigational hints.

As the ELAI architecture makes use of the xAPI protocol, tools for learning analytics can be attached. For instance, this allows to report on the number of successfully completed game sessions or on the frequency of some interactions. Such type of reports are already included in some xAPI *Learning Record Stores* (LRS) or in some xAPI tools (e.g., xAPI Dashboard). For the ELAI we added the functionality to manually control the adaptivity parameters via a web-based interface, e.g., control on the difficulty, helping or skill level.

Evidence of a first evaluation of the prototype show that the adaptivity mechanisms are positively recognized by the participants. Further work has to address issues with the current realization of the virtual agent - it should be triggered on-demand only. However, the adaptively adjusted helping level and the quality of the hints showed to be appropriate. The web-based tutor interface was well accepted and rated as helpful to interpret the learners' progress.

3 Summary

This paper presents the interoperable adaptivity framework for simulations and serious games, called "E-Learning A.I." (ELAI). The solution approach is a decentralized software architecture which decouples game engines from internal adaptivity components which typically are monolithically built into (adaptive) simulations or serious games. The architecture consists of a game engine adapter and a communication layer to capture data and to present adapted content. At its core is an intelligent tutoring controller (the ELAI controller) which interprets the collected data to adjust the simulations or games. The architecture has been verified in a seek-and-find game for image interpretation. Future work will address other games and simulations as well as further analysis of usage data.

Acknowledgments. The underlying project to this article is funded by the Federal Office of Bundeswehr Equipment, Information Technology and In-Service Support under promotional references. The authors are responsible for the content of this article.

References

1. Chen, J.: Flow in games (and everything else). ACM **50**(4), 31–34 (2007)
2. Csikszentmihalyi, M., Abuhamdeh, S., Nakamura, J.: Flow and the Foundations of Positive Psychology. Springer, Berlin (2014)
3. Henning, P., Heberle, F., Fuchs, K., Swertz, C.: INTUITEL - Intelligent tutoring interface for technology enhanced learning. In: PALE Workshop (2014)
4. Magerko, B., Stensrud, B.S., Holt, L.S.: Bringing the schoolhouse inside the box - a tool for engaging individualized training. In: 25th Army Science Conference (2006)
5. Noseworthy, J.R.: The test and training enabling architecture (TENA) supporting the decentralized development of distributed applications and LVC simulations. In: IEEE/ACM DS-RT Symposium, pp. 259–268 (2008)
6. Oijen, J., Vanhée, L., Dignum, F.: CIGA: a middleware for intelligent agents in virtual environments. In: Beer, M., Brom, C., Dignum, F., Soo, V.-W. (eds.) AEGS 2011. LNCS (LNAI), vol. 7471, pp. 22–37. Springer, Heidelberg (2012). doi:10.1007/978-3-642-32326-3_2
7. Peirce, N., Conlan, O., Wade, V.: Adaptive educational games: providing non-invasive personalised learning experiences. In: DIGITEL, pp. 28–35. IEEE (2008)
8. Roller, W., Berger, A., Szentes, D.: Technology based training for radar image interpreters. In: RAST, pp. 1173–1177. IEEE (2013)
9. Streicher, A., Roller, W.: Towards an interoperable adaptive tutoring agent for simulations and serious games. In: MCCSIS TPMC, pp. 194–197. IADIS (2015)
10. Streicher, A., Smeddinck, J.D.: Personalized and adaptive serious games. In: Dörner, R., Göbel, S., Kickmeier-Rust, M., Masuch, M., Zweig, K. (eds.) Entertainment Computing and Serious Games. LNCS, vol. 9970, pp. 332–377. Springer, Cham (2016). doi:10.1007/978-3-319-46152-6_14
11. Van Der Vegt, W., Westera, W., Nyamsuren, E., Georgiev, A., Ortiz, I.M.: RAGE architecture for reusable serious gaming technology components. Int. J. Comput. Games Technol. (2016)

Opeka and Ropeka, the Self-assessing Services for Teachers and Principals

Erika Tanhua-Piiroinen(✉) and Jarmo Viteli

University of Tampere, Kanslerinrinne 1, 33014 Tampere, Finland
{erika.tanhua-piiroinen,jarmo.viteli}@uta.fi

Abstract. Digitalization has strongly arrived to school communities. Teachers and principals are the key players on changing the school culture, so it is important to find out their views on the school's digital ecosystem. For getting a joint picture on the matter, self-assessment tools Opeka and Ropeka have been developed. Opeka has been in use five years now and Ropeka for principals has been launched in the beginning of year 2017. To make the analysis of school's digital ecosystem more accurate, we have put at least one question from Opeka into Ropeka's every theme section. Doing this we can connect the views of these two respondent groups and get richer point of view to the phenome in hand. How well are teachers and principals prepared to the digital environment change at schools? How do they assess themselves and how do they experience the changing modus operandi with, for example, digital books and tests as well as new teaching practices? In our poster, we will introduce the tools and show the first results from both of the key respondent groups.

Keywords: Teachers' and principals' self-evaluation · Digital skills and attitudes · Evidence based school development · Differences among teachers' and principals' self-evaluation

1 Digitalization in School Environment

Digitalization is reaching to every part of the societies and has strongly arrived to school communities too. It is a constant process. Many kinds of skills are needed in education, when available technologies continuously change (See for example The NMC Horizon Project reviews[1]), and new generations of pupils and students arrive to school. In Finland, "digital literacy" is included into the national curriculum (Finnish National Agency for Education 2014) and the Finnish government has raised for example "*New learning environments and digital materials to comprehensive schools*" for one of the key projects during the government term (Finnish government 2015).

Teachers act usually quite independent with their pupils in classes, though teamwork and collaboration between colleagues have increased recently. They may share their impressions and experiences during every day work with each other but still cannot easily see the full picture of the whole organization. As for the principals, having a

[1] https://www.nmc.org/nmc-horizon/.

É. Lavoué et al. (Eds.): EC-TEL 2017, LNCS 10474, pp. 602–605, 2017.
DOI: 10.1007/978-3-319-66610-5_72

different job description from teachers, they might not be so well aware of every part of teachers' working environment in practice. For getting a joint picture of the school ecosystem (Zhao and Frank 2003), special self-assessment tools called Opeka[2] (Sairanen et al. 2013) and Ropeka[3] have been developed. Other tools have been made or are being planned Europe-wide, too, for helping reflection on digitalization in educational contexts, like The Joint Research Centre (JRC) with SELFIE[4] or Mentep from Europen Schoolnet[5]. However, in this presentation we introduce Opeka, which has been utilized in a large scale in Finland already 5 years now, together with "newcomer" Ropeka. We show the first results where both teachers' and principals' answers on self-assessment tools are put side by side.

2 Self-assessment Tools

The idea behind the service has been scaffolding the self-reflection according to the Kolb's (1984) learning cycle (Sairanen et al. 2013). In this context it means that information and communication technology (ICT) use is first evaluated with the help of the web service, then the results are reflected on school and organizational level, after which plans are made in form of ICT development strategies and then the plans are executed in practice. Thus, when the self-assessment results will be made visible in the school and the municipality level, both the people in the management team and the whole school community are able to develop together their digital learning and working environment. Transparent self-assessment results help in decision making for stakeholders and planning of in-service training for different occupational groups.

2.1 Opeka for Teachers

Opeka is an online tool with background questions and four questionnaires with different themes. Those themes are *Digital operating environment, Organizational culture, Pedagogical activities* and *Competences*. After completing the background questions other questionnaires, including mainly numerical questions can be finished in free order. When at least one of the questionnaires has been finished, the respondent gets his or her own results and feedback compared with other respondents. Opeka has been in use from year 2012 and the reports from every year after that can be compared easily as the data is saved in one single database.

2.2 Ropeka for Principals

Ropeka questionnaire has been developed according to the same philosophy as Opeka, but where Opeka is a tool for teachers and educators, Ropeka is targeted for principals.

[2] http://opeka.fi.
[3] http://ropeka.fi.
[4] https://ec.europa.eu/jrc/en/digcomporg/selfie-tool.
[5] http://mentep.eun.org/.

Ropeka has been developed in collaboration with a focus group of principals and school leaders and it has been open from January 2017 forward. The service consists of four themes, each having one so-called rubric question and some statements in 5 points Likert-scale. Each section has also one open-ended question. With the description in rubric question, the respondent is asked to position his or her school to the level he or she is thinking they in this moment are (in the beginning, under way, advanced or in target). The Likert-scale questions then complement the picture.

Themes of Ropeka are *Strategy, Engagement in change, Creating a new organizational culture* and *Competence development*. In addition to the foregoing there is a section called *My school's digital operating environment*, which collect data about devices in use, network resources, available tutor teachers and helpdesk services. After finishing at least one of the questionnaires, the respondent receives feedback about his or her results and comparison is available with other respondents.

2.3 Reports in School and Municipality Level

Both Opeka and the newer Ropeka give also reports for administration and ICT-personnel in municipality or school level. Reports for managers (like principals or ICT development team members) include graphs, visualizations and analyzes of the data. There are also links to associated reports, as school in the municipality, which managers can share to relevant quarters. Reports are structured hierarchically too:

> *"– municipality report contains all the data collected from respondents that have selected the particular municipality as their primary place of work; school report contains the data with the particular municipality and school; office report contains data with the particular municipality, school and office. In addition, region report contains data from a group of municipalities and area report contains data from a group of schools."* (Sairanen et al. 2013).

Altogether, these reports give a rich view on the digitalization process in school community and they can be utilized in developing the learning environment to better meet the conditions of modern digitized society.

2.4 What We Can Research with Opeka and Ropeka?

With the self-assessing tools, we can explore the changes in (1) school cultures and strategies, (2) pedagogical activities, (3) digital operating environments and (4) personnel's digital competence. For making the analysis more accurate, we have put at least one question from Opeka into every Ropeka's theme section. Doing this we can compare the views of these two respondent groups on same questions and get richer viewpoint to the phenome in hand. The exactly same questions and the results on them are presented in Table 1. There is also an item: "Choose the level that best describes your competence in terms of ICT use." in both questionnaires.

Table 1. Teachers' and principals' answers on same questions.

Positive answers (agree or strongly agree)		
Question	Opeka	Ropeka
"Our school has a jointly agreed goal for utilizing ICT in teaching"	45%	73%
"In my school it is easy to start developing new procedures"	64%	87%
"My school has peer teachers offering ICT instruction"	78%	89%
"ICT skills are discussed as part of performance reviews"	54%	91%

3 First Results: Teachers' and Principals' Views

In the first findings from data collected in 2017 (N (Opeka) = 7771, N (Ropeka) = 511) we have seen that the principals seem to assess their digital school culture more positively than the teacher respondents do (Table 1).

One of the reasons may be that the principals possibly describe their school from the visions they have and the teachers more practically as they have experienced themselves. This is, however, an interesting observation, and in our poster, we will describe the results from Opeka and Ropeka more detailed.

References

Finnish government: Finland, a land of solutions. Strategic Programme of Prime Minister Juha Sipilä's Government, 29 May 2015. Government Publications 12/2015. Traslated in English 2016 (2016). http://valtioneuvosto.fi/en/sipila/government-programme. Accessed 26 June 2017

Finnish National Agency for Education: The new curricula in a nutshell (2014). http://www.oph.fi/english/curricula_and_qualifications/basic_education/curricula_2014. Accessed 22 June 2017

Kolb, D.: Experiential Learning: Experience as the Source of Learning and Development. Prentice Hall, Englewood Cliffs (1984)

Sairanen, H., Vuorinen, M., Viteli, J.: Collecting and using data to develop digital learning culture at school. Presented in TEPE 2013 conference (2013). http://blogs.helsinki.fi/tepe-2013/files/2013/12/Sairanen_Vuorinen_Viteli_Collecting-and-Using-data-to-Develop-Digital-Learning-Culture-at-School.pdf. Accessed 22 June 2017

Zhao, Y., Frank, K.A.: Factors affecting technology uses in schools: an ecological perspective. Am. Educ. Res. J. **40**(4), 807–840 (2003)

Semantic Boggle: A Game for Vocabulary Acquisition

Irina Toma[1], Cristina-Elena Alexandru[1], Mihai Dascalu[1,2(✉)], Philippe Dessus[3], and Stefan Trausan-Matu[1,2]

[1] Faculty of Automatic Control and Computers, University "Politehnica" of Bucharest, 313 Splaiul Independenţei, 60042 Bucharest, Romania
irina_toma@rocketmail.com, elena.cristina.alexandru@gmail.com, {mihai.dascalu,stefan.trausan}@cs.pub.ro

[2] Academy of Romanian Scientists, Splaiul Independenţei 54, 050094 Bucharest, Romania

[3] Laboratoire des Sciences de l'Éducation, Univ. Grenoble Alpes, F38000 Grenoble, France
philippe.dessus@univ-grenoble-alpes.fr

Abstract. Learning a new language is a difficult endeavor, the main encountered problem being vocabulary acquisition. The learning process can be improved through visual representations of coherent contexts, best represented in serious games. The game described in this paper, *Semantic Boggle*, is a serious game that exercises vocabulary. It is based on the traditional word-guessing game, but it brings educational value by identifying semantically-related words. The words are found using the *ReaderBench* framework and are placed in the game grid using a greedy algorithm. The assigned score is computed as the semantic similarity value multiplied by the normalized length of the seed. Our preliminary validation consisted of 20 users, who emphasized its interest and playability.

Keywords: Serious games · Vocabulary acquisition · Semantic games · Word-guessing · Boggle · Language learning

1 Introduction

When learning a new language, people are overwhelmed by the amount of information they should assimilate. This lowers the learners' confidence in their progress and their ability to communicate in a certain language. In order to overcome this, different techniques for vocabulary acquisition have been developed. Traditional techniques focus on memorizing words, using them for translating sentences and expressing grammatical rules, while newer ones propose visual support (i.e., flashcards), group listening activities, or pre-reading activities [1].

Learners, whatever their learning habits and skills are, memorize words used to express their ideas and understand conversations, develop strategies for coping with unknown words and take responsibility for vocabulary expansion [2]. However, each learning technique should be personalized for each individual, and previous knowledge should be integrated with new concepts through comparison, combination, matchmaking and visual concept representation [3].

É. Lavoué et al. (Eds.): EC-TEL 2017, LNCS 10474, pp. 606–609, 2017.
DOI: 10.1007/978-3-319-66610-5_73

2 Vocabulary Games – Serious Games Focused on Language

Vocabulary games help learners assimilate words. This process is influenced by the number of times learners are exposed to a word and to its different definitions. If words are not exercised, they do not end up in long-term memory and are easily forgotten [4]. We believe these two challenges can be solved with serious games that behave as a tool for revising vocabulary, in order to adapt its difficulty level to the learner's background.

A game of particular interest for this paper is *MagicWord* [5], a word searching, Boggle-like game that exercises the inflection forms of one language. An alternative gameplay was probed within the E-LOCAL project (https://e-localcourses.unibo.it/) [6], which focuses on the meaning of words, instead of morphology. The experiments with the latter approach showed the need to personalize the game; therefore, an authoring tool was created, allowing teachers and learners to create their own games with user generated content.

3 Semantic Boggle

Boggle is a word game in which players connect neighboring letters in a 4 × 4 grid. The game is won by the player who finds the longest words. This is a board game, played for fun, but it can be added educational value by looking for specific words or relations between words. The letter arrangement in the 4 × 4 grid must be predefined and, at the same time, various versions of the grid must be generated. This is a difficult task to be done manually and *Semantic Boggle*, our serious game, was created for that purpose. The main idea of the game is that the grid is populated with semantically-related words, starting from a given word. The algorithm behind the game is described below.

1. *Choose the starting word* (*seed*). The word is chosen randomly from a given lexicon, with the condition that its word length is less than 5 characters.
2. *Populate the game grid with the seed* (see Fig. 1). First, a random cell is selected as the starting point for generating the word. Then, each move is randomly generated, with the conditions that the cells are neighbors and an already filled-in cell cannot be occupied. If the algorithm reaches a dead end, where at least one cell cannot be filled-in, the grid is rolled-back to the previous step.
3. *Find and filter semantically similar concepts*. For this step, we use a dedicated web service offered by *ReaderBench*, a framework designed for advanced text analysis [7, 8], to find semantically similar concepts. This service takes as input: a) the seed (the start word), b) the used language (English or French), c) the employed method (e.g., semantic distances in lexical databases – WordNet and WOLF (Wordnet Libre du Français) –, Latent Semantic Analysis – LSA and Latent Dirichlet Allocation – LDA) and d) the corresponding corpus (e.g., TASA or "*Le Monde*" – http://lsa.colorado.edu/spaces.html). The web service outputs a list of similar words and their semantic similarity score using LSA as a semantic model. For the next step only words less than 8 characters, with a similarity score higher than .3 are retained.
4. *Populate the game grid*. The same greedy algorithm used during the second step is used for the other words. If, by any chance, the word cannot be filled-in in 20 moves,

the current word is abandoned. In a next iteration of our game, an improvement will be made, similar to the *MagicWord* grid population algorithm [6]. It consists of identifying a common substring, regardless of its position, in the words from the grid and the current word, enabling the re-usage of letters.

5. *Score words selected by the user*. Each selected word is scored as in Eq. (1), which takes into account the normalized length of the identified words, as well as their semantic similarity. Words that are not similar to the game seed are scored 0, thus guiding the user to converge towards the initial seed word.

$$Score = (1 + ln(length\_lemma)) \text{ x } semantic\_similarity(seed, selected\_word) \quad (1)$$

6. *Finish condition*. The goal of our game consists of identifying the lexical field of the seed word. Once users discover this seed, they have the option of going to the next round, or continuing the game to find additional semantically-related words.

Graphical User Interface. *Semantic Boggle* is a minimalistic web application, where the user forms words by selecting letters from the 4 x 4 grid. The current word is sent to the *ReaderBench* web server together with the seed in order to compute a semantic similarity score. This latter value is then added to the initial score. For keeping track of the used words, checked words are available in the list under *Used Words* and are highlighted based on the similarity with the seed (see Fig. 1).

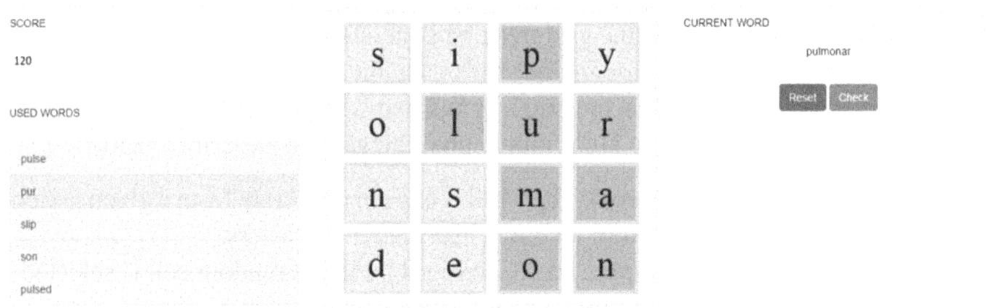

Fig. 1. *Semantic Boggle* – Gameplay print-screen.

4 Results and Discussions

A group of 20 users (60% males) aged 20–27 were asked to play *Semantic Boggle* and provide feedback regarding the gameplay. The users were asked to answer a 10 questions survey with ratings on a 5-point Likert Scale (1 – completely disagree; 5 – completely agree) covering users' perspective on *Semantic Boggle*. Based on all participants' ratings, average intra-class correlation (ICC) was .908 and Cronbach's alpha was .911 denoting a high agreement among the raters. Of particular interest were two questions that demonstrated the adequacy and appeal of our approach: '*Did you enjoy the game?*' (mean = 4.66; SD = 0.478) and '*Did the list of wrong/correct words helped you?*' (mean = 4.26; *SD* = 0.593). From the three free-answer questions, the general feedback was players appreciated the simplicity of the game and considered it challenging and educative. Two users even agreed it is addictive. As improvements, 50% of the users suggested enhancing the graphical interface, 20% considered adding more complicated words and making them harder to find, and three users proposed personalizing the game based on the background players' knowledge.

Considering the feedback, the most important aspect to improve is the graphical interface, which will be enhanced in terms of usability and design. Second, the algorithm will search for common stubs in order to better fill-in the grid. This will enable teachers to set a list of predefined words to be used, based on the concepts taught and the similar words inferred using *ReaderBench*.

Summing up, *Semantic Boggle* brings a new flavor to the classic *Boggle* game, where an educational aspect is added to the old gameplay. This consists of populating the 4 x 4 grid with semantically-related words, plus scoring learners based on their ability to identify a cohesive context around the seed word. Suggestions for similar words are provided by the dedicated web service available from *ReaderBench* framework, which also includes the capability to assess semantic relatedness. Preliminary validation proved that the concept of the game was appealing to learners. Based on their feedback, a more attractive graphical interface will be implemented, together with a modification of the grid generation algorithm.

Acknowledgment. This work was partially funded by the FP7 2008-212578 LTfLL project, by the 644187 EC H2020 *Realising an Applied Gaming Eco-system* (RAGE) project and by University Politehnica of Bucharest through the Excellence Research Grants Program UPB–GEX 12/26.09.2016. We want also to thank Mathieu Loiseau for all his helpful insights.

References

1. Common European Framework of Reference for Languages: Learning, Teaching, Assessment. Council of Europe. Cambridge University Press, Cambridge (2000)
2. Přibilová, L.: Teaching vocabulary to young learners. English Language and Literature, p. 46. Masaryk University, Brno (2006)
3. Thornbury, S.: How to teach vocabulary, vol. 1. Pearson Education India, Longman, Harlow (2006)
4. Carter, R., McCarthy, M.: Vocabulary and language teaching. Routledge, NY (2014)
5. Loiseau, M., Zampa, V., Rebourgeon, P.: Magic Word – premier jeu développé dans le cadre du projet Innovalangues. In: ALSIC, vol. 18, no. 2 (2015)
6. Roccetti, M., Salomoni, P., Loiseau, M., Masperi, M., Zampa, V., Ceccherelli, A., Cervini, C., Valva, A.: On the design of a word game to enhance Italian language learning. In: International Conference on Computing, Networking and Communications (ICNC), pp. 1–5. IEEE (2016)
7. Dascalu, M., Dessus, P., Bianco, M., Trausan-Matu, S., Nardy, A.: Mining texts, learner productions and strategies with *ReaderBench*. In: Peña-Ayala, A. (ed.) Educational Data Mining. SCI, vol. 524, pp. 345–377. Springer, Cham (2014). doi: 10.1007/978-3-319-02738-8_13
8. Dascalu, M.: Analyzing Discourse and Text Complexity for Learning and Collaborating. SCI, vol. 534. Springer, Cham, Switzerland (2014)

NAPP: Connecting Mentors and Students at Técnico Lisboa

Pedro Veiga(✉), Alberto Sardinha(✉), Ana Moura Santos(✉), and Carla Boura(✉)

Instituto Superior Técnico, Universidade de Lisboa,
Taguspark Av. Prof. Dr. Cavaco Silva, 2744-016 Porto Salvo, Portugal
{pedro.veiga,alberto.sardinha,ana.moura.santos,
carla.boura}@tecnico.ulisboa.pt
https://tecnico.ulisboa.pt/en/

Abstract. In the past five years, a successful first-year mentoring programme at Técnico Lisboa's Taguspark campus promoted by Núcleo de Apoio ao Estudante - Taguspark (NAPE-TP) was brought into play. Nevertheless, the relationship between mentors (mostly second-year students) and mentees (first-year students) tends to weaken after the first academic weeks of the semester. This problem can be addressed with the creation of a consistent and unique communication channel between all the parties involved in this programme. This work presents NAPP, a novel mentoring software solution for first-year mentorship programmes, that enhances the communication between mentors and mentees while providing study guidance tools for mentees. NAPP is composed of two key components, a cross-platform mobile application and a web application that is used as a high level performance analysis tool by the programme's coordinator. These components were developed using state of the art technologies like the Ionic Framework using AngularJS, and the NoSQL databases CouchDB and PouchDB.

Keywords: Mentoring program · Student support systems · Mobile application · NoSQL databases

1 Context

Núcleo de Apoio ao Estudante - Taguspark (NAPE-TP)[1] main student support service is the mentoring programme. The main focus of this programme is the welcoming, integration and assistance of students that are admitted for the first time in Técnico Lisboa[2], mainly first-year and international students, into academic life. In the Taguspark campus in particular, with the help of NAPE-TP's mentors, mostly second/third year students, the newcomers get personalized assistance during their first steps in Técnico Lisboa's academic life. Even though

[1] https://nape.tecnico.ulisboa.pt/en/.
[2] https://tecnico.ulisboa.pt/en/.

É. Lavoué et al. (Eds.): EC-TEL 2017, LNCS 10474, pp. 610–613, 2017.
DOI: 10.1007/978-3-319-66610-5_74

the programme is well organized, there is a recognized communication problem between the three parties involved on it: NAPE-TP, mentors and mentees. Therefore, there was a need for a software solution that supports the information flow between these parties and also integrates study guidance tools that help students throughout their academic life.

Looking at the related work on the topic of mentoring programmes, we paid special attention to MIT Sloan School Of Management[3] the mentoring programme that is based in the relationship between students and alumni. This programme is powered by Chronus [1], a software dedicated to support mentoring. Also, between other mentoring programmes, we could identify in TU Delft[4], there are two different mentoring programmes, one for first-year students and another for master students [2].

While MIT's mentoring programme has a mentoring support software solution tailored for last-year students that are planning their career path, TU Delft's has the same focus of NAPE-TP's programme but without the technological support. Hence, NAPP is the first software solution to support first-year mentoring programmes.

1.1 NAPE-TP Communication Problem

NAPE-TP mentoring program is aimed at helping first-year students to achieve academic success and to support their integration within the first year. Figure 1 presents the information exchange between the three parties in the programme, namely NAPE-TP, mentees and mentors.

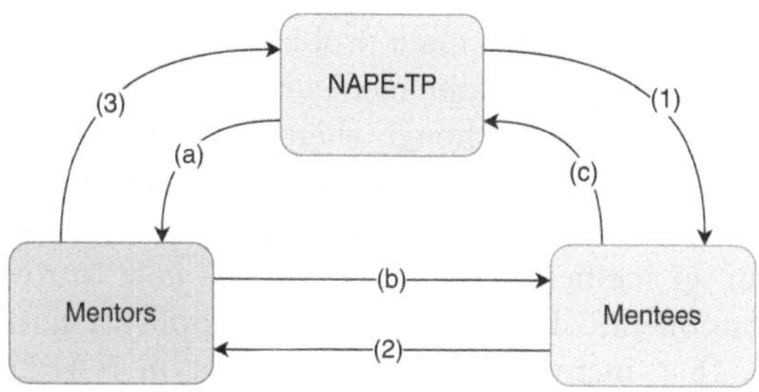

Fig. 1. NAPE-TP mentoring program communication channels for academic success and integration

In what concerns academic issues, the flow starts in direction (1) where NAPE-TP provides psychological and/or academic personalized support to mentees; in direction (2) mentees report their academic performance to the corresponding mentor; and in direction (3) mentors report their mentee's grades to

[3] http://mitsloan.mit.edu/.
[4] https://www.tudelft.nl/en/.

the NAPE-TP coordinator. Concerning academic integration, the flow starts at direction (a) where NAPE-TP invites and distributes mentors to all first-year students; in direction (b) mentors provide academic and campus-related support to their mentees; and in (c) mentees report problems and give suggestions to NAPE-TP related with the mentoring program.

If a mentor reports a particular case of a mentee with poor academic performance (fail in three or more evaluations), the mentee will then be invited to an interview with NAPE-TP's coordinator in order to find a quick solution. Until now, the process of reporting mentee's grades to mentors is entirely dependent on the exchanging of e-mails between the two parties in communication channel (2), or oral communication in case there is a personal relationship. The part of the communication process is usually very delayed, and mentors have to pressure their mentees in order to get their feedback. The delay referred in (2) cascades to channel (3), leading to a desynchronised communication which results in the overburden of the programme's coordinator.

Moreover, the distribution referred in channel (a) is a manual process in which the NAPE-TP's coordinator matches every first-year student (300 students in total) with a mentor, from a pool of around 90 mentor-students. Analysing channel (b), the experience of several annual editions of the NAPE-TP mentoring programme indicates that a relationship of trust is not always possible to establish during the enrolment week. It also happens in direction (c) that NAPE-TP seldom receives any direct feedback on the mentoring programme from mentees, only from mentor's reports.

1.2 Proposed Software Solution

As described above (Sect. 1.1), the main problem in NAPE-TP's mentoring programme is caused by undefined and inefficient communication channels used in both processes (see Fig. 1). Although there was an attempt to improve the exchange of information based on emails and Slack, the programme coordinator always resorted to other methods to reach mentors and mentees because these were being used in an inefficient way. We propose now to divide the software solution in two components. The first is a mobile application, designed for mentors and mentees, that increases their engagement in NAPE-TP's mentoring programme through the implementation of well-timed and relevant push notifications [3]. This app also provides mentors with academic performance tracking reports of their mentees and key study guidance tools. The second component is a web application, which is designed for NAPE-TP's coordinator, that enables a high level view of the mentees' academic performance evolution and the mentoring activities carried out by mentors.

1.3 Solution's Architecture

NAPP's architecture is based mainly on three technologies: Ionic Framework, PouchDB and CouchDB (see Fig. 2).

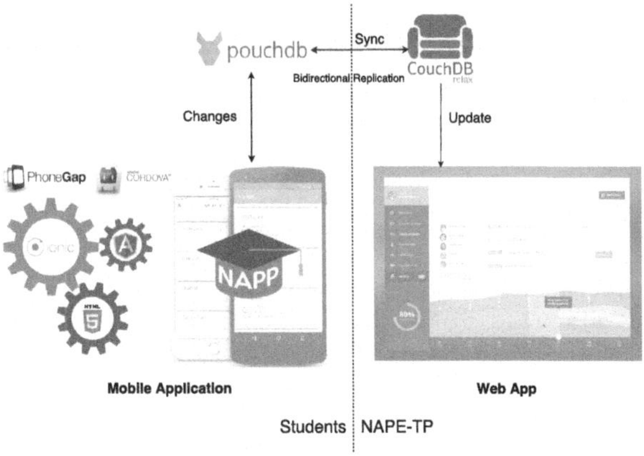

Fig. 2. NAPP's architecture

On the client side (student's side), the multiple NAPP mobile applications, built with Ionic Framework, are able to keep their local PouchDB database up-to-date even when the users are offline. On the server side (NAPE-TP's side), NAPP web application provides access to the information on the CouchDB server that is synchronized with all PouchDB instances.

2 Conclusion and Further Work

It is our conviction that this framework modernizes the mentoring programme, reducing the number of manual processes that are still part of it, while increasing its impact and fostering the engagement of first-years students through a mobile approach. We present here a work in progress, the next step of which consists of the validation and the testing of the software solution, both in what concerns its impact in the communication between mentors and mentees, and its overall performance while on high load of usage.

Acknowledgements. This work was supported by national funds through Fundação para a Ciência e a Tecnologia (FCT) with reference UID/CEC/50021/2013.

References

1. Chronus, Mobile Applications. http://chronus.com/news-and-events/chronus-introduces-industrys-comprehensive-mobile-experience. Accessed 22 November 2016
2. TU Delft - TPM, EPA and MOT Mentoring System. http://studenten.tudelft.nl/en/students/faculty-specific/tpm/academic-counsellors/mentor-system/. Accessed 10 November 2016
3. Pham, X.L., Nguyen, T.H., Hwang, W.Y., Chen, G.D.: Effects of push notifications on learner engagement in a mobile learning app. In: 2016 IEEE 16th International Conference on Advanced Learning Technologies (ICALT), pp. 90–94, July 2016

Designing Learning Experiences Outside of Classrooms with a Location-Based Game Avastusrada

Terje Väljataga(✉), Ulla Moks, Anne Tiits, Tobias Ley, Mihkel Kangur, and Jaanus Terasmaa

Tallinn University, Narva Road 25, 10120 Tallinn, Estonia
{terje.valjataga,ulla.moks,anne.tiits,tobias.ley,mihkel.kangur, jaanus.terasmaa}@tlu.ee

Abstract. Mobile technology with numerous affordances provides opportunities to take learning outside of classrooms, into authentic contexts. This paper presents a location-based tool – Avastusrada - which allows teachers to easily create learning tracks by developing different types of tasks connected to specific locations. The paper reports preliminary results of teachers' experiences with the tool and their perceived affordances of the tool for various educational purposes. In addition, emerged shortcomings of the tool and further suggestions for improvements will be outlined. The first pilot study with K-12 school teachers and students demonstrated that the tool has a great potential to be used in outdoor formal learning contexts because of its ease of use and its potential to enhance numerous competencies outlined in the national curriculum.

Keywords: Outdoor learning · Location-based application

1 Introduction

The most important developments in the area of education in formal and informal settings in Estonia is defined by The Estonian Lifelong Learning Strategy 2020, which in addition to other aspects stresses the importance of achieving concordance between learning content, objectives and learning outcomes outlined in curricula as well as taking formal and informal learning activities outside of the school environments, into authentic settings to enrich learning processes. The strategy also emphasises the use of digital technology (including bring your own device concept) and availability of digital learning resources as catalysts to make learning more engaging and efficient. Numerous studies have demonstrated that learning scenarios and tools with competitive and gamified components arouse learners' interest and motivation to engage in learning tasks [2, 4, 6, 7]. However, a variety of applications have been developed mainly for classroom settings. Without a question taking learning outdoors creates challenges for teachers on many different levels: orchestrating distributed learning settings [1]; managing technology and BYOD; letting students to take hold of their culture of learning and shaping it to be more participatory, communicative, collaborative and digital [3]; designing learning scenarios in which knowledge building [5] happens through outdoor adventure tracks. The paper presents a location-based tool, which provides teachers an option to

É. Lavoué et al. (Eds.): EC-TEL 2017, LNCS 10474, pp. 614–617, 2017.
DOI: 10.1007/978-3-319-66610-5_75

easily and quickly design adventure tracks outside of physical classrooms. The results from the first pilot study with teachers and students will be reported.

2 Avastusrada - A Location-Based Tool

Avastusrada is a web-based tool, which allows creating location-based learning tracks. Using it requires a smart-phone or a tablet, which has an Internet connection (WiFi, 3G or 4G) that allows making use of the GPS location service (Fig. 1a).

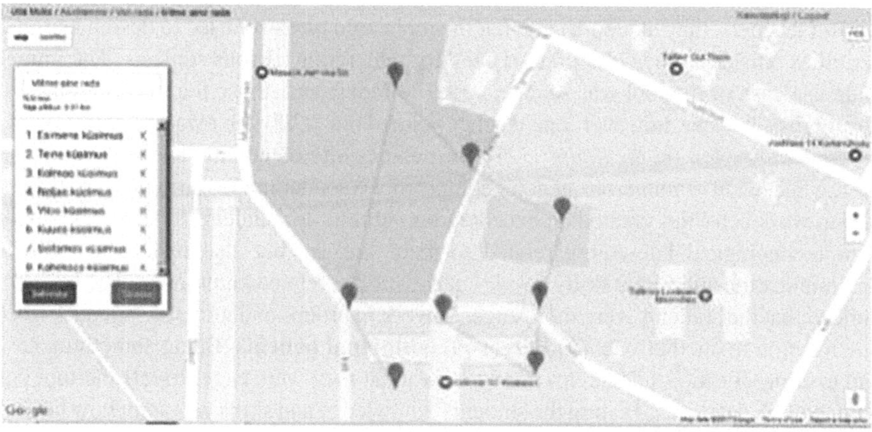

Fig. 1. a, b. An example of a track in Avastusrada.

The tool offers a list of templates for creating different types of tasks, such as multiple choice answers, free form answers, etc. In order to monitor what is going on in the track and how students have progressed, the teacher can see submitted answers of every location point by every student (or student groups) and provide feedback. The tool also currently displays simple statistics (the number of players, location points, time for completing the track etc.). The location points with tasks get activated when students reach close enough to the particular location and will be turned to blue as soon as the answer to the task has been submitted (Fig. 1b). In that way the tool helps to keep track on which points have been solved already. Depending on how the track has been defined, the students can visit location points randomly or in a predefined order.

3 Piloting Avastusrada with Teachers

The study presented here is the first phase of a more comprehensive research on gamified learning and knowledge building on the move in authentic contexts with the help of a simple, light-weight location-based tool. The overall research design follows a design-based research approach with the emphasis on exploring the use cases and possibilities for designing and implementing learning scenarios with mobile devices in formal educational outdoor settings. 6 teachers of a K-12 school participated in the pilot study. During the participatory design sessions 4 different tracks (physical education, technology (materials), science and an integrated track encompassing various subjects such as science, math, art and Estonian) were developed in the neighborhood of the school territory and implemented in the lessons. Subsequently, the teachers' experiences and ideas were collected through recorded semi-structured interviews. The main focus of the interviews was to explore: What are the perceived possibilities of making use of Avastusrada in formal educational settings and integrating subjects into coherent learning scenarios? What is the perceived added value of Avastusrada? To what extent Avastusrada can support the achievement of learning goals? The following main themes emerged from the interview data: (1) **Suitability for different subjects**. Being different subject teachers, they all confirmed that the tool could be easily used to design learning activities outside of the classroom or even for integrating various subjects. The immediate use case of the tool was seen as a way to repeat and revise the material covered during the semester, however, one teacher pointed out "*Only the teacher's fantasy and creativity are what set the limits*". (2) **Competence advancement**. The tool supported the advancement of numerous general competencies set out in the National Curriculum. Group work activities created an excellent opportunity for students to share and apply their technological know-how related to their devices, but also make use of their communication and social skills besides of the subject related knowledge. The teachers noticed that the students were more eager to work in groups and move as "squads" from one location to another one. (3) **Perceived additional benefits**. Being something new and exciting for the students, teachers noticed that they were eager to test the tool out with their own devices. Testing the students' knowledge and skills was somehow hidden in the overall learning activity, thus reducing the pressure on students. Using the tool, it created an internal desire for the students to outperform each other, creating a gamified experience. Two of the teachers claimed that the tool takes far less preparation time for an outdoor lesson, for instance in comparison to other similar initiatives. Yet another important aspect for the teachers was its option to receive immediate feedback from the students' submissions. (4) **Challenges.** As expected, some common usability and technical issues emerged as well, such as batteries running empty, not having data packages (in our case, the school WIFI didn't cover the whole area where the tracks had been planned) or not knowing how to turn on geo-location services in one's phone. In addition to teachers' time concern, some of them acknowledged that they themselves were the greatest obstacle because of their limited technological knowledge and rather fixed mindset of what makes a good lesson design. (5) **Suggestions for tool improvements.** One of the teachers proposed: "*It would be nice to have a notification appearing when arriving at the next location point*", another suggested that the tool could form student groups automatically and enable to create more complicated problem-solving tasks. These suggestions have been forwarded to the developers and are in consideration.

4 Conclusions and Future Steps

The first phase of the presented study shows promising results to continue with the tool development for formal learning purposes. Being a subject-neutral tool, Avastusrada can be used to design meaningful learning experiences for different (integrated) subjects on the move. Quite a lot depends here on teachers' mindsets and what makes up a good lesson design (accepting that learning can happen through gaming and fun activities). The study showed the teachers and students' curiosity and excitement, however, there is a chance to be one time effect. We believe, that the wide range of task types and the opportunity to change locations of the tracks should reduce this concern tremendously. The second phase of the study will be focusing on a bigger group of teachers attempting to create coherent meaningful learning tracks while integrating different subjects. Another challenge we foresee is to design orchestration tools that could provide teachers with data that help them to cope with 20 or 30 students in distributed outdoor settings. Our ultimate goal is to design interventions that intend to facilitate learner-generated design, i.e. to give students the role of the creator and let them learn through designing their own learning experiences, i.e. choose locations, create tasks and turn them into tracks.

Acknowledgement. *This project has received funding from the European Union's Horizon 2020 research and innovation programme under grant agreement No. 669074.*

References

1. Dillenbourg, P., Jermann, P.: Designing integrative scripts. In: Fischer, F., Mandl, H., Haake, J., Kollar, I. (eds.) Scripting Computer-Supported Collaborative Learning – Cognitive, Computational, and Educational Perspectives. CULS, vol. 6, pp. 275–301. Springer, New York (2007). doi:10.1007/978-0-387-36949-5_16
2. Huang, W.H.: Evaluating learners' motivational and cognitive processing in an online game-based learning environment. Comput. Hum. Behav. **27**(2), 694–704 (2011)
3. Kim, B., Tan, L., Bielaczyc, K.: Learner-generated designs in participatory culture: What they are and how they are shaping learning. Interact. Learn. Environ. **23**(5), 545–555 (2015)
4. Papastergiou, M.: Digital game-based learning in high school computer science education: Impact on educational effectiveness and student motivation. Comput. Educ. **52**(1), 1–12 (2009)
5. Scardamalia, M., Bereiter, C.: Knowledge building. In: Encyclopedia of Education. 2nd edn., pp. 1370–1373. Macmillan Reference, New York (2003)
6. Woo, J.-C.: Digital game-based learning supports student motivation, cognitive success, and performance outcomes. Educ. Technol. Soc. **17**(3), 291–307 (2014)
7. Yang, Y.-T.C.: Building virtual cities, inspiring intelligent citizens: Digital games for developing students' problem solving and learning motivation. Comput. Educ. **59**(2), 365–377 (2012)

Author Index

The manufacturer's authorised representative in the EU is Springer Nature Customer Service Centre GmbH, Europaplatz 3, 69115 Heidelberg, Germany. If you have any concerns regarding our products, please contact ProductSafety@springernature.com

Printed and bound by CPI Group (UK) Ltd, Croydon, CR0 4YY
22/09/2026
02220983-0011